High Impact Data Visualization in Excel with Power View, 3D Maps, Get & Transform and Power BI

Second Edition

Adam Aspin

Apress®

High Impact Data Visualization in Excel with Power View, 3D Maps, Get & Transform and Power BI

Adam Aspin
Stafford
United Kingdom

ISBN-13 (pbk): 978-1-4842-2399-4   ISBN-13 (electronic): 978-1-4842-2400-7
DOI 10.1007/978-1-4842-2400-7

Library of Congress Control Number: 2016959188

Managing Director: Welmoed Spahr
Lead Editor: Jonathan Gennick
Development Editor: Laura Berendson
Editorial Board: Steve Anglin, Pramila Balan, Laura Berendson, Aaron Black, Louise Corrigan, Jonathan Gennick, Todd Green, Robert Hutchinson, Celestin Suresh John, Nikhil Karkal, James Markham, Susan McDermott, Matthew Moodie, Natalie Pao, Gwenan Spearing
Coordinating Editor: Jill Balzano
Copy Editor: Kim Wimpsett
Compositor: SPi Global
Indexer: SPi Global
Artist: SPi Global

Distributed to the book trade worldwide by Springer Science+Business Media New York, 233 Spring Street, 6th Floor, New York, NY 10013. Phone 1-800-SPRINGER, fax (201) 348-4505, e-mail orders-ny@springer-sbm.com, or visit www.springer.com. Apress Media, LLC is a California LLC and the sole member (owner) is Springer Science + Business Media Finance Inc (SSBM Finance Inc). SSBM Finance Inc is a Delaware corporation.

For information on translations, please e-mail rights@apress.com, or visit www.apress.com.

Apress and friends of ED books may be purchased in bulk for academic, corporate, or promotional use. eBook versions and licenses are also available for most titles. For more information, reference our Special Bulk Sales–eBook Licensing web page at www.apress.com/bulk-sales.

Any source code or other supplementary materials referenced by the author in this text are available to readers at www.apress.com. For detailed information about how to locate your book's source code, go to www.apress.com/source-code/. Readers can also access source code at SpringerLink in the Supplementary Material section for each chapter.

Printed on acid-free paper

For Hannah

Contents at a Glance

About the Author xxvii

Acknowledgments xxix

Introduction xxxi

■ Chapter 1: Self-Service Business Intelligence with Excel 2016 1

■ Chapter 2: Power View and Tables 17

■ Chapter 3: Filtering Data in Power View 57

■ Chapter 4: Charts in Power View 87

■ Chapter 5: Advanced Charting with Power View 121

■ Chapter 6: Interactive Data Selection in Power View 143

■ Chapter 7: Images and Presentation in Power View 175

■ Chapter 8: Mapping Data in Power View 205

■ Chapter 9: 3D Maps 225

■ Chapter 10: Discovering and Loading Data with Get & Transform
in Excel 2016 279

■ Chapter 11: Transforming Data Sets Using Get & Transform 321

■ Chapter 12: Data Cleansing with Get & Transform 349

■ Chapter 13: Data Mashup with Get & Transform 371

■ Chapter 14: Extending the Excel Data Model Using Power Pivot 411

■ Chapter 15: Extending the Data Model with Calculated Columns 463

■Chapter 16: Adding Measures to the Data Model 495

■Chapter 17: Analyzing Data over Time with DAX 529

■Chapter 18: Self-Service Business Intelligence with PowerBI.com 565

Index 591

Contents

About the Author xxvii

Acknowledgments xxix

Introduction xxxi

■Chapter 1: Self-Service Business Intelligence with Excel 2016 1

The Excel BI Toolkit 2
  The Self-Service Business Intelligence Universe in Excel 2016... 2
  Get and Transform 3
  Power Pivot.. 3

Power View..4
  3D Maps... 5
  The Power BI Service 5

Preparing the Excel BI Toolkit...5
  Enabling the Excel BI Toolkit... 6
  Power View.. 8
  Get and Transform 10
  3D Maps... 11

Corporate BI or Self-Service BI? 11

The Excel Data Model...12

How This Book Is Designed to Be Read..13
  Discovering Data 14
  Creating a Data Model 14
  Taking Data and Preparing It for Output 14
  Delivering Geodata 14

Taking Existing Excel BI and Sharing It..14

Delivering Excel BI to Mobile Devices..14

Learning the Product Suite Following a Real-World Path.......................................15

Conclusion 15

■Chapter 2: Power View and Tables 17

The Power View Experience 18

Adding a Power View Sheet to an Excel Workbook 18

The Power View Interface 18

The Power View Ribbon..19

The Field List 21

Using the Field List 21

Renaming or Deleting a Power View Report..23

Tables in Power View 23

Adding a Table 23

Deleting a Table 26

Changing the Table Size and Position..26

Changing Column Order..27

Removing Columns from a Table 27

Types of Data..28

Data and Aggregations 29

Enhancing Tables 30

The Design Ribbon..30

Row Totals 32

Formatting Columns of Numbers..33

Default Formatting..34

Changing Column Widths..34

Font Sizes in Tables 36

Copying a Table..36

Sorting by Column 36

Table Granularity 37

Matrix Tables 38

    Row Matrix 38

    Column Matrix 40

    Sorting Data in Matrix Tables 43

Drilling Through with Matrix Tables 44

    Drilling Down 45

    Drilling Up 46

    Reapplying Matrix Visualization 47

    Drilling Through with Column Hierarchies 47

Card Visualizations 49

    Card Visualization Styles 52

    Sorting Data in Card-View Tables 53

Switching Between Table Types 53

Key Performance Indicators 54

Creating Power View Reports and Tables Without a Data Model 54

Conclusion 55

Chapter 3: Filtering Data in Power View 57

Filters 57

View Filters 59

    Adding Filters 59

    Using the (All) Filter 61

    Clearing Filters 61

    Deleting Filters 62

    Expanding and Collapsing Filters 62

    Subsetting Large Filter Lists 63

Filtering Different Data Types 66

    Range Filter Mode 66

    List Filter Mode 68

    Quickly Excluding Outliers 69

Date and Time Data 69

Other Data Types 71

Multiple Filters 71

Advanced Filters 71

    Applying an Advanced Filter 72

    Clearing an Advanced Filter 73

    Advanced Wildcard Filters 74

    Numeric Filters 75

Date and Time Filters 76

Complex Filters 78

    Advanced Text Filter Options 79

    Advanced Numeric Filter Options 79

    Advanced Date Filter Options 80

Visualization-Level Filters 80

Filter Hierarchy 81

Filtering Tips 83

    Don't Filter Too Soon 83

    Drill-Down and Filters 84

    Annotate, Annotate, Annotate 85

Conclusion 86

■Chapter 4: Charts in Power View 87

A First Chart 87

Deleting a Chart 91

Basic Chart Modification 92

Basic Chart Types 93

    Column Charts 93

    Line Charts 94

    Pie Charts 94

    Essential Chart Adjustments 96

Resizing Charts 96

Repositioning Charts 97

Sorting Chart Elements 97

Font Size... 100

Applying Color to Bar and Column Charts 100

Multiple Data Values in Charts 101

The Layout Ribbon.. 105

Enhancing Charts 106

    Chart Legends 106

    Chart Title 107

    Chart Data Labels 107

Drilling Down in Charts.. 109

Popping Charts Out and In.. 113

Chart Filters.. 115

Conclusion.. 119

■Chapter 5: Advanced Charting with Power View 121

Multiple Charts 121

    Multiple Bar or Column Charts 121

    Specifying Vertical and Horizontal Selections 123

Specifying the Layout of Multiple-Chart Visualizations 124

    Creating Horizontal Multiples 124

    Defining the Multiples Grid.. 124

    Multiple Line Charts... 126

    Multiple Pie Charts 128

    Drilling Down with Multiple Charts 130

Scatter Charts 131

    Drilling Down with Scatter Charts 132

    Scatter Charts to Display Flattened Hierarchies.. 133

    Scatter Chart Multiples.. 134

Bubble Charts 135

    Bubble Chart Data Labels and Legend 137

    Multiple Bubble Elements 138

    Bubble Chart Multiples 139

Play Axis 140

Conclusion 142

■Chapter 6: Interactive Data Selection in Power View 143

Tiles 144

    Creating a Tiled Visualization from Scratch 144

    Adjusting Tile Display 145

Some Variations on Ways of Creating Tiled Visualizations 146

    Creating a Tiled Visualization from Scratch—Another Variant 146

    Adding Tiles to an Existing Visualization 146

    Adding Tiles to an Existing Visualization—Another Variant 147

    Modifying an Existing Visualization Inside a Tile Container 147

Re-creating a Visualization Using Existing Tiles 148

Removing Tiles from a Visualization 149

Deleting a Tile Visualization 149

Tile Types 150

Using Tiles 151

Filtering Tiles 151

Tiles with No Data 152

Changing the Inner Visualization 153

Tiles and Multiple Charts 154

Slicers 154

    Adding a Slicer 155

    Applying a Slicer 156

Clearing a Slicer 157

Deleting a Slicer 157

Modifying a Slicer 158

Using Charts as Slicers 158

Highlighting Chart Data 160

Cross-Chart Highlighting 161

Highlighting Data in Bubble Charts 163

Charts as Filters 165

    Column and Bar Charts as Filters 167

    Choosing the Correct Approach to Interactive Data Selection 171

Filter Granularity 171

Conclusion 174

Chapter 7: Images and Presentation in Power View 175

Titles 175

    Adding a Title 176

    Moving and Resizing Titles 176

    Formatting a Title 177

The Text Ribbon 177

Adding Text Boxes to Annotate a Report 178

The Context Menu 179

Altering the Font Used in a Report 181

Changing the Text Size 182

Altering the Theme of a Report 182

Deciphering Themes 185

Applying a Report Background 186

Images 189

Image Sources 189

Background Images 190

    Adding a Background Image 190

    Fitting a Background Image 191

Removing a Background Image 192

Setting an Image's Transparency 193

Images in Tables 194

Images in Slicers 195

Images in Tiles 196

Independent Images 197

Layering Visualizations 199

Some Uses for Independent Images 200

Image File Format 202

Conclusion 203

■Chapter 8: Mapping Data in Power View 205

Bing Maps 205

Maps in Power View 206

Adjusting Map Display in Power View 208

Positioning the Map Elements 208

Zooming In or Out 209

Removing or Adding a Map Title 209

Modifying the Map Background 209

Filtering Map Data 211

Multivalue Series 212

Highlighting Map Data 214

Adjusting a Legend 216

Adding Tiles to Maps 217

Multiple Maps 218

Multiple Maps by Region 219

Drilling Down in Maps 221

Conclusion 223

Chapter 9: 3D Maps 225

Bing Maps 225

Running 3D Maps 226

The 3D Maps Window 227

The 3D Maps Ribbon 228

Region Maps 230

3D Maps Source Data 232

Refreshing Data 232

Geographical Data Types 232

Using the Layer Pane 233

Showing and Hiding the Layer Pane 233

Layer Pane Elements 234

The Data Area 234

Data Operations 235

Adding a Field 236

Removing a Field 236

Moving Around in 3D Maps 236

Moving Around a Map 237

Zooming In or Out 237

Flat Map and 3D Globe 238

Adjusting the Pitch 238

Going to a Specific Location 238

3D Maps Aggregations 239

Map Types 239

The Various Map Types, by Example 240

Bubble Maps 240

Column Maps 244

Heat Maps 247

Region Maps 248

Presentation Options 250

   The Settings View 250

   Applying Specific Colors to Data Elements.. 254

3D Maps Themes.. 255

Text Boxes 256

Customizing the Data Card.. 257

Timelines 259

   Adding a Timeline 259

   Using a Timeline 261

Using Layers 265

   2D Charts 268

   2D Chart Types 269

3D Maps Tours... 269

   Creating 3D Maps Tours.. 270

   Deleting a 3D Maps Tour... 271

   Existing 3D Maps Tours in Excel 272

3D Maps Movies... 272

   Scene Transitions 274

   Managing Scenes.. 274

   Exporting a Movie... 275

Custom Regions 277

Conclusion.. 277

■Chapter 10: Discovering and Loading Data with Get & Transform
in Excel 2016 279

Data Sources 280

   File Sources... 281

   Databases.. 281

   Other Sources 283

Loading Data 285

   Web Pages 285

   CSV Files... 289

   Understanding CSV Files 292

   Text Files... 292

   XML Files 293

   Excel 295

   Adding Data from Excel Tables inside the Current Workbook.................................... 296

   Microsoft Access Databases.. 297

Relational Databases: SQL Server 298

   Automatically Loading Related Tables 301

   Database Options 301

Editing Existing Queries 308

Microsoft SQL Server Analysis Services Data Sources 308

   Add Items 311

   Collapse Columns 313

Microsoft SQL Server Analysis Services Tabular Data Sources.......................... 313

Other Data Sources 313

Reusing Recent Data Sources 313

   Reusing a Data Source 314

   Pinning a Data Source 315

   Old Data 315

Connection Security 315

Modifying Data Sources 318

Conclusion.. 319

■Chapter 11: Transforming Data Sets Using Get & Transform 321

Get & Transform Queries 322

   Editing Data After a Data Load... 322

   Transforming Data Before Loading 324

Query or Load? 324

The Get & Transform Query Editor 325

    The Applied Steps List 326

    The Get & Transform Query Editor Ribbons 327

Data Set Shaping 332

    Renaming Columns 332

    Reordering Columns 333

    Removing Columns 334

    Merging Columns 334

    Removing Records 336

    Removing Duplicate Records 339

    Sorting Data 340

    Reversing the Row Order 341

Filtering Data 342

    Selecting Specific Values 342

    Finding Elements in the Filter List 343

    Filtering Text Ranges 344

    Filtering Numeric Ranges 344

    Filtering Date and Time Ranges 344

    Filtering Data 345

Counting the Rows in a Data Set 346

Conclusion 347

■Chapter 12: Data Cleansing with Get & Transform 349

Viewing a Full Record 349

Get & Transform Query Editor Context Menus 350

Changing Data Type 351

Detecting Data Types 353

Replacing Values 353

Transforming Column Contents 355

    Text Transformation 355

    Removing Leading and Trailing Spaces 357

    Number Transformations 357

    Calculating Numbers 358

    Date Transformations 360

    Time Transformations 362

    Duration 362

Filling Down 363

Using the First Row As Headers 366

Grouping Records 366

Conclusion 369

Chapter 13: Data Mashup with Get & Transform 371

The Get & Transform View Ribbon 371

Extending Data 372

Duplicating Columns 373

Splitting Columns 373

    Splitting Column by a Delimiter 374

    Splitting Columns by Number of Characters 376

Merging Columns 376

Custom Columns 377

Index Columns 379

Merging Data 381

    Adding Data 381

    Aggregating Data During a Merge Operation 384

    Types of Join 388

    Joining on Multiple Columns 389

    Preparing Data Sets for Joins 390

    Correct and Incorrect Joins 391

Examining Joined Data 391

The Expand and Aggregate Buttons 393

Appending Data 394

Adding the Contents of One Query to Another 394

Adding Multiple Files from a Source Folder 395

Changing the Data Structure 397

Unpivoting Tables 398

Pivoting Tables 399

Transposing Rows and Columns 401

Managing the Transformation Process 401

Modifying a Step 402

Renaming a Step 402

Deleting a Step or a Series of Steps 402

Adding a Step 403

Altering Process Step Sequencing 403

An Approach to Sequencing 404

Error Records 404

Removing Errors 404

Duplicating Part of a Query 405

Managing Queries 405

Organizing Queries 406

Grouping Queries 406

Duplicating Queries 408

Referencing Queries 408

Add a Column As a New Query 408

Pending Changes 409

Copying Data from Get & Transform 409

Conclusion 410

■**Chapter 14: Extending the Excel Data Model Using Power Pivot**......................**411**

Power Pivot 412

   Launching Power Pivot 412

   The Power Pivot Window 413

Data Model or Query? 414

The Power Pivot Ribbons 414

   The Home Ribbon 414

   The Design Ribbon 416

   The Advanced Ribbon 417

Managing Power Pivot Data 418

   Manipulating Tables 419

   Manipulating Columns 419

Power Pivot Data Types 422

   Formatting Power Pivot Data 422

   Currency Formats 423

Preparing Data for Analysis 424

   Categorize Data 425

   Apply a Default Summarization 426

   Define Sort by Columns 427

Sorting Data in Power Pivot Tables 428

Designing a Data Model 429

   Data View and Diagram View 430

   Creating Relationships 433

   Creating Relationships Manually 434

   Creating Relationships Automatically 435

   Deleting Relationships 436

   Managing Relationships 436

Preparing the Data Model 439

Default Field Set 440

Defining Table Behavior 442

    Row Identifier 442

    Keep Unique Rows 444

    Default Label 444

    Set a Default Aggregation (Summarize By) 445

Preparing Images for Power View 447

Image URLs 447

Default Image 448

Preparing Hyperlinks for Power View 448

Creating Hierarchies 448

Modifying Hierarchies 450

    Adding a Level to a Hierarchy 450

    Removing a Level from a Hierarchy 450

    Altering the Levels in a Hierarchy 451

    Deleting a Hierarchy 451

    Hiding the Original Field 451

Key Performance Indicators 451

    Creating a KPI 452

    KPI Options 453

    KPI Descriptions 454

    Calculated KPI Targets 456

    Modifying a KPI 456

    Deleting a KPI 456

Perspectives 457

    Creating a Perspective 457

    Applying a Perspective 458

Optimizing File Size 459

Copying Data from Power Pivot 460

Conclusion 461

Chapter 15: Extending the Data Model with Calculated Columns 463

Types of Calculations... 464

New Columns 464

Naming Columns 465

Concatenating Column Contents 466

Tweaking Text... 468

Simple Calculations 470

    Math Operators.. 471

    Rounding Values 472

Calculating Across Tables... 473

Choosing the Correct Table for Linked Calculations 474

Cascading Column Calculations 475

Refreshing Data.. 475

Using Functions in New Columns.. 476

    Safe Division.. 476

    Counting Reference Elements 478

    Statistical Functions 479

    Applying a Specific Format to a Calculation... 480

Correcting and Removing Errors 483

Simple Logic: The IF() Function 483

    Exception Indicators 483

    Creating Alerts 484

    Comparison Operators... 485

    Flagging Data 485

    Nested IF() Functions... 486

    Creating Custom Groups Using Multiple Nested IF() Statements 488

    Multiline Formulas... 489

Complex Logic 489

Formatting Logical Results 493

Making Good Use of the Formula Bar 494

Conclusion 494

■Chapter 16: Adding Measures to the Data Model 495

Introducing Measures 495

A First Measure: Number of Cars Sold 495

Basic Aggregations in Measures 498

Using Multiple Measures 500

Cross-Table Measures 503

More Advanced Aggregations 505

Filter Context 508

Row Context 508

Query Context 508

Filter Context 509

Filtering Data in Measures 509

Simple Filters 509

Text Filters 509

Numeric Filters 511

More Complex Filters 512

Multiple Criteria in Filters 513

Using Multiple Filters 514

Calculating Percentages of Totals 515

A Simple Percentage 515

Removing Multiple Filter Elements 517

Visual Totals 518

The ALLEXCEPT() Function 519

Filtering on Measures 521

Displaying Rank 522

A Few Comments and Notes on Using Measures 524

Managing Measures 524

Formatting Measures 525

    Formatting Measures 525

    Hiding Measures 526

Calculation Options 527

Conclusion 527

■Chapter 17: Analyzing Data over Time with DAX 529

Simple Date Calculations 529

    Date and Time Formatting 532

    Calculating the Age of Cars Sold 535

    Calculating the Difference Between Two Dates 535

Adding Time Intelligence to a Data Model 538

Creating and Applying a Date Table 538

Creating a Date Table in Excel 539

    Marking a Table as a Date Table 541

Creating the Date Table in Power Pivot 542

    Adding Sort By Columns to the Date Table 546

    Date Table Techniques 546

    Adding the Date Table to the Data Model 547

Applying Time Intelligence 548

    YearToDate, QuarterToDate, and MonthToDate Calculations 549

    Analyze Data As a Ratio over Time 551

    Comparing a Metric with the Result from a Range of Dates 553

Comparisons with Previous Time Periods 556

Comparison with a Parallel Period in Time 558

    Comparing Data from Previous Years 558

    Comparing with the Same Date Period from a Different Quarter, Month, or Year 560

Rolling Aggregations over a Period of Time 562

Conclusion 564

■Chapter 18: Self-Service Business Intelligence with PowerBl.com 565

Create a Power BI Account 565

Publish Excel Files to Power BI 569

Work with Reports on PowerBl.com 572

Printing PowerBl.com Reports 573

Creating Reports in PowerBl.com 573

Uploading Excel Workbooks Without OneDrive for Business 575

Creating PowerBl.com Dashboards 577

Creating a New Dashboard 578

Adding Tiles to PowerBl.com Dashboards 579

Editing Dashboard Tiles 580

Modifying Dashboards 583

Sharing Dashboards 587

The Power BI App on Tablet Devices 588

Conclusion 590

Index 591

About the Author

Adam Aspin is an independent business intelligence consultant based in the United Kingdom. He has worked with SQL Server for more than 20 years. During this time, he has architected and developed several dozen reporting and analytical systems based on the Microsoft BI product suite.

A graduate of Oxford University, Adam began his career in publishing before moving into IT. Databases soon became a passion, and his experience in this arena ranges from dBase to Oracle and from Access to MySQL, with occasional sorties into the world of DB2. He is, however, most at home in the Microsoft universe when using SQL Server Analysis Services, SQL Server Reporting Services, SQL Server Integration Services, SharePoint, and Power BI.

Business intelligence has been his principal focus for the last 20 years. He has applied his skills for a range of clients in industry sectors from finance to utilities and telecoms to insurance.

Adam is a frequent contributor to Simple-Talk.com and SQLServerCentral. He has written numerous articles for various French IT publications. A fluent French speaker, Adam has worked in France and Switzerland for many years.

He is the author of *SQL Server Data Integration Recipes* (Apress, 2012), *High Impact Data Visualization with Power View, Power Map, and Power BI* (Apress, 2014), *Business Intelligence with SQL Server Reporting Services* (Apress, 2015), and *Pro Power BI Desktop* (Apress, 2016).

Acknowledgments

Writing a technical book can be a lonely occupation. So, I am all the more grateful for the help and encouragement that I have received from so many fabulous friends and colleagues.

First, my considerable thanks go to Jonathan Gennick, the commissioning editor of this book. Throughout the publication process Jonathan has been both a tower of strength and an exemplary mentor. He has always been available to share his vast experience selflessly and courteously.

Heartfelt thanks go to Jill Balzano, the Apress coordinating editor, for managing this book through the production process. She succeeded, once again, in the well-nigh impossible task of making a potentially stress-filled trek into a pleasant journey filled with light and humor. Her team also deserves much praise for their calm under pressure.

My thanks also go to Kim Wimpsett for her tireless and subtle work editing and polishing the prose, and to SPi Global for the hours spent preparing the book for publishing.

Once again my deepest gratitude is reserved for the two people who have given the most to this book. They are my wife and son. Timothy has put up with a mentally absent father for months while nonetheless providing continual encouragement to persevere. Karine has not only given me the support and encouragement to persevere but also the love without which nothing would be worth any effort. I am a very lucky man to have both of them.

Introduction

Business intelligence (BI) is a concept that has been around for many years. Until recently it has all too often been a domain reserved for large corporations with teams of dedicated IT specialists. All too frequently this has meant developing complex solutions using expensive products on timescales that rarely met real business needs.

All this has now changed with the advent of self-service business intelligence. Now, a user with a reasonable knowledge of Microsoft Excel can leverage their skills to produce accurate and meaningful analysis with little or no support from central IT.

The democratization has been made possible by four extensions to the Excel ecosystem that are all now integral parts of the core product. These elements combine to revolutionize the way that data is discovered, structured, and shaped so that it can be sliced, chopped, queried, and presented in an interactive and intensely visual way.

These are the four components of the Excel BI Toolkit:

- *Get & Transform*: To find, manage, morph, and load external data

- *Power Pivot*: To design and extend a coherent data model for analysis

- *Power View*: To present your findings interactively

- *3D Maps*: To display insights with a geographical slant

All of these tools have been around in various guises for a while. However, they are now completely integrated into Excel 2016. This allows an Excel user to take their business intelligence analysis to a whole new level. When used together, these tools empower the user as never before. They provide you with the capability to analyze and present your data and to shape and deliver your results easily and impressively. All this can be produced in a fraction of the time and cost that would be necessary when implementing a corporate solution.

These tools are enhanced by the Power BI service, a simple way of sharing your analyses and insights on PCs and mobile devices from the Microsoft cloud.

The aim of this book, therefore, is to introduce the Excel user to the brave new world of self-service BI using the Excel BI Toolkit. Although I assume you have a basic knowledge of Excel, no previous knowledge of the components described in this book is required. Indeed, this book will describe Get & Transform, Power Pivot, Power View, and 3D Maps from the ground up. If you read the book and follow the examples, you will arrive at a level of practical knowledge and confidence that you can subsequently apply to your own BI requirements.

This book is, in effect, an updated version of my previous book *High Impact Data Visualization with Power View, Power Map, and Power BI*. It describes these products in their latest integrated incarnation in Excel 2016. I have also expanded the chapter on DAX into three chapters on this analytical language to give you a head start when adding your own metrics and calculations to your analytical models.

This book should prove invaluable to business intelligence developers, Excel power users, IT managers, and financial analysts—indeed anyone who needs to deliver telling business intelligence to their audience. Whether your aim is to develop a proof of concept or to deliver a fully fledged BI system, this book will be your guide and mentor.

This book comes with full sample data that can be downloaded from the Apress web site. The data set is small (which may seem paradoxical when used with a product that can handle even big data), but I prefer to use a simple data set so that you can concentrate on the essence of what is being explained rather than the data itself.

Inevitably not every question can be answered and not every issue resolved in a single book. I truly hope that I have anticipated most of the essential self-service BI conundrums that you will encounter and have provided solutions to many of the challenges that you will meet when delivering self-service BI.

I wish you the best of luck in using the Excel BI Toolkit. I hope also that you have as much fun using these tools as I had writing this book.

—Adam Aspin

CHAPTER 1

Self-Service Business Intelligence with Excel 2016

If you are reading this book, it is most likely because you need to use data. More specifically, it may be that you need to make a journey from data to insight in which you have to take quantities of facts and figures, shape them into comprehensible information, and give them clear and visual meaning.

This book is all about that journey. It covers the many ways that you, an Excel user, can transform raw data into high-impact analyses delivered by Microsoft's self-service business intelligence (BI) tools that are integrated into the analysis platform that you use on a daily basis—Excel 2016. This approach is based on enabling you to handle industrial-strength quantities of data using familiar tools and to share stunning output in the shortest possible time frame.

The keywords in this universe are

- Fast
- Decentralized
- Intuitive
- Interactive
- Delivery

Using the tools and techniques described in this book, you can discover and load your data, create all the calculations you need, and then develop and share stylish interactive presentations.

It follows that this book is written from the perspective of the user. Essentially it is all about empowerment—letting users define their own requirements and satisfy their own needs simply and efficiently by building on their existing Excel skills.

You may find that you do not need all these products all the time. Indeed, you may find that you use them independently or in certain combinations. This is because self-service business intelligence is designed to be flexible and respond to a variety of needs. Nonetheless, we will be exploring all of these tools in the course of this book so that you can handle most, if not all, of the challenges that you may meet.

Taken together, this combination of tools and technologies creates a unique solution to the challenges of creating and sharing analytical insights. However, let me say again that you may not need *all* that the solution can offer. If all you need to do is share workbooks, then you do not need to share queries. The advantage of self-service BI is that it is a smorgasbord of potential solutions, where each department or enterprise can choose to implement the tools and technologies that suit its specific requirements.

Electronic supplementary material The online version of this chapter (doi:10.1007/978-1-4842-2400-7_1) contains supplementary material, which is available to authorized users.

© Adam Aspin 2016

A. Aspin, *High Impact Data Visualization in Excel with Power View, 3D Maps, Get & Transform and Power BI*, DOI 10.1007/978-1-4842-2400-7_1

The Excel BI Toolkit

Self-service business intelligence has always been possible with Excel. However, it is with Excel 2016 that all the elements that make up what we call the Excel BI Toolkit have united in a harmonious and easy-to-use way.

To understand how all these elements fit together, it will probably help if I begin with a more detailed overview of the various technologies that are employed. This should help you see how they can let you discover and load your data and then calculate and shape your data model so that you can create and share presentations and insights.

The Excel self-service BI toolkit consists of Excel (inevitably) and four built-in extensions that allow you to import, model, prepare, and display your analyses.

- *Get and Transform*: To import and transform data

- *Power Pivot*: To model data and carry out all necessary calculations

- *Power View*: To display your results interactively

- *3D Maps*: To show your data from a geographical perspective

The Self-Service Business Intelligence Universe in Excel 2016

The amalgam of products and technologies that make up the world of Microsoft self-service business intelligence can seem complex and even confusing at first glance. This is, to some extent, because some Excel tools and options seem to have overlapping aims. Also, you have to remember that Excel is a mature product that has evolved over time—and is continually moving forward. Consequently, there are both older and newer ways of solving problems that are still core parts of the product. While I have no intention of comparing and contrasting (or criticizing) the various aspects of Excel that you can choose to apply to an analytical challenge, I firmly believe that the Excel 2016 BI tools are the way forward.

Figure 1-1 provides a more comprehensible vision of the total toolset so that you can better see how all the pieces work together.

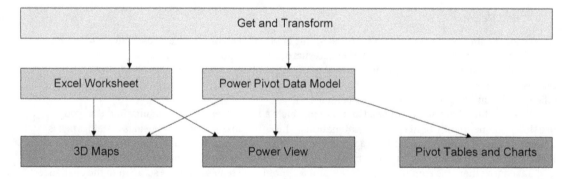

Figure 1-1. *The self-service business intelligence universe*

Get and Transform

Get and Transform (which used to be called Power Query) is one of the most recent additions to the self-service Excel BI Toolkit. It allows you to discover, access, and consolidate information from varied sources. Once your data is selected, cleansed, and transformed into a coherent structure, you can then place it in an Excel worksheet or, better still, load it directly into the Excel data model, which is a natural source for data when you are using Power View and 3D Maps. This data model is accessed and shaped using Power Pivot.

Get and Transform allows you to do many things with source data, but the four main steps are likely to be as follows:

- *Import* data from a wide variety of sources. This includes everything from corporate databases to files and from social media to big data.

- *Merge* data from multiple sources into a coherent structure.

- *Shape* data into the columns and records that suit your uses.

- *Cleanse* your data to make it reliable and easy to use.

There was a time when these processes required dedicated teams of IT specialists. Well, not any more. With Get and Transform, you can mash up your own data so that it is the way you want it and is ready to use as part of your self-service BI solution.

It is worth noting that you can also load data into Power Pivot directly without using Get and Transform. As you will see in this book, you have the choice. Whether you want or need to use Get and Transform at all will depend on the complexity of the source data and whether you need to cleanse and shape the data first. However, Get and Transform is certainly a fabulous tool when it comes to ingesting large quantities of data from a wide variety of sources, cleansing the data, and then giving it a clear, clean initial structure that you can build on. It is certainly generations ahead of the data ingestion tools that were part of previous versions of Excel. So even if you are used to connecting to external databases or data warehouses to source your data, you could be well advised to consider upgrading your existing processes to use Get and Transform instead. You could be pleasantly surprised by the reduction in both data refresh times and quantities of data that you transfer using this amazing tool.

Get and Transform is discussed in more depth in Chapters 10 through 13.

Power Pivot

Power Pivot is essentially the data store for your information. Indeed, many people refer to the Excel *data model* when they talk about data in Power Pivot. Get and Transform lets you import data and make it usable; Power Pivot then takes over and lets you extend and formalize the cleansed data. More specifically, it allows you to do the following:

- Create a data model by joining tables to develop a coherent data structure from multiple separate sources of data. This data model will then be used by Power View and 3D Maps.

- Enrich the data model by applying coherent names and data types.

- Create calculations and prepare the core metrics that you want to use in your analyses and presentations.

- Add hierarchies to enhance the user experience and guide your users through complex data sets.

- Create key performance indicators (KPIs) to allow benchmarking.

At the heart of Power Pivot are two core elements.

- The Excel data model

- DAX

As I will be referring to these throughout this book, I prefer to explain them here at the outset.

The Excel Data Model

The Excel data model is a way of storing large amounts of data in Excel but not in worksheets. The Excel data model is an in-memory engine that takes source data and compresses it (often by orders of magnitude) so that you can handle millions of rows of data. Indeed, a data model can be seven to ten times smaller than the source data. So if you are loading data into the Excel data model, you are less likely to hit the sort of restrictions (in row numbers and memory usage) that you will encounter if using "normal" Excel tables.

It is worth noting that you are not restricted to using Power View or 3D Maps if you have stored data in the Excel data model. You can use—or continue using—pivot tables and pivot charts that are based on Power Pivot data stored in the Excel in-memory data model. Yet your pivot tables and charts will likely become even more powerful and insightful if you learn to prepare the data that they display using Get and Transform and data analysis expressions (DAX).

DAX

DAX is a formula language that you can use to add functionality to your Excel data models. It is particularly adapted to business intelligence calculations. Fortunately, it is similar to Excel formulas. Indeed, some 80 DAX formulas are identical to their Excel counterparts. So, most Excel users will have little difficulty learning to use DAX to extend their analyses using the Excel BI toolkit.

Power Pivot, the Excel data model, and DAX are discussed in Chapters 14 through 17.

Power View

I think of Power View as the "jewel in the crown" of the 2016 Excel BI Toolkit. It is a dynamic analysis and presentation tool that lets you create professional-grade

- Tables

- Matrixes

- Charts

- KPIs

- Maps

Not only that, but it is incredibly fast and highly intuitive. It provides advanced interactivity through the use of

- Slicers

- Filters

- Highlighting

A Power View report is a special type of Excel worksheet, and you can have many reports in an Excel file. In most cases, users tend to create Power View reports using a Power Pivot data model, but you can also create Power View reports using data tables in an Excel worksheet if you prefer. However (at the risk of belaboring the point), an in-memory data set can be tweaked to make Power View reports much easier to create and modify than can a table in Excel.

Power View is discussed in Chapters 2 through 8.

3D Maps

3D Maps is, as its name implies, a mapping tool. As long as your data contains some form of geographical data and you can connect to Bing Maps, you can use 3D Maps to create geographical representations of the data.

The types of presentation that you can create with 3D Maps include the following:

- Maps

- Automatic presentations of geographical data

- Time-based representations of geographical data

As is the case with Power View, 3D Maps is at its best when you use the data in an in-memory data set. However, you can use data in Excel if you prefer.

3D Maps is discussed in Chapter 9.

The Power BI Service

The Power BI service is a cloud-based data-sharing environment. Power BI leverages existing Excel 2016 Power Pivot, Get and Transform, and Power View functionality and adds new features that allow you to do the following:

- Share presentations and queries with your colleagues.

- Update your Excel file from data sources that can be onsite or in the cloud.

- Display the output on multiple devices. This includes PCs, tablets, and HTML5-enabled mobile devices as well as Windows tablets that use the Power BI app.

- Query your data using natural language processing (or Q&A, as it is known).

How Excel 2016 leverages the Power BI service is discussed in Chapter 18.

Preparing the Excel BI Toolkit

Before you can begin to use the Excel BI Toolkit, you need to make sure that your PC is set up correctly and that everything is in place. This is not difficult, but it is probably less frustrating if you get everything set up correctly before you leap into the fray rather than get annoyed if things do not work flawlessly the first time. If you are working in a corporate environment where these add-ins are the norm, then all your problems are probably solved already. If not, you might have a few tweaks to perform. So, let's see how to ensure that your version of Excel is ready to fly with self-service BI.

However, before ensuring that Excel is configured correctly, you need to know that not all aspects of the Excel BI Toolkit are available with all versions of Excel. At the time of writing, Microsoft has split the available tools as follows:

- Basic business analytics features are available in Office 365 and Office 2016.

- All business analytics features are available in Office 365 ProPlus, Office 2016 Professional Office 2016 Professional Plus, and Excel 2016 Standalone.

Table 1-1 shows which features are currently available across the Excel 2016 product line.

Table 1-1. *Excel Business Analytics Feature Availability*

Feature	Office 365 or Office 2016	Office 365 ProPlus, Office 2016 Professional, Office 2016 Professional Plus, and Excel 2016 Standalone
3D Maps	X	X
Import data with Get and Transform from CSV, text, Excel, Access, SQL Server, Analysis Services, the Web, oData, ODBC, and Facebook	X	X
Import data with Get and Transform from Oracle, Teradata, DB2, MySQL, PostgreSQL, SharePoint, Azure, Hadoop, Dynamics CRM, and SharePoint (and more)		X
Transform data with Get and Transform	X	X
Basic data model support	X	
Power Pivot		X
DAX measure creation	X	
DAX calculated columns		X
Create KPIs in the data model		X
Create hierarchies in the data model		X
Power View		X
Search and share Get and Transform queries		X

Enabling the Excel BI Toolkit

Assuming that you have a version of Excel that allows access to all the components that make up the Excel BI Toolkit, the first thing to do is to ensure that these components are enabled.

To do this, follow these steps:

1. In the File menu, click Options.

2. Click Add-Ins on the bottom of the menu on the left. The Excel Options dialog will look like Figure 1-2.

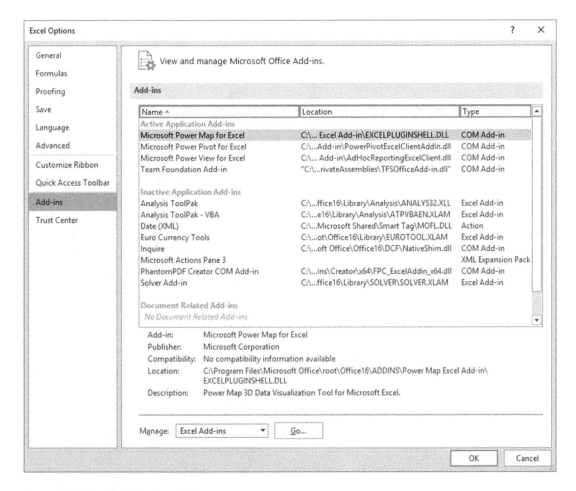

Figure 1-2. *The Excel Options dialog*

3. In the Manage pop-up list, select COM Add-ins.

4. Click Go. The COM Add-ins dialog will appear, as shown in Figure 1-3.

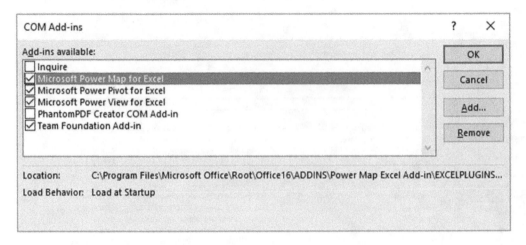

Figure 1-3. *The COM Add-ins dialog*

5. Select the following check boxes:

   a. Microsoft Power Pivot for Excel

   b. Microsoft Power Map for Excel (this is the old name for 3D Maps)

   c. Microsoft Power View for Excel

6. Click OK.

The Power Pivot menu and ribbon should now be available in Excel. Also, you will be able to see the 3D Map button in the Insert ribbon.

■ **Note**   Depending on your exact configuration of Excel, you may see more or fewer add-ins displayed in the COM Add-ins dialog on your PC.

Power View

Power View is an integral part of Excel. However, it is not immediately accessible even if you have enabled it. So, you will have to follow these steps to make Power View easy to access:

1. In Excel, click File ➤ Options. The Excel Options dialog will open, as shown in Figure 1-4.

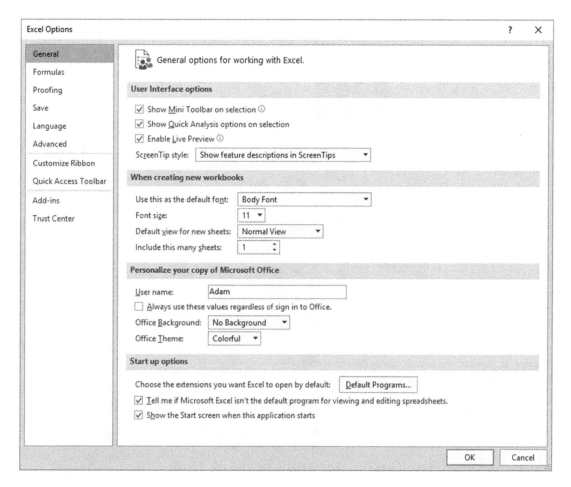

Figure 1-4. *The Excel Options dialog*

2. Click Customize Ribbon in the left pane.

3. In the Main Tabs section on the right, expand the Insert hierarchy.

4. Click the bottom item of those available in the Insert hierarchy.

5. Click the New Group button. A new empty group will be added to the list.

6. Click Rename.

7. Change the display name to **Power View**.

8. Select a symbol from those available in the dialog. The Rename dialog will look like the one shown in Figure 1-5.

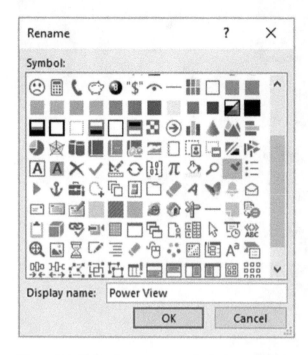

Figure 1-5. *Renaming a new group in the Insert ribbon*

9. Click OK.

10. In the list on the left of the Customize the Ribbon dialog, select commands not in the ribbon from the Choose Commands From pop-up.

11. Scroll down the list and select Insert A Power View Report.

12. Drag Insert A Power View Report over the new Power View group that you created in step 5.

13. Click OK.

Now, if you open Excel and activate the Insert ribbon, you will see the Power View button, as shown in Figure 1-6.

Figure 1-6. *The Power View button in the Excel Insert ribbon*

Get and Transform

Get and Transform is now an integral part of Excel 2016. You should therefore see the group that is displayed in Figure 1-7 in the Excel 2016 Data ribbon.

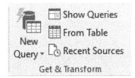

Figure 1-7. *The Get and Transform group in the Excel Data ribbon*

3D Maps

As of Microsoft Office 2016, 3D Maps is now an integral part of Excel. If you have 3D Maps already installed, you will have an active Map button in the Excel Insert ribbon, as shown in Figure 1-8.

Figure 1-8. *The 3D Maps button in the Excel Insert ribbon*

Corporate BI or Self-Service BI?

This book is all about self-service business intelligence. Although this concept stands in opposition to corporate business intelligence, the two interact and relate. However, the distinctions are not only blurred, they are evolving along continually changing lines.

In any case, I do not want to describe these two approaches as if they are mutually antagonistic. They are both in the service of the enterprise, and both exist to provide timely analysis. The two can, and should, work together as much as possible. After all, much self-service business intelligence needs corporate data, which is often the result of many months (or years) of careful thought and intricate data processing and cleansing. So, it is really not worth rejecting all that a corporate IT department can provide for avid users of self-service BI. At the same time, the speed at which a purely self-service approach can deliver rapid discovery, analysis, and presentation can relieve hard-pressed IT departments from the kind of ad hoc jobs that distract from larger projects. Therefore, it pays for central IT to see self-service BI as a friend and for users to appreciate all the support and assistance that an IT department can provide.

Self-service business intelligence, then, is part of an equation. It is not a total solution—and neither is it a panacea. Anarchic implementation of self-service BI can lead to massive data duplication and so many versions of "the truth" that all facts become mere opinions. Consequently, I advise a measured response. When managers, users, or, heaven forbid, external consultants announce in tones of hyperactive excitement that Microsoft has produced a new miracle-working solution to replace all your existing BI solutions, I suggest you take a step backward and a deep calming breath. I would never imply that you use Power VIew to replace "canned" corporate reports, for instance (to solve this requirement, see *Business Intelligence with SQL Server Reporting Services* [Apress, 2015] by Adam Aspin). Yet, if you need interactive reports based on volatile and varied data sources, then the Excel BI Toolkit and Power View could be a perfect solution.

The Excel Data Model

When introducing Power Pivot toward the start of this chapter, I made a passing reference to the Excel data model. As this is fundamental to the practice of self-service BI using Excel 2016, you really need to understand what this data model is and how it helps you to create valid analyses.

The data model is a collection of one or more tables of data that are loaded into the Excel in-memory data model and then joined together in a coherent fashion using Power Pivot. The data can come via Get and Transform, be obtained from existing Excel tables or worksheets, or be imported from a variety of sources. There can be only a single data model for an Excel file.

Admittedly, you can place all your data in a single "flat" table in Excel and use that as the basis for Power View reports and 3D Maps output. However, it is highly likely that you will want to develop a data model using Power Pivot if you intend to use data sets of any complexity. There are occasions when building a good data model can take a while to get right, but there are many valid justifications for spending the time required to build a coherent data model using Power Pivot. The reasons for this investment include the following:

- You can go way beyond the million-row limit of an Excel worksheet if you are using the Excel data model in Power Pivot. Indeed, in Power Pivot, tables of tens of millions of rows are not unknown.

- A coherent data model makes understanding and visualizing your data easier.

- A well-thought-out data model means less redundant information stored in a single table when it can be referenced from another table rather than repeated endlessly.

- The data model saves space on disk and in memory because it uses a highly efficient data compression algorithm to store the data set. This means that a workbook using a data set will take up considerably less space than storing data in Excel worksheets.

- Since a data set is loaded entirely into the PC's memory, calculations are faster.

- A data model can be prepared for data output. More specifically, you can apply formatting and define data types (such as geographical types, for instance) for specific columns so that Power View and 3D Maps will recognize them instantly and make the correct deductions as to the best ways to use them.

- A data model can contain certain calculations (some of which can get fairly complex) that are designed to ensure that the correct results are returned when slicing and filtering data in Power View and 3D Maps.

- A data model can contain hierarchies and KPIs.

- A data model can be used to create complex pivot tables in Excel if you do not want to use Power View or 3D Maps.

- A data model can be the basis, or the proof of concept, for a fully fledged SQL Server Analysis Services (SSAS) tabular data warehouse.

As an example of a data set, this book will use a simple model that uses the sales data for an imaginary company that sells classic and modern British sports cars throughout Europe and that is starting to expand into the United States. This fictitious corporation is called Brilliant British Cars, and it has been going for a couple of years. Their data is relatively simple, and you can see the data model for the company in Figure 1-9.

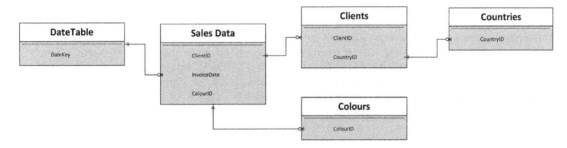

Figure 1-9. *The Excel data model used by Brilliant British Cars*

The art and science of developing data models could easily be the subject of a separate tome. It is, in fact, not unrelated to basic relational database design, which has been described exhaustively in dozens (or hundreds) of books over the last couple of decades. As a reader, you can breathe a sigh of relief as I have no intention of attempting to cover this subject in this book. As far as this sample data model is concerned, I will just take it as is and suggest that you consult one of the many excellent resources already available should you need further guidance when developing your own specific data model.

Throughout this book I will be using the established best practice, which is to use the Excel data model as the basis for self-service BI. However, as I remarked earlier, you can use plain old Excel tables as a source of data for both Power View reports and 3D Maps deliverables if you want.

How This Book Is Designed to Be Read

The suite of technologies that makes up the Microsoft self-service business intelligence offering essentially consists of independent products. It follows that you may need to focus on only one or two of them to solve a particular problem. Or it may be that you already know how to use part of the toolset but need to learn, or revise, other elements.

Because we are looking at a set of tools, each of which can be learned individually, this book is not designed to be read *only* in a linear fashion. Given that the primary focus of this text is on delivering output that has the "wow" factor, it begins with Power View to show what can be done with the new presentation tool that is now integrated into Excel.

The chapters on Power View, however, do not presume any knowledge of how to assemble or develop an underlying data set. Their aim is to get you up and running with interactive presentations as fast as possible. Nevertheless, it is likely that you will one day need a data model to use as the basis for your reports. So, after the chapters on Power View, you learn how to use Power Pivot to create data sets and get them ready to be the bedrock of your Power View deliverables.

Frequently Power Pivot is all you need to connect to source data. Yet sometimes you need something more advanced to load and prepare data from multiple varied sources. If this is the case, you can learn how to perform these tasks using Get and Transform.

You can then see all that 3D Maps can do for you in a single chapter and learn, in the final chapter, how to pull it all together by sharing your data and insights with the Power BI service.

There are, however, other possible reading paths, if you prefer. So, depending on your requirements, you may want to try one of the following approaches.

Discovering Data

If your primary focus is on discovering data and then preparing it for later use—that is, you need to load, mash up, rationalize, and cleanse data from multiple diverse sources—then Chapters 10 through 13, which introduce Get and Transform, should be your first port of call. Chapter 13 explains how to connect to many of the data sources that Get and Transform can read. Chapter 11 gives you a thorough grounding in how to transform source data to make it coherent and usable by Power Pivot as part of a logical data set. Chapter 12 introduces key data cleansing techniques, and Chapter 13 explains how to "mash up" your data into accessible structures.

Creating a Data Model

Conversely, if the source data that you are using is already clean and accessible, then you may be more interested in learning how to create a valid and efficient data model that is clean and comprehensible and contains all the calculations that you need for your presentations. In this case, you should start by reading Chapter 14.

Taking Data and Preparing It for Output

If you are faced with the task of finding, cleansing, and modeling data that is ready to be used for reporting, then you will probably need to use both Get and Transform and Power Pivot. If this is the case, you may be best served by reading Chapters 10 through 13 on Get and Transform (to import and shape the source data) and then Chapters 14 on Power Pivot (to model the data).

Delivering Geodata

It is not just tables and charts that create the "Eureka!" moment. Sometimes an insight can come from seeing how data is dispersed geographically or how geographic data evolves over time. If this is what you are looking for, then you need to look at Chapter 8 (which covers maps in Power View) and at Chapter 9 (which covers 3D Maps) to learn how these two tools can create and deliver new insights into your data.

Taking Existing Excel BI and Sharing It

You may well be a Power Pivot expert already and have possibly learned to use Power View in its initial incarnation as part of SharePoint. If this describes your situation, you may want to move straight to the part where you learn to share your reports in the cloud. This means that Chapter 18 on the Power BI service is for you. Here you will learn how best to load and share Excel BI workbooks and Get and Transform queries as well as how to update workbooks in the cloud with the latest data from on-premises data sources.

Delivering Excel BI to Mobile Devices

If you need to ensure that you and your colleagues can access their data on mobile devices, then Chapter 18 on Power BI is the one for you. Here you will see how to use the Power BI app on a Windows tablet, as well as how to use Power View on many other mobile devices.

Learning the Product Suite Following a Real-World Path

If you are coming to self-service BI as a complete novice, then one way to learn it is by taking the path that you would need to follow in a real-world situation. If this suits you, then you could try reading the entire book, but in this order:

- *Discover and prepare data*: Start with Chapters 10 to 13 on Get and Transform.

- *Create a data model*: Next, read Chapter 14 on Power Pivot.

- *Extend a data model using DAX*: Look at Chapters 15 through 17 that introduce DAX.

- *Create visualizations*: Continue with Chapters 2–7 on Power View.

- *Add geodata outputs*: Move on to Chapter 8 and Chapter 9, which cover maps in Power View and 3D Maps.

- *Share Excel with Power BI*: Finish with Chapter 18 and learn how to integrate Excel 2016 with the Power BI service.

Anyway, these proposed reading paths are only suggestions. Each chapter is designed to cover a complete aspect of self-service BI in as thorough a fashion as possible. Feel free to jump in and pick and choose the path that best suits you.

Conclusion

Microsoft self-service business intelligence using the 2016 Excel BI Toolkit, then, is not an application but a suite of tools and technologies that allow you to find, import, join, and structure data that you then extend with any necessary calculations; you then use this data as the basis for interactive presentations that you can subsequently share in the cloud and access using a variety of devices.

More precisely, you will be using a set of Excel tools and possibly a cloud-based subscription service to create and share data and high-impact analyses with your colleagues. The output can be viewed using a PC or a mobile device and can allow your public to select and filter the reports to discover their own insights.

In any case, that is enough of a preamble. The best way to learn any instrument is to practice using it. So, it is time for you to move on to the chapters that interest you and start your journey into the wonderful world of self-service business intelligence.

CHAPTER 2

Power View and Tables

Welcome to Power View! This chapter, along with the next six, aims to give you a comprehensive introduction to Microsoft's presentation and analysis tool for Excel. You will learn how to use this to do the following:

- Delve deep into data and produce valuable information from the mass of facts and figures you have available

- Create interactive views of your insights, where you can test your analyses quickly and easily

- Enhance the presentation of your results to grab your audience's attention

Power View may be easy to use, but it can present your insights in many and varied ways. So, to provide some structure, I have decided on an approach that mimics the analysis and presentation process (for many of us, at least). As data analysis often begins with a look at the data itself, presenting the facts will be the immediate focus. More precisely, you will learn the following in this chapter:

- How to use the Power View interface.

- How to create and enhance tabular visualizations of your data. This covers simple lists and more advanced matrix-style tables.

- How to drill down into your tables to dig into the meaning of the numbers.

- How to use cards as a new and innovative way to display facts and figures.

- How to display tabular key performance indicators (KPIs).

I realize that it may seem contradictory to spend time on things that are generally described as intuitive. I can only say to this that while getting up and running is easy, attaining an in-depth understanding of all the potential of this powerful tool does require some explanation. The approach in this book is to go through all the possibilities of each aspect being handled as thoroughly as possible. So, feel free to jump ahead (and back) if you don't need all the details just yet.

In the chapters on Power View, I will be using a set of data from an Excel data model. This data is in the sample Excel worksheet CarSales.xlsx in the directory C:\DataVisualisationInExcel2016 (assuming that you have followed the instructions in Appendix A). As I explained in Chapter 1, accessing the right source data and ensuring that this data is coherent and in a valid data model are vital tasks for successful self-service business intelligence. However, I feel that preparing the data is a separate (although clearly related) subject, so I will be treating it separately in Chapters 9, 10, 11, and 12. For the moment I want to concentrate on all that Power View has to offer, so I will use this sample data set as a basis for all the data visualizations that you will learn to produce in the next few chapters.

© Adam Aspin 2016

A. Aspin, *High Impact Data Visualization in Excel with Power View, 3D Maps, Get & Transform and Power BI*, DOI 10.1007/978-1-4842-2400-7_2

As Power View is now a core part of Excel, I will assume you have some basic Excel knowledge. You do not need to be an Excel maestro by any stretch of the imagination, however. Indeed, one of the major aspects of Power View is that it really is highly intuitive and requires only basic familiarity with its host application.

Anyway, that is enough said to set out the ground rules. It is time to get started. So, on to Power View.

The Power View Experience

I realize that you probably just want to start creating punchy presentations straightaway. Well, that is fair enough. Feel free to jump ahead to the next section if you can't wait. However, if you are the sort of person who prefers to have concepts and terms explained first, then this section will describe the Power View interface so you know what is available, what it does, and, possibly most important of all, what everything is called. Of course, you can always refer to this section at a later time, whatever your approach to learning Power View.

Adding a Power View Sheet to an Excel Workbook

Assuming you have launched Excel and that Power View is enabled (as described in Chapter 1), then this is how you start using Power View:

1. Open the CarSales.xlsx sample workbook (or any workbook where you have prepared a data model).

2. Click Insert to activate the Insert ribbon.

3. Click Power View (assuming you have customized the ribbon as I described in Chapter 1).

You will find yourself face to face with an empty Power View report.

The Power View Interface

The Power View interface—as with everything about it—is designed for simplicity so that you can use it almost instantaneously rather than learn how to use it. However, as you can see, being simple does not make it austere. Essentially, you are looking at four main elements, as illustrated in Figure 2-1:

- The *Power View report* (where most things happen) in the center of the screen.

- The *Filters area*, to the right of the Power View report. This lets you select the data that will appear in the report and even in specific parts of the report.

- The *field list*, at the right of the screen. Here you will see all the available data for your report and any data that you're using for a selected visualization.

- Finally—not to say inevitably—the *Power View ribbon*, at the top of the screen.

Figure 2-1. *The Power View interface*

Now that you have an overall feeling for the Power View interface, two initial aspects need some further explanation: the ribbon and the field list.

The Power View Ribbon

The Power View ribbon is something that you will be seeing a lot of, so it is probably worth getting to know it sooner rather than later. Table 2-1 describes the buttons in the Power View ribbon. Don't worry, I will not be explaining what each one can do in detail straightaway, as I prefer to let you see how they can be used in the context of certain operations; you will see what each one can do over the course of the next few chapters.

Table 2-1. *Buttons Available in the Power View Ribbon*

Button	Description
Paste	Pastes a copied element from the clipboard
Cut	Removes the selected element and places it in the clipboard
Copy	Copies the selected element and places it in the clipboard
Undo	Undoes the last action
Redo	Undoes the last undo action
Themes	Lets you select a theme (color palette and font) for your report
Font	Lets you choose a font from the pop-up menu of those available
Text Size	Allows you to set a text size percentage
Background	Displays a selection of backgrounds to add to the report
Set Image	Lets you insert a background image into your report
Image Position	Lets you alter the dimensions of the background image in the report
Transparency	Sets the transparency of an image

(*continued*)

Table 2-1. (*continued*)

Button	Description
Refresh	Refreshes the source data for a Power View report
Relationships	Enables you to add, modify, or delete joins between source data tables
Fit To Window	Fits the report to the screen window
Field List	Displays or hides the list of data fields
Filters Area	Displays or hides the Filter area
Power View	Inserts a new, blank Power View report
Text Box	Adds a free-form text box to the report
Picture	Lets you add a free-form image into the report
Arrange	Allows you to alter the way in which objects are placed on top of each other in the report

Figure 2-2 shows you how the buttons are grouped in the Power View ribbon.

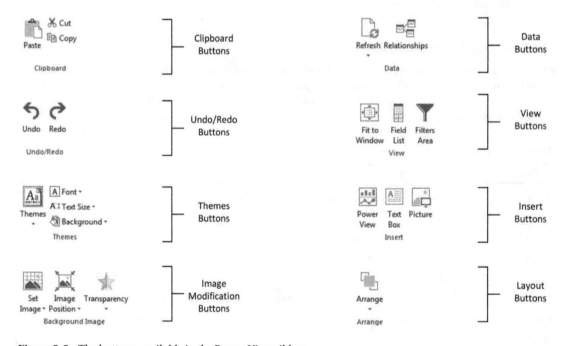

Figure 2-2. *The buttons available in the Power View ribbon*

The Power View ribbon can be minimized just like any other Microsoft Office ribbon to increase the screen space available for report creation. To hide the ribbon, do the following:

1.   Click the Minimize icon (the small upward-facing caret at the bottom right of the ribbon).

Once the Power View ribbon has been minimized, all Excel ribbons are minimized. You can, however, make a ribbon reappear temporarily by clicking the ribbon name in the menu bar at the top of the Excel application. Once you have finished with a ribbon option, the ribbon will be minimized once more.

To make the ribbon reappear permanently, just click the small pin icon that has replaced the initial caret at the bottom right of any ribbon.

The Field List

The field list, as I mentioned earlier, is where you can see and select all the fields that contain the data in the underlying data model.

To display the field list, do this:

1.   In the Power View ribbon, click the Field List icon.

The field list will (re)appear to the right of the Power View canvas.

The Field List icon will also hide the field list—it is a simple on/off switch. The field list also has a Close icon, just like a normal window. So, you can hide the field list by clicking the Close button (the small X at the top-right corner of the field list) if you want.

You can also adjust the width of the field list. While the default width is probably suitable in most circumstances, you may want to

- Widen the field list to display particularly long field names

- Narrow the field list to increase the size of the Power View canvas

To resize the field list, do the following:

1.   Place the mouse pointer over the left border of the field list. The cursor will become a two-headed lateral arrow.

2.   Drag the mouse pointer left or right until the field list is the width you want.

Once you have resized the field list, it will remember the size that you set, even if you hide and redisplay it.

Remember that to create any visualization or to modify the data behind an existing visualization, you will need to have the field list visible. My advice is to leave it visible, at least in the initial stages of developing Power View reports.

Using the Field List

The field list is possibly one of the most fundamental parts of Power View. Consequently, it is well worth making its acquaintance earlier rather than later.

Figure 2-3 shows you part of a Power View field list, using the data model from the CarSales.xlsx workbook. Only some of the available data tables are visible, and the layout section may look very different from what you see onscreen. Moreover, the pop-up menus can vary depending on the context of the current operation. However, this figure enables you to get an idea of what the field list has to offer.

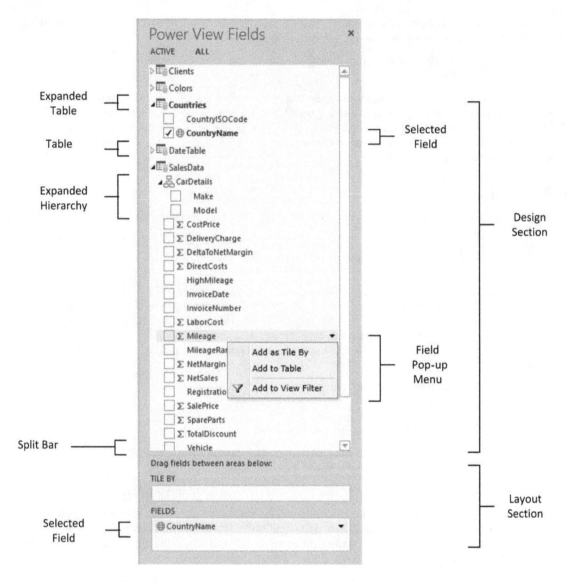

Figure 2-3. *The field list*

The field list is divided into two parts. The upper part (known as the design section) is the available data, displayed as tables that you can expand to view the fields, and possibly any hierarchies that they contain. The lower part is the layout section, which contains any selected fields. The layout section will change considerably depending on which visualization is being used. You can alter the relative sizes of the upper and lower parts of the field list by dragging the split bar up and down.

■ **Note**   You can see whether you are using data from a data table in the current report because the name of the table will be in **bold** in the field list.

Renaming or Deleting a Power View Report

So, you have created a Power View report. This new report has been added as a new Excel sheet, as you can guess from looking at the tabs at the bottom of the screen. This report is now part and parcel of the Excel workbook in which it was created. You can save it with the Excel .xlsx file extension (it cannot be saved independently). A Power View report is an Excel sheet like any other (worksheet, chart, and so on) and can be manipulated like any other sheet. This means it can be hidden, deleted, or renamed using standard Excel techniques. Just in case, here is a quick refresher on deleting or renaming an Excel tab:

1. Right-click the tab at the bottom of the screen.

2. Select Rename (for instance).

3. Enter the new Power View sheet name.

4. Press Enter to confirm.

If you chose to delete the Power View report, then you will see a dialog asking for confirmation that you really want to delete the report.

Tables in Power View

Now that you understand the Power View interface, let's look at getting some data from the data model into a report. I suggest a progression that begins with the simplest type of list first—a standard table. From there I will move on to matrix tables and, finally, cards and KPIs. Tables are an essential starting point for any Power Pivot visualization. Indeed, everything that is based on data (which is to say virtually everything) in Power View starts out as a table. So, it is worth getting to know how tables work—and how to get them into action the fastest possible way.

Let's start with the simplest possible type of table: a list. This is what you could well find yourself using much of the time to create visualizations in your Power View reports.

Adding a Table

Adding a basic table is probably the simplest thing you can do in Power View. After all, a table is the default visualization that Power View will create. So, here is how you can create a table that shows total sales to date by make of car from the sample data set:

1. Display the field list, unless it is already visible.

2. Expand the table containing the field that you want to display (SalesData to begin with). You do this by clicking the hollow triangle to the left of the table name. The triangle becomes a black triangle, and the field names are displayed, slightly indented, underneath the table name.

3. Find the hierarchy named CarDetails and expand this, too, by clicking the triangle to its left. The fields that make up the hierarchy will be displayed.

4. Select the check box to the left of the field name for the first field that you want to display in a table. In this example, this is Make. When you do this, a table containing a list of all the makes of car in the data set appears in the Power View canvas. The field you selected will also appear in the FIELDS well (or box if you prefer) in the layout section (the lower part) of the field list.

5. Repeat steps 2 through 4 for all the fields that you want to display. In this simple example, the SalePrice field will suffice. You will see that any field that you add appears in the existing table.

The table immediately displays the data that is available from the source, and all the new fields appear to the right of any existing fields. If there is a lot of data to display, then a vertical scroll bar appears at the right of the table, allowing you to scroll up and down to view the data. Totals will be added automatically to the bottom of the table—though you may have to scroll down to see them. Figure 2-4 shows the basic list-type table that you created.

Make	SalePrice
Aston Martin	10686040
Bentley	4998000
Jaguar	6319000
MGB	1011000
Rolls Royce	7356900
Triumph	925500
TVR	542750
Total	**31839190**

Figure 2-4. A first table

This is, self-evidently, a tiny table. In the real world, you could be looking at tables that contain thousands, or tens of thousands, of records. Power View accelerates the display of large data sets by only loading the data that is required as you scroll down through a list. So, you might see the scroll bar advance somewhat slowly as you progress downward through a large table.

■ **Note** In this example, I leapt straight into a concept that might be new to you—that of *hierarchies*. These are essentially an organizational technique you can use to help you manage access to data. You will learn how to create them in Chapter 14.

You can always see which fields have been selected for a table either by selecting the table or by clicking inside it. The fields used will be instantly displayed in both the field list (as checked fields) and the FIELDS well in the layout section of the field list. To get you used to this idea, see Figure 2-5, which shows the field list for the table you just created.

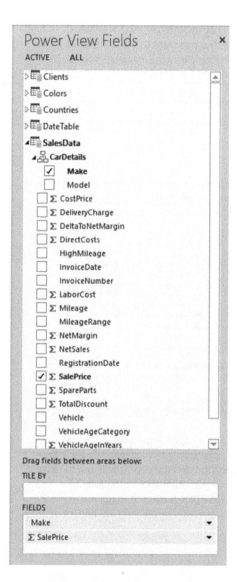

Figure 2-5. *The field list for the table of sales by make*

As befits such a polished product, Power View does not limit you to just one way of adding fields to a table. The following are other ways in which you can add fields to a table:

- By dragging the field name into the Fields section at the bottom of the field list.

- By hovering the mouse pointer over a field in the Fields section (the upper part) of the field list. When you do this, the field is highlighted, and a down-facing triangle appears on the right of the field name. You can then click the down-facing triangle and select Add To Table from the pop-up menu.

You can add further fields to an existing table at any time. The key thing to remember (if you are using the two techniques just described) is that you must select the table that you want to modify first. This is as simple as clicking inside it. After you click, you instantly see that the table is active because tiny handles appear at the corners of the table as well as in the middle of each side of the table.

■ **Note**   If you do not select an existing table before adding a field, Power View will create a new table using the field that you are attempting to add to a table.

To create another table, all you have to do is click outside any existing visualizations in the Power View report and begin selecting fields as described earlier. A new table will be created as a result. Power View will always try to create new tables in an empty part of the canvas. You will see how to rearrange this default presentation shortly.

Deleting a Table

Suppose that you no longer need a table in a Power View report. Well, that is simple; just do the following:

1. Choose the table. You can do this by hovering the pointer over any of the table borders (in practice the left, right, and bottom borders are easiest).

2. Click to select; the table will briefly flash another color, and the borders will remain visible, even if you move the mouse pointer away from the table.

3. Press Delete.

Another way to select a table is to click inside it. This is a bit like selecting a cell in Excel. You will even see the "cell" that you selected appear highlighted.

If you are used to controlling your software through avid use of the right mouse button, then you can also remove a table by right-clicking it. You will not get a Delete menu choice, but you can use the Cut option. This will store the table in the clipboard for later use, leaving it deleted if you choose not to reuse it.

Deleting a table is so easy that you can do it by mistake, so remember that you can restore an accidentally deleted table by pressing Ctrl+Z or clicking the Undo icon (the large left-facing arrow) in the Power View ribbon. And, yes, you guessed it—you can undo an Undo action by clicking the Redo icon (the large right-facing arrow) in the Power View ribbon.

■ **Note**   You will have to return to the Power View ribbon to use the Power View Undo and Redo buttons. Interestingly, the Excel Undo and Redo buttons in the Quick Access toolbar do not work with Power View. Also, you need to be aware that Power View offers significantly fewer levels of undo than standard Excel.

Changing the Table Size and Position

A table can be resized just like any other visualization in a Power View report. All you have to do is to click any of the table handles and drag the mouse.

Moving a table is as easy as placing the pointer over the table so that the edges appear and, once the cursor changes to the hand shape, dragging the table to its new position. You will know that the table is correctly selected as it will be highlighted in its entirety as long as the mouse button is depressed.

Changing Column Order

If you have built a Power View table, you are eventually going to want to modify the order in which the columns appear from left to right. To do this, follow these steps:

1. Activate the field list—unless it is already displayed.

2. In the FIELDS well in the layout section (the lower part) of the field list, click the name of the field (which, after all, is a column in a table) that you want to move.

3. Drag the field vertically to its new position. This can be between existing fields, at the top or at the bottom of the field list. A thick gray line indicates where the field will be positioned. A small right-facing blue arrow icon under the field name tells you that the field can be moved there.

Figure 2-6 shows how to drag a field from one position to another.

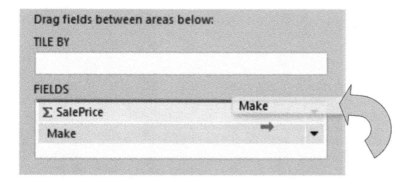

Figure 2-6. *Changing column order by moving fields*

■ **Note**   You cannot change the position of a column in a table by dragging it sideways inside the table itself.

Removing Columns from a Table

Another everyday task in Power View is removing columns from a table when necessary. As is the case when rearranging the order of columns, this is not done directly in the table but is carried out using the field list. There are, in fact, at least five ways of removing columns from a table, so I will begin with the way that I think is the fastest and then describe the others.

1. Activate the field list—unless it is already displayed.

2. Uncheck the field name in the design section of the field list.

The other three ways to remove a field are

- Hover the mouse pointer over the field you want to remove. Click the pop-up menu icon (the downward-facing triangle at the right of the field name) and select Remove Field.

- Drag the field from the FIELDS well back up into the upper area (the design section) of the field list. You will see that the field name is dragged with the mouse pointer and that the pointer becomes an X when you are over the field list. Just release the mouse button to remove the field.

- Click, in the FIELDS well in the lower area (the layout section) of the field list, the name of the field (or column) that you want to remove; then press the Delete key.

Figure 2-7 shows how to remove a field (or column if you prefer) by dragging it out of the layout section of the field list.

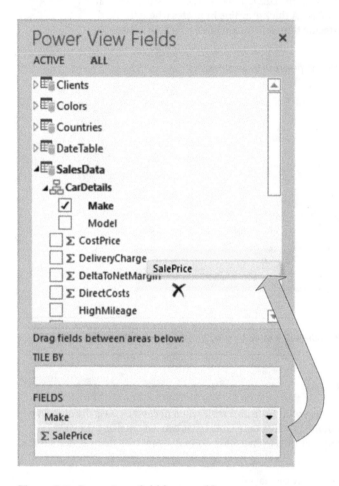

Figure 2-7. *Removing a field from a table*

Types of Data

Not all data is created equal, and the data model that underlies Power View will provide you with different types of data. The initial two data types are

- Descriptive (non-numeric) attributes

- Values (or numeric measures)

Power View indicates the data type by using a descriptive icon beside many of the fields that you can see when you expand a data table in the field list. Table 2-2 describes these data types.

Table 2-2. *Data Types*

Data Type	Icon	Comments
Attribute	None	This is a descriptive element and is non-numeric. It can be counted but not summed or averaged.
Aggregates	Σ	This is a numeric field whose aggregation type can be changed.
Calculation	▦	This is a numeric field whose aggregation type cannot be changed as it is the result of a specific calculation.
Geography	⊕	This field can potentially be used in a map to provide geographical references.
Binary Data	▤	This field contains data such as images.
Hierarchy	▷	This indicates that a hierarchy needs to be expanded to see any fields that it contains.
KPI	▷ 🚦	This indicates a KPI has been defined as the source data.

■ **Note**   Numeric fields are not the only ones that can be added as aggregates. If you add an attribute field by clicking its pop-up triangle in the field list and then selecting Add To Table As Count, you will get the number of elements for this attribute.

Data and Aggregations

When you create a table, Power View will always aggregate the data to the highest possible level. Not only will it do this, but it will add up (sum) the data, if it can, by default. This is not, however, the only possible way to aggregate data in Power View.

Selecting the type of aggregation required is a useful way to fine-tune the final output. As this is done on a column-by-column basis, you will need to do the following:

1. Click inside the column whose aggregation you want to change.

2. Display the pop-up menu for the relevant field name in the Fields section at the bottom of the field list by clicking the small black triangle at the right of the field.

3. Select the type of aggregation you want.

There are seven available aggregation types, as explained in Table 2-3.

Table 2-3. *Data Aggregation Options*

Aggregation Type	Description
Do not Summarize	No aggregation is applied, and every record is displayed.
Sum	The total of the values is displayed.
Average	The average of the values is displayed.
Minimum	The smallest value is shown.
Maximum	The largest value is shown.
Count (Not Blank)	The number of all records/rows/elements is displayed, providing that there is data available.
Count (Distinct)	The number of all unique data elements in the column is returned.

Enhancing Tables

So, you have a basic table set up and it has the columns you want in the correct order. Quite naturally, the next step is to want to spice up the presentation of the table a little. Let's see what Power View has to offer here. Specifically, I will cover the following:

- Adding and removing totals
- Formatting columns of numbers
- Changing columns widths
- Sorting rows by the data in a specific column
- A few other aspects of table formatting

The Design Ribbon

The starting point for modifying the appearance of a table is the Design ribbon. You will be using this much of the time to tweak the presentation of your tables, so it is well worth getting to know. This ribbon will appear whenever a visualization is selected. It is likely to become your first port of call when you are enhancing the look and feel of Power View reports.

Figure 2-8 shows you the buttons in the Design ribbon.

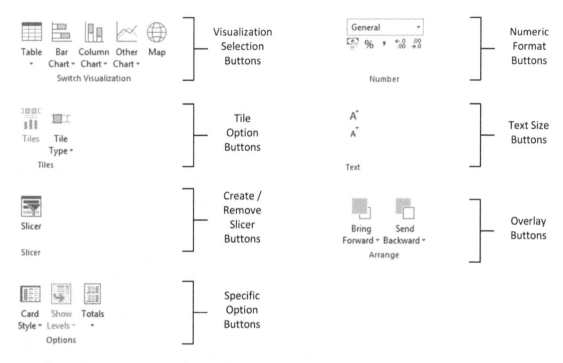

Figure 2-8. *The Design ribbon*

It is not my intention to go through all the options that the Design ribbon offers in detail straightaway. I prefer to explain things as required over the course of the next few chapters. Nonetheless, as a succinct overview (and as a reference, should you require it), Table 2-4 explains the options available in all the Design ribbon buttons.

Table 2-4. *Buttons Available in the Design Ribbon*

Button	Description
Table	Lets you select the table type, including the card type of visualization.
Bar Chart	Converts the visualization to one of the available Bar Chart types.
Column Chart	Converts the visualization to one of the available Column Chart types.
Other Chart	Displays the other available chart types.
Map	Converts the visualization to a map.
Tiles	Adds tiles to a visualization. This is explained in Chapter 6.
Tile Type	Lets you choose the tile type. This is explained in Chapter 6.
Slicer	Adds a slicer to a report. This explained in Chapter 6.
Card Style	Lets you choose the card style. This is explained in Chapter 6.
Show Levels	Lets you switch between grouping and drill-down in a matrix table.
Totals	Shows or hides the totals.
Number Format Selector	Lets you select a number format for a column from the pop-up list of those available.
Currency	Applies the Currency format.
Percentage	Applies the Percentage format.
Thousands Separator	Adds a thousands separator.
Increase Number of Decimal places	Increases the number of decimal places displayed.
Decrease Number of Decimal places	Decreases the number of decimal places displayed.
Increase Text Size	Increases the text size in the selected visualization.
Decrease Text Size	Decreases the text size in the selected visualization
Bring Forward	Brings a visualization, text, image, or other object to the top/front.
Send Backward	Sends a visualization, text, image, or other object to the bottom/back.

Row Totals

Row totals are added automatically to all numeric fields. You may, however, want to remove the totals. Conversely, you could want to add totals that were removed previously. In any case, to remove all the totals from a table, follow these steps:

1. Select the table, or click anywhere inside it. In this example I will use the table you saw earlier in Figure 2-4.

2. Click Totals - None in the ribbon.

To add totals where there are none, merely click Totals - Rows in the Design ribbon (with the table selected). You can see the table you created previously—without totals—in Figure 2-9.

Make	SalePrice
Aston Martin	10686040
Bentley	4998000
Jaguar	6319000
MGB	1011000
Rolls Royce	7356900
Triumph	925500
TVR	542750

Figure 2-9. *The initial table without totals*

■ **Note** You can add or remove totals only if a table displays multiple records. If a table is displaying the highest level of aggregation for a value, then no totals can be displayed, as you are looking at the grand total already. In this case, the Totals button will be grayed out.

Formatting Columns of Numbers

Power View will make an educated guess as to the correct type of numeric formatting to apply to a column of numbers in a table based on the source data type. More specifically, if you have applied a format in an Excel table that has been added to the data model or if you have formatted a column in the data model using PowerPivot, then these formats will be carried into Power View. However, there could well be times when you want to override the formatting that Power View has chosen and apply your own. Once again, this is an extremely intuitive process, which consists of doing the following:

1. Click anywhere in the column you want to reformat—except on the title.

2. Switch to the Design ribbon (unless it is already active).

3. Click one of the available formatting icons (or click the pop-up menu in the Number section of the Design ribbon and select the type of formatting you require).

Power View will apply the formatting to the entire column, including totals if there are any. You can then increase or decrease the number of decimal places displayed by clicking the Increase Decimal places and Decrease Decimal places icons.

■ **Tip** Clicking the Increase Decimal places or Decrease Decimal places icons will apply the Number style if the current style is General. Any other style will remain in force if these icons are clicked—but the number of decimal places will be changed, of course.

You may well be familiar with the available number formatting options, as they are essentially a subset of the Excel formatting options, and you may be extremely well acquainted with this tool already. Alternatively, if you have used PowerPivot, then you could have a strong sense of déjà vu. In the interest of completeness, Table 2-5 describes the available options.

Table 2-5. *Number Formatting Options*

Format Type	Icon	Description	Example
General		Does not apply any uniform formatting and leaves the current number of decimal places in place.	100000.011
Number		Adds a thousands separator and two decimal places. This is also called Comma style.	100,000.01
Currency		Adds a thousands separator and two decimal places as well as the current monetary symbol.	£100,000.01
Accounting		Adds a thousands separator and two decimal places as well as the current monetary symbol at the left of the column.	£ 100,000.01
Percentage		Multiplies by 100, adds two decimal places and prefixes with the percentage symbol.	28.78%
Scientific		Displays the numbers in Scientific format.	1.00E+05
Long Date		Displays a date column as a long date, that is, with the month name in full.	25 July 2014
Short Date		Displays a date column as short date, that is, in figures.	25/07/14
Time		Displays the time part of a date or date/time field.	16:55:01
Increase Decimal places		Adds another decimal place to the display of the figure.	
Decrease Decimal places		Removes a decimal place from the figure's display.	

Default Formatting

Power View will apply the Date, Time, and Currency formats that are set for your PC. For an Excel-based Power View worksheet, you can use Control Panel to set the regional defaults and select the appropriate settings for the Long Date, Short Date, and Time (Short Time) format. Remember the following:

- Altering the Date, Time, and Number formats using Control Panel will take effect only once you close and reopen any open Power View reports.

- Modifying the default Date, Time, and Number formats using Control Panel will affect all applications that use these formats—that is, not just all past and future Power View reports, but many other applications as well.

Changing Column Widths

Power View will automatically set the width of a column so that all the data is visible. Here also, at times you may want to narrow or widen columns to suit the aesthetics of a particular table or report.

To alter the column widths, which is shown in Figure 2-10, follow these steps:

1. Hover the mouse pointer over the column title. The column title will be highlighted.

2. Place the mouse pointer on the right edge of the column. The pointer will become a two-headed sideways arrow.

3. Drag left or right to increase or decrease the column width.

Make	SalePrice
Aston Martin	10686040
Bentley	4998000
Jaguar	6319000
MGB	1011000
Rolls Royce	7356900
Triumph	925500
TVR	542750
Total	**31839190**

Figure 2-10. Altering column width

There are, inevitably, a few points to consider once you start overriding Power View's default column sizing.

- If you widen one or more columns to the point that all the columns of data are not visible in the table, then the horizontal scroll bar will appear at the bottom of the table. Power View will *not* resize the table as you resize a column.

- If you reduce a column's width so that text or numbers will no longer fit, then Power View will add ellipses (…) to indicate that data has been truncated.

- You cannot reduce a column's width to zero and hide the column, as Power View will always leave a narrow sliver of a column (and its contents) visible.

- Double-clicking the right edge of the column will set the column width automatically to the width of the widest element that is currently visible. If there is a wider element further up or down in the data set, then you might have to widen the column again.

- You can, of course, adjust the width of your table to take the new column widths into account by making the table larger; this is done by dragging the left or right lateral handles or the corner handles.

- If you subsequently change the size of the text in a table, then the column widths will not change. You may have to resize certain columns, however, if you think this is required for the general appearance of the report.

- Applying a different theme from the Power View ribbon can apply different fonts to the table and thus cause the column widths to change, as Power View will continue to display the same number of characters per column as were visible using the previous theme. For more information on themes, please see Chapter 7.

Font Sizes in Tables

You may prefer to alter the default font size that Power View applies when a table is first created. Follow these simple steps:

1. Click anywhere inside the table (or select the table).

2. Switch to the Design ribbon if it is not active already.

3. Click the Increase Font Size and Decrease Font Size icons until the table text size suits your requirements.

I really should add these points to conclude the topic of font sizes in tables:

- You cannot select a font size; you can only use the Increase Font Size and Decrease Font Size icons until you have found a size that suits you. My impression is that the available range is from 6 to 36 point.

- Altering the font size can cause the table to grow or shrink, as Power View will continue to display the same number of characters per column as were visible using the previous font size. So, you may end up having to alter the column widths or the table size (as described previously) to make your table look exactly the way you want it.

Copying a Table

You will need to copy tables on many occasions. There could be several reasons for this.

- You are creating a new visualization on the Power View report and need the table as a basis for the new element, such as a chart, for instance.

- You are copying visualizations between reports.

- You want to keep an example of a table and try some fancy tricks on the copy, but you want to keep the old version as a fail-safe option.

In any case, all you have to do is the following:

1. Select the table (as described previously).

2. Right-click and select Copy (or press Ctrl+C).

To paste a copy, click outside any visualization in a current or new Power View report, right-click, and select Paste (or press Ctrl+V).

Sorting by Column

Any column can be used as the sort criterion for a table, whatever the type of table. To sort the table, merely click the column header. Once the rows in the table have been sorted according to the elements in the selected column, a small triangle will appear to the right of the column header to indicate that this column has been used to sort the data, as you can see in Figure 2-11. A downward-facing triangle tells you that the sort order is A to Z (or lowest to highest for numeric values). An upward-facing triangle tells you that the sort order is Z to A (or highest to lowest for numeric values).

Once a table has been sorted, you cannot unsort it. You can, however, use another column to re-sort the data. As an example of sorting a column, look at Figure 2-11 (once again I will use the table you created at the beginning of this chapter).

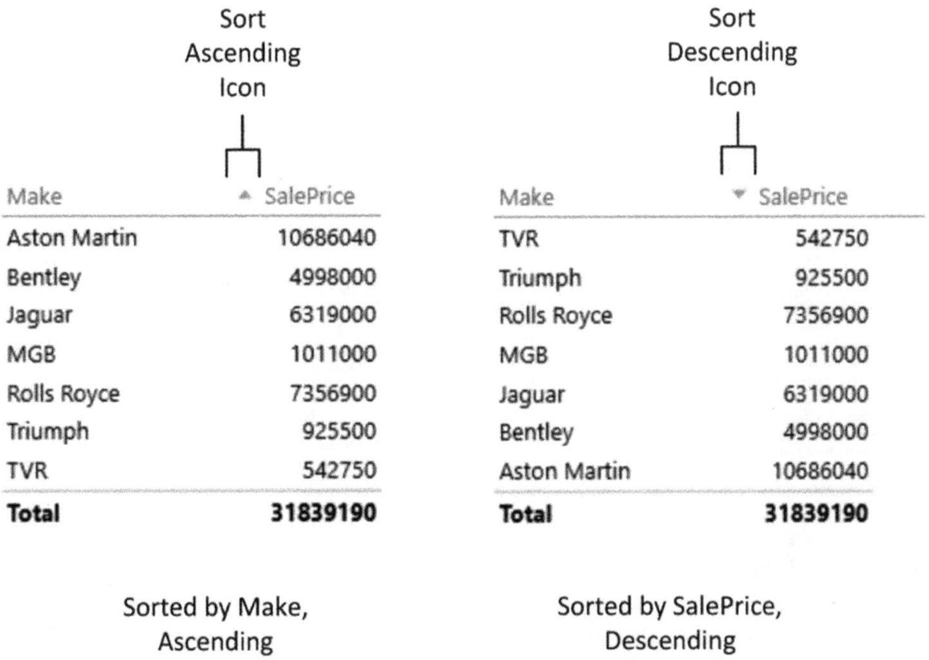

	Sort Ascending Icon			Sort Descending Icon

Make	▲ SalePrice		Make	▼ SalePrice
Aston Martin	10686040		TVR	542750
Bentley	4998000		Triumph	925500
Jaguar	6319000		Rolls Royce	7356900
MGB	1011000		MGB	1011000
Rolls Royce	7356900		Jaguar	6319000
Triumph	925500		Bentley	4998000
TVR	542750		Aston Martin	10686040
Total	**31839190**		**Total**	**31839190**

Sorted by Make,
Ascending

Sorted by SalePrice,
Descending

Figure 2-11. *Sorting a table by column*

Sometimes you are sorting a column on one field (as was the case in all the examples so far), but the actual sort uses another column as the basis for the sort operation. For example, you could sort by month name but see the result by the month number (so that you are not sorting months alphabetically but numerically). You can see how this is set up in Chapter 11.

Table Granularity

A Power View table will automatically aggregate data to the lowest available level of grain. Put simply, this means it is important to select data at the lowest useful level of detail but not to add pointlessly detailed elements.

This is probably easier to understand if I use an example. Suppose you start with a high level of aggregation—the country, for instance. If you create a table with the CountryName and Sales columns, it will give you the total sales by country. If you use the sample data given in the examples for this book (the file CarSales.xlsx on the Apress web site), this table will contain only half a dozen or so lines.

Then add the ClientName after the country. When you do this, you will then obtain a more finely grained set of results, with the aggregate sales for each client in each country. If you (finally) add the InvoiceNumber, you will get an extremely detailed level of data. Indeed, adding such a fine level of grain to your table could produce an extremely large number of records. Figure 2-12 shows this example.

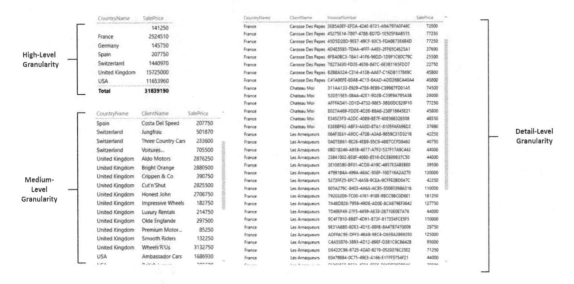

Figure 2-12. *Progressive table granularity*

Power View will always attempt to display the data using the information available to it in the underlying data model. Exactly how this can be optimized for the best possible results is described in Chapter 11.

■ **Note** You can see in the data that some vehicles are not associated with a country. In cases like this, Power View groups all empty (or *null*) elements together and leaves a blank where there is no country.

Matrix Tables

So far in this chapter we have limited ourselves to tables that display the information as full columns of lists, just like the source data in an Excel spreadsheet or database, for instance. Lists, however, do not always give an intuitive feeling for how data should be grouped at various levels. Presenting information in a neat hierarchy with multiple grouped levels is the task of a matrix-type table.

Row Matrix

When creating a matrix table, I find that it helps to think in terms of a hierarchy of information and to try to visualize this information as flowing from left to right. For instance, suppose you want to create a matrix with the country name as the highest level in the hierarchy (and consequently the leftmost item). Then you want the make of car to be the second level and the next element in from the left. (In Figure 2-13, I've labeled this Make.) Finally, you want the color of car sold, followed by all the numeric fields that interest you.

Figure 2-13. *An information hierarchy*

Figure 2-13 shows this hierarchy.

When creating a matrix, it is important to have the field list reflect the hierarchy. Put another way, you must ensure that the order of the fields that you select for the table follows the display hierarchy that you want for the matrix. Consequently, to create a matrix table like the one just described, you will need to do the following:

1. Click outside any existing visualizations (or start with a new Power View report).

2. Add the fields CountryName, Make (from the CarDetails hierarchy), and Color (in this order) to the field selection. (Remember that you can drag them onto the Power View canvas, drag them into the FIELDS well in the layout section at the bottom of the field list, or select them using the pop-up menu for each field.) Then add the fields SalePrice and NetMargin. The table will be very long, but do not worry about that at this point. The table should look something like Figure 2-14.

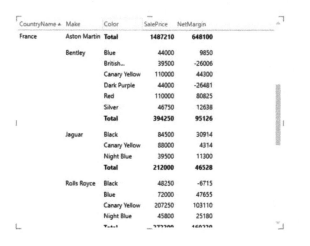

Figure 2-14. *A table before conversion to a matrix*

3. In the ribbon, select Table-Matrix. The layout section of the field list changes to add two new boxes: COLUMNS and ∑ VALUES. The table and the layout section of the field list will now look like those shown in Figure 2-15.

Figure 2-15. *A matrix table*

As you can see, a matrix display not only makes data easier to digest but automatically groups records by each element in the hierarchy and also adds totals. What is more, each level in the hierarchy is sorted in ascending order.

You can also add fields directly to a table by dragging them onto the table. However, you need to remember that Power View will always add a field to the right of existing fields. In a matrix, this means that any aggregate/numeric field will be added to the right of existing aggregate fields (and appear in the Σ VALUES well), whereas any text or date/time fields will be added to the right of any existing hierarchy fields (and appear in the ROWS well). However, it is always a simple matter to reorganize them by dragging the required fields up and down in the ROWS and Σ VALUES wells.

When creating matrix tables, my personal preference is to drag the fields that constitute the hierarchy of non-numeric values into the ROWS well, which means I am placing them accurately above, below, or between any existing elements. This ensures that your matrix looks right the first time, which can help you avoid some very disconcerting double takes!

Column Matrix

Power View does not limit you to adding row-level hierarchies; you can also create column-level hierarchies or mix the two. Suppose you want to get a clear idea of sales and gross margin by country, make, and vehicle type and how they impact one another. To achieve this, I suggest extending the matrix you created previously in the following ways:

- Remove the Color level from the row hierarchy

- Add a VehicleType level as a column hierarchy

Here is how you can do this:

1. Click inside the table that you created previously to select it. The field list will update to display the fields that are used for this table.

2. Drag the Color field from the FIELDS well in the layout section (the lower part of the field list) back up into the upper part of the field list. This will remove it from the table.

3. Drag the VehicleType field down into the COLUMNS well in the layout section of the field list. This will add a hierarchy to the columns in the table. The field list will look like it does in Figure 2-16.

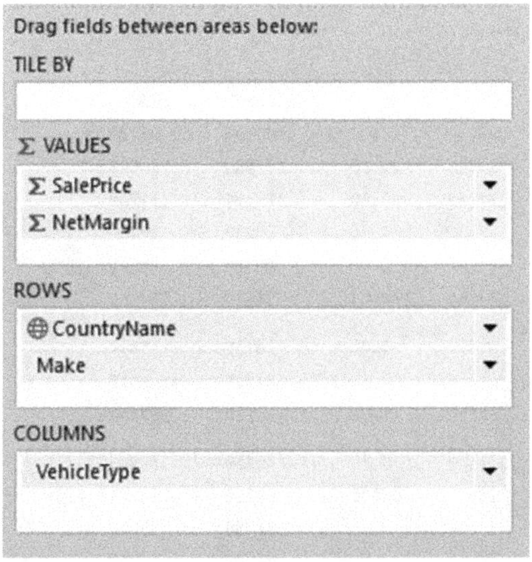

Figure 2-16. *The field list for a row and column matrix table*

The table will now look like the one in Figure 2-17. As you can see, you now have the sales and gross margin by country name, make, and vehicle type, but it is in a cross-matrix, where the data is broken down by both rows and columns.

CountryName ▲	Make	Convertible		Coupe		Saloon		Total	
VehicleType		SalePrice	NetMargin	SalePrice	NetMargin	SalePrice	NetMargin	SalePrice	NetMargin
France	Aston Martin	267570	117870	1219640	530230			1487210	648100
	Bentley			44000	-26481	350250	121607	394250	95126
	Jaguar			86250	25139	125750	21389	212000	46528
	Rolls Royce			77250	38030	296050	131200	373300	169230
	Triumph			28000	4450			28000	4450
	TVR			29750	-8525			29750	-8525
	Total	**267570**	**117870**	**1484890**	**562843**	**772050**	**274196**	**2524510**	**954909**
Germany	Jaguar			32500	-10911	42250	-1000	74750	-11911
	TVR			71000	-5550			71000	-5550
	Total			**103500**	**-16461**	**42250**	**-1000**	**145750**	**-17461**
Spain	Bentley	46750	12969					46750	12969
	Jaguar			29750	-8686	39500	1225	69250	-7461
	Triumph			47750	15875			47750	15875
	TVR			44000	750			44000	750
	Total	**46750**	**12969**	**121500**	**7939**	**39500**	**1225**	**207750**	**22133**
Switzerland	Aston Martin	153500	61695	389670	156830			543170	218525
	Bentley					222750	158068	222750	158068
	Jaguar	120000	81725	39500	-1387	290750	106852	450250	187190
	Rolls Royce			74500	40255	117800	73285	192300	113540
	TVR			32500	-10750			32500	-10750
	Total	**273500**	**143420**	**536170**	**184948**	**631300**	**338205**	**1440970**	**666573**
United...	Aston Martin			4933500	1645357			4933500	1645357
	Bentley	390750	90946	577500	175231	1439500	480355	2407750	746532
	Jaguar			1044250	12669	1717500	301215	2761750	313884

Figure 2-17. *A row and column matrix table*

To conclude the section on creating matrix tables, here are a few things to note:

- If you add totals, then every level of the hierarchy will have totals.

- Adding non-numeric data to the aggregated data will make Power View display the Count aggregation.

- Matrix tables can get very wide, especially if you have a multilevel hierarchy. Power View matrix tables reflect this in the way in which horizontal scrolling works. A matrix table will freeze the nonaggregated data columns on the left and will allow you to scroll to the right to display aggregated (numeric) data.

- Moving the fields in the VALUES well of the field list (using drag and drop as described previously) will reorder the aggregated data columns in the table.

Sorting Data in Matrix Tables

When you sort data in a matrix table, the sort order will respect the matrix hierarchy. This means that if you sort on the second element in a hierarchy (Make, in the example table you just created), then the primary element in the hierarchy (CountryName, the leftmost column) will not be altered, but all the subgroupings by Make for each country will be sorted. This means, in effect, that you can carry out multiple sort operations, by sorting on several columns, and in any order. The net result will be independent sorts on multiple elements.

As an example of this, look at Figure 2-18, which is based on the matrix table displayed in Figure 2-15. Here I sorted on make, country name, and color. Power View even indicates that there was a multiple sort operation by displaying the sort triangles to the right of all the fields. CountryName and Make are sorted in ascending order and Color in descending order.

CountryName ▲	Make ▲	Color ▼	SalePrice	NetMargin	
France	Aston Martin	Silver	155380	74315	
		Red	450300	300360	
		Night Blue	165600	14425	
		Green	108990	24925	
		Canary Yellow	284440	90395	
		British Racing Green	181250	48355	
		Blue	141250	95325	
		Total	**1487210**	**648100**	
	Bentley	Silver	46750	12638	
		Red	110000	80825	
		Dark Purple	44000	-26481	
		Canary Yellow	110000	44300	
		British Racing Green	39500	-26006	
		Blue	44000	9850	
		Total	**394250**	**95126**	
	Jaguar	Night Blue	39500	11300	
		Canary Yellow	88000	4314	

Figure 2-18. *Sorted matrix table*

If you sort by an aggregate figure, then the total for the highest level of the hierarchy will be used to reorder the whole table. You can see this in Figure 2-19, where the matrix from the previous figure has been sorted on gross margin in descending order. This has made the best-selling country move to the top of the table. As well, if you have a column matrix (as in this example), then you must sort on the grand total of the columns (the two rightmost columns in this example) to make the matrix sort by numeric values.

CountryName	Make	Color	SalePrice	NetMargin ▼
United Kingdom	Rolls Royce	Red	1118750	530702
		Silver	685000	352382
		British Racing Green	830250	298317
		Black	521750	234720
		Dark Purple	359750	199087
		Green	401500	80506
		Blue	310750	62751
		Canary Yellow	92000	25450
	Aston Martin	Blue	858250	459008
		Dark Purple	582500	300896
		Silver	670250	242987
		Red	732500	205512
		Green	251750	118207
		Black	665250	101973
		British Racing Green	288500	82877
		Canary Yellow	438250	75346
		Night Blue	446250	58551
	Bentley	Red	508000	208135
		Green	222750	159700
		Canary Yellow	629750	149966
		Night Blue	404250	141389
		British Racing Green	152250	51737
		Blue	167000	42790
		Dark Purple	233000	38052
		Black	90750	-45237

Figure 2-19. *Matrix table sorted by value*

Drilling Through with Matrix Tables

By default a matrix table will show all the levels in the hierarchy of information that you have selected. With smaller data sets there is not usually a problem in displaying and finding the records that interest you. However, with larger data sets (or if you want to isolate a subset of data to drive a point home), you may prefer not to display all the levels at once but to drill down, level by level, until you reach the figures that interest you.

A drill-down approach can be particularly useful with large and complex data sets. As an extension to matrix tables, it can avoid having to display too many columns at once, which makes the table easier to view (and consequently easier to scroll through). Using drill-down matrix tables, you can display only one key column at a time with all the correctly aggregated data visible for each level of information.

Drilling Down

To switch from the default overall view of the grouping hierarchy and then drill down through the data, follow these steps:

1. Click Show Levels in the Design ribbon and select Rows - Enable Drill-Down One Level At A Time. The matrix will hide all but the first grouping level (the leftmost column, CountryName) in the hierarchy. If you take the matrix table you saw in Figure 2-15 as a basis for this, you will now see a drill-down table like the one in Figure 2-20.

CountryName	SalePrice	NetMargin ▼
United Kingdom	15725000	5060288
USA	11653960	3556075
France	2524510	954909
Switzerland	1440970	666573
	141250	35919
Spain	207750	22133
Germany	145750	-17461

Figure 2-20. *The topmost level of a drill-down matrix table*

2. Double-click an element (the United Kingdom in this example), and the next level down in the hierarchy (Make) will be displayed, as in Figure 2-21. This was, if you remember, the second column in the matrix.

Drill-Down
Arrow

Make	SalePrice	NetMargin ▼
Rolls Royce	4319750	1783915
Aston Martin	4933500	1645357
Bentley	2407750	746532
MGB	663000	438750
Jaguar	2761750	313884
Triumph	530250	152600
TVR	109000	-20750

Figure 2-21. *The second level of a drill-down table*

3. To drill down to the next level (if there is one), double-click an element of the current grouping level, and so on, until the lowest level is reached. Figure 2-22 shows the lowest level for Aston Martin—the color of the cars sold. This was the third column from the left in the original matrix.

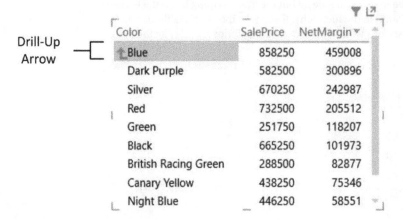

Figure 2-22. *The final level of drill-down in a matrix table*

■ **Tip** The easy way to see whether there are further drill-down levels available is to click any descriptive element in the leftmost column of the table. If Power View displays a downward-facing arrow to the right of the selected element, then you can continue drilling down into the data. Power View will indicate when no further drill-down is possible by not displaying the downward-facing arrow when you click an element at the lowest available level.

You can continue drilling down through a grouping hierarchy until you have reached the lowest available level. You can drill down in a hierarchy without double-clicking if you prefer. The alternative solution is as follows (assuming that you have already enabled drill-down):

1. Click any non-numeric element in the drill-down table. A small downward-facing arrow appears at the right of the selected element.

2. Click the downward-facing arrow.

You can see an example of an element in a table, just before clicking the downward-facing arrow in the earlier Figure 2-21.

Drilling Up

Drilling back up through a hierarchy is as easy as clicking the upward-facing arrow that appears at the top of the column of data on the left of the table. Power View will move up to the previous level of data in the hierarchy.

You can see the drill-up arrow earlier in Figure 2-22.

Reapplying Matrix Visualization

To switch back to the default view of all the hierarchy of grouping levels, follow these steps:

1. Click Show Levels in the ribbon and select Rows - Show All Grouping Levels At Once.

2. The drill-down table will revert to a matrix table. All the columns in the table will be visible once more.

Drilling Through with Column Hierarchies

Drill-through is not limited to rows. It can also be applied to columns either together with row-based drill-through or on its own.

I prefer to use different data to show you a table that will use row-based drill-through and column-based drill-through together. This will also serve as a revision of the matrix and drill-through possibilities that Power View offers. So, here are the steps:

1. Add a new Power View report by clicking the Power View button in the Power View ribbon.

2. Create a table based on the following fields, and in this order:

   a. CountryName

   b. Color

   c. VehicleType

   d. VehicleAgeCategory

   e. SpareParts

3. Convert the table to a matrix by selecting Matrix from the Table button in the Design ribbon.

4. Drag the fields VehicleType and VehicleAgeCategory from the ROWS well to the COLUMNS well in the layout section of the field list. You now have a column-based matrix to extend the row matrix.

5. Add a Matrix filter to allow only data for 2014.

6. Select Both Groups from the Totals button in the Design ribbon. The table should look like Figure 2-23, after a little bit of resizing and aesthetic adjustment.

CountryName	Color	Conv 6-10	Conv >30	Conv Total	Coupe 6-10	Coupe 11-15	Coupe 16-20	Coupe 21-25	Coupe >30	Coupe Total	Saloon 6-10	Saloon 16-20	Saloon 26-30	Saloon >30	Saloon Total	Total
France	Black											1950			1950	1950
	Night Blue							750		750						750
	Red						900			900						900
	Silver										1950				1950	1950
	Total						900	750		1650	1950	1950			3900	5550
Switzerland	British Racing Green										2570	1950			4520	4520
	Canary Yellow											2570			2570	2570
	Total										2570	4520			7090	7090
United...	Black					600				600						600
	Blue				600				900	1500	2570		85		2655	4155
	British Racing Green											2570		4000	6570	6570
	Canary Yellow	2570	2570	4520			3900		750	9170	4520	1950			6470	18210
	Dark Purple						2570		900	3470						3470
	Green						1950			1950	3320				3320	5270
	Red										5140				5140	5140
	Silver							750	600	1350				3000	3000	4350
	Total	2570	2570	5120	600		8420	750	3150	18040	15550	4520	85	7000	27155	47765
USA	Black					600				600	3900	1950			5850	6450
	Blue				600				900	1500	2570	5140	85		7795	9295
	British Racing Green										2570	4520		4000	11090	11090
	Canary Yellow	2570	895	3465	4520		3900		750	9170	4520	4520			9040	21675
	Dark Purple						6470		900	7370						7370
	Green						1950			1950	3320				3320	5270
	Night Blue							750		750						750
	Red							900	3900	4800	5140				5140	9940

Figure 2-23. *A column and row matrix table*

7. Click Show Levels in the Design ribbon and select Rows - Enable Drill-Down One Level At A Time.

8. Click Show Levels in the Design ribbon and select Columns - Enable Drill-Down One Level At A Time.

You now have a table where you can drill down both by column and by row. It should look like the one in Figure 2-24.

CountryName	Convertible	Coupe	Saloon	Total
France		1650	3900	**5550**
Switzerland			7090	**7090**
United Kingdom	2570	18040	27155	**47765**
USA	3465	27490	47185	**78140**
Total	6035	47180	85330	**138545**

Figure 2-24. *A matrix table ready for row and column drill-down*

Now if you double-click any row or column header, you will drill down to the next level in the corresponding hierarchy. Figure 2-25 shows you the same table after drilling down by country (United Kingdom) and vehicle type (saloon).

Color	↑6-10	16-20	26-30	>30	Total
↑Blue	2570		85		2655
British Racing Green		2570		4000	6570
Canary Yellow	4520	1950			6470
Green	3320				3320
Red	5140				5140
Silver				3000	3000
Total	**15550**	**4520**	**85**	**7000**	**27155**

Figure 2-25. *A matrix table after drill-down by row and column*

As you can see, the principles for drilling up and down through a column hierarchy are the same as those that you used with a row hierarchy.

Card Visualizations

Tabular data can also be displayed in an extremely innovative way using the Power View card style of output. As is the case with matrix tables, you begin by choosing the fields that you want to display as a basic table, and then you convert this to another type of visualization. Here is an example of how this can be done:

1. Create a new Power View report or select a report with some available space.

2. Add the following fields, in this order (as before, this can be done by selecting the relevant check boxes in the upper part of the field list, by dragging fields into the FIELDS well in the layout section of the field list, or by dragging the fields onto the Power View report and into an existing table if you are adding fields):

    a. CountryName

    b. CostPrice

    c. TotalDiscount

    d. LaborCost

    e. SpareParts

3. Set all the numeric fields to be the average of the value by clicking the pop-up menu for each field (the small black triangle to the right of the field name in the FIELDS well in the layout section of the field list) and selecting Average.

4. Select Table ➤ Card in the ribbon; you now have a card-type table, as shown in Figure 2-26.

Figure 2-26. *A card visualization*

Card-type tables will display the selected fields in the order in which they appear in the Fields section at the bottom of the field list, and it is here that they can be reordered, as with any table. This makes each card into a data record. The fields will flow left to right and then on to the following line in each card. What is interesting here is that adjusting the size of the table can change the appearance of the table quite radically. A narrow table will list the fields vertically, one above the other. If you can fit all the fields onto a single row, then you will get a highly original multiple record display.

In the initial example of a card visualization, you added only one attribute (or non-numeric) field. Power View correspondingly took this to be the title of each card and made its text larger than that of the other elements. However, try adding a second descriptive element to the FIELDS well in the layout section of the field list (I used vehicle type); as you can see from Figure 2-27, this resets all the fonts in each card to the same size.

sort by CountryName ▾ asc   ▼ ↗

CountryName	Convertible	30700
	VehicleType	CostPrice
200.00	486	2570
TotalDiscount	LaborCost	SpareParts

CountryName	Coupe	69500
	VehicleType	CostPrice
700.00	975	1200
TotalDiscount	LaborCost	SpareParts

France	Convertible	134750
CountryName	VehicleType	CostPrice
5,850.00	5650	4475
TotalDiscount	LaborCost	SpareParts

France	Coupe	864750
CountryName	VehicleType	CostPrice
22,750.00	19767	19105
TotalDiscount	LaborCost	SpareParts

France	Saloon	460600
CountryName	VehicleType	CostPrice
10,700.00	11054	18850
TotalDiscount	LaborCost	SpareParts

Germany	Coupe	117500
CountryName	VehicleType	CostPrice
500.00	1136	1200
TotalDiscount	LaborCost	SpareParts

Germany	Saloon	42500
CountryName	VehicleType	CostPrice
200.00	325	400
TotalDiscount	LaborCost	SpareParts

Figure 2-27. *A card visualization with multiple non-numeric fields*

In any case, card-style tables will only scroll vertically, unlike basic tables and matrix tables. If you add multiple fields to a table, you will note that Power View will always attempt, initially, to keep the data for a record on one line, shrinking the text as more fields are added. Once there is simply too much data to fit on a single row, Power View will flow the data onto the next line in a card and possibly alter the font size.

A card-style table will always display the column headers for each field in the record. Cards are also a perfect vehicle for images. This is described in Chapter 7. Also, there is a technique to set a field as the title field; however, many non-numeric fields are added. This is part of the way that the underlying data set is prepared for Power View, and it is described in Chapter 14.

Card Visualization Styles

Just to make things even more interesting—and diversified—Power View lets you switch card styles if you want. The style of cards that you have seen up until now is called simply Card. However, there is another card style that is completely different, called Callout. To switch the existing card visualization to the Callout style, follow these steps:

1. Click inside, or select, the card visualization.

2. Remove the VehicleType field from the field area.

3. Select Callout from the Card Style button in the Design ribbon. Your card visualization should look like Figure 2-28.

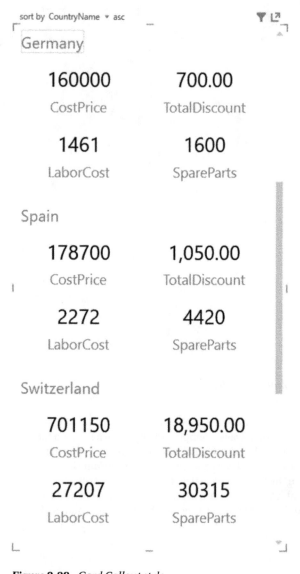

Figure 2-28. *Card Callout style*

Callout cards do take up a lot of space, which makes them ideal candidates for pop-out display should you want a detailed look at the figures that they contain. This is explained in Chapter 4.

Sorting Data in Card-View Tables

You sort data in card-type tables slightly differently than the way you saw previously for basic and matrix tables. As you can see in Figure 2-29, when you hover the mouse pointer over a card-type table Sort By, a field name will appear above the top left of the table. If the table is not yet ordered, then Power View will display the first field in the table. If the table is already ordered, then the column used to sort the data will be displayed.

To sort the records, you have two choices.

- Click the downward-facing triangle to the right of the sort field and select the field that you want to order the data by from the pop-up list that will appear. This is shown in Figure 2-29.

Figure 2-29. *Sorting cards in a card visualization*

- If you prefer, you can simply click the sort field, which will then display the next field in the table, and order the data by this field.

To change the sort order—that is, to switch between ascending and descending order—simply click Asc (or Desc) that appears to the right of the sort field when you hover the mouse pointer over a card-type table. As you can see, this is similar to the way in which you sorted data in table columns.

Switching Between Table Types

One of the fabulous things about Power View is that it is designed from the ground up to let you test ideas and experiment with ways of displaying your data quickly and easily. So, quite naturally, you can switch table types easily to see which style of presentation is best suited to your ideas and the message you want to convey. To switch table types, all you have to do is click Table in the ribbon and select one of these options:

- Table
- Matrix
- Card

What is even more reassuring is that Power View will remember the attributes of the previous table type you used. So, for instance, if you set up a matrix with a carefully crafted hierarchy and then switch to a card-type table, Power View will remember how you set up the matrix should you want to switch back to it.

Key Performance Indicators

There is a tabular presentation that can be considered a little special, and consequently, it is worthy of being looked at separately. This kind of table is a KPI table, and it contains a visual indication of how an objective is being met (if at all). A KPI does require that the underlying data has been prepared to display the data as a KPI, so this is explained in Chapter 14. Fortunately, we have KPI data in the sample file, so here is how to display it:

1. Drag the Make field to the FIELDS well in the field list.

2. Expand the KPI field (AverageNetMargin) and drag the field's Value and Status to the FIELDS well in the field list.

A table will be created, but the columns will be named AverageNetMargin and AverageNetMarginStatus. The AverageNetMarginStatus field will contain the KPI indicators (Xs and check marks or exclamations in this case) to indicate whether the metric is on track. You can see this in Figure 2-30.

Make	AverageNetMargin	AverageNetMargin Status
Aston Martin	33,697.77	✅
Bentley	21,574.42	🔽
Jaguar	8,743.67	❌
MGB	17,930.56	🔽
Rolls Royce	48,878.41	✅
Triumph	6,841.67	❌
TVR	-5,383.33	❌
Total	**22,295.96**	✅

Figure 2-30. A KPI

Creating Power View Reports and Tables Without a Data Model

So far in this chapter I have shown you how to start using Power View using data that exists in an Excel in-memory data model. However, you do not need to have created such a model to use Power View (even if it is the more traditional approach). This is because you can base your Power View report on the data in an existing Excel table, providing that this table contains *all* the data you require.

As an example of this, follow these steps:

1. Open the sample Excel file SalesDataList.xlsx, in the C:\DataVisualisationInExcel2016 folder.

2. Click inside the table of data in the worksheet named SalesData.

3.   In the Insert ribbon, click the Power View button.

Excel will add a new Power View report that uses the data from the SalesData table. What is more, it will automatically create a table in the new report, as you can see in Figure 2-31.

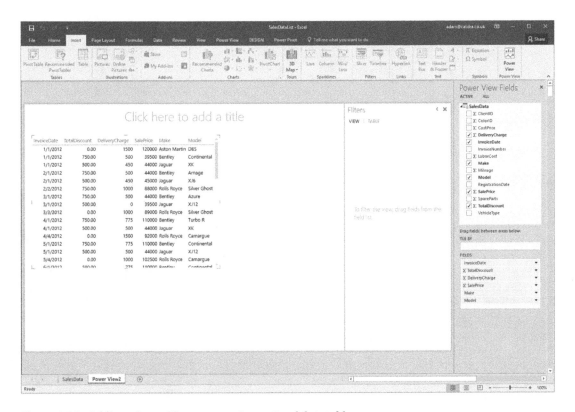

Figure 2-31. *Adding a Power View report using an Excel data table*

Conclusion

I hope that you are now comfortable with the Power View interface and are relaxed about using it to present your data, whether you are using standard tables, matrix tables, KPIs, or the new and innovative card visualizations that Power View offers. Equally, I hope that you are at ease sorting your tables using the various techniques that are available. Finally, never forget that you can, if you prefer, set up tables so that you can drill down into the data—and back up, of course.

This chapter is just a taster of the many ways in which Power View can help you analyze and display the information that you want your audience to appreciate. Yet, as tables are the basis for just about every other form of visualization, it is well worth mastering the techniques and tricks of table creation. This way you will be well on the way to a fluent mastery of Power View, which will lay the foundations for some truly impressive presentations.

CHAPTER 3

■ ■ ■

Filtering Data in Power View

Power View is built from the ground up to enable you, the user, to sift through mounds of facts and figures so that you can deliver meaningful insights. Consequently, what matters is being able to delve into data and display the information it contains quickly and accurately. This way, you can always follow up on a new idea or simply follow your intuitions without needing either to apply complex processes or to struggle with an impenetrable interface. After all, Power View is there to help you come up with new analyses that could give your business an edge on the competition.

Filtering the potentially vast amounts of data that stand between you and the insights that could make all the difference to your business is profoundly important. The people who developed Power View recognized this, which is why you can filter on any field or set of fields in the underlying data model. Not only is this intuitive and easy, it is also extremely fast, which ensures that you almost never have to wait for results to be returned.

You can add filters before, after, or during the creation of a Power View report. If you add filters before creating a table, say, then your table will display only the data that the filter allows through. If you add a filter to an existing report, then the data visualization will alter before your eyes to reflect the new filter. If you modify a filter when you have visualizations on a Power View report, then (as you probably guessed by now), all the visualizations will also be updated to reflect the new filter criteria—instantaneously.

You can filter any type of data.

- Text

- Numeric values

- Dates

Each data type has its own ways of selecting elements and setting (where possible) ranges of values that can be included—or excluded. This chapter will explain the various techniques for isolating only the data that you want to display. You will then be able to create Power View reports based only on the data that you want them to show.

This chapter, like the previous one, will presume you have downloaded the file `CarSales.xlsx` into the folder `C:\DataVisualisationInExcel2016`, assuming you want to try the filtering techniques for yourself.

Filters

Subsetting data in Power View is based on applying filters correctly. Consequently, the first thing that you need to know about filters is that they work at two levels.

- View-level filters

- Visualization-level filters

© Adam Aspin 2016

A. Aspin, *High Impact Data Visualization in Excel with Power View, 3D Maps, Get & Transform and Power BI*, DOI 10.1007/978-1-4842-2400-7_3

57

Table 3-1 describes the characteristics of these two kinds of filter.

Table 3-1. *Power View Filters*

Filter Type	Application	Comments
View-level	Applies to every visualization in the current report	This kind of filter will filter data for every visualization in the current view.
Visualization-level	Applies only to the selected visualization	This kind of filter will apply only to the selected visualization (table, chart, and so on).

When you first open Power View, you will probably see the Filters area displayed to the immediate right of the Power View report; it looks like a narrow empty sheet of paper. There could be times when you will not be filtering data, so you may prefer to hide the Filters area to increase the available screen space you need to hone your report. So, if you want to remove the Filters area from view, follow these steps:

1. Activate the Power View ribbon (if it is not already active).

2. Click the Filters Area button and the Filters area will slide out of view.

To display the Filters area, follow these steps:

1. Activate the Power View ribbon (if it is not already active).

2. Click the Filters Area button and the Filters area will reappear.

Alternatively, to hide the Filters area, you can click the Close Filters Area button (the small X in the top-right corner of the Filters area), and it will obligingly remove itself from view.

If you prefer to collapse the Filters area while leaving a thin strip visible to the immediate right of the Power View report, you can click the Minimize icon (a lesser-than symbol in the top-right corner of the Filters area), and the Filters area will collapse nearly completely out of sight. You can make it reappear at any time by clicking the Expand icon (a greater-than symbol) in the top-right corner of the slimmed-down Filters area. Figure 3-1 shows the elements of a typical Filters area.

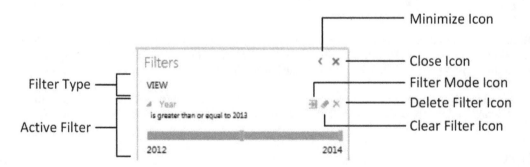

Figure 3-1. *The essential parts of the Filters area*

View Filters

Saying that there are two types of filter available in Power View is a purely descriptive distinction. For Power View, any filter is a filter, and all filters work in the same way. However, as there is a clear hierarchy in their application, I will begin with view filters and then move on to their descendants—the visualization filters. Given the general similarity between the two, it is probably worth noting that it is important that you check that you are creating or modifying the appropriate filter. As this is not always obvious, at least when you are starting out with Power View, you need to look out for the word *View*, which is at the top of the view area. If it is not grayed out, this will tell you that you are working on a view filter. To be really sure that you are creating or modifying a view filter, a good trick is to ensure that no visualizations are selected in the Power View report—or even to click a blank part of the report canvas to be extra sure that you are dealing with a view filter. In this case, only the word *View* will be displayed at the top of the view area.

Adding Filters

The Filters area helpfully advises you as follows: To Filter The View, Drag Fields From The Fields List. And yes, it really is that simple. Here is how to add a filter to select only a couple of countries from those available in the source data. In this case, you will add the filter before creating a Power View table.

1. In the Power View field list, expand the table containing the field that will be a filter criterion (Countries in this example).

2. Drag the CountryName field into the Filters area. The Filters area will display all the unique elements in the source table; in this case, it will be a list of countries.

3. Select two or three elements by clicking the appropriate check boxes (France, Germany, and Spain, in this example). The Filters area will look like Figure 3-2.

Figure 3-2. *A simple filter to select specific countries*

■ **Note** The filter will include the number of elements in the data table for each filter element. For a reference-style table such as this one for countries, this will probably always be 1. For a table containing metrics, the figures will be much larger.

To see the filter working, I suggest creating a table using the following fields:

- CountryName (from the Country table)
- Color (from the Colors table)
- SalePrice (from the SalesData table)

You will see that data is displayed only for the countries that were selected in the filter. Of course, you do not need to display the CountryName field in the table just because it is used to filter the data. In a real-world Power View report, you will probably not display a field in a table or chart if it is being used to filter data. However, if you want to confirm to yourself that filters work, then you can always display them in a table or chart, and once you are happy that the results are what you expect, you can remove the filtering field from the table. The resulting table should look like Figure 3-3.

CountryName	Colour	SalePrice
France	Black	£22,750.00
France	Blue	£69,250.00
France	British Racing Green	£39,500.00
France	Canary Yellow	£491,190.00
France	Green	£60,440.00
France	Night Blue	£131,100.00
France	Red	£355,300.00
France	Silver	£67,440.00
Germany	Blue	£41,250.00
Germany	Silver	£29,750.00
Spain	Canary Yellow	£22,500.00
Spain	Green	£39,500.00
Spain	Red	£29,750.00
Total		**£1,399,720.00**

Figure 3-3. *A simple filtered table*

You will have noticed that when the filter was first applied, every check box was empty, including the (All) check box. The default is (fairly logically) to set up a filter ready for tweaking, but not actually to filter any data until the user has decided what filters to apply. Once you start adding filter elements, they will be displayed in the Filters area just above the name of the field that is being used to filter data. Well, as many filters as will fit on one line will be displayed to indicate that filters are active.

■ **Tip** There is a subtle difference that you need to watch out for when selecting filter elements. If you click the check box, then an element is added to the filter (or removed if the check box was already selected). If, however, you click the name of an element, then all the currently selected elements are deselected, and only the element that you clicked is active in filtering the data.

You modify filters the same way you apply them. All you have to do to remove a selected filter element is to click the check box with the check mark to clear it. Conversely, to add a supplementary filter element, just click an empty check box.

Using the (All) Filter

The only subtlety concerning simple filters is that you also have the (All) check box. This acts as a global on/off switch to select, or deselect, all the available filter elements for a given filter field. The (All) filter field has three states.

- *Empty*: No filters are selected for this field.

- *Checked*: All filters are selected for this field.

- *Filled-in*: Some (but not all) filters are selected for this field.

Clicking a filled-in (All) filter field will deselect all filter elements for this field, in effect rendering the filter inactive. Checking the (All) filter field will select all filter elements for this field, also rendering the filter inactive. Removing the check mark from the (All) filter field will deselect all filter elements for this field, also rendering the filter inactive. Clicking multiple times on the (All) filter field will cycle through the available options.

The (All) filter field is particularly useful when you want not only to remove multiple filter selections in order to start over but also want to select all elements in order to deselect certain elements individually (and avoid manually selecting reams of elements).

The (Blank) filter field allows you to select—or exclude—any records where there is no data for a particular field.

■ **Note** When selecting multiple elements in lists, you may be tempted to apply the classic Windows keyboard shortcuts that you may be in the habit of using in, for instance, Excel or other Windows applications. Unfortunately, Ctrl+ or Shift+clicking to select a subset of elements will simply not work. In addition, although you can select and deselect a check box using the spacebar, it is not possible to use the cursor keys to pass from one element to another in a filter list.

Clearing Filters

Setting up a finely honed filter so that you are drilling through the noise in your data to the core information can take some practice. Fortunately, the virtually instantaneous application of filters means that you can see almost immediately if you are heading down the right path in your analysis. However, there are frequent occasions when you want to start over and remove any settings for a particular filter. This can be done as follows:

1. Click the Clear Filter icon to the right of the selected filter. This icon is shown in Figure 3-4.

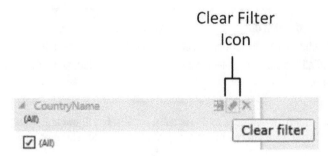

Figure 3-4. *Clearing a filter*

Once a filter has been cleared, the only way to get it back to its previous state is to click Undo (or press Ctrl+Z) immediately. Otherwise, you will have to rebuild it from the ground up.

■ **Tip**   An interesting trick to note is that if you click the filter field in the Filters area, you can expand and collapse the filter.

Deleting Filters

When working with filters, at times you may want to clear the decks and start over. The fastest way to do this is to delete a filter; once a filter is deleted, it produces no effect on the data in the Power View report. This can be done as follows:

1. Click the Delete Filter icon to the right of the selected filter. This icon is shown in Figure 3-5.

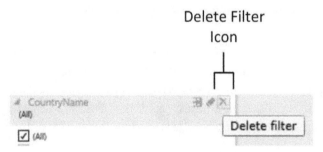

Figure 3-5. *Deleting a filter*

Once a filter has been deleted, the only way to get it back is to click Undo (or press Ctrl+Z) immediately. Otherwise, you will have to rebuild it from scratch. Interestingly, although you can add filters by dragging elements into the Filters area, you cannot drag them out of the Filters area to remove them.

Expanding and Collapsing Filters

When you have only a few filters active in a Power View report and when those filters contain only a few elements, then having all the filter elements visible at the same time is no real problem. However, when you are using multiple filters or are employing filters that contain dozens, or hundreds, of elements, then managing filters may require a little attention.

To give a more uncluttered aspect to the Filters area, the simplest thing to do is to collapse any filters once you have defined them. To do this, follow these steps:

1. Click the Collapse icon (a filled triangle facing down and to the right situated to the left of the filter title). The filter elements will disappear, leaving only the filter title and the list of selected elements.

Note that if no elements are selected for a filter, then (All) will be displayed under the filter title. A collapsed filter is shown (with some selected elements) in Figure 3-6.

Figure 3-6. *Collapsing a filter*

To expand a filter and continue refining the selection, follow these steps:

1. Click the Expand icon (an empty triangle facing right, situated to the left of the filter title). The filter elements will reappear, as you saw previously in Figure 3-2.

Subsetting Large Filter Lists

Depending on the source data you are using, you could have only a few elements making up each filter. If so, then you should probably consider yourself lucky, because many data sets can contain dozens, or hundreds, of filter elements. If this is the case, then you will probably need to know a few simple techniques for handling long lists of filter elements.

First, you need to specify what exactly a "large" filter list is. Fortunately, Power View helps you here, as it will start helping to manage lists once there are more than ten (or so) elements in the list. If more than 20 elements are in a filter (this will depend on several factors including your screen resolution and how many filters you have placed in the Filters area), then Power View will limit the number of elements displayed and will display a vertical scroll bar. This way you can scroll through the available filter elements.

Searching for Specific Elements in a Filter

So, assuming you have a large list of filter elements, just how can Power View help you?

Simply, you can search for any text inside a list of elements. For instance, assuming you have added a filter on ClientName (by dragging the ClientName field from the Clients table into the Filters area), you will see immediately that for Power View, this is a large set of filter elements, because it adds a search box between the filter name and the filter detail (this is the box with a magnifying glass to the right). To search for a specific element, follow these steps:

1. Click inside the search box.

2. Enter the (ideally few) characters that are enough to isolate the element that you are looking for. I suggest entering the word **England**.

3. Click the magnifying glass to the right of the search box (or press Enter).

Power View will return only a subset of the filter elements that contain the characters you have searched on. The characters you entered will be highlighted inside each of the filter elements that is returned. It is worth noting that the character string you entered will be found anywhere inside the filter elements. Figure 3-7 shows an example of this search facility.

Figure 3-7. *Searching inside a filter*

Once you have returned the subset of filter elements, you can select the ones you want as described earlier. Do remember that when searching in a filter, you can find only the elements that are available. So, if there are other active filters, you might not get all the results you were expecting.

Clearing a Filter Subset

To clear the filter on a filter that you created using the search box, all you have to do is the following:

1.   Click the small X to the right of the search box. This X replaced the magnifying glass once you activated the filter search.

The search string will be removed, as will the filter on the filter elements. All the filter elements (or at least, as many as can be displayed) will reappear in the filter. Be aware that just deleting the contents of the search box might not produce the result you were expecting!

Filtering with Wildcards

When searching through a large and varied set of filter elements, you might want to bring back elements based not on a specific search string but on a string containing certain letters or combinations of letters. This is called a *wildcard search*. For instance, when searching car colors, you could indicate to Power View that you want all filter elements that contain the letter *a* followed anywhere further in the element by the letter *e*. So, if you take this as an example of a subset of filter elements that you want to isolate, this is what you have to do:

1.   Add the ClientName field to the Filters area (unless you have already done so).

2.   Enter the search string **a*e** in the search box, as shown in Figure 3-8.

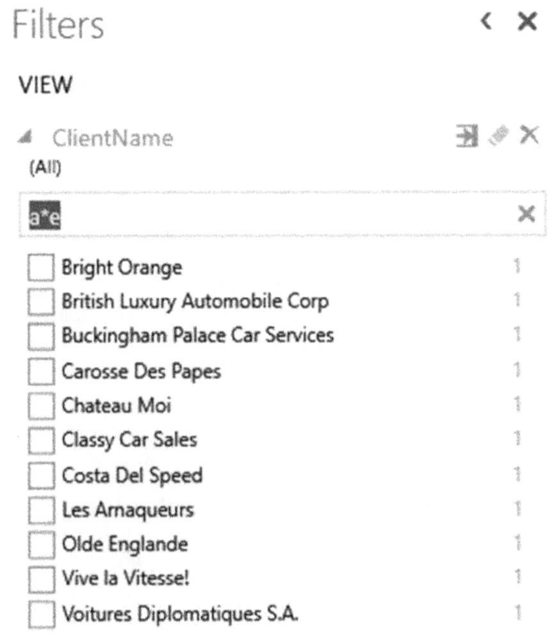

Filters ‹ ✕

VIEW

◢ ClientName ⤒ ✎ ✕
(All)

| a*e | ✕ |

☐	Bright Orange	1
☐	British Luxury Automobile Corp	1
☐	Buckingham Palace Car Services	1
☐	Carosse Des Papes	1
☐	Chateau Moi	1
☐	Classy Car Sales	1
☐	Costa Del Speed	1
☐	Les Arnaqueurs	1
☐	Olde Englande	1
☐	Vive la Vitesse!	1
☐	Voitures Diplomatiques S.A.	1

Figure 3-8. Wildcard filter search

3. Click the magnifying glass to the right of the search box (or press Enter).

4. Select the elements from the filter subset to which you want to apply the filter. Only cars of the selected colors will appear in any visualization.

As you can see, the wildcard search returned only the clients that you can see in Figure 3-8.

All of these clients contain the letter *a* followed further in the element by the letter *e*. Of course, this example is not necessarily very practical, but it shows how you can extend the search facility for filter elements to widen a search by using the asterisk wildcard. This will return any number of characters in the place of the asterisk.

Finally, if you want a slightly narrower search—for just one character—you can use the question mark (?) character. Entering the search string **c?a** in the search box will return the following:

- Chateau Moi

- Classy Car Sales

Using the question mark wildcard character will force Power View to find a single character.

▨ **Note**   This search facility is not case sensitive.

Clearing a Filter Element Search

To cancel a filter element search (and remove the search string from the search box), click the X (which replaces the magnifying glass when a filter element search is active). The search string will be removed, and the subset of filter elements will be replaced with the available filter elements—or at least by as many elements as Power View can display.

Filtering Different Data Types

So far you have seen only how Power View can filter text elements in a view. Although text-based elements are a major part of many data filters, they are far from the only available type. There are also the following:

- Numeric data

- Date and time data

You can filter on numeric elements just as you can filter on text-based elements in Power View. However, although the core principles are the same, there are some interface differences and tricks that you probably need to know.

Range Filter Mode

The first trick worth knowing is that when filtering on numeric data, you do not only have the choice of selecting elements from a list. You also have a *range selector*, which is the default filter for numeric filters. The range selector is a slider, which allows you to set the lower and upper limits of the range of numbers that you want to display in a Power View report.

To set the range of figures for which data will be displayed, follow these steps:

1. Drag a numeric field into the Filters area (CostPrice in this example). The field title and a blue range slider bar appear in the Filters area. The initial range filter is given in Figure 3-9. You can see that the range filter starts with the lowest available value and ends with the highest available value.

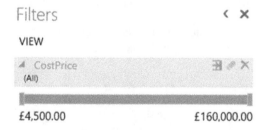

Figure 3-9. A range filter for numeric values

2. Place the mouse pointer over the left (lower) extremity of the blue range slider bar for the selected filter. The mouse pointer becomes a two-headed arrow.

3. Slide the left-hand range limiter to the right. You will see the constituent elements of the field appear above the slider and below the field title, preceded by Is Greater Than Or Equal To *X*, where *X* is the figure from the source data. The figures will increase from smaller to larger the farther to the right you slide the range boundary. Stop when you have reached a suitable lower bound for the data. This is shown in Figure 3-10.

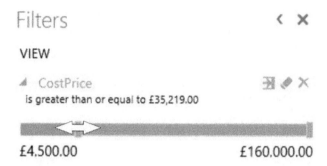

Figure 3-10. *Setting a range filter*

4. Place the mouse pointer over the right (upper) extremity of the blue range slider bar for the selected filter. The mouse pointer becomes a two-headed arrow.

5. Slide the upper range limiter to the left. You will see the constituent elements of the field appear above the slider and below the field title, preceded by Is Between *lower range boundary* And *X*, where *X* is the figure from the source data. Stop when you have reached a suitable upper bound for the data.

That is it; you have set a range for all data in the Power View report corresponding to the selected field. It should look like Figure 3-11.

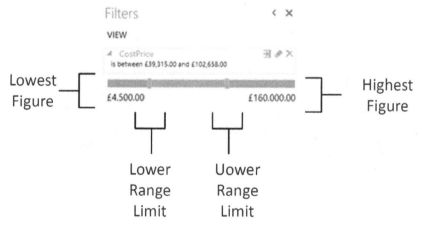

Figure 3-11. *A filter range*

When selecting a range of numeric data, you do not, of course, have to set both upper and lower bounds. You may set one, the other, or both. Also, you will have noticed that the figures that are displayed as you alter the boundaries are not in any regular progression. This is because they are extrapolated from the actual data, as it is in the data source.

■ **Note** Numeric filters seem to support 400-plus increments—fewer if the data has a smaller range.

List Filter Mode

In some cases, you may prefer to select real values to filter numeric data. This is, in my experience, more rarely required, but it can be useful when you want to exclude outliers at either end of the data spectrum.

To switch a numeric list to List Filter mode (I will use the CostPrice filter, which you just set up), follow these steps:

1. Hover the mouse pointer over the filter title (the field name you selected when you created the filter). The filter title will turn blue.

2. Click the Filter Mode icon to the right of the filter title. This is the first of the three icons at the top right of the filter. You should see something like Figure 3-12.

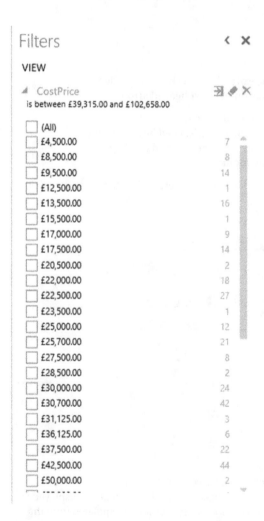

Figure 3-12. *A list filter*

That is it; you will now see the numeric data in list mode, and you can select specific values.

■ **Tip**   Be warned, however, that it is not because no values are selected that the filter is inactive. You need to be careful and check the filter title, which could still say Is Between *value* and *value*. This indicates that a filter is active. To reset the filter so that the range filter is deactivated, you need to click the (All) filter field, twice, preferably. This will select, and then clear, all the check boxes for all the elements in the list.

You can then select, or exclude, any specific elements, as you did earlier in the chapter for colors. In practice, you may want to exclude any values that are suspiciously high or low and presume that they are outliers that need to be filtered out of the data set. Alternatively, you may want to select any suspicious-looking values to take a closer look at them.

To flip back to Range Filter mode, follow these steps:

1. Hover the mouse pointer over the filter title (the field name you selected when you created the filter). The filter title will turn blue.

2. Click the Filter Mode icon twice to the right of the filter title. This is the first of the three icons at the top right of the filter.

You will see that the list filter disappears, and in its place the range filter reappears.

When cycling through the filter modes (by clicking the Filter Mode icon to the right of the filter title), you will see that there is also an Advanced Filter mode. As this will be described shortly, I will not describe it here. Power View is also helpful in providing a tooltip when you hover the mouse pointer over the Filter Mode icon that tells you what the next filter mode will be if you click the icon.

Quickly Excluding Outliers

A few paragraphs ago I mentioned the possibility of excluding outliers. Here is a quick trick to getting this done efficiently that you may find useful:

1. Drag the filter for the field containing the outlier value to the Filters area.

2. Click the Filter Mode button to switch to List Filter mode.

3. Click (All) to select all the values in the list filter.

4. Uncheck the values that are at the upper and lower limits of the filter elements and that you consider to be outliers.

By definition, there should be only a few outliers, so this process should take only a few seconds.

Date and Time Data

At its simplest, date and time data is merely list data, like the List Filter mode for numeric data. Consequently, dragging a Date, Time, or DateTime field into the Filters area will add a list of discrete elements from the data source. You can then select all, none, or a chosen subset of elements from the list as was described for text-based data. If your data has a Date table (or as data warehousing people would call it, a *date dimension*), then you could well be using this to select date filter criteria. Let's see this in action.

1. Expand the Date table in the field list.

2. Expand the YearHierarchy hierarchy.

3. Drag the MonthAbbr, QuarterFull, and Year fields into the Filters area. Figure 3-13 demonstrates this.

Filters   ‹ ✕

VIEW

◢ MonthAbbr   ⊒ ✎ ✕
   (All)

   | Search... | 🔍 |

   ☐ (All)
   ☐ (Blank)   1
   ☐ Apr   90
   ☐ Aug   93
   ☐ Dec   93
   ☐ Feb   85
   ☐ Jan   93
   ☐ Jul   93
   ☐ Jun   90
   ☐ Mar   93
   ☐ May   93
   ☐ Nov   90
   ☐ Oct   93
   ☐ Sep   90

◢ QuarterFull   ⊒ ✎ ✕
   (All)

   ☐ (All)
   ☐ (Blank)   1
   ☐ Quarter 1   271
   ☐ Quarter 2   273
   ☐ Quarter 3   276
   ☐ Quarter 4   276

◢ Year   ⊒ ✎ ✕
   (All)

   ▐▬▬▬▬▬▬▬▬▬▬▬▬▬▬▬▬▬▬▬▬▬▬▬▬▐

   2012   2014

Figure 3-13. *A date filter based on a hierarchy*

What you are looking at is, in essence, multiple filters, where you can select elements from each of the different filters: Year, Quarter, and/or Month. Alternatively, if you will be filtering on successive elements in a date hierarchy (Year, followed by Month, for instance), you may find it more intuitive to drag the filter elements from the date hierarchy to the Filters area in the temporal order in which you will be using them (that is, Year followed by Month, and probably not even Quarter). This way, you can proceed in a logical manner, from top to bottom in the Filters area, to apply the date criteria that interest you.

■ **Note**   If, or when, you want to delete filters that were added as a hierarchy, you will have to delete them individually, as you cannot remove all the fields that make up the hierarchy together. Fortunately, this takes only a few seconds.

However, if you are faced with multiple dates that are taken directly from source data and you do not have a time table in your PowerPivot data, it is frequently easier to set ranges for dates. This is best dealt with by using the advanced filters for all the available data types. These kinds of filters are explained later in the chapter.

Other Data Types

There are, of course, other data types in the source data that you are likely to be handling. You might have Boolean (True or False) data, for instance. However, for Power View, this is considered, for all intents and purposes, to be a text-based filter. So, if you filter on Boolean data, Power View will display True and False in the expanded filter for this data type. You can see this if you expand the Client table and drag IsCreditWorthy to the Filters area. On the other hand, there are some data types that you cannot use to filter on and that will not even appear in the Filters area. Binary data (such as images) is a case in point.

Multiple Filters

So far you have treated filters as if only one was ever going to be applied at a time. Believe me, when dealing with large and intricate data sets, it is unlikely that this will be the case. As a matter of course, Power View will let you add multiple filters to a report. This entails some careful consideration of the following possible repercussions:

- All filters will be active at once (unless you have cleared a filter), and their effect is cumulative. That is, data will be returned only if the data matches all the criteria set by all the active filters. So, for example, if you have requested data between a specified date range and above a certain sales figure, you will not get any data back where the sale figure is lower than the figure that you specified or the sales date is before or after the dates that you set.

- It is easy to forget that filters can be active. Remember that all active filters in the Filters area will remain operational whether the Filters area itself is expanded or collapsed. If you are going to collapse filters to make better use of the available space on the screen, then it is worth getting into the habit of looking at the second line below any filter title that will give you a description of the current filter state. It will display something like Contains Rolls. Of course, the exact text will vary according to the filter you have applied.

- Filters can interact in the Filters area. The time hierarchy is a case in point. If you select Quarter 3, for instance, you will only see the months for that quarter in the Months filter.

Advanced Filters

In many cases, when you are delving into your data, merely selecting a "simple" filter will be enough to highlight the information that interests both you and your audience. There will, however, inevitably be cases when you will need to filter your data more finely to return the kinds of results that sort the wheat from the chaff. This is where Power View's advanced filters come to the fore. Advanced filtering lets you search inside field data with much greater precision, and it is of particular use when you need to include, or exclude, data based on parts of a field (if it is text) or a precise range (if it is a number or a date).

Advanced filters, just like standard filters, are adapted to the three main data types that Power View handles, as follows, so it is best to look at each of these separately:

- Text

- Numbers

- Dates

However, before going through all the details, you first need to know how to switch to Advanced Filter mode in Power View.

Applying an Advanced Filter

Let's begin with a simple example of how to apply an advanced filter to a text field.

1. Add a field on which you want to filter to the Filters area (unless, of course, the filter is already in place). In this example, it will be the ClientName field.

2. Expand the filter field (you can see a list of individual data elements from the field) unless it has already been done.

3. Click the Advanced Filter Mode icon to the right of the filter header. The body of the filter switches to show the Advanced Filter boxes, and the text under the filter title now reads Show Items For Which The Value. This is shown in Figure 3-14.

Figure 3-14. *Advanced filters*

4. Click inside the filter text box (under the "contains" box) and enter the text to filter on (**Aldo** in this example).

5. Click Apply Filter, or press the Enter key, and all objects in the Power View report will only display data where the client contains the text *Aldo*. The result (a sample table) is shown in Figure 3-15; the advanced filter used to produce it is also shown.

CountryName	ClientName	Color	SalePrice
United Kingdom	Aldo Motors	Black	146500
United Kingdom	Aldo Motors	Blue	392750
United Kingdom	Aldo Motors	British Racing Green	179250
United Kingdom	Aldo Motors	Canary Yellow	426250
United Kingdom	Aldo Motors	Dark Purple	231250
United Kingdom	Aldo Motors	Green	277000
United Kingdom	Aldo Motors	Night Blue	143250
United Kingdom	Aldo Motors	Red	541250
United Kingdom	Aldo Motors	Silver	538750
Total			2876250

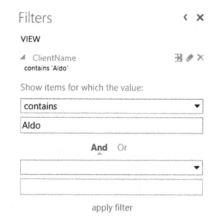

Figure 3-15. *The results of applying an advanced filter*

Here are some important points:

- Advanced filtering is *not* case sensitive. You can enter uppercase or lowercase characters in the filter box; the result will be the same.

- Spaces and punctuation are important, as they are taken literally. If you enter, for instance, **A** with a space after the *A*, then you will only find elements containing an *A* (uppercase or lowercase) followed by a space.

- Advanced filters, just like standard filters, are cumulative in their effect. So, if you have applied a filter and do not get the results you were expecting, be sure to check that no other filter is active that might be narrowing the data returned beyond what you want.

- If your filter excludes all data from the result set, then any tables in the Power View report will display This Table Contains No Rows.

- Similarly, if your filter excludes all data, charts will be empty, and multiple charts will display Contains No Small Multiples To Display.

In any case, if you end up displaying no data or data that does not correspond to what you wanted to show, just clear the filter and start over!

Clearing an Advanced Filter

Inevitably you will also need to know how to remove an advanced filter. The process is the same as for a standard filter.

1. Click the Clear Filter icon (the middle icon of the three to the right of the filter field name). The filter elements are removed for this filter.

You can, of course, if you have no further need for the entire filter, delete the filter by clicking the Delete Filter icon (the right one of the three to the right of the filter field name). This will not only clear the filter settings but also delete the entire filter.

Advanced Wildcard Filters

A few pages previously you saw how to use wildcards to create a subset of filter elements that would then be used to select specific values. Well, you can also use wildcards directly to filter data using the Advanced Filter mode. To apply a wildcard filter to your data, follow these steps:

1. Add a field on which you want to apply a wildcard filter to the Filters area (unless, of course, the filter is already in place). I suggest using the ClientName field.

2. Expand the filter field (you can see a list of individual data elements from the field) unless this has already been done.

3. Click the Advanced Filter Mode icon to the right of the filter header. The body of the filter switches to show the Advanced Filter boxes, and the text under the filter title now reads Show Items For Which The Value.

4. Click inside the filter text box (under the box displaying Contains) and enter the filter text containing one or more wildcards. In this example it will be **u*e**.

5. Click Apply Filter, or press the Enter (Return) key, and all visualizations in the Power View report will only display data where the client contains the character *u* followed anywhere by the character *e*.

As you can see in Figure 3-16, the result is that the Power View report only displays clients containing a *u* followed by an *e* further on in the client name.

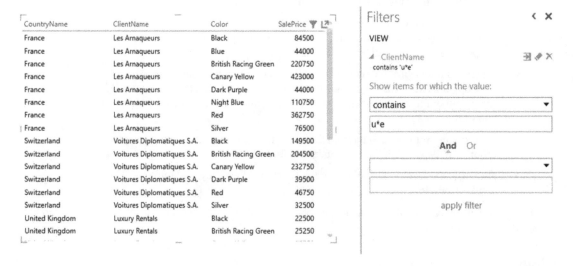

Figure 3-16. *Applying an advanced wildcard filter*

Table 3-2 describes the wildcard variations that you can apply.

Table 3-2. *Wildcard Filter Options*

Wildcard Character	Description	Comments
*	Asterisk	Searches for zero or more characters in the data
?	Question mark	Searches for a single character in the data

Note that using the question mark wildcard character will force Power View to find at least one character. Also, using wildcards in advanced filtering is not case sensitive.

Numeric Filters

Setting an advanced filter for a numeric value is, if anything, easier than when instantiating a filter for a text-based value—and it is similar. Here is the process to filter Gross Margin so that only sales for makes of car with a gross margin value above £50,000 are displayed in the report.

1. Create a new Power View report (this way you know that no other filters are active).

2. Create a table based on the ClientName and SalePrice fields.

3. Drag the field GrossMargin to the Filters area.

4. Click the Advanced Filter Mode icon to the right of the filter header. The body of the filter switches to show the Advanced Filter boxes, and the text under the filter title now reads Show Items For Which The Value. The filter option is Greater Than Or Equal To. Do not change this as it suits the requirements as is.

5. Click inside the box under the filter option text and enter **50000**. Do not add formatting elements to this figure.

6. Click Apply Filter (or press the Enter key).

The report, including the Filters area, looks like the one in Figure 3-17. The filter title now says Gross Margin Is Greater Than Or Equal To 50,000.00. As you can see, the filter title adopts the formatting used in the source data.

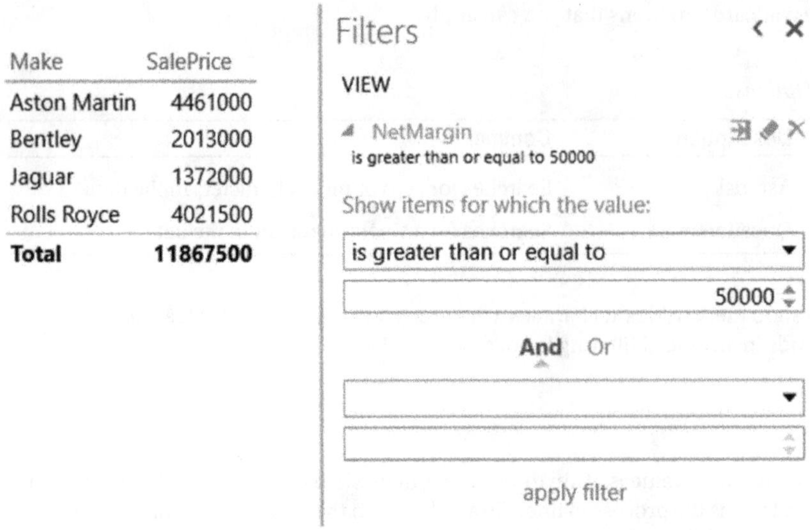

Make	SalePrice
Aston Martin	4461000
Bentley	2013000
Jaguar	1372000
Rolls Royce	4021500
Total	**11867500**

Filters   ‹ ✕

VIEW

◢ NetMargin   ⊞ ✎ ✕
   is greater than or equal to 50000

Show items for which the value:

is greater than or equal to ▼

50000 ↕

And   Or

▼

↕

apply filter

Figure 3-17. *Using numeric filters*

When you have added a numeric filter, you can increase and decrease the value by clicking the tiny up and down triangles that appear to the right of the value box. This saves you from having to reenter figures. It will, however, change only by single increments.

Date and Time Filters

If you are filtering on a Date or DateTime field, then you will quickly notice that Power View adds a couple of pop-up elements to the advanced filter to help you select dates and times more easily. These additions are as follows:

- A calendar pop-up, which lets you click a day of the month (and scroll through the months of the year, forward and backward)

- A time series pop-up, which lets you select times preset to every five minutes throughout the day

Figure 3-18 shows the calendar pop-up.

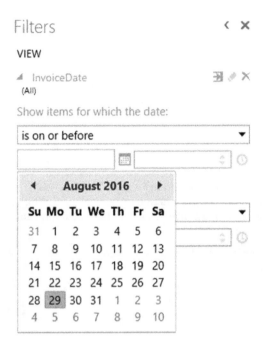

Figure 3-18. *The calendar pop-up*

Here are a couple of tricks that may save you time when you are selecting dates from the calendar pop-up (you may be used to these techniques already in other desktop packages, so forgive me if I add them anyway in the interests of completeness):

- When using the calendar pop-up, clicking the right-facing triangle to the right of the month and year will display the following month.

- When using the calendar pop-up, clicking the left-facing triangle to the left of the month and year will display the previous month.

- When using the calendar pop-up, clicking the month and year will display a Year pop-up, in which you can click the right-facing triangle to the right of the year to display the following year, and then you can select the month from those displayed.

- When using the calendar pop-up, clicking the month and year will display a Year pop-up, in which you can click the left-facing triangle to the left of the year to display the previous year, and then you can select the month from those displayed.

- When using the time pop-up, clicking inside any constituent part of the time (hour, minute, or second) and then clicking the up and down scroll triangles to the right of the time field allows you to scroll rapidly through the available options.

- Clicking the clock icon to the right of the time box lets you scroll through the time of day in five-minute intervals.

If you do not want to select a date using the calendar pop-up, then you can enter a date directly in the date box of the advanced filter for a Date (or DateTime) field. Just remember that you must enter the date in the date format corresponding to the environment you are using. That is to say, it must be formatted exactly as a Date field appears in a Date column in any Power View table.

■ **Note**   If you enter a date where the format does not correspond to the system format or the date is purely and simply invalid (the February 30, for instance), then Power View will not let you apply the filter. In this case, the Apply Filter link will remain grayed out, and pressing the Enter key will not apply the filter. To correct this, merely select a correct date using the calendar pop-up. Similarly, if you enter a nonexistent time, the Power View will refuse to accept it and will revert to the previous (acceptable) time that was chosen.

Complex Filters

All the examples I've given so far in this chapter have used a single filter criterion for each filter that was applied, even if multiple filters were used. You can, however, add a second criterion to a single filter (using the Advanced Filter mode) if you want to extend or limit the effect of the filter. Each filter that you apply can contain two possible criteria at most. This is how it can be done:

1. Add an advanced filter as described in steps 1–4 of the "Applying an Advanced Filter" section earlier. Enter only an **A** in the upper filter text box. Do not apply the filter.

2. Click And under the filter text box.

3. Select Does Not Contain from the lower filter type pop-up.

4. Enter **O** in the lower filter text box.

5. Click Apply Filter, or press the Enter key, and all objects in the Power View report will display data only where the client's name contains an *A* but not an *O*.

    This filter should look like the one given in Figure 3-19.

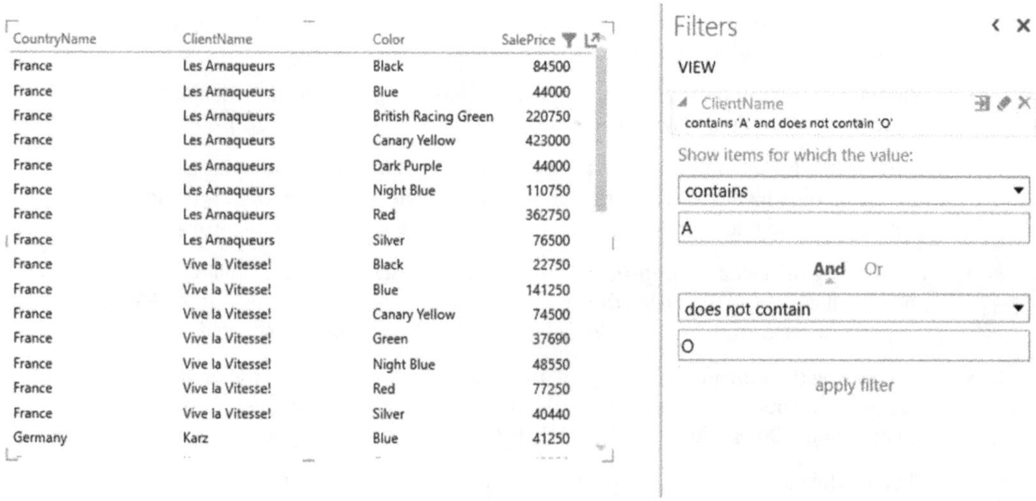

Figure 3-19. *A complex filter*

In this past example, you selected an *And* filter. In fact, as you can see from the Power View screen, you have two choices of complex filter. They are explained in Table 3-3.

Table 3-3. *Complex Filter Options*

Filter Type	Comments
And	Applies both filter elements to reduce the amount of data allowed through the filter
Or	Applies either of the filter elements separately to increase the amount of data allowed through the filter

Advanced Text Filter Options

When filtering on the text contained in a data field, you can apply the string you are filtering on to the underlying data in several ways. These are the same for both the upper and lower of the two advanced filter options for a text field. They are described in Table 3-4.

Table 3-4. *Advanced Text Filter Options*

Filter Option	Description
Contains	The selected field contains the search text anywhere in the field data.
Does Not Contain	The selected field does not contain the search text anywhere in the field data.
Starts With	The selected field begins with the search text, followed by any data.
Does Not Start With	The selected field does not begin with the search text, followed by any data.
Is	The selected field matches the search text exactly.
Is Not	The selected field does not match the search text exactly.
Is Blank	The selected field is blank.
Is Not Blank	The selected field is not blank.

Advanced Numeric Filter Options

Numbers cannot be filtered in the same ways as text. Consequently, the advanced filtering options are slightly different from those you use when filtering text. They are described in Table 3-5.

Table 3-5. *Advanced Numeric Filter Options*

Filter Option	Description
Is Less Than	The selected field is less than the number you are searching for.
Is Less Than Or Equal To	The selected field is less than or equal to the number you are searching for.
Is Greater Than	The selected field is greater than the number you are searching for.
Is Greater Than Or Equal To	The selected field is greater than or equal to the number you are searching for.
Is	The selected field matches exactly the number you are searching for.
Is Not	The selected field does not exactly match the number you are searching for.
Is Blank	The selected field is blank.
Is Not Blank	The selected field is not blank.

When applying a numeric filter, you must—not altogether surprisingly—enter a numeric value. If you enter text by mistake, you will get the following message: "The value is not valid. Enter a valid number between -Infinity and Infinity."

In this case, you will have to delete the characters that you entered and enter a numeric value in the place of the erroneous text. You can, if you really want, format numbers (by adding a thousands separator, for instance), but Power View will remove all number formatting.

Advanced Date Filter Options

Dates also cannot be filtered in the same ways as text or numbers. Consequently, the advanced filtering options for date filters are slightly different from those used when filtering other data types. They are described in Table 3-6.

Table 3-6. Advanced Date Filter Options

Filter Option	Description
Is	The selected field contains the date you are searching for.
Is Not	The selected field does not contain the date you are searching for.
Is After	The selected field contains dates after the date that you entered, that is, later dates that do not include the date you entered.
Is On Or After	The selected field contains dates beginning with the date that you entered or later.
Is Before	The selected field contains dates before the date that you entered, that is, earlier dates, not including the date you entered.
Is On Or Before	The selected field contains dates on or before the date that you entered, that is, earlier dates, up to and including the date you entered.
Is Blank	The selected field is blank.
Is Not Blank	The selected field is not blank.

Visualization-Level Filters

So far in this chapter you have looked at View filters, that is, filters that will be applied to the entire view (or report or dashboard if you prefer) and every visualization it contains. Although filtering the source data at a global level will certainly ensure coherence among the tables, charts, and other visualizations that you are using, there will inevitably be times when you want to filter a specific visualization at a finer level. This is where visualization-level filters come in.

Fortunately, visualization-level filters are virtually identical to view filters. The essential thing to remember is that you must select (or click inside) a visualization to apply a visualization-level filter. You will see when this option is available, as the word *Table* or *Chart* will appear at the top right of the Filters area to the immediate right of the word *View*.

As with nearly everything in Power View, this is probably best experienced in practice, so to apply a visualization-level filter, follow these steps:

1. Return to an existing Power View report.

2. Display the Filters area (unless it is already visible).

3. Click an existing visualization. In this example, I will be using the initial table created in this chapter, which you can see in Figure 3-3.

4. Click the word *Table*, which has appeared at the top right of the Filters area to the immediate right of the word *View* in the View area. You will see that all the fields that are used by the selected table appear in the View area.

5. Expand any filter fields that you want to use, or add any further fields from the Power View field list, and apply any filters that you require, as described previously in this chapter. I suggest selecting a couple of the colors for this example. This is shown in Figure 3-20.

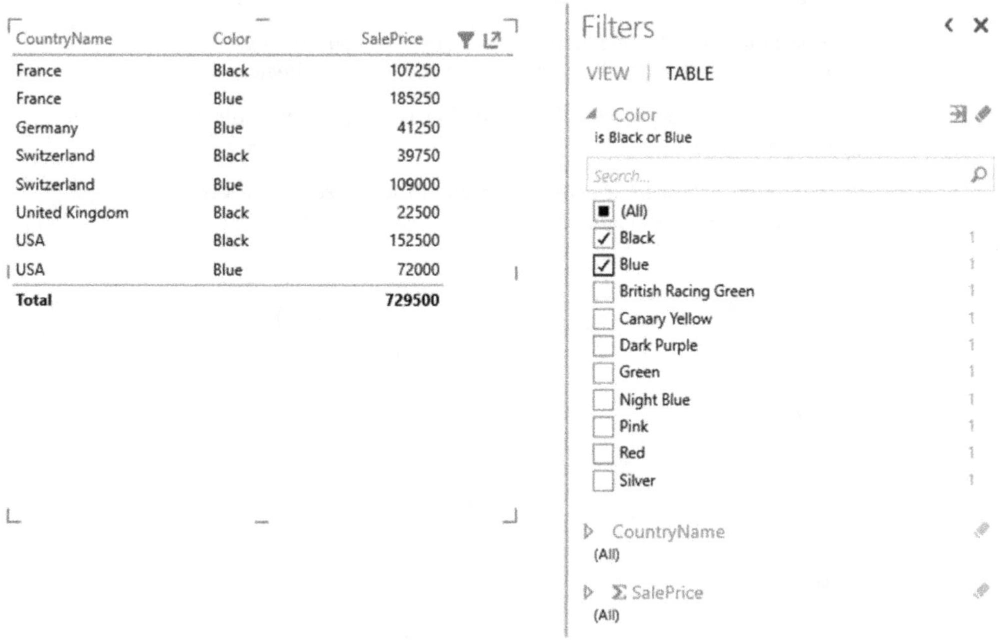

Figure 3-20. *A visualization-level filter*

You will notice right away that the filter(s) that you have applied only affect the selected visualization (the table in this example). When you create more complex reports that contain several visualizations, you will see that no other visualizations in the report have their underlying data modified in any way.

You can clear any filter at the visualization level just as you can at the view level—by clicking the Clear icon at the top right of the filter name. You can also delete any filter that you have added to the Filters area for a visualization (but not those that are based on the fields used by the visualization) by clicking the Delete icon at the top right of the filter name. Adding and removing fields from a visualization will automatically add and remove the corresponding filters from the Filters area for the visualization. This will include any filters that you added manually before you add them to the list of fields used by the visualization.

Filter Hierarchy

As I mentioned previously, a hierarchy of filters is applied in Power View.

- **First**, at the data level, any selections or choices you apply to the underlying data will restrict the data set that Power View can use to visualize your information.

- **Second**, at the report or view level, any view-level filters that you apply will affect all visualizations in the view, using the (possibly limited) available source data.

- **Finally**, for each visualization, any visualization-level filters that you apply will further limit the data that is allowed through the view-level filter—but only for the specific visualization.

As a quick example of this, you could do the following:

1. Apply a country filter to the view (which means you would either deselect any selected visualization or, alternatively, click the word *View* at the top of the view area).

2. Drag the CountryName field into the Filters area and select all countries except the UK. You will see that all current visualizations are updated to reflect the new filter.

3. Click the table for which you added a table filter earlier. Click the Table indicator at the top of the Filters area.

4. Now expand the CountryName filter in the Filters area. You will see that UK is not available to filter on, as shown in Figure 3-21.

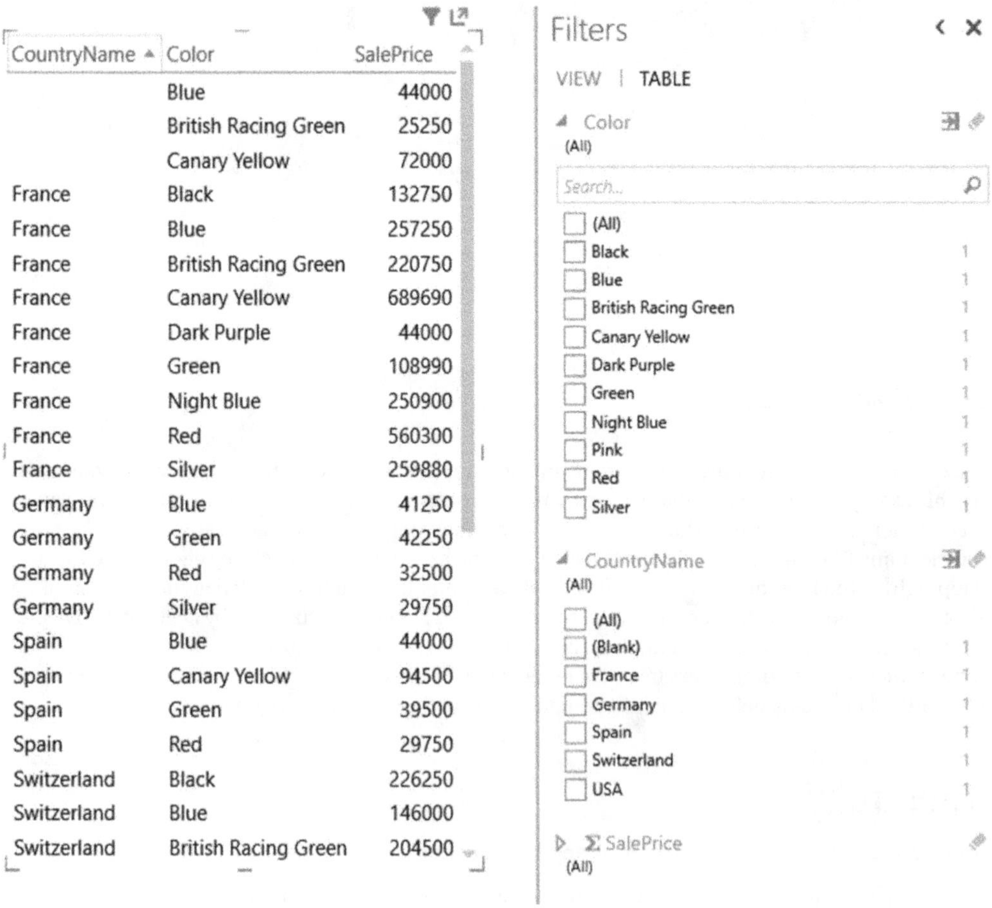

CountryName ▲	Color	SalePrice
	Blue	44000
	British Racing Green	25250
	Canary Yellow	72000
France	Black	132750
France	Blue	257250
France	British Racing Green	220750
France	Canary Yellow	689690
France	Dark Purple	44000
France	Green	108990
France	Night Blue	250900
France	Red	560300
France	Silver	259880
Germany	Blue	41250
Germany	Green	42250
Germany	Red	32500
Germany	Silver	29750
Spain	Blue	44000
Spain	Canary Yellow	94500
Spain	Green	39500
Spain	Red	29750
Switzerland	Black	226250
Switzerland	Blue	146000
Switzerland	British Racing Green	204500

Filters

VIEW | TABLE

⊿ Color
(All)

Search...

- ☐ (All)
- ☐ Black — 1
- ☐ Blue — 1
- ☐ British Racing Green — 1
- ☐ Canary Yellow — 1
- ☐ Dark Purple — 1
- ☐ Green — 1
- ☐ Night Blue — 1
- ☐ Pink — 1
- ☐ Red — 1
- ☐ Silver — 1

⊿ CountryName
(All)

- ☐ (All)
- ☐ (Blank) — 1
- ☐ France — 1
- ☐ Germany — 1
- ☐ Spain — 1
- ☐ Switzerland — 1
- ☐ USA — 1

▷ Σ SalePrice
(All)

Figure 3-21. *The filter hierarchy*

It is worth noting the following points:

- You have no way to apply a selection to a visualization filter if it has been filtered out at the view level. Clicking (All) will select only from the subset of previously filtered elements.

- If you apply a filter at the visualization level and then reapply the same filter at the view level but with different elements selected, you will still be excluding all nonselected elements from the filter at the visualization level. I stress this because Power View will remember the previously selected elements at the visualization level and leave them visible even if they cannot be used in a filter because they have already been excluded from the visualization-level filter by being ruled out at the view level. This, in my opinion, adds a certain visual confusion, even if the hierarchical selection logic is applied.

Ideally this shows you that Power View is rigorous in applying its hierarchy of filters. Should you need to apply a filter at the visualization level when the filter choice is excluded at the view level, you have no choice but to remove the filter at the view level and then reapply visualization-level filters to all necessary visualizations to apply the view filter individually to each visualization.

Filtering Tips

Power View makes it incredibly easy to filter data and to exclude any and all data that you feel is not helpful in your data analysis. However, like many powerful tools, this ability to apply filters so quickly and easily can be something of a double-edged sword. So, here are a few words of advice and caution when applying filters to your data.

Don't Filter Too Soon

As an initial point, I would say that a key ground rule is "Don't filter too soon." By this, I mean that if you are examining data for trends, anomalies, and insights, you have to be careful not to exclude data that could contain the very insights that can be game-changing.

The problem is, of course, that when you first delve into a haystack of data in search of needles of informational value, you have no idea what you could be looking for. So, I can only suggest the following approaches:

- Begin with no filters at all, and see what the data has to say in its most elemental form.

- Apply filters one at a time, and remember to delete a filter before trying another one.

- Try to think in terms of "layers" of filters. So, once you have defined an initial set of filters, add further filters sequentially.

- Go slowly. The temptation is to reach a discovery in order to shout about it from the rooftops. This can lead to inaccurate analysis.

- Always remove any filters that are not absolutely necessary.

- Be careful when hiding the Filters area. It is too easy to forget that there are active filters.

- Remember that you can have filters specific to a visualization that cannot be visible in the Filters area. So, always check whether any visualization filters are active for each table and chart in a report.

Drill-Down and Filters

In Chapter 2 you saw how to drill down in a matrix table. In the following chapter, you will see how to drill down into charts. In either case, you need to know that performing a drill-down operation (or indeed a drill-up) will have a subtle effect on the Filters area.

What happens is that the Filters area for the visualization will reflect the selected drill-down element. As an example, you could try the following (I will not give all the details for all the steps as a bit of revision for you):

1. Create a matrix based on the following fields, in the following order:

   a. Color

   b. CountryName

   c. ClientType

   d. CostPrice

2. Remove the totals.

3. Set the matrix to be a drill-down table (by rows).

4. Drill down to the second level by double-clicking Night Blue and then Dealer.

5. Expand the Filters area (if necessary) and click Matrix to see the visualization-level filters.

6. Expand the Color and ClientType filters.

The table, and the Filters area, will look like Figure 3-22.

Figure 3-22. *Drill-down and filters*

As you can see, the filters indicate the drill-down elements, both by indicating the selected elements and by selecting the appropriate check boxes. So, drilling down is essentially a filter operation.

Annotate, Annotate, Annotate

If you are presenting a key finding based on a data set, then it can save a lot of embarrassment if you make it clear in every case what the data does, and does not, contain. You could, for instance, be so pleased with the revelatory sales trend that you have discovered that you forget to note an important exclusion in the underlying data. Now, no one is suggesting that you are doing anything other than making a point, but your audience needs to know what has been excluded, and possibly why—just in case it makes a difference. After all, you don't want a rival using this point to try to invalidate your findings in the middle of a vital meeting, do you?

Annotation techniques are described in Chapter 7 if you need to jump ahead to check this out now.

Conclusion

This chapter showed you how to apply and fine-tune a series of techniques to enable you to select the data that will appear in your Power View reports. The main thing to take away is that you can filter data at two levels: the overall report and each individual visualization.

You have also seen a variety of selection techniques that allow you to subset data. These range from the avowedly simple selection of a few elements to the specification of a more complex spread of dates or values. Finally, it is worth remembering that you can filter data using any fields in the underlying data set, whether the field is displayed in a report or not.

CHAPTER 4

■ ■ ■

Charts in Power View

It is one thing to have a game-changing insight that can fundamentally alter the way your business works. It is quite another to be able to convince your colleagues of your vision. So, what better way to show them—intuitively and instantaneously—that you are right than with a chart that makes your point irrefutably?

Power View is predicated on the concept that a picture is worth many thousands of words. Its charting tools let you create clear and convincing visualizations that tell your audience far more than a profusion of figures ever could. This chapter, therefore, will show you how simple it can be not just to make your data explain your analysis but to make it seem to leap off the screen. You will see over the next few pages how a powerful chart can persuade your peers and bosses that your ideas and insights are the ones to follow.

A little more prosaically, Power View lets you make a suitable data set into the following:

- Pie charts

- Bar charts

- Column charts

- Line charts

- Scatter charts

- Bubble charts

- Multiple charts

In this chapter, you will get up and running by looking at creating pie, bar, column, and line charts. The other chart types will be discussed in the next chapter. Once you have decided upon the most appropriate chart type, you can then enhance your visualization with titles, data labels, and legends, where appropriate. You will also see how to apply drill-down techniques to charts and how to filter the data that underlies them.

The sample file for this chapter is `CarSales.xlsx`, which you should find in the directory `C:\ DataVisualisationInExcel2016`—assuming you have installed the samples as described in Appendix A.

A First Chart

As with so much in Power View, it is easier to appreciate its simplicity and power by doing rather than talking. So, I suggest leaping straight into creating a first chart straightaway. In this section, you will look only at "starter" charts that all share a common thread—they are based on a single column of data values and a single column of descriptive elements. This data will be the following:

- A list of clients

- Car sales for a given year

© Adam Aspin 2016
A. Aspin, *High Impact Data Visualization in Excel with Power View, 3D Maps, Get & Transform and Power BI*,
DOI 10.1007/978-1-4842-2400-7_4

So, let's get charting!

Any Power View chart begins as a data set. So, let me introduce you to the world of charts; this is how to begin:

1. Create a new Power View report by clicking Power View in the Insert ribbon.

2. Display the field list by clicking the Field List button in the Power View ribbon (unless the field list is already visible).

3. Drag the field ClientName from the Clients table onto the Power View report canvas.

4. Drag the field SalePrice from the SalesData table onto the table that was created in the report canvas during the previous step.

5. Expand the YearHierarchy in the Date table and add the Year field to the Filters area. Select the year 2013 (I'll let you refer to Chapter 3 if you need a refresher on how this is done). The data table should look something like Figure 4-1.

ClientName	SalePrice
Aldo Motors	637750
Bright Orange	1034250
Carosse Des Papes	152040
Chateau Moi	157990
Costa Del Speed	91750
Crippen & Co	123000
Cut'n'Shut	964250
Honest John	914000
Impressive Wheels	87250
Jungfrau	301740
Karz	71000
Les Arnaqueurs	348750
Luxury Rentals	103250
Olde Englande	143750
Premium Motor Vehicles	41250
Rocky Riding	150000
Smooth Riders	64750
Three Country Cars	111000
Vive la Vitesse!	204190
Voitures Diplomatiques S.A.	159500
Wheels'R'Us	1297250
Total	**7158710**

Figure 4-1. *A source data table for charting*

6. Leaving the table selected, click Bar Chart and then Clustered Bar in the Design ribbon. Your chart should look like Figure 4-2.

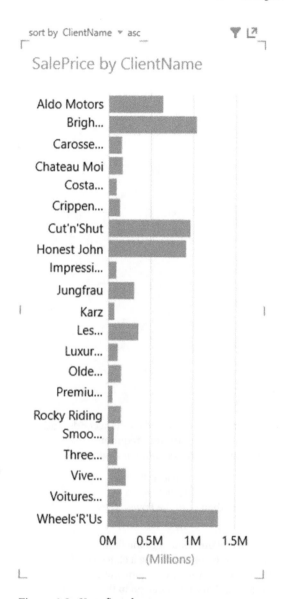

Figure 4-2. *Your first chart*

7. Resize the chart—I suggest widening it—by dragging the handle in the middle of the right edge to the right until the axis labels are clearly visible, as shown in Figure 4-3.

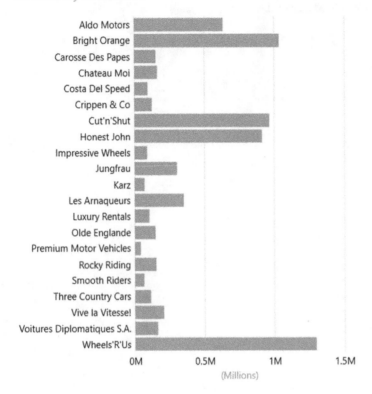

Figure 4-3. *A basic chart after resizing*

That is all there is to creating a simple starter chart. This process might take only a few seconds, and once it is complete, it is ready to show to your audience or be remodeled to suit your requirements. Nonetheless, a few comments are necessary to clarify the basics of chart creation in Power View.

- First, when creating the table on which a chart is based, you can use any of the techniques described in Chapter 2 to create a table. You can drag fields into the FIELDS well of the design section of the field list rather than onto the Power View canvas if you prefer.

- Second, when you transform a table into a chart, the layout section of the field list changes to reflect the options available when creating or modifying a chart. If you select the chart that you just created, you will see that the ClientName field has been placed in the AXIS well and the SalePrice field has been placed in the VALUES well. Neither of these wells existed when the visualization was a table. You can see this in Figure 4-4.

Figure 4-4. *The layout section of the field list for a clustered bar chart*

- Third, when using only a single data set, you can choose either clustered or stacked as the chart type for a bar or column chart; the result will be the same in either case. As you will see as you progress, this will not be the case for multiple data sets.

- Fourth, Power View will add a title at the top left of the chart explaining what data the chart is based on. You can see an example of this in Figure 4-3.

- Fifth, you can disregard the totals in the initial table. These are not used in a chart.

- Finally, creating a chart is very much a first step. You can do so much to enhance a chart and accentuate the insights that it can bring. However, all of this will follow later in this chapter and in the next one.

Deleting a Chart

Deleting a chart is as simple as deleting a table. All you have to do is

1. Click inside the chart.

2. Press the Delete key.

If you remove all the fields from the layout section of the field list (with the chart selected), then you will also delete the chart.

Basic Chart Modification

So, you have an initial chart. Suppose, however, that you want to change the actual data on which the chart is based. Well, all you have to do to change both the axis elements, the client names, and the values represented, is the following:

1. Click on, or inside, the chart you created previously. Avoid clicking any of the bars in the chart for the moment.

2. In the field list, click the pop-up menu for SalePrice in the VALUES well and select Remove Field. The bars will disappear from the chart.

3. Drag the field NetMargin from the SalesData table into the VALUES well.

4. In the field list, click the pop-up menu for ClientName in the AXIS well and select Remove Field. The client names will disappear from the chart, and a single bar will appear.

5. Click the pop-up menu for the Color field in the Colors table and select Add As Axis (or drag the Color field from the Colors table into the AXIS well). The list of colors will replace the list of clients on the axis, and a series of bars will replace the single bar. Look at Figure 4-5 to see the difference.

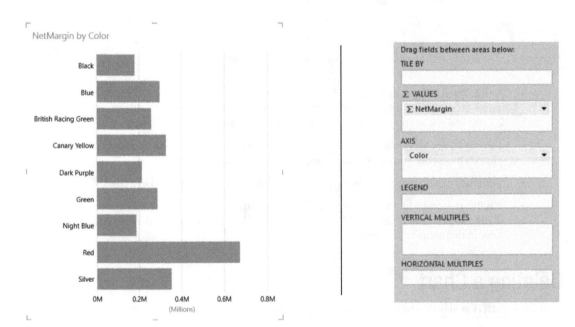

Figure 4-5. *A simple bar chart with the corresponding layout section*

That is it. You have changed the chart completely without rebuilding it. Power View has updated the data in the chart and the chart title to reflect your changes.

Basic Chart Types

When dealing with a single set of values, you will probably be using the following four core chart types:

- Bar chart
- Column chart
- Line chart
- Pie chart

Let's see how you can try these types of chart using the current data set—the colors and gross margin that you applied previously.

Column Charts

A column chart is, to all intents and purposes, a bar chart where the bars are vertical rather than horizontal. So, to switch your bar chart to a column chart, follow these steps:

1. Click on, or inside, the bar chart that you created previously. Avoid clicking any of the bars in the chart for the moment.

2. Click Column Chart and then Clustered Column in the Design ribbon. Your chart should look like Figure 4-6.

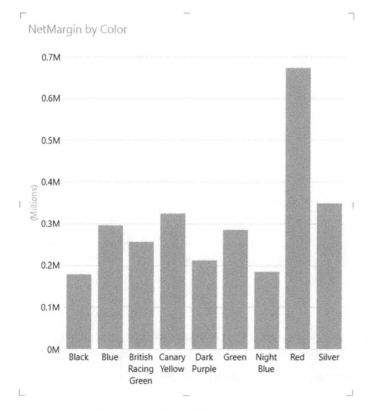

Figure 4-6. *An elementary column chart*

Line Charts

A line chart displays the data as a set of points joined by a line. To switch your column chart to a line chart, follow these steps:

1. Click on, or inside, the bar chart you created previously. Avoid clicking any of the bars in the chart for the moment.

2. Click Other Charts and then Line in the Design ribbon. Your chart should look like Figure 4-7.

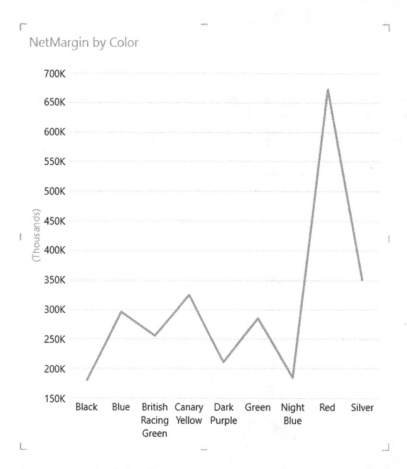

Figure 4-7. *A simple line chart*

Pie Charts

Pie charts can be superb at displaying a limited set of data for a single series—like you have in this example. To switch the visualization to a pie chart, follow these steps:

1. Click on, or inside, the line chart that you created previously. Avoid clicking the line in the chart for the moment.

2. Click Other Charts and then Pie in the Design ribbon. Your chart should look like Figure 4-8. You will notice that the layout section has changed slightly for a pie chart, and the AXIS well has been replaced by a COLOR well.

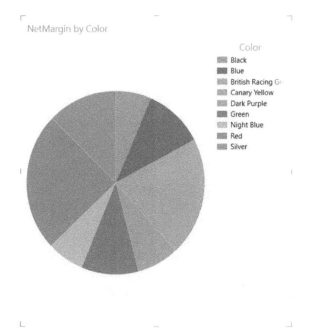

Figure 4-8. *A basic pie chart*

A pie chart will be distorted if it includes negative values at the same time as it contains positive values. What Power View will do is display the negative values as if they were positive because otherwise the values cannot be displayed. This is probably not the effect you were hoping for. If your data set contains a mix of positive and negative data, then Power View will display an alert above the chart warning you as follows: Pie Chart Contains Positive And Negative Values. You can see which pie slices contain negative values by hovering the mouse pointer over each slice and reading the values in the pop-up that appears.

In practice, you may prefer not to use pie charts when your data contains negative values, or you may want to separate out the positive and negative values into two data sets and display two charts, as explained in the "Chart Filters" section later in this chapter.

░ **Note** Juggling chart size and font size to fit in all the elements and axis and/or legend labels can be tricky. One useful trick is to prepare "abbreviated" data fields in the source data, as has been done in the case of the QuarterAbbr field in the Date table that contains Q1, Q2, and so on, rather than Quarter 1, Quarter 2, and so on, to save space in the chart. Chapter 17 gives techniques for this sort of data preparation.

Essential Chart Adjustments

Creating a chart in Power View is, I hope you will agree, extremely simple. Yet the process of producing a telling visualization does not stop when you take a table of data and switch it into a chart. At the least, you will want to make the following tweaks to your new chart:

- Resize the chart

- Reposition the chart

- Sort the elements in the chart

- Alter the size of the fonts in the chart

None of these tasks is at all difficult. Indeed, it can take only a few seconds to transform your initial chart into a compelling visual argument—when you know the techniques to apply.

Resizing Charts

A chart is like any other visualization on the Power View report and can be resized to suit your requirements. To resize a chart, follow these steps:

1. Place the mouse pointer over any of the eight handles that appear at the corners and in the middle of the edges of the chart that you want to adjust. The pointer becomes a two-headed arrow.

2. Drag the mouse pointer. As you are resizing the chart, its background changes color to indicate that it is selected.

■ **Note**   You do not have to select or click inside a chart before you resize it. Remember that the lateral handles will let you resize the chart only horizontally or vertically and that the corner handles allow you to resize both horizontally and vertically.

When resizing a chart, you will see that this can have a dramatic effect on the text that appears on an axis. Power View will always try to keep the space available for the text on an axis proportionate to the size of the whole chart.

For bar charts, this can mean that the text can be

- Adjusted to spread over two or more lines

- Cut, with words split over two rows

- Truncated, with an ellipsis (three dots) indicating that not all the text is visible

For column and line charts, this can mean that the text can be

- Adjusted to spread over two or more lines

- Angled at 30, 60, or 90 degrees

- Truncated, with an ellipsis (three dots) indicating that not all the text is visible

If you reduce the height (for a bar chart) or the width (for a column or a line chart) below a certain threshold, Power View will stop trying to show all the elements on the non-numeric axis. Instead, it will show only a few elements and will add a scroll bar to allow you to scroll through the remaining data. You can see an example of this for a bar chart in Figure 4-9.

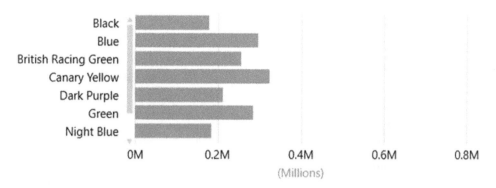

Figure 4-9. *A chart with a scroll bar visible*

All this means is that you might have to tweak the size and the height to width ratio of your chart until you get the best result. If you are in a hurry to get this right, I advise using the handle in the bottom-right corner to resize a chart, as dragging this up, down, left, and right will quickly show you the available display options.

Repositioning Charts

You can move a chart anywhere inside the Power View report.

1. Place the mouse pointer over the border of the chart. The pointer changes into a hand. As you are repositioning the chart, its background changes color to indicate that it is selected.

2. Drag the mouse pointer.

Sorting Chart Elements

Sometimes you can really make a point about data by changing the order in which you have it appear in a chart. Up until this point you have probably noticed that when you create a chart, the elements on the axis (and this is true for a bar chart, column chart, line chart, or pie chart) are in alphabetical order by default. If you want to confirm this, then just take a look at Figures 4-5 to 4-8 on the preceding pages.

Suppose now, for instance, you want to show the way that sales are affected by the color of the vehicle. In this case, you want to sort the data in a chart from highest to lowest so that you can see the way in which the figures fall, or rise, in a clear order. Here is how to do this:

1. Select the Clustered Bar chart type, as described earlier (and shown in Figure 4-5).

2. Place the mouse pointer over the chart. You will see that Sort By Color Asc appears over the chart on the top left. This is shown in Figure 4-10.

Sort Options

Figure 4-10. The sort area in a chart

3. Click the word *Color*. This will change to NetMargin, and the sort order of the elements in the chart will change.

4. Let's suppose now that you want to see the sales by color in descending order. Place the mouse pointer over the chart. You will see that Sort By NetMargin Asc appears over the chart on the top left.

5. Click Asc. This becomes Desc, and the chart changes to become like it is in Figure 4-11.

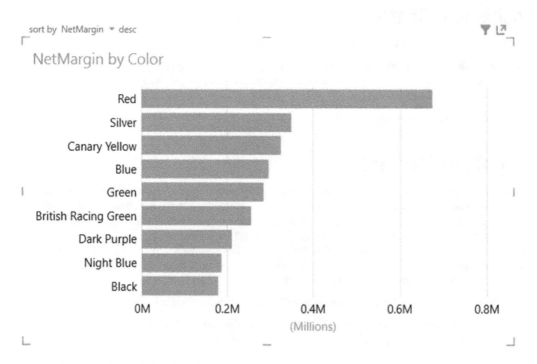

Figure 4-11. Sorting data in a bar chart

If a chart has multiple values, as will be the case for some of the charts that you will see later in this chapter, then you have two options when selecting the field on which the chart will be ordered.

- Click the field name that appears above the top left of the chart when the mouse pointer is placed over the chart (as you did a moment ago). Each click will change the sort to the next available field used by the chart and then continue to cycle through the fields.

- Click the downward-facing triangle to the right of the currently selected sort field to get a pop-up list of available fields to sort on. Then click the field you want to use as a basis for the sort. This is shown in Figure 4-12.

Figure 4-12. *Selecting the sort element in a chart*

I should add just a short remark about sorting pie charts. When you sort a pie chart, the pie chart will be sorted clockwise, starting at the top of the chart. So, if you are sorting colors by NetMargin in descending order, the top-selling color will be at the top of the pie chart (at 12 o'clock), with the second bestselling color will be to its immediate right (3 o'clock, for example), and so on. Figure 4-13 shows an example of this.

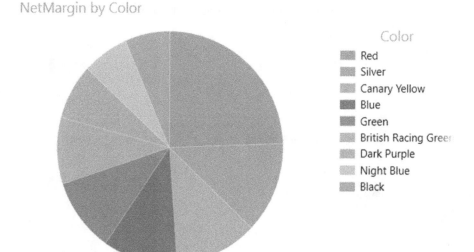

Figure 4-13. *Sorting data in a pie chart*

Font Size

When a chart is initially created, Power View will apply a default font size. This font size will not change proportionally if you resize the chart. This does not, however, mean that Power View fixes font sizes definitively. You can influence matters by choosing proportionally to reduce, or increase, the size of the fonts used on both axes of the chart. You can do this in the following way:

1. Select the chart (but do not click any of the bars, columns, or lines).

2. In the Design ribbon, click the Increase Font Size button to make the fonts in the chart larger or click the Decrease Font Size button to make the fonts in the chart smaller.

Adjusting the font size will produce many of the same effects that you saw when you were resizing a chart; namely, text on the axes will be as follows:

*   Adjusted to spread over two or more lines

*   Truncated, with an ellipsis (three dots) indicating that not all the text is visible

*   Angled at 30, 60, or 90 degrees

If Power View considers the text too large to display all the elements in the chart, then it will show only a few elements and will add a scroll bar to allow you to scroll through the remaining data.

Applying Color to Bar and Column Charts

The bar and column charts that you have created so far are a little lacking in color, as every bar or column is the same shade. If you want to add a splash of color, then you can override the default and make Power View apply a palette of colors to the bars and columns for a chart based on a single data element.

For example, take the column chart shown in Figure 4-5; all you have to do is the following:

1. Drag the Color field from the AXIS well into the LEGEND well in the layout section of the field list.

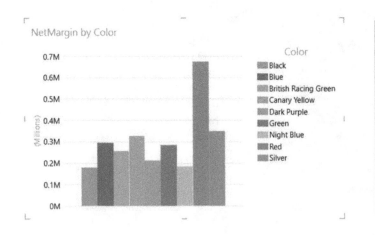
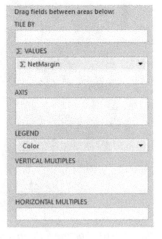

Figure 4-14. *Applying a color palette to individual columns*

You can see the result in Figure 4-14. The axis titles are now the legend elements, and the bars are in different colors. Admittedly, on the printed page you cannot see the colors, but the shading indicates that your changes have worked! You can get a similar result for a bar chart.

■ **Note**　You cannot sort a chart like this one—one that does not have any axis values.

Multiple Data Values in Charts

So far in this chapter you have seen simple charts that display a single value. Life is, unfortunately, rarely that simple, so it is time to move on to slightly more complex, but possibly more realistic, scenarios where you need to compare and contrast multiple data elements.

For this set of examples, I will presume that you need to take an in-depth look at the indirect cost elements of your car sales to date. These are

- Parts

- Delivery

- Labor

All of these can be found in the CarSalesData table.

Consequently, to begin with a fairly simple comparison of these indirect costs, let's start with a clustered column chart.

1. Starting with a clean Power View report, create a table that displays the following fields:

   a. ClientName (from the Clients table)

   b. SpareParts (from the SalesData table)

   c. DeliveryCharge (from the SalesData table)

   d. LabourCost (from the SalesData table)

2. Filter to include only data for the year 2013 as described for the initial chart that you created at the start of this chapter.

3. Leaving the table selected, click Bar Chart and then Clustered Bar in the Design ribbon.

4. Resize the chart to make it clear and comprehensible, as shown in Figure 4-15 (I have included the field list so that you can see this too).

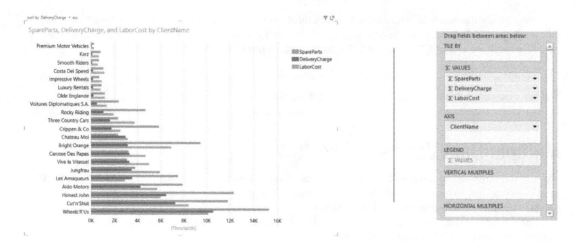

Figure 4-15. *Multiple data values in charts—a clustered bar chart with the layout section shown*

You will notice that a chart with multiple data sets has a legend by default and that the automatic chart title now says SpareParts, DeliveryCharge, And LaborCost By ClientName.

The same data set can be used as a basis for other charts that can effectively display multiple data values. These are as follows:

- Stacked bar

- Clustered column and stacked column

- Line charts

As column charts are essentially bar charts pivoted through 90 degrees, I will not show examples of these here. However, in Figures 4-16 and 4-17, you will see examples of a stacked bar chart and a line chart. You will also see that when creating these types of visualization, the layout section of the field list remains the same for all these charts.

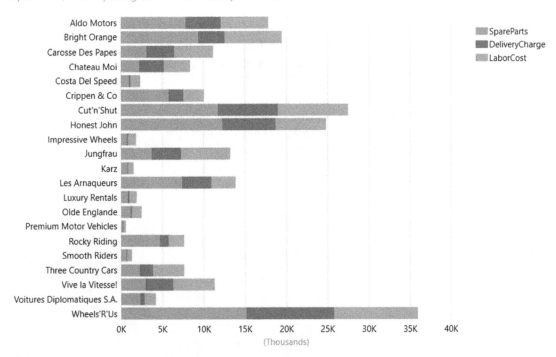

Figure 4-16. *A simple stacked bar chart*

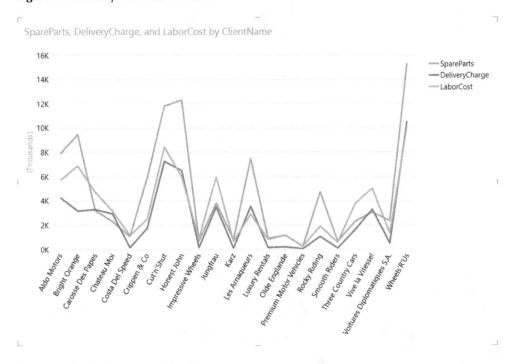

Figure 4-17. *An introductory line chart*

■ **Note** You cannot create a stacked bar or stacked column chart directly from a table that has multiple numeric data values, so you have two choices: either you start with a table containing only one numeric data value and then drag the other numeric fields that you want to use onto the stacked chart (or into the $\sum$ VALUES well) or you start with a clustered chart that you then convert into a stacked chart.

To conclude the tour of basic charts, I just want to make a couple of comments.

First, you can always see exactly what the figures behind a bar, column, line, point, or pie segment are just by hovering the mouse pointer over the bar (or column or line or pie segment). This will work whether the chart is its normal size or whether it has been popped out to cover the Power View report area. Figure 4-18 shows an example of this.

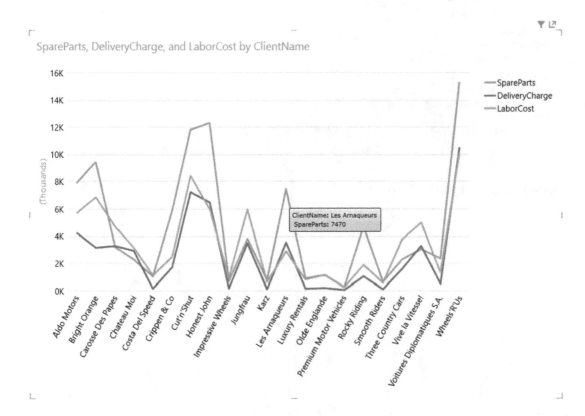

Figure 4-18. *A clustered bar chart with the pop-up displayed*

Second, however much work you have done to a chart, you can always switch it back to a table if you want. Simply select the chart, and select the required table type from the Table button in the Design ribbon. If you do this, you will see that the table attempts to mimic the design tweaks that you applied to the chart, keeping the font sizes the same as in the chart and the size of the table identical to that of the chart. Should you subsequently switch back to the chart, then you should find virtually all of the design choices that you applied are still present—unless, of course, you made any changes to the table before switching back to the chart visualization.

The Layout Ribbon

You have already seen most of the basic charting techniques. I hope that you found them as simple as I promised they would be. So, before moving on to the next level, I will explain a new Power View ribbon that appears every time you click a chart. It is the Layout ribbon.

The Layout ribbon is largely devoted to enhancing charts in Power View. Figure 4-19 outlines the buttons it contains.

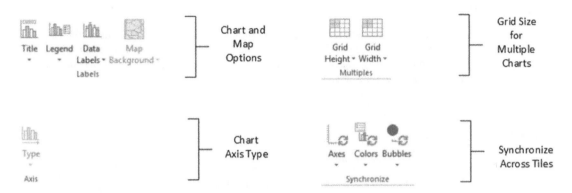

Figure 4-19. *The Layout ribbon*

There are only a few buttons in the Layout ribbon, and they are, fortunately, largely intuitive. Should you need a reference, Table 4-1 gives a detailed explanation of their use.

Table 4-1. *The Layout Ribbon Buttons*

Button	Description
Title	Adds or removes a title from the chart.
Legend	Lets you choose where (if at all) the legend is placed on a chart.
Data Labels	Lets you decide to add or hide data labels and choose where they are placed.
Map Background	Adds a thematic background to a map. This is explained in Chapter 7.
Axis Type	Lets charts have continuous or interrupted axes.
Grid Height	Allows you to choose the number of vertical charts that can be displayed if multiples are selected.
Grid Width	Allows you to choose the number of horizontal charts that can be displayed if multiples are selected.
Axes	Synchronizes chart axes when tiles are added to a chart.
Colors	Synchronizes chart colors across the tiles when tiles are added to a chart.
Bubbles	Synchronizes chart bubble sizing when tiles are added to a chart.

Enhancing Charts

Now that you have been introduced to the Layout ribbon and have mastered basic charts, it is time to move on to the next step and learn how to tweak your charts to the greatest effect. The next few sections are, consequently, devoted to the various techniques available in Power View to give your charts real clarity and power.

Chart Legends

If you have a chart with more than one field that provides the values on which the chart is based, then you will see a legend appear automatically. The default for the legend is for it to be placed on the right of the chart. However, you can choose where to place the legend, or even whether to display it at all, by choosing from one of the options that appear when you click the Legend button in the Layout ribbon.

Table 4-2 describes the available options.

Table 4-2. *Legend Position Options*

Legend Option	Comments
None	No legend is displayed for this chart.
Show Legend At Right	The legend is displayed at the right of the chart.
Show Legend At Top	The legend is displayed above the chart.
Show Legend At Left	The legend is displayed at the left of the chart.
Show Legend At Bottom	The legend is displayed below the chart.

If one of the legend options is grayed out, it is because this is the option that is currently active.

Legends can require a little juggling until they display their contents in a readable way. This is because the text of the legend is often truncated when it is initially displayed. If this is the case, you have two options.

- Decrease the font size for the chart (as described earlier)

- Modify the chart size

Do not hesitate to try both these methods and to switch between the two, as Power View will often end up by displaying the legend in a way that suits your requirements as you adjust these two aspects of the chart display.

▦ **Note**   A legend can contain a scroll bar (vertical for legends to the left or right or horizontal in the case of legends above or below the chart). This can be both extremely useful if you are dealing with many elements in a legend and extremely disconcerting if you are not expecting it!

Chart Title

Each chart is created with a title explaining what the chart is displaying, that is, the fields on which it is based. Here, the available options are fairly simple, as you can only choose between displaying the title or not.

1. To hide the chart title, all you have to do is click the Title button in the Layout ribbon and select None.

2. To make a title reappear, click the Title button in the Layout ribbon, and select Above Chart.

You can always add further annotations to a chart using free-form text boxes. This is described in Chapter 7.

Chart Data Labels

As you have seen already, you can display the exact data behind a column, bar, or point in a line chart simply by hovering the mouse pointer over the data that interests you. Yet there could be times when you want to display the values behind the chart permanently on the visualization. This is where data labels come into play.

To add data labels to a chart (in this example I will use the chart shown in Figure 4-11, which you created previously), all you have to do is follow these steps:

1. Click inside the chart to which you want to add data labels.

2. Go to the Layout ribbon.

3. Select Outside End from the Data Labels button.

Power View will add data labels to the chart, as shown in Figure 4-20.

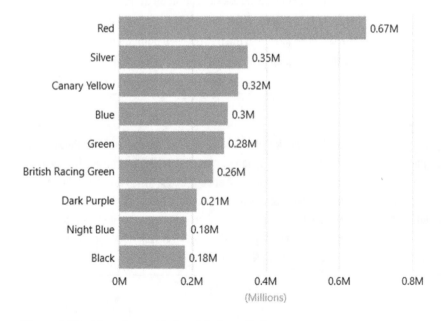

NetMargin by Color

Figure 4-20. *A bar chart with data labels applied*

As you will have seen when you were clicking the Data Labels button, Power View gives you several options concerning the placement of data labels in a chart. Table 4-3 explains these options.

Table 4-3. *Data Labels for Column and Bar Charts*

Data Label Option	Comments
None	No data labels will be superimposed on the chart.
Center	The data label will be displayed (if possible) inside the data area.
Inside End	The data label will be displayed (if possible) inside the data area, at the top end of the bar or column.
Inside Base	The data label will be displayed (if possible) inside the data area, at the top end of the bar or column.
Outside End	The data label will be displayed (if possible) outside the data area, at the top end of the bar or column.

When applying data labels to line charts, the possible options are somewhat different from those offered for bar and column charts. Table 4-4 gives the options for line charts.

Table 4-4. *Data Labels for Line Charts*

Data Label Option	Comments
None	No data labels will be superimposed on the chart.
Auto	Power View will place the data labels as it sees best.
Center	Data labels will be placed across each point on the chart.
Left	Data labels will be placed to the left of each point on the chart.
Right	Data labels will be placed to the right of each point on the chart.
Above	Data labels will be placed above each point on the chart.
Below	Data labels will be placed below each point on the chart.

■ **Note**   When applying data labels to column, bar, and line charts, you will notice that sometimes Power View cannot, physically, place all the data labels exactly where the option that you have selected implies that they should appear. This is because on some occasions there is simply not enough space inside a bar or column at the upper or lower end of a chart to fit the figures because the bar or column is too small. In these cases, Power View will place the data outside the bar or column. On other occasions, the data cannot fit outside a line, column, or bar without being placed above the upper end of the axis. Here again, Power View will tweak the presentation to get as close as possible to the effect that you asked for.

There are a few final points to note on the subject of data labels:

- If one of the data label options is grayed out when you click the Data Labels button on the Layout ribbon, it is because this is the option that is currently active.

- Pie charts cannot display data labels, so the Data Labels button is grayed out on the Layout ribbon.

- Scatter charts and balloon charts can also display data labels. However, they will not display figures; instead, they will display the labels (the descriptive text) for the point or balloon in a chart.

Drilling Down in Charts

In Chapter 2, you saw that Power View lets you drill down into tables, level by level, to pursue your analyses of the underlying data. Well, it probably comes as no surprise to discover that you can also drill down into the data that is displayed as charts, as well as drill back up again. As an example of this, let's imagine that you want to take a look at average direct costs and average sale costs. Yet you want to see these:

- At the top level, by country

- Then, for a given country, by car age bucket (this is explained in Chapter 10 and is a way of grouping car ages into a set of thresholds)

Let's see how this can be done:

1. Start with a new Power View report, where the report filter is set to allow data only for the year 2013.

2. Add the following fields to the FIELDS well in the field list:

    a. CountryName (from the Countries table)

    b. VehicleAgeCategory (from the SalesData table)

    c. DirectCosts (from the SalesData table)

    d. SpareParts (from the SalesData table)

3. Click the pop-up triangle at the right of the DirectCosts and SalesCosts fields and set the aggregation to Average for each of these fields.

4. Switch the visualization from Table to Matrix, using the Table button in the Design ribbon.

5. Also in the Design Ribbon, click Show Levels and select Rows, Enable Drill Down One Level At A Time.

6. Switch the visualization to clustered column (using the Column button in the Design ribbon). You will see a column chart with only the top level of axes (CountryName) visible. It should look like Figure 4-21. Note that the title is Average Of DirectCosts, Average Of SpareParts By CountryName.

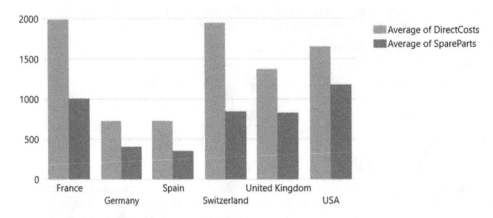

Figure 4-21. *The top level in a drill-down chart*

7. Double-click either of the columns for the United Kingdom. You will drill down to the next axis level, VehicleAgeCategory. The chart should look like Figure 4-22. Note that the title is now Average of DirectCosts, and Average Of SpareParts by VehicleAgeCategory.

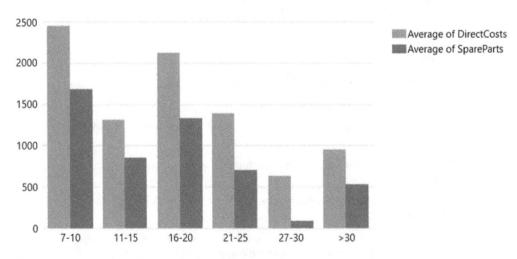

Figure 4-22. *A lower level in a drill-down chart*

8. To drill back up to the preceding level, click the Drill-Up icon, which appears at the top right of the chart (as shown in Figure 4-23).

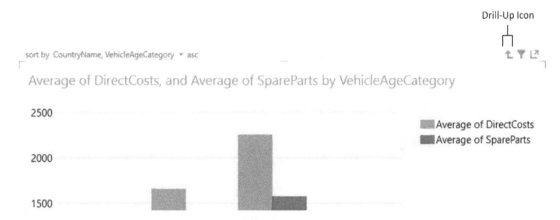

Figure 4-23. The Drill-Up icon in a chart visualization

Drilling up will return you to the initial chart, as shown in Figure 4-20.

Now, the technique that I just explained is not the only way to create a drill-down chart. I would argue that it is probably the easiest to do when you are new to Power View or when you are testing things as you try to find a suitable visualization to express your findings in visual form. However, and in the interests of completeness, there is another way that I tend to use in practice. It consists of the following:

- Creating a single-level chart

- Adding a second level (or indeed, several more levels) to this chart

To create a drill-down chart using this alternative approach, follow these steps:

1. Add the following fields to the FIELDS well in the field list in a Power View report:

   a. CountryName (from the Countries table)

   b. NetSales (from the SalesData table)

   c. CostPrice (from the SalesData table)

■ **Note**   As you can see, you did not add VehicleAgeCategory (from the SalesData table) yet. Also, you need to make sure that the values are set to use the Average aggregation type.

---

2. Add a view-level filter for the year 2013.

3. Switch the visualization to a clustered bar chart (to ring the changes a little). You should see a chart like Figure 4-24.

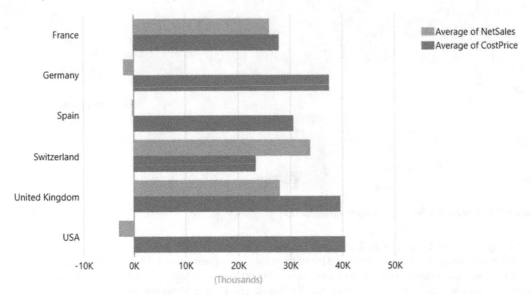

Figure 4-24. *A clustered bar chart using average aggregations*

4. Leaving the chart selected, add the VehicleAgeCategory (from the SalesData table) to the AXIS well in the field list Design area, under the CountryName field. The field list Design area should look like Figure 4-25.

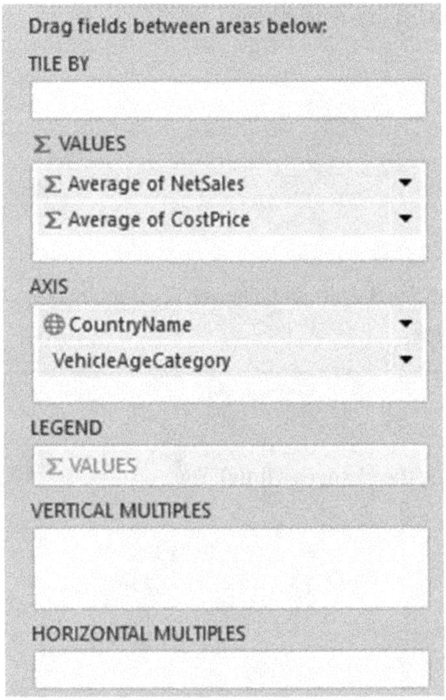

Figure 4-25. *The field list's layout section for a clustered bar chart and average aggregations*

Nothing in the chart has changed; yet, if you double-click any bar, you drill down to the next level. If you were to try this with Switzerland, for instance, you would see what appears in Figure 4-26.

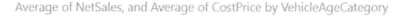

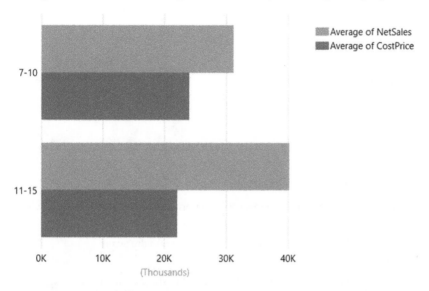

Figure 4-26. *Drilling down inside a chart*

You can add multiple levels to the axis of a chart into which you want to drill down. If you want to change the order of the elements used to provide the levels you use to drill down, then all you have to do is alter the arrangement of the field names in the AXIS well of the field list's design area by dragging them up or down.

You can remove a level in this hierarchy in one of two ways.

- Clicking the pop-up icon for the level at the right of the field name and selecting Remove Field

- Dragging the field out of the AXIS well of the field list's design area and up into the field list area

As it is all too easy to get lost when using charts with multiple hierarchical levels, I advise you to take a look at the chart title before drilling up or down. This way you can always see which level in the data hierarchy is currently displayed. Also, you can always see whether you are at the top of a hierarchy—the Drill-Up icon will never appear at the top right of a chart.

Popping Charts Out and In

Once you have perfected the appearance of a chart, you can zoom in to the chart for a detailed look.

1. Move the mouse pointer over the chart (I will use the one you saw in Figure 4-15). You will see two tiny icons appear over the top right of the chart. You can see these icons in Figure 4-27.

Figure 4-27. *The Pop Out icon*

2. Click the rightmost of these icons—the Pop Out icon.

The chart will expand to cover the entire area of the Power View report. Not only that, but the following changes will be visible:

- The axis text will be adjusted and should not contain ellipses (unless the text is extraordinarily long).

- The number of elements displayed will be adjusted to attempt to show as much data as clearly as possible. This can mean that any scroll bars that are visible in the chart before you clicked Pop Out could disappear.

- The major gridline on the values axis could change to allow finer increments.

Take a look at the chart you created previously in Figure 4-15; once it has been popped out, you can see that a much clearer representation of the underlying data is available. Indeed, to get the full effect of a pop-out, it is probably better to see the entire Power View report, as shown in Figure 4-28.

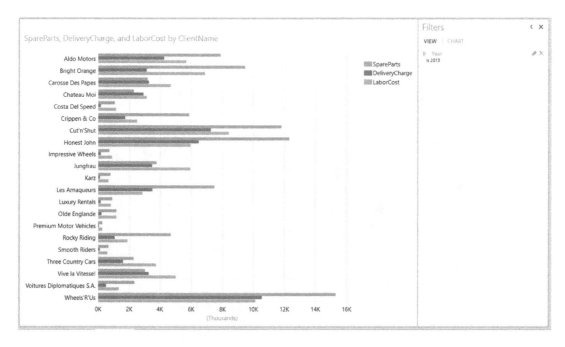

Figure 4-28. *A pop-out chart*

▪ **Note** A pop-out visualization cannot be saved in its expanded version. A Power View report will always open with all visualizations in their normal state. Interestingly, you cannot delete a chart that is expanded, either.

Chart Filters

Any chart can be filtered to show a subset of the data that you want to display. Fortunately, applying filters is easy, as all the filtering techniques are identical to those that I described in the previous chapter. So, I will assume that you have already taken a look at Chapter 3, and here I will build on the knowledge you have already acquired and explain how it can be used effectively when creating chart visualizations with Power View.

To give a practical example of this, let's take up a point that I made earlier about negative values in pie charts. To avoid giving the idea that negative gross margin is somehow positive, it would be a good idea to display two pie charts that show, respectively, clients where you made money and clients where you lost money in 2013. This is how you can do it:

1. Create a new Power View report and set the report filter to include data for the year 2013 only.

2. Drag the field ClientName from the Clients table onto the report area.

3. Drag the field NetMargin from the SalesData table onto the table containing the client names.

4. Make this table into a pie chart. You will see the warning that the chart contains negative data, as shown in Figure 4-29.

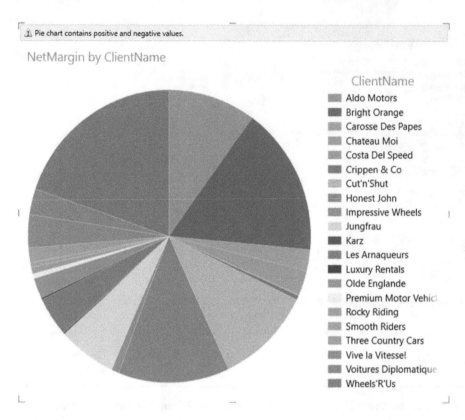

⚠ Pie chart contains positive and negative values.

NetMargin by ClientName

ClientName
- Aldo Motors
- Bright Orange
- Carosse Des Papes
- Chateau Moi
- Costa Del Speed
- Crippen & Co
- Cut'n'Shut
- Honest John
- Impressive Wheels
- Jungfrau
- Karz
- Les Arnaqueurs
- Luxury Rentals
- Olde Englande
- Premium Motor Vehic
- Rocky Riding
- Smooth Riders
- Three Country Cars
- Vive la Vitesse!
- Voitures Diplomatique
- Wheels'R'Us

Figure 4-29. *A pie chart containing negative values*

5. Sort the chart by NetMargin, in descending order (hover the mouse pointer over the chart, and when Sort By ClientName, Asc appears at the top of the chart, click ClientName and Asc to switch them to NetMargin and Desc).

6. Click inside this chart (but not on any pie segment) and display the Filter pane (unless it is already visible).

7. Click Chart in the Filters area, expand NetMargin, and click the Advanced Filter Mode icon.

8. From the pop-up Show Items For Which The Value, select Is Greater Than Or Equal To.

9. From the box under this selection, enter **0** (zero), and press Enter. This will prevent negative numbers from being displayed.

10. Tweak the font size, and resize the chart if you want to, to give it the allure that you prefer.

11. Copy the pie chart and ensure that the copy is selected.

12. Click Chart in the Filters area; NetMargin should be expanded and in Advanced Filter mode.

13. In the pop-up Show Items For Which The Value in the Filter pane, select Is Less Than 0, and press Enter.

14. Sort the values in the second stacked bar chart by NetMargin, Ascending (as these are negative values, you want to see the biggest loss-maker first).

15. Tweak the font sizes and adjust the legend position for the second chart.

16. Position the two pie charts on the Power View report.

The report should look like Figure 4-30. You can always see the exact figures that underlie the visualization by floating the mouse pointer over a pie segment.

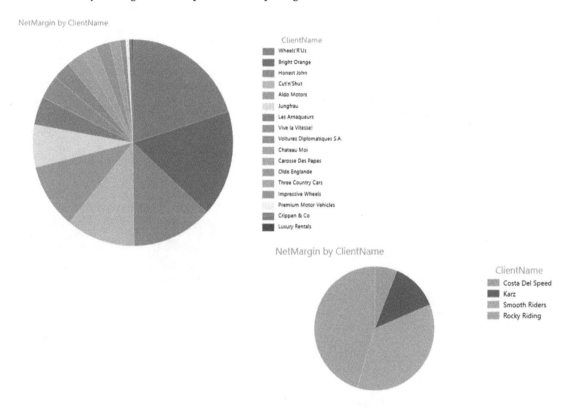

Figure 4-30. *Pie charts with separate filters for each chart*

Data visualization purists are, I imagine, looking at the pie chart of positive sales and muttering that there are too many elements for a single pie chart and that there are too many clients for whom the sales figures are too small to be read easily. I agree, and the solution is to split the pie chart of positive values into two charts: one for major clients and one for the smaller clients. I will also set the chart of all middle-sized clients to be a bar chart, as there are (in my opinion) too many elements for a pie chart. So, to separate out the clients with sales less than 200,000.00 (I came up with this figure by looking at the sales figures in the pop-up for the pie slices; I chose what seemed to be a good break point between major sales and lower sales figures), you will extend the chart filter used previously to set a filter of upper and lower boundaries for the data in the chart.

1. Click the initial pie chart for positive sales.

2. Click Chart in the Filter pane.

3. Change the value for Is Greater Than Or Equal To to **200000**, and press Enter.

4. Copy the initial pie chart for positive sales and ensure that the copy is selected.

5. Convert this chart to a clustered bar chart by selecting Clustered Bar from the Bar Chart button in the Design ribbon. This is to show you that filters are applied independently of the chart type.

6. In the Filter pane for the third (clustered bar) chart, change the value for Is Greater Than Or Equal To to **0** and press Enter.

7. Click And under the box where you entered the value 0.

8. Select Is Less Than Or Equal To from the second pop-up.

9. From the box under this selection, enter **200000** and press Enter.

10. Set Chart Type to Clustered Column.

11. Tweak the layout of all three charts until you have a telling presentation.

Figure 4-31 gives an example of how the data can be filtered to create three separate charts.

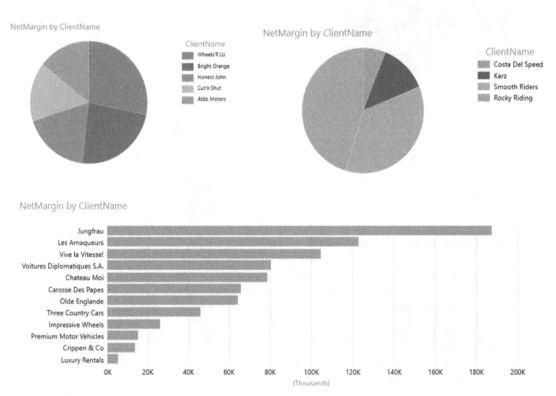

Figure 4-31. *Individual charts with separate filters*

I have jumped ahead slightly here by adding a title to the dashboard. This technique is explained in Chapter 7 if you want to flip a few pages and find out. However, what matters here is that you have seen how to fine-tune individual visualizations so that they display only the data you want them to show.

Conclusion

The techniques described in this chapter should help you produce a real "wow" effect on your audience. You can now deliver punchy presentations where crisp clear charts help you make your point with definite panache.

You have seen how to create a set of basic chart types (pie charts, bar charts, column charts, and line charts) using one or more data values. You have also seen how to filter charts using the same filtering techniques that you learned previously.

However, charts do not end at this in Power View. There is a further range of more advanced charting possibilities that you can learn to exploit; they are the subject of the next chapter.

CHAPTER 5

■ ■ ■

Advanced Charting with Power View

Now that you have mastered the core skills required to create simple but powerful charts with Power View, the time has come to extend your knowledge and discover some of the more advanced charting possibilities that are open to you. The techniques that you will look at in this chapter are as follows:

- Multiple charts

- Scatter charts

- Bubble charts

- Using a play axis to animate charts

These more advanced charting techniques are well worth learning, in my opinion, as they allow you to make your point with greater subtlety and originality. Used effectively, they can enhance considerably the clarity of a presentation and can make your analysis stand out in the crowd.

In this chapter, too, you will be using the sample file CarSales.xlsx from the folder C:\ DataVisualisationInExcel2016. How to download the contents of this folder is explained in Appendix A.

Multiple Charts

Teasing out real meaning from a mass of data occasionally requires an approach that goes beyond the traditional charts that you may be used to using. Power View comes to your aid in this area by giving you the possibility of creating multiple charts simultaneously, which can allow you to see individual details and trends as well as comparative distinctions. These types of visualization are also known as *trellis* or *lattice* charts.

Multiple-chart visualizations, as is the case with single-chart visualizations, display and enhance data differently according to the chart type. So, to give you a flavor of what you can achieve using Power View, here are a few examples of multiple-chart visualizations using different chart types. This way, you can decide on the type that best suits your data.

Multiple Bar or Column Charts

Let's assume that you want to see a comparative breakdown of dealer sales compared to wholesaler sales, but you want them split into multiple bar charts (which could just as easily be column charts), one for each car age range. This is how you can do it:

© Adam Aspin 2016

A. Aspin, *High Impact Data Visualization in Excel with Power View, 3D Maps, Get & Transform and Power BI*, DOI 10.1007/978-1-4842-2400-7_5

1. Insert a new Power View report, or open an uncluttered report, as you will need a certain amount of space for a multiple-chart visualization.

2. Create a table using the following fields:

   a. Make (from the CarDetails hierarchy in the SalesData table)

   b. NetMargin (from the SalesData table)

3. Convert the table to a bar chart (in the Design ribbon, select Bar Chart and then Clustered Bar).

4. Drag the Color field from the Colors table into the VERTICAL MULTIPLES well in the design area of the field list.

5. Apply a filter to include data only for the year 2013 (as described for the initial chart shown in Figure 4-1 in the previous chapter).

6. Resize your visualization with the multiple bar charts, which, as it stands, is probably too small to be really effective.

7. Tweak the font sizes if you want.

Your Power View report should look something like Figure 5-1. This figure includes the layout section of the field list so that you can see what it looks like for a multiple-chart visualization.

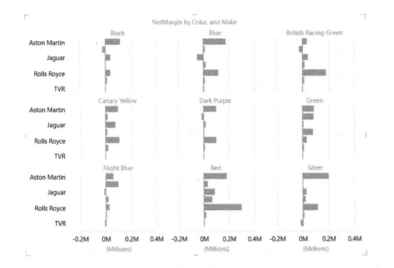

Figure 5-1. *Multiple bar charts*

You will notice that the title of the visualization is now NetMargin By Color And Make, which draws viewers' attention to the fact that they are looking at the multiple bar charts as a whole, not as a separate set of unconnected analyses. Also, if you chose to resize the visualization, you will have seen that Power View will not only alter the size of the overall chart "container" but also resize the individual charts inside it. However, all the charts inside the outer container will stay the same size.

■ **Tip** There is just one point to add specifically about multiple pie charts. Multiple pie charts can contain slices, just as single pie charts can. So, if you place the mouse pointer over a bar chart segment (color) or slice, you will get a pop-up that gives you the exact details of the data you are examining.

Specifying Vertical and Horizontal Selections

In the previous section, you saw how to visualize multiple charts to see how the color and make of a car affected the gross margin. Now let's take this one step further, by adding another element of comparison. Suppose that now you want to extend the analysis by adding the car age range to the mix to see whether this can tell you anything about your margins and how to improve them.

To do this, follow these steps:

1. Click inside the visualization that you made previously (NetMargin By Color And Make).

2. Drag the field VehicleAgeCategory into the HORIZONTAL MULTIPLES well of the design area of the field list.

And that is it! Your visualization now has colors on the vertical axis on the left side and the age range groups on the horizontal axis across the top. Yet each individual bar chart shows you the gross margin by make for each combination of color and car age group. It should look something like Figure 5-2.

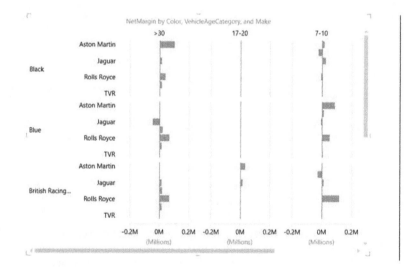

Figure 5-2. *Horizontal and vertical multiple charts*

Power View has added vertical and horizontal scroll bars to the visualization, so you can scroll through the available charts. You can also define the number of charts that are visible, which is described in the next section.

Specifying the Layout of Multiple-Chart Visualizations

In the first multiple-chart visualization you created, it was Power View that decided how the charts would be set out together—in two rows of three charts. This layout will change depending on the number of charts that are created, which will depend on the source data—specifically the number of elements in the field that you use to define the vertical multiples. However, you can override the default chart layout so you have the final word as to how your multiple charts are displayed.

Creating Horizontal Multiples

First, be aware that if you choose to place the field where the charts will be expanded into multiple charts into the VERTICAL MULTIPLES well, Power View will distribute the charts as best it can. If you add this field to the HORIZONTAL MULTIPLES well instead, then Power View will place all the separate charts in a single row and add a scroll bar to allow you to scroll through the set of "sub" charts that make up the complete visualization. Figure 5-3 shows an example of this layout (with the chart type set to Column).

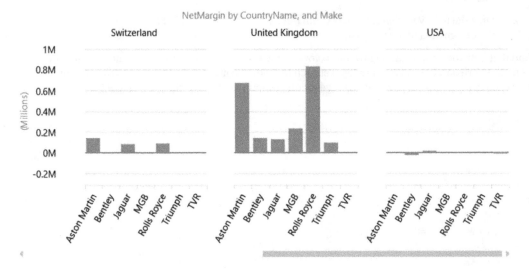

Figure 5-3. *Default use of horizontal multiples*

Defining the Multiples Grid

Depending on the complexity of your individual charts and the density of the information they contain, you may prefer to specify the dimensions of the grid that contains the individual charts in a multiple-chart visualization. Put simply, you can set the number of rows and columns that make up the matrix that holds the individual charts. If there are too many charts to be displayed at once, then scroll bars will be displayed to let you navigate, vertically and horizontally, through the set of available charts.

To show you how to define the number of charts that will be displayed at once in each row or column, let's assume that you have created a multiple-column chart based on the following data:

- *∑ SIZE*: NetMargin
- *LEGEND*: ClientType
- *VERTICAL MULTIPLES*: Color

This chart should look like that shown in Figure 5-4.

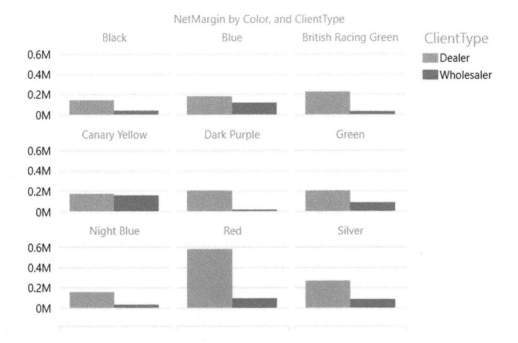

Figure 5-4. *Default use of vertical multiples*

Now, let's alter the layout and tell Power View to show the individual column charts in a 2×2 matrix. To do this, follow these steps:

1. Click inside the multiple-chart visualization or select it. Remember not to click an individual column.

2. Switch to the Layout ribbon.

3. Click the Grid Height button and choose 2 from the pop-up.

4. Click the Grid Width button and choose 2 from the pop-up.

The visualization will change and should look like Figure 5-5. As you can see, a vertical scroll bar has appeared to let you scroll down through the set of charts.

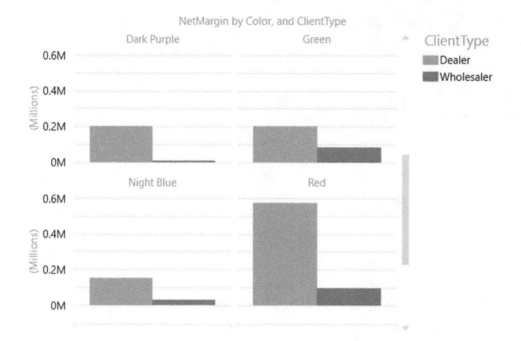

Figure 5-5. *Multiple charts with horizontal and vertical multiple grids set*

If you resize this visualization, it will never display more than a 2×2 matrix of charts. You can, of course, alter the number of charts per row or column at any time by selecting a different grid height or grid width.

■ **Tip** An interesting aspect of playing with the grid size for multiple charts is that once you have overridden the default grid and specified the required number of rows and columns, you cannot revert to it later unless you undo the operation immediately. From then on, Power View will not automatically try to fit all the charts as best it can in a grid that it decides is best for the number of charts. So, once you have "switched to manual," you will have to make all the decisions yourself.

Multiple Line Charts

Adding a visualization that displays multiple line charts is virtually identical to displaying multiple bar or column charts. They too can show several data series. However, they are particularly suited to showing how data evolves over time, so that is what I propose to look at in this example. Anyway, now that you have seen how it is done, it might be worth clarifying the principles before creating the visualization. The process follows these steps:

1. Create the core chart that displays the data that you want repeated across multiple charts.

2. Add the elements that will separate the charts into multiples—either horizontally, vertically, or both.

3. Set the number of charts in the grid, horizontally and vertically.

4. Resize the chart, adjust any legend, and tweak the font sizes.

To see this, let's create a visualization with multiple line charts, showing the average SalesCost and average DirectCosts for all the months in the year. To give you some insights, you will also compare these figures by client type—dealer and wholesaler.

1. Delete the existing multiple-chart visualization, leaving an empty Power View report, filtered to display data only for the year 2013. Alternatively, create a new report.

2. Create a line chart with the following fields:

   a. *Σ VALUES*: SalePrice and CostPrice

   b. *AXIS*: VehicleAgeCategory

   I won't repeat all the instructions again, as it is definitely time for you to try this on your own. Do, however, set the fields to return the average of the values. At this point, you should see a chart like Figure 5-6.

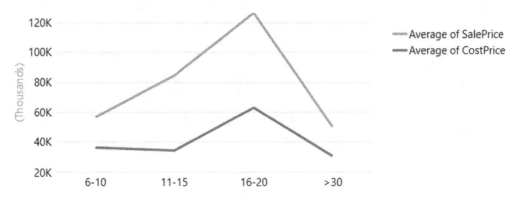

Average of SalePrice, and Average of CostPrice by VehicleAgeCategory

Figure 5-6. *A simple line chart ready for multiples*

3. Drag the MonthFull field from the Date table into the VERTICAL MULTIPLES well.

4. Set Grid Height to 4 and Grid Width to 3 in the Layout ribbon.

5. Resize the visualization and adjust the font sizes for the best effect.

Your visualization should now look like Figure 5-7.

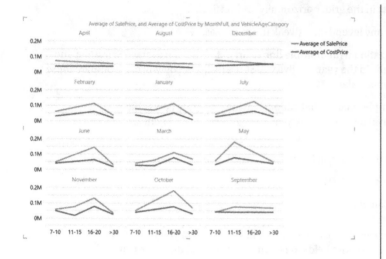
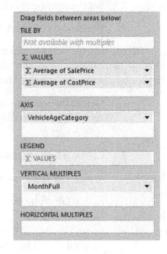

Figure 5-7. *Multiple line charts*

You can switch between all the available bar and column types (clustered, stacked, 100% stacked) and see which type of visualization best gets your insights across to your audience.

Multiple Pie Charts

Multiple pie charts are, in their turn, similar to multiple bar, line, and column charts.

Let's imagine that you want to look at the cost of spare parts and see whether this varies significantly depending on the age of the car; you also want to see these costs in multiple charts by car age group. Here is how this can be done:

1. Delete the existing multiple-line visualization, leaving an empty Power View report.

2. Create a pie chart with the following fields:

   a. ∑ *SIZE*: SpareParts (from the SalesData table)

   b. *COLOR*: QuarterFull (from YearHierarchy in the DateTable table)

3. Filter the year to 2014.

4. Set the legend under the chart (select Show Legend At Bottom from the Layout button in the Design ribbon). You should see a chart like Figure 5-8.

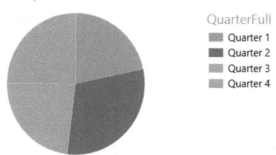

Figure 5-8. *A simple pie chart before setting the vertical multiples*

5. Drag the VehicleAgeCategory field from the SalesData table into the VERTICAL MULTIPLES well.

6. As there are virtually no spare parts sold in the 21–25 bracket, display the Filter pane and click Chart. Expand VehicleAgeCategory, check (All), and then uncheck 21–25. (This is to remind you about filters; you might not exclude data in such a cavalier fashion in reality.)

7. Resize the visualization and adjust the font sizes for the best effect.

Your visualization should look like Figure 5-9.

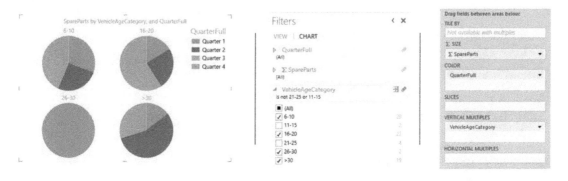

Figure 5-9. *Multiple pie charts with a filter*

Ideally these examples will give you ideas of how you can use the power of comparative charts—first to analyze and discover the information hidden in your data and then to present it clearly to your audience. The type of chart that you use will depend on your data, of course, and some data sets are better suited to certain types of presentation. One thing to remember is that multiple charts are inevitably small, so I really advise you not to overload them with data or you could end up by hiding rather than clarifying your analysis.

Drilling Down with Multiple Charts

One solution to the problem of data overload is to use drill-down with multiple charts just as you did with single charts in Chapter 4. All you have to do to add a drill-down hierarchy to a multiple chart is to add another descriptive element to the fields used. Here is a short example:

1. Create the multiple pie chart example given previously.

2. Add a VehicleType field to the COLOR well in the design area of the field list under the existing QuarterFull field. The charts in the multiple chart will not change.

3. Double-click any pie slice for (say) the age range 6–10 in one of the charts. You will drill down to the vehicle types for that VehicleAgeCategory.

Your visualization should look like Figure 5-10.

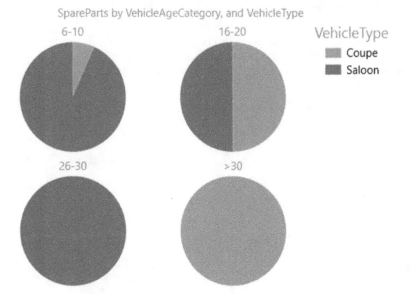

Figure 5-10. *Drilling down with chart multiples*

To return to the previous level of the data (the previous set of multiple charts), just click the Drill Up icon at the top right of the set of multiple charts. The legend (assuming you have kept one) will indicate the drill-down level that is currently displayed.

▦ **Note**   A final thing to note with multiple charts is that the Tile By option is not available. This really interesting feature will be covered in Chapter 6.

Scatter Charts

You are near the end of your tour of Power View chart types and charting possibilities. What I want to look at now is the penultimate chart type Power View offers—the scatter chart. A *scatter chart* is a plot of data values against two numeric axes, so by definition you will need two sets of numeric data to create a scatter chart. To appreciate the use of these charts, let's imagine you want to see the sales and margin for all the makes and models of car you sold in 2013. Ideally this will allow you to see where you really made money. Here is how you can do this:

1. Create a new Power View report or go to an existing report with plenty of available space.

2. Set the report filter to include data only for the year 2013, as described previously.

3. Create a table with the following fields from the SalesData table in this order:

   a. Vehicle

   b. NetMargin

   c. LaborCost

4. Convert the table to a scatter chart by clicking Other Chart and then Scatter from the Design ribbon.

5. Power View will display a scatter chart that looks like the one shown in Figure 5-11. Resize the chart to suit your taste.

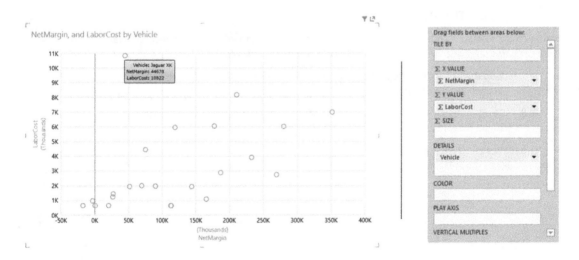

Figure 5-11. *A scatter chart*

If you look at the design area of the field list (which is also shown in Figure 5-11), you will see that Power View has used the fields that you selected like this:

- *Vehicle*: Placed in the DETAILS well.

- *NetMargin*: Placed in the Σ X VALUE well. This is the vertical axis.

- *LaborCost*: Placed in the Σ Y VALUE well. This is the horizontal axis.

If you hover the mouse pointer over one of the points in the scatter chart, you will see, as you are probably expecting by now with Power View, the data for the specific car model.

■ **Note** By definition, a scatter chart requires numeric values for both the x- and y-axes. So, if you add a non-numeric value to either the Σ X VALUE or Σ Y VALUE well, then Power View will convert the data to a Count aggregation.

You made this chart by adding all the required fields to the initial table first, and you also made sure that you added them in the right order so the scatter chart would display correctly the first time. In the real world of interactive data visualization, things may not be quite this coherent, so it is good to know that Power View is very forgiving, and it lets you build a scatter chart (just like any other chart) step by step if you prefer. In practice, this means that you can start with a table containing just two of the three fields that are required at a minimum for a scatter chart, convert the table to a scatter chart, and then add the remaining data field. Power View will always attribute numeric or time fields to the x- and y-axes (in the order in which they appear in the FIELDS well) and place the first descriptive field into the DETAILS well.

Once a scatter chart has been created, you can swap the fields around and replace existing fields with other fields from the tables in the data to your heart's content.

You can also add data labels to a scatter chart, just as you did for column charts earlier. However, unless you have few data points (which rather goes against the raison d'être of a scatter chart in the first place), you may find that data labels just clutter up the visualization.

Drilling Down with Scatter Charts

Scatter charts also let you drill down into the data. For example, to add a second level of analysis to the existing chart and to see sales and margin by color, follow these steps:

1. Add the Color field (from the Colors table) to the DETAILS well, under Vehicle. The scatter chart will not alter.

2. Double-click the data point for Aston Martin DB9 (currently the car achieving the highest net margin and the data point that is at the right of the x-axis).

The scatter chart will drill down to show the labor cost and net margin for this type of vehicle but by color. This is shown in Figure 5-12.

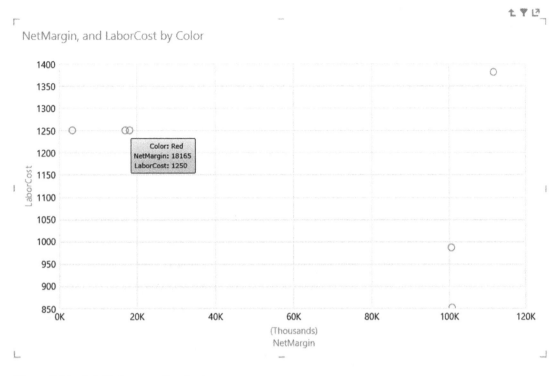

Figure 5-12. *A drill-down scatter chart*

To return to the root level of the data (the initial chart), all you have to do is to click the Drill Up icon at the top right of the chart.

Scatter Charts to Display Flattened Hierarchies

Scatter charts generically are designed to show many, many data points. This makes them useful in, paradoxically, avoiding the need to drill down through a predefined hierarchy of data. Let's see how to display multiple data sets on one level, rather than drilling down for them. For this to happen, of course, the source data must lend itself to the type of analysis that is required. Fortunately, the source data has a field named Vehicle that combines the make and model of each car and that suits this kind of analysis. The following is what you have to do:

1. Create a new Power Pivot report.

2. Add the following fields (in this order) to the Fields List VALUES well:

    a. Vehicle

    b. Color

    c. NetMargin

    d. Mileage

3. Convert the resulting table to a scatter chart (click Other Chart and then Scatter from the Design ribbon, with the table selected).

As you can see in Figure 5-13, every data point appears multiple times, once for every time there is a sale for a different color. Placing the mouse pointer over a data point will let you see exactly which model of vehicle and color is being represented. I have, as you have probably guessed, tweaked the size and display of the chart to show the data in its best light.

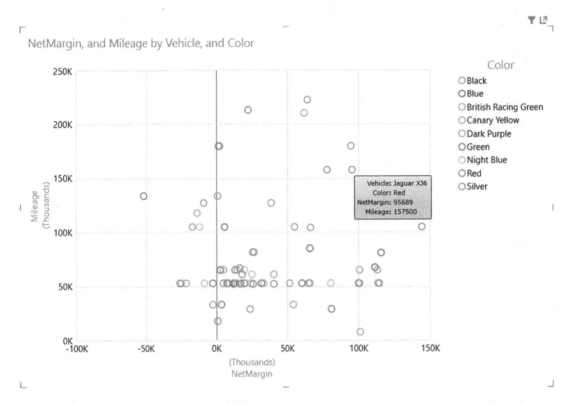

Figure 5-13. *Flattened hierarchies in a scatter chart*

In the case of some scatter charts, this technique can make the chart hard to decipher. However, if your scatter chart contains relatively few data points, this technique can be useful. What is more, Power View has the ability to highlight data by the elements that compose the legend; this is explained in Chapter 6.

Scatter Chart Multiples

Scatter charts, just like bar, column, and pie charts, allow you to display the data as multiple charts. Personally, I do not always find them easy to read, but in the interests of completeness (and because all forms of visualization do, after all, depend on the data as well as each user's preferences and taste), here is how to display the sales and gross margin by color:

1.   Select the chart that you made previously.

2.   In the design area of the field list, drag the Color field from the COLOR well to the VERTICAL MULTIPLES well.

The scatter chart will divide into a series of smaller charts, rather like the example shown in Figure 5-14.

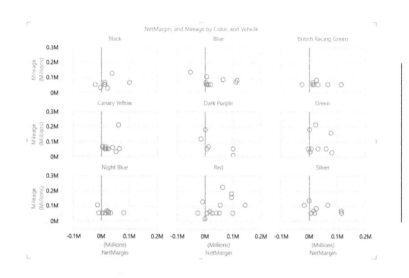

Figure 5-14. *Multiple scatter charts*

You can tailor the display of the grid—the number of charts shown horizontally and laterally—by selecting the required value from the Grid Height and Grid Width buttons in the Layout toolbar, as was described earlier for pie, column, and bar charts.

Bubble Charts

The final chart type available to you in Power View is the bubble chart. This is one of my favorite chart types, though of course you cannot overuse it without losing some of its power. A bubble chart is, essentially, a scatter chart with a third piece of data included. So, whereas a scatter chart shows you two pieces of data (one on the x-axis and one on the y-axis), a bubble chart lets you add a third piece of information, which becomes the size of the point. Consequently, each point becomes a bubble.

The best way to appreciate a bubble chart is to create one. So, here I will assume that you want to look at the following for all makes of car sold in a single chart:

- The Net Sales

- The Average Net Margin

- The Mileage

Here is how a bubble chart can do this for you:

1. Create a new Power View report or go to an existing report with plenty of available space.

2. Set the report filter to include data only for the year 2013, as described previously.

3. Create a table with the following fields from the SalesData table, in this order:

    a. Make (from the CarDetails hierarchy)

    b. NetSales

    c. Average NetMargin

    d. Mileage

4. Convert the table to a bubble chart by clicking Other Chart and then Scatter from the Design ribbon. Yes, a bubble chart is a scatter chart, with a fresh tweak added.

5. Power View will display a bubble chart that looks like that shown in Figure 5-15. Resize the chart if you need to do so.

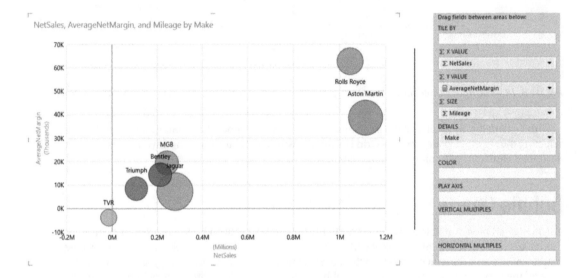

Figure 5-15. *An initial bubble chart*

If you look at the design area of the field list (also shown in Figure 5-15), you will see that Power View has used the fields that you selected like this:

- *Make*: Placed in the DETAILS well.

- *NetSales*: Placed in the Σ X VALUE well. This is the vertical axis.

- *AverageNetMargin*: Placed in the Σ Y VALUE well. This is the horizontal axis.

- *Mileage*: Placed in the SIZE well. This defines the size of the points, which have consequently become bubbles.

If you hover the mouse pointer over one of the points in the bubble chart, you will see all the data that you placed in the field list's layout section for each make, including the NetMargin.

Bubble Chart Data Labels and Legend

Apart from the points becoming bubbles, you will notice that a bubble chart automatically displays the data labels. If this is something you want to remove, then all you have to do is the following:

1. Click in the bubble chart.

2. Select None from the options available when you click the Data Labels button in the Layout ribbon.

If you want to keep the data labels but alter their position relative to each bubble, then instead of None, you can choose one of the other data label options when you click the Data Labels button in the Layout ribbon.

If you have chosen not to display the data labels but still need an indication of what element each bubble represents, then add a legend to a bubble chart. This is how:

1. Select the bubble chart.

2. Drag the field used for the DETAILS of the bubble chart to the COLOR well (Make, in this example).

3. Power View will add a legend to your visualization. It should look something like Figure 5-16.

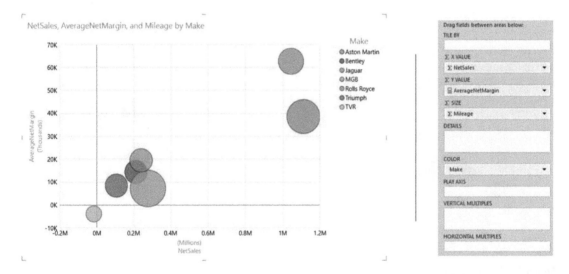

Figure 5-16. *A bubble chart with legend added*

Note Be careful not to add the field twice to the field list in two different wells. The trap that awaits the unwary here is that the chart will remain apparently the same. Yet, if you hover the mouse pointer over a bubble, you will see the field that appears in both the DETAILS and COLOR wells *twice* in the pop-up.

If you were to add further fields to the DETAILS well (except if it is a field, which is in another well in the field list, as mentioned earlier), then your bubble chart will become a drill-down chart, like any other chart type shown in this chapter. You can double-click any bubble to drill down and click the Drill Up arrow to return to a previous level, exactly as you have done for other chart types.

Multiple Bubble Elements

Provided that your bubble chart is not already swamped with data points, you may be able to display multiple data elements simultaneously. Imagine that you want to see not only bubbles for each make but also each make by age range (or age bucket if you prefer) in the same visualization without needing to drill down to a second level in the chart.

This can be done by using a combination of the DETAILS and COLOR wells in the layout section of the field list. Here is how you can split the existing bubbles into multiple bubbles, while still identifying the make of each car:

1. Click inside the bubble chart that you created previously (or create it exactly as described earlier with the Make field placed in the COLOR well).

2. Add the VehicleAgeCategory field to the DETAILS well.

3. Click the DataLabels button in the Layout ribbon and select Center.

Your visualization will look like Figure 5-17. As you can see, each bubble has become multiple bubbles, one for each set of cars in each age range. You will see that each car make is always represented in the same color. In this case, a good way to see which age range a bubble represents is to add data labels.

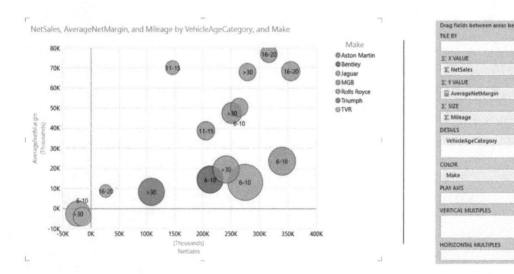

Figure 5-17. *Multiple bubble elements in a bubble chart*

If all this information clutters up your visualization, you can remove the data labels and the legend and display only the Make and VehicleAgeCategory when you hover the mouse pointer over a bubble.

To remove all the labels and legend, follow these steps:

1. Click inside the chart.

2. Click Layout to activate the Layout ribbon (unless this has already been done).

3. Select DataLabels, None.

4. Select Legend, None.

The bubble chart will look like Figure 5-18 (with a pop-up visible to show you how to see the details of the data).

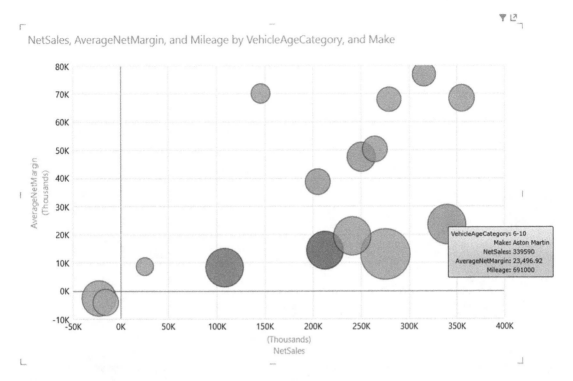

Figure 5-18. A bubble chart without a legend or data labels

Bubble Chart Multiples

Bubble charts can adapt well to multiple-chart visualizations. I realize that this has been described earlier in this chapter, but I think that it is worthwhile to look at multiples of bubble charts as a separate topic. This will take only a few seconds, in any case. So, to display multiple bubble charts, follow these steps:

1. Create (or revert to) the bubble chart, as shown in Figure 5-15. This shows the following:

    a. *∑ X VALUE*: NetSales

    b. *∑ Y VALUE*: AverageNetMargin

    c. *SIZE*: Mileage

    d. *COLOR*: Make

2. Add VehicleAgeCategory (also from the SalesData table) to the VERTICAL MULTIPLES well.

3. Select None from the Data Labels button in the Layout ribbon.

4. Adjust the grid height and the grid width if you want or need, and possibly alter the placement of the legend if you add one. The visualization will look something like Figure 5-19.

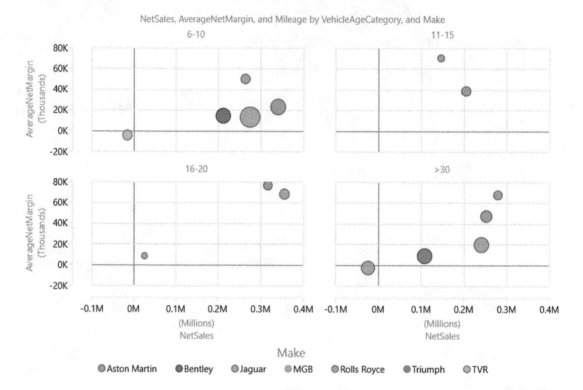

Figure 5-19. *Multiple bubble charts*

Play Axis

So far in this chapter you have seen various ways of presenting data as charts and how to select, compare, and drill into the data using a variety of techniques. A final trick with Power View, but one that can be extremely effective at riveting your audience, is to apply a play axis to the visualization. This will animate the chart and, ideally, is suited to showing how data evolves over time. It is, unfortunately, harder to get the "wow" effect using these printed pages, so this really is a technique that you will have to try for yourself.

You need to know that a play axis can be applied only to scatter or bubble charts. Similarly, adding a play axis will not suit or enhance all types of data. However, if you have a time-dependent element that can be added to your chart as the y-axis (such as sales to date, for instance), then you can produce some powerful and revelatory effects.

To close this chapter, then, here is how to create a bubble chart that shows the net margin ratio for colors of car sold against the sales for the year to date:

1.   Create a new Power View report with a report filter so that you can see the years 2012 and 2013.

2.   Create a table with the following fields from the SalesData table, in this order:

    a.   Color

    b.   SalesYTD

    c.   DirectCosts

    d.   Mileage

3. Convert the table to a bubble chart by clicking Other Chart and then Scatter from the Design ribbon.

4. The data fields will be placed in wells for a bubble chart, but the default is to place the initial field (Color) in the DETAILS well. As a legend would be useful, drag the Color field from the DETAILS well to the COLOR well.

5. Adjust the presentation (size, legend placement, data labels, and so on) to obtain the best effect.

6. Drag the QuarterAndYear field from the DateTable (after expanding the YearHierarchy) into the PLAY AXIS well.

The visualization will look like that shown in Figure 5-20.

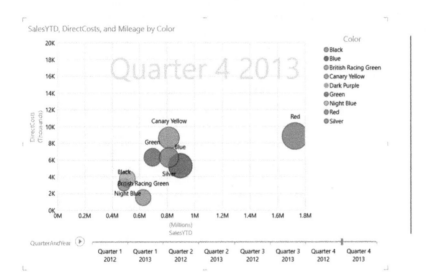

Figure 5-20. *The play axis*

Click the Play icon to the left of the play axis, and you will see the bubbles reveal how sales progress throughout the year.

Here are a few points worth noting about the play axis:

- You can pause the automated display by clicking the Pause icon, which the Play icon has become, while the animation is progressing. You can stop and start as often as you like.

- You can click any month (or any element) in the play axis to display the data just for that element, without playing the data before that point. This essentially means you can use the play axis as a filter for your data.

- A play axis need not be time-based. However, it can be harder to see any coherence or progression in the data if time is not used as a basis for a play axis. As an example, try using NetSales (instead of SalesYTD) and VehicleAgeCategory as the play axis in the visualization that you just created for a play axis example. The data is still visible, but it is probably less indicative of underlying trends.

141

- You can use a play axis as another interactive filter for your data, but doing this makes you miss out on a fabulous animation technique!

- You cannot add tiles to a visualization that has a play axis.

- You cannot convert a visualization that has a play axis to display multiple charts.

You can also apply tiles to any chart type (unless there is a play axis). However, this is described alongside the general use of tiles in Chapter 6.

Conclusion

If you apply the techniques that you saw in this chapter, you should be able to create bubble charts, scatter charts, and also multiple chart visualizations using any of the available chart types. You can even animate certain types of chart using a play axis to show how data evolves over time. With this gamut of possibilities at your fingertips, you can, ideally, take your analysis and presentation skills to a higher level.

CHAPTER 6

Interactive Data Selection in Power View

In Chapter 3 you saw how to define filters both for Power View reports and for specific visualizations in a report. Filtering data in this way is extremely powerful and is perfectly suited to tweaking your analysis and trying out differing scenarios. However, altering filter elements is not really suitable for the interactive presentations to which Power View lends itself so ideally. When facing your audience, you need to be able to deliver your insights in a single click. It probably comes as no surprise to discover that making dynamic selections in a report is part of the DNA of Power View. Learning these approaches is the subject of this chapter.

The other techniques that you can apply above and beyond filters in Power View reports to subset or isolate data have the following characteristics:

- Always visible in the Power View report

- Instantly accessible

- Interactive

- Clearly indicate which selections are being applied

So, what are the effects that you can add to a Power View report to select and project your data? Essentially they boil down to these three main approaches:

- Slicers

- Tiles

- Highlighting

These interactive elements can be considered to function as a supplementary level of filtering. That is, they take the current filters that are set in the Filter pane (both at the report level and those tailored to a specific visualization) and then provide further fine-grained selection on top of the data set that has been allowed through the existing filters. Each approach has its advantages and limitations, but used appropriately, each gives you the ability not only to discover the essence of your data but also to make your point clearly and effectively.

You will see how these three approaches work in detail in the rest of this chapter. In any case—and as is so often the case with Power View—it is easier to grasp these ideas by seeing them in practice than by talking about them, so let's see how tiles, slicers, and highlighting work. This chapter will follow the trend of all the Power View chapters in this book and use the sample file CarSales.xlsx from the folder C:\DataVisualisationInExcel2016.

© Adam Aspin 2016
A. Aspin, *High Impact Data Visualization in Excel with Power View, 3D Maps, Get & Transform and Power BI*,
DOI 10.1007/978-1-4842-2400-7_6

Tiles

So far you have seen how one or more filters will let you exclude data from an entire Power View report as you make your point about the insights that you have unearthed. Sometimes, however, you may need to provide interactive filtering on the data in a specific visualization (whether it is a table or a chart) without affecting all the other visualizations in a report. This is where tiles come in.

A *tile* is a filter that applies only to a selected visualization. In fact, tiles are "containers" for the visualization. Not only that, but tiles look really cool and can help you review a set of data, item by item, which can make anomalies and essentials stand out in a clear and telling fashion. There are four main ways to add tiles to a visualization, so I will explain all four; then you can decide which you prefer.

Creating a Tiled Visualization from Scratch

When you want to create a visualization, which exists, so far, only in your mind's eye, I suggest that you first try to imagine all aspects of the visualization except the tile elements and build the "core" visualization. Then all you have to do is add the tiles to enable interactive data visualization. As a starting point, you could try the following:

1. Create a table or chart that displays all the fields you want to display in your Power View report. In this example, I suggest adding Year and MonthFull from the Date table and adding the fields SalePrice and CostPrice from the SalesData table.

2. Drag the ClientName field from the Clients table into the TILE BY well in the layout section of the field list.

That is it; you have a tiled visualization, as shown in Figure 6-1.

Figure 6-1. *Tiles applied to a table*

Clicking any tile will filter the visualization to display only data for the selected tile. I suggest that you try clicking a few of the client names in the tiles to appreciate just how fast Power View displays only the figures for the selected client. For the moment, admittedly, the tiled visualization may look a little cramped, but you will see how to adjust that in the next section.

■ **Tip** When you hover the mouse pointer over the scroll triangle at the left or right of the tile display, it will indicate exactly how many tiles there are and how many are displayed. You may see (2 – 6 / 6), for instance; this tells you that there are six tiles in all and that you can currently see the second to the sixth.

Adjusting Tile Display

When you add tiles to a visualization, you may not always achieve a perfect display of the data instantly. So, be prepared to do the following:

- Adjust the dimensions and proportion of the "outer" tile container
- Adjust the dimensions and proportion of the "inner" visualization

This is as simple as dragging the handles at the corners or in the middle of the sides of, respectively, the following:

- The outer tile container
- The inner visualization

Figure 6-2 outlines these elements. As you can see, each has corner and lateral handles and can be resized, and moved, independently.

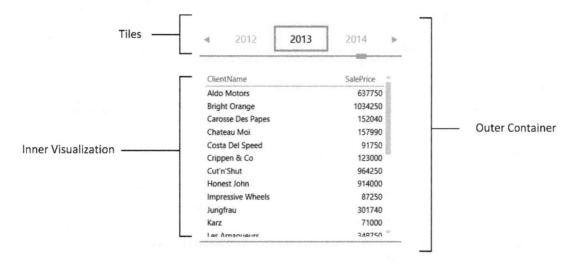

Figure 6-2. *A tiled visualization—container and inner visualization*

When resizing these visualizations, you will soon notice that it is impossible to make the inner visualization larger than the tile container, so you will always have to resize the tile container first. Then you can adjust the inner visualization as a function of its container. Just to make the point, the inner visualization is a standard Power View visualization and can be fine-tuned using all the techniques that you would use to modify a table or chart that was not part of a tile view.

Some Variations on Ways of Creating Tiled Visualizations

You just saw one way of creating tiled visualizations. There are, however, several other ways of achieving this objective. Indeed, you have quite a variety of choices. In any case, here are some of the other techniques that you could use, if you so choose.

Creating a Tiled Visualization from Scratch—Another Variant

An alternative to the technique just discussed is to create a visualization, probably as a simple table, that also contains the field that will be used for the tiles. Providing that the field destined to become the tiles is the first field in the field list, you can create a tiled visualization with a single click. Assuming, then, that you have created a table with the following fields in this order:

- The ClientName field from the Clients table

- The YearHierarchy field from the Date Table

- The SalePrice field from the SalesData table

then you do the following:

1. Click the Tile button in the Power View Design ribbon.

This approach will take the first field in the visualization as the tile element and give you a "tiled" visualization using the ClientName field as the basis for the tiles. However, unfortunately, Power View will leave this field in the visualization as well, which makes it redundant in most cases. So, presuming that you do not want to display this information twice, follow these steps:

1. Click the pop-up menu for the first field in the FIELDS well in the field list's layout section (ClientName in this example).

2. Select Remove Field.

The field will be removed from the visualization but remain in the tiles above the visualization.

Adding Tiles to an Existing Visualization

If you have created a visualization already and you want to add a layer of interactive filtering specific to this visualization, all you have to do is drag the field that will be used for the tiles into the TILE BY well in the layout (upper) section of the field list. To see this, let's extend the use of tiles to charts. Here, you will revise the process of creating a chart and then extend it by adding tiles:

1. Create a table using the fields Color (from the Colors table) and GrossMargin (from the SalesData table).

2. Convert this table to a Clustered Bar chart.

3. Add the VehicleAgeCategory field to the TILE BY well in the design (lower) area of the field list.

4. Resize the chart. This could involve adjusting the size of both the inner chart and the outer container that displays the tiles as was explained previously.

The chart will look something like the one in Figure 6-3. If you prefer, an alternative to dragging a field to the TILE BY well is to select the chart, click the pop-up menu for the field that you want to tile by in the field list, and select Add As Tile By.

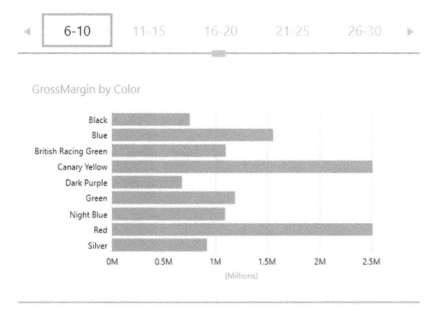

Figure 6-3. *Adding tiles to a bar chart*

Adding Tiles to an Existing Visualization—Another Variant

If you have created a visualization already that contains the fields that you want to use for the tiles, then you can do the following:

1. Drag the field that will be used for the tiles from the ROWS (or possibly COLUMNS) well into the TILE BY well in the layout section of the field list.

Once again you have created a tiled visualization, but without the duplicate data this time.

Modifying an Existing Visualization Inside a Tile Container

Once you have added tiles to a visualization, you can alter the inner visualization in any of the ways that you learned in previous chapters. Put simply, you can do any of the following:

- Add and remove data fields

- Switch from table to chart, and vice versa

- Change table types from table to matrix to card

- Alter the chart types

- Switch between card styles

All this only goes to show that a tiled visualization is only a standard visualization wrapped inside a selection container.

■ **Note** You can alter the font size of the tiles and the nested visualization separately. Just remember to click inside either the tiles or the inner visualization before adjusting the font size.

Re-creating a Visualization Using Existing Tiles

Once you have built a tile-based visualization, you may decide that the tiles are perfect but that the "inner" visualization needs a total revamp. After reaching this conclusion, you may even decide that a complete rebuild of the "inner" visualization is necessary because simply adding or removing a field and altering the visualization type is harder than starting over.

So, to delete and re-create the visualization inside a tile container, simply follow these steps:

1. Click on or inside the inner visualization (the chart or table).

2. Press the Delete key. You will be left with a disconcertingly empty outer tile container, as shown in Figure 6-4.

Figure 6-4. *The outer tile container*

3. Drag the fields that you want to use as the basis for the new tiled visualization inside the existing tile container.

4. Modify the style of visualization as described in previous chapters.

This way you can fill the container with a new visualization.

■ **Tip**   What is important to remember is that the outer container remains completely independent of the inner visualization. Consequently, you can tweak, or change completely, the inner visualization without altering the outer container.

Another way to re-create a visualization inside an existing tile container is as follows:

1. Ensure that the Tile visualization remains selected.

2. Drag the fields on which you want to base your visualization into the FIELDS well in the design area of the field list on the right.

3. Modify the style of visualization as described in previous chapters.

You will notice that in the design area of the field list on the right the TILE BY well has remained populated with the choice of tile field. Consequently, you do not need to modify this—unless, of course, you decide to alter the field that supplies the data to the tiles themselves.

Removing Tiles from a Visualization

Tiles do not always suit every type for visualization, or indeed every data set. So, you may well end up deciding that the tiles that you have applied to a table or chart are just not appropriate and need to be removed but you want to leave the rest of the visualization in place. To do this, follow these steps:

1. Select the tile-based visualization from which you want to remove the tiles.

2. Display the field list, unless it is already visible.

3. Drag the field currently in the TILE BY well of the field list's design area out of the design area and back into the field list. An X on the field that you are dragging away will indicate that this tile field is the one that will be deleted.

Once the field used to add the tiles has been removed from the TILE BY well in the design area, then the tiles will also be removed from the visualization. Remember that if you have made a mistake, a quick Ctrl+Z will restore the tiles to their former glory.

If you attempt to delete tiles by dragging the Tile By field anywhere other than back into the field area (the upper part of the field list), then a warning icon, as shown in Figure 6-5, will appear to alert you to the fact that the field cannot be dragged anywhere but to specific areas.

Deleting a Tile Visualization

Despite your efforts, it may simply turn out that tiles are not suited to the kind of data, analysis, or presentation that you are making. So, you may need to remove a tiled visualization completely (that is, from both the container and its content).

1. Click inside the tiled visualization but outside the inner table or chart (or whatever the inner visualization is).

2. Press the Delete key.

The tile-based visualization will disappear in its entirety—though, of course, a rapid click on Undo in the Power View ribbon (or Ctrl+Z) will restore it instantly.

Tile Types

When you first add tiles to a visualization, the default is to apply a set of tiles above the inner visualization. Power View calls this the Tab Strip tile type. However, there is a second tile type available—Tile Flow. To switch between the two types of tile, follow these steps:

1. Ensure that a tiled visualization is selected.

2. In the Design ribbon, click the Tile Type button and select Tile Flow.

You can see an example of a tile flow in Figure 6-5.

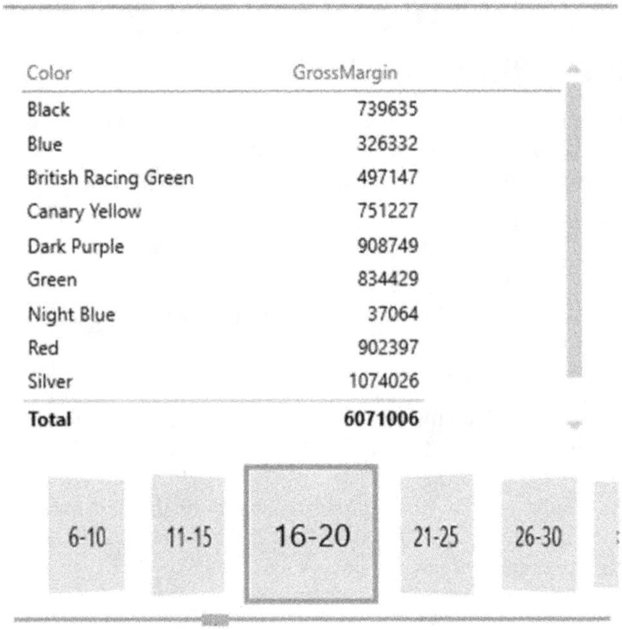

Color	GrossMargin
Black	739635
Blue	326332
British Racing Green	497147
Canary Yellow	751227
Dark Purple	908749
Green	834429
Night Blue	37064
Red	902397
Silver	1074026
Total	**6071006**

6-10   11-15   **16-20**   21-25   26-30

Figure 6-5. *A tile flow visualization*

To switch back to the Tab Strip tile type, follow these steps:

1. Ensure that a tiled visualization is selected.

2. In the Design ribbon, click the Tile Type button and select Tab Strip.

The differences between the two types of tile are purely visual and are described in Table 6-1.

Table 6-1. *Tile Types*

Tile Type	Position	Comments
Tab Strip	Top of visualization	Displays a set of identically sized tiles above the visualization
Tile Flow	Bottom of visualization	Displays a carousel of tiles beneath the visualization

■ **Note**   You can scroll through all the available elements in a tile flow just as you can in a tab strip.

Using Tiles

Given that tiles are a selection tool, all you have to do to apply filtering based on a tile is to click the relevant tile. This tile will then be displayed in boldface, and the data visible in the inner visualization will be filtered so that only data for the selected tile will be displayed.

Unless all the elements in a set of tiles can be displayed at once, you will have to scroll through the tile set. Whatever the tile type (Tab Strip or Tile Flow), you will see a scroll bar at the bottom of the tile set. Sliding this left or right will scroll through the tile set.

A Tab Strip tile set also has scroll icons at the right and left of the tiles. Clicking these will cause the tile set to scroll in the direction of the scroll icon. You will notice that Power View does not jump from tile to tile but moves fluidly through the tile set. A Tile Flow tile set, however, does not have scroll icons at the right and left of the tiles. Clicking any tile will cause that tile to move to the center of the tile set.

■ **Note**   You cannot select multiple tiles simultaneously, no matter what type of tile you are using.

Filtering Tiles

A tiled visualization is essentially just another visualization. Consequently, it too can have a visualization-level filter applied. For instance, suppose you want to reuse the initial tiled chart from Figure 6-3, earlier in this chapter, but you want to display only some of the car age ranges. Here is how this can be done:

1. Click inside the inner (chart) visualization—anywhere except on a bar in the chart.

2. Click Chart in the Filters pane.

3. In the Design ribbon, click the Tile Type button and select Tile Flow (unless you have already done this).

4. Click inside the chart inside the tiled visualization (but not on a bar).

5. Click Chart in the Filters pane.

6. Expand the filter VehicleAgeCategory.

7. Select the following elements:

    a. 11–15

    b. 16–20

    c. 26–30

You will see that the tiles also display only the elements that you selected. In most cases, this means a reduced number of tiles in the tile set. For this to work, by the way, the option Show Items With No Data described in the following section must *not* be activated. Figure 6-6 shows the result of this process.

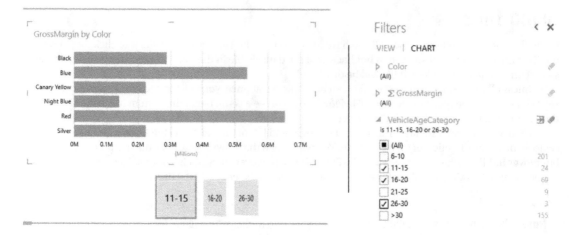

Figure 6-6. *Tiles once a filter has been applied*

Tiles with No Data

One point of note is that a tile set will, by default, not contain any elements for which there is no data available. At times you may want tiles to be displayed, even if they have no relevant data, possibly to make the point that nothing was sold. If this is your wish, then you can try the following example:

1. Create a new Power View report.

2. Add the following fields:

    a. ClientName from the Clients table

    b. SalePrice from the SalesData table

    c. The VehicleType field from the SalesData Table

3. Drag the VehicleType field from the FIELDS well to the TILE BY well.

4. Drag the CountryName field to the Filters pane and select only the USA.

5. In the Layout section of the field list, click the pop-up option for the VehicleType field in the TILE BY well.

6. Select Show Items With No Data.

This will cause the tiles to contain every element to be displayed from the field that you are using to tile by—even if there is no data for this selection. Initially, when you created this visualization, you did not see a tile for Convertible or Saloon. Once Show Items With No Data was selected, these vehicle types appeared in the tiles. Figure 6-7 shows the before and after effects of this choice.

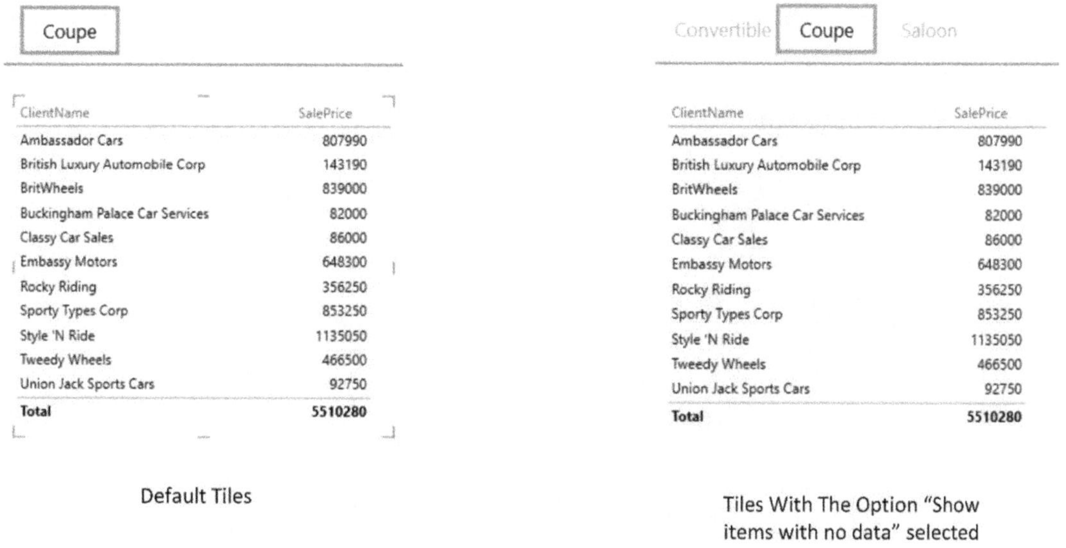

Coupe

ClientName	SalePrice
Ambassador Cars	807990
British Luxury Automobile Corp	143190
BritWheels	839000
Buckingham Palace Car Services	82000
Classy Car Sales	86000
Embassy Motors	648300
Rocky Riding	356250
Sporty Types Corp	853250
Style 'N Ride	1135050
Tweedy Wheels	466500
Union Jack Sports Cars	92750
Total	**5510280**

Convertible	Coupe	Saloon

ClientName	SalePrice
Ambassador Cars	807990
British Luxury Automobile Corp	143190
BritWheels	839000
Buckingham Palace Car Services	82000
Classy Car Sales	86000
Embassy Motors	648300
Rocky Riding	356250
Sporty Types Corp	853250
Style 'N Ride	1135050
Tweedy Wheels	466500
Union Jack Sports Cars	92750
Total	**5510280**

Default Tiles

Tiles With The Option "Show items with no data" selected

Figure 6-7. *The effects of selecting Show Items With No Data*

■ **Note**   Remember that the items in the tiles are filtered by any view filters (such as table, matrix, and chart filters) and slicers that are active in the report. So, if you modify any of these, you could see the items making up the tiles change dramatically. Indeed, you could remove all the existing tile elements and replace them with a completely different set, if the filters and slicer (or slicers) that you have applied exclude the existing tile items. If this happens (and there are no common tile items shared between the filters that you switch from and the new filters that you apply), then Power View will default to selecting the first tile in the set.

Changing the Inner Visualization

You can change the visualization that is inside a tile container at any time, just as you would change it if it were a stand-alone visualization. For instance, to switch the chart from a bar chart to a pie chart (using the example you saw earlier in Figure 6-6), all you have to do is the following:

1.   Click the inner chart visualization.

2.   Click Other Chart and then Pie in the Design ribbon.

As you can see from Figure 6-8, only the chart type has altered and the tiles have remained unchanged. So, you can flip between chart and table visualizations and switch chart types independently of the tiles in place.

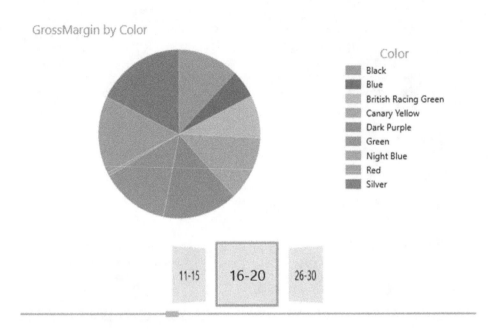

Figure 6-8. *Pie chart using tiles*

Tiles and Multiple Charts

Tiles can be added to any chart as they can be to any table. The only restriction is that tiles cannot be added to charts if the chart has horizontal or vertical multiples. You will have to decide which of the two approaches you prefer to use.

Tiles can be a perfect use for images. This process, along with other uses for images, is described in Chapter 7.

■ **Tip** As a final comment on tiles in Power View, tiled visualizations cannot be *popped out*, that is, expanded to allow for a more detailed view.

Slicers

Another form of interactive filter is the slicer. This is, to all intents and purposes, a standard multiselect filter, where you can choose one or more elements to filter data in a report. The essential difference is that a slicer remains visible on the Power View report, whereas a filter is normally hidden. So, this is an overt rather than a hidden approach to data selection. Moreover, you can add multiple different slicers to a Power View report and consequently slice and dice the data instantaneously and interactively using multiple criteria. Slicers can be text-based, or indeed, they can be simple charts, as you will soon see.

Adding a Slicer

To appreciate all that slicers can do, you need to see one in action. To add a slicer, follow these steps:

1. From the Power View Fields pane (which you need to display if it is hidden), drag the field name you want to use as a slicer to an empty part of the report. In this example, I am using the VehicleAgeCategory field from the SalesData table. Power View creates a single-column table.

2. Click the Slicer button in the Design ribbon. The table becomes a slicer.

3. Adjust the size of the slicer to suit your requirements using the corner or lateral handles. Power View will add a vertical scroll bar to indicate that there are further elements available or will add a horizontal scroll bar if the text is truncated.

You can recognize a slicer by the small squares to the left of each element in the list. This way you know that it is not just a single-column table. Figure 6-9 shows a slicer using the VehicleAgeCategory field from the SalesData table.

VehicleAgeCategory

■ 6-10

■ 11-15

■ 16-20

■ 21-25

■ 26-30

■ >30

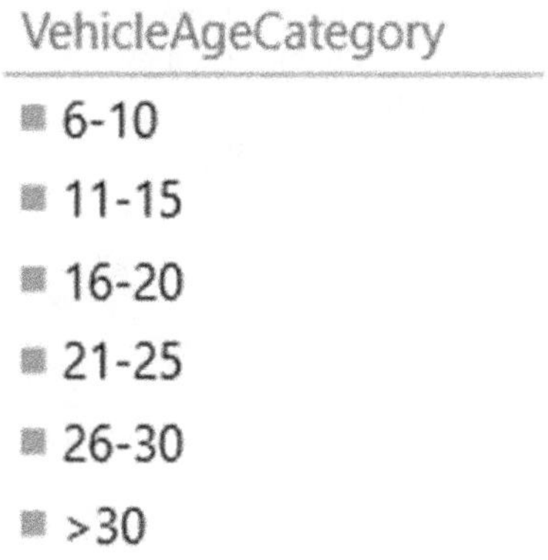

Figure 6-9. *A slicer*

■ **Note** If the Slicer icon is grayed out, then check that the table you are trying to convert to a slicer has only one column (that is, one field in the FIELDS well of the layout area of the field list).

You can create multiple slicers for each view. All you have to do is repeat steps 1 through 3 for adding a slicer using a different field as the data for the new slicer.

When you start applying slicers to your Power View reports, you will rapidly notice one important aspect of the Power View filter hierarchy. A slicer can only display data that is not specifically excluded by a view-level filter. For instance, if you add a Color filter at the view level and select only certain colors in this filter, you will only be able to create a slicer that also displays this subset of colors. The slicer is, in fact, dynamic and will reflect the elements selected in a view-level filter. Consequently, adding or removing elements in a filter will cause these elements to appear (or disappear) in a slicer that is based on the same field.

■ **Note**   You cannot, however, apply a filter specifically to a slicer. You can see this if you click a slicer and then look at the Filters area. There is no visualization-level filter available (you cannot see Table, Chart, Matrix, or Slicer to the right of the word *Filter* at the top of the Filter pane). In addition, if you applied a table-level filter to a single-column table before you converted it to a slicer, the filter would be removed, and all the field elements would be displayed in the slicer, including those previously removed by the table-level filter.

Applying a Slicer

To apply a slicer and use it to filter data in a view, follow these steps:

1. Click a single element in the slicer, or Shift+click (or Ctrl+click) multiple elements.

All the objects in a Power View report will be filtered to reflect the currently selected slicer list. In addition, each element in the slicer list that is active (and consequently used to filter data by that element) now has a small rectangle to its left, indicating that this element is selected. The color of this rectangle is dictated by the Power View theme that is applied, but this is described in more detail in Chapter 7.

Figure 6-10 shows what happens when the slicer defined for Figure 6-8 is applied to the tiled visualization shown in Figure 6-8.

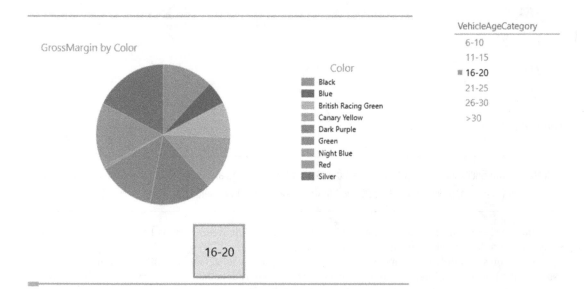

Figure 6-10. *Applying a slicer*

When you apply a slicer, think filter. That is, if you select a couple of elements from a slicer based on the CountryName field, as well as three elements based on the Color fields, you are forcing the two slicers (filters) to limit all the data displayed in the view to two countries that have any of the three colors that you selected. The core difference between a slicer and a filter is that a slicer is always visible—and that you have to select or unselect elements, not ranges of values.

If you experiment, you will also see that you cannot create a slicer from numeric fields in the source data. A slicer has to be based on a text field. If you need slicers based on ranges of data, then you will need to prepare these ranges in the data model. The VehicleAgeCategory field is an example of this, and Chapter 7 explains how to add these sorts of fields to a data model.

■ **Tip**   You can (if you Shift+click or Ctrl+click all the elements in a slicer) unselect all the data it represents. This will not, however, clear the Power View report. Unselecting everything is the same as selecting everything—despite that the selection squares are no longer visible to the left of each element in the slicer.

Clearing a Slicer

To clear a slicer and stop filtering on the selected data elements in a view, follow this step:

1.   Click the Clear Filter icon at the top right of the slicer.

Any filters applied by the slicer to the view are now removed. You will see that each element in the slicer list now has a small rectangle to its left, indicating that this element is not selected. As this is the same thing as saying that all of the elements are selected, no data is filtered out of the report.

■ **Tip**   Another technique to clear a slicer completely is to Shift+click (or Ctrl+click) the last remaining active element in a slicer. This will leave all elements active. So, in effect, removing all slicer elements is the same as activating them all.

Deleting a Slicer

To delete a slicer and remove all filters that it applies for a view, do this:

1.   Select the slicer and press the Delete key.

Any filters applied by the slicer to the view as well as the slicer itself are now removed. Another technique to delete a slicer is to select the slicer and then, in the Power View Fields pane, click the pop-up triangle to the right of the field name toward the bottom of the pane. Then select Remove Field, and the slicer will disappear.

You can even copy and paste slicers if you want. Although, since modifying a slicer is virtually impossible, this is largely useful only when you are copying slicers across different Power View reports.

■ **Note**   If you intend to use the field that was the basis for a slicer in a table or chart, you do not need to delete the slicer and re-create a table based on the same underlying field. You can merely do the following:

1.   Select the slicer.

2.   Click the Table button in the Design ribbon and select the type of table (table, matrix, or card) to which you want to convert the slicer.

The instant that a slicer becomes a table, it also ceases to subset the data in the Power View report.

Modifying a Slicer

If all you want to do is replace the field that is used in a slicer with another field, then it is probably simplest to delete the slicer and re-create it.

■ **Note** When you save an Excel workbook containing Power View reports with active slicers, the slicer is reopened in the state in which it was saved.

Using Charts as Slicers

You have seen how a table can become a slicer, which is, after all, a kind of filter. Well, charts can also be used as slicers. Knowing how charts can affect the data in a Power View report can even influence the type of chart that you create or your decision to use a chart to filter data rather than a standard slicer. Charts can be wonderful tools to grab and hold your audience's attention—as I am sure you will agree once you see the effects that they can produce.

To begin with, let's see how a chart can be used to act as a slicer for all the visualizations in a Power View report. Initially, let's assume you are aiming to produce a report using these two objects:

- A table of Net Margin by Color

- A column chart of Net Sales by Make

I will start with the table of Net Margin by Color. This will principally be used to show the effect using a chart as a slicer in a Power View report has on other objects.

1. Create a new Power View report. You will need a whole uncluttered report for this example.

2. Filter the report to display only data for 2013, as described in the previous chapter.

3. Add a table based on the following fields:

   a. Color (from the Colors table)

   b. NetMargin (from the SalesData table)

4. Add a clustered bar chart based on the following fields:

   a. Make (from the SalesData table in the CarDetails hierarchy)

   b. NetSales (from the SalesData table)

5. Adjust the layout of the two visualizations so that it looks something like Figure 6-11. This includes sorting the bar chart by NetSales, in descending order.

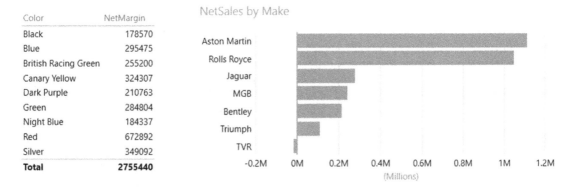

Color	NetMargin
Black	178570
Blue	295475
British Racing Green	255200
Canary Yellow	324307
Dark Purple	210763
Green	284804
Night Blue	184337
Red	672892
Silver	349092
Total	**2755440**

Figure 6-11. *Preparing a chart for use as a slicer*

Now let's see how to use a chart as a slicer.

1. Click any column in the chart of NetSales by Make. I will choose Jaguar in this example.

The Power View report will look something like Figure 6-12.

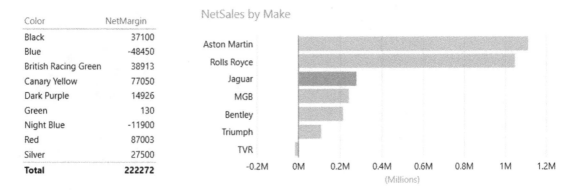

Color	NetMargin
Black	37100
Blue	-48450
British Racing Green	38913
Canary Yellow	77050
Dark Purple	14926
Green	130
Night Blue	-11900
Red	87003
Silver	27500
Total	**222272**

Figure 6-12. *Slicing data using a chart*

You will see that not only is the make that you selected highlighted in the chart (and the bars for other makes are dimmed) but that the figures in the table also change. They, too, display only the net margin (for each color) for the selected make.

To slice on another make, merely click the corresponding column in the column chart. To cancel the effect of the chart acting as a slicer, all you have to do is click for a second time on the highlighted column.

Any bar chart, pie chart, or column chart can act like a slicer in this way. The core factor is that for a simple slice effect, you need to use a chart that contains only one axis; that is, there will be only a single axis in the source data and no color or legend. What happens when you use more evolved charts to slice, filter, and highlight data is explained next.

■ **Tip** It is perfectly possible to select multiple bars in a chart to highlight data in the same way that you can select multiple elements in a slicer.

Highlighting Chart Data

So far you have seen how a chart can become a slicer for all the visualizations in a report. However, you can also use another aspect of Power View interactivity to make data series in charts stand out from the crowd when you are presenting your findings. This particular aspect of data presentation is called *highlighting*.

Once again, highlighting is probably best appreciated with a practical example. So, first you will create a stacked bar chart of costs by CountryName; then you will use it to highlight the various costs inside the chart.

1. In a new Power View report (so you do not get distracted), create a clustered column chart based on the following fields:

    a. CountryName

    b. DeliveryCharge

    c. SpareParts

    d. LaborCost

2. Click DeliveryCharge in the legend. All the delivery charges will be highlighted (that is, remain the original color) in the column for each country, whereas the other two costs will be grayed out.

The chart, after highlighting has been applied, will look like Figure 6-13.

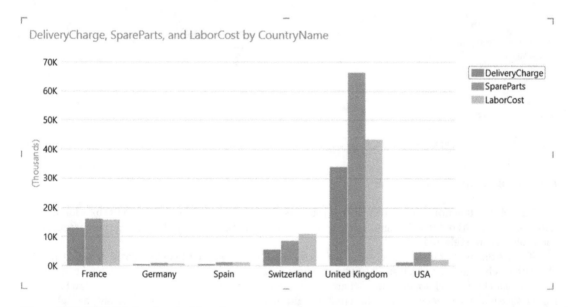

Figure 6-13. *Highlighting data inside a chart*

To remove the highlighting, all you have to do is click a second time on the same element in the legend. Or, if you prefer, you can click another legend element to highlight this aspect of the visualization instead. Yet another way to remove highlighting is to click inside the chart, but not on any data element.

Highlighting data in this way should suit any type of bar or column chart as well as line charts. It can also be useful in pie charts where you have added data to both the COLOR and SLICES wells, which, after all, means you have multiple elements in the chart just as you can have with bar, column, and line charts. You might find it less useful with scatter charts.

Cross-Chart Highlighting

Cross-chart filtering adds an interesting extra aspect to chart highlighting and filtering. If you use one chart as a filter, the other chart will be updated to reflect the effect of selecting this new filter not only by excluding any elements (slices, bars, or columns) that are filtered out but also by showing the proportion of data excluded by the filter.

As an example of this, create a pie chart of net sales by color and a column chart of sales costs by vehicle type. You will then cross-filter the two charts and see the results. The steps to follow are as follows:

1. Create a pie chart using the following fields:

    a. Color

    b. NetSales

2. Sort the pie chart by NetSales in descending order.

3. Create a (clustered) column chart using the following fields:

    a. VehicleType

    b. SalesCost

For charts that are this simple, Power View will automatically attribute the fields to the correct wells in the field list once the source tables are converted into charts. Figure 6-14 shows the result.

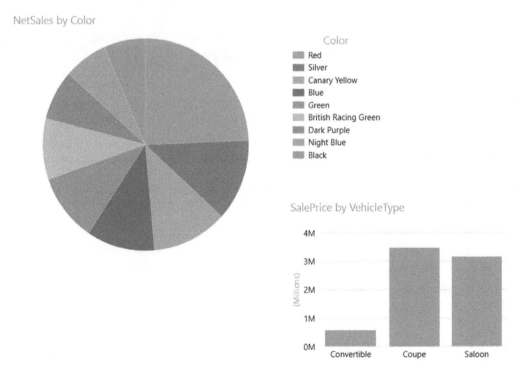

Figure 6-14. *Preparing charts for cross-chart highlighting*

Now click the largest slice in the pie chart (or the legend element: Red). You should see the result given in Figure 6-15.

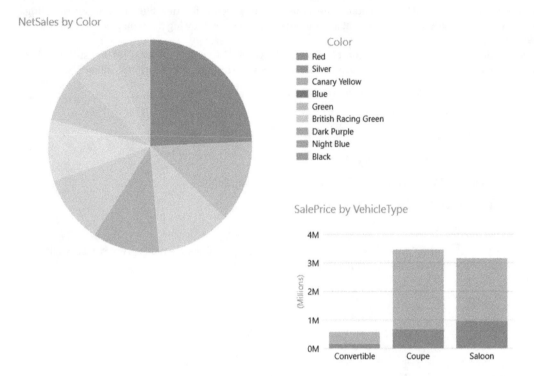

Figure 6-15. *Cross-chart highlighting*

Not only has the pie chart been updated to show the filter effect that it produces, but the bars in the bar chart have been highlighted to show the proportion of the selected color of the total sales cost per vehicle cost.

Now click the bar in the bar chart corresponding to the vehicle type Convertible. You are now using the bar chart as a slicer. As you can see (the output is given in Figure 6-16), the pie chart displays the proportion of convertible sales for each color.

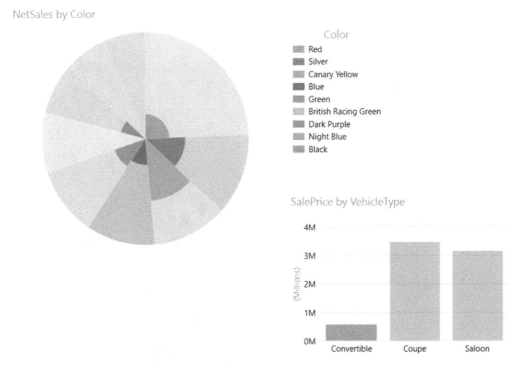

Figure 6-16. *Cross-chart highlighting applied to a pie chart*

■ **Note**   When you use a filter, you will not highlight a chart but will actually filter the data that feeds into it—and consequently, you will remove elements from the chart.

Highlighting Data in Bubble Charts

Often when developing a visualization whose main objective, after all, is to help you to see through the fog of data into the sunlit highlands of comprehension, profit, or, indeed, whatever is the focus of your analysis, you may feel that you cannot see the forest for the trees. This is where Power View's ability to highlight data in a chart visualization can be so effective.

Let's take a visualization that contains a lot of information; in this example, it will be a bubble chart of vehicle types. Indeed, in this example, an audience might think that there is so much data that it is difficult to see the bubbles for specific makes of car and so analyze the uniqueness for sales data by make. Power View has a solution to isolate a data series in such a chart. To see this in action and to make the details clearer, follow these steps:

1. Create a bubble chart using the following elements:

    a. *∑ X VALUE*: RatioNetMargin

    b. *∑ Y VALUE*: SalePrice

    c. *∑ Y SIZE*: NetSales

    d. *DETAILS*: Color

    e. *COLOR*: VehicleType

2. In the legend for the chart where you want to highlight the data for one element (the make of car in this example), click a vehicle type. I will use saloon in this example.

The data for this vehicle type is highlighted in the chart, and the data for all the other vehicle types are dimmed, making one set of information stand out. This is shown in Figure 6-17.

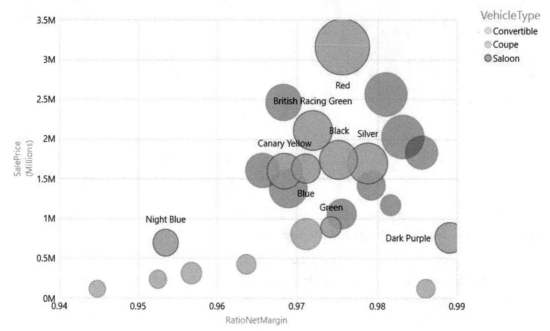

Figure 6-17. *Highlighting data in bubble charts*

This technique needs a few comments:

- To highlight another data set, merely click another element in the legend.

- To revert to displaying all the data, click the selected element again in the legend.

Highlighting data in this way will also filter data in the entire report. The filter effect is described in detail in Chapter 5.

■ **Tip**   You can add drill-down to charts and still use chart highlighting in the same way as you would use it normally. The chart will highlight an element at a drill-down sublevel normally as well as apply filtering to the Power View report.

Charts as Filters

Now that you have seen how charts can be used as slicers, let's take things one step further and see them used as more complex filters. To show this, I will build on the principles shown in the previous example but add a bubble chart that will filter on two elements at once.

To make this second chart, I will do the following:

1. Build a Power View report that has the following:

    a. A matrix of net margin by CountryName and Color

    b. A chart of net sales by Make

2. Create a bubble chart using the following data:

    a. *∑ X VALUE*: NetMargin (from the SalesData table)

    b. *∑ Y VALUE*: NetSales (from the SalesData table)

    c. *SIZE*: DeliveryCharge (from the SalesData table)

    d. *DETAILS*: CountryName (from the Countries table)

    e. *COLOR*: Color (from the Colors table)

3. Resize and tweak the bubble chart so that it is displayed under the existing column chart and table.

4. Click one of the bubbles in the bubble chart (Blue in this example). The Power View report should look like Figure 6-18.

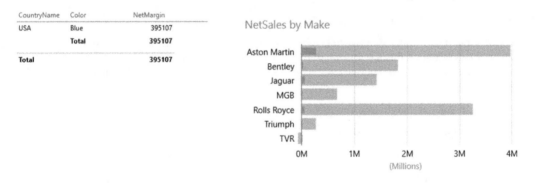

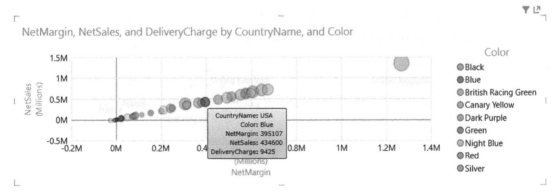

Figure 6-18. *Highlighting and filtering using a chart*

You can see that the other visualizations are filtered so that both the elements that make up the individual bubble (CountryName and Color) are used as filters (or double-slicers if you prefer to think of them like that). This means the following:

- The table shows colors only where there are sales for this country and this color.

- The chart highlights data for this country and this color as a percentage of the total for each make.

As was the case with simple chart slicers, you can cancel the filter effect merely by clicking for a second time on the selected bubble. Or you can switch filters by clicking another bubble in the bubble chart. You will also see the chart itself has data highlighted, but this is explained a little later.

Clearly, you do not have to display the fields on which you are filtering and highlighting in all the visualizations in a report. I chose to do it in this example to make the outcome clearer. In the real world, all other visualizations in a report will be filtered on the elements in the DETAILS and COLOR wells of the bubble chart.

Bubble charts are not, however, the only chart type that lets you apply two simultaneous filters. All chart types will allow this. However, I am of the opinion that some charts are better suited than others to this particular technique. Specifically, I am not convinced that line charts are always suited to being used as filters for a Power View report and that scatter charts may work—visually, that is—but it is just as likely that they will not.

To show this in action, the following sections give examples of how to use the following as chart filters:

- Scatter charts

- Clustered column charts

- Clustered bar charts

- Scatter chart filtering

As a scatter chart is virtually identical to a bubble chart (except for the third data value used to add the size of the bubbles), it follows that a scatter chart can also be used as a filter.

To see this in action, it is probably easiest to create a Power View report described earlier with the following three elements:

- A matrix of net margin by CountryName and Color

- A bar chart of net sales by Make

- A scatter chart using

    a. $\sum X\ VALUE$: NetMargin (from the SalesData table)

    b. $\sum Y\ VALUE$: NetSales (from the SalesData table)

    c. DETAILS: CountryName (from the Countries table)

    d. COLOR: Color (from the Colors table)

The net result should look virtually identical to the bubble chart, except that the bubbles are now small points. If you now click a point in the scatter chart, you will see something like Figure 6-19.

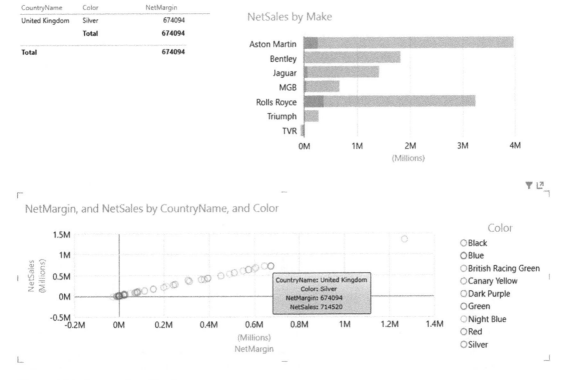

CountryName	Color	NetMargin
United Kingdom	Silver	674094
	Total	674094
Total		674094

Figure 6-19. Scatter chart filtering

I suggest that using scatter charts to filter the rest of the report is slightly less intuitive, as it is harder to see exactly what you are filtering on, given that the points are so small that they make the colors hard to distinguish. Nonetheless, it certainly works! Of course, you can always hover the mouse pointer over a data point to see from the pop-up which elements you will be filtering on.

Column and Bar Charts as Filters

Column charts and bar charts can also be used to filter a Power View report on two elements simultaneously. The only limitation is that you can have only one set of numeric data as the ∑ values for the chart. If the bar or column chart is a stacked bar, then you can click any of the sections in the stacked bar. In addition, if the chart is a clustered bar or column, you can click any of the columns in a group to slice by the elements represented in that section.

If this limitation is not a problem, then here is how you can use bar or column charts (whether they are clustered, stacked, or 100% stacked) to apply double filters to a report.

1. Create a Power View report with the following two elements:

    a. A table based on color, country name, net sales, net margin, and cost price

    b. A bar chart of net sales by CountryName

2. Then create a stacked column chart using the following data:

    a. *∑ VALUES*: NetMargin (from the SalesData table)

    b. *AXIS*: CountryName (from the Countries table)

    c. *LEGEND*: VehicleAgeCategory (from the SalesData table)

Once tweaked to clarify the appearance of the chart, the net result should look like Figure 6-20.

Color	CountryName	NetSales	NetMargin	CostPrice
Black	France	35250	24199	£97,500.00
Black	Switzerland	125550	115364	£100,700.00
Black	United Kingdom	403790	366549	£1,086,960.00
Black	USA	488730	452555	£811,770.00
Blue		1500	825	£42,500.00
Blue	France	164050	152830	£93,200.00
Blue	Germany	3750	2975	£37,500.00
Blue	Spain	1500	750	£42,500.00
Blue	Switzerland	88500	80790	£57,500.00
Blue	United Kingdom	626950	574293	£1,335,300.00
Blue	USA	434600	395107	£851,900.00
British Racing Green		11750	10975	£13,500.00
British Racing Green	France	28750	22349	£192,000.00
British Racing Green	Switzerland	93800	81675	£110,700.00

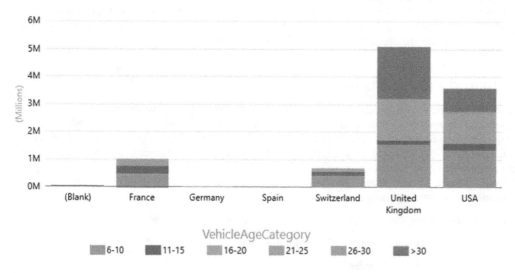

Figure 6-20. A report ready for chart-based filtering and highlighting

Clicking any segment of a bar will filter and highlight other visualizations on the same report for that country and car age range. An example of this is given in Figure 6-21, where the car age range of 6–10 has been selected for the United Kingdom bar.

Color	CountryName	NetSales	NetMargin	CostPrice
Black	United Kingdom	-11250	-21387	£141,500.00
Blue	United Kingdom	203950	176170	£527,300.00
British Racing Green	United Kingdom	302550	287479	£251,700.00
Canary Yellow	United Kingdom	264850	221221	£662,900.00
Dark Purple	United Kingdom	77950	62327	£236,800.00
Green	United Kingdom	193850	173235	£328,900.00
Night Blue	United Kingdom	218420	195040	£441,080.00
Red	United Kingdom	431750	379339	£687,500.00
Silver	United Kingdom	82500	71480	£164,500.00
Total		**1764570**	**1544904**	**£3,442,180.00**

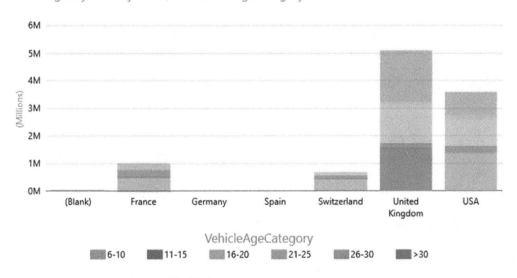

Figure 6-21. *Applying filters and highlights*

Clicking any car age range in the legend will filter by car age range only. You can see this in Figure 6-22 where the age range 21–25 is selected.

Color	CountryName	NetSales	NetMargin	CostPrice
British Racing Green	France	51250	48355	£130,000.00
British Racing Green	United Kingdom	53500	50830	£125,000.00
British Racing Green	USA	51250	48430	£130,000.00
Red	France	200750	195875	£52,000.00
Red	USA	99250	96900	£28,500.00
Silver	United Kingdom	-4030	-9005	£156,780.00
Silver	USA	-3140	-5540	£80,890.00
Total		**448830**	**425845**	**£703,170.00**

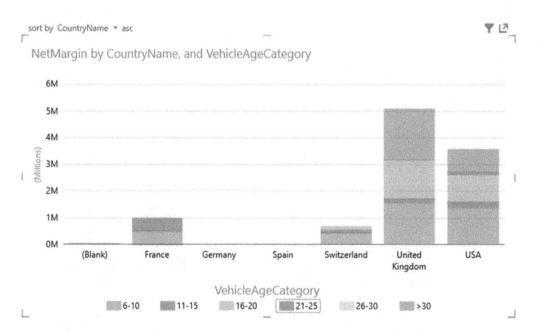

Figure 6-22. *Filtering using a legend element*

So, in fact, you can choose to filter on a single element or multiple elements, depending on whether you use the chart or the legend as the filter source. It is interesting to note, finally, that if you have added tiles to a chart, then the tiles will only filter the chart itself and reduce the available possibilities for further slicing and highlighting. The choice of tile will not affect other visualizations on the same report directly.

▦ **Note** A line chart will not produce the same effect, however. If you click a series in a line chart, you are highlighting that series, which is numeric data, and so it cannot be used as a slicer. Similarly, if you click an element in the legend of a column or bar chart, you are selecting a data series, and this, too, cannot serve as a slicer (even though it will highlight the series in the chart).

Choosing the Correct Approach to Interactive Data Selection

Now that you have taken a tour of the interactive options that Power View offers, it is worth remembering that there is a fundamental difference between slicers and chart filters and tiles.

- Slicers and chart filters apply to the entire Power View report.

- Tiles affect only the visualization to which they are applied.

- Highlighting will apply only to the selected chart, although it will filter data in other tables and highlight the percentage of this element in other charts.

Filter Granularity

It is worth noting that tiles do not override filters or slicers. They simply apply a further selection at an even lower level of granularity—that of a single visualization. So, remember that you could be, in effect, applying the following filters (in the order in which they are given):

- View filter

- Visualization filter

- Slicer

- Tile

This is probably best explained with an example. I propose to create a simple Power View report that will contain all of these elements. It will take a few steps to complete, but if you follow this exercise all the way through, you should certainly not only understand the hierarchy of filtering in Power View but also be able to handle slicers and tiles with ease.

So, this is what you have to do, beginning with creating the report filter even before adding any visualizations:

1. Create a new Power View report by selecting the Insert ribbon in the Excel workbook containing the CarSales data and subsequently clicking Power View (or by clicking Power View in the Power View ribbon).

2. Display the field list by clicking Field List in the Power View ribbon (unless it is already visible).

3. In the field list, expand the Date table.

4. In the Date table, expand Year Hierarchy.

5. Drag the Year field into the Filters area (if this is not visible, click Filters Area to display it).

6. Adjust the slider endpoints so that only the years 2012 and 2013 are selected.

   You will now create a table that will display costs and sales by client.

7. Drag the ClientName field from the Clients table into the Fields section of the field list.

8. Drag the CostPrice and SalePrice fields from the SalesData table into the Fields section of the field list.

   You will now add a filter to the table only.

9. Click inside the table that was created in steps 7 and 8.

10. In the Filters area, click Table.

11. Drag the ClientType field from the Clients table into the Filters area.

12. Select the Dealer element. This will show only the clients who are dealers.

   To prove the points about which filters apply to which elements, you need a visualization that will have no filters applied specifically to it, nor any tiles applied. I suggest a simple column chart of sales by country.

13. Click inside the Power View report canvas outside the table that you just created (ensuring that no visualization is selected).

14. Drag the VehicleAgeCategory field from the SalesData table onto the Power View report.

15. Drag the CostPrice field onto the list of car age ranges that you just created in step 14.

16. In the Design ribbon, click the Column Chart button and select Clustered Column.

   The table will become a column chart. Now you will move from filters to interactive selections, adding a slicer first.

17. Click inside the Power View report outside the visualizations that you just created (ensuring that no visualization is selected).

18. Drag the CountryName field from the Country table onto the Power View report.

19. Click Slicer in the Design ribbon. The table of countries becomes a slicer.

   Finally, you will add tiles to the table of client sales.

20. Select (or click inside) the table you created in steps 7 and 8.

21. In the field list, drag Color from the Colors table to the TILE BY well.

And that is it! At the highest level, you have selected data only for 2012 and 2013. Then you filtered the table so that it will display only dealer data. This filter does not apply to the chart. Then you added a country slicer. Selecting one or more countries will affect both the table and the chart; however, selecting an item from the tiles applied to the table will have no effect on the chart. For a final confirmation of how Power View filters data, try clicking one of the chart columns, and you will see that this too will filter the data elsewhere in the report, complementing both the filters and the slicer selections.

Assuming that all went well—and after, perhaps, a little tweaking to make things look good in Power View—you should have a report that looks something like Figure 6-23.

◄ | Black | Blue | British Racing G | ►

ClientName	CostPrice	SalePrice
Bright Orange	£155,000.00	95000
Crippen & Co	£12,500.00	39500
Cut'n'Shut	£75,890.00	178500
Luxury Rentals	£8,500.00	22500
Olde Englande	£25,700.00	39500
Three Country Cars	£22,500.00	37000
Vive la Vitesse!	£22,500.00	22750
Wheels'R'Us	£62,000.00	44000
Total	**£384,590.00**	**478750**

CountryName
- (Blank)
- France
- Germany
- Spain
- Switzerland
- United Kingdom
- USA

Figure 6-23. *A filtered report ready for slicing, filtering, and tile-based selection*

Now try slicing and highlighting. I will click United Kingdom in the slicer, click the column for the car age range 11–15, and then choose the color Red from the tiles in the table. The result is shown in Figure 6-24.

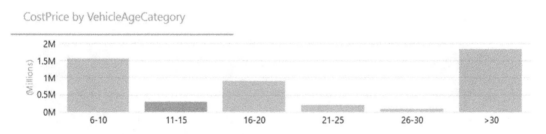

Figure 6-24. *Slicing, filtering, highlighting, and tiles applied*

Believe me, this is just the start of what you can do. In a single click, you can change the country you are slicing the data on. You can examine each car age range in turn, or out of sequence. Then you can see dealer sales by car color and cycle through the colors.

Conclusion

In this chapter, you saw how to use the interactive potential of Power View to enhance the delivery of information to your audience. You saw how to add slicers to a report and then how to use them to filter out data from the visualizations it contains. Then you saw how to add tiles to any table or chart to select a subset of data with a single click. Finally, you learned how to highlight data in charts and tables using charts to isolate specific elements in a presentation.

So, all that remains is for you to start applying these techniques using your own data. Then you can see how you too can impress your audiences using all the interactive possibilities of Power View.

■ ■ ■

CHAPTER 7

Images and Presentation in Power View

After spending a little time working with Power View, let's assume you have analyzed your data. In fact, I imagine that you have been able to tease out a few extremely interesting trends and telling facts from your deep dive into the figures—and you have created the tables and charts to prove your point. To finish the job, you now want to add the final touches to the look and feel of your work so that it will come across to your audience as polished and professional.

Fortunately, Power View is on hand to help you here, too. It can propel your effort onto a higher level of presentation—without you needing to be a graphic artist—so that your audience is captivated. With a few clicks, you can do the following:

- Add and format a report title

- Apply a report background

- Change the color scheme and fonts used in a report (which, taken together, are called the *theme* of a report)

- Alter the font used in a report

- Add free-form text and annotations (or text boxes in Power View speak)

- Add images (which Power View calls *pictures*) to a report

- Use images in tables

- Use image-based slicers

- Apply images to tiles

This chapter will take you through these various techniques and explain how to use them to add real pizzazz to your analysis. You will use the CarSales.xlsx file as the source data and also the image files, which you can download to the folder C:\DataVisualisationInExcel2016\Images from the Apress web site, as described in Appendix A.

Titles

You have spent quite a while digging into data and have found effective ways of drawing your audience's attention to the valuable information that it contains. However, you need the one final cherry on the cake—a title for the report.

© Adam Aspin 2016
A. Aspin, *High Impact Data Visualization in Excel with Power View, 3D Maps, Get & Transform and Power BI*, DOI 10.1007/978-1-4842-2400-7_7

Adding a Title

Adding a title is so easy that it takes longer to describe than to do, but nonetheless, here is how you do it:

1. Click in the section at the top of the report with the helpful label Click Here To Add A Title.

2. Type in an appropriate title. I have entered **2013-2014 Key Sales Data**.

3. Click outside the title anywhere in the blank report canvas.

Figure 7-1 shows you a before and after snapshot of a title added to a report. Moreover, should you want to modify a title, it is as easy as clicking inside the title box and altering the existing text. You can find this example in C:\DataVisualisationInExcel2016\PVPresentation.xlsx.

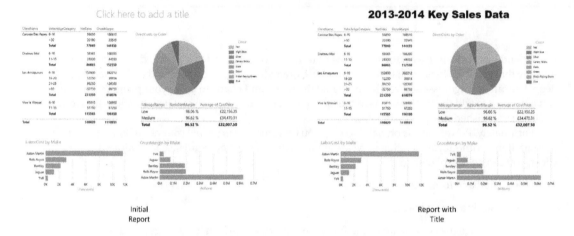

Figure 7-1. *Adding a title to a report*

Moving and Resizing Titles

Titles are a Power View visualization like any other, and consequently, they can be moved and resized just as if they were a table or a chart. This is all you have to do to move a title is:

1. Hover the mouse pointer over the title. The corners and centers of the title box will appear.

2. Place the mouse pointer over the edges of the title box and drag the title to a new position.

To resize a title (should this ever be necessary), follow these steps:

1. Hover the mouse pointer over the title. The corners and centers of the title box will appear.

2. Place the mouse pointer over either the corner or lateral central indicators of the title box and drag the mouse to resize the title box.

Formatting a Title

The title of a Power View report can be formatted specifically so that you can give it the weight and power that you want.

To give the title some emphasis, follow these steps:

1. Hover the mouse pointer over the title and select the title box (or select the text of the title).

2. Activate the Text ribbon, unless it is already active.

3. Select the text attributes that you want to modify. These are described in the next section.

The aspects of a title that you can change are

- Font

- Font attribute (bold, underline, italic)

- Font size

- Alignment (horizontal and vertical)

■ **Note**   If you really do not want a title and you don't want the Power View prompt Click Here To Add A Title to be visible, then you can delete a title just like you can delete a text box. This is described shortly.

The Text Ribbon

As its name suggests, the Text ribbon allows you to modify text display in Power View. It is specifically used with text boxes, such as the title box that you just saw or free-form text boxes, which are explained in the next section.

Figure 7-2 describes the buttons available in the Text ribbon.

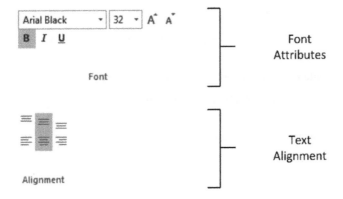

Figure 7-2. *The Text ribbon*

■ **Note**   You cannot enter a font size; you have to select a size from those available in the Font Size pop-up list. You also cannot change the color of the title. Table 7-1 describes the options available for text modification.

Table 7-1. *Text Ribbon Options*

Text Option	Description
Font	Lets you choose the font to apply from those installed on the computer
Font Size	Allows you to select a font size from those in the list
Increase Font Size	Increases the font to the size of the next available size in the list of font sizes
Decrease Font Size	Decreases the font to the size of the next available size in the list of font sizes
Bold	Switches the font to boldface
Italic	Switches the font to italic
Underline	Underlines the selected text
Align Top	Aligns the text at the top of the text box
Align Middle	Aligns the text in the middle (horizontally) of the text box
Align Bottom	Aligns the text at the bottom of the text box
Align Left	Aligns the text at the left of the text box
Align Center	Aligns the text in the center (vertically) of the text box
Align Right	Aligns the text at the right of the text box

Adding Text Boxes to Annotate a Report

Now that you have seen how to add and modify a title, it is probably a good time to extend the knowledge acquired to the close relative of the title—the text box. A *text box* is a floating text entity that you can place anywhere inside a Power View report. They are especially useful for annotating specific parts of a presentation. To add a text box, follow these steps:

1. Switch to the Power View ribbon, unless it is already active.

2. Click the Text Box button. A new text box is added to the report, and the text cursor will flash inside this box.

3. Type in the text you want to add. I entered **Clear Market Leader** in this example.

4. Click outside the text box, preferably in an empty part of the report canvas, to finish.

5. Move and resize the text box to produce the effect you are looking for.

Figure 7-3 shows a text box added to a chart visualization.

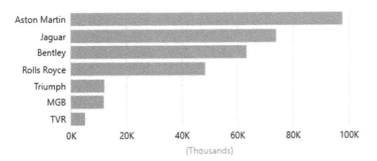

Figure 7-3. *Adding a text box*

A text box can be moved and resized exactly as a title can. Consequently, I will not explain this again; just go back a couple of pages to the section called "Moving and Resizing Titles."

The text inside a text box can be formatted as well. Here, too, the steps to take are identical to those you follow when formatting a title. So once again, just flip back a couple of pages, and it is all explained.

■ **Tip**   Remember that you can highlight only part of the text if you want to format only one or two words. If you select the text box itself, then you will be formatting all the text in the text box.

If you want to delete a text box, then be sure to do the following:

1. Hover the mouse pointer over the text box until you see the corner and lateral handles.

2. Select the text box.

3. Press the Delete key.

■ **Note**   Merely selecting and deleting the text inside the text box will not remove the text box itself, so to be sure that you do not leave any unnecessary clutter in a report, delete any unwanted and empty text boxes.

The Context Menu

Although I have not mentioned it so far, there is a context menu available when you use Power View. This menu is particularly useful when you are adding the final tweaks to a report, so now is probably a good time to look at what it can do. Right-clicking any visualization, text, or image, in a Power View report will display the menu shown in Figure 7-4.

Figure 7-4. The context menu for visualizations

If you click the canvas of a Power View report (that is outside any existing visualization), you will see a slightly different context menu, as shown in Figure 7-5.

Figure 7-5. The context menu for reports

The two available context menus are largely similar. Table 7-2 outlines the available options in the context menus.

Table 7-2. *Context Menu Options*

Menu Option	Context Menu	Description
Cut	Visualization/canvas	Removes the selected visualization, text, or image and places it in the clipboard
Copy	Visualization/canvas	Copies the selected visualization, text, or image to the clipboard
Paste	Visualization/canvas	Adds the selected visualization, text, or image from the clipboard
Refresh Sheet	Visualization/canvas	Updates the data for the current Power View report
Bring To Front	Visualization	Lets you move the selected visualization, text, or image to the top, or forward, above/in front of any others
Send To Back	Visualization	Lets you move the selected visualization, text, or image to the bottom, or backward, below/behind any others
Hide/Show Field List	Canvas	Hides the field list if it is visible; displays it if it is not
Hide/Show Filters Area	Canvas	Hides the Filters area if it is visible; displays it if it is not

■ **Note** The Cut, Copy, and Paste options are visible but not accessible in the context menu for the Power View canvas.

Altering the Font Used in a Report

If you work in a corporate environment, then you probably have to follow enterprise guidelines on presentation. Even if this is not the case, you may have preferences when it comes to the choice of fonts that you use. In any case, Power View will let you choose the font used in a presentation. The following are the things you can change:

- Font family
- Font size
- Font family

To change the font used in an entire Power View presentation (that is, in every Power View report in an Excel workbook), this is all you have to do:

1. Switch to the Power View tab (unless it is already active).

2. Click the downward-facing triangle to the right of Font in the Themes section.

3. Select the font that you want to apply from those available.

The only thing to remember is that this will affect every Power View report in an Excel workbook. Changing the font this way will not, however, override any font settings made to a specific text box using the Font ribbon.

Changing the Text Size

You can also change the proportional text size in an entire presentation. Now I really mean *proportional*. Remember that when you created individual tables and charts you set the size of the text in each visualization—at least relative to the other visualizations since you could not set exact font sizes? Well, this can be overridden at the level of the entire presentation, where you can proportionally increase or decrease the size of the text in every visualization, whether it is a table, a chart, or a text box.

To do this, follow these steps:

1. Switch to the Power View tab (unless it is already active).

2. Click the downward-facing triangle to the right of Text Size in the Themes section.

3. Select the proportional text size from those available.

■ **Note** This can produce some quite devastating results and can render a report—or indeed an entire presentation—unreadable. So, it is probably best if you use it at an appropriate stage in the creation process and *before* you have spent valuable time tweaking individual visualizations to get them to appear exactly the way that you want them.

You cannot enter a specific percentage for the text size and have to restrict your choice to the selection on offer. Currently, you can choose between the following:

- 200%
- 175%
- 150%
- 125%
- 100%
- 75%

Altering the Theme of a Report

Power View understands that you may not have a lot of time to spend on the presentation of your report. Consequently, many of the visual aspects of a report work using a few simple, yet sophisticated, preset values. Central to these is the notion of the report theme. Basically, what you do is choose a set of colors and fonts from a palette that Power View offers, and the software does the rest.

Rather than discuss the theory, I propose seeing themes in action. So, to apply a theme to a Power View report, whether it is a blank report or an existing one, this is what you do:

1. Click the Themes button in the Power View ribbon; the available themes will appear in a scrollable list, as shown in Figure 7-6.

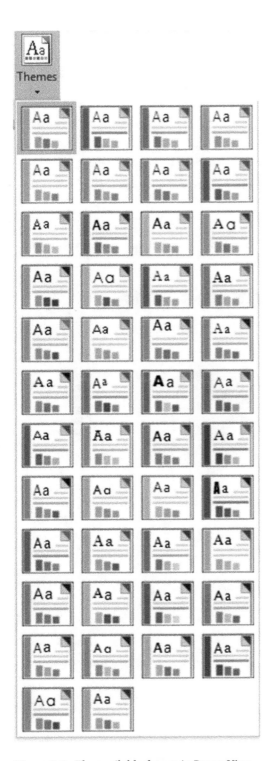

Figure 7-6. *The available themes in Power View*

2.   Select a theme by clicking it.

Yes, it really is as simple as it sounds. However, as the changes can be subtle, you may not see much change to begin with. What you have probably noticed (assuming that your Power View report has a table, a couple of charts, and a slicer, like the Power View sheet StylesExample in the example workbook entitled PVPresentation.xlsx) is that the following have changed:

- The font used in the entire report—tables, charts, titles, slicers—everything!

- The color used as a principal highlight. You will see it change in the line under table titles and above totals as well as in the bullets to the left of slicer items, for instance.

- The palette of colors used by charts. This is the basis for bars, columns, pie slices, bubbles, and lines.

- The report background.

As an example, Figure 7-7 shows the Power View sheet StylesExample from the sample workbook with the Concourse theme applied.

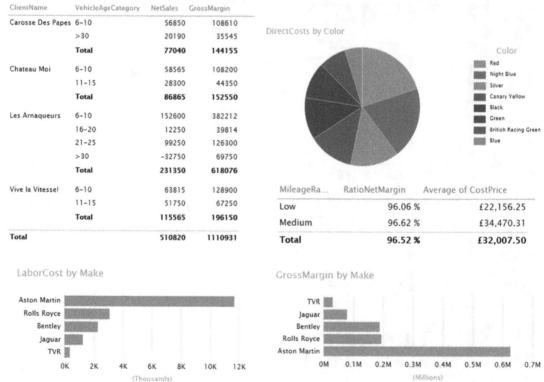

Figure 7-7. *The theme Concourse applied to a Power View report*

Although the color change is not immediately obvious in a book printed in black and white, the change of font family is clear, as is the modification of the font size. In fact, I had to resize the matrix and pie chart very slightly, as well as the column widths in the matrix and table, to achieve an optimum presentation. So, to avoid lots of last-minute retweaking of your reports, I advise you to decide on a theme earlier rather than later in your creative cycle.

■ **Note**   You have 46 presentation styles to choose from, so the best advice that I can give is that you spend some time trying them. This way you will see which one is best suited to your presentation style and the type of information you are delivering.

Deciphering Themes

Testing the available themes can be great fun, but it does not have to be a process based entirely on trial and error. This is because each image of a theme in the Themes list is, in fact, a preview of what it contains. Each tiny image of a theme indicates the display elements, which are explained in Table 7-3.

Table 7-3. Themes

Theme Element	Description
Dark Background Color	The color applied to the canvas if the dark background is selected
Light Background Color	The color applied to the canvas if the light background is selected
Highlight Color	The color used as bullets for slicer elements and general highlighting, as well as being the color used when chart highlighting is applied
Font	The font that will be applied
Chart Color 1	The first color in the chart color palette
Chart Color 2	The second color in the chart color palette
Chart Color 3	The third color in the chart color palette

Figure 7-8 explains exactly how these elements are contained in a theme image.

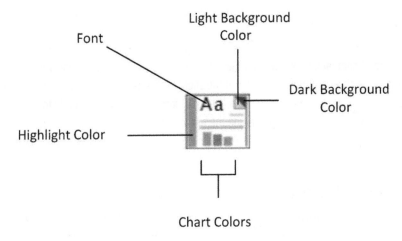

Figure 7-8. Theme elements

The chart color scheme does not stop with three colors, of course, but the colors given in the theme image give you a pretty good idea of the palette that will be used by the theme you have chosen.

If (or ideally, when) you become a regular user of Power View, you may find that you frequently want to use the same themes over and over. This can, of course, provide consistency and an impression of coherence to your reports. So, rather than having to remember that the last time you used the "second column third row" theme in the pop-up list of themes, it is probably easier to try to remember the theme name. To see a theme name, follow these steps:

1. Hover the mouse pointer over a theme image in the Themes pop-up, as shown in Figure 7-9.

Figure 7-9. *The theme name*

2. If you cannot remember which theme you used, then look closely at the theme images in the Themes list. An active theme has a subtle border around it to indicate that it is selected. Figure 7-10 shows an example of this.

Figure 7-10. *The active theme*

The themes are in alphabetical order in the Themes menu. They flow from left to right, and the first two rows rejoice in the names Theme 1, Theme 2, and so on.

■ **Note**   If you add a theme to a report containing a slicer, then the slicer will adopt the highlight color from the theme for the square to the left of the slicer element (or the bar if the slicer is an image). However, if you then apply a different theme, the highlight color will not change. If you want to force Power View to apply the new highlight color, you have to switch the slicer back to a table and then revert to a slicer.

Applying a Report Background

Power View does not condemn you to presenting every report with a white background. To avoid monotony, you can choose from a predefined set of 12 report backgrounds that you can add to every report in a presentation with a couple of clicks.

To apply a background to a report, all you have to do is the following:

1. On the Power View menu, click the pop-up triangle for Background (in the Themes section). The choice of available backgrounds will appear, as shown in Figure 7-11.

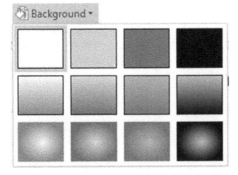

Figure 7-11. *The Background pop-up menu*

2. Select the background you want to apply. The sample report that you have been using so far looks like Figure 7-12, if you apply the Dark 1 Solid background (the image on the top right of the set of choices).

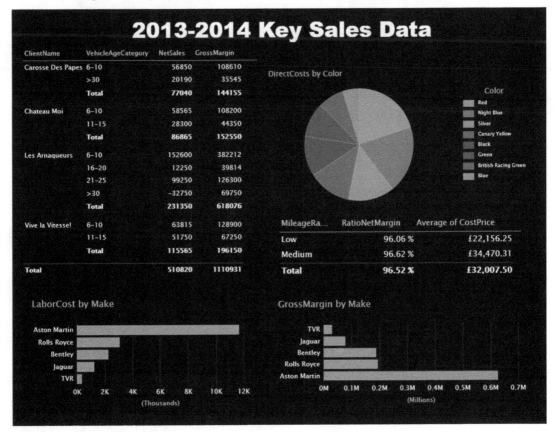

Figure 7-12. *Applying a background to a report*

These three families of background are available:

- Solid

- Vertical gradient

- Central gradient

One of each of these is essentially light in tone; it is based on predominantly white coloring. Another set is based on black, so it is consequently dark in tone. The two other sets are based on the two background colors defined in the report theme—one light, the other dark. The actual colors are displayed as the two tiny color triangles at the top right of each theme image in the Theme pop-up menu.

To explain how the backgrounds are set out, take a look at Figure 7-13.

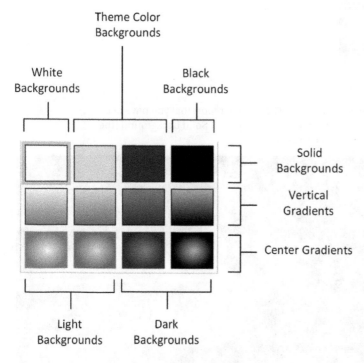

Figure 7-13. *The available report backgrounds*

If you apply any of the dark backgrounds, then Power View will automatically switch the text to white or a light color. Applying a light background will switch all the text in a presentation to black, or a dark color.

If you want a color-based background, then you will have to choose one of the options available in the two central columns in the Background pop-up menu. However, to choose a color, you must apply a theme to the presentation. As you will discover, there are only a limited set of background colors available.

You can always see which background has been applied by looking at the images in the Background pop-up menu. The current background has a subtly thicker line around it. The default background is always the top-left background called Light 1 Solid, which is, in effect, a clear background.

Images

We all know what a picture is worth. Well, so does Power View. Consequently, you can add pictures, or images, as they are generically known, to a Power View report to replace words and enhance your presentation. The images that you insert into a Power View report can come from the Web or from a file on a disk—either local or on an available network share. Once an image has been inserted, it is not linked to the source file. So if the source image changes, you will have to reinsert it to keep it up to date. So, although you can have images from databases appear in tables via Power Pivot, you cannot place these same images outside a table in Power View.

The following are some of the uses for images in Power View:

- As a background image for a report.

- Images in tables instead of text. An example could be to use product images.

- Images in slicers. These could be flags of countries, for instance.

- Images in tiles. These could be flags or products.

- Independent images— a logo, for instance, or a complement to draw the viewer's attention to a specific point.

Once you have looked at the types of image formats available, you will see how images can be used in all these contexts.

Image Sources

A multitude of image formats exist. Power View, however, will accept only two of them.

- *JPEG (pronounced "jay-peg")*: This is a venerable standard image file format.

- *PNG*: This is a standard file format for Internet images.

The former generally has the extension .jpg or .jpeg. The latter generally has the .png extension. Both can deliver reasonable-quality images that should certainly suffice for Power View reports.

If you attempt to insert an image that is not in a format that Power View can handle (this is difficult, but it can be done), you will get the alert shown in Figure 7-14.

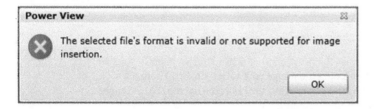

Figure 7-14. *Invalid image format alert dialog*

■ **Note** When you attempt to insert an image from a file, the Open dialog will filter the files so that only files with a .jpeg, .jpg, or .png extension are visible. You can force the dialog to display other file formats, but Power View will not be able to load them.

Background Images

One major, and frequently striking, use of images is as a background to a report—and possibly even to a whole series of reports. Let's take a look at how to use images for report backgrounds and some of the things you can do with them.

Adding a Background Image

Before anything else, you need to add a background image. This is, once again, extremely simple.

1. In the Power View ribbon, select Set Image from the Set Image button. A classic Windows dialog will appear; it lets you choose the source image, as shown in Figure 7-15.

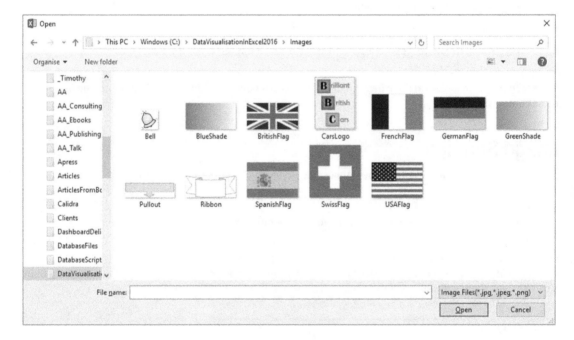

Figure 7-15. *Navigating to a background image file*

2. Navigate to the directory containing the image you want to insert. There are several sample images in the folder C:\DataVisualisationInExcel2016\Images that you can install, as described in Appendix A.

3. Click the image file. I will use the example image GreenShade in this example.

4. Click Open.

The selected image will be loaded as a report background. By default it will be adjusted proportionally until it covers the width of the report. The Power View report that you have been developing in this chapter (and that you last saw in Figure 7-12) should look like Figure 7-16.

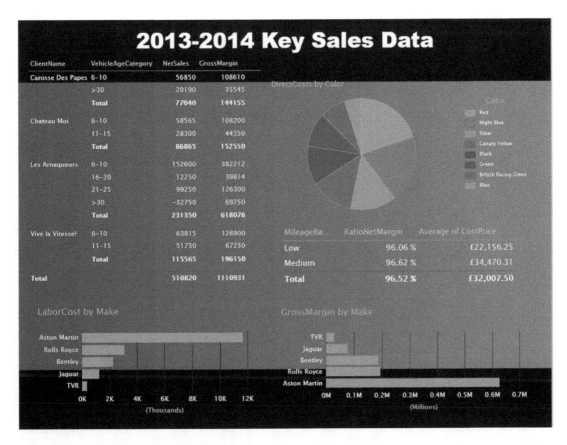

Figure 7-16. *An initial background image*

Fitting a Background Image

Frequently an image can need a little tweaking until it truly enhances a Power View report. To help you control the final display of a background image, Power View offers you several ways to resize the image— both proportionally and nonproportionally—in a report.

For example, to make an image cover an entire report, follow these steps:

1. In the Power View menu, click the Image Position button.

2. Select Stretch.

The image will be stretched (and possibly distorted) to fit the entire Power View report canvas, as shown in Figure 7-17.

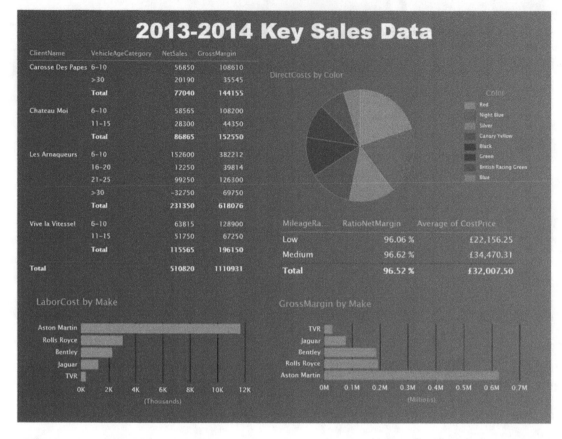

Figure 7-17. *A stretched background image*

There are other options you can use when fitting an image to a report canvas, as outlined in Table 7-4.

Table 7-4. *Background Image Fit Options*

Image Option	Description
Fit	Enlarges the image proportionally until either the sides or top and bottom of the report canvas are reached
Stretch	Enlarges the image nonproportionally to cover the entire report canvas
Tile	Repeats the image (keeping it at its original size) to cover the entire report canvas
Center	Places the image at the center of the report canvas

Removing a Background Image

To remove a background image, all you have to do is the following:

1. In the Power View ribbon, select Remove Image from the Set Image button.

The existing background image will disappear from the report.

Setting an Image's Transparency

A background image sits on top of the background of the actual report, assuming you have applied one. This lets you achieve some interesting effects by combining the image with the background. What Power View lets you do, in the interest of greater readability, is set the transparency of the image. Put simply, a largely transparent image will let the background show through, whereas a completely opaque image will not let any of the background underneath the image be visible in the report.

To make this clearer, I suggest altering the transparency of the image that you added to create Figure 7-17.

1.   In the Power View button, click Transparency.

2.   Select a transparency percentage from those available.

Figure 7-18 shows an example of this, using 10 percent transparency. The image is as close as possible to the original, and it completely hides any background that was set. If you compare this with the report where the default transparency of 50 percent was applied (in Figure 7-17), you can see that the underlying dark background is now virtually hidden by the background image.

You cannot choose a transparency setting other than those offered. However, as the selection varies from 0 to 100 percent, you should always be able to find a setting to suit your needs.

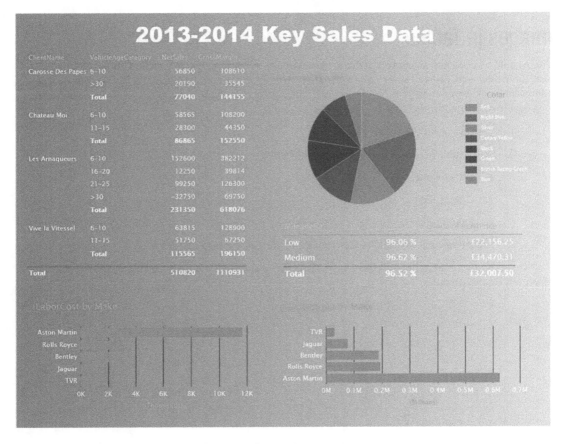

Figure 7-18. *Adjusting the transparency of a background image*

■ **Tip**   Even if you hide a background almost completely (as you have done here), it can have an effect. If you select one of the light backgrounds, then the font color will be dark, and if you choose a dark background, the font color is set to a light color. So, selecting the appropriate, but invisible, background can change the font color to make the text more readable. This is what has been applied in Figure 7-18.

The next question that you may be asking is "What purpose can this option possibly serve?" Well, consider the case where you have applied an image over a report where all the presentation's backgrounds are dark, so the text is, consequently, white. When you apply a fairly clear image, this could make the text hard to read. So, adjusting the image's transparency could enable you to "darken" the image, making the text readable.

■ **Note**   It is worth noting that a background image will be applied only to the current report. This is unlike what happens when you set a background, for instance, which will be applied to all reports (Power View worksheets) in an Excel workbook.

Images in Tables

There could be occasions when you prefer to use an image rather than text in a table. This is a technique that, if not overused, can add some color and variety to a report. As an example of this, let's create a list of clients and their home country using the flag of each country to indicate the geographical zone where the sale occurred. The following is one way to do this:

1. Create a new Power View report.

2. Add a table based on the following three fields:

    a. ClientName

    b. CountryFlag

    c. SalePrice

3. Adjust the table size and column widths to get the best result.

The resulting table should look like Figure 7-19. As you can see, the effect is instantaneous—and extremely easy to produce.

Figure 7-19. *Using images in tables*

The images that are used in tables can be resized globally but not individually. To adjust the size of all the images, all you have to do is to increase or decrease the width of the column containing the images. This will not, however, cause the row height to change.

Images in Slicers

The use of slicers is one area where images can be a really powerful presentation tool. Suppose that you have a report where you want to add a slicer by country. Now consider how it would look if, instead of the country name, you use the country's flag. Let's see this in action.

1. Choose a report, such as ReadyForSlicer in the sample PVPresentation.xlsx workbook.

2. Drag the CountryFlag field onto the report canvas. A table of flags will appear.

3. Click Slicer in the Power View ribbon.

The table of flags becomes a slicer, as shown in Figure 7-20. If you click any of the flags, you will filter the report to display only data for that country. The slicer is, to all intents and purposes, an ordinary slicer. Consequently, you can slice on multiple elements, clear the selection, and, in fact, use all the slicer techniques explained in Chapter 6.

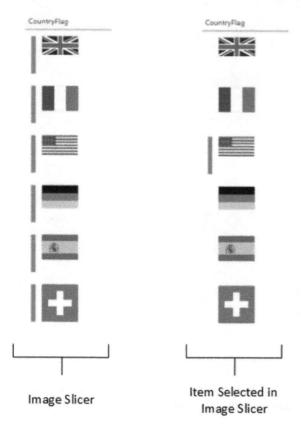

Figure 7-20. Images in slicers

Images in Tiles

As I mentioned in Chapter 6, you can also use images in tiles. This is a selection technique that you can often use to great effect. As an example (which still uses the country flags, since we have images for them), I suggest creating a table of clients showing their sales and net margin tiled by country. To create this visualization, follow these steps:

1. In a new or existing Power View report, add a table based on the following fields:

    a. ClientName

    b. SalePrice

    c. NetMargin

2. Drag the CountryFlag field to the TILE BY well in the layout section of the field list.

The resulting tiled table should look like Figure 7-21 (Switzerland is the selected country). As you can see, tiles with images can be larger than text-based tiles.

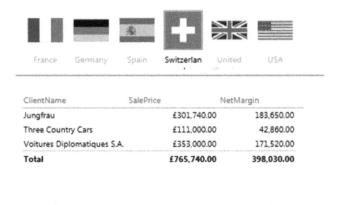

ClientName	SalePrice	NetMargin
Jungfrau	£301,740.00	183,650.00
Three Country Cars	£111,000.00	42,860.00
Voitures Diplomatiques S.A.	£353,000.00	171,520.00
Total	£765,740.00	398,030.00

Figure 7-21. *Using images in tiles*

The tiles act in the same way as tiles based on a text field. You will also notice that if you use an image in tiles, the tiles will automatically add the name field as a title. Although you cannot make this field disappear, you can reduce its font size if you find it superfluous.

___

■ **Note**   If you want a more polished final effect, then spend a little time making sure that all the source images are the same size. This way you will avoid one image setting the height for the other images and having empty space above and below the images.

___

Independent Images

Whether you have added a background image or not, you may still want to add completely free-form floating images to a report. However, before getting carried away with all that can be done with images, remember that Power View is not designed as a high-end presentation package. If anything, it is there to help you analyze and present information quickly and cleanly. Inevitably you will find that there are things you cannot do in Power View that you are used to doing in, say, PowerPoint. Consequently, there are many presentation tricks and techniques that you may be tempted to achieve in Power View using images to try to get similar results. Indeed, you can achieve many things in a Power View report by adding images. Yet the question that you must ask yourself is "Am I adding value to my report?" I am a firm believer that less is more in a good presentation. Consequently, although I will be showing you a few tricks using images, many of them go against the grain of fast and efficient Power View report creation and can involve considerable adjustment whenever the data in a visualization changes. So, I advise you not to go overboard using images to enhance your presentations unless it is really necessary.

In any case, let's add a floating, independent image to a Power View report. In this example, it will be a company logo—that of Brilliant British Cars, the company whose metrics you are analyzing throughout the course of this book.

1. Click the Picture button in the Power View ribbon. The Open dialog will display as a result.

2. Navigate to the image file that you want to insert (CarsLogo.png in this example, from the samples in C:\DataVisualisationInExcel2016\Images).

3. Click Open.

4. Resize or reposition the image.

Figure 7-22 shows a Power View report with a logo added.

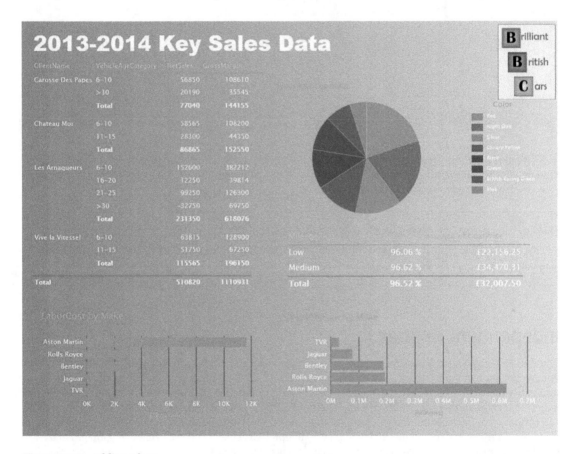

Figure 7-22. *Adding a logo*

■ **Tip** If you use the corner handles to resize an image, you will keep the image in proportion; that is, the height to width ratio will stay the same. Resizing an image using the lateral handles will distort the image.

Layering Visualizations

As a report gets more complex, you will inevitably need to arrange the elements that it contains not only side by side but also one on top of the other. Power View lets you do this simply and efficiently.

As an example of this, let's create a chart with another chart superposed on it.

1. Create a bar chart using the following two fields:

   a. Make

   b. LaborCost

2. Order the bar chart by LaborCost, in ascending order.

3. Create a pie chart using the following two fields:

   a. DirectCosts

   b. CountryName

4. Reduce the size of the font in the pie chart and set the legend to appear on the right.

5. Place the pie chart in the top-right corner of the bar chart.

6. With the pie chart selected, choose Arrange ➤ Bring To Front from the Power View ribbon.

Your composite chart should look like Figure 7-23. If you did not set the pie chart to be at the front (in the topmost layer), the vertical lines of the bar chart would have overlaid the pie chart, making it harder to appreciate.

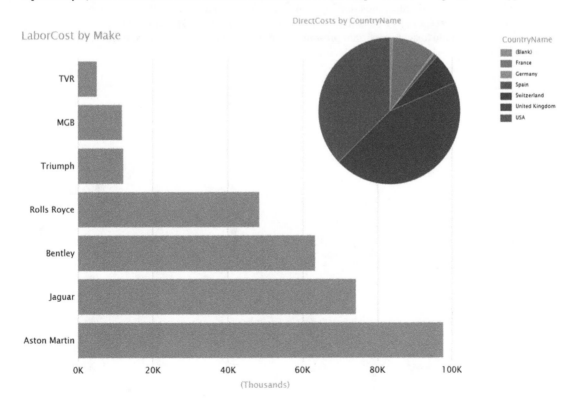

Figure 7-23. *Layering charts*

This technique is particularly useful when you are adding independent images, as described in the previous section. It is also handy when you are combining elements such as images and text boxes, as you will see in the next section.

Some Uses for Independent Images

The limits of what images can do to a report are only those of your imagination, so it is impossible to give a comprehensive list of suggestions. Nonetheless, these are a few uses that I have found for free-form images:

- Company logos, as you have just seen.

- Images added for a purely decorative effect. I would hesitate, however, before doing this at all, as it can distract from the analysis rather than enhance it. Nonetheless, at times, this may be precisely what you want to do (to turn attention away from some catastrophic sales figures, for instance). So, add decoration if you must, but please use sparingly!

- To enhance the text in a text box by providing shading that is in clear relief to the underlying image or background.

- As a background to a specific column in a table. Be warned, however, that the image cannot be made to move with a column if it is resized.

- Pullout arrows.

Figure 7-24 shows several of these techniques. This example will ideally clearly indicate the limits of such techniques, as they detract (considerably, in my opinion) from the simplicity and style of an uncluttered Power View report, as well as make it extremely laborious to make any modifications. Nonetheless, it is possible to achieve certain presentation effects using images. So, if your boss insists, you can push the boundaries between added effects and visual overload.

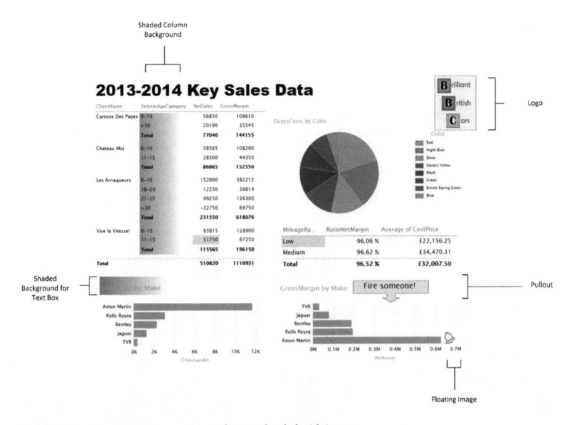

Figure 7-24. A Power View report somewhat overloaded with images

■ **Tip**   When adding images to a Power View report, you should avoid shaded backgrounds, or you may end up spending a lot of time manipulating your images in an attempt to make them conform to the Power View shading.

Image File Format

Earlier in this chapter I mentioned that Power View can accept only two image formats. This is, however, not the limitation that it sounds like it could be because changing the format of an image file is usually easy.

So—and without going too far off on a tangent about the subject of image file formats—here is a simple technique to try in order to adapt a file to the PNG format.

Let's assume you have received the file for a client logo that you have to include in your Power View presentation. This file has the `.gif` extension, and Power View has refused to load it. Now, if your PC or laptop has a fairly standard Windows installation, you should have Microsoft Paint installed. As there have been many versions of Paint over the years, the instructions given here are fairly generic. To create a copy of the client logo file in the PNG file format, follow these steps:

1. Open Microsoft Paint (for instance, open the Windows menu, enter **Paint** in the search/run box, and press Enter).

2. In Paint, open the original GIF file.

3. Choose Save As from the File menu. Depending on the version of Paint that you are using, you may need to select Save As followed by PNG Picture in the submenu.

4. Ensure that the Save As type is set to PNG (*.Png).

5. Modify the file name if you need to and select the appropriate directory.

6. Click Save.

You can now insert the file that you received into a Power View report.

As I stressed earlier, it is easy to try to use images to produce effects that Power View does not provide out of the box. So, even if this may take a disproportionate amount of time compared to producing your analysis, at times you simply have to add some visual effects. In other words, here are a few suggestions for those moments when the boss can't spell "overkill."

- For backgrounds, especially if you want a good shading effect, take a look at one of the free graphic design programs that are around. I have a weakness for Pixlr, which I used for many of the sample images that accompany this book.

- If you need to resize an image, remember that there is a Resize option in Paint and that Pixlr (or several other web sites and free products) can do this too.

- Take a look at the many, many web sites that offer royalty-free stock images. There are so many that I suggest using your favorite search engine for this. Then you can convert them to PNG or JPG as described previously (if this is necessary).

- As you are using Excel, then you could well be a PowerPoint user. Remember that PowerPoint has a vast image library and that you can export selected images in PNG format.

- If your company uses Microsoft Visio, then you may find lots of images to use from among the shapes that come with the product. To export a shape as a PNG file, just select it, choose File ➤ Save As, and select Save As Type Portable Network Graphics. You may recognize one or two of the images used in this chapter as coming from Visio, if you look carefully!

Conclusion

In this chapter, you saw how to push the envelope when using Power View to deliver especially compelling presentations. This covers not only the general aspect of a report, such as its background and color scheme, but also the enhancements that you can add by tweaking the font attributes for individual elements.

Finally, you saw how adding images can turbo-charge the impression that your analysis can give when you add graphic elements to tables, slicers, and tiles. And, used sparingly, images and free-form text elements can draw your audience's attention to the most salient features of your presentation. So, now it is up to you to use these powerful Power View features to deliver some really compelling interactive analyses to your audience.

■ ■ ■

CHAPTER 8

Mapping Data in Power View

Data visualization in Power View is not limited to tables and charts. Another powerful technique that you can use to both analyze and present your insights is to display the data in map form. All that this requires is that your source data contains information that can be used for geographical representation. So, if you have country, state, town, or even latitude and longitude in the data set, then you can get Power View to add a map to your report and show the selected data using the map as a background.

Better yet, a Power View map behaves just like any other visualization. This means you can filter the data that is displayed in a map, as well as highlighting it, just like you can do for charts, tables, and matrices. Indeed, you can even drill down into maps just like you can with matrices and charts. Not only that, but a map is an integral and interactive part of a Power View report. So, if you highlight data in a chart, a map in the same report will also be highlighted.

The aim of this chapter is to show you some of the ways in which you can add real spice to your reports by using maps. Then, when presenting your analyses, you can interact with the maps and really—no, really—impress your audience.

Bing Maps

Before adding a first map, I want to explain how mapping works in Power View. The geographical component is based on Bing Maps. So, to add a map, you need to be able to connect to the Internet and use the Bing Maps service. Second, the underlying data set must contain fields that are recognized by Bing Maps as geographical data. In other words, you need country, state, town, or other information that Bing Maps can use to generate the plot of the map. Fortunately, Power View will indicate whether it recognizes a field as containing data that it can use (ideally) to create a map, as it will display a tiny icon of a globe in the field list for every field in the underlying data set that apparently contains geographical data.

To avoid the risk of misinterpreting data, you can add metadata to the underlying PowerPivot data model that will define geographical field types. This is explained in Chapter 14 where you will see how to apply data categories to fields. Power View maps will then use these categories to interpret geographical data for mapping.

Preparing data so that any fields used by Bing Maps not only are recognizable as containing geographic data but are also uniquely recognizable is vital. You must help Bing Maps so that if you are mapping data for a city named Paris, Bing can see whether you mean Paris, France, or Paris, Texas. Chapter 14 explains some of the ways in which you can prepare your data for use by Bing Maps and consequently use it to add map visualizations to Power View.

Although preparing the data may be necessary, it is certainly a lot simpler than the alternatives that involve finding, loading, and understanding shape files for geographical representation or manipulating geospatial data in a database such as SQL Server.

© Adam Aspin 2016

A. Aspin, *High Impact Data Visualization in Excel with Power View, 3D Maps, Get & Transform and Power BI*, DOI 10.1007/978-1-4842-2400-7_8

■ **Note**   There are some areas of the world that cannot use Bing Maps. So, if you attempt to use Power View mapping in these geographical zones, you will not see any map appear when you attempt to create a map.

Maps in Power View

Let's begin by creating a map of sales by country. Fortunately, the sample data set contains the country where the sale was made. This means you can use this data to make Power View display a map of worldwide sales. Here is how to create an initial map:

1. Insert a new Power View sheet. You need to do this because maps tend to need most, if not all, of the available space in a Power View report.

2. Add the following fields to the FIELDS well in the layout section of the field list. You will see a table appear in the Power View canvas containing the data.

    a. CountryName

    b. GrossMargin

3. Filter the report to show only data for 2013 (this is described in Chapter 3 if you have started the book at the current chapter).

4. Click Map in the Design ribbon.

5. If this is the first time you are using the Map function, then Power View will display the alert shown in Figure 8-1.

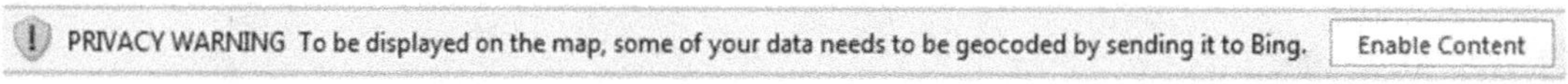

ⓘ PRIVACY WARNING To be displayed on the map, some of your data needs to be geocoded by sending it to Bing.   Enable Content

Figure 8-1. *The Bing Maps privacy warning*

6. Click Enable Content to allow Bing Maps to be used.

7. The table will be replaced by a map representing the data for each country. You can now resize the map to make it easier to read. It should look something like Figure 8-2.

GrossMargin by CountryName

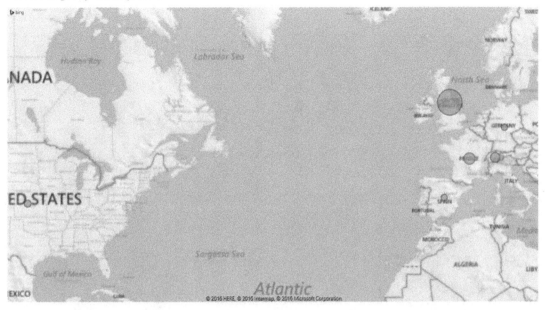

Figure 8-2. *An initial Power View map*

It is probably worth clarifying a few points about maps in Power View before going any further.

- A map is a visualization like any other. You can resize and move it anywhere on the Power View canvas.

- The map will apply any filters that have been set for the report.

- Each data point (or bubble) in a map is proportional to the relative size of the underlying data.

You can hover the mouse pointer over a data "bubble" to display a pop-up showing the exact data that is represented. Figure 8-3 shows an example of this.

Figure 8-3. *Displaying the exact data in a Power View map*

Adjusting Map Display in Power View

Creating a map is, as you have seen, extremely easy. However, the initial map is not necessarily the finalized version that you want to show to your audience. You may want to do the following:

- Position the map elements more precisely inside the visualization

- Zoom in or out of the map

- Remove or add a map title

- Select a different type of map background

- Filter the underlying data

In the next few sections, you will look at these various modifications that you can make to Power View maps. Ideally, you will find these tweaks both intuitive and easy to implement. In any case, with a little practice, you should find that these modifications take only a few seconds to accomplish.

Positioning the Map Elements

If the area displayed in a map is not quite as perfect as you would prefer, then you can alter the area (whether it is a country or a region) that appears in the map visualization. To do this, follow these steps:

1. Place the mouse pointer over the map. The Zoom and Pan icons will appear at the top right of the map.

2. Click the Pan Right icon (the right-facing triangle) to alter the geographical area displayed in the map visualization.

The icons used to pan a map appear in Figure 8-4.

Figure 8-4. *Panning around a Power View map*

■ **Tip**   You can also click inside a map and drag the mouse to pan around.

Zooming In or Out

It is conceivable that the map that is displayed is not at a scale that you would prefer. Fortunately, this is extremely easy to fix.

1. Place the mouse pointer over the map. The Zoom and Pan icons will appear at the top right of the map.

2. Click the Zoom Out button (the minus sign) to zoom out, or click the Zoom In button (the plus sign) to zoom in.

■ **Tip**   You can also move the mouse scroll wheel to zoom in or out of a map.

Removing or Adding a Map Title

A map adds a title automatically to explain what data you are seeing. You can remove (or add back) a title like this:

1. Click the map visualization to select it.

2. In the Layout ribbon, click Title.

3. Select None.

The title will be removed from the map. To add a title back to a map, all you have to do is to carry out the first two steps and then select Above Map instead of None.

Modifying the Map Background

You can choose between any one of five map types when using maps in Power View. By default, a map is displayed using Grayscale Road Map Background. Yet you can alter the map display in the following way:

1. Click the map to select it.

2. In the Layout ribbon, click Map Background and select Aerial (Satellite Photo) Map Background.

Your map will now look like Figure 8-5.

Figure 8-5. *Changing the background of a Power View map*

Power View allows you to choose from five available map backgrounds. These are explained in Table 8-1.

Table 8-1. *Map Background Options*

Map Background Option	Description
Road Map Background	Displays the classic road map with colors
Grayscale Road Map Background	Shows the road map using a monochrome representation of the geographical data and colors for the display data
Reverse Grayscale Road Map Background	Shows the road map but using dark grayscale for the geographical data and colors for the display data
Aerial (satellite photo) Map Background	Shows a satellite view of the map
Grayscale Aerial Map Background	Shows a satellite view of the map using a monochrome representation of the geographical data

Filtering Map Data

A map can be filtered to display only specific data, just like any other Power View visualization. This is virtually identical to the way in which you saw how to filter data in Chapter 3, but as a quick revision, here is how to exclude, say, data for the United States from the list of countries in a Power View map.

1. Display the Filters area (unless it is already visible).

2. Click a map; you will see the word *Map* at the top of the Filters area.

3. Click the word *Map*. You will see the filters for the fields that are used in the map visualization.

4. Expand the CountryName field.

5. Click (All). A check mark will appear for each country.

6. Uncheck the boxes for United States and the United Kingdom.

The data bubbles for the United States and the United Kingdom will be removed from the map, leaving the other countries visible. This is shown in Figure 8-6 (after a little repositioning).

Figure 8-6. *Filtering data for a Power View map*

You can use all the filtering techniques described in Chapter 3 to filter a map. Rather than reiterate all the options here, I suggest you refer to that chapter for full details.

■ **Tip** If you know that you will want to see the data only for a subset of geographical locations, then it can be worth defining a filter to display only the areas that interest you before you switch to a map visualization. This way the initial map will show only the selected locations, which could save you from having to zoom and pan the map.

Multivalue Series

So far you have seen how you can add a single data series to a map and have the data represented as a data point. Power View can extend this paradigm by allowing you to display the data bubble as a pie that contains a second data series—and consequently display the data broken down by a specific data set per geographical entity.

As an example of this (and to revise the some of the map creation techniques that you have seen so far), let's try to analyze European car sales by age range.

1. Insert a new Power View sheet.

2. Display the Filters area (if necessary) and add the Year field from YearHierarchy in the Date table.

3. Adjust the Year slider to select only the year 2014.

4. Add the following fields to the FIELDS well in the layout section of the field list:

   a. CountryName

   b. VehicleAgeCategory

   c. SalePrice

5. Filter the table to exclude the United States as described in the previous section.

6. Click Map in the Design ribbon.

7. Resize the map visualization.

The map now contains a legend for VehicleAgeCategory and has added the VehicleAgeCategory field to the COLOR well of the field list's layout section. Each bubble is now a pie of data. The overall size of the pie represents, proportionally, the sum total data compared to the other pies. The map should now look like Figure 8-7.

SalePrice by CountryName, and VehicleAgeCategory

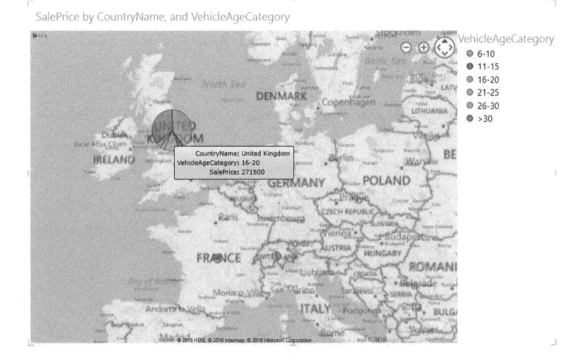

Figure 8-7. Displaying pie charts in a Power View map

It is worth remarking that if you hover the mouse pointer over the data representation (the pie) for a country, it will expand slightly, and as you pass the pointer over each pie segment, you will see a tooltip giving the details of the data, including which car age range it refers to.

■ **Tip** The colors of a pie in a Power View map can be modified by selecting a different theme from the Power View menu. This can help the pie stand out against the map background.

Highlighting Map Data

If you have added data to the COLORS well of the field list and a legend is displayed, you can highlight segments of data in a map, much as you saw how to do in a chart in Chapter 5. This allows you to draw the audience's attention to specific trends in your data.

1. Using the map you created and can see in Figure 8-7, click 6-10 (the first element) in the legend.

The segment of each pie corresponding to the car age range from 6-10 years will be highlighted, as you can see in Figure 8-8.

Figure 8-8. *Highlighting map data*

To remove highlighting from a map, all you have to do is click again on the legend element that you are using to highlight data, or you can simply click the title of the legend.

Using a map as a basis for highlighting data follows the same logic you saw in Chapter 5 for charts. That is, if you highlight a data element in a map, all other objects in the current report will be filtered by that selection.

For example, suppose you have created the original map of net sales per country shown in Figure 8-6 (filtered to show only data for 2013), which you have resized to allow for space to one side and have adjusted to show only European countries. You have also added a table composed simply of the Color and NetSales fields. This report should look something like Figure 8-9, where you can see a bubble representing the sales figures for European countries where you have clients.

SalePrice by CountryName

Color	NetSales
Black	194660
Blue	319050
British Racing Green	275410
Canary Yellow	350025
Dark Purple	228820
Green	310275
Night Blue	203810
Red	726495
Silver	371590
Total	**2980135**

Figure 8-9. *Sales in Europe before highlighting a specific country*

Now, click the data point for Switzerland. The map will highlight this country's sales, and the table will also be updated to reflect the fact that you are, in effect, filtering out all data except for Switzerland. This report should now look like Figure 8-10.

SalePrice by CountryName

Color	NetSales
Black	14500
Blue	71250
Canary Yellow	125875
Dark Purple	2000
Green	28300
Red	20190
Silver	76500
Total	**338615**

Figure 8-10. *Sales in Europe after highlighting Switzerland*

■ **Tip** If you click a segment of a pie for a country in a report where you have added a field for the Color element of a map as you did to create Figure 8-7, then you will be filtering on both elements that make up the segment—the country *and* the car age range.

Adjusting a Legend

If you are coming to maps in Power View after you have used charts, then you will feel a strong sense of déjà vu when modifying the map legend. Suppose you want to move the legend from the right side of the map to the bottom of the map. Here is how:

1. Revert to the map displayed in Figure 8-7.

2. Click the map to select it.

3. In the Layout ribbon, click Legend.

4. Select Show Legend At Bottom.

The map should now look like Figure 8-11, where I have zoomed out a little to make the pie charts appear more clearly.

SalePrice by CountryName, and VehicleAgeCategory

VehicleAgeCategory

● 6-10   ● 11-15   ● 16-20   ● 21-25   ● 26-30   ● >30

Figure 8-11. *Adjusting the position of the legend in a Power View map*

Table 8-2 describes the options available for positioning a legend.

Table 8-2. *Legend Placement Options for Power View Maps*

Legend Option	Description
None	The legend is removed.
Show Legend At Right	The legend is displayed on the right side the map (this is the default).
Show Legend At Top	The legend is displayed at the top of the map.
Show Legend At Left	The legend is displayed on the left side of the map.
Show Legend At Bottom	The legend is displayed at the bottom of the map.

Adding Tiles to Maps

Another similarity between maps and charts or tables is their capacity for interactive filtering using tiles. Let's suppose you want to be able to see worldwide car sales by the color of car sold, as well as by car age range. Here is how:

1.   Take the map visualization you created earlier for Figure 8-11.

2.   Drag the VehicleAgeCategory field from the Colors table to the TILE BY well in the layout section of the field list. Alternatively, you can click the pop-up menu for the VehicleAgeCategory field and select Add As Tile By.

Tiles will appear above the map, with the first tile element selected, as shown in Figure 8-12.

217

Figure 8-12. *Adding tiles to a map*

Tiles for maps act in the same way as tiles for tables or charts. Clicking a tile element will restrict the data in the map to the selected element. This means the pie segments and the corresponding legend will display only available data. When applied to a map, this has the added effect of swapping the mapped region to show only the geographical areas that have data corresponding to the selected tile. To see this effect, try clicking these tiles:

- 6-10
- 21-25
- >30

You will see the map "jump" to reflect the selected data. Since you are in the realm of geography, you could also try using the CountryName field to tile the map. This way, when you select a country, there is a real visual effect as the map moves to display the selected country.

In all other respects, the tiles will act in the same way as described in Chapter 6. If this is your first experience of tiles, I suggest you refer to the section on tiles in that chapter for further details.

Multiple Maps

Maps can also be displayed as multiples or "trellis" visualizations, just like charts can. To see this in action, let's return to the map of car sales by car age range, as shown in Figure 8-11 earlier, and see how to display multiple maps—one per car color sold.

1. Open the map visualization that you created for Figure 8-11.

2. Drag the VehicleAgeCategory field from the COLOR well to the VERTICAL MULTIPLES well in the layout section of the field list. Alternatively, you can click the pop-up menu for the VehicleAgeCategory field and select Add To Vertical Multiples.

The map will be split into multiple maps, as shown in Figure 8-13.

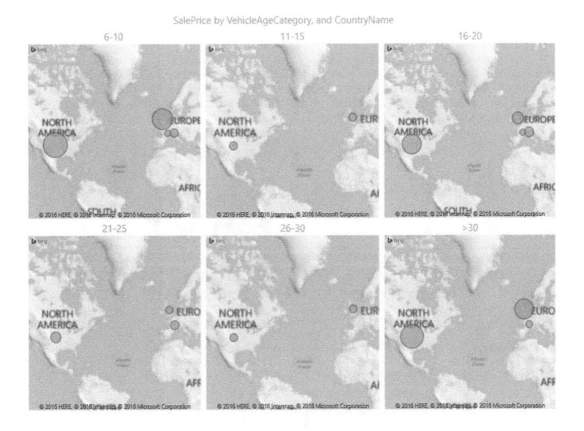

Figure 8-13. *Multiple map visualization*

Multiples, like tiles, behave in the same way for maps as for charts. So, once again, I will not be repeating all the techniques and tricks here; instead, I'll refer you to the appropriate sections of Chapter 5 for full details. The only new point that is probably worth taking into consideration is that zooming and panning are now possible for each individual map.

Multiple Maps by Region

One interesting trick when working with multiple maps is to use the same geographical data that is used as the location as the multiple. This is a purely visual effect, but it allows you to see the data per region (country, in this example), while comparing sales per region using the size of the data point.

Here is how you can do this:

1. Open the map visualization you created for Figure 8-11 earlier.

2. Drag the CountryName field from the Countries table to the VERTICAL MULTIPLES well in the layout section of the field list. Alternatively, you can click the pop-up menu for the CountryName field and select Add To Vertical Multiples.

3. If required, zoom in a little for certain individual maps so that the country fills the available space in the grid.

The map will be split, once again, into multiple maps, as shown in Figure 8-14. This time you can see the country map as a background for the country data. You will also note that the pie charts are proportional to the sales for each country. The only drawback when using this trick is that the title will repeat the field name that you applied to both the COLOR well and the VERTICAL MULTIPLES well. However, you can always remove the title.

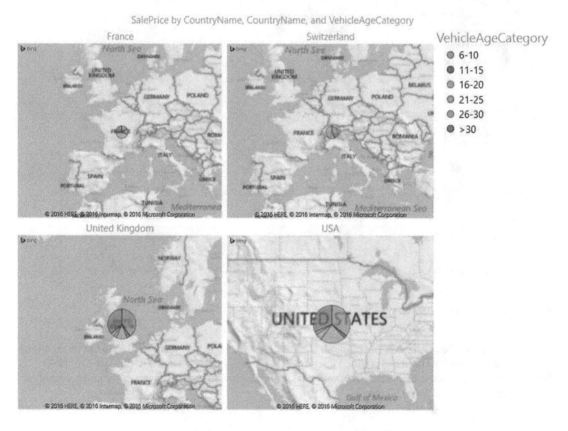

Figure 8-14. *Multiple maps defined by geography*

Drilling Down in Maps

Another extremely interesting interactive aspect of using Power View maps is the ability to drill down into a map to see further levels of detail. This will require, inevitably, source data that contains a geographical hierarchy. Fortunately, you have hierarchical data available in the form of country and town, even if these are not specifically defined as a hierarchy in the underlying data set.

To create a drill-down map, you need to follow these steps:

1. Insert a new Power View sheet.

2. Create a table based on the following fields:

   a. CountryName from the Countries table

   b. NetSales from the SalesData table

3. Convert the table to a map by clicking the Map button in the Design ribbon.

4. Resize the map to improve visibility.

5. Pan and zoom to place the United Kingdom in the center of the map. You should see something like the map given in Figure 8-15.

Figure 8-15. *An initial map ready for drill down*

6. Add the Town field from the Clients table to the LOCATIONS well under the
    ClientCountry field. The map should remain the same, as shown in Figure 8-15.

7. Double-click the bubble for a country. I suggest the data for the United Kingdom
    in this example. The map will drill down to show the data for each town where
    sales occurred.

8. Adjust the map display to show only the area where there is data for a town. You
    can see this in Figure 8-16.

NetSales by Town

Figure 8-16. Drill-down for the United Kingdom

The map shown in Figure 8-15 has a drill-up icon on the top right, just like a chart or matrix with drill-down enabled. You can see this icon if you place the mouse pointer over the map. Clicking this will drill back up to the previous level. You can create as many levels of drill-down as your data allows.

Conclusion

Few things add the "wow" factor to a presentation in the way that a carefully crafted interactive map can. In this chapter, you saw how to add a map to a Power View report and then how to apply the techniques that you learned for other types of visualization to filter and highlight data in maps.

You then explored how to use a Power View map interactively to highlight data in other visualizations in the report. Finally, you saw how you can drill down into map data just as you can with matrices and charts.

Remember also that you can manipulate maps just like any other Power View element. Consequently, you can superimpose a chart on a map. Indeed, you can add slicers, as well, to add to the interactivity. Finally, you can enhance the map with text boxes and pictures to underscore the points that you are making about the data the map contains.

So, used judiciously, maps can become a vital part of your analytical and presentation toolkit. Have fun creating geographical representations of your data, and I hope that your audience is suitably impressed with your newfound skills.

CHAPTER 9

3D Maps

An addition to the panoply of self-service BI tools that Excel now makes available is 3D Maps. As its name implies, it is a powerful mapping tool that can generate some exceedingly cool three-dimensional geospatial representations of your data. Specifically, it can do the following:

- Create various types of map to represent geospatial data

- Add multiple layers of information to each map to show different data representations

- Add a time dimension to a map and display how the data evolves over time

- Chain several maps together into a dynamic visualization that can then be exported as a multimedia file

3D Maps will use the data that you have prepared in the Excel data model, or it can add data from a spreadsheet table to a data model for geographical representation. So, once again, it can be important to spend a certain amount of time creating and finalizing an accurate and coherent data model before you try and display—or discover—new insights using 3D Maps.

You may well be wondering why you have the choice between adding a map to Power View or using 3D Maps to display your data. Well, they have two quite different uses. Power View maps let you use all of the interactive filtering and slicing techniques that you learned in earlier chapters; however, if you want to create rich multilayered visualizations or the stunning exportable "movies," then you will need to use 3D Maps. In any case, once you master both approaches, you will be able to choose the Excel add-in that best suits your needs.

3D Maps is now part of Excel and should be available in the Insert ribbon. If you cannot see the 3D Maps button, then please ensure that you have followed the instructions in Chapter 1 to enable this add-in.

This chapter will use a sample file named PowerMapSample.xlsx, which is in the C:\DataVisualisationInExcel2016 folder, assuming you have downloaded the sample files as described in Appendix A.

Bing Maps

3D Maps, just like maps created with Power View, uses Bing Maps to provide the geographical data. Consequently, you will need to allow 3D Maps access to Bing Maps or maps simply cannot be created. 3D Maps currently needs an Internet connection to function correctly.

■ **Note** Some areas of the world cannot use Bing Maps. If you attempt to use 3D Maps in these geographical zones, nothing will appear when you attempt to create a map.

© Adam Aspin 2016

A. Aspin, *High Impact Data Visualization in Excel with Power View, 3D Maps, Get & Transform and Power BI*, DOI 10.1007/978-1-4842-2400-7_9

Running 3D Maps

It's time to get started! Clearly the first thing you need to do is to launch 3D Maps, which is similar to the way you learned to launch Power View. Do the following:

1. In Excel, click Insert to activate the Insert ribbon.

2. Click the 3D Maps button. The Launch 3D Maps window will open, as you can see in Figure 9-1.

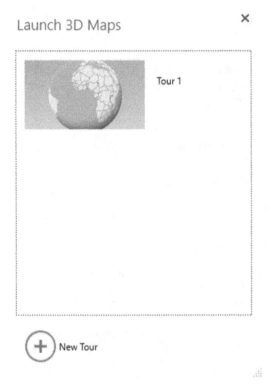

Figure 9-1. The Launch 3D Maps window

3. Click Tour 1.

4. The 3D Maps window will open, looking (most probably) like Figure 9-2.

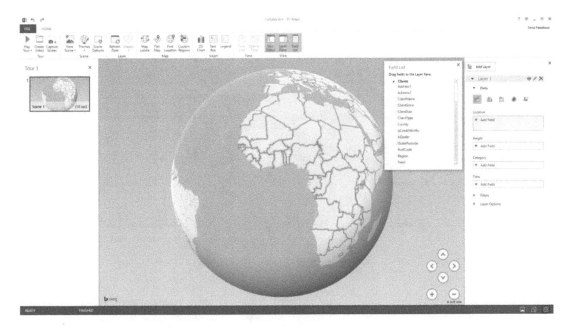

Figure 9-2. *The 3D Maps window*

⬛ **Note** 3D Maps needs data to work. Consequently, it is important you have either an Excel data model in the workbook from which you launch 3D Maps or a table of data that you have selected or clicked in before you run 3D Maps.

The 3D Maps Window

Even if the 3D Maps window and many of the elements that you will use are largely intuitive, I prefer to continue with the logic applied throughout this book and explain the 3D Maps window and the objects that it contains from the outset. This way (I hope) the terms and elements that you will be using will be as clear as possible.

The 3D Maps window consists of the following five main elements:

- *The map visualization*: This is the core of 3D Maps and where your audience will see your analysis and the geographical representation of your insights.

- *The Layer pane*: This is the area where you select data (both geographical data and the metrics that you want to overlay on the map) as well as modify many of the presentation aspects of the map.

- *The Tour Editor*: This panel is where you can put together an automated slideshow, or film, of the data for your audience.

- *The 3D Maps ribbon*: This is where you will find many of the available options for adding elements or enhancing the map that you are creating and modifying.

Figure 9-3 shows the main elements of the 3D Maps window.

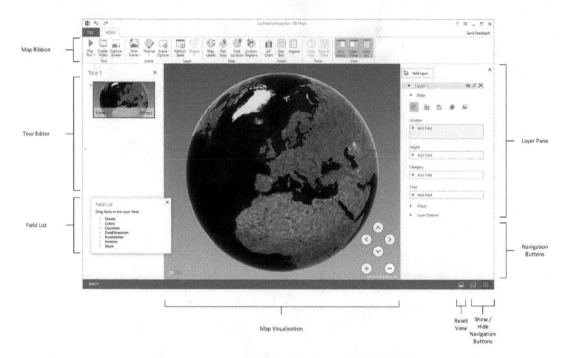

Figure 9-3. *The principal elements of the 3D Maps window*

The 3D Maps Ribbon

One of the key features of the 3D Maps window is the 3D Maps ribbon. Table 9-1 outlines the buttons that it contains and their uses.

Table 9-1. *The 3D Maps Ribbon*

Button	Description
Play Tour	Plays a 3D Maps tour
Create Video	Exports a 3D Maps tour as a stand-alone video
Capture Screen	Creates a screen capture of the map
New Scene	Adds a new scene to a 3D Maps tour
Themes	Alters the 3D Maps presentation style
Scene Options	Adds effects to scene transitions and lets you specify the duration of each scene
Refresh Data	Refreshes the source data
Shapes	Chooses the bar chart shape
Map Labels	Adds country, region, and town labels to the map
Flat Map	Switches between a flat (two-dimensional) and curved (three-dimensional) map
Find Location	Finds a location on the map by entering a map reference or a town or county name
Custom Regions	Lets you import data to define custom regions
2D Chart	Adds an independent 2D chart based on the data in a layer on the map
Text Box	Adds a floating text box
Legend	Adds one or more legends
Time Line	Shows or hides the timeline
Date And Time	Shows or hides the date and time
Tour Editor	Displays or hides the Tour Editor
Layer Pane	Displays or hides the Layer pane
Field List	Displays or hides the field list

Region Maps

As a first, and admittedly simple, map, suppose you want to see the cumulative sales for the various countries where Brilliant British Cars has hawked its wares. This example will introduce the core mapping concepts that you will build on later in this chapter to develop some more complex geographical visualizations.

1. In the field list, expand the Countries table and drag the CountryName field to the Location well in the Layer pane. The map of the globe could swivel to display the area of the world where the majority of the data can be found.

2. At the top of the Layer pane, click the rightmost icon to switch to the region visualization type. The countries where there are sales will appear colored in on the map.

3. In the field list, expand the InvoiceLines table. Drag the SalePrice field to the Value well of the Layer pane. The field name followed by *(Sum)* will indicate that the aggregation that has been applied is Sum. The countries will be shaded at different levels of intensity on the map to represent the proportion of sales by country. 3D Maps will also add a legend.

4. Click the plus (+) icon a few times to zoom in on the map.

5. Resize the legend by dragging the circle icon in the bottom right (or left) of the legend.

6. Reposition the legend by dragging the legend window. The map might look something like Figure 9-4.

Figure 9-4. *A simple regional sales map*

This short example did quite a few things and introduced several concepts. To make some of the ideas easier to reapply in the future, here is a quick overview of the key points to note.

3D Maps Source Data

As I mentioned in the introduction to this chapter, 3D Maps uses the Excel data model (or data from a worksheet added to the data model) as the source for the data that you will deliver as a map. It is important, then, to consider 3D Maps as you consider Power View—that is, as a final output medium and not as a data management solution. You will probably need to import data with Get & Transform and will then almost certainly have to mold the data set into a coherent data model before you start using 3D Maps. When you launch 3D Maps, it will display the current data model, and this is what you will be using to create your maps.

Refreshing Data

If your data has changed (and remember that it could have changed in a source database or a shared worksheet on a network drive), you could both need and want to refresh the data so that 3D Maps will redraw the visualization to display the latest version of events. To do this, follow these steps:

1.   Click the Refresh Data button in the 3D Maps ribbon.

The data will be updated from the source, and the maps will be redrawn. If the path to the source data involves a Get & Transform process and a Power Pivot data model, then the entire chain of data will be updated.

Geographical Data Types

In this first 3D Maps example, you added a single geographical data field. What is more, this field was recognized instantly for what it was—country names. In the real world of mapping data, however, you may not only have to add several fields but also specify which type of geographical data each field represents. Put simply, 3D Maps needs to know what the data you are supplying represents. Not only that, it needs to know what it is looking at without ambiguity. Consequently, it is up to you to define the source data as clearly and unambiguously as possible. This can involve one or more of several possible approaches.

Define the Data Category in the Data Model

As you will see in Chapter 14, you can define a data category for each column of data in Power Pivot. Although this is not an absolute prerequisite for accurate mapping with 3D Maps, it can help reduce the number of potential anomalies. This means attributing a specific geographical data type (country, town, region, and so on) to a column.

Add Multiple Levels of Geographical Information

3D Maps lets you add several levels of geographical information from a data model. For instance (and as you will see in a few pages), you can add not just a country but also a town if you want. The advantage of adding as many relevant source data fields as possible is that by working in this way, you are helping 3D Maps dispel possibly ambiguous references. For instance, if you add only a field for Town, 3D Maps might not know if you are referring to Birmingham, Alabama, or England's second city. If, however, you add a Country field and a Town field, then 3D Maps has a much better chance of detecting the correct geographical location. This principle can be extended to adding states, counties, and other geographical references. Remember, you can add multiple source fields, but you should select only the one you want to display in a map.

Select the Correct Geographical Data Type in 3D Maps

3D Maps will indicate in the Location well of the Layer pane the geographical data type that it is using for each selected field. If you have applied the right data category in the data model, then your life is made easier because the correct geographical data type will be displayed. If you have *not* attributed a data category, then 3D Maps will try to guess the correct geographical data type. On most occasions, it will guess right; sometimes, however, you will need to override its choice to ensure that the mapping is applied correctly. Selecting another geographical data type is as easy as clicking the pop-up (the downward-facing triangle) for each geographic data field in the Location well whose data type you want to change and selecting the appropriate data type.

Table 9-2 explains the available geographical data types.

Table 9-2. *Geographical Data Types*

Data Type	Comments
Latitude	Indicates that the source data contains the latitude
Longitude	Indicates that the source data contains the longitude
X Coordinate	Specifies the precise X coordinate reference
Y Coordinate	Specifies the precise Y coordinate reference
City	Tells 3D Maps that the data is a town or city
Country/Region	Tells 3D Maps that the data defines a country or region
County	Indicates that the source data defines a county
State/Province	Indicates that the source data defines a state or province
Street	Provides street-level data
Postal Code	Contains a ZIP (postal) code
Full Address	Contains a full address
Custom Region	Specifies a custom region defined using a shape file
Custom Region Set	Specifies a custom region defined using a shape file
Other	Indicates other geographical data that can be interpreted by Bing Maps

Using the Layer Pane

The Layer pane is where much of the work is done both to specify the data that will be displayed in a map and to tweak the available options for the map. To be sure you are at ease with this key facet of the 3D Maps interface, let's take a more in-depth look at what it has to offer.

Showing and Hiding the Layer Pane

If you have finished, temporarily or permanently, with the Layer pane, you can hide it (or make it reappear) by clicking the Layer Pane button in the Power View ribbon. Alternatively, to make it disappear entirely, you can click the Close icon (the small X) at the top right of the panel.

Layer Pane Elements

The Layer pane contains these three main areas:

- The Data area (geographical and metrics)
- The Filters area
- The Layer Options area

You can expand or reduce each of these areas by clicking the small triangle to the left of the area header in the Layer pane.

For the next few pages you will be looking only at the Data area; I will introduce the Layer Options area a little later in this chapter. I will not describe the Filters area, as it is virtually identical to the filtering techniques that you learned to apply to Power View in Chapter 3.

The Data Area

The Data area has five subdivisions:

- *The visualization type*: This lets you select from one of the five possible types of data mapping display.
- *The location*: This is where you add geographical data.
- *The values*: This is where you add the data that will be displayed on the map.
- *The category*: This contains a second data element to add categorization to the data representation.
- *The time element*: This can be used to show how data evolves over time.

Figure 9-5 shows these elements.

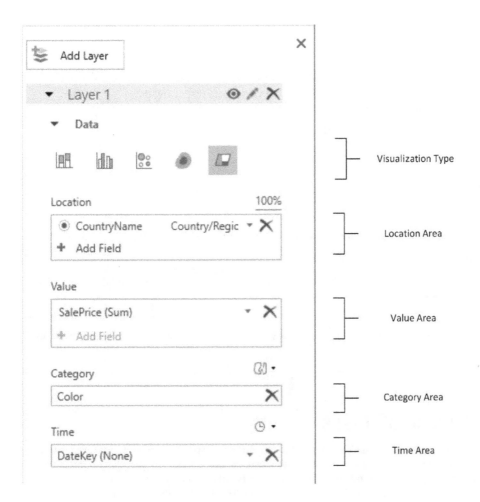

Figure 9-5. *The Location area of the Layer pane*

Data Operations

Clearly, as a geographical representation of data, a 3D map needs data to work with. Consequently, you will spend a large amount of the time that you spend creating maps adding and removing data. These operations are mercifully simple in 3D maps.

Adding a Field

As you have seen, you can add fields from the underlying data simply by dragging a field from the Fields pane to the appropriate well in the Layer pane. There is, however, an alternative method if you prefer.

1. In the Layer pane, click Add Field. A pop-up list will appear displaying the available tables and the fields that they contain.

2. Scroll through the list and expand the table containing the data that you want to add.

3. Click the required field name.

Removing a Field

Inevitably there will be times when you want to remove a field from the Layer pane. The technique is simple.

1. Click the X to the right of the field name.

The field will be removed from the map (but not from the underlying data model), and the map will be redrawn to reflect the modification.

■ **Note** This operation cannot be undone—so if you have removed the wrong field, you will just have to add it again.

Moving Around in 3D Maps

When you first add geographical data, 3D Maps will adjust the map to display the geographical area with the greatest concentration of data. However, you may need to tweak the continents, countries, or counties that are displayed to make your point. If the area displayed in a map is not quite as perfect as you would prefer, then you can alter the area that appears in the map visualization. This involves the following:

- *Zooming in and out*—to get closer to the detail of the data—or inversely taking a bird's eye view

- *Panning around*, which essentially means moving to the area that interests you

- *Altering the pitch*, which can enhance the visual experience by changing the 3D view of the map

Figure 9-6 explains the icons used to zoom in or out and alter the pitch of a map.

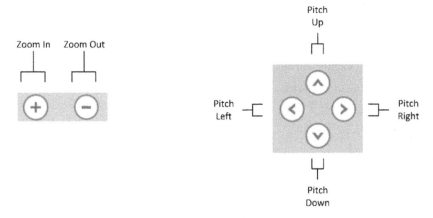

Figure 9-6. *Zoom and Pan icons*

You can hide the Zoom and Pan icons by clicking the Show/Hide Navigation Buttons icon at the bottom right of the 3D Maps window. This icon is shown in Figure 9-2, earlier.

Moving Around a Map

Moving around a map (without altering the pitch) is, as you would probably expect, extremely easy. All you have to do is to click the globe (or the map if you have already zoomed in) and drag the mouse. The map will move in the direction that you drag the mouse pointer.

■ **Tip**   You can also use the cursor keys to move up, down, left, or right without altering the pitch.

Zooming In or Out

It is conceivable that the map that is displayed is not at a scale that you would prefer. All you have to do is this:

1.   Click the Zoom Out button (the minus sign) to zoom out or click the Zoom In button (the plus sign) to zoom in.

■ **Tip**   You can also move the mouse scroll wheel or use the Page Up and Page Down keys to zoom in or out of a map.

Flat Map and 3D Globe

Although the 3D Maps default is to show a three-dimensional globe, you can flip to a flattened view if you prefer. This view will show more data and will allow you to avoid having parts of the map disappear over the horizon. To switch between 3D and flat mapping, do this:

1. Click the Flat 3D Maps button in the 3D Maps ribbon.

Adjusting the Pitch

To adjust the pitch of a map, follow these steps:

1. Click the Pan Up or Pan Down icon (the up- or down-facing symbols) to alter the geographical area displayed in the map visualization.

2. Click the Pan Left or Pan Right icon (the left- or right-facing symbols) to swivel the map left or right.

Going to a Specific Location

Sometimes all you want to do is move to a particular location. You can do this in a couple of ways. If you can see the place where you want to take a closer look, simply double-click it and 3D Maps will zoom in. If you want to jump straight to a particular region or town, then do this:

1. Click Find Location in the 3D Maps ribbon. The Find Location dialog will appear.

2. Enter the place you want to find. The Find Location dialog will look like Figure 9-7.

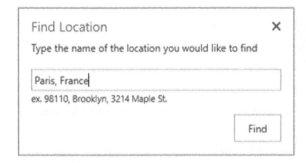

Figure 9-7. *The Find Location dialog*

3. Click Find. 3D Maps will jump to the location.

4. If 3D Maps has found the place that you are looking for, you can close the Find Location dialog by clicking the Close icon (the X at the top right). If not, enter a new location and click Find again.

■ **Tip**   You can move the Find Location dialog around the screen—and essentially away from the center of the map—to get a better view of the area that it has found. Remember that you can zoom in and out while searching for a specific place to ensure that you have found the right one. This can help to ensure that you are not looking at Paris, Texas, when you really wanted the French capital.

3D Maps Aggregations

When you used the SalePrice field in the first example in this chapter as the basis for shading the regions in the map, 3D Maps automatically used the default aggregation for the field that you chose. This probably comes as no surprise since it is exactly what Power View does. Similarly, 3D Maps does not limit you to using the default aggregation for a numeric field or a count for an attribute field. To select another aggregation, follow these steps:

1. Switch to the Geography view of the Data area of the Layer pane (unless it is already active).

2. Click the pop-up icon (the downward-facing triangle to the right of the selected metric name) for the metric. The pop-up list should look like Figure 9-8.

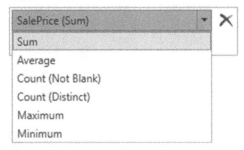

Figure 9-8. *Aggregations*

3. Click the required aggregation.

The map will be updated to reflect the new metric. Table 9-3 outlines the available aggregations.

Table 9-3. *Aggregation Types*

Aggregation	Description
Sum	Returns the total of the numeric field
Average	Returns the average of the numeric field
Count (Not Blank)	Counts all the nonblank records
Count Distinct	Counts all unique values in the data
Maximum	Returns the maximum value from a numeric field
Minimum	Returns the minimum value from a numeric field

Map Types

3D Maps is not limited to shading in countries—far from it. In the current version, there are five main map types. These are described in Table 9-4, and you will take a look at each map type to see how they can best be used in the next few sections.

Table 9-4. *Map Types in 3D Maps*

Chart Type	Description
Stacked Column	Adds a stacked column chart to the map
Column	Adds a column chart to the map
Bubble	Adds a bubble (or pie) chart to the map
Heat Map	Adds a heat map indicator (concentric colored circles) to the map
Region	Shades geopolitical entities by country or region

You change the type of map that you want to display using the icons in the Layer pane. Figure 9-9 explains these icons.

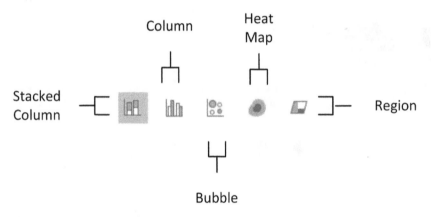

Figure 9-9. *Map types*

The Various Map Types, by Example

Now that you understand the basic elements of 3D Maps, it is time to move on to the various ways in which data can be displayed and overlaid onto a geographical background. I feel that the best way to do this is to explain the data used, step-by-step, to give you an idea of what you can achieve. So, on that note, here are the five types of mapping data that 3D Maps can display. Let me just add that these map types are not explained in any particular order; it is up to each user to apply the type of visualization that makes their point most clearly and effectively.

Bubble Maps

A simple, yet effective, way of displaying data is to use a bubble map. This is simply a circular representation of the data for each data point, where the relative size of each dot (or bubble or point; there are many synonyms used to describe this) gives an idea of the proportional extent of the underlying data.

Bubble maps in 3D Maps come in two distinct flavors:

- Simple bubbles.

- Bubbles with multiple "subdivisions" or categories. These look like pie charts superimposed upon the map.

Let's look at each in turn. To begin with, here is how to create a simple bubble map:

1. Starting with the `PowerMapSample.xlsx` file, click Map in the Insert tab to launch 3D Maps.

2. Select Bubble as the visualization type (the middle icon).

3. In the field list, expand the Countries table and drag the CountryName field to the Location well in the Layer pane.

4. In the field list, expand the Invoices table. Drag the TotalDiscount field to the Size well of the Layer pane. Your map should look like Figure 9-10.

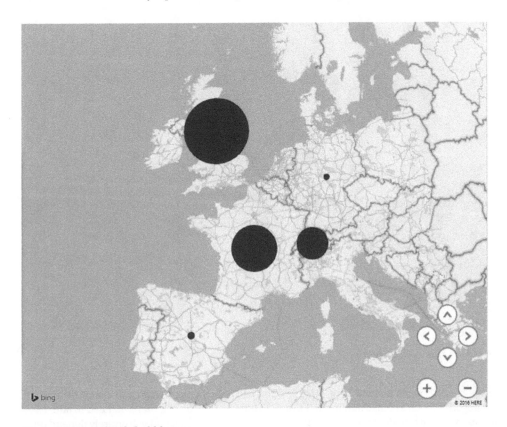

Figure 9-10. *A simple bubble map*

Now let's extend this by adding a further breakdown—and consequently further information—by adding categories to the map.

1. In the bubble map you just created, click the Legend button in the ribbon to add a legend.

2. Resize and place the legend where it does not hide any data.

3. In the Layer pane, add the Make field from the Stock table to the Category well.

4. Hover the cursor over one of the segments for the pie in the United Kingdom. A pop-up (called the data card) will appear explaining what the segment represents.

The map should now look like the one in Figure 9-11. As you can see, each bubble is now a pie chart.

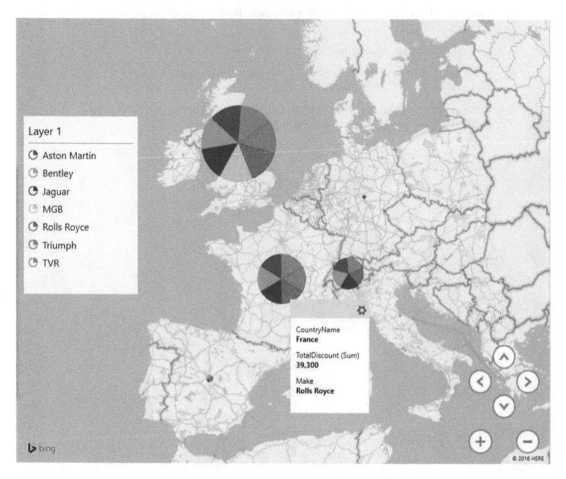

Figure 9-11. A bubble map with categories

I have a couple of comments to make here. First, you can add only a single category to a map. So, if you need multiple categories (such as make and model) to subdivide the data further, then you need to add a calculated column to the data model first. Second, the aesthetics of having a legend will entirely depend on your requirements and circumstances.

An alternative to analysis by sector in a pie-style bubble map is to compare multiple values. As an example, let's suppose you want to see the proportional costs (Parts, Labor, and Discount) for each country.

1. Starting with the PowerMapSample.xlsx file, click Map in the Insert tab to launch 3D Maps.

2. In the field list, expand the Countries table and drag the CountryName field to the Location well in the Layer pane.

3. In the field list, expand the Stock table. Drag the following fields to the Size well of the Layer pane. Remember to add a new field in the well before dragging the field over.

   a. SpareParts

   b. LaborCost

   c. CostPrice

4. Select Bubble as the type.

5. Click Flat Map in the 3D Maps ribbon to remove the 3D view.

6. Resize and reposition the legend.

7. To anticipate a little (and to ring the changes), click the Themes button and select the first theme on the second row. The map should look like Figure 9-12.

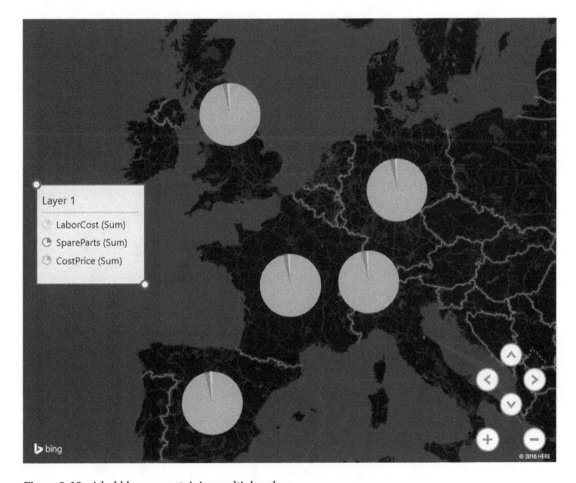

Figure 9-12. *A bubble map containing multiple values*

I will explain the use of themes in more detail a little later in this chapter. Nonetheless, I wanted to add a little variety to the presentation. As you can see, you have displayed the costs, and their proportional representation, for each country.

Column Maps

To take the example a little further but still using simple data, let's now see how you can use columns to display the data for each geographical element. Here again there are two main options:

- Clustered columns
- Stacked columns

In both cases the height of the column represents the scale of the data. In the case of clustered columns, you can see the data points side by side; in the case of stacked columns, you can get an idea not only of the relative values but also of the totals for each geographical point.

Clustered Columns

I will begin by showing you how a clustered column could look.

1. Create a 3D map using Country as the location, LaborCost as the height, and Make as the category.

2. Select Column as the type from the five available icons.

3. Add a legend by clicking the Legend button in the ribbon.

4. Tweak the presentation using the Zoom and Pan icons for greater effect. Specifically try altering the pitch to get a more persuasive fly-over effect.

The map should look like Figure 9-13.

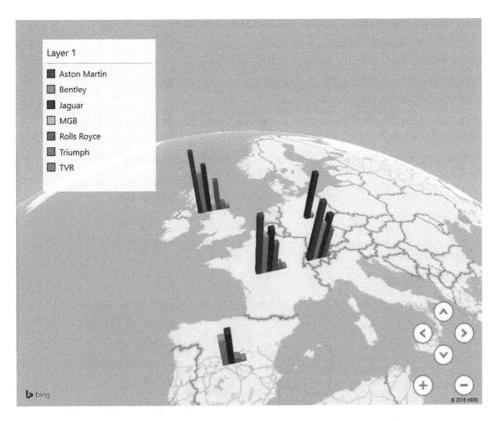

Figure 9-13. *A clustered column map*

▨ **Note** Here again, you may, or may not, want a legend. It is entirely up to you.

Stacked Columns

An alternative to clustered columns is to use stacked columns. Which you choose to use will depend on your requirements and the available data. I merely suggest that when you have multiple data points, stacked columns can be easier to read and can avoid clutter in the presentation. As an example of this, let's see sales for each town by make.

1. Starting with the `PowerMapSample.xlsx` file, click Map in the Insert tab to launch 3D Maps.

2. Click the Stacked Bar icon in the Data area of the Layer pane.

3. In the field list, expand the Countries table and drag the CountryName field to the Location well in the Layer pane.

4. Add the Town field from the Clients table to the Location well in the Layer pane under the Country field.

5. In the field list, expand the Stock table. Drag the CostPrice field to the Height well of the Layer pane.

6. Drag the Color field to the Category well from the Stock table in the field list.

7. Resize and reposition the legend.

8. Adjust the zoom and panning to get the best effect, focusing on the East Coast of the United States.

The map should look like Figure 9-14.

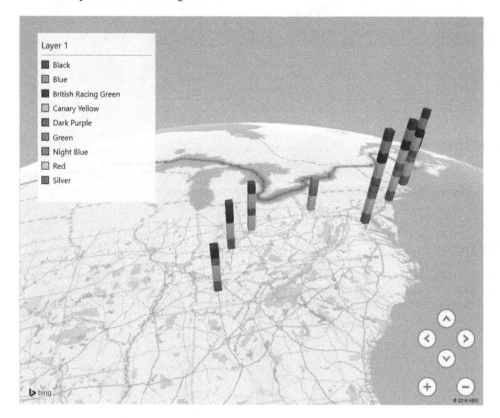

Figure 9-14. *A stacked column map*

Heat Maps

The term *heat map* can mean many different things to different people. In 3D Maps it means a colored bubble where the intensity and shading of the color represents the scale of values that is represented. To see this, let's look at the costs of sales for UK towns.

1. Follow steps 1 to 8 that you used to create a stacked column map; however, set the Value field to be the SalePrice from the InvoiceLines table.

2. In the pop-up menu to the right of the SalePrice field, select Average.

3. Select Heat Map as the type from the icons at the top of the Data area of the Layer pane.

4. Adjust the zoom, pan, and pitch to get the best effect, thus centering the map on the entire United States.

5. Resize and reposition the legend.

The map should look similar to Figure 9-15.

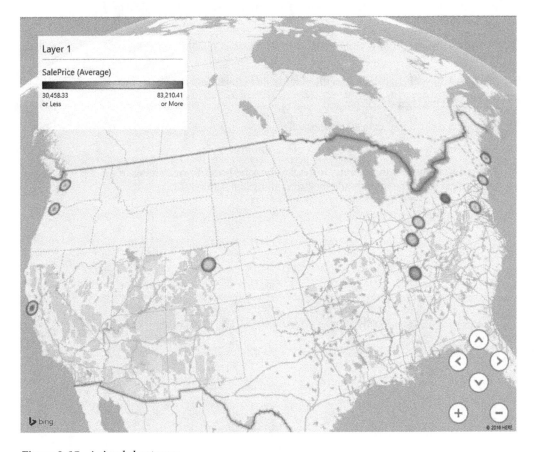

Figure 9-15. *A simple heat map*

■ **Note**   A heat map is somewhat more limited than some of the other map types. For instance, you cannot choose a category; neither can you add multiple metrics.

Region Maps

The first map you created in this chapter was a region map, and the example you created covers much of what you can do when you use this map type. Nonetheless, there is an interesting variation on a theme that deserves to be explained—using categories with region maps.

Suppose, for instance, that you want to see the sales by country, but you also want the colors of car sold to shape the data. Here is how:

1. Starting with the `PowerMapSample.xlsx` file, click Map in the Insert tab to launch 3D Maps.

2. Set the map type as Region from the available icons.

3. In the field list, expand the Countries table and drag the CountryName field to the Location well in the Layer pane.

4. In the field list, expand the Stock table. Drag the CostPrice field to the Value well of the Layer pane.

5. Drag the MileageRange field from the Stock table to the Category well.

6. Ensure that the legend is displayed.

7. Adjust the zoom and pan to get the best effect.

8. Click Germany to highlight the borders of the country.

9. Hover the cursor over this country to display the sales breakdown by mileage range of car sold. The map should look something like Figure 9-16.

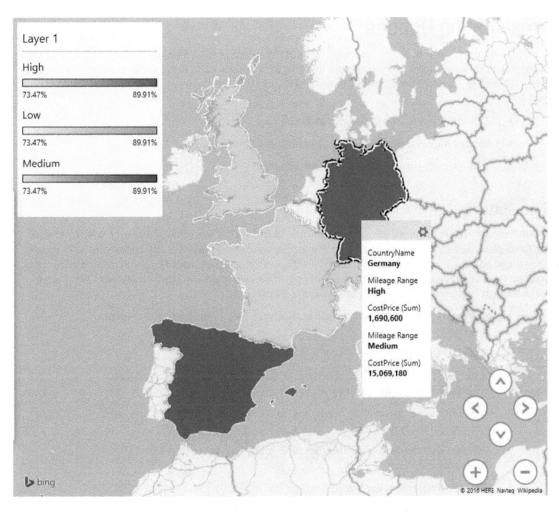

Figure 9-16. A region map with categories applied

When you see the result in a black-and-white book, the effect is probably less immediate. On the screen, however, the change is profound as each country is now a different color. If you look at the pop-up for each country, you will see that the top-selling category for each country has forced the choice of color for the country.

Presentation Options

Great! You have now seen how to create maps using 3D Maps, and you've also taken a look at the major types of geographical visualization that you can put together with this powerful extension to your self-service BI armory. Now it is time to move on to look at some of the presentation options that are available and that will help you.

- Adjust the way in which metrics are displayed

- Change the colors used for charts, bubbles, and heat maps

- Tweak the size of charts, bubbles, and heat maps

The Settings View

The first thing to retain is that all the map options that I listed earlier are adjusted from the Settings view of the Layer pane. As a result, you will have to make sure that the Layer pane is visible before you can proceed. The second point is that the settings will vary slightly depending on the type of map you have chosen. So, as an example, let's suppose I want to display a heat map of sales of spare parts by country, but I also want to make the heat "bubbles" larger and alter the shading. Here is how:

1. Starting with the `PowerMapSample.xlsx` file, click Map in the Insert tab to launch 3D Maps.

2. Choose the Heat Map type.

3. In the field list, expand the Countries table and drag the CountryName field to the Location well in the Layer pane.

4. Add the Town field from the Clients table to the Location well in the Layer pane under the Country field.

5. Add the CostPrice field from the Stock table in the field list to the Value well in the Layer pane.

6. Resize and reposition the legend.

7. Adjust the zoom and panning to get the best effect, focusing on Great Britain.

8. Expand the Layer Options area in the Layer pane.

9. Set Color Scale to 50 percent (or drag the slider to the right to get the effect you need).

10. Set Radius Of Influence to 125 percent (or drag the slider to the right to get the effect you need).

11. Set Opacity to 75 percent. The Layer Options area of the Layer pane should look like Figure 9-17.

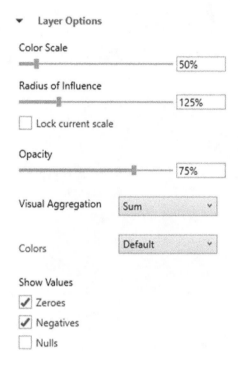

Figure 9-17. The Layer pane Settings view

The map should look like Figure 9-18.

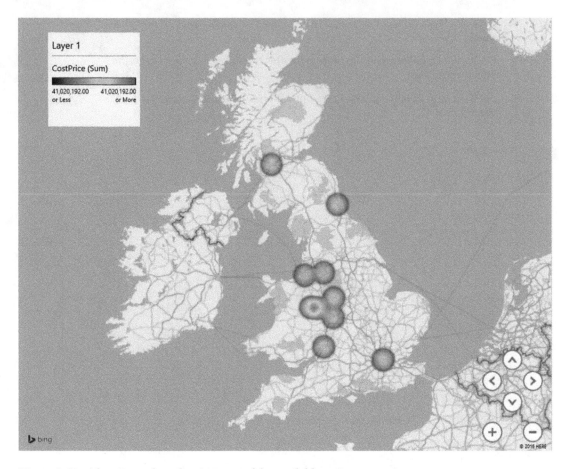

Figure 9-18. *A heat map after adjusting some of the available options*

Now that you have seen the principles, it is probably easiest to outline the options for each map type rather than give examples for each variation on a theme. As there are certain common options, I will begin with those first. Table 9-5 gives the shared settings.

Table 9-5. *Common Map Settings*

Option	Explanation
Color Scale	Adjusts how the range of colors is weighted on the scale of values
Show Zeroes	Displays attributes even when the value is zero
Show Negatives	Displays attributes even when the value is a negative number
Show Nulls	Displays attributes even when the value is null
Lock Current Scale	Freezes the current scale

Bubble Map Settings

Bubble maps allow you to tweak the settings outlined in Table 9-6.

Table 9-6. *Bubble Map Settings*

Option	Explanation
Color	For a bubble map *without* categories or multiple metrics, this option lets you choose the color of each data point.
Radius Of Influence	This extends the size of the bubble.
Thickness	This specifies the height of the bubble when viewed in 3D. This effectively turns the bubble into a cylinder.

Column Map Settings

Column maps allow you to alter the options given in Table 9-7.

Table 9-7. *Column Map Settings*

Option	Explanation
Height	Sets the height of the column
Thickness	Sets the width of the column
Opacity	Adjusts the transparency of the data elements

Region Map Settings

Region maps allow you to tweak the options shown in Table 9-8.

Table 9-8. *Region Map Settings*

Option	Explanation
Color	This option lets you choose the color used for the shading.
Color Scale	This option allows you to adjust the balance (from the center to the periphery) of the color shading.
Opacity	This option adjusts the transparency of the data elements.

Heat Map Settings

Heat maps allow you to adjust the options outlined in Table 9-9.

Table 9-9. *Heat Map Settings*

Option	Explanation
Radius Of Influence	This lets you set the size of the heat bubble.
Color Scale	This option allows you to adjust the balance (from the center to the periphery) of the color shading.
Opacity	This option adjusts the transparency of the data elements.

Applying Specific Colors to Data Elements

One truly powerful setting is the ability to set specific colors for elements in the data display. How this is done varies slightly according to the type of visualization.

Column Charts, Clustered Column Charts, and Bubble Charts

To set the color that you want to display for each value element (the height in the case of Column charts and Clustered Column charts), you need to do the following:

1. Expand the Layer Options area of the Layer pane.

2. Select the data element that you want to modify from the pop-up list under the Color heading.

3. Select a color from the palette to the right of the pop-up list of data elements.

Heat Maps

In the case of heat maps, you are, in effect, setting the upper and lower colors for the range of values that will be represented.

1. Expand the Layer Options area of the Layer pane.

2. Select the data element that you want to modify from the pop-up list under the Color heading.

3. Select Custom from the Colors pop-up menu.

4. Select a color from the palette to the right of the pop-up list of those available for the Low color.

5. Select a color from the palette to the right of the pop-up list of those available for the Low color.

6. If you want, you can extend the set of colors that are displayed in the heat map by clicking the Add Color button in the Layer pane and selecting another color from the palette.

■ **Note**　You need to add any new intermediate colors in the order in which they must be displayed. It is not possible to alter the color order; just delete colors and add them again. Alternatively, you can reattribute different colors to each element in the list.

3D Maps Themes

Certain types of data require a different type of geographical presentation. Sometimes you may want a simple political map that shows countries and towns. At other times, you may need a satellite image. At still others, you may want to see some physical geography such as forests and rivers in your presentation. This is where 3D Maps themes come into play. 3D Maps comes with eight types of map, in both monochrome and color. Some themes contain generic road maps, and some contain high-fidelity satellite images. The theme you choose to apply is independent of the way in which data is plotted, so you can consider it as a geographical backdrop, if you prefer. As you saw when creating the bubble map shown in Figure 9-12, applying a theme is as easy as selecting the required theme from the pop-up that appears when you click the Themes button in the 3D Maps ribbon. Themes are described in Figure 9-19 and Table 9-10.

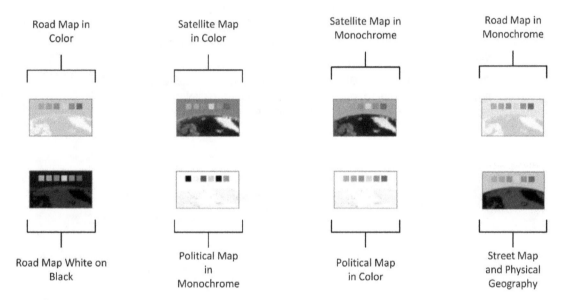

Figure 9-19. *3D Maps themes*

Table 9-10. *3D Maps Themes Explained*

Theme	Description
Theme 1	Road map in color
Theme 2	Satellite map in color
Theme 3	Satellite map in monochrome
Theme 4	Road map in monochrome
Theme 5	Road map, white on black
Theme 6	Political map in monochrome
Theme 7	Political map in color
Theme 8	Street and physical geography map in color

Text Boxes

A picture (or even a map) may be worth many words, but on occasion, you still need a few comments to make a point. Consequently (or inevitably), you can add one or more text boxes to your 3D Maps visualizations to drive home the message. So, let's suppose you're the national sales manager for the UK and you want to crow about your success. Here is how you might add a text box to Figure 9-14:

1. Once you have created the 3D map that displays the data, click the Text Box button in the 3D Maps ribbon. The Edit Text Box dialog will appear.

2. Click inside the TITLE box and enter a title. I will add **UK Sales Key To Success!** in this example.

3. Click inside the DESCRIPTION box and enter a description. I will use **More Sales Of More Makes To More Customers!** as an example.

4. Click inside the TITLE box and select the font, font size, and font attributes that you want to apply. I will choose Arial, 20pt, bold.

5. Click inside the DESCRIPTION box and select the font, font size, and font attributes that you want to apply. I will choose Andalus, 14, italic. The content preview box will display the text as it will appear. The Add Text Box dialog should look like Figure 9-20.

Figure 9-20. *The Add Text Box dialog*

6. Click Create. The Add Text Box dialog will close, and the text box will appear on the map.

7. Reposition the text box by dragging its title bar (the colored bar that appears when the pointer is placed over the text box).

8. Resize the text box by dragging its resize handles (the circles that appear at the top left and bottom right when the pointer is placed over the text box).

9. Click the map to deselect the text box. The text box might look something like Figure 9-21.

UK Sales Key To Success!

More Sales Of More Makes To More Customers!

Figure 9-21. *A text box in 3D Maps*

To alter the properties of a text box, all you have to do is right-click a text box and select Edit from the context menu. The Edit Text Box dialog will be displayed, and you can alter the text of the title and/or the description as well as modify the font attributes.

To remove a text box, you can do the following:

- Right-click a text box and select Remove from the context menu.

- Place the cursor over the text box so that the title bar and resize handles appear and then click the Close icon in the top-right corner of the text box.

Table 9-11 explains the various options available for text boxes.

Table 9-11. *Text Box Options*

Aggregation	Description
Font Family	This lets you choose the font family from those available.
Font Size	This lets you choose the font size from those available.
Bold	This makes all the text in the text box appear in boldface.
Italic	This makes all the text in the text box appear in italics.
Font Color or Shade	This lets you apply a color or shade of gray (depending on the theme) to the text.
Text	This is where you enter the text here.
Description	This is where you add more descriptive text under the text box title.
Background Color	This lets you choose the background color from the palette of available colors.

Customizing the Data Card

As you have seen, placing the pointer over the data on a map will display a pop-up that provides more detail of the data that you are interested in. This is called the *data card*, and while it defaults to displaying the fields that are used to create the 3D map, it can be extended to include further data elements.

To customize the data card, follow these steps:

1. At the bottom of the Layer pane, click Customize. The Customize Data Card dialog will appear.

2. Click the Add field on the left of the dialog. The list of all available tables and fields will appear.

3. Select a field to add. This field will be added to the data card.

4. Click the sigma icon at the right of the new field. The pop-up list of possible aggregations will appear.

5. Select the required aggregation.

6. Click the pencil icon at the right of the new field. This allows you to edit the field name.

7. Modify the field name.

8. On the right of the dialog, click the arrows to the left or right of the word *Template*. Cycle through the available templates until you find the one you are happiest with. The Customize Data Card dialog should look like the one in Figure 9-22.

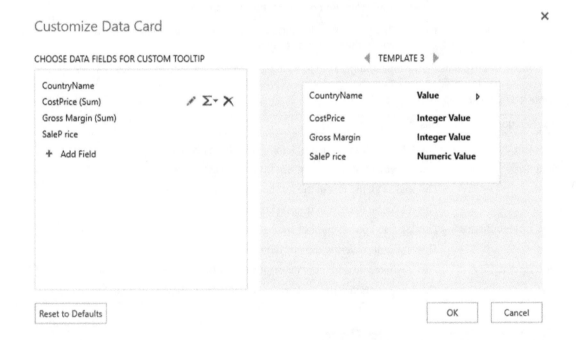

Figure 9-22. *The Customize Data Card dialog*

9. Click OK.

The dialog will close, and now when you place the pointer over a data element, you will see the pop-up containing the elements that you defined and using the chosen template. You can see an example of this in Figure 9-23.

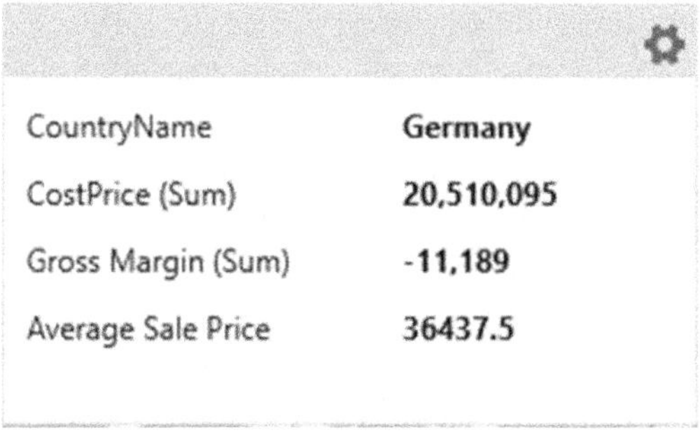

	⚙
CountryName	**Germany**
CostPrice (Sum)	**20,510,095**
Gross Margin (Sum)	**-11,189**
Average Sale Price	**36437.5**

Figure 9-23. *A modified data card*

▓ **Note**   You can alter the data card presentation at any time by clicking the gear icon in the data card. This will display the Customize Data Card dialog.

Timelines

Up until now all the metrics that you have seen have been static. They have been a snapshot taken at a specific moment. 3D Maps, however, can add another dimension to geographic visualization by adding a time element. If the source data contains a time field (or, better still, a date table as part of the data model), then you can do any of the following:

- Show the evolution of data over time, both automatically and manually

- Display the data for a specific date or time in a single click

This is done by adding a Timeline element to the map you are creating. Adding a timeline will add a *time decorator*, as 3D Maps calls it, to the visualization. This object allows you to display the exact date and/or time when the data was in a certain state. What is more, you can set the map to display the data changes over a range of dates (or times) that you specify if you want to concentrate on a subset of data. You can also define the playback settings for a timeline to set the duration of the display. This is probably best appreciated through an example, so let's see first how to add a timeline to a map and then look at some of the cool effects that you can add once you have implemented a timeline.

Adding a Timeline

Rather than add a timeline to an existing map, I prefer to re-create a map so that you can see the whole process. The following is what you do:

1. Starting with the PowerMapSample.xlsx file, click Map in the Insert tab to launch 3D Maps.

2. Select Stacked Column as the visualization type in the Layer pane.

3. In the field list, select the CountryName field from the Countries table.

4. Drag this field into the Location well in the Layer pane.

5. Select the Town field from the Clients table.

6. Drag this field into the Location well in the Layer pane under the Country field.

7. Drag CostPrice from the Stock table into the Height well in the Layer pane.

8. Drag Make from the Stock table into the Category well in the Layer pane.

9. Adjust the zoom and panning to get the best effect—focus on Europe.

10. Resize and reposition the legend.

11. In the Layer pane, expand the DateDimension table and select the DateKey field. This will be added to the Time well in the Layer pane. The timeline slider and a time decorator will appear on the map.

12. Right-click the time decorator (this is a date and time element that normally appears at the top left of the map) and select Edit. The Edit Time Decorator dialog will appear.

13. Select June 2010 (the month and year format) from the Time Format pop-up. The Edit Time Decorator dialog will look like Figure 9-24.

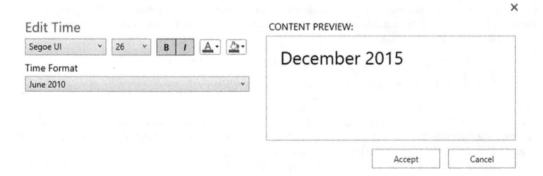

Figure 9-24. The Edit Time Decorator dialog

14. Click Accept to close the Edit Time Decorator dialog.

15. Resize and reposition the time decorator just as you learned to do with a text box. The map should look something like Figure 9-25.

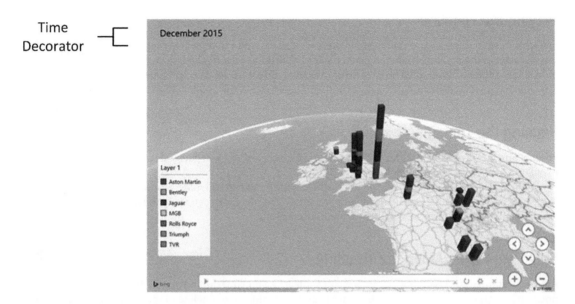

Figure 9-25. *A map with a timeline added*

And that is it. You have a map that can display the evolution of your data over time. Interestingly, when you add a timeline, the map does not change; this is because a timeline's default setting is to show the data at the *end* of the time period. Now, in the next section, you will see how you can use the timeline to enhance your presentation.

■ **Note** Modifying the font attributes for a time decorator is, to all intents and purposes, identical to tweaking a text box, so I will not repeat the options here and instead refer you to Table 9-11.

Using a Timeline

So, what can you do now that your map has a timeline, and what does it bring to the party? Perhaps the first thing is to understand the timeline itself. Figure 9-26 explains the various parts of a timeline.

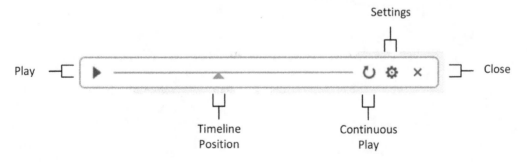

Figure 9-26. *Timeline elements*

Playing the Timeline

Probably the first thing that you will want to do is see the evolution of your data over time. To do this, click the Play icon in the timeline (the triangle on the left). The data will initially disappear from the map, and then it will reappear, developing progressively over time until the final date is reached. Not only that, but the time decorator will scroll through the dates and/or times to show the linear evolution of the data over time.

Pausing the Timeline

When a timeline is playing, the Play icon becomes a Pause icon. Yes, you guessed it, clicking this will halt the playback so that you can take a closer look at the data.

When a timeline is paused (or even if it is still playing), you can still move around the map as well as zoom and pan. With a little practice and once you know your data, you can apply these techniques to draw your audience into the heart of what you are communicating.

Selecting Points Along the Timeline

Although a timeline is linear, you do not have to apply it in a linear fashion. You can drag the timeline position icon (the triangle under the timeline) to any point along the timeline to show the data at a chosen point in time. As you slide the timeline position icon left and right, the time decorator will change to show the exact date and/or time you have selected.

Figure 9-27 shows you a bird's-eye view of how the timeline used in this example progresses from start to finish. The time decorator at the top left of each image illustrates how the data is changing over time.

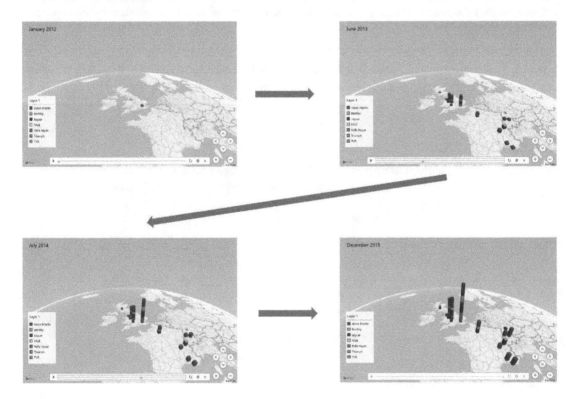

Figure 9-27. *Timeline progression*

Setting Timeline Duration

I mentioned earlier in passing that you can modify the duration of a timeline. You may find yourself needing to do this since the default is only ten seconds, which could be much too short in many cases. To do this, follow these steps:

1.   Click the Settings icon in the timeline (the cog at the right). The Scene Options settings pane of the Layer pane will be displayed.

2.   Enter a scene duration or use the up and down triangles for the Scene Duration box to set a number of seconds for the playback time. I have set 45 seconds in this example, as you can see in Figure 9-28.

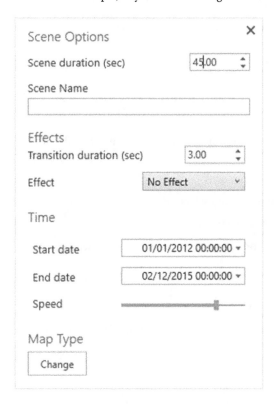

Figure 9-28.   Timeline options

That is all that you have to do. When you next play the timeline, the display will last for 45 seconds.

___

■ **Tip**   If you prefer a more intuitive approach, drag the vertical bar in the Speed section left or right to set the playback speed, which is another way of defining the playback time.

___

Hiding the Time Decorator

You can choose one of the following ways to remove a time decorator:

- Click the Date And Time button in the 3D Maps ribbon.

- Right-click a time decorator and select Remove from the context menu.

- Place the cursor over the time decorator so that the title bar and resize handles appear; then click the Close icon in the top-right corner of the time decorator.

Hiding the Timeline

Hiding a timeline is similar to hiding a time decorator. There are two possible techniques.

- Click the Timeline button in the 3D Maps ribbon.

- Click the Close icon in the right corner of the timeline.

Setting the Date Range for Playback

A final aspect of a timeline is that it can become a kind of date filter, in that you can set the start and end dates for the display. To do this, follow these steps:

1. Click the Settings icon in the timeline (the cog at the right).

2. Click the pop-up triangle at the right of the start date and select a date.

3. Click the pop-up triangle at the right of the end date and select a date.

It is really that easy. If you now play back the timeline, you will see that the metrics begin with the start date and the timeline progression stops at the end date.

Date and Time Formats in the Time Decorator

In step 13 of the process where you added a timeline earlier in the chapter, you set a date format to override the default date and time format. Several date and time formats were available. These are explained in Table 9-12.

Table 9-12. *Date and Time Formats*

Description	Format
Short date and time	01/04/2015 12:00
Short date	01/04/2015
Long date	01 April 2015
Long date and time	01 12:00
Long date and time with seconds	01 April 2015 12:00:10
Short date and time with seconds	01 April 2015 12:00:10
Day and month	01 April
Short date in ISO format with fractions of a second	01 April 2015T12:00:10.0000000
Weekday, short date and time with seconds and time zone reference	Wed, 01 April 2015 12:00:10 GMT
Short date in ISO format with seconds	01 April 2015T12:00:10
Time	12:00
Time with seconds	12:00:10
Month and year	April 2015

Using Layers

In the next part of this chapter, you will start creating more complex—and I hope more impressive—map-based visualizations. More complex, and consequently more telling, map visualizations use layers in 3D Maps. Each layer is a separate map that uses different metrics and possibly different geographical elements. However, using multiple layers is merely an extension of the techniques that you have learned so far. As an example, let's produce a map that uses the following:

- *Layer 1*: Sales by country

- *Layer 2*: A heat map of profit per town

- *Layer 3*: A stacked column of town sales by color

Let's see this in action. The process is a little long since you are creating three maps in one, but I am essentially revising techniques that you have already used. The result is, I hope you will agree, well worth it.

1. Starting with the PowerMapSample.xlsx file, click Map in the Insert tab to launch 3D Maps.

2. Drag the CountryName field from the Countries table into the Location well in the Layer pane.

3. Select the Region Map type.

4. Drag the SalePrice field in the InvoiceLines table into the Height well in the Layer pane.

5. Delete the legend if it appears.

6. Place the cursor over the layer name (Layer 1) at the top of the Layer pane.

7. Click the Rename icon that appears at the right of the layer name (a pencil).

8. Enter the name **CountrySales** and press Enter.

   The first layer is now created and displays sales for each country. The next layer will be a heat map of profit per town.

9. Click the Add Layer button.

10. Rename the layer **ProfitByTown** as described in steps 6 and 7.

11. Add the Town field to the Location well in the Layer pane.

12. Choose HeatMap as the type.

13. Add the GrossMargin field from the InvoiceLines table in the field list to the Value well in the Layer pane.

14. Resize and reposition the legend to the left of the map.

    The second layer is now created. All that remains is to create a clustered column map of sales by make for the third and final layer and to tweak the presentation.

15. Click the Add Layer button.

16. Rename the new layer **SalesByMake** as described in steps 6 and 7.

17. Select the Heat Map visualization type.

18. Add the CountryName and Town fields, in this order, to the Location well in the Layer pane.

19. Add the SalePrice and Make fields from the Stock table in the field list to the Value well in the Layer pane.

20. Choose Clustered Column as the visualization type.

21. Resize and reposition the legend to the left of the map under the existing legend.

22. Zoom, pan, and swivel the map to display the data to best effect.

    Now you need to adjust a couple of settings to enhance the readability of the map.

23. Close the SalesByMake layer and expand the ProfitByTown layer.

24. Expand the Layer Options area in the Layer pane and tweak the height and thickness of the column.

25. Close the ProfitByTown layer and expand the SalesByMake layer.

26. Expand the Layer Options area in the Layer pane.

27. Tweak the Color Scale and Radius Of Influence settings to make the profit more visible.

That is it. The multilayered map should look something like Figure 9-29.

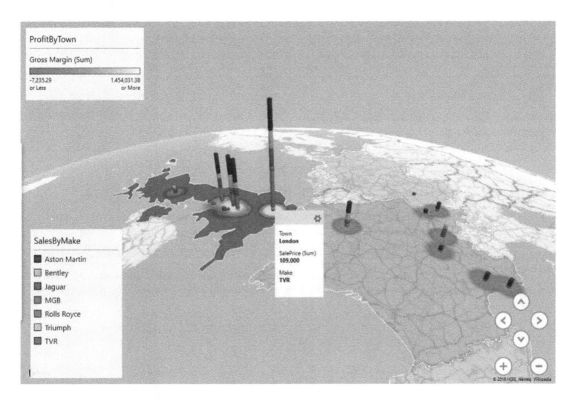

Figure 9-29. A multilayered map

As you have seen, each layer is quite simply a standard 3D map just like all those that you have developed thus far. The trick is to add further maps (in practice they will nearly always be of different types) to get the desired effect. Each layer is then visible in the Layer pane. You can see this in Figure 9-30.

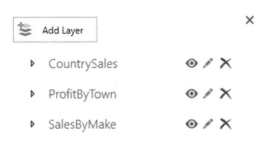

Figure 9-30. Multiple layers

■ **Note** When creating layered maps, I find that it really helps to have an idea of what I want initially. However, nothing will stop you from creating different layers and experimenting as you go.

These are just a few final comments to make about using layers:

- You can hide, or display, the details of an existing layer by clicking the expand icon in the Layer pane for the selected layer.

- To delete a layer, simply click the Delete icon in the Layer pane for that layer. 3D Maps will show an alert that warns you that this operation cannot be undone.

■ **Tip** You can adjust the map presentation by zooming and panning at any time. However, 3D Maps will always create a new layer from a global map, so I find it easier to adjust the map display right at the end of the process, once and for all.

2D Charts

In some cases you may want to enhance a purely geographical representation of data with a more classic visualization. 3D Maps can let you do this, without distracting from its core aim, by letting you add a two-dimensional chart to a map. This chart will apply to an existing layer of that map and will use the data that the selected layer already represents on the map.

As an example, when shading is used, such as in the case of Region maps, I find that a chart can give a more accurate grasp of the underlying figures. So, let's see how to add a 2D chart to the map that you just created.

1. Click the 2D Chart button in the 3D Maps ribbon. The Insert 2D Chart dialog will appear, looking like the one in Figure 9-31.

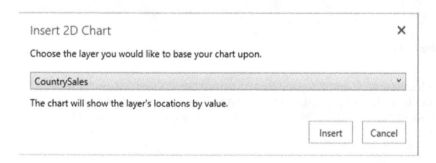

Figure 9-31. *The Insert 2D Chart dialog*

2. Select a layer to base the chart on. In this example, I will use CountrySales. A chart will be added to the map.

3. Select the Horizontal chart type from the pop-up list of available chart types at the right of the chart name.

4. Resize the chart and position it so that the country data is not obscured.

The map should now look like Figure 9-32.

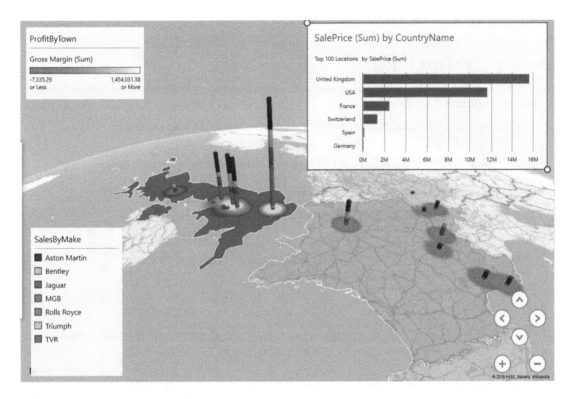

Figure 9-32. *A map with a 2D chart superimposed*

2D Chart Types

There are only four available 2D charts.

- Column charts

- Stacked column charts

- Bar charts

- Stacked bar charts

As these chart types are identical to the Power View charts described in Chapter 4, I will not describe them again here.

The trick here is to find a shade (it need not be gray) that will scarcely show a difference on the map but will be visible in the 2D chart.

3D Maps Tours

Up until now you have treated each map that you have created as a completely separate entity. Indeed, you have acted as if an Excel workbook could contain only a single map, even if it was composed of multiple layers. Nothing could be further from the truth, because you can add as many separate maps to an Excel workbook as you like. However, you will not see separate worksheets as you did when using Power View in Excel; Excel handles maps in a slightly different way. Each map is called a *tour*, and you can choose which map (or tour) you want to use when you launch 3D Maps.

Creating 3D Maps Tours

To see this in action, you will create (or re-create) a couple of independent maps in a single Excel workbook and see how to manage these elements.

1. Starting with the sample file `PowerMapSample.xlsx`, create the map you first made for Figure 9-4 at the start of this chapter.

2. Assuming that the Tour Editor is visible on the left (and if it is not, click the Tour Editor button in the 3D Maps ribbon to display it), click the tour name (it is probably called Tour 1) and enter a name. I suggest **SalesByRegion**.

3. Press Enter to confirm the new name for the tour.

4. Click File ➤ Close to close 3D Maps.

5. From inside Excel, click 3D Map in the Insert ribbon. The Launch 3D Maps dialog will be displayed, as shown in Figure 9-33.

Launch 3D Maps   ✕

SalesByRegion

 New Tour

Figure 9-33. *The Launch 3D Maps dialog*

6. Click the New Tour icon (the plus sign in a circle). A new, blank map will be created.

7. Create the map shown in Figure 9-10.

8. Name this tour **GrossProfit**.

9. Click File ➤ Close to close 3D Maps.

That is it. You now have two separate maps inside the Excel workbook. Whenever you click the 3D Map button in the Excel Insert ribbon, you will see the existing tours. You can launch a tour directly simply by clicking the preview of the tour, which is visible in the Launch 3D Maps dialog.

Deleting a 3D Maps Tour

Sometimes you will want to delete a tour. This is how to do so:

1. From inside Excel, click Map in the Insert ribbon; the Launch 3D Maps dialog will be displayed.

2. Hover the pointer over one of the tours. An X will appear to the upper right of the map image, as shown in Figure 9-34.

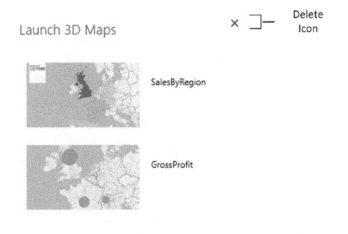

Figure 9-34. *Deleting a tour*

3. Click the X. Excel will display a confirmation dialog, as in Figure 9-35.

271

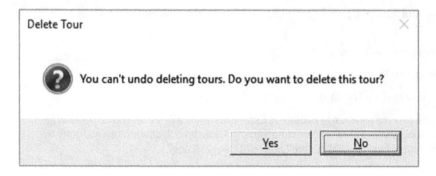

Figure 9-35. *Confirming tour deletion*

4.   Click OK. The tour will be deleted.

Existing 3D Maps Tours in Excel

When you open an Excel worksheet, you may not know that it contains 3D Maps tours. After all, both the data in the data model and the maps themselves are not immediately visible. Fortunately, the software team at Microsoft has thought of this. Any time you open an Excel workbook that contains 3D Maps tours, you will see the alert shown in Figure 9-36.

Figure 9-36. *The Excel alert that 3D Maps tours are present in the current workbook*

3D Maps Movies

A final, but extremely impressive, 3D Maps function is the way that you can create and replay "movies" of geographical data. This technique can extend maps (with or without layers and timelines) to create a sequence of views of the data that can be played back either from within 3D Maps or as separate multimedia files. A multimedia file created by 3D Maps does not even need Excel to work.

A 3D Maps movie is a 3D Maps tour that can contain several scenes. Each scene is a copy of an existing scene that is then modified to display a different visualization. You can also add transition effects so that each scene flows into the following scene. As always, this is best visualized by using an example. Let's imagine that you want to begin with an initial map of European sales and then take a closer look at UK sales. The example 3D Maps movie will have only two scenes, whereas in reality, you can create much more complex scenarios. Here is how to do it:

1.   Create a map of Country Sales as you did at the start of this chapter (you can see this in Figure 9-3).

2.   Set the map type to Flat Map in the 3D Maps ribbon.

3.   Add a timeline using the MonthAndYear field from the Date table and tweak the time decorator for best effect.

4. Click the Scene Options button in the 3D Maps ribbon.

5. Enter a scene name in the Scene Name box and press Enter. I suggest **European Sales** as the name.

6. In the Scene Duration (sec) box, set the duration to **10**.

7. Set Effect to Circle from the effects pop-up list.

   You have finished the first scene. Now you will add a second scene.

8. In the 3D Maps ribbon, click Add Scene. A second scene thumbnail will appear in the Tour Editor on the left. This scene will be a copy of the initial scene (or the selected scene if there are already several scenes in the movie).

9. Ensure that the second scene is selected, and rename it **UK Sales by Make**.

10. Set the scene duration to 30 seconds.

11. Remove the MonthAndYear field from the data to delete the timeline.

12. Add the Town field to the geographical data.

13. Add the Make field to the metric data.

14. Zoom in on the United Kingdom only.

15. Remove the legend.

16. Click the Settings icon in the Layer pane and select Scene Options.

17. Set the duration to **20** seconds.

18. Set the effect to Push In.

19. Set the map type to Curved (Not Flat) Map.

20. Click Play Tour in the 3D Maps ribbon.

3D Maps will play the two scenes and run one into the other. It will play the timeline from the first scene and then remove the legend and timeline as well as change the map type and the data displayed to show the second scene.

■ **Note**   You can add scenes that are, in effect, existing 3D Maps tours. You do this by clicking the small triangle at the bottom of the New Scene button in the ribbon and selecting the required tour from the pop-up list of existing tours.

This movie was only a tiny sample of what you can do with 3D Maps to create fluid and extremely impressive automated visualizations. You can create movies containing as many scenes as you want. Set the following for each one:

- A duration in seconds

- A transition effect

- The map type and data

- A timeline

- Multiple map layers

As always, it is your data and the points that you want to emphasize that will make or break a good 3D Maps movie. Just remember that less is frequently more when creating effects and that you can add and remove legends and text boxes to each separate scene if you want to clarify certain aspects of the data. You can even use text boxes to create your own silent movie.

You can pause a movie at any time by clicking the Pause icon that appears in the status bar at the bottom of a movie. Clicking this icon again (it will have become a Play icon) will continue with the playback. You can jump from scene to scene by clicking the Next and Previous icons in the movie status bar. Pressing the Esc key will cancel a movie and return you to 3D Maps.

Scene Transitions

When creating this example, you tried a couple of transitions. A transition is always the visual effect that introduces a scene—and that will link a scene to its predecessor. The available transitions are explained in Table 9-13. You can alter the duration of a transition in the Options dialog.

Table 9-13. *Transition Options*

Aggregation	Description
Circle	The map will pivot around a central axis for the duration of the scene.
Dolly	The map will move to the center of the frame.
Figure 8	The map will move its central point around an imaginary horizontal figure eight, as if tracing an infinity symbol.
Fly Over	The map will move from top to bottom as if a camera were flying over the map.
Push In	The map will zoom in progressively.
Station	The map will not move.

Managing Scenes

To complete your education as far as 3D Maps scenes are concerned, there are a few easy points to note.

Deleting Scenes

To delete a scene, all you have to do is to hover the cursor over a scene. Three small icons will appear at the bottom of the scene. Click the small X and the scene will be deleted. Be warned that 3D Maps does not ask for any confirmation of this, although you can undo the operation if you deleted a scene by mistake.

Modifying Scene Options

You can modify all the options that you set for a scene either by selecting the scene in the scenes list on the left and clicking the Scene Options button in the ribbon or by clicking a scene and then clicking the small cog icon that appears at the bottom of the scene.

Playing a Scene

You can play an individual scene by clicking a scene and then clicking the small triangle icon that appears at the bottom of the scene.

Exporting a Movie

Once you have created and perfected a movie, you are not limited to using 3D Maps to display your artwork. You can export a 3D Maps movie as a Windows multimedia file (in MP4 format) so that it can be played back without a user needing Excel 2013 or Office 356. To create a movie file, follow these steps:

1. Create a movie as described earlier.

2. Click Create Video from the 3D Maps toolbar. The Create Video dialog will be displayed, as shown in Figure 9-37.

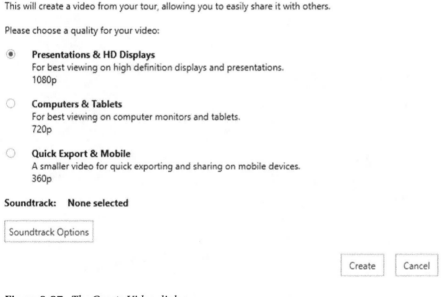

Create Video   ✕

This will create a video from your tour, allowing you to easily share it with others.

Please choose a quality for your video:

⦿ **Presentations & HD Displays**
    For best viewing on high definition displays and presentations.
    1080p

◯ **Computers & Tablets**
    For best viewing on computer monitors and tablets.
    720p

◯ **Quick Export & Mobile**
    A smaller video for quick exporting and sharing on mobile devices.
    360p

Soundtrack: None selected

Soundtrack Options

Create   Cancel

Figure 9-37. *The Create Video dialog*

3. Select the appropriate resolution as a function of the output device that you expect to be used.

4. Click Create. The Save Movie dialog will appear.

5. Enter a file name, select a destination directory, and click Save.

6. The Creating Video message box will appear as in Figure 9-38.

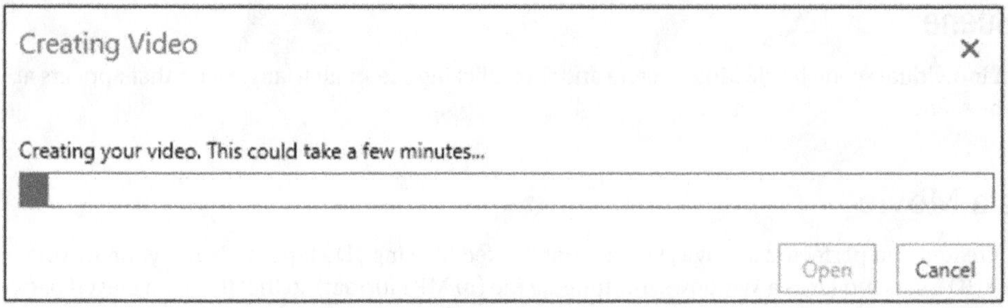

Creating Video   ✕

Creating your video. This could take a few minutes...

[   ]

                                                Open   Cancel

Figure 9-38. Exporting a 3D Maps movie

7. As a final note, you can also add soundtracks to your movies. To do this, just click the Soundtrack options button in the Create Video dialog and you will see the dialog displayed in Figure 9-39.

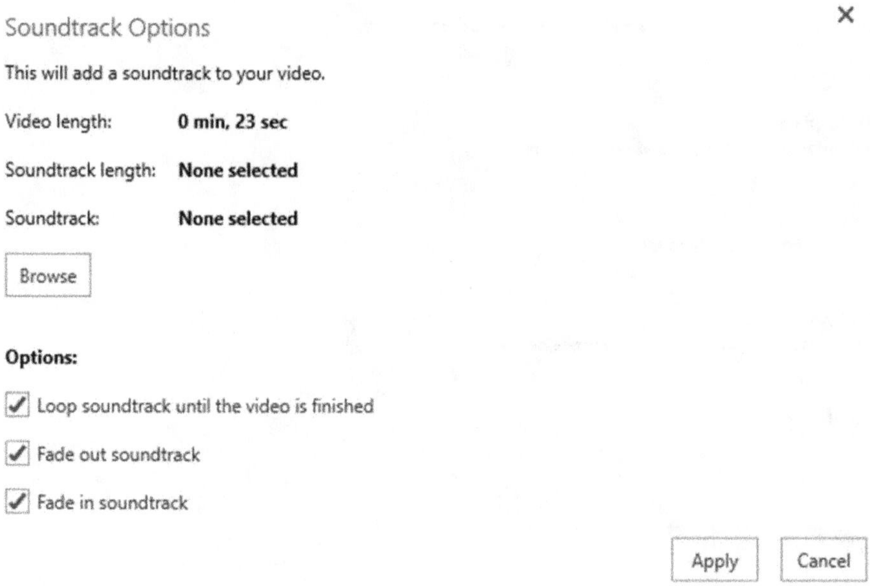

Soundtrack Options   ✕

This will add a soundtrack to your video.

Video length: **0 min, 23 sec**

Soundtrack length: **None selected**

Soundtrack: **None selected**

Browse

Options:

☑ Loop soundtrack until the video is finished

☑ Fade out soundtrack

☑ Fade in soundtrack

                                        Apply   Cancel

Figure 9-39. Soundtrack options for movies

8. Click the Browse button to select a suitable sound file to accompany the movie.

9. Click Apply.

10. Click Close.

You can now open the 3D Maps movie file in a multimedia player—or you can double-click it in Windows Explorer to play back the movie.

Custom Regions

If the built-in geospatial possibilities of 3D Maps are not enough, or possibly not precise enough for you, then you can have 3D Maps use custom mapping data to present your data the way you want.

Custom data presentation like this requires you to have found or purchased geospatial data in a specific format: the .shp file. Creating these files is a specialized science that is outside the scope of this book.

However, if you have been able to procure such data, here is how you can use it in 3D Maps:

1. Open 3D Maps.

2. Click the Custom Regions button in the ribbon. The Import Custom Region Set dialog will appear.

3. Click Import New Set, and browse to the shape (.shp) file containing the geospatial data. There is a folder named C:\DataVisualisationInExcel2016\ GEoData that contains the sample file Regions.shp file in the sample data.

4. Click Open. The Import Custom Region Set dialog will look like Figure 9-40.

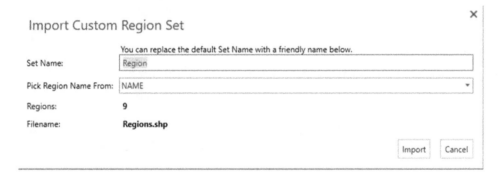

Figure 9-40. *The Import Custom Region Set dialog*

5. Click Import. The external data will be added to the available mapping data for you to use when creating 3D maps.

Conclusion

This, then, is 3D Maps. You can now push the creation of geospatial data representation to places that previously you could not achieve without using specialized software. Now, with just Excel 2016, you can achieve some stunning effects and data displays. In this chapter, you saw how to create maps, alter map types, and even add multiple varieties of maps and overlay them to produce succinct and clear insight into your data. Finally, you saw how to merge distinct visualizations into a movie that you can export as a file and send to colleagues.

CHAPTER 10

▓ ▓ ▓

Discovering and Loading Data with Get & Transform in Excel 2016

Before you can present any analysis or insight, you need data. Your sources could be in many places and in many formats. Nonetheless, you need to access them, look at them, select them, and quite possibly clean them up to some extent. You may also need to join many separate data sources before you shape the data into a coherent model that you can use as the foundation for your dashboards and reports. The amazing thing is that you can do all of this using Excel 2016 without needing any other tools or utilities thanks to the Get & Transform function. What is more, you can feed the output from Get & Transform either into a spreadsheet (if the data is not too voluminous) or into the in-memory data model for larger—and even extremely large—data sets.

Get & Transform was available for previous versions of Excel as an optional add-in called Power Query. Now, however, it is completely integrated into Excel 2016. Indeed, you may find Get & Transform referred to as Power Query from time to time. The good news is that if you have already used Power Query, then you will find Get & Transform to be similar. Moreover, if you have used Power BI—Microsoft's self-service BI tool—then you will surely experience a strong sense of déjà vu, as the query editor in Power BI and Get & Transform both share a common ancestor in Power Query.

If you are an Excel user who has imported data from text files, Access databases, SQL Server, Analysis Services, or other sources for several years already, then you may be wondering why, exactly, you might need to move to another data ingestion tool for Excel. The answer is simple. Anything you have done so far when importing data into Excel can be taken to a whole new level with Get & Transform. You will learn in this chapter (and the next three) some of the amazing things that you can do with this powerful, intuitive, and agile tool.

Discovering, loading, cleaning, and modifying source data are areas where Get & Transform in Excel 2016 really shines. Using this part of the Excel analysis toolkit, you can carry out the following:

- *Data discovery*: Find and connect to a myriad of data sources containing potentially useful data. This can be from both public and private data sources.

- *Data loading*: Select the data you have examined and load it into Excel 2016 for shaping.

- *Data modification*: Modify the structure of each data table that you have imported, filter and clean the data itself, and then join any separate data sources (you will look at this in detail in Chapters 11 through 13).

Although I have outlined these three steps as if they are completely separate and sequential, the reality is that they often blend into a single process. Indeed, there could be many occasions when you will examine the data *after* it has been loaded into Excel 2016—or join data tables *before* you clean them. The core objective will, however, always remain the same: find some data and then load it into Excel 2016 where you can tweak, clean, and shape it.

© Adam Aspin 2016   279
A. Aspin, *High Impact Data Visualization in Excel with Power View, 3D Maps, Get & Transform and Power BI*,
DOI 10.1007/978-1-4842-2400-7_10

This process could be described simplistically as "First, catch your data." In the world of data warehousing, the specialists call it ETL, which is short for extract, transform, and load. Despite the reassuring confidence that the acronym brings, this process is rarely a smooth logical progression through a clear-cut series of steps. The reality is often far messier than that. You may often find yourself importing some data, cleaning it, importing some more data from another source, combining the second data set with the first one, removing some rows and columns, and then repeating many of these operations several times over.

In this chapter and the following three, I will try to show you how the process can work in practice using Excel 2016. I hope that this will make the various steps that comprise an ETL process clearer. All I am asking is that you remain aware that the range of options that Get & Transform in Excel 2016 includes make it a multifaceted and tremendously capable tool. The science is to know *which* options to use. The art is to know *when* to use them.

In this chapter, you will often load data into Excel 2016 Get & Transform before adding it to the data model or a spreadsheet. This "detour" is the part of the process that allows you to cleanse and transform the data before it is added Excel. Of course, if your data is perfect, then you can add it straight into a spreadsheet or the data model and start building reports. Indeed, if you are connecting to cleansed corporate data, you may want to jump straight to Chapter 14 and learn how to structure the data model. However, if your data needs any adjustment at all, then Excel 2016 Get & Transform will likely soon become a trusted tool.

This chapter begins by seeing how to find and load data from a variety of sources. Once again, I will be using a set of example files that you can find on the Apress web site. If you have followed the instructions in Appendix A, then these files will be in the `C:\DataVisualisationInExcel2016` folder.

Data Sources

It is now time to take a wider look at the *types* of data that Excel 2016 can ingest and manipulate.

As the sheer wealth of possible data sources can seem overwhelming at first, Excel 2016 groups potential data sources into the following categories:

- *File*: Includes Excel files, comma-separated values (CSV) files, text files, and XML files.

- *Database*: A fairly comprehensive collection of relational databases that are currently in the workplace and in the cloud, including (among others) SQL Server, Microsoft Access, and Oracle. The full list is given later in this chapter.

- *Azure*: This option lets you see all available data that is hosted in the Microsoft cloud. This covers a range of data formats, from SQL Server to big data sources.

- *Other*: A considerable and ever-growing range of data sources, from Facebook to Microsoft Exchange. The full list (at least at the time this book was printed) is given later in this chapter.

It is perfectly possible that this list will evolve over time, and you need to be aware that you have to look closely at the version of Excel 2016 that you are using if you want an exhaustive list of the available data sources. Given that Power BI Desktop now embraces several additional data sources, it might be the case that some of these other sources will have been added to Excel by the time you read this book. However, you also need to know that not all IT departments allow these updates to take place and that they can appear many, many months after they are generally available in Power BI.

You can also list the contents of folders on any available local disk or network share (even if it is not always a data source) and then leverage this to import several files at once. Similarly (if you have the necessary permissions), you can list the databases and data available on the database servers you connect to. This way, Excel 2016 can provide not only the data but also the metadata—or data about data—that can help you to take a quick look at potential sources of data and choose only those that you really need.

Unfortunately, the sheer range of data sources from which Excel 2016 can read data is such that I do not have space here to examine the minutiae of every one. Consequently, I will take you on a rapid tour of *some* of the most frequently used data sources in the next few pages. Fortunately, most of the data sources that Excel 2016 can read are used in a similar way. The Excel 2016 interface does a wonderful job of making the arcane connection details as unobtrusive as possible. So, even if you are not using the data sources that are described in this chapter, you will nonetheless see a variety of techniques that can be applied to virtually any of the data sources that Excel 2016 can connect to.

File Sources

Sending files across networks and over the Internet or via e-mail has become second nature to most of us. As long as the files you have obtained conform to some of the widely recognized standards currently in use (of which you will learn more later), you should have little difficulty loading them into Excel 2016.

Table 10-1 gives the file sources that Excel 2016 can currently read and from which it can load data.

Table 10-1. *File Sources*

File Sources	Comments
Excel	Allows you to read Microsoft Excel files (versions 97 to 2016) and load worksheets, named ranges, and tables
CSV	Lets you load text files that conform to the CSV format
XML	Allows you to load XML data
Text	Lets you load text files using a variety of separators
Folder	Lets you load the information about all the files in a folder

Databases

Much corporate data currently resides in relational databases. It follows that being able to look at this data is essential for much of today's business intelligence. In the real world, connecting to corporate data could require you to have a logon name and possibly a password that will let you connect (unless the database can recognize your Windows login). I imagine that you will also require permissions to read the tables and views that contain the data. So, the techniques described here are probably the easy bit. The hard part is convincing the guardians of corporate data that you actually *need* the data and you should be allowed to see it.

Table 10-2 gives the databases that Excel 2016 can currently connect to and can preview and load data from.

Table 10-2. *Database Sources*

Database	Comments
SQL Server	Lets you connect to a Microsoft SQL Server on-premises database and import records from all the data tables and views that you are authorized to access.
Access database	Lets you connect to a Microsoft Access file on your network and load queries and tables.
SQL Server Analysis Services database	Lets you connect to a SQL Server Analysis Services (SSAS) database. This can be either an online analytical processing (OLAP) cube or an in-memory tabular data warehouse.
Oracle database	Lets you connect to an Oracle database and import records from all the data tables and views that you are authorized to access.
IBM DB2 database	Lets you connect to an IBM DB2 database and import records from all the data tables and views that you are authorized to access.
MySQL database	Lets you connect to a MySQL database and import records from all the data tables and views that you are authorized to access.
PostgreSQL database	Lets you connect to a PostgreSQL database and import records from all the data tables and views that you are authorized to access.
Sybase database	Lets you connect to a Sybase database and import records from all the data tables and views that you are authorized to access.
Teradata database	Lets you connect to a Teradata database and import records from all the data tables and views that you are authorized to access.

Connecting to Oracle, DB2, MySQL, PostgreSQL, Sybase, or Teradata requires not only that the database administrator has given you the necessary permissions but also that connection software (known as *drivers* or *providers*) has been installed on your PC. Moreover, these databases are available only when you are using certain versions of Excel, as I explained in Chapter 1. Given the "corporate" nature of the requirements, it may help if you talk directly to your IT department to get this set up in your enterprise IT landscape.

Azure

Azure is the Microsoft cloud. Table 10-3 gives the Azure data sources that Excel 2016 can currently connect to and can preview and load data from.

Table 10-3. *Azure Sources*

Source	Comments
Microsoft Azure SQL database	Lets you connect to a Microsoft SQL Server cloud-based database and import records from all the data tables and views that you are authorized to access.
Microsoft Azure SQL data warehouse	Lets you connect to Microsoft's cloud-based, elastic, enterprise data warehouse.
Windows Azure Marketplace	Lets you load data that you are authorized to access on the Windows Azure Marketplace. It requires a Windows Azure Marketplace subscription.
Windows Azure HDInsight	Reads cloud-based Hadoop files in the Microsoft Azure environment.
Windows Azure blob storage	Reads from a cloud-based unstructured data store.
Windows Azure table storage	Reads from Windows Azure tables.

Other Sources

Up until now, you have seen some of the more traditional sources of data that you might need for your analysis. As the world changes, the available sources evolve. The current trend is toward less "structured" (and controlled) data sources and more varied and often less corporate sources.

Excel 2016 can connect to, and read data from, a whole host of these less classic sources. Table 10-4 lists some of the most used other sources that it can currently connect to.

Table 10-4. *Other Sources*

Source	Comments
Web	Connects to a web page and reads tables of data.
SharePoint list	Loads a SharePoint list as a data table. You will need SharePoint permissions to access SharePoint data.
OData feed	Connects to an OData feed to read and load the data it contains. OData is a standardized protocol for creating and consuming data, especially over the Internet.
Hadoop Distributed File System (HDFS)	Reads Hadoop ("big data") files.
Active Directory	Reads data from the enterprise Active Directory. This will probably require custom access rights.
Dynamics CRM Online	Reads data from Microsoft Dynamics business solutions.
Facebook	Connects to a Facebook profile and downloads the data.
Microsoft Exchange	Reads data from the Microsoft Exchange e-mail system.
Facebook	Reads Facebook data.
Google Analytics	Connects to Google Analytics so that you can monitor your web site usage.
Salesforce objects	Connects to Salesforce objects and downloads data for analysis.
Salesforce reports	Connects to Salesforce reports and downloads data for analysis.
ODBC	Connects to an ODBC driver. This is a standard data interface that can connect to an extremely wide range of data sources.

These data sources are so varied, and so often customized or uniquely personal, that I will not be going through anything other than web page sources in this chapter.

■ **Note**   The list of data sources that Excel 2016 can access is growing all the time. Consequently, you will probably find even more sources than those described so far by the time that this book is published.

Loading Data

It is time to start looking at the heavy-lifting aspect of Excel 2016 and how you can use it to load data from a variety of different sources. I will begin on the bunny slopes with a simple example of "scraping" data from a web page. Then, given the plethora of available data sources and to make the process a clearer structure, you will load data from several of the ubiquitous data sources that are found in most workplaces. These data sources are the basis of the data that you will learn to tweak and "mash up" in the following chapters. These sources are as follows:

- *CSV*: This file type will be the source of the Countries table.

- *Text*: Here you will use the Stock table.

- *XML*: You will use an XML file containing the Colors data.

- *Excel*: You will use the Invoices and InvoiceLines tables from an Excel file.

- *Access*: You will load the Clients table from an Access database file.

After you have loaded these six tables, you will look into getting data from a relational database (SQL Server will be the example here) because in my experience, databases are a frequent source of core data for analysis. Here you will see how to apply several tricks and techniques to database sources.

Finally, you will load data from a couple of "all-in-one" sources that contain *all* the data that you need in one place to create dashboards without any extensive data preparation. These sources are

- *SQL Server Analysis Services OLAP cube*: You will load a simplified subset of data from an enterprise data warehouse "cube."

- *SQL Server Analysis Services Tabular data warehouse*: You will read data directly from an in-memory data warehouse.

Finally, you will look at a technique for loading multiple files of the same format, as this can be a frequent requirement in the real world.

Web Pages

As a first and extremely simple example, let's grab some data from a web page. Since I want to concentrate on the method rather than the data, I will use a web page that has nothing to do with the sample data in the book. You will not be using this other than as a simple introduction to the process of loading data from web pages using Excel 2016.

Assuming that you have launched Excel 2016 and closed the splash screen, follow these steps:

1. In the Data ribbon, click the small triangle at the bottom of the New Query button.

2. Select From Other Sources.

3. Select From Web from the menu that appears, as shown in Figure 10-1.

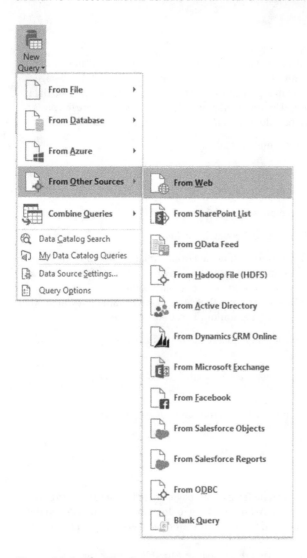

Figure 10-1. *The New Query menu*

4. Enter the following URL (it is a Microsoft help page for Excel 2016 that contains a
    few tables of data): **http://office.microsoft.com/en-gb/excel-help/guide-
    to-the-power-query-ribbon-HA103993930.aspx**. I am, of course, hoping that
    it is still available when you read this book. Of course, if you have a URL that you
    want to try, then feel free! The dialog will look something like Figure 10-2.

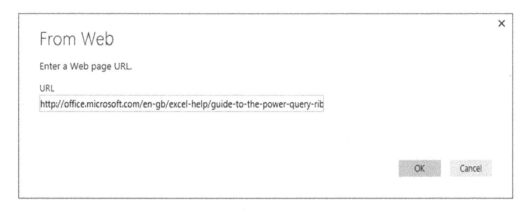

Figure 10-2. *The From Web source dialog*

5. Click OK. The Navigator dialog will appear. After a few seconds, during which Excel 2016 is connecting to the web page, the list of available tables of data in the web page will be displayed.

6. Click one of the table names on the left of the Navigator dialog. The contents of the table will appear on the right of the Navigator dialog to show you what the data in the chosen table looks like, as shown in Figure 10-3.

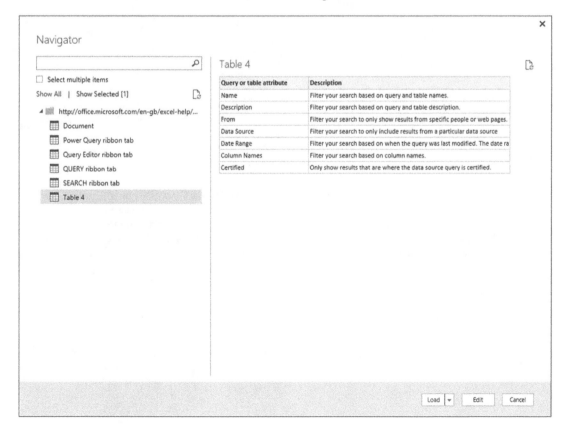

Figure 10-3. *The Navigator dialog previewing the contents of a table on a web page*

7.   Click Edit at the bottom of the window. The Excel 2016 Get & Transform Query Editor window opens to display the table of data. It should look like Figure 10-4. (You will look at this window in detail in the next chapter.)

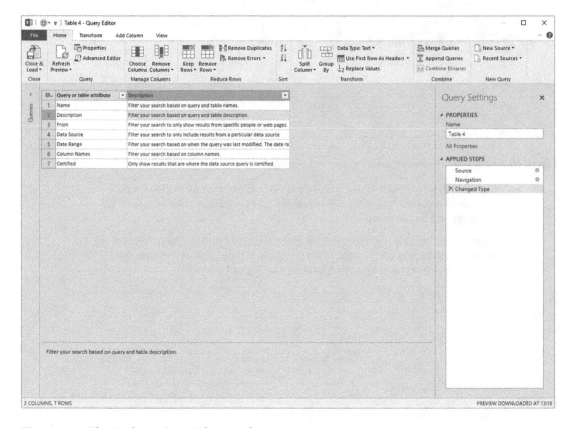

Figure 10-4.   *The Excel 2016 Query Editor window*

8.   Click Close & Load in the Query Editor ribbon. The Excel 2016 Query Editor window will close and copy the data into a new Excel 2016 worksheet. You can see this in Figure 10-5, where you can also see that the Workbook Queries pane has appeared at the right of the screen. This pane contains the list of all the Get & Transform queries that you have added to Excel.

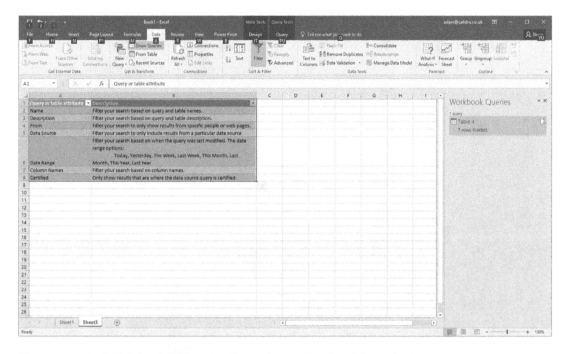

Figure 10-5. *An initial data load from a web page into an Excel worksheet*

9. Because you will not be using this data (it was only an example of how to load data from a table on a web page), delete the worksheet that contains the data that you just loaded from the Web.

This simple example showed how you can access data from a supported data source and load it into Excel 2016 Get & Transform. You have also met the Excel 2016 Get & Transform Query Editor window, where you can modify and transform the queries that access the original data.

CSV Files

The scenario is as follows: you have been given a comma-separated text file (also known as a *CSV file*) containing a list of data. You now want to load this into Excel 2016 so that you can look at the data and consider what needs to be done (if anything) to make it usable. The following explains what you have to do:

1. In the Data ribbon, click the small triangle at the bottom of the New Query button, select From File, and then click From CSV. The Import Data dialog will appear.

2. Navigate to the folder containing the file you want to load and select it (C:\ DataVisualisationInExcel2016\Countries.csv, in this example).

3. Click Import. The Excel 2016 Get & Transform Query Editor window appears; it contains the contents of the entire CSV file. You can see this in Figure 10-6.

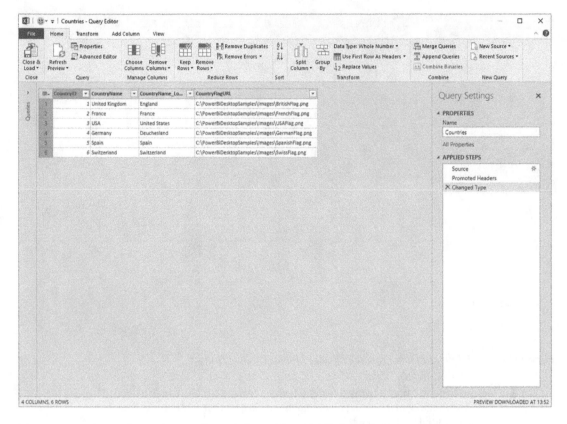

Figure 10-6. *The Excel 2016 Query Editor window with a CSV file loaded*

4. Click the small triangle at the bottom of the Close & Load button in the Query Editor window.

5. Select Load To. The Load To dialog will appear.

6. Select Only Create Connection and check the Add This Data To The Data Model check box. The Load To dialog will look like the one shown in Figure 10-7.

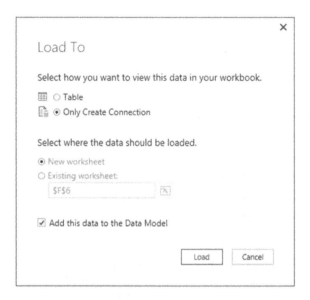

Figure 10-7. *The Load To dialog*

7. Click Load. The data will be loaded into the data model (but not into a worksheet), and the Workbook Queries pane will appear on the right of the current workbook containing the query you just created.

And that, for the moment, is that. You have loaded the file into the in-memory data model in a matter of a few clicks, and it is ready for use in dashboards and reports. The data itself is not visible for the moment, but it can be accessed using Power Pivot, as you will discover in Chapter 14. Alternatively, you can use it immediately to create Power View dashboards.

The important thing to note here is that although you used two completely different data sources in these first two examples, the process that you applied was virtually identical. This really is one of the great strengths of Get & Transform.

Understanding CSV Files

Before moving on to other file types, there are a few comments I need to make about CSV files. There is a technical specification of what a "true" CSV file is, but I won't bore you with that. What's more, many programs that generate CSV files do not always follow the definition exactly. What matters is that Excel 2016 can handle text files that have the following characteristics:

- Have a .csv extension (it uses this by default to apply the right kind of processing).

- Use a comma to separate the elements in a row. This, too, is a default that can be overridden.

- End with a line feed, carriage return, or line feed/carriage return.

- Can, optionally, contain double quotes to encapsulate fields. These will be stripped out as part of the data load process. If there are double quotes, they do not have to appear for every field, nor even for every record in a field that can have occasionally inconsistent double quotes.

- Can contain "irregular" records; that is, rows that do not have every element found in a standard record. However, the first row (whether it contains titles) must cover every element found in all the remaining records in the list. Put simply, any other record can be shorter than the first one but cannot be longer.

- Do not contain anything other than the data table. If the file contains header rows or footer rows that are not part of the data, then Excel 2016 cannot load the data table without further work. There are workarounds to this all-too-frequent problem; one (parsing data) is given in Chapter 12.

Text Files

If you followed the process for loading a CSV file in the previous section, then you will find that loading a text file is similar. This is not surprising. Both are, in essence, text files, and both should contain a single list of data. The following are the core differences:

- A text file can have something *other* than a comma to separate the elements in a list. You can specify the delimiter when defining the load step.

- A text file should normally have the extension .txt (though this, too, can be overridden).

- A text file *must* be perfectly formed; that is, every record (row) must have the same number of elements as every other record.

- A text file, too, *must not* contain anything other than the data table if you want a flawless data load the first time.

- If a text file encounters difficulties, it should import the data as a single column that you can then try to split up into multiple columns, as described in Chapter 12.

Here, then, is how to load a text file into Excel 2016:

1. In the Data ribbon, click New Query ➤ From File ➤ From Text. The Import Data dialog will open.

2. Navigate to the folder containing the file and select the file (C:\ DataVisualisationInExcel2016\CountryList.txt, in this example).

3. Click Import. The Excel 2016 Get & Transform Query Editor window appears; it contains the contents of the text file.

4. Click the Close icon for the Query Editor window (because after a quick look at the contents of the file, you have decided that you do not really need it). A confirmation dialog like the one in Figure 10-8 will appear.

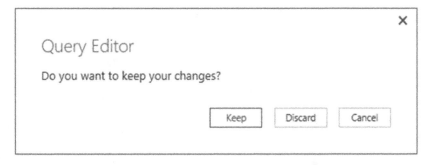

Figure 10-8. *The Query Editor cancellation confirmation dialog*

5. Click Discard. The data will not be loaded anywhere, and the query will not be created. Consequently, it will not appear in the Workbook Queries pane.

Where Excel 2016 is really clever is that it can make an educated guess as to how the text file is structured; that is, it can nearly always guess the field separator (the character that isolates each element in a list from the other elements). So, not only will it break the list into columns, but it will also avoid importing the column separator. If it does not guess correctly, then don't despair. You will learn how to correct this in Chapter 12.

Looking at the contents of a file and then deciding not to use it is part and parcel of the *data discovery* process that you will find yourself using when you work with Excel 2016. The point of this exercise is to show you how easy it is to glance inside potential data sources and then decide whether to import them into the data model.

■ **Tip**   At the risk of stating the obvious, you can press Enter to accept a default choice in a dialog and press Esc to cancel out of the dialog.

XML Files

Extensible Markup Language (XML) is a standard means of sending data between IT systems. Consequently, you have every chance of having to load an XML file one day. Although an XML file is just text, it is text that has been formatted in a specific way, as you can see if you ever open an XML file in a text editor such as Notepad. Do the following to load an XML file:

1. In the Data ribbon, click New Query and then click From File and then From XML.

2. Navigate to the folder containing the file and select the file (C:\ DataVisualisationInExcel2016\ColoursTable.xml, in this example).

3. Click Import. The Navigator dialog will open.

4. Click the Colors table in the left pane of the Navigator dialog. The contents of the XML file will be displayed on the right of the Navigator dialog, as shown in Figure 10-9.

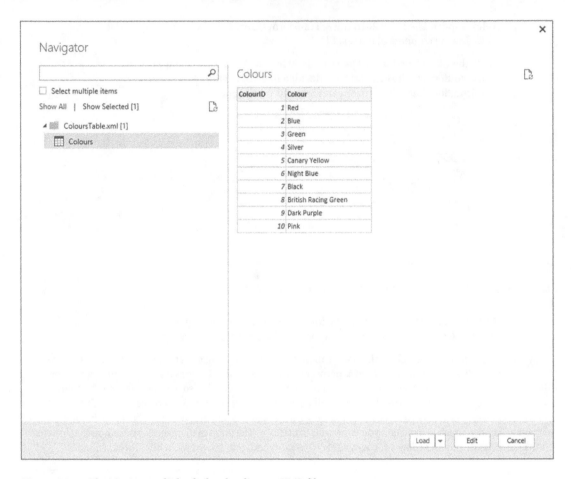

Figure 10-9. *The Navigator dialog before loading an XML file*

5. Click the check box to the left of the Colors table on the left.

6. Click the Edit button. The Get & Transform Query Editor window will display the contents of the XML file.

7. Click the downward-facing triangle on the Load button and select Load To. The Load To dialog will appear.

8. Select Only Create Connection and check the Add This Data To The Data Model check box.

9. Click Load. The data will be loaded into the data model but not into a worksheet, and the query that you just created will be added to the Workbook Queries pane.

The actual internal format of an XML file can get extremely complex. Sometimes an XML file will contain only one data table; sometimes it will contain many separate data tables. On other occasions, it will contain one table whose records contain nested levels of data that you need to handle by expanding or aggregating. These techniques are described later in this chapter in the context of database sources.

■ **Note**   Certain types of data sources allow you to load multiple sets of data simultaneously. XML files (unlike CSV and text files) can contain multiple independent data sets. You can load several "tables" of data simultaneously by selecting the check box to the left of each data set that you want to load from the XML file *if* you have checked the Select Multiple Items check box in the Navigator dialog.

Excel

You are probably already a major Excel user and have many, many spreadsheets full of data that you want to rationalize and use for analysis and presentation. So, let's see how to load the contents of an Excel file.

1. In the Data ribbon, click the small triangle at the bottom of the New Query button and then click From File ➤ From Workbook.

2. Navigate to the directory containing the file that you want to look at (C:\ DataVisualisationInExcel2016, in this example).

3. Select the source file (InvoicesAndInvoiceLines.xlsx, in this example) and click Import. The Navigator dialog will appear, showing the worksheets, tables, and ranges in the workbook file, as shown in Figure 10-10.

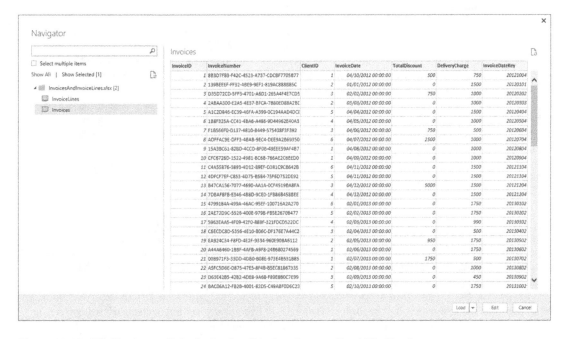

Figure 10-10. The Navigator dialog before loading data from an Excel Workbook

4. Click one of the tables listed on the left of the Navigator dialog. The top few rows of the selected spreadsheet will appear on the right of the dialog to show you what the data in the chosen table looks like.

5. Check the Select Multiple Items check box.

6.   Click the check boxes to the left of the Invoices and InvoiceLines tables on the left.

7.   Click the downward-facing triangle in the Load button of the Navigator dialog.

8.   Select Load To. The Load To dialog will appear.

9.   Select Only Create Connection, check the Add This Data To The Data Model check box, and click Load. The selected worksheets will be loaded into the Excel 2016 data model and will appear in the Workbook Queries pane.

As you can see from this simple example, having Get & Transform read Excel data is really not difficult. You could have edited this data in the Get & Transform Query Editor before loading it, but as the data seemed clean and ready to use, I preferred to load it straight into Excel 2016 (or rather the Excel 2016 data model). As well, you saw that Excel 2016 can load multiple tables at the same time from a single data source. Finally, you saw that you can load data into the data model directly from the Navigator dialog without having to open the Get & Transform Query Editor as was the case in the previous examples.

However, you might still be wondering about a couple of things that you saw during this process, so here are some anticipatory comments.

The Navigator dialog displays the following:

- Worksheets

- Named ranges

- Named tables

Each of these elements is represented by a different icon in the Navigator dialog. Sometimes these can, in effect, be duplicate references to the same data, so you should really use the most precise data source that you can. For instance, I advise using a named table or a range name rather than a worksheet source, as the latter could easily end up containing "noise" data (that is, data from outside the rows and columns that interest you), which would make the load process more complex than it really needs to be.

Get & Transform will list and use data connections to external data sources in a source Excel workbook *if* the data connection is active and has returned data to the workbook. Once a link to Excel 2016 has been established, you can delete the data table itself in the source Excel workbook—and still use Get & Transform to load the data over the data connection in the source workbook.

Get & Transform will not take into account any data filters on an Excel data table. Consequently, you will have to reapply any filters (of which you'll learn more in the next chapter) in Get & Transform if you want to subset the source data.

Adding Data from Excel Tables inside the Current Workbook

There could well be occasions when you need to add a small amount of data to a data model to complete it. Perhaps you have some lookup data that is needed or maybe a time dimension like the one that you will meet in Chapter 17.

In any case, Get & Transform offers a fast and easy way to add data from the current Excel workbook. As an example, imagine that you have some data already in Excel and you want to cleanse it using Get & Transform. To load the data directly from a worksheet, follow these steps:

1.   Open the sample file `C:\DataVisualisationInExcel2016\ BrilliantBritishCars.xlsx`.

2.   Click anywhere inside the table of data.

3.   In the Data ribbon, click From Table. The Create Table dialog will appear, as shown in Figure 10-11. (Of course, if your data is already an Excel table, then you will not see this dialog.)

Figure 10-11. *The Create Table dialog*

4. Click OK. The Get & Transform Query Editor window will open and display the data from the Excel table. You can then proceed to cleanse and mash up the data or load it directly into the in-memory data model.

Microsoft Access Databases

Another well-used data repository that proliferates in many corporations today is Microsoft Access. It is a powerful relational desktop database and can contain multiple tables, each containing millions of records. So, you need to see how to load data from this particular source. Because this process uses the same dialogs that you saw previously, I will not show them again here.

1. In the Data ribbon, click New Query ➤ From Database ➤ From Microsoft Access Database.

2. Navigate to the Microsoft Access database containing the data that you want to load (C:\DataVisualisationInExcel2016\ClientsDatabase.accdb in this example).

3. Select the Access file and click Import. The Navigator dialog appears; it lists all the tables and queries in the Access database.

4. Select the ClientList table (or select the check box for this table if the Select Multiple Items check box is selected). The "tables" can also be Access queries.

5. Click the downward-facing triangle in the Load button of the Navigator dialog.

6. Select Load To. The Load To dialog will appear.

7. Select Only Create Connection, check the Add This Data To The Data Model check box, and click Load. The selected Access data tables or queries will be loaded into the Excel 2016 data model and will appear in the Workbook Queries pane.

I am sure that you can see a pattern emerging here. Indeed, this pattern will continue as you progress to loading tables from relational databases in a few pages. The process nearly always consists of the following:

•   Knowing the type of source data that you want to look at

•   Finding the file, database, or connection that lets you access the data

•   Examining the data tables and selecting the ones you want to load

■ **Note**   Excel 2016 cannot see linked tables, only imported tables or tables that are actually in the Access database. It can, however, read queries overlaid upon native, linked, or imported data.

Once you have loaded the Excel, XML, CSV, and Microsoft Access data, the Workbook Queries pane should look something like the one in Figure 10-12.

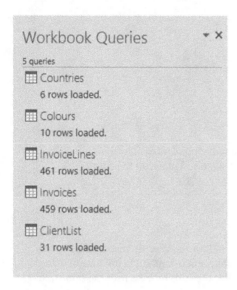

Figure 10-12. *The Workbook Queries pane after loading several different data sources*

To conclude this short introduction, save the Excel 2016 file as `CarSalesFirstDashboard.xlsx`.

Relational Databases: SQL Server

Enterprise-grade relational databases still hold much of the world's data, so you really need to know how to tap into the vast mines of information that they contain. The bad news is that there are many, many databases out there, each with their intricacies and quirks. The good news is that once you have learned to load data from *one* of them, you should be able to use *any* of them.

Here I will use the Microsoft enterprise relational database—SQL Server—as an example to show you how to load data from a database into Excel 2016. The first advantage of this setup is that you probably do not need to install any software to enable access to SQL Server (although this is not always the case, so talk this through with your IT department). A second advantage is that the techniques are pretty similar to those used and applied by Oracle, DB2, and the other databases to which Get & Transform in Excel 2016 can connect. Furthermore, you can load multiple tables or views from a database at once. To see this in action (and presuming that you have created the database CarSalesData as described in Appendix B), take the following steps:

1. Open a new Excel 2016 workbook.

2. In the Data ribbon, click the small triangle at the bottom of the New Query button and then click From Database ➤ From SQL Server Database. The SQL Server Database dialog will appear.

3. Enter the server name in the Server text box. This will be the name of your SQL Server or one of the SQL Server resources used by your organization.

4. Enter the database name; if you are using the sample data, it will be CarSalesData. The dialog will look like Figure 10-13.

Figure 10-13. *The Microsoft SQL Database dialog*

5. Click OK. The Access A SQL Server Database dialog will appear. Assuming that you are authorized to use your Windows login to connect to the database, leave Use My Current Credentials selected, as shown in Figure 10-14.

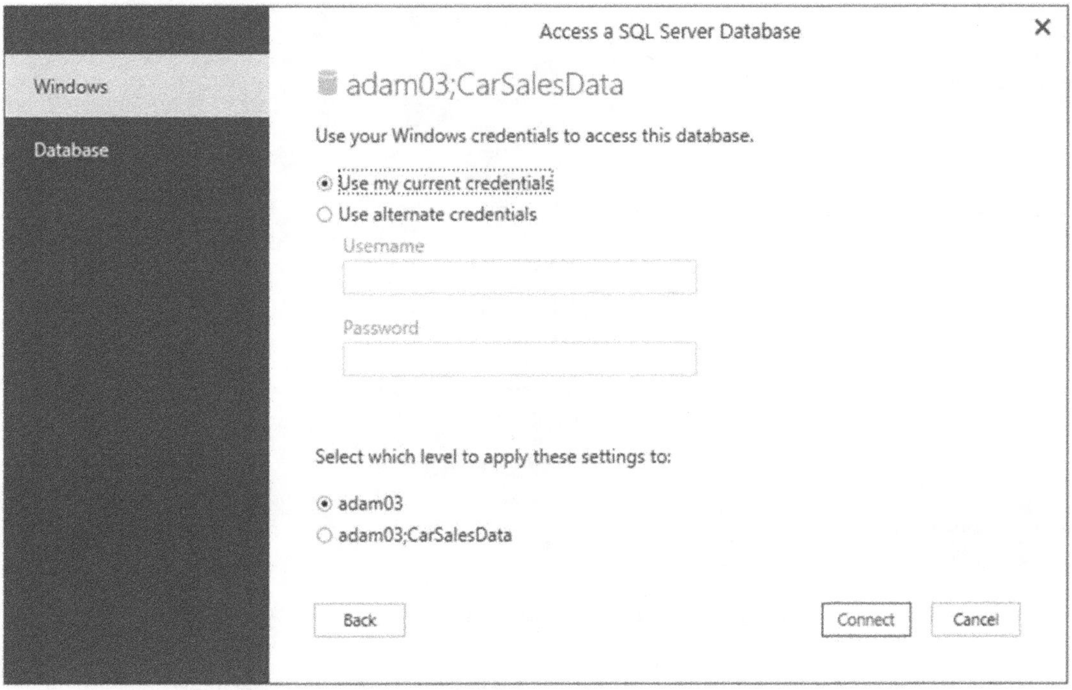

Figure 10-14. *The Access A SQL Server Database dialog*

6. Click Connect. Excel 2016 will connect to the server and display the Navigator dialog containing all the tables and views in the database that you have permission to see on the server you selected. In some cases, you could see a dialog saying that the data source does not support encryption. If you feel happy with an unencrypted connection, then click the OK button for this dialog.

7. Click the Select Multiple Items check box.

8. Click the check boxes for the Clients, Colors, Countries, Invoices, InvoiceLines, and Stock tables. The data for the most recently selected data appears on the right of the Navigator dialog, as shown in Figure 10-15.

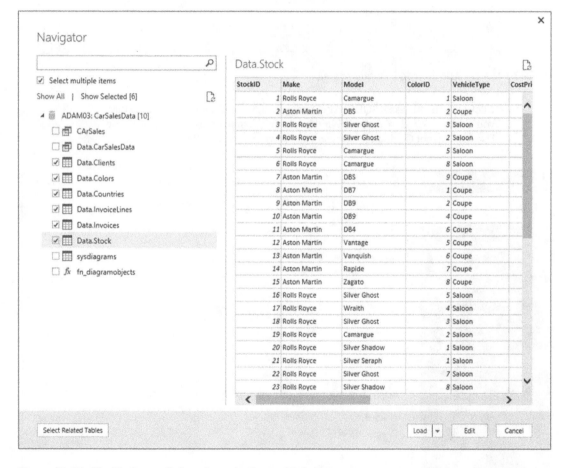

Figure 10-15. *The Navigator dialog when selecting multiple items*

9. Click the downward-facing triangle in the Load button of the Navigator dialog.

10. Select Load To. The Load To dialog will appear.

11. Ensure that the Only Create Connection radio button and the Add This Data To The Data Model check box are selected and click Load. The selected SQL Server data tables or views will be loaded into the Excel 2016 data model, and a query for each table or view will appear in the Workbook Queries pane.

Since this is similar to the way in which you loaded data from Access, I imagine that you are getting the hang of things by now. Interestingly, Get & Transform defaults to loading data from databases into the data model, which is understandable as you could be ingesting large amounts of data when using database sources.

▓ **Tip** When selecting multiple tables or views, you will only ever see the contents of a single data source in the Navigator dialog. However, you can preview the contents of any of the selected data sources (or even any that are not selected) simply by clicking the table or view name. This will not affect the choice of selected tables and views that you want to load into Excel 2016.

Automatically Loading Related Tables

Relational databases are nearly always intricate structures composed of many interdependent tables. Indeed, you will frequently need to load several tables to obtain all the data you need.

Knowing which tables to select is not always easy. Excel 2016 tries to help you by automatically detecting the links between tables in the source database; this way, you can rapidly isolate the collections of tables that have been designed to work together.

Do the following to see a related group of tables:

1. Connect to the source database as described in the previous section.

2. In the Navigator dialog, click a table that contains data you need.

3. Click the Select Related Tables button.

Any tables that are linked in the database are selected. You can deselect any tables that you do not want, of course. More importantly, you can click the names of the selected tables to see their contents.

Database Options

The world of relational databases is—fortunately or unfortunately—a little more complex than the world of files or Microsoft Access. Consequently, there are a few comments to make about using databases as a data source, specifically, how to connect to them.

First, let's cover the initial connection to the server. The options are explained in Table 10-5.

Table 10-5. *Database Connection Options*

Option	Comments
Server	You cannot browse to find the server, and you need to type or paste the server name. If the server has an instance name, you need to enter the server and the instance. Your IT department will be able to supply this if you are working in a corporate environment.
Database	If you know the database, then you can enter (or paste) it here. This restricts the number of available tables in the Navigator dialog and makes finding the correct table or view easier.
SQL statement	You can enter a valid snippet of T-SQL that returns data from the database.

▓ **Note** These options apply to most databases and certainly to SQL Server. However, they vary slightly depending on the make of database you are connecting to.

These options probably require a little more explanation. So, let's look at each one in turn.

Server Connection

It is fundamental that you know the exact connection string for the database you want to connect to. This could be the following:

- The database server name

- The database server name, a backslash, and an instance name (if there is one)

- The database server IP address

- The database server IP address, a backslash, and an instance name (if there is one)

■ **Note**   A database instance is a separate SQL Server service running alongside others on the same physical or virtual server. You will always need both the server and this instance name (if there is one) to successfully connect.

■ **Tip**   If you are connecting to a SQL Server database on your PC (as might be the case if you have installed the sample database available with this book), then you can simply enter a period (.) or the word **localhost** as the server name.

Most SQL Server instances host many, many databases. Sometimes these can number in the hundreds. Sometimes, inevitably, you cannot remember which database you want to connect to. Fortunately, Excel 2016 can let you browse the databases on a server. For this, do the following:

1. In the Data ribbon, click the small triangle at the bottom of the New Query button and then click From Database ➤ From SQL Server Database. The SQL Server Database dialog will appear.

2. Enter the server name in the Server text box and click OK. The Navigator window opens, as shown in Figure 10-16. Of course, the actual contents depend on the server you are connecting to.

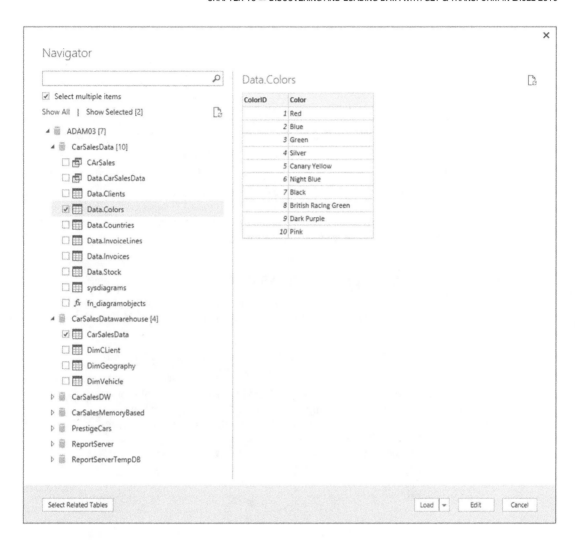

Figure 10-16. *The Navigator dialog when selecting databases*

You can see from Figure 10-11 that if you click the small triangle to the left of a database, then you are able to see all the tables and views that are accessible to you in this database. Although this can mean an overabundance of possible choices when looking for the table(s) or view(s) that you want, it is nonetheless a convenient way of reminding you of the name of the data set that you require.

■ **Tip**　If you are swamped by the sheer number of tables in the Navigator dialog, then you can always click Show Selected above the list of tables. This displays only selected tables in the Navigator window. Inversely, clicking Show All reverts to the display of all the available tables in the database.

As a final point when loading data from databases (be they SQL Server or any of the other databases that Get & Transform can use), remember that you can load data from *multiple databases on the same server* at the same time. You can see this in Figure 10-15 where data tables in two separate databases are selected and will load in a single process, but as separate queries, of course.

Searching for Databases, Tables, and Views in Navigator

If you are swamped by the sheer volume of table(s) and view(s) that appear in the left panel of the Navigator dialog, then you can use Navigator's built-in search facility to help you to narrow down the set of potential data sources. For this, do the following:

1. Carry out steps 1 and 2 in the earlier "Relational Databases: SQL Server" section to connect to a SQL Server instance *without* specifying a database.

2. Enter a few characters that you know are contained in the name of the table or view that you are looking for in the empty field on the top left of the Navigator dialog. This is called the *search box*. Entering, for example, **car** on my server gives the result that you see in Figure 10-17. As you can see, the characters that you entered are highlighted in the database objects that are listed.

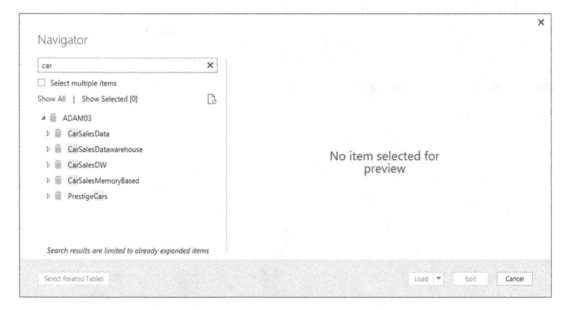

Figure 10-17.　*Using search with Navigator*

You can enter the text in uppercase or lowercase, and the text can appear anywhere in the names of the tables or views—not just at the start of the name. With every character that you type, the list of potential matches get shorter and shorter. Once you have found the data set that you are looking for, simply proceed as described earlier to load the data into Excel 2016.

If your search does not return the subset of tables in any views that you were expecting, all you have to do is to click the X at the right of the search box. This cancels the search and displays all the available tables, as well as clears the search box.

If you are not convinced that you are seeing all the tables and views that are in the database, then click the small icon at the bottom right of the search box (it looks like a small page with two green circular arrows). This is the Refresh button, which refreshes the connection to the database and displays all the tables and views that you have permission to see.

■ **Note** Navigator search also looks for database names.

Database Security

Remember that databases are designed to be extremely secure. Consequently, you only see servers, databases, tables, and views if you are authorized to access them. You might have to talk to your IT department to ensure that you have the required permissions; otherwise, the table you are looking for could be in the database but remain invisible to you.

■ **Tip** If you experience a connection error when first attempting to connect to SQL Server, simply click the Edit button to return to the Microsoft SQL Database dialog and correct any mistakes. This avoids having to start over.

Using a SQL Statement

If there is a downside to using a relational database such as SQL Server as a data source, it is that the sheer amount of data that the database stores—even in a single table—can be dauntingly huge. Fortunately, all the resources of SQL Server can be used to filter the data that is used by Excel 2016 before you even load the data. This way, you do not have to load entire tables of data at the risk of drowning in information before you have even started to analyze it.

The following are SQL Server techniques that you can use to extend the partnership between SQL Server and Excel 2016:

- SQL SELECT statements

- Stored procedures

- Table-valued functions

These are, admittedly, fairly technical solutions. Indeed, if you are not a database specialist, you could well require the services of your IT department to use these options to access data in the server. Nonetheless, it is worth taking a quick look at these techniques in case they are useful one day.

Any of these options can be applied from the SQL Server Database dialog. Here is an example of how to filter data from a database table using a SELECT statement:

1. In the Excel 2016 ribbon, click the small triangle at the bottom of the New Query button and then click SQL Server. The SQL Server Database dialog will appear.

2. Enter the server name and the database.

3. Click the triangle to the left of SQL Statement (Optional). This opens a box where you can enter an SQL command.

4. Enter the SQL command that you want to apply. In this case, it is SELECT ClientName, Town, Region FROM Data.Clients ORDER BY ClientID. The dialog will look like Figure 10-18.

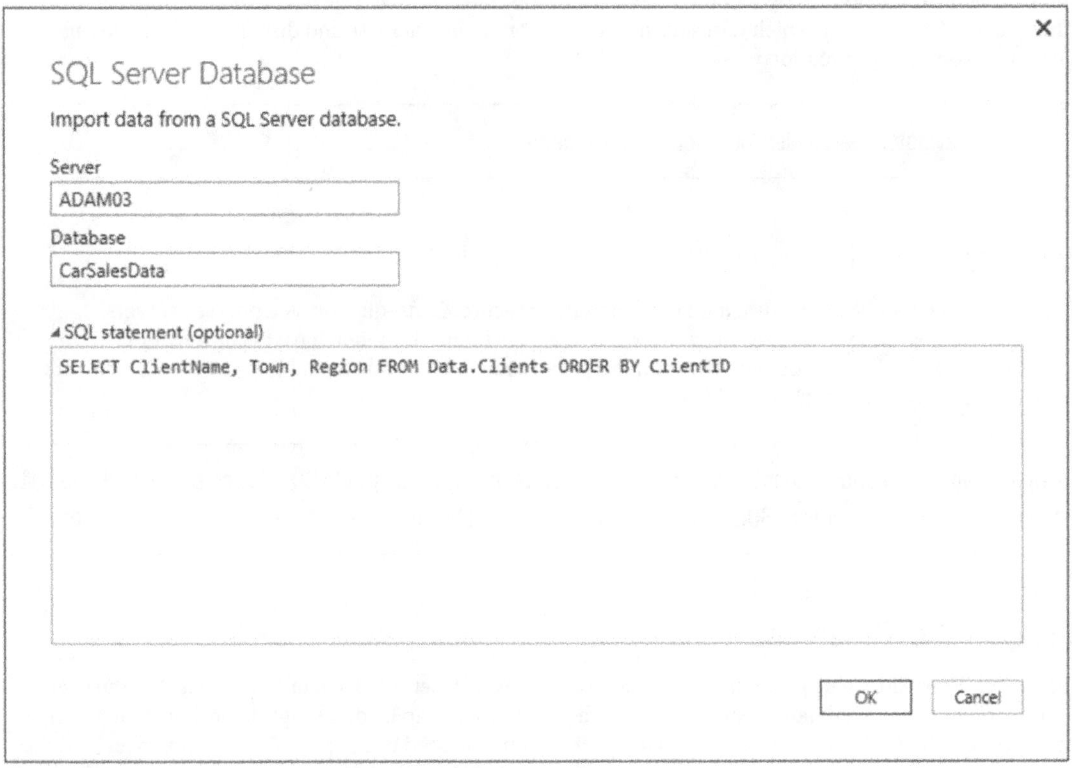

Figure 10-18. Using SQL to select database data

5. Click OK. The Get & Transform Query Editor will open, looking like the one shown in Figure 10-19.

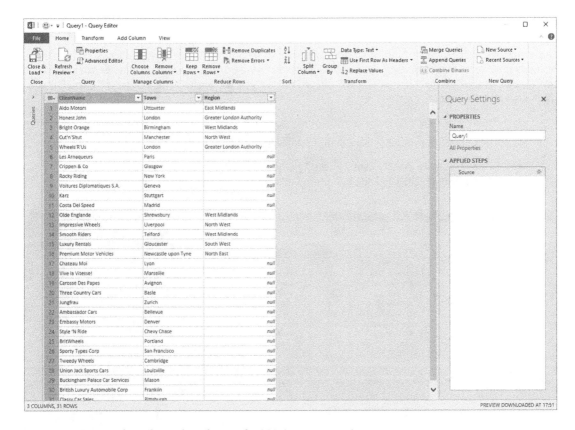

Figure 10-19. *Database data selected using the SQL Statement option*

6.   Click Close & Load or Edit to continue with the data load process. Alternatively, you can close the window and discard the connection to start a different data load.

The same principles apply when using stored procedures of functions to return data from SQL Server. You will always use the SQL Statement option to enter the command that will return the data. Unfortunately, the world of relational databases is huge; much, much more could be said at this point. I am afraid that I simply do not have the space to devote to all the subtleties of how you can use the available relational database sources, however. Just remember that to call a SQL Server stored procedure or function, you would enter the following elements into the Microsoft SQL Database dialog:

- *Server*: <your server name>

- *Database*: <the database name>

- *SQL statement*: EXEC <enter the schema (if there is one, followed by a period) and the stored procedure name, followed by any parameters

This way, either you or your IT department can create complex and secure ways to allow data from the corporate databases to be read into Excel 2016 from enterprise databases.

Editing Existing Queries

Clearly you will not spend all your time creating new queries using Get & Transform. Indeed, you will probably spend a lot of your time working with data in modifying existing queries. So, you need to know how to edit existing queries. Once you have displayed the Workbook Queries pane, Get & Transform lets you choose from the following:

- Double-click a query.

- Right-click a query and select Edit from the context menu.

- Hover the mouse pointer over a query. The "peek" window will appear (as you can see in Figure 10-20). Click the Edit button in the peek window.

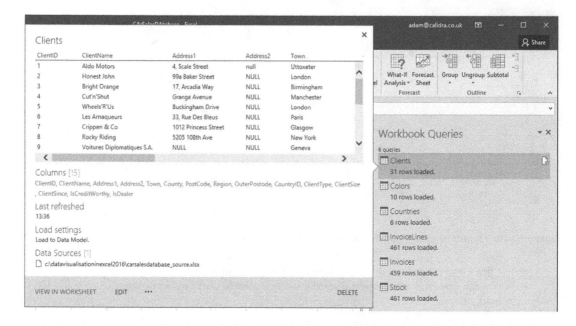

Figure 10-20. *The peek window*

As you can see, the peek window is a great way to take a sneak look at the data that will be returned by a query.

Microsoft SQL Server Analysis Services Data Sources

An Analysis Services database is a data warehouse technology that can contain a vast amount of data that has been optimized to enable decision-making. *SSAS cubes* (as these databases are also called) are composed of facts (measures or values) and dimensions (descriptive attributes). If your enterprise uses Analysis Services databases, you can access them by following these steps:

1. In the Excel 2016 Data ribbon, click New Query ➤ From Database ➤ From SQL Server Analysis Services Database in the New Query dialog.

2. Click Connect. The SQL Server Analysis Services Database dialog will appear.

3. Enter the Analysis Services server name and the database (or *cube*) name, if you know it. If you are using the sample data from the Apress site for this book, the database is CarSalesOLAP; otherwise, you have to specify your own SSAS server name. The dialog will look like Figure 10-21.

Figure 10-21. Connecting to the SSAS (multidimensional) database

4. Click OK. If this is the first time you are connecting to the cube, then the Access SQL Server Analysis Service dialog will appear so that you can define the credentials that you are using to connect to the Analysis Services database, as shown in Figure 10-22.

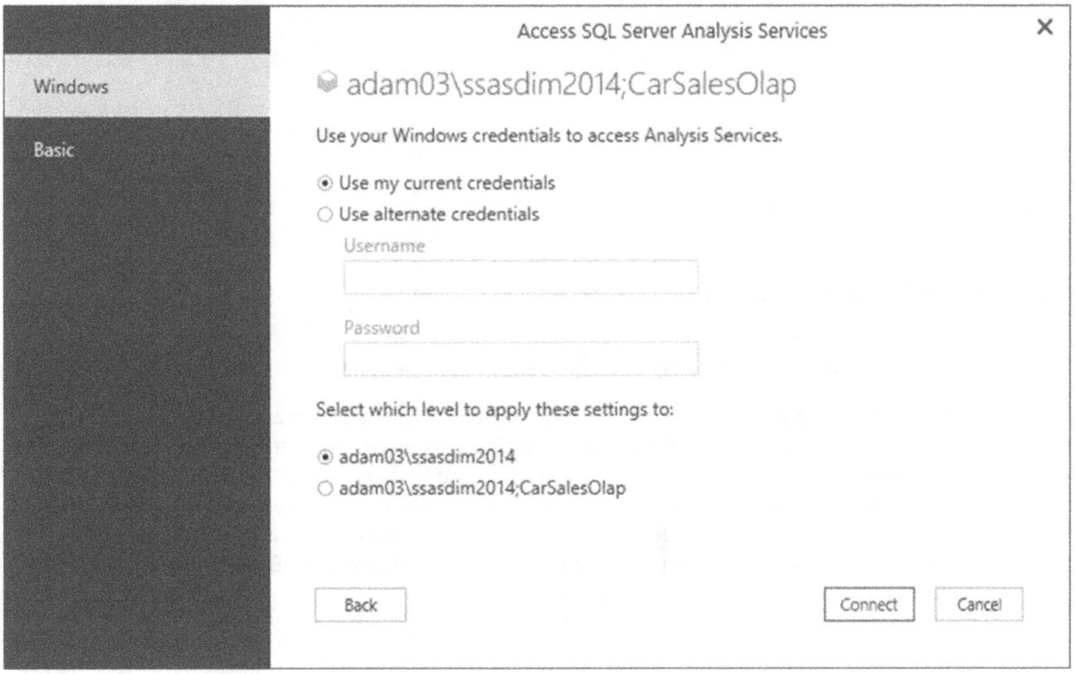

Figure 10-22. SQL Server Analysis Services credentials dialog

5.   Accept or alter the credentials and click Connect. The Navigator dialog will appear.

6.   Expand the folders on the left pane of the dialog. This way, you can see all the fact tables and dimensions contained in the data warehouse.

7.   Select the fact tables, dimensions, or even only the dimension elements and measures that you want to load. The dialog will look something like Figure 10-23.

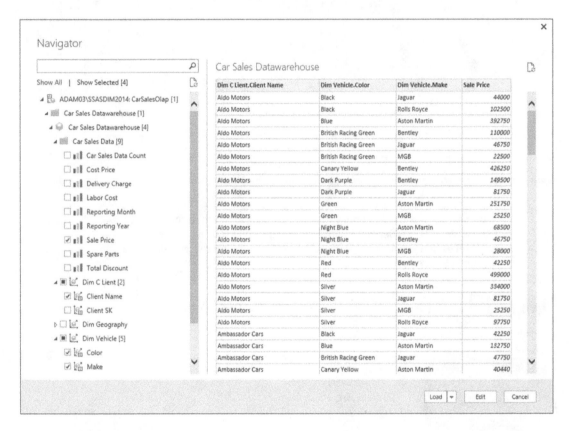

Figure 10-23. *Selecting attributes and measures from the SSAS cube*

8.   Click Load. The data will be loaded into a new worksheet in Excel.

SSAS cubes are potentially huge. They can contain dozens of dimensions, many fact tables, and hundreds of measures and attributes. Understanding multidimensional cubes and how they work is beyond the scope of this book. Nonetheless, it is important to understand that for Excel 2016 a cube is just another data source. This means you can be extremely selective as to the cube elements that you load into Excel 2016 and load only the elements that you need for your analysis. You can load entire dimensions or just a few attributes, just like you can load whole fact tables or just a selection of measures. Equally you can search for elements in SSAS cubes just as you can in relational databases.

Note You can filter the data that is loaded from an SSAS cube by expanding the MDX Or DAX Query (Optional) item in the SQL Server Analysis Services Database dialog. Then you can enter an MDX query in the box that appears before clicking OK. Be warned that SSAS cubes use queries written in MDX—a specialist language that is considered not always easy to learn.

Analysis Services data sources allow you to tweak the selection of source elements in a way that is not available with other data sources. Essentially, you have two extra options.

- Add Items
- Collapse Columns

Add Items

When using an SSAS data source, you can at any time add any attributes or measures that you either forgot or thought that you would not need when setting up the initial connection.

1. In the Workbook Queries pane, double-click the SSAS query that you previously established. The Query Editor window will open, and the Manage ribbon will appear, as shown in Figure 10-24.

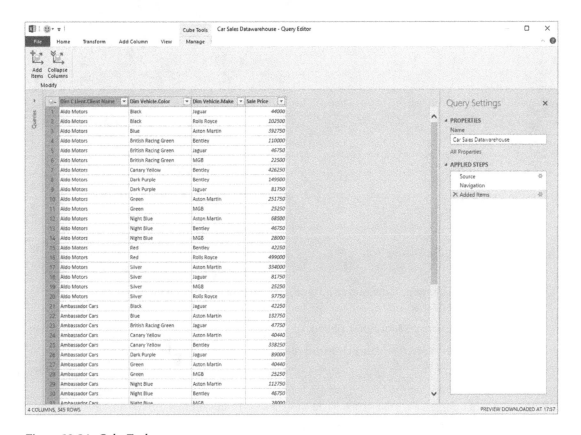

Figure 10-24. *Cube Tools*

2. In the Manage ribbon, click the Add Items button. The Add Items dialog will appear.

3. Expand any measure groups and select all the measures and attributes that you want to add, as shown in Figure 10-25.

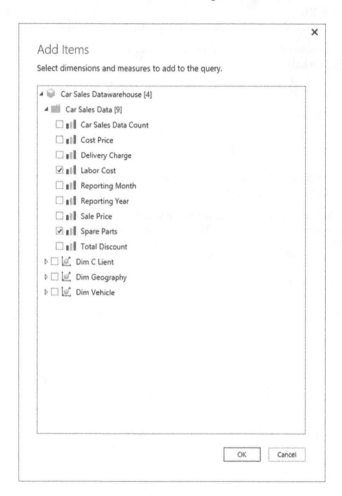

Figure 10-25. The Add Items dialog

4. Click OK. The selected measures and attributes are added as new columns at the right of the data set.

5. Display the Query Editor Home ribbon.

6. Click Close & Load. The data in the worksheet will be extended to include the elements you have added.

▪ **Note** Get & Transform will not detect if any new measures and attributes that you add are already in the data set. So, if you add an element twice, it will appear *twice* in the query.

Collapse Columns

Do the following to remove any columns that you no longer require from the data source (which can accelerate data refresh):

1. In the Get & Transform Query pane, double-click the SSAS query that you previously established. (The sample data for this connection will be displayed in the center of the Query window.) The Manage ribbon will appear.

2. In the Manage ribbon, click the Collapse Columns button.

The columns are removed from the connection to the SSAS cube and, consequently, from the Fields list at the right of the Query Editor window. They are also removed from any visualizations that use them.

■ **Note**   Removing columns from a Get & Transform query can have a serious domino effect on reports and dashboards. Consequently, you need to be careful when removing them.

Microsoft SQL Server Analysis Services Tabular Data Sources

A SQL Server Analysis Services tabular database is another technology that is used for data warehousing. It is different from the more traditional dimensional data warehouse in that it is entirely stored in the server memory and, consequently, is usually much faster to use.

Connecting to a tabular data warehouse is identical to connecting to a traditional SSAS cube, so I will not explain it here. All you have to do is follow the steps that you used in the previous section to connect to a SQL Server Analysis Services data source; you just enter the tabular database server and database. If you want to filter the data that is returned, then you can use the DAX language to return only a subset of the available data.

Other Data Sources

So far in this chapter, you saw how to load data from a handful of the more frequently used available sources. The good news is that Excel 2016 can read data from dozens more sources. The bad news is that it would take a whole book to go into all of them in detail.

So, I will not be describing any other data sources in this book. This is because now that you have come to appreciate the core techniques that make up the extremely standardized approach that Get & Transform in Excel 2016 takes to loading data, you can probably load any possible data type without needing much more information from me.

Reusing Recent Data Sources

Given the myriad of data sources that Excel 2016 can connect to, it is easy to lose track of which data set is contained in what database. This could make returning to a previous connection a matter of trial and error. Fortunately, the Excel 2016 team has sought to make your life easier. Excel 2016 remembers the last couple of dozen connections that you have made, whatever the data source, and allows you to reconnect to a data source from any Excel 2016 application.

Reusing a Data Source

Do the following to reuse a data source that you have connected to recently:

1. In the Excel 2016 Data ribbon, click the Recent Sources button. A dialog of recently used data sources will appear. On my laptop, the list looks like the one shown in Figure 10-26.

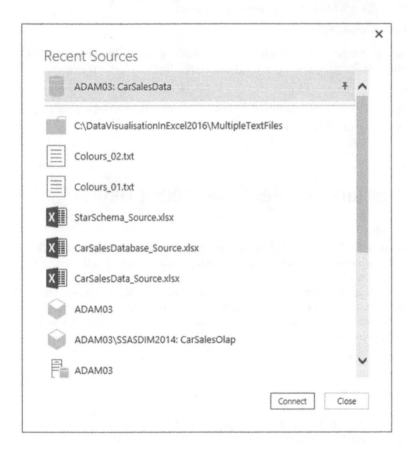

Figure 10-26. *The Recent Sources list*

2. Click the data source that you want to use again and click Connect.

From here, you can continue to select the data that you want from the data source, just as if you had reestablished a connection. As you can see, Excel 2016 has memorized any security information and will not ask you to reenter passwords or choose a security method. It is worth noting that it is only the data source that is memorized by Excel 2016. The application does not remember the selected tables, views, spreadsheets, named ranges, fact tables, or dimensions that you used previously. Consequently, you have to reselect them.

If you cannot see the connection that you were hoping for in the menu of recent sources, then do not despair. If you scroll to the bottom of the list of recent sources, you will find a More option. Clicking this displays the Recent Sources dialog, which contains a much bigger list of recently used data sources.

Pinning a Data Source

If you look closely at Figure 10-22, you see that the database connection ADAM03:CarSalesData is pinned to the top of both the Recent Sources menu and the Recent Sources dialog. This allows you to make sure that certain data sources are always kept on hand and ready to reuse.

Do the following to pin a data source that you have recently used to the menu and dialog of recent sources:

1. Click the Recent Sources button in the Excel 2016 Home ribbon.

2. Scroll down to the bottom of the menu and click More. The Recent Sources dialog will appear.

3. Hover the mouse over a recently used data source. A pin icon will appear at the right of the data source name.

4. Click the pin icon. The data source is pinned to the top of both the Recent Sources menu and the Recent Sources dialog. A small pin icon remains visible at the right of the data source name.

■ **Note**   To unpin a data source from the Recent Sources menu and the Recent Sources dialog, all you have to do is click the pin icon for a pinned data source. This unpins it, and it reappears in the list of recently used data sources.

Old Data

When you open a Excel 2016 file that you have not used in some time, you could well see a message above the data pane indicating that the data ingested using Get & Transform is old and potentially out of date.

Simply click the Refresh button (if that is what you want to do). The preview data is refreshed, and the latest data is loaded.

■ **Tip**   You do not have to exit the Get & Transform Query Editor to create a new query. All you have to do is to switch to the Home ribbon and click the New Source button (or even the Recent Sources button) to add a new query.

Connection Security

BI with Excel 2016 is not just about accessing data when you want and creating awesome dashboards. It is also about speed. One way that it can help you to work faster is by remembering the security information that you entered when connecting to secure data sources such as databases and data warehouses.

Secure credentials can evolve, and consequently, you may need to change your login or password occasionally. You could even want to remove security information from Excel 2016 from time to time. Here is how you can do this:

1. In the Data ribbon, click the New Query button and select Data Source Settings. The Data Source Settings dialog will appear, as shown in Figure 10-27.

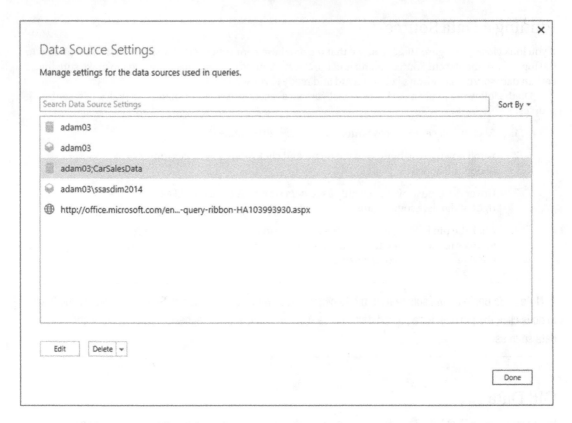

Figure 10-27. *The Data Source Settings dialog*

2. Select a data source that you want to modify and click Edit. The Edit Data Source Settings dialog will appear, as shown in Figure 10-28.

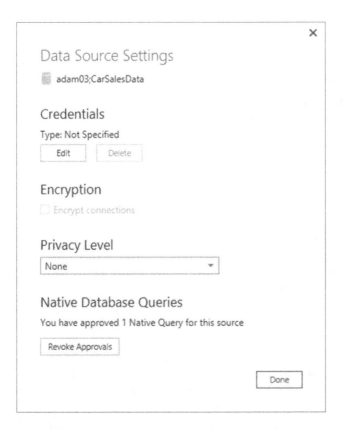

Figure 10-28. *The Edit Data Source Settings dialog*

3. Click Edit to display the credentials dialog (as shown in Figure 10-16). You can modify your login and password here.

4. Once you have finished any necessary modifications, click Done.

The Edit Data Source Settings dialog also lets you do the following:

- Delete (revoke, if you prefer) the existing credentials

- Force encryption of the data over the connection

- Define a privacy level

- Revoke approval for native database queries

The Data Source Settings dialog also lets you delete the data source settings for any selected data source—or all of them.

Modifying Data Sources

Follow these steps:

1.   Click the File menu option in Get & Transform.

2.   Select Options and Settings ➤ Data Source Settings. The Data Source Settings dialog will appear showing your recently used data sources. You can see an example of this in Figure 10-29.

Figure 10-29.   *The Data Source Settings dialog*

3.   Click one of the data sources and click Edit (or double-click the data source if you prefer). The Data Source Settings details dialog will appear. You can see an example of this in Figure 10-30.

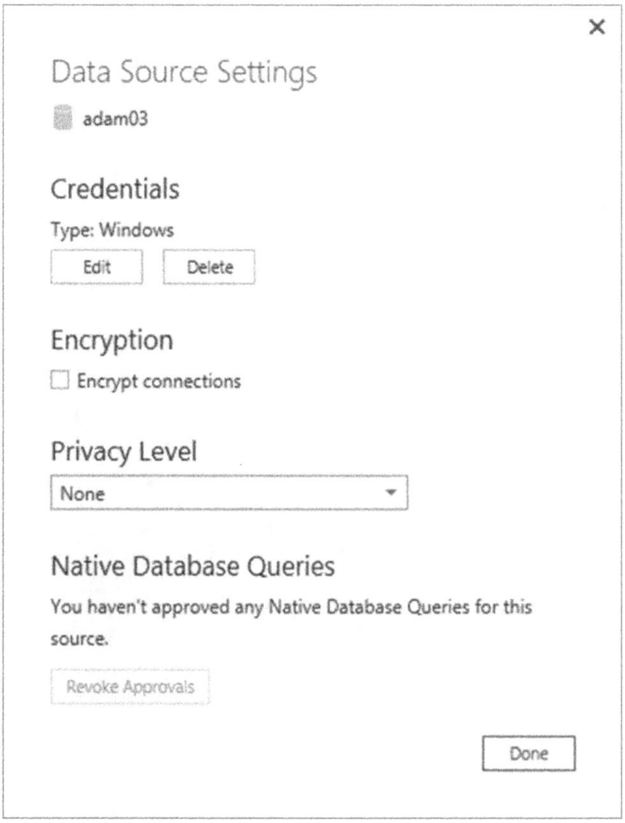

Figure 10-30. *The Data Source Settings options dialog*

4.   Make any changes that you need to the available options and click Done twice.

Conclusion

In this chapter, you saw how the coolest addition to the Microsoft business intelligence toolset, Get & Transform in Excel 2016, can help you find and load data from a variety of sources. These sources can be more traditional—such as Access, Excel, or text files—or they could come from corporate databases, data warehouses, or even big data repositories or social media sources. Indeed, data could even be found in public data repositories or from commercial cloud-based sources. Get & Transform can even help you find available data (from both inside and outside the enterprise) and remember any recent searches that you have made. Yet this is only the first part of the story. Now you need to learn how to shape and tweak the data to prepare it for further use. This is the subject of the next three chapters.

CHAPTER 11

Transforming Data Sets Using Get & Transform

In the previous chapter, you saw some of the ways in which you can find and load data into either Excel worksheets or the Excel in-memory data model using Get & Transform. Inevitably, this is the first part of any process that you create to extract, transform, and load data. Yet it is only a first step. Once the data is made accessible using Get & Transform, you need to know how to adapt it to suit your requirements in a multitude of ways. This is because not all data is ready to be used immediately. Quite often, you have to do some initial work on the data to make it more easily usable in Get & Transform. Tweaking source data is generally referred to as *data transformation*, which is the subject of this chapter.

The transformations that you can apply to the raw data are many and varied. Given the vast range of ways that you can chop, change, and tweak your data, you will concentrate on the following transformations in this chapter:

- Renaming, removing, and reordering columns

- Removing groups or sets of rows

- Deduplicating data sets

- Excluding records by filtering the data

- Sorting the data

These transformations (or modifications, if you prefer another term) are potentially extensive and varied. Learning to apply the techniques that Get & Transform makes available enables you to take data as you find it and push it as a series of coherent and structured data tables in the data model (or into worksheets if the data is not too voluminous) so that it is ready to be used to create Get & Transform dashboards.

As it is all too easy to be overwhelmed (at least initially) by the extent of the data transformation options that Get & Transform has to offer, I have grouped the possible modifications into four categories. These are my own and are merely a suggestion to facilitate understanding.

These categories are as follows:

- *Transforming data sets*: This includes adding and removing columns and rows, renaming columns, and filtering data.

- *Data modification*: This covers altering the actual data in the rows and columns of a data set.

- *Extending data sets*: By this, I mean adding further columns, possibly expanding existing columns into more columns or rows and adding calculations.

- *Joining data sets*: This involves combining multiple separate data sets—possibly from different data sources—into a single data set.

© Adam Aspin 2016

A. Aspin, *High Impact Data Visualization in Excel with Power View, 3D Maps, Get & Transform and Power BI*, DOI 10.1007/978-1-4842-2400-7_11

This chapter covers the first option in this list and introduces you to how you can use Get & Transform to chop and change source data. In the next chapter, you learn how to cleanse and modify data. In Chapter 13, you learn how to subset columns to extract part of the available data in a column, calculate columns, merge data from separate queries, and add further columns containing different types of calculations, and you learn about pivoting and unpivoting data. So, if you cannot find what you are looking for in this chapter, there is a good chance that the answer is in the next one or the one after that.

In this chapter, I will also use a set of example files that you can find on the Apress web site. If you have followed the instructions in Appendix A, then these files are in the `C:\DataVisualisationInExcel2016` folder.

Get & Transform Queries

In Chapter 10, you saw how to load source data directly into Get & Transform where you can use it immediately to create deliver analysis from data output to worksheets or loaded into the in-memory data model. Clearly, this approach presumes that the data you are using is perfectly structured, clean, and error-free. Source data is nearly always correct and ready to use when it comes from "corporate" data sources such as data warehouses (held in relational, dimensional, or tabular databases). This is not always the case when you are faced with multiple disparate sources of data that have not been precleansed and prepared by an IT department. The everyday reality is that you could have to cleanse and transform much of the source data that you will use for your data analysis and visualization.

The really good news is that the kind of data transformation that used to require expensive servers and industrial-strength software is now available for free. Yes, Get & Transform is an awesome extract, transform, and load (ETL) tool that can rival many applications that cost hundreds of thousands of dollars.

Get & Transform data transformation is carried out using *queries*. As you saw in Chapter 10, you do not have to modify source data. You can load it directly if it is ready for use. Yet if you need to cleanse the data, you add an intermediate step between connecting the data and loading it into the Get & Transform data model. This intermediate step uses the Get & Transform Query Editor to tweak the source data.

So, how do you apply queries to transform your data? You have two choices.

- Load the data first from one or more sources and then transform it later

- Edit each source data element in a query before loading it

Get & Transform is extremely forgiving. It does not force you to select one or the other method and then lock you in to the consequences of your decision. You can load data first and then realize that it needs some adjustment, switch to the Query Editor and make changes, and then return to creating your dashboard. Or you can first focus on the data and try to get it as polished and perfect as possible before you start delivering analysis. The choice is entirely up to you.

To make this point, let's take a look at both of these ways of working.

■ **Note**   At risk of being pedantic and old-fashioned, I advise you to make notes when creating really complex transformations because going back to a solution and trying to make adjustments later can be painful when they are not documented at all.

Editing Data After a Data Load

Now let's presume that you want to make some changes to the data structure of the data that you have already loaded. Specifically, you want to rename the CostPrice column in the sample file set as `CarSalesData.xlsx`. This file contains a data set loaded into an Excel worksheet from an external data source using Get & Transform. Before anything else, note that the header for column F reads CostPrice.

1. In the Data ribbon, click the Show Queries button to display the workbook queries that were used to import the data.

2. Double-click the query CarSalesData. The Get & Transform Query Editor will open and display the source data as a table. The window will look like Figure 11-1.

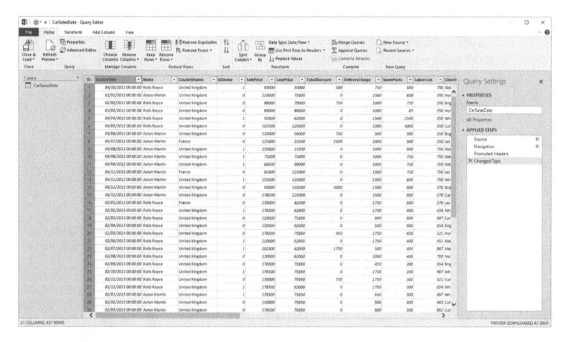

Figure 11-1. The Get & Transform Query Editor

3. Right-click the title of the CostPrice column. The column will be selected.

4. Select Rename from the context menu.

5. Type **VehicleCost** and press Enter. The column title will change to VehicleCost.

6. In the Get & Transform Query Editor Home ribbon, click the Close & Load button. The Get & Transform Query Editor will close, upload the data to the previously selected destination, and return you to the initial Excel worksheet. Column F now has the header VehicleCost.

I hope that this simple example makes it clear that transforming the source data is a quick and painless process. The technique you applied— renaming a column— is only one of many dozens of possible techniques that you can apply to transform your data. However, it is not the specific transformation that is the core idea to take away here. What you need to remember is that the data that underpins your pivot table or dashboard is always present and only a single click away. At any time, you can "flip" to the data and make changes, simply by double-clicking the query name in the Workbook Queries pane to open the Query Editor window. Any changes that you make and confirm will update your worksheets, pivot tables, dashboards, and reports instantaneously.

Transforming Data Before Loading

On some occasions, you might prefer to juggle with your data before you load it. Do the following to transform your data before it appears in the Get & Transform window:

1. Open a new, blank Excel worksheet.

2. In the Data ribbon, click the New Query button.

3. Select From File ➤ From Workbook and open the Excel file `C:\ DataVisualisationInExcel2016\CarSalesData_Source.xlsx`.

4. In the Navigator window, select the CarSalesData worksheet.

5. Click the Edit button (*not* the Load button). The Get & Transform Query Editor will open and display the source data as a table.

6. Carry out steps 3 through 6 from the previous example to rename the CostPrice column.

7. In the Get & Transform Query Editor Home ribbon, click the Close & Load button. The Get & Transform Query Editor will close and return you to Excel where the source data has now been added to a new worksheet.

This time, you have made a simple modification to the data *before* loading the data set into a worksheet. The data modification technique was the same. The only difference between loading the data directly and taking a detour via the Query window was clicking Edit instead of Load in the Navigator dialog.

Query or Load?

Get & Transform always gives you the choice of loading data directly into the Excel data model (or a spreadsheet) or taking a constructive detour via the Query Editor. The path that you follow is entirely up to you and clearly depends on each set of circumstances. Nonetheless, there are a few basic principles that you might want to consider when faced with a new dashboarding challenge using unfamiliar data.

- Are you convinced that the data is ready to use? That is, is it clean and well structured? If so, then you can try loading it directly into the Excel data model.

- Are you faced with multiple data sources that need to be combined and molded into a coherent structure? If this is the case, then you really need to transform the data using Get & Transform.

- Does the data come from an enterprise data warehouse? This could be held in a relational database, a SQL Server Analysis Services cube, or even an in-memory tabular data warehouse. As these data sources are nearly always the result of many hundreds—or even thousands—of hours of work cleansing, preparing, and structuring the data, you can probably load these straight into the data model.

- Does the data need to be preaggregated and filtered? Think Get & Transform.

- Are you faced with lots of lookup tables that need to be added to a "core" data table? Then Get & Transform is your friend.

- Does the data contain many superfluous or erroneous elements? Then use Get & Transform to remove these as a first step.

- Does the data need to be rationalized and standardized to make it easier to handle? In this case, the path to success is via Get & Transform.

These kinds of questions are only rough guidelines. Yet they can help to point you in the right direction when you are working with Get & Transform. Inevitably, the more you work with this application, the more you will develop the reflexes and intuition that will help you make the correct decisions. Remember, however, that Get & Transform is there to help and that even a directly loaded data set is based on a query. So, you can always load data and then decide to tweak its structure later if you need to do so. Alternatively, editing data in a Query window can be a great opportunity to take a closer look at your data before loading it into the data model—and it adds only a couple of clicks.

So, feel free to adopt a way of working that you feel happy with. Get & Transform will adapt to your style easily and almost invisibly, letting you switch from data to output so fluidly that it will likely become second nature.

The remainder of this chapter will take you through some of the techniques that you need to know to cleanse and shape your data. However, before getting into all the detail, let's take a quick, high-level look at the Get & Transform Query Editor and the way it is laid out.

The Get & Transform Query Editor

All of your data transformation will take place in the Get & Transform Query Editor. It is a separate window from the Excel or Power Pivot windows, and it has a slightly different layout.

The Get & Transform Query Editor consists of six main elements.

- The four ribbons (Home, Transform, Add Columns, and View)

- The Query list pane containing all the queries that have been added to a Get & Transform file

- The Data window, where you can see a sample of the data for a selected query

- The Query Settings pane that contains the list of steps used to transform data

- The formula bar above the data that shows the code (written in the M language) that performs the selected transformation step

- The status bar (at the bottom of the window) that indicates useful information, such as the number of rows and columns in a query table and the date when the data set was downloaded

Figure 11-2 shows the callouts for these elements.

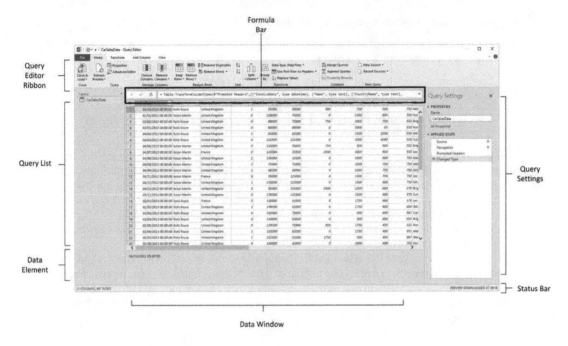

Figure 11-2. The Get & Transform Query Editor, explained

The Applied Steps List

Data transformation is by its very nature a sequential process. So, the Query window stores each modification that you make when you are cleansing and shaping source data. The various elements that make up a data transformation process are listed in the Applied Steps list of the Query Settings pane in the Query Editor.

The Get & Transform Query Editor does not number the steps in a data transformation process, but it certainly remembers each one. They start at the top of the Applied Steps list (nearly always with the Source step) and can extend to dozens of individual steps that trace the evolution of your data until you load it into the data model. Indeed, as you click each step in the Applied Steps list, the data in the Data window changes to reflect the results of each transformation, giving you a complete and visible trail of all the modifications that you have applied to the data set.

The Applied Steps list gives a distinct name to the step for each and every data modification option covered in this chapter and the next. As it can be important to understand exactly what each function actually achieves, I will always bring to your attention the standard name that Get & Transform applies.

There are just a couple of fundamental functions that you need to know when using the Applied Steps list, as explained next.

Renaming a Step

You can rename any step really simply.

1. Right-click the step you want to rename.

2. Select Rename from the context menu.

3. Change the existing name.

4. Press Enter.

Deleting a Step

Simply click the X to the left of the step name in the Applied Steps list.

■ **Note** Be aware that deleting a step can have serious consequences for any steps that follow the step that you delete. Indeed, Get & Transform warns you if removing a step will disrupt the processing sequence. If you need to alter a series of steps to change a sequence of data modifications, it is often easiest to delete steps from the bottom upward, in reverse order, and then rebuild a sequence of transformations from a stable starting point.

The Get & Transform Query Editor Ribbons

Get & Transform Query Editor uses (in the current version, at least) four ribbons. They are fundamental to what you will learn in the course of this chapter.

- The Home ribbon

- The Transform ribbon

- The Add Column ribbon

- The View ribbon

I am not suggesting for a second that you need to memorize what all the buttons in these ribbons do. What I hope is that you are able to use these brief descriptions of the query ribbon buttons to get an idea of the amazing power of Get & Transform in the field of data transformation. So, if you have an initial data set that is not quite as you need it, you can take a look at the resources that Get & Transform has to offer and how they can help. Once you find the function that does what you are looking for, you can jump to the relevant section for the full details on how to apply it.

The Home Ribbon

Since you will be making intense use of the Get & Transform Home ribbon to transform data, it is important to have an idea of what it can do. I explain the various options in Figure 11-3 and in Table 11-1.

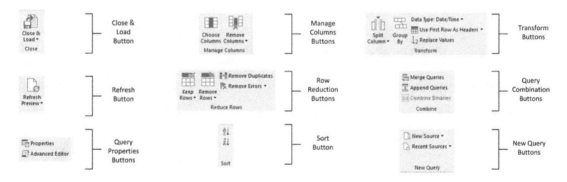

Figure 11-3. *The Query Editor Home ribbon*

Table 11-1. *Query Editor Home Ribbon Options*

Option	Description
Close & Load	Finishes the processing steps; saves and closes the query.
Refresh Preview	Refreshes the source data and reprocesses all the steps.
Properties	Displays the query properties and lets you add a description and inhibit or enable data load and refresh.
Advanced Editor	Displays the complete M language code for all the transformation steps that have been used in a query.
Choose Columns	Lets you select the columns to retain from all the columns available in the source data.
Remove Columns	Removes one or more columns.
Keep Rows	Keeps the specified number of rows at the top of the table.
Remove Rows	Removes a specified number of rows from the top of the data table.
Remove Duplicates	Removes all duplicate rows, leaving only unique rows.
Remove Errors	Removes all rows that contain processing errors.
Sort	Sorts the table using the selected column as the sort key.
Split Column	Splits a column into one or many columns at a specified delimiter or after a specified number of characters.
Group By	Groups the table using a specified set of columns and aggregates any numeric columns for this grouping.
Data Type	Applies the chosen data type to the column.
Use First Row As Headers	Use the first row as the column titles.
Replace Values	Carries out a search-and-replace operation on the data in a column or columns. This only affects the complete data in a column.
Merge Queries	Joins a second query table to the current query results and aggregates or adds data from the second to the first.
Append Queries	Adds the data from another query to the current query in the current Get & Transform file.
Combine Binaries	Merges all the binary data from another column into a single binary column.
New Sources	Lets you discover and add a new data source to the set of queries.
Recent Sources	Lists all the recent data sources that you have used.

The Transform Ribbon

The Transform ribbon, as its name implies, contains a wealth of functions that can help you to transform your data. The various options it contains are explained in Figure 11-4 and Table 11-2.

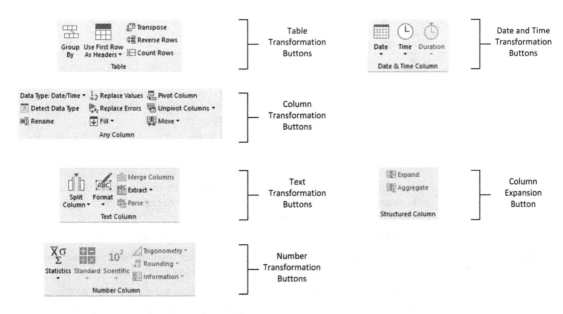

Figure 11-4. *The Query Editor Transform ribbon*

Table 11-2. *Query Editor Transform Ribbon Options*

Option	Description
Group By	Groups the table using a specified set of columns; aggregates any numeric columns for this grouping.
Use First Row As Headers	Uses the first row as the column titles.
Transpose	Transforms the columns into rows and the rows into columns.
Reverse Rows	Displays the source data in reverse order, showing the final rows at the top of the window.
Count Rows	Counts the rows in the table and replaces the data with the row count.
Data Type	Applies the chosen data type to the column.
Rename	Renames a column.
Detect Data Type	Detects the correct data type to apply to multiple columns.
Replace Values	Carries out a search-and-replace operation inside a column, replacing a specified value with another value.
Replace Errors	Replaces error values with a specified value.
Fill	Copies the data from cells above or below into empty cells in the column.
Pivot Column	Creates a new set of columns using the data in the selected column as the column titles.
Unpivot Columns	Takes the values in a set of columns and unpivots the data, creating two new columns using the column headers as the descriptive elements.
Move	Moves a column.

(continued)

329

Table 11-2. (*continued*)

Option	Description
Split Column	Splits a column into one or many columns at a specified delimiter or after a specified number of characters.
Format	Modifies the text format of data in a column (uppercase, lowercase, capitalization) or removes trailing spaces.
Merge Columns	Takes the data from several columns and places it in a single column, adding an optional separator character.
Extract	Replaces the data in a column using a defined subset of the current data. You can specify a number of characters to keep from the start or end of the column, set a range of characters beginning at a specified character, or even list the number of characters in the column.
Parse	Creates an XML or JSON document from the contents of each cell in a column.
Statistics	Returns the Sum, Average, Maximum, Minimum, Median, Standard Deviation, Count, or Distinct Value Count for all the values in the column.
Standard	Carries out a basic mathematical calculation (add, subtract, divide, multiply, integer-divide, or return the remainder) using a value that you specify applied to each cell in the column.
Scientific	Carries out a basic scientific calculation (square, cube, power of n, square root, exponent, logarithm, or factorial) for each cell in the column.
Trigonometry	Carries out a basic trigonometric calculation (Sine, Cosine, Tangent, ArcSine, ArcCosine, or ArcTangent) using a value that you specify applied to each cell in the column.
Rounding	Rounds the values in the column either to the next integer (up or down) or to a specified factor.
Information	Replaces the value in the column with simple information: Is Odd, Is Even, or Positive/Negative.
Date	Isolates an element (day, month, year, and so on) from a date value in a column.
Time	Isolates an element (hour, minute, second, and so on) from a date/time or time value in a column.
Duration	Calculates the duration from a value that can be interpreted as a duration in days, hours, minutes, and so forth.
Expand	Adds the (identically structured) data from another query to the current query.
Aggregate	Calculates the sum or product of numeric columns from another query to the current query.

The Add Column Ribbon

The Add Column ribbon does a lot more than just add columns. It also contains functions to break columns down into multiple columns and to add columns containing dates and calculations based on existing columns. The various options it contains are explained in Figure 11-5 and Table 11-3.

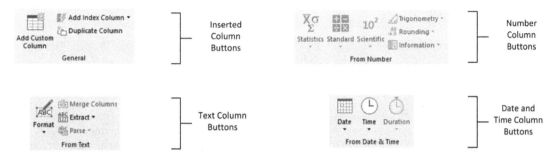

Figure 11-5. *The Query Editor Add Column ribbon*

Table 11-3. *Query Editor Add Column Ribbon Options*

Option	Description
Add Custom Column	Adds a new column using a formula to create the columns' contents.
Add Index Column	Adds a sequential number in a new column to uniquely identify each row.
Duplicate Column	Creates a copy of the current column.
Format	Modifies the text format of data in a column (uppercase, lowercase, capitalization) or removes trailing spaces.
Merge Columns	Takes the data from several columns and places it in a single column, adding an optional separator character.
Extract	Replaces the data in a column using a defined subset of the current data. You can specify a number of characters to keep from the start or end of the column, set a range of characters beginning at a specified character, or even list the number of characters in the column.
Parse	Creates an XML or JSON document from the contents of each cell in a column.
Statistics	Returns the Sum, Average, Maximum, Minimum, Median, Standard Deviation, Count, or Distinct Value Count for all the values in the column.
Standard	Carries out a basic mathematical calculation (add, subtract, divide, multiply, integer-divide, or return the remainder) using a value that you specify applied to each cell in the column.
Scientific	Carries out a basic scientific calculation (square, cube, power of n, square root, exponent, logarithm, or factorial) for each cell in the column.
Trigonometry	Carries out a basic trigonometric calculation (Sine, Cosine, Tangent, ArcSine, ArcCosine, or ArcTangent) using a value that you specify applied to each cell in the column.
Rounding	Rounds the values in the column either to the next integer (up or down) or to a specified factor.
Information	Replaces the value in the column with simple information: Is Odd, Is Even, or Positive/Negative.
Date	Isolates an element (day, month, year, and so on) from a date value in a column.
Time	Isolates an element (hour, minute, second, and so on) from a date/time or time value in a column.
Duration	Calculates the duration from a value that can be interpreted as a duration in days, hours, minutes, and so forth.

The View Ribbon

The View ribbon lets you alter some of the query settings and see the underlying data transformation code. The various options that it contains are explained in the next chapter.

Data Set Shaping

So, you are now looking at a data table that you have loaded into Get & Transform. For argument's sake, let's assume it is the C:\DataVisualisationInExcel2016\CarSalesData.xlsx file from the sample data directory and that you have clicked the Edit Queries button to display the Get & Transform Query Editor. What can you do to the CarSalesData data table that is now visible? It is time to take a look at some of the core techniques that you can apply to shape the initial data set. These include the following:

- Renaming columns

- Reordering columns

- Removing columns

- Merging columns

- Removing records

- Removing duplicate records

- Filtering the data set

I have grouped these techniques together as they affect the initial size and shape of the data. Also, it is generally not only good practice but also easier for you, the data modeler, if you begin by excluding any rows and columns that you do not need. I also find it easier to understand data sets if the columns are logically laid out and given comprehensible names from the start. All in all, this makes working with the data easier in the long run.

Renaming Columns

Although you took a quick look at renaming columns in the first pages of this chapter, let's look at this technique again in more detail. I admit that renaming columns is not actually modifying the form of the data table. However, when dealing with data, I consider it vital to have all data clearly identifiable. This implies meaningful column names being applied to each column. Consequently, I consider this modification to be fundamental to the shape of the data and also an essential best practice when importing source data.

To rename a column, follow these steps:

1. Click inside the column that you want to rename.

2. Click Transform to activate the Transform ribbon.

3. Click the Rename button. The column name will be highlighted.

4. Enter the new name or edit the existing name.

5. Press Enter or click outside the column title.

The column will now have a new title. The Applied Steps list on the right will now contain another element, Renamed Columns. This step will be highlighted.

■ **Note** As an alternative to using the Transform ribbon, you can right-click the column title and select Rename.

Reordering Columns

Get & Transform will load data as it is defined in the data source. Consequently, the column sequence will be entirely dependent on the source data (or by a SQL query if you used a source database, as described earlier). This need not be definitive, however, and you can reorder the columns if that helps you understand and deal with the data. Do the following to change column order:

1. Click the header of the column you want to move.

2. Drag the column left or right to its new position. You will see the column title slide laterally through the column titles as you do this, and a thicker gray line will indicate where the column will be placed once you release the mouse button. Reordered Columns will appear in the Applied Steps list.

Figure 11-6 shows this operation.

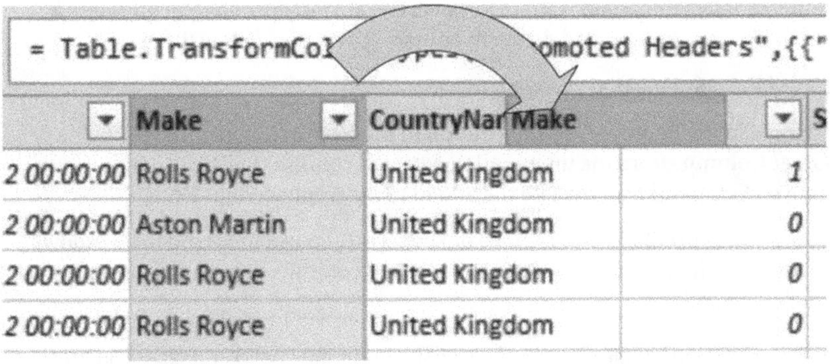

Figure 11-6. *Reordering columns*

If your query contains dozens—or even hundreds—of columns, you may find that dragging a column around can be slow and laborious. Equally, if columns are extremely wide, it can be difficult to "nudge" a column left or right. Get & Transform can come to your aid in these circumstances with the Move button in the Transform ribbon. Clicking this button gives you the menu options that are outlined in Table 11-4.

Table 11-4. *Move Button Options*

Option	Description
Left	Moves the currently selected column to the left of the column on its immediate left
Right	Moves the currently selected column to the right of the column on its immediate right
To Beginning	Moves the currently selected column to the left of all the columns in the query
To End	Moves the currently selected column to the right of all the columns in the query

The Move command also works on a set of columns that you have selected by Ctrl+clicking and/or Shift+clicking. Indeed, you can move a selection of columns that is not contiguous if you need to do so.

■ **Note**   You need to select a column (or a set of columns) before clicking the Move button. If you do not, then the first time that you use Move, Get & Transform selects the column (or columns)—but does not move them.

Removing Columns

So, how do you delete a column or series of columns? Like this:

1. Click inside the column you want to delete or if you want to delete several columns at once, Ctrl+click the titles of the columns that you want to delete.

2. Click the Remove Columns button in the Home ribbon. The column (or columns) will be deleted, and Removed Columns will be the latest element in the Applied Steps list.

When working with imported data sets over which you have had no control, you may frequently find that you need only a few columns of a large data table. If this is the case, you will soon get tired of Ctrl+clicking numerous columns to select those you want to remove. Get & Transform has an alternative method. Just select the columns you want to keep and delete the others. To do this, follow these steps:

1. Ctrl+click the titles of the columns that you want to keep.

2. Click the small triangle in the Remove Columns button in the Home ribbon. Select Remove Other Columns from the menu. All unselected columns will be deleted, and Removed Other Columns will be the added to the Applied Steps list.

When selecting a contiguous range of columns to remove or keep, you can use the standard Windows Shift+click technique to select from the first to last column in the block of columns that you want to select.

■ **Note**   Both of these options for removing columns are also available from the context menu, if you prefer. It shows Remove (or Remove Columns, if there are several columns selected) when deleting columns, as well as Remove Other Columns if you right-click a column title.

Merging Columns

Source data is not always exactly as you wish it could be (and that is sometimes a massive understatement). Certain data sources could have data spread over many columns that could equally well be merged into a single column. So, it probably comes as no surprise to discover that Get & Transform can carry out this kind of operation too. Here is how to do it:

1. Ctrl+click the headers of the columns that you want to merge (Make and Model in the CarSalesData table in this example).

2. In the Transform ribbon, click the Merge Columns button. The Merge Columns dialog will be displayed.

3. From the Separator pop-up menu, select one of the available separator elements. I chose Colon in this example.

4. Enter a name for the column that will be created from the two original columns (I am calling it MakeAndModel). The dialog should look like Figure 11-7.

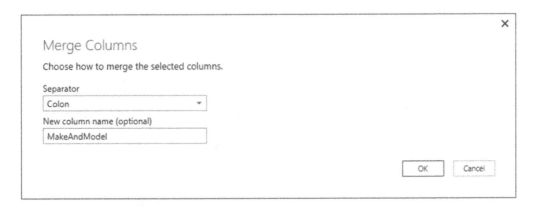

Figure 11-7. *The Merge Columns dialog*

5. Click OK. The columns that you selected will be replaced by the data from all the original columns, as shown in Figure 11-8.

		fx	= Table.CombineColumns(#"Changed Type",{"Make", "Model"},Combiner.C

LaborCost ▼	ClientName ▼	MakeAndModel ▼	Color ▼
750	Aldo Motors	Rolls Royce:Camargue	Red
550	Honest John	Aston Martin:DBS	Blue
550	Bright Orange	Rolls Royce:Silver Ghost	Green
550	Honest John	Rolls Royce:Silver Ghost	Blue
550	Wheels'R'Us	Rolls Royce:Camargue	Canary Yellow
550	Cut'n'Shut	Rolls Royce:Camargue	British Racing Green
550	Bright Orange	Aston Martin:DBS	Dark Purple
550	Les Arnaqueurs	Aston Martin:DB7	Red
750	Aldo Motors	Aston Martin:DB9	Blue
750	Aldo Motors	Aston Martin:DB9	Silver

Figure 11-8. *The result of merging columns*

Here are a few comments about this process:

- You can select as many columns as you want when merging columns.

- If you do not give the resulting column a name in the Merge Columns dialog, it will simply be renamed Merged. You can always rename it later if you want.

- The order in which you select the columns affects the way that the data is merged. So, always begin by selecting the column whose data must appear at the left of the merged column, then the column whose data should be next, and so forth. You do not have to select columns in the order that they initially appeared in the data set.

- If you do not want to use any of the standard separators that Get & Transform suggests, you can always define your own. Just select --Custom-- in the pop-up menu in the Merge Columns dialog. A new box will appear in the dialog, in which you can enter your choice of separator. This can be composed of several characters if you really want.

- Merging columns from the Transform ribbon removes all the selected columns and replaces them with a single column. The same option is also available from the Add Column ribbon—only in this case, this operation adds a new column and leaves the original columns in the data set.

▓ **Note**   This option is also available from the context menu if you right-click a column title.

Table 11-5 describes the available merge separators.

Table 11-5. *Merge Separators*

Option	Description
Colon	Uses the colon (:) as the separator
Comma	Uses the comma (,) as the separator
Equals Sign	Uses the equal sign (=) as the separator
Semi-Colon	Uses the semicolon (;) as the separator
Space	Uses the space ( ) as the separator
Tab	Uses the tab character as the separator
Custom	Lets you enter a custom separator

▓ **Tip**   You can split, remove, and duplicate columns using the context menu if you prefer. Just remember to right-click the column title to display the correct context menu.

Removing Records

You may not always need *all* the data you have loaded into Get & Transform. There could be several possible reasons for this.

- You are taking a first look at the data and you need only a sample to get an idea of what the data is like.

- The data contains records that you clearly do not need and that you can easily identify from the start.

- You are testing data cleansing and you want a smaller data set to really speed up the development of a complex data extractions and transformation process.

- You want to analyze a reduced data set to extrapolate theses and inferences and to save analysis on a full data set for later, or even using a more industrial-strength toolset such as SQL Server Integration Services.

To allow you to reduce the size of the data set, Get & Transform proposes two basic approaches out of the box.

- Keep certain rows

- Remove certain rows

Inevitably, the technique you adopt will depend on the circumstances. If it is easier to specify the rows to sample by inclusion, then the keeping certain rows is the best option to take. Inversely, if you want to proceed by exclusion, then removing certain rows is best. Let's look at each of these in turn.

Keep Rows

This approach lets you specify the rows that you want to continue using. It is based on the application of one of the following three choices:

- Keep the top n records

- Keep the bottom n records

- Keep a specified range of records—that is, keep n records every y records

Most of these techniques are similar, so let's start by imagining that you want to keep the top 50 records in the sample `C:\DataVisualisationInExcel2016\CarSalesData.xlsx` file.

1. In the Home ribbon of the Get & Transform Query Editor, click the Keep Rows button. The menu will appear.

2. Select Keep Top Rows. The Keep Top Rows dialog will appear.

3. Enter **50** in the Number Of Rows box, as shown in Figure 11-9.

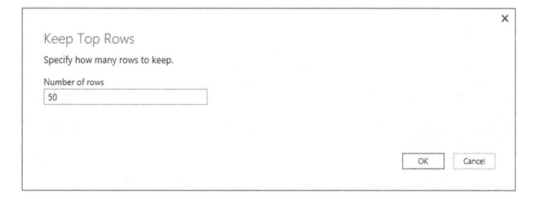

Figure 11-9. The Keep Top Rows dialog

4. Click OK. All but the first 50 records are deleted, and Kept First Rows is added to the Applied Steps list.

To keep the bottom *n* rows, the technique is virtually identical. Follow the steps in the previous example, but select Keep Bottom Rows in step 2. In this case, the Applied Steps list displays Kept Last Rows.

To keep a range of records, you need to specify a starting record and the number of records to keep from then on. For instance, suppose you want to lose the first 10 records but keep the following 25. This is how to go about it:

1. In the Home ribbon, click the Keep Rows button.

2. Select Keep Range Of Rows. The Keep Range dialog will appear.

3. Enter **11** in the First Row box.

4. Enter **25** in the Number Of Rows box, as shown in Figure 11-10.

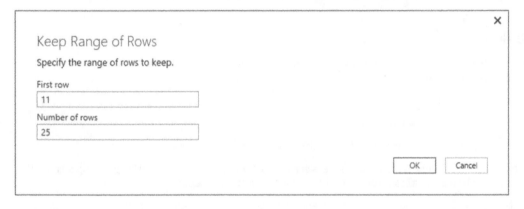

Figure 11-10. *The Keep Range dialog*

5. Click OK. All but records 1–10 and 36 to the end are deleted and Kept Range Of Rows is added to the Applied Steps list.

Remove Rows

Removing rows is a nearly identical process to the one you just used to keep rows. As removing the top or bottom *n* rows is highly similar, I will not go through it in detail. All you have to do is click the Remove Rows button in the Home ribbon and follow the process as if you were keeping rows. The Applied Steps list will read Removed Top Rows or Removed Bottom Rows in this case, and rows will be removed instead of being kept in the data set, of course.

The remove rows approach does have one useful option that can be applied as a sampling technique. It allows you to remove one or more records every few records to produce a subset of the source data. To do this, you need to do the following:

1. Click the Remove Rows button in the Query window Home ribbon. The menu will appear.

2. Select Remove Alternate Rows. The Remove Alternate Rows dialog will appear.

3. Enter **10** as the first row to remove.

4. Enter **2** as the number of rows to remove.

5. Enter **10** as the number of rows to keep.

The dialog will look like Figure 11-11.

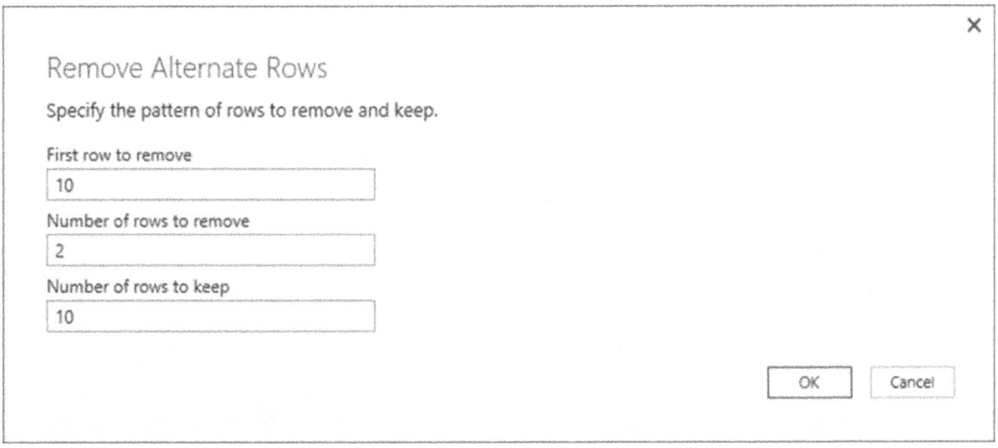

Figure 11-11. *The Remove Alternate Rows dialog*

6. Click OK. All but the records matching the pattern you entered in the dialog are removed. Removed Alternate Rows is then added to the Applied Steps list.

■ **Note**   If you are really determined to extract a sample that you consider to be representative of the key data, then you can always filter the data before subsetting it to exclude any outliers. Filtering data is explained later in this chapter.

Remove Blank Rows

If your source data contains completely blank (empty) rows, you can delete these as follows:

1. Click the Remove Rows button in the Query window Home ribbon. The menu will appear.

2. Select Remove Blank Rows.

This results in empty rows being deleted. Removed Blank Rows is then added to the Applied Steps list.

Removing Duplicate Records

An external source of data might not be quite as perfect as you might hope. One of the most annoying features of poor data is the presence of duplicates. These are insidious since they falsify results and are not always visible. If you suspect that the data table contains strict duplicates (that is, where every field is identical in two or more records), then you can remove the duplicates like this:

1. Click the Remove Duplicates button in the Home ribbon. All duplicate records are deleted and Removed Duplicates are added to the Applied Steps list.

■ **Note**   I must stress that this approach will remove only *completely* identical records. If two records have just one character or a number different but everything else is identical, then they are *not* considered duplicates by Get & Transform.

So, if you suspect or are sure that the data table you are dealing with contains duplicates, what are the practical solutions? This can be a real conundrum, but these are some basic techniques that you can apply:

- Remove all columns that you are sure you will not be using later in the data-handling process. This way, Get & Transform will be asked only to compare essential data across potentially duplicate records.

- Group the data on the core columns (this is explained in the next chapter).

■ **Note**   As you have seen, Get & Transform can help you to home in on the essential elements in a data set in just a few clicks. If anything, you need to be careful that you are *not excluding* valuable data—and consequently skewing your analysis—when excluding data from the query.

Sorting Data

Although not strictly a data modification step, sorting an imported table will probably be something that you want to do at some stage, if only to get a clearer idea of the data you are dealing with. Do the following to sort the data:

1. Click inside the column you want to sort by.

2. Click Sort Ascending (the A/Z icon) or Sort Descending (the Z/A icon) in the Home ribbon.

The data is sorted in either alphabetical (smallest to largest) or reverse alphabetical (largest to smallest) order. If you want to carry out a complex sort operation (that is, first by one column and then by another if the first column contains the same element over several rows), you do this simply by sorting the columns one after another. Get & Transform Query Editor adds a tiny 1, 2, 3, and so on, to the right of the column title to indicate the sort sequence. You can see this in Figure 11-12.

Make	1 ▾↑	Model	2 ▾↑
Aston Martin		DB4	
Aston Martin		DB4	
Aston Martin		DB4	
Aston Martin		DB4	
Aston Martin		DB4	
Aston Martin		DB4	
Aston Martin		DB4	
Aston Martin		DB4	
Aston Martin		DB7	

Figure 11-12. *Sorting multiple columns*

As sorting data is considered part of the data modification process, it also appears in the Applied Steps list as Sorted Rows.

■ **Note** An alternative technique for sorting data is to click the pop-up menu for a column (the downward-facing triangle at the right of a column title) and select Sort Ascending or Sort Descending from the context menu.

Reversing the Row Order

If you find that the data you are looking at seems upside-down (that is, with the bottom rows at the top and vice versa), you can reverse the row order in a single click, if you want. To do this, do the following:

1. In the Transform ribbon, click the Reverse Rows button.

The entire data set will be reversed, and the bottom row will now be the top row.

Filtering Data

The most frequently used way of limiting a data set is, in my experience, the use of filters on the table that you have loaded. Now, I realize that you may be coming to Get & Transform after years with Excel, or after some time using PowerPivot, and that the filtering techniques you are about to see probably look much like the ones you have used in those two tools. However, because it is fundamental to include and exclude appropriate records when loading source data, I will thoroughly handle Get & Transform filters, even if this means that certain readers will experience a strong sense of déjà vu.

Here are two basic approaches for filtering data in Get & Transform:

- Select one or more specific values from the unique list of elements in the chosen column

- Define a range of data to include or exclude

The first option is common to all data types, whether they are text, number, or data/time. The second approach varies according to the data type of the column you are using to filter data.

Selecting Specific Values

Selecting one or more values present in a column of data is as easy as this (assuming that you are still using the Excel file CarSalesData.xlsx and are in the Get & Transform Query Editor):

1. Click a column's pop-up menu. (I used Make in the sample data set in this example.) The filter menu appears.

2. Check all elements that you want to retain and uncheck all elements that you want to exclude. In this example, I kept Bentley and Rolls-Royce, as shown in Figure 11-13.

Figure 11-13. *A filter menu*

3. Click OK. The Applied Steps box adds Filtered Rows.

░ **Note** You can deselect all items by clicking the (Select All) check box; reselect all the items by selecting this box again. It follows that, if you want to keep only a few elements, it may be faster to unselect all of them first and then select only the ones you want to keep.

Finding Elements in the Filter List

Scrolling up and down in a filter list can get extremely laborious. A fast way of limiting the list to a subset of available elements is to do the following:

1. Click the pop-up menu for a column. (I use Model in the sample data set in this example.) The filter menu appears.

2. Enter a letter or a few letters in the Search box. The list shortens with every letter or number that you enter. If you enter **ar**, then the filter pop-up will look like Figure 11-14.

Figure 11-14. *Searching the filter menu*

To remove a filter, all that you have to do is click the X that appears at the right of the search box.

Filtering Text Ranges

If a column contains text, then you can apply specific options to filter the data. These elements are found in the filter pop-up of any text-based column in the Text Filters submenu. Table 11-6 gives the choices.

Table 11-6. *Text Filter Options*

Filter Option	Description
Equals	Sets the text that must match the cell contents
Does Not Equal	Sets the text that must not match the cell contents
Begins With	Sets the text at the left of the cell contents
Does Not Begin With	Sets the text that must not appear at the left of the cell contents
Ends With	Sets the text at the right of the cell contents
Does Not End With	Sets the text that must *not* appear at the right of the cell contents
Contains	Lets you enter a text that will be part of the cell contents
Does Not Contain	Lets you enter a text that will *not* be part of the cell contents

Filtering Numeric Ranges

If a column contains numbers, then there are also specific options that you can apply to filter the data. You'll find these elements in the filter pop-up of any text-based column in the Number Filters submenu. Table 11-7 gives the choices.

Table 11-7. *Numeric Filter Options*

Filter Option	Description
Equals	This sets the number that must match the cell contents.
Does Not Equal	This sets the number that must not match the cell contents.
Greater Than	The cell contents must be greater than this number.
Greater Than Or Equal To	The cell contents must be greater than or equal to this number.
Lesser Than	The cell contents must be less than this number.
Lesser Than Or Equal To	The cell contents must be less than or equal to this number.
Between	The cell contents must be between the two numbers.

Filtering Date and Time Ranges

If a column contains dates or times (or both), then specific options can also be applied to filter the data. These elements are found in the filter pop-up of any text-based column in the Date/Time Filters submenu. Table 11-8 gives the choices.

Table 11-8. *Date and Time Filter Options*

Filter Element	Description
Equals	Filters data to include only records for the selected date
Before	Filters data to include only records up to the selected date
After	Filters data to include only records after the selected date
Between	Lets you set an upper and a lower date limit to exclude records outside that range
In the Next	Lets you specify a number of days, weeks, months, quarters, or years to come
In the Previous	Lets you specify a number of days, weeks, months, quarters, or years up to the date
Day ➤ Tomorrow	Filters data to include only records for the day after the current system date
Day ➤ Today	Filters data to include only records for the current system date
Day ➤ Yesterday	Filters data to include only records for the day before the current system date
Week ➤ Next Week	Filters data to include only records for the next calendar week
Week ➤ This Week	Filters data to include only records for the current calendar week
Week ➤ Last Week	Filters data to include only records for the previous calendar week
Month ➤ Next Month	Filters data to include only records for the next calendar month
Month ➤ This Month	Filters data to include only records for the current calendar month
Month ➤ Last Month	Filters data to include only records for the previous calendar month
Quarter ➤ Next Quarter	Filters data to include only records for the next quarter
Quarter ➤ This Quarter	Filters data to include only records for the current quarter
Quarter ➤ Last Quarter	Filters data to include only records for the previous quarter
Year ➤ Next Year	Filters data to include only records for the next year
Year ➤ This Year	Filters data to include only records for the current year
Year ➤ Last Year	Filters data to include only records for the previous year
Year ➤ Year To Date	Filters data to include only records for the calendar year to date
Custom Filter	Lets you set up a specific filter for two possible date ranges

Filtering Data

Filtering data uses a similar approach, whatever the type of filter that is applied. As a simple example, here is how to apply a number filter to the sale price to find vehicles that sold for less than £5,000.00.

1. Click the pop-up menu for the SalePrice column.

2. Click Number Filters. The submenu will appear.

3. Select Less Than. The Filter Rows dialog will be displayed.

4. Enter **5000** in the box next to the Is Less Than box, as shown in Figure 11-15.

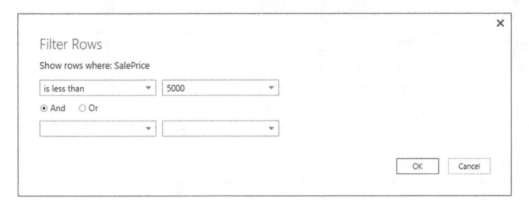

Figure 11-15. *The Filtered Rows dialog*

    5.   Click OK. The data set only displays rows that conform to the filter that you have defined.

Although extremely simple to apply, filters do require these comments:

- You can combine up to two elements in a filter. You can say that both must be applied together (an AND filter) or they can be an alternative (an OR filter).

- You should not apply any formatting when entering numbers.

- Any text that you filter on is not case-sensitive.

- If you choose the wrong filter, you do not have to cancel and start over. Simply select the correct filter type from the pop-up in the left boxes in the Filter Rows dialog.

■ **Note** If you set a filter value that excludes all the records in the table, Get & Transform displays an empty table except for the words *This table is empty*. You can always remove the filter by clicking the X to the left of Filtered Rows in the Applied Steps list.

Counting the Rows in a Data Set

Occasionally you may want to use Get & Transform to check data quality. One core technique that you may need to apply is to count the number of records in a source data set. This data may help you decide if it is worth proceeding with an ETL process.

    1.   In the Transform Ribbon of Get & Transform, click the Count Rows button.

The Get & Transform data grid will display the number of records in the data source. Figure 11-16 shows an example of this.

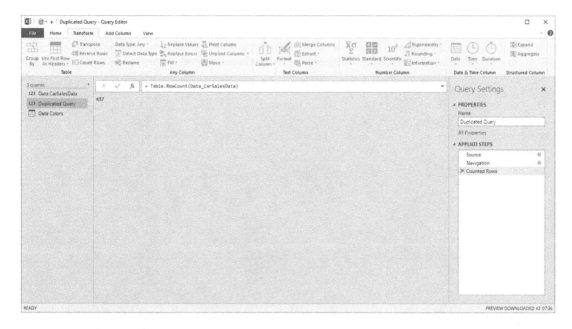

Figure 11-16. *Applying a row count to source data*

Conclusion

This chapter started you on the road to transforming data sets with Get & Transform. You saw how to trim data sets by removing rows and columns. You also saw how to subset a sample of data from a data source by selecting alternating groups of rows.

You saw how to move columns around in the data set and how to rename columns so that your data is easily comprehensible when you use it later in dashboards and reports. Finally, you saw how to filter and sort data, as well as how to remove duplicates to ensure that your data set only contains the precise rows that you need for your upcoming visualizations.

Preparing raw data for use in dashboards and reports is not always easy and can take a while to get right. However, Get & Transform can make this task really easy with a little practice.

So, now that you have grasped the basics, it is time to move on and discover some further data transformation techniques. Specifically, you will see how to cleanse the data that you have imported. This is the subject of the next chapter.

CHAPTER 12

Data Cleansing with Get & Transform

Once a data set has been shaped and filtered, it probably still needs a good few modifications to make it ready for consumption. Many of these modifications are, at their heart, a selection of fairly simple yet necessary techniques that you apply to make the data cleaner and more standardized. I have chosen to group these approaches under the heading *data cleansing*.

The sort of things that you may be looking to do before finally loading source data into the data model can include the following:

- Change the data type for a column—by telling Get & Transform that the column contains numbers, for example

- Replace the values in a cell with other values

- Transform the column contents—by making the text uppercase, for instance, or by removing decimals from numbers

- Apply math or statistical (or even trigonometric) functions to columns of numbers

- Convert date or time data into date elements such as days, months, quarters, years, hours, or minutes

- Fill data down or up over empty cells to ensure that records are complete

- Ensure that the first row is used as headers (if this is required)

- Group record sets and aggregate numbers

This chapter will take you on a tour of these kinds of essential data transformations. Once you have finished reading it, you should be confident that you can take a rough and ready data source as a starting point and convert it into a polished and coherent data table that is ready to become a pivotal part of your Get & Transform data model. Not only that, but you will have carried out really heavy lifting much faster and more easily than you could have done using enterprise-level tools.

Viewing a Full Record

Before even starting to cleanse data, you probably need to take a good look at it. While the Get & Transform Query Editor is great for scrolling up and down columns to see how data compares for a single field, it is often less easy to appreciate the entire contents of a single record.

© Adam Aspin 2016
A. Aspin, *High Impact Data Visualization in Excel with Power View, 3D Maps, Get & Transform and Power BI*,
DOI 10.1007/978-1-4842-2400-7_12

So to avoid having to scroll frenetically left and right across rows of data, the Query Editor has another brilliantly simple solution. If you click a row (or more specifically, on the number of a row in the grid on the left), the Get & Transform Query Editor will display the contents of an entire record (or at least as much as the screen real estate will allow) in a single window under the data set. You can see an example of this in Figure 12-1.

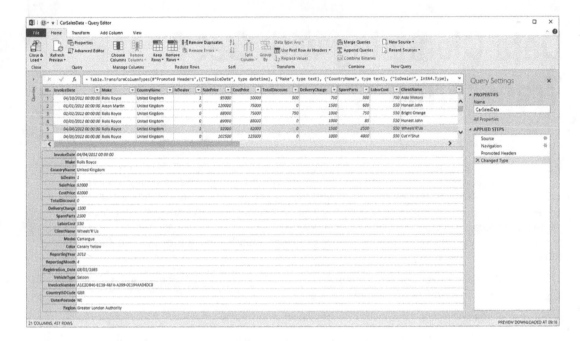

Figure 12-1. *Viewing a full record*

Get & Transform Query Editor Context Menus

As is normal for Windows programs, the Get & Transform Query Editor makes full use of context (or "right-click") menus as an alternative to using the ribbons. When transforming data sets, there are three main context menus that you will probably find yourself using.

- *Table menu*: This menu appears when you right-click the top corner of the grid containing the data.

- *Column menu*: This menu appears when you right-click a column title.

- *Cell menu*: This menu appears when you right-click a data cell.

While I have referred copiously to the context menus when explaining how to transform data, it is probably easier to take a quick look at them now so that you can see the various options. Figure 12-2 gives you a quick overview of these three context menus.

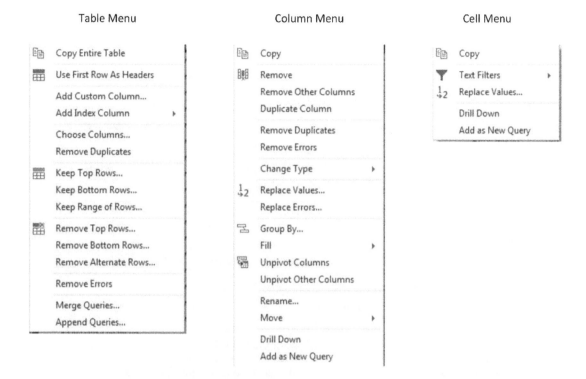

Figure 12-2. *The Get & Transform Query Editor context menus*

■ **Note**   The elements in the context menus are, well, contextual. So, they can vary depending on circumstances. For instance, the cell context menu will display Text Filters, Number Filters, or Date/Time Filters depending on the data type of the selected cell.

Changing Data Type

A truly fundamental aspect of data modification is ensuring that the data is of the appropriate type; that is, if you have a column of numbers that are to be calculated at some point, then the column should be a numeric column. If it contains dates, then it should be set to one of the date or time data types. I realize that this can seem arduous and even superfluous; however, *if you want to be sure that your data can be sliced and diced correctly further down the line,* then setting the right data types at the outset is *vital.* An added bonus is that if you validate the data types early on in the process of loading data, you can see from the start whether the data has any potential issues—dates that cannot be read as dates, for instance. This allows you to decide what to do with poor or unreliable data early in your work with a data set.

The good news here is that for many data sources, Get & Transform applies an appropriate data type. Specifically, if you have loaded data from a database, then Get & Transform will recognize the data type for each column and apply a suitable native data type. Unfortunately, things can get a little more painful with file sources, specifically CSV, text, and Excel files, as well as some XML files. In the case of these file types, Get & Transform often tries to guess the data type, but there are times when it does not succeed. If it has made a stab at deducing data types, then you see a Changed Type step in the Applied Steps list. Consequently, if you are obtaining your data from these sources, then you could well be obliged to apply data types to many of the columns manually.

■ **Note**   In some cases, numbers are not meant to be interpreted as numerical data. For instance, a French postal code is five numbers, but it will never be calculated in any way. So, it is good practice to let Get & Transform know this by changing the data type of fields like these to Text.

Do the following to change the data type for a column or a group of columns, once you have loaded the file SalesData.xlsx:

1. Open the sample file C:\DataVisualisationInExcel2016\CarSalesData.xlsx.

2. Display the Workbook Queries pane, unless it is already visible.

3. Double-click the query CarSalesData in the Workbook Queries pane. The Query Editor will open.

4. Click inside the column whose data type you want to change. If you want to modify several columns, then Ctrl+click the requisite column titles. In this example, you could select the CostPrice and TotalDiscount columns.

5. Click the Data Type button in the Transform section of the Get & Transform Query Home ribbon. A pop-up menu of potential data types will appear.

6. Select an appropriate data type. If you have selected the CostPrice and TotalDiscount columns, then Whole Number is the type to choose.

After a few seconds, the data type will be applied. Changed Type will appear in the Applied Steps pane. Table 12-1 outlines the data types that you can apply.

Table 12-1. *Data Types in Get & Transform*

Data Type	Description
Decimal Number	Converts the data to a decimal number.
Fixed Decimal Number	Converts the data to a decimal number with a fixed number of decimals.
Whole Number	Converts the data to a whole (integer) number.
Date/Time	Converts to a date and time data type.
Date	Converts to a date data type.
Time	Converts to a time data type.
Duration	Sets the data as being a duration. These are used for date and time calculations.
Text	Sets to a text data type.
True/False	Sets the data type to Boolean (True or False).
Binary	Defines the data as binary, and consequently, it is not directly visible.

Inevitably, there will be times when you try to apply a data type that simply cannot be used with a certain column of data. Converting a text column (such as Make in this sample data table) into dates will simply not work. If you do this, then Get & Transform will replace the column contents with Error. This is not definitive or dangerous, and all you have to do to return the data to its previous state is to delete the Changed Type step in the Applied Steps list.

It can help to alter data types at the same time for a *set* of columns where you think that this operation is necessary. There are a couple of good reasons for this approach.

- You can concentrate on getting data types right, and if you are working methodically, you are less likely to forget to set a data type.

- Applying data types for many columns (even if you are doing this in several operations, to single or multiple columns) will add only a single step to the Applied Steps list.

■ **Note**   Don't look for any data formatting options in the Get & Transform Query Editor; there aren't any. This is deliberate since this tool is designed to structure, load, and cleanse data, but not to present it. You carry out the formatting in the in-memory data model using Power Pivot, as you will see in Chapter 14. Alternatively, if you are loading data directly into an Excel worksheet, then format it as you would normally.

Detecting Data Types

Applying the correct data type to dozens of columns can be more than a little time-consuming. Fortunately, Get & Transform now contains an option to apply data types automatically to a whole table.

1. In the Transform ribbon, click the Detect Data Type button.

2. Changed Type will appear in the Applied Steps list. Most of the columns will have the correct data type applied.

This technique does not always give perfect results, and there will be times when you want to override the choice of data type that Get & Transform has applied. Yet it is nonetheless a welcome addition to the data preparation toolset that can save you considerable time when preparing a data set.

Replacing Values

Some data that you load will need certain values to be replaced by others in a kind of global search-and-replace operation—just as you would in a document. For instance, perhaps you need to standardize spellings where a make of car (to use the current sample data set as an example) has been entered incorrectly. To carry out this particular data cleansing operation, do the following:

1. Click the title of the column that contains the data that you want to replace. The column will become selected. In this example, I used the Model column as an example.

2. In the Home ribbon, click the Replace Values button. The Replace Values dialog will appear.

3. In the Value To Find box, enter the text or number that you want to replace. I used Ghost in this example.

4. In the Replace With box, enter the text or number that you want to replace. I used Fantôme in this example, as shown in Figure 12-3.

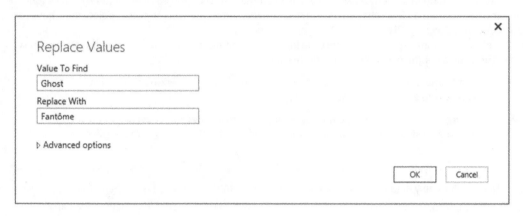

Figure 12-3. The Replace Values dialog

5. Click OK. The data is replaced in the entire column. Replaced Values are added to the Applied Steps list.

I have these few comments about this technique:

-   The Replace Values process searches for every occurrence of the text that you are looking for in each record of the selected columns. It does not look for the entire contents of the cell unless you specifically request this by checking the Match Entire Cell Contents check box in the advanced options.

-   If you click a cell containing the contents that you want to replace (rather than the column title, as you just did), before starting the process, Get & Transform automatically places the cell contents in the Replace Values dialog as the value to find.

-   You can only replace text in columns that contain text elements. This does not work with columns that are set as a numeric or date data type.

-   If you really have to replace parts of a date or figures in a numeric column with other dates or numbers, then you can do the following:

    -   Convert the column to a text data type

    -   Carry out the replace operation

    -   Convert the column back to the original data type

The Replace Values dialog also has a few advanced options that you can apply. You can see these if you expand the Advanced Options item by clicking the triangle to its left. Table 12-2 explains these options.

Table 12-2. *Advanced Replace Options*

Option	Description
Match Entire Cell Contents	Replaces the search value only if it makes up the entire contents of the column for a row
Replace Using Special Characters	Replaces the search value with a nonprinting character
Tab	Replaces the search value with a tab character
Carriage Return	Replaces the search value with a carriage return character
Line Feed	Replaces the search value with a line feed character
Carriage Return And Line Feed	Replaces the search value with a carriage return and line feed

■ **Note** Replacing words that are subsets of another is dangerous. When replacing any data, make sure that you don't damage elements other than the one you intend to change.

As a final and purely spurious comment, I must add that I would never suggest rebranding a Rolls-Royce, as it would be close to automotive sacrilege.

Transforming Column Contents

Get & Transform has a powerful toolbox of automated data transformations that allow you to standardize the contents of a column in several ways. These include the following:

- Setting the capitalization of text columns

- Rounding numeric data or applying math functions

- Extracting date elements such as the year, month, or day (among others) from a date column

Get & Transform is strict about applying transformations to appropriate types of data. This is because transforms are totally dependent on the data type of the selected column. This is yet another confirmation that applying the requisite data type is an operation that should be carried out early in any data transformation process—and certainly *before* transforming the column contents. Remember, you will only be able to select a numeric transformation if the column is a numeric data type, and you will only be able to select a date transformation if the column is a date data type. Equally, the text-based transformations can be applied only to columns that are of the text data type.

Text Transformation

Let's look at a simple transformation operation in action. As an example, I will get Get & Transform to convert the Make column to uppercase characters.

1. Still using the file CarSalesData.xlsx, click anywhere in the column whose contents you want to transform (Make, in this case).

2. In the Transform ribbon, click the Format button. A pop-up menu will appear.

3. Select UPPERCASE, as shown in Figure 12-4.

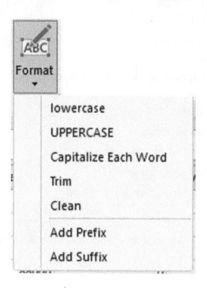

Figure 12-4. *Transforming a text to uppercase*

The contents of the entire column will be converted to uppercase. Uppercased Text will be added to the Applied Steps list.

As you can see from the menu for the Format button, you have seven possible options when formatting (or transforming) text. Table 12-3 explains these options.

Table 12-3. *Text Transformations*

Transformation	Description	Applied Steps Definition
Lowercase	Converts all the text to lowercase	Lowercased Text
Uppercase	Converts all the text to uppercase	Uppercased Text
Capitalize Each Word	Converts the first letter of each word to a capital	Capitalized Each Word
Trim	Removes all spaces before and after the text	Trimmed Text
Clean	Removes any nonprintable characters	Cleaned Text
Add Prefix	Adds text that precedes the cell contents	Added Prefix
Add Suffix	Adds text that follows the cell contents	Added Suffix

■ **Note**   I realize that Get & Transform Query calls text transformations *formatting*. Nonetheless, these options are part of the overall data transformation options.

If you choose to add a prefix or a suffix to the cell contents, the dialog that you can see in Figure 12-5 will appear, where you can enter the text that you want to add.

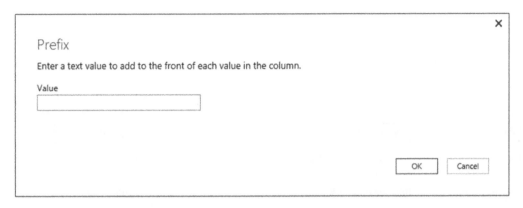

Figure 12-5. *The Prefix dialog*

Removing Leading and Trailing Spaces

There will inevitably be occasions when you inherit data that has extra spaces before, after, or before *and* after the data itself. This can be insidious, as it can cause the following:

- Data duplication, because a value with a trailing space is *not* considered identical to the same text without the spaces that follow

- Sort issues, because a leading space causes an element to appear at the *top* of a sorted list

- Grouping errors, because elements with spaces are not part of the same group as elements without spaces

Fortunately, Get & Transform has a ruthlessly efficient solution to this problem.

1. Click anywhere in the column whose contents you want to transform (Make, in this case).

2. In the Transform ribbon, click the Format button. A pop-up menu will appear.

3. Select Trim from the menu.

All superfluous leading and trailing spaces will be removed from the data in the column. This should help with sorting, grouping, and deduplicating records.

Number Transformations

Just as you can transform the contents of text-based columns, you can also apply transformations to numeric values. As an example, suppose you want to round up all the figures in a column to the nearest whole number.

1. Click anywhere in the column whose contents you want to transform (TotalDiscount, in this case).

2. In the Transform ribbon, click the Rounding button. A pop-up menu will appear.

3. Select Round Up.

The values in the entire column will be rounded up to the nearest whole number. Rounded Up will be added to the Applied Steps list.

Table 12-4 describes the other possible numeric transformations that are available. Because these numeric transformations use several buttons in the Transform ribbon, I have indicated which button to use to get the desired result.

Table 12-4. *Number Transformations*

Transformation	Description	Applied Steps Definition
Rounding ➤ Round Up	Rounds each number to the specified number of decimal places.	Rounded Up
Rounding ➤ Round Down	Rounds each number up.	Rounded Down
Round...	Rounds each number to the number of decimals that you specify. If you specify a negative number, you round to a given decile.	Rounded Off
Scientific ➤ Absolute Value	Makes the number absolute (positive).	
Scientific ➤ Power ➤ Square	Returns the square of the number in each cell.	Calculated Square
Scientific ➤ Power ➤ Cube	Returns the cube of the number in each cell.	Calculated Cube
Scientific ➤ Power ➤ Power	Raises each number to the power that you specify.	Calculated Power
Scientific ➤ Square Root	Returns the square root of the number in each cell.	Square Root
Scientific ➤ Exponent	Returns the exponent of the number in each cell.	Calculated Exponent
Scientific ➤ Logarithm ➤ Base 10	Returns the base 10 logarithm of the number in each cell.	Calculated Base 10 Logarithm
Scientific ➤ Logarithm ➤ Natural	Returns the natural logarithm of the number in each cell.	Calculated Natural Logarithm
Scientific ➤ Factorial	Gives the factorial of numbers in the column.	Calculated Factorial
Trigonometry ➤ Sine	Gives the sine of the numbers in the column.	Calculated Sine
Trigonometry ➤ Cosine	Gives the cosine of the numbers in the column.	Calculated Cosine
Trigonometry ➤ Tangent	Gives the tangent of the numbers in the column.	Calculated Tangent
Trigonometry ➤ ArcSine	Gives the arcsine of the numbers in the column.	Calculated ArcSine
Trigonometry ➤ ArcCosine	Gives the arccosine of the numbers in the column.	Calculated ArcCosine
Trigonometry ➤ ArcTangent	Gives the arctangent of the numbers in the column.	Calculated ArcTangent

■ **Note**   Get & Transform will not even let you try to apply numeric transformation to text or dates. The relevant buttons remain grayed out if you click inside a column of letters or dates.

Calculating Numbers

The Get & Transform Query can also apply simple arithmetic to the figures in a column. Suppose, for instance, that you want to multiply all the sale prices by 110 percent as part of your forecasts. This is how you can do just that:

1. Click inside any column of numbers. In this example, I used the column SalePrice.

2. Click the Standard button in the Transform ribbon. The menu will appear.

3. Click Multiply. The Multiply dialog will appear.

4. Enter **1.1** in the Value box. The dialog will look like the one shown in Figure 12-6.

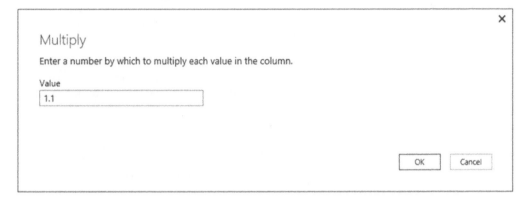

Figure 12-6. Applying a calculation to a column

5. Click OK.

All the numbers in the selected column will be multiplied by 1.1. In other words, they are now 110 percent of the original value. Table 12-5 describes the possible math operations that you can carry out in Get & Transform.

Table 12-5. Applying Basic Calculations

Transformation	Description	Applied Steps Definition
Add	Adds a selected value to the numbers in a column	Added to Column
Multiply	Multiplies the numbers in a column by a selected value	Multiplied Column
Subtract	Subtracts a selected value from the numbers in a column	Subtracted from Column
Divide	Divides the numbers in a column by a selected value	Divided Column
Integer-Divide	Divides the numbers in a column by a selected value and removes any remainder	Integer-Divided Column
Modulo	Divides the numbers in a column by a selected value and leaves only the remainder	Calculated Modulo

> ■ **Note** You can also carry out many types of calculations in Power Pivot or even in Excel worksheets and avoid carrying out calculations in the Query Editor. Indeed, many Get & Transform purists seem to prefer that anything resembling a calculation should take place inside the data model rather than at the query stage. As ever, I will let you decide which approach you prefer. Yet I would advise you to read Chapters 15 through 17 to get a clearer understanding of how to add calculated elements using DAX. This is because some transformations need to adjust to the situation (the context) in which they are used and consequently need to be done using DAX. Be aware that some heavy transforms can slow the reports down if calculated at run time, whereas others can be effective only as part of a well-thought-out calculation process.

Finally, it is important to remember that you are altering the data when you carry out this kind of operation. In the real world, you might be safer duplicating a column before profoundly altering the data it contains.

Date Transformations

Transforming dates follows similar principles to transforming text and numbers. As an example, here is how to isolate the year from a date:

1. Click inside the InvoiceDate column.

2. In the Transform ribbon, click the Date button. The menu will appear.

3. Click Year. The submenu will appear.

4. Select Year. The year part of the date will replace all the dates in the InvoiceDate column.

Table 12-6 gives the other possible date transformations that are possible.

Table 12-6. *Date Transformations*

Transformation	Description	Applied Steps Definition
Age	Calculates the date and time difference (in days and hours) between the original date and the current local time	Calculated Age
Date Only	Converts the data to a date without the time element	Calculated Date
Year ➤ Year	Extracts the year from the date	Calculated Year
Year ➤ Start of Year	Returns the first day of the year for the date	Calculated Start of Year
Year ➤ End of Year	Returns the last day of the year for the date	Calculated End of Year
Month ➤ Month	Extracts the number of the month from the date	Calculated Month
Month ➤ Start of Month	Returns the first day of the month for the date	Calculated Start of Month
Month ➤ End of Month	Returns the last day of the month for the date	Calculated End of Month
Month ➤ Days in Month	Returns the number of days in the month for the date	Calculated Days in Month
Day ➤ Day	Extracts the day from the date	Calculated Day
Day ➤ Day of Week	Returns the weekday as a number (Monday is 1, Tuesday is 2, and so on)	Calculated Day of Week
Day ➤ Day of Year	Calculates the number of days since the start of the year for the date	Calculated Day of Year
Day ➤ Start of Day	Returns the start of the day	Calculated Start of Day
Day ➤ End of Day	Returns the end of the day	Calculated End of Day
Quarter ➤ Quarter	Returns the calendar quarter of the year for the date	Calculated Quarter
Quarter ➤ Start of Quarter	Returns the first date of the calendar quarter of the year for the date	Calculated Start of Quarter
Quarter ➤ End of Quarter	Returns the last date of the calendar quarter of the year for the date	Calculated End of Quarter
Week ➤ Week of Year	Calculates the number of weeks since the start of the year for the date	Calculated Week of Year
Week ➤ Week of Month	Calculates the number of weeks since the start of the month for the date	Calculated Week of Month
Week ➤ Start of Week	Returns the date for the first day of the week (Monday) for the date	Calculated Start of Week
Week ➤ End of Week	Returns the date for the last day of the week (Monday) for the date	Calculated End of Week

Time Transformations

You can also transform date/time or time values into their component parts using the Get & Transform Query. This is extremely similar to how you apply date transformations, but in the interest of completeness, the following explains how to do this:

1. Click inside the InvoiceDate column.

2. In the Transform ribbon, click the Time button. The menu will appear.

3. Click Hour. The hour part of the time will replace all the values in the InvoiceDate column.

Table 12-7 gives the range of time transformations.

Table 12-7. *Time Transformations*

Transformation	Description	Applied Steps Definition
Time Only	Isolates the time part of a date and time	Extracted Time
Local Time	Converts time from other time zones to the local time	Local Time
Parse	Converts times stored as text to time values	Parsed Time
Hour	Isolates the hour from a date/time or date value	Extracted Hour
Minute	Isolates the minute from a date/time or date value	Extracted Minute
Second	Isolates the second from a date/time or date value	Extracted Second
Earliest	Returns the earliest time from a date/time or date value	Calculated Earliest
Latest	Returns the latest time from a date/time or date value	Calculated Latest

■ **Note** In the real world, you could well want to leave a source column intact and apply number or date transformations to a copy of the column. You learn how to apply these transformations to copies of columns in the next chapter.

Duration

If you have values in a column that can be interpreted as a duration (in days, hours, minutes, and seconds), then the Get & Transform Query can extract the component parts of the duration as a data transformation. For this to work, however, the column *must* be set to the duration data type. This means that the contents of the column have to be interpreted as a duration by Get & Transform. Any values that are incompatible with this data type will be set to error values.

If you have duration data, you can extract its component parts like this:

1. Click inside the column.

2. In the Transform ribbon, click the Duration button. The menu will appear.

3. Click Hour. The hour part of the time will replace all the values in the InvoiceDate column.

Table 12-8 gives the range of duration transformations.

Table 12-8. *Duration Transformations*

Transformation	Description	Applied Steps Definition
Days	Isolates the day element from a duration value	Extracted Days
Hours	Isolates the hour element from a duration value	Extracted Hours
Minutes	Isolates the minutes element from a duration value	Extracted Minutes
Seconds	Isolates the seconds element from a duration value	Extracted Seconds
Total Days	Displays the duration value as the number of days and a fraction representing hours, minutes, and seconds	Calculated Total Days
Total Hours	Displays the duration value as the number of hours and a fraction representing minutes and seconds	Calculated Total Hours
Total Minutes	Displays the duration value as the number of minutes and a fraction representing seconds	Calculated Total Minutes
Total Seconds	Displays the duration value as the number of seconds and a fraction representing milliseconds	Calculated Total Seconds
Multiply	Multiplies the duration (and all its component parts) by a value that you enter	Multiplied Column
Divide	Divides the duration (and all its component parts) by a value that you enter	Divided Column
Statistics ➤ Sum	Returns the total for all the duration elements in the column	Calculated Sum
Statistics ➤ Minimum	Returns the minimum value of all the duration elements in the column	Calculated Minimum
Statistics ➤ Maximum	Returns the maximum value of all the duration elements in the column	Calculated Maximum
Statistics ➤ Median	Returns the median value for all the duration elements in the column	Calculated Median
Statistics ➤ Average	Returns the average for all the duration elements in the column	Calculated Average

░ **Note** If you multiply or divide a duration, the Get & Transform Query displays a dialog so that you can enter the value to multiply or divide the duration by.

Filling Down

Imagine a data source where the data has come into Get & Transform from a matrix-style structure. The result is that some columns contain only a single example of an element and then a series of empty cells until the next element in the list. If this is difficult to imagine, then suppose you have loaded the sample file CarMakeAndModelMatrix.xlsx into Get & Transform (the easiest way is to click inside the table and then click the From Table button in the Data ribbon) and you are looking at the table shown in Figure 12-7 in the Get & Transform Query Editor.

⊞▾	Make	▼	Marque	▼	Sales	▼
1	Aston Martin		DB4		391000	
2		null	DB7		500740	
3		null	DB9		915070	
4		null	DBS		230000	
5		null	Rapide		225000	
6		null	Vanquish		746500	
7		null	Vantage		320850	
8		null	Zagato		178500	
9	Bentley		Arnage		44000	
10		null	Azure		239250	
11		null	Continental		991250	
12		null	Turbo R		347500	
13	Jaguar		XJ12		303500	
14		null	XJ6		602000	
15		null	XK		1092250	
16	MGB		GT		315000	
17	Rolls Royce		Camargue		810300	
18		null	Phantom		178500	
19		null	Silver Ghost		649500	
20		null	Silver Seraph		288500	
21		null	Silver Shadow		308500	
22		null	Wraith		178500	
23	Triumph		TR4		140500	
24		null	TR5		98250	
25		null	TR7		47750	
26	TVR		Cerbera		89250	
27		null	Tuscan		112250	

Figure 12-7. *A matrix data table*

Since you need a full data table, all these blank cells are a problem—or rather, they would be, if Get & Transform did not have a really cool way of overcoming this particular difficulty. Do the following to solve this problem:

1. Click in the column that contains the empty cells; make sure you click where you want to replace the empty cells with the contents of the first nonempty cell above.

2. In the Transform ribbon, click Fill. The menu will appear.

3. Select Down. The blank cells will be replaced by the value in the first nonempty cell above. Filled Down will be added to the Applied Steps list.

The table will now look like Figure 12-8.

▦▾	Make	▾	Marque	▾	Sales	▾
1	Aston Martin		DB4		391000	
2	Aston Martin		DB7		500740	
3	Aston Martin		DB9		915070	
4	Aston Martin		DBS		230000	
5	Aston Martin		Rapide		225000	
6	Aston Martin		Vanquish		746500	
7	Aston Martin		Vantage		320850	
8	Aston Martin		Zagato		178500	
9	Bentley		Arnage		44000	
10	Bentley		Azure		239250	
11	Bentley		Continental		991250	
12	Bentley		Turbo R		347500	
13	Jaguar		XJ12		303500	
14	Jaguar		XJ6		602000	
15	Jaguar		XK		1092250	
16	MGB		GT		315000	
17	Rolls Royce		Camargue		810300	
18	Rolls Royce		Phantom		178500	
19	Rolls Royce		Silver Ghost		649500	
20	Rolls Royce		Silver Seraph		288500	
21	Rolls Royce		Silver Shadow		308500	
22	Rolls Royce		Wraith		178500	
23	Triumph		TR4		140500	
24	Triumph		TR5		98250	
25	Triumph		TR7		47750	
26	TVR		Cerbera		89250	
27	TVR		Tuscan		112250	

Figure 12-8. *A data table with empty cells replaced by the correct data*

▨ **Note** This technique is built to handle a fairly specific problem and really works only if the imported data is grouped by the column containing the missing elements.

Although it's rare, you can also use this technique to fill empty cells with the value from below. If you need to do this, just select Fill ➤ Up from the Transform ribbon. In either case, you need to be aware that the technique is applied to the entire column.

Using the First Row As Headers

Get & Transform is good at guessing if it needs to take the first record of a source data set and have it function as the column headers. This is fundamental for two reasons.

- You avoid leaving the columns named Column1, Column2, and so on. Leaving them named generically like this would make it needlessly difficult for a user (or even yourself) to understand the data.

- You avoid having a text element (which should be the column title) in a column of figures, which can cause problems later. This is because a whole column needs to have the same data type for another data type to be applied. Having a header text in the first row prevents this for numeric and data/time data types, for instance.

Yet there could be—albeit rare—occasions when Get & Transform guesses incorrectly and assumes that the first record in a data set is data when it is really the header information. So, instead of headers, you have a set of generic column titles such as Column1, Column2, and so forth. Fortunately, correcting this and using the first row as headers is simple.

1. Click Use First Row As Headers in the Transform section of the Get & Transform Query window Home ribbon.

After a few seconds, the first record disappears and the column titles become the elements that were in the first record. On the right now contains a Promoted Headers element, indicating which process has taken place. This step is highlighted.

■ **Note** Get & Transform is often able to apply this step automatically when the source is a database. It can often correctly guess when the source is a file. However, it cannot always guess accurately, so sometimes you have to intervene. You can see if Get & Transform has had to guess this if it has added a Promoted Headers element to the Applied Steps list.

In the rare event that Get & Transform gets this operation wrong and presumes that a first row consists of column titles when it is not, you can reset the titles to be the first row by clicking the tiny triangle to the right of the Use First Row As Headers button. This displays a short menu where you can click the Use Headers As First Row option. The Applied Steps list on the right now contains a Demoted Headers element, and the column titles are Column1, Column2, and so forth. You can subsequently rename the columns as you see fit.

Grouping Records

At times, you will need to transform your original data in an extreme way—by grouping the data. This is very different from filtering data, removing duplicates, or cleansing the contents of columns. When you group data, you are altering the structure of the data set to "roll up" records where you do the following:

- Define the attribute columns that will become the unique elements in the grouped data table

- Specify which aggregations are applied to any numeric columns included in the grouped table

Grouping is frequently an extremely selective operation. This is inevitable, since the more attribute (that is, non-numeric) columns you choose to group on, the more records you are likely to include in the grouped table. However, this will always depend on the particular data set you are dealing with, and grouping data efficiently is always a matter of flair, practice, and good old-fashioned trial and error. As an example, you could try the following:

1. Edit the Sales Workbook query from the Excel workbook `C:\DataVisualisationInExcel2016\SalesData2012_2013.xlsx`.

2. Select the following columns (by Ctrl+clicking the column headers):

   a. Make

   b. Model

3. In the Get & Transform Query Editor's Home ribbon, click the Group By button. The Group By dialog will appear.

4. In the New Column Name box, enter **TotalSales**.

5. Select Sum as the operation.

6. Choose SalePrice as the source column in the Column pop-up list.

7. Click the plus (+) icon to the right of the new column elements that you just entered and repeat the operation; only this time, use the following:

   a. *New Column Name*: AverageCost

   b. *Operation*: Average

   c. *Column*: CostPrice

The dialog should look like the one in Figure 12-9.

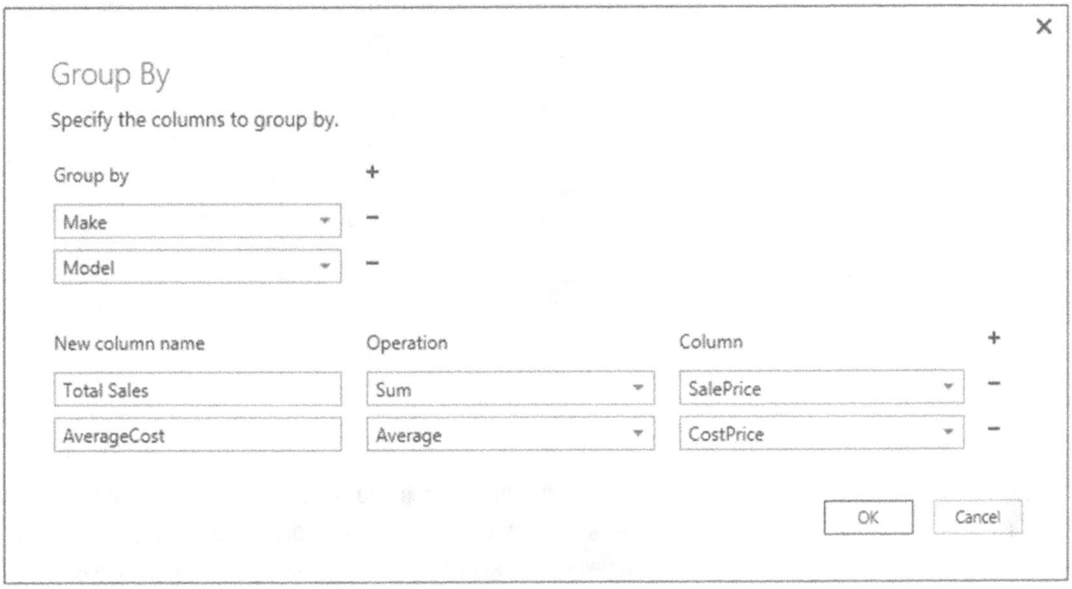

Figure 12-9. The Group By dialog

8. Click OK. All columns, other than those that you specified in the Group By dialog, are removed, and the table is grouped and aggregated, as shown in Figure 12-10. Grouped Rows will be added to the Applied Steps list. I have also sorted the table by the Make and Model columns to make the grouping easier to comprehend.

▦▾	Make	Model	Total Sales	AverageCost
1	Rolls Royce	Camargue	4116900	61002.69231
2	Aston Martin	DBS	465500	68000
3	Rolls Royce	Silver Ghost	1315500	75630
4	Aston Martin	DB7	1023480	23703.125
5	Aston Martin	DB9	5423860	59132.96296
6	Aston Martin	DB4	793000	84167.5
7	Aston Martin	Vantage	658200	38750
8	Aston Martin	Vanquish	1506750	89700
9	Aston Martin	Rapide	455500	142500
10	Aston Martin	Zagato	359750	127500
11	Rolls Royce	Wraith	359750	64500
12	Rolls Royce	Silver Shadow	622500	71445
13	Rolls Royce	Silver Seraph	582500	71445
14	Rolls Royce	Phantom	359750	64500
15	Jaguar	XK	4431500	39827.65957
16	Jaguar	XJ6	1239750	32630.76923
17	Jaguar	XJ12	618000	33750
18	Bentley	Continental	3662250	49256.86275
19	Bentley	Arnage	90750	28200
20	Bentley	Azure	489500	28200
21	Bentley	Turbo R	708750	35460
22	TVR	Tuscan	374250	41000
23	TVR	Cerbera	154250	39500
24	MGB	GT	1011000	9500
25	Triumph	TR4	566500	18704.54545
26	Triumph	TR5	207500	19500
27	Triumph	TR7	101000	15250

Figure 12-10. *Grouping a data set*

■ **Note** You do not have to Ctrl+click to select the grouping columns. You can add them one by one to the Group By dialog by clicking the plus button to the top right of the list of grouped columns. Equally, you can remove grouping columns (or added and aggregated columns) by clicking the minus icon to the right of a column name.

Conclusion

In this short chapter, you learned some essential techniques that you can use to cleanse and standardize data sets. You saw how to round numbers up and down, how to deliver conformed text presentation, and how to remove extraneous spaces from columns of data.

You also saw how to replace values inside columns, as well as ways of applying mathematical, statistical, and trigonometric functions to numbers. Other techniques covered extracting date, time, and duration elements from date/time and duration columns. Finally, you saw how to group and aggregate data that is ready to load into the data model.

It is now time to see how you can join separate data sets into single queries and, more generally, how to manage the multiple queries that often underpin a data model. This will be the subject of the next chapter.

CHAPTER 13

■ ■ ■

Data Mashup with Get & Transform

In the previous two chapters, you saw how to hone your data set so that you used only the rows and columns of data that you really need and then how to cleanse and complete the data that they contain. In this chapter, you will learn how to build on these foundations to deliver data that is ready to be molded into a structured and usable data model.

The generic term for this kind of data preparation in Get & Transform is *data mashup*. It covers the following:

- *Extending data sets by adding further columns*: These will nearly always be derived from existing columns of data. You could extract years or months from a date column into separate columns, for instance. Alternatively, you could create calculated columns based on existing data—or even take lists of data from a single column and present the data across several columns.

- *Joining data sets (or queries, if you prefer)*: This involves taking two queries and linking them so that you display the data from both sources as a single data set.

- *Pivoting and unpivoting data*: If you need to switch data in rows to display as columns—or vice versa—then you can get the Get & Transform Query Editor to help you do this. This means you can guarantee that the data in all the tables that you are using conforms to a standardized tabular structure.

I want to be clear that separating data preparation into these two apparently contradictory approaches—reducing data sets only to augment them later—is not necessarily the way you will work in practice. Given the range of features available in Get & Transform, I have simply tried to apply some structure to the way they are explained. Ideally, this will make the data-handling toolkit that is the Get & Transform Query Editor a little easier to understand. I imagine that when you are delving into data with Get & Transform, you will mix and alternate many of the techniques that are outlined in Chapters 10 through 13 in any order. After all, one of the great strengths of Get & Transform is that it does not impose any strict way of working and lets you experiment freely. So, remember that you are at liberty to take any approach you want when transforming source data. The only thing that matters is that it gives you the result you want.

Creating a good data model can mean using a large variety of source data queries. So, you will also need to know how to manage the queries that you create to use them efficiently. Consequently, I will end this chapter with a short overview of query management so that you can get an idea of some of the techniques that you might need to keep your queries under control in real-world situations.

The Get & Transform View Ribbon

Until now, you have concentrated your attention on the Get & Transform Home, Transform, and Add Columns ribbons. This is for the simple reason that this is where nearly all the action takes place. There is, however, a fourth Get & Transform ribbon—the View ribbon. Figure 13-1 shows the buttons that it contains, and Table 13-1 explains the options.

© Adam Aspin 2016

A. Aspin, *High Impact Data Visualization in Excel with Power View, 3D Maps, Get & Transform and Power BI*, DOI 10.1007/978-1-4842-2400-7_13

Figure 13-1. *The Get & Transform View ribbon*

Table 13-1. *Get & Transform View Ribbon Options*

Option	Description
Query Settings	Displays or hides the Query Settings pane at the right of the Get & Transform window. This includes the Applied Steps list.
Advanced Editor	Displays the Advanced Editor dialog containing all the code for the steps in the query.
Formula Bar	Shows or hides the formula bar.
Monospaced	Displays data in a monospaced font.

Possibly the only option that is not immediately self-explanatory is the Advanced Editor button. It displays the code for all the transformations in the query as a single block of M language script.

■ **Tip**   Personally, I find that the Query Settings pane and the formula bar are too vital to be removed from the Get & Transform Query window when transforming data. Consequently, I tend to leave them visible. If you need the screen real estate, however, then you can always hide them for a while.

Extending Data

Transforming data does not only consist of reducing it. Sometimes you may have to *extend* the data to make it usable. This normally means adding further columns to a data table. The techniques to do this cover the following:

- Duplicating columns and possibly altering the format of the data in the copied column

- Extracting part of the data in a column into a new column

- Parsing the data in a column so that each data element appears in a separate column

- Merging columns into a new column

Let's take a look at these techniques and see how you can apply them to prepare data for the reports and dashboards that you will create using Get & Transform.

- Adding custom columns that possibly contain calculations or extract part of a column's data into a new column, or even concatenate columns. This can be crucial given that Get & Transform tries to aggregate anything remotely looking like a number. Consequently, you must ensure that you have provided it with the columns of numbers that you need to work with.

- Adding "index" columns to ensure uniqueness or memorize a sort order.

Duplicating Columns

Sometimes you just need a simple copy of a column, with nothing added and nothing taken away. This is where the Duplicate Column button comes into play.

1. Load the C:\DataVisualisationInExcel2016\CarSales_Tables.xlsx sample file.

2. Display the Workbook Queries pane (if it is not yet visible) and right-click the SalesData query.

3. Select Edit. The Get & Transform Query Editor will open and display the data underlying this query.

4. Click inside (or on the title of) the column you want to duplicate. I will use the Make column in this example.

5. In the Add Column ribbon, click the Duplicate Column button. After a few seconds, a copy of the column is created at the right of the existing table. Duplicated Column will appear in the Applied Steps list.

6. Scroll to the right of the table and rename the existing column; it is currently named Make-Copy.

■ **Note**   The duplicate column is named Original Column Name-Copy. I find that it helps to rename copies of columns sooner rather than later in a data mashup process.

Splitting Columns

Sometimes a source column contains data that you really need to break up into smaller pieces across two or more columns. The following are classic cases where this happens:

- A column contains a list of elements, separated by a specific character (known as a *delimiter*).

- A column contains a list of elements, but the elements can be divided at specific places in the column.

- A column contains a concatenated text that needs to be split into its composite elements (a bank account number or a Social Security number are examples of this).

The following short sections explain how to handle such eventualities where it cannot be handled by the initial data load.

Splitting Column by a Delimiter

Here is another requirement that you may encounter occasionally. The data that has been imported
has a column that needs to be further split into multiple columns. Imagine a text file where columns are
separated by semicolons, and these subdivisions each contain a column that holds a comma-separated list
of elements. Once you have imported the file, you then need to further separate the contents of this column
that uses a different delimiter.

Here is what you can do to split the data from one column over several columns:

1. Load the C:\DataVisualisationInExcel2016\CarSales_Tables.xlsx sample
    file.

2. Display the Workbook Queries pane (if it is not yet visible) and right-click the
    SalesData query.

3. Select Edit. The Get & Transform Query Editor will open and display the data
    underlying this query.

4. Click inside the InvoiceNumber column.

5. In the Transform ribbon, click the Split Column button. The menu will appear.

6. Select By Delimiter in the pop-up menu. The Split A Column By Delimiter dialog
    appears.

7. Select Custom from the list of available options in the Select Or Enter Delimiter
    pop-up. A new box will appear in the dialog.

8. Enter a hyphen (-) in the new box.

9. Click At Each Occurrence Of The Delimiter. The dialog should look like
    Figure 13-2.

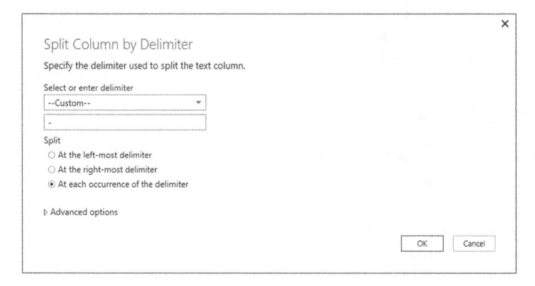

Figure 13-2. *Splitting a column using a delimiter*

10. Click OK. Split Column By Delimiter will appear in the Applied Steps list.

The initial column is replaced, and all the new columns are named InvoiceNumber.1, InvoiceNumber.2, and so forth. As many additional columns as there are delimiters are created; each is named (Column.n) and is sequentially numbered. Figure 13-3 shows the result of this operation.

InvoiceNumber.1 ▼	InvoiceNumber.2 ▼	InvoiceNumber.3 ▼	InvoiceNumber.4 ▼	InvoiceNumber.5 ▼
8B3D7F83	F42C	4523	A737	CDCBF7705B77
139BEEEF	FF32	4BE9	9EF1	819AC888B85C
D35D72CD	5FF3	4701	A6D1	265A4F4E7CD5
2ABAA300	E2A5	4E37	BFCA	7B80ED88A2BD
A1C2D846	EC39	46FA	A399	0C194AAD4DC8
1B8F325A	CC41	4BA6	A486	9D44962E40A3
F1B566F0	D137	4810	B449	575438F3F392
ADFFAC9E	DFF3	4BAB	9EC4	DEE9A2B69350
15A3BC61	82BD	4CCD	8F0B	49EEE59AF4B7
CFC6726D	1522	4981	BC6B	766AE2C6EED0

Figure 13-3. *The results of splitting a column*

This particular process has several options, and their consequences can be fairly far-reaching as far as the data is concerned. Table 13-2 describes the available options followed by a few comments.

Table 13-2. *Delimiter Split Options*

Option	Description
Colon	Uses the colon (:) as the delimiter.
Comma	Uses the comma (,) as the delimiter.
Equals Sign	Uses the equal sign (=) as the delimiter.
Semi-Colon	Uses the semicolon (;) as the delimiter.
Space	Uses the space ( ) as the delimiter.
Tab	Uses the tab character as the delimiter.
Custom	Lets you enter a custom delimiter.
At the Left-Most Delimiter	Splits the column once only at the first occurrence of the delimiter.
At the Right-Most Delimiter	Splits the column once only at the last occurrence of the delimiter.
At Each Occurrence of the Delimiter	Splits the column into as many columns as there are delimiters.
Advanced Options ➤ Number of Columns to Split Into	Allows you to set a maximum number of columns into which the data is split in chunks of the given number of characters. Any extra columns are placed in the rightmost column.
Advanced Options ➤ Quote Style ➤ CSV	Separators inside a text that is contained in double quotes are not used to split the text into columns.
Advanced Options ➤ Quote Style ➤ None	Quotes are not taken into consideration when splitting text into columns.

Splitting Columns by Number of Characters

Another variant on this theme is when text in each column is a fixed number of characters and needs to be broken down into constituent parts at specific intervals. Suppose, for instance, that you have a field where each group of (a certain number of) characters has a specific meaning and you want to break it into multiple columns. Alternatively, suppose you want to extract the leftmost or rightmost n characters and leave the rest. A bank account or Social Security number are examples of this. This is where splitting a column by the number of characters can come in handy. As the principle is similar to the process you just saw, I will not repeat the whole thing again. All you have to do is choose the By Number Of Characters menu option at step 4 in the previous exercise. Table 13-3 gives options for this type of operation.

Table 13-3. *Options When Splitting a Column by Number of Characters*

Option	Description
Number Of Characters	Lets you define the number of characters of data before splitting the column.
Once, As Far Left As Possible	Splits the column once only at the given number of characters in from the left.
Once, As Far Right As Possible	Splits the column once only at the given number of characters in from the right.
Repeatedly	Splits the column as many times as necessary to cut it into segments every defined number of characters.
Advanced Options ➤ Number Of Columns To Split Into	Allows you to set a maximum number of columns into which the data is split in chunks of the given number of characters. Any extra columns are placed in the rightmost column.

Here are a couple of things to note when splitting columns:

- When splitting by a delimiter, Get & Transform makes a good attempt at guessing the maximum number of columns into which the source column must be split. If it gets this wrong (and you can see what its guesstimate is if you expand the Advanced Options box), you can override the number here.

- If you select a Custom Delimiter, Get & Transform displays a new box in the dialog where you can enter a specific delimiter.

- Not every record has to have the same number of delimiters. Get & Transform simply leaves the rightmost column (or columns) blank if there are fewer split elements for a row.

■ **Note**   You can split columns only if they are text data. The Split Column button remains grayed out if your intention is to try to split a date or numeric column.

Merging Columns

You may be feeling a certain sense of déjà-vu when you read the title of this section. After all, you saw how to merge columns (that is, how to fuse the data from several columns into a single, wider column) in a previous chapter, did you not?

Yes, you did indeed. However, this is not the only time in this chapter that you will see something that you have tried previously. This is because the Get & Transform Query Editor repeats several of the options that are in the Transform menu in the Add Column menu. While these functions all work in much the same way, there is one essential difference. If you select an option from the Transform menu, then the column (or columns) that you selected is *modified*. If you select a similar option from the Add Column menu, then the original column (or columns) will not be altered, but a *new column* is added containing the results of the data transformation.

Merging columns is a case in point. Now, as I went into detail as to how to execute this kind of data transformation in the previous chapter, I will not describe it all over again here. Suffice it to say, if you Ctrl+click the headings of two or more columns and then click Merge Columns in the Add Column ribbon, you will still see the data from the selected columns concatenated into a single column. However, this time the original columns *remain* in the data set. The new column is named Merged, exactly as was the case for the first of the columns that you selected when merging columns using the Transform ribbon.

The following are other functions that can either overwrite the data in existing columns *or* display the result as a new column:

- *Format*: Trims or changes the capitalization of text

- *Extract*: Takes part of a column and creates another column from this data

- *Parse*: Adds a column containing the source column data as JSON or XML strings

- *Statistics*: Creates a new column of aggregated numeric values

- *Standard*: Creates a new column of calculated numeric values

- *Scientific*: Creates a new column by applying certain kinds of math operations to the values in a column

- *Trigonometry*: Creates a new column by applying certain kinds of trigonometric operations to the values in a column

- *Rounding*: Creates a new column by rounding the values in a column

- *Information*: Creates a new column indication arithmetical information about the values in a column

- *Date*: Creates a new column by extracting date elements from the values in a date column

- *Time*: Creates a new column by extracting time elements from the values in a time or datetime column

- *Duration*: Creates a new column by calculating the duration between two dates or date/times

When transforming data, the art is to decide whether you want or need to keep the original column before applying one of these functions. Yet, once again, it is not really fundamental if you later decide that you made an incorrect decision because you can always backtrack. Alternatively, you can always decide to insert new columns as a matter of principle and delete any columns that you really do not need at a later stage in the data transformation process.

Custom Columns

Another way to extend the original data table is to add more columns. Although these are known as *custom columns* in Get & Transform, they are also known more generically as *derived columns* or *calculated columns*. Although they can do many things, their essential role is to do the following:

- Concatenate (or join, if you prefer) existing columns

- Add calculations to the data table

- Extract a specific part of a column

- Add flags to the table based on existing data

The best way to understand these columns is probably to see them in action. I've provided an initial example that should explain the basics, and you can see further techniques in Table 13-8. You can then extend these principles in your own processes.

Initially, let's perform a column join and create a column named Vehicle, which concatenates the Make and Model columns with a space in between.

1. Load the C:\DataVisualisationInExcel2016\CarSales_Tables.xlsx sample file.

2. Display the Workbook Queries pane (if it is not yet visible) and right-click the SalesData query.

3. In the Add Column ribbon, click Add Custom Column. The Add Custom Column dialog is displayed.

4. Click the Make column in the column list on the right and then click the Insert button. =[Make] will appear in the Custom Column Formula box at the left of the dialog.

5. Enter & " " & in the Custom Column Formula box after =[Make].

6. Click the Model column in the column list on the right and then click the Insert button.

7. Click inside the New Column Name box and enter a name for the column. I call it **CarType**. The dialog will look like Figure 13-4.

Figure 13-4. The Add Custom Column dialog

8. Click OK. The new column is added to the right of the data table; it contains the results of the formula. InsertedColumn appears in the Applied Steps list.

You can always double-click a column to insert it into the Custom Column Formula box if you prefer. To remove a column, simply delete the column name (including the square brackets) in the Custom Column Formula box.

▓ **Note** You must always enclose a column name in square brackets.

Rather than take you step-by-step through other examples, I prefer to show you some of the formulas that you can use to calculate columns and extract data into a new column. These code snippets are given in Table 13-4. As an Excel user, you can probably see a distinct similarity with how you build formulas in Excel and Power Pivot, except that here (as in Power Pivot) you use column names rather than cell references.

Table 13-4. *Custom Column Code Examples*

Output	Code Snippet	Description
Column calculations	`= [SalePrice]-[CostPrice]`	Subtracts the cost price from the sale price to give the gross margin
Column arithmetic	`=[SalePrice] * 1.2`	Adds the UK sales tax (20 percent) to the net sale price
Left	`Text.Start([Make],3)`	Returns the first three characters from the Make column
Right	`Text.End([Make],3)`	Returns the last three characters from the Make column
Up to a specific character	`Text.Start([Make],Text.PositionOf([Make]," "))`	Returns the leftmost characters up to the first space

If you look ahead to Chapter 14, then you are probably wondering why you carry out operations like this in Get & Transform Query when you can do virtually the same thing in the data model. Well, it is true that there is some overlap, so you have the choice of which to use. You can perform certain operations at multiple stages in the data preparation and analysis process. It all depends on how you are using the data and with what tool you are carrying out the analyses.

The last three examples in Table 13-4 probably seem a little abstruse for the moment. This is because they are examples of how to use the Get & Transform/Power Query data transformation language. This language is normally referred to as M. Because an in-depth description of this language is beyond the scope of this book, I suggest you refer to the Microsoft documentation available at `https://msdn.microsoft.com/en-us/library/mt211003.aspx` if you require further information.

Index Columns

An index column is a new column that numbers every record in the table sequentially. This numbering scheme applies to the table because it is currently sorted and begins at zero. There are many situations where an index column can be useful. The following are some examples:

- Reapply a previous sort order.
- Create a unique reference for every record.

- Prepare a recordset for use as a dimension table in a Get & Transform data model.
  In cases like this, the index column becomes what dimensional modelers call a
  surrogate key.

This list is not intended to be exhaustive in any way; you will almost certainly find other uses as you work with Get & Transform. Whatever the need, here is how to add an Index column (assuming that you are using the SalesData query in the CarSales_Tables.xlsx file that you have been using so far in this chapter):

1. In the Add Column ribbon, click Add Index Column. The new, sequentially
   numbered column is added at the right of the table, and Added Index is added to
   the Applied Steps list.

2. Scroll to the right of the table and rename the index column; it is currently
   named Index.

As you can see, the new column begins at 0. If you prefer to start the sequence at 1 (or indeed, at any other number), then you can click the small downward-facing triangle in the Add Index Column button and select one of the following options:

- From 0

- From 1

- Custom

You have a fairly free hand when it comes to deciding how to begin numbering an index column. The choices are as follows:

- Start at 0 and increment by a value of 1 for each row

- Start at 1 and increment by a value of 1 for each row

- Start at any number and increase by any number

As you saw in this example, the default is for the Get & Transform query to begin numbering rows at 0. However, you can choose another option by clicking the small triangle to the right of the Add Index Column button. This displays a menu with the three options outlined.

Selecting the third option, Custom, displays the dialog shown in Figure 13-5.

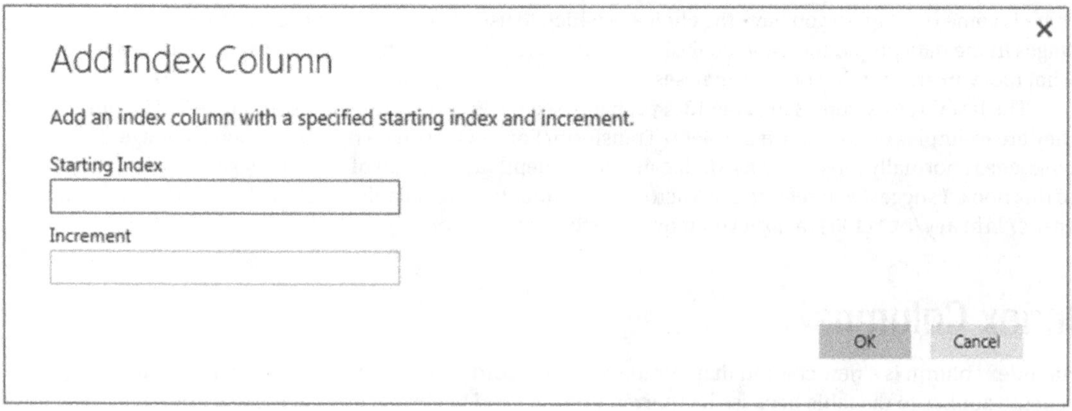

Figure 13-5. The Add Index Column dialog

This dialog lets you specify the start number for the first row in the data set as well as the increment that is added for each record.

▪ **Note** It is a good idea to sort the data set before adding an index column if you have a specific need for the records to be numbered in a certain order. Indeed, you can add multiple indexes to varied columns in differing sort orders. This lets you switch sort orders by sorting on different index columns.

Merging Data

Until now, I have treated each individual query as if it existed in isolation. The reality, of course, is that you will frequently be required to use the output of one query in conjunction with the output of another to join data from different tables in various ways. Assuming that the results of one query share a common field with another query, you can "join" queries into a single data table. Get & Transform calls this a merge operation, and it enables you, among other things, to do the following:

- Look up data elements in another "reference" table to add lookup data. This could be where you want to add a client name where only the client code exists in your main table, for instance.

- Aggregate data from a "detail" table (such as invoice lines) into a higher-grained table, such as a table of invoices.

Here, again, the process is not difficult. The only fundamental factor is that the two tables, or queries, that you are merging must have a shared field or fields that enable the two tables to match records coherently. Let's look at a couple of examples.

Adding Data

First, let's try looking up extra data that you will add to a query.

1. In a new, empty Excel workbook, use Get & Transform to load all the worksheets in the CarSalesDatabase_Source.xlsx Excel file into the data model. This will create six queries in the Workbook Queries pane. If you don't need to practice loading data, then you can open the Excel file CarSalesDatabase.xlsx instead, where the six queries have been created for you.

2. Edit the query named Invoices in the Workbook Queries pane.

3. Click the Merge Queries button in the Home ribbon. The Merge dialog will appear.

4. In the upper part of the dialog—where an overview of the output from the current query is displayed—click the ClientID column title. This column is highlighted.

5. In the pop-up under the upper table, select the Clients query. The output from this query will appear in the lower part of the dialog.

6. In the lower table, select the column title for the column—the join column—that maps to the column that you selected in step 4. This will also be the ClientID column. This column is then selected in the lower table. You may be asked to set privacy levels for the data sources. If this is the case, set them to Public.

7. Select the Join Kind Inner (only matching rows) from the pop-up. The dialog will look like Figure 13-6.

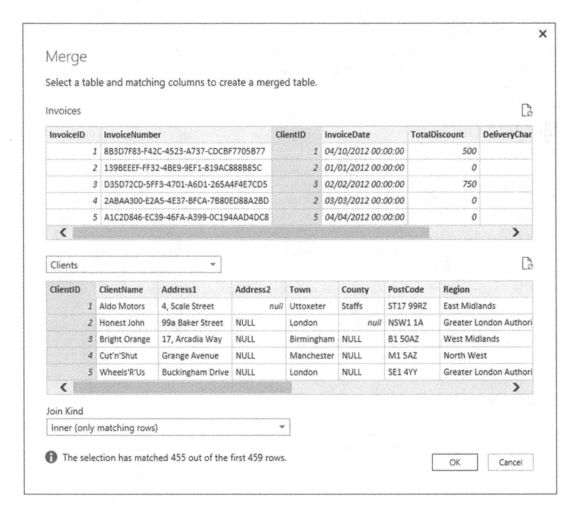

Figure 13-6. The Merge dialog

8. Click OK. A new column is added to the right of the existing data table.

9. Scroll to the right of the existing data table and click the Expand icon to the right of the column name (it has probably been named New Column and every row contains the word *Table*). The pop-up list of all the available fields in this data table (or query, if you prefer) is displayed, as shown in Figure 13-7.

Figure 13-7. *The fields available in a joined query*

10. Ensure that the Expand radio button is selected.

11. Clear the selection of all the columns by unchecking the (Select All Columns) check box.

12. Select the following columns:

   a. ClientName

   b. ClientSize

   c. ClientSince

13. Click OK. The selected columns from the linked table are merged into the main table, and the link to the reference table (New Column) is removed.

14. Rename the columns that have been added and apply and close the query.

You now have a single table of data that contains data from two linked data sources. Reprocessing the Sales query will also reprocess the dependent *client's* query and result in the latest version of the data being reloaded.

■ **Note**   You probably noticed that the Merge dialog indicated how many matching records there were in the two queries. This can be a useful indication that you have selected the correct column (or columns) to join the two queries. Specifically, if you see few matches in the Merge dialog, then you could be attempting to join queries on inappropriate fields.

Aggregating Data During a Merge Operation

If you are not just looking up reference data but need to aggregate data from a separate table and then add the results to the current query, then the process is largely similar. This second approach, however, is designed to suit another completely different requirement. Previously, you saw the case where the current query had many records that mapped to a *single* record in the lookup table. This second approach is for when your current (or main) query has a single record where there are *multiple* linked records in the second query. Consequently, you need to aggregate the data in the second table to bring the data across into the first table. Here is a simple example, using some of the sample data from the C:\DataVisualisationInExcel2016 folder:

1. Find the CarSalesDatabase.xlsx Excel source file in the C:\ DataVisualisationInExcel2016 folder.

2. Edit the query named Invoices in the Queries pane on the left.

3. In the Home ribbon, click the Merge Queries button. The Merge dialog will open. You will see some of the data from the Invoices data set in the upper part of the dialog.

4. Click anywhere inside the InvoiceID column. This column is selected.

5. In the pop-up, select the InvoiceLines query. You will see some of the data from the Invoices data set in the lower part of the dialog.

6. Click anywhere inside the InvoiceID column for the lower table. This column is selected.

7. Select Inner (only matching rows) from the Join Kind pop-up menu. The dialog will look like Figure 13-8.

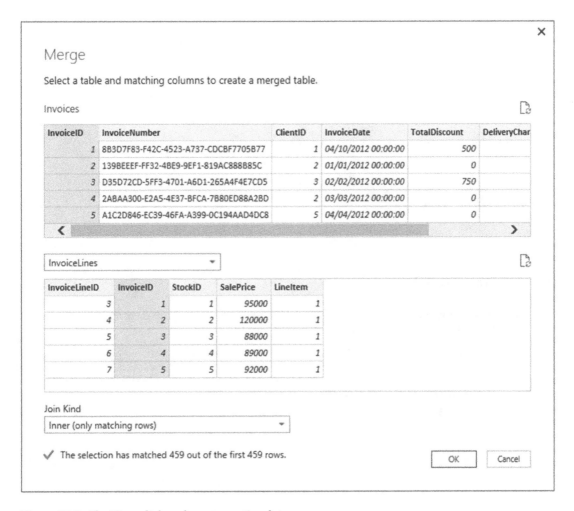

Figure 13-8. The Merge dialog when aggregating data

8. Click OK.

9. Scroll to the right of the existing data table. You will see a new column (named NewColumn) that contains the word *Table* in every cell. This column will look something like Figure 13-9.

DeliveryCharge ▼	InvoiceDateKey ▼	NewColu... ⇆
750	20121004	Table
1500	20120101	Table
1000	20120202	Table
1000	20120303	Table
1500	20120404	Table
1000	20120504	Table
500	20120604	Table
1000	20120704	Table
1000	20120804	Table
1000	20120904	Table
1500	20121104	Table

Figure 13-9. *A merged column*

10. Click the Expand icon to the right of the new column title. The pop-up list of all the available fields in the InvoiceLines query is displayed.

11. Select the Aggregate radio button. The dialog will look like Figure 13-10.

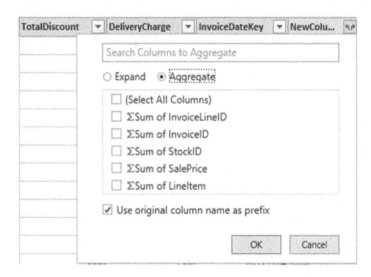

Figure 13-10. *The available fields from a merged data set*

12. Select the Sum Of SalePrice field.

13. Uncheck Use Original Column Name As Prefix and click OK.

Get & Transform will add up the total sale price for each invoice and add this as a new column. Naturally, you can choose the type of aggregation that you want to apply (before clicking OK), if the sum is not what you want. To do this, place the cursor over the column that you want to aggregate (see step 11 in the preceding exercise) and click the pop-up menu that appears at the right of the field name. Get & Transform will suggest the following options:

- Sum

- Average

- Minimum

- Maximum

- Count (All)

- Count (Not Blank)

Figure 13-11 shows an example of this.

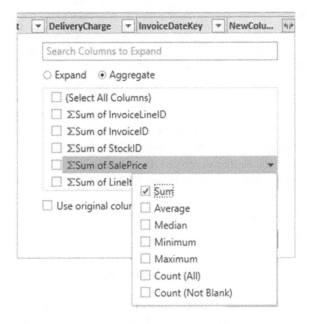

Figure 13-11. *Aggregation options when merging data sets*

The merge process that you have just seen, while not complex in itself, suddenly opens up many new horizons. It means that you can now create multiple separate queries that you can then use together to expand your data in ways that allow you to prepare quite complex data sets.

Here are a couple of comments I need to make about the merge operation:

- Only queries that have been previously created in the Get & Transform Query window can be used when merging data sets. So, remember to prepare all the data sets (or queries if you prefer) that you require before attempting a merge operation.

- Refreshing a query will cause any other queries that are upstream of this query to be refreshed also. This way you will always get the most up-to-date data from all the queries in the process.

■ **Note**   When merging (or joining) tables, you can select columns in the lower table first if you prefer.

Types of Join

When merging queries—either to join data or to aggregate values—you were faced with a choice when it came to how the two queries could be linked. The choice of join can have a profound effect on the resulting data set. Consequently, it is important to understand the six join types that are available. These are described in Table 13-5.

Table 13-5. *Join Types*

Join Type	Explanation
Left Outer	Keeps all records in the upper data set in the Merge dialog (the data set that was active when you began the Merge operation). Any matching rows (those that share common values in the join columns) from the second data set are kept. All other rows from the second data set are discarded.
Right Outer	Keeps all records in the lower data set in the Merge dialog (the data set that was not active when you began the Merge operation). Any matching rows (those that share common values in the join columns) from the upper data set are kept. All other rows from the upper data set (the data set that was active when you began the Merge operation) are discarded.
Full Outer	All rows from both queries are retained in the resulting data set. Any records that do not share common values in the join field (or fields) contain blanks in certain columns.
Inner	Only joins queries where there is an exact match on the column (or columns) that are selected for the join. Any rows from either query that do not share common values in the join column (or columns) are discarded.
Left Anti	Keeps only rows from the upper (first) query.
Right Anti	Keeps only rows from the lower (second) query.

When you are expanding the column that is the link to a merged data set, you have a couple these useful options that are worth knowing about.

- Use Original Column Name As Prefix
- Search Columns To Expand

Use the Original Column Name As the Prefix

You will probably find that some columns from joined queries can have the same names in both source data sets. It follows that you need to identify which column came from which data set. If you leave the check box selected for the Use Original Column Name As Prefix merge option (which is the default), any merged columns will include the source query name to help you identify the data more accurately.

If you find that these longer column names only get in the way, you can unselect this check box. This will leave the added columns from the second query with their original names. However, because Get & Transform cannot accept duplicate column names, any new columns will have .1, .2, and so forth, added to the column name.

Search Columns to Expand

If you are merging a query with a second query that contains a large number of columns, then it can be laborious to search for the columns you want to include. To narrow your search, you can enter a few characters from the column that you are looking for. The more characters you type, the fewer matching columns are displayed in the Expansion pop-up dialog.

■ **Note** When you use any of the *outer* joins, you are keeping records that do not have any corresponding records in the second query. Consequently, the resulting data set contains empty values for some of the columns.

Joining on Multiple Columns

In the examples so far, you joined queries on only a single column. While this may be possible if you are looking at data that comes from a clearly structured source (such as a relational database), you may need to extend the principle when joining queries from diverse sources. Fortunately, Get & Transform allows you to join queries on multiple columns when the need arises.

As an example of this, the sample data contains a file that I have prepared as an example of how to join queries on more than one column. This sample file contains data from the sources that you saw in Chapter 10. However, they have been modeled as a data warehouse star schema. To complete the model, you need to join a dimension named Geography to a fact table named Sales so that you can add the field GeographySK to the fact table. However, the Sales table and the Geography table share three fields (Country, Region, and Town) that must correspond for the queries to be joined. The following explains how to perform a join using multiple fields:

1. Open the `C:\DataVisualisationInExcel2016\StarSchema.xlsx` Excel file.

2. Edit the Sales query from the list of existing queries in the Workbook Query window (you can double-click to edit a query).

3. In the Home ribbon, click the Merge Queries button. The Merge dialog will appear.

4. In the pop-up list of queries, select Geography as the second query to join to the first (upper) query.

5. Select Inner (only matching rows) as the join kind.

6. In the upper list of fields (taken from the Sales table), Ctrl+click the fields CountryISOCode, Region, and Town, in this order. A small number will appear to the right of each column header indicating the order that you selected the columns.

7. In the lower list of fields (taken from the Sales table), Ctrl+click in the fields CountryISOCode, Region, and Town, in this order. A small number will appear to the right of each column header indicating the order that you selected the columns.

8. Verify that you have a reasonable number of matching rows in the information message at the bottom of the dialog. The dialog will look like Figure 13-12.

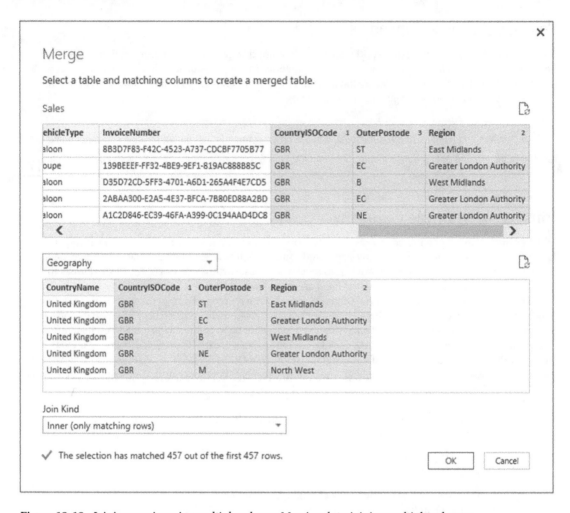

Figure 13-12. *Joining queries using multiple columnsMerging data:joining multiple columns*

9. Click OK.

You can then continue with the data mashup. In this example, that would be adding the GeographySK field as an index field to the Sales query and then removing the Country, Region, and Town fields from the Sales query. This would then become the core of a "star" schema.

There is no real limit to the number of columns that can be used when joining queries. It will depend entirely on the shape of the source data.

Preparing Data Sets for Joins

You could have to carry out a little preparatory work on real-world data sets before joining queries. More specifically, any columns that you join have to be the same basic data type. Put simply, you need to join text-based columns to other text columns, number columns to numbers, and dates to dates. If the columns are *not* the same data type, you receive a warning message when you try to join the columns in the Merge dialog.

Consequently, it is nearly always a good idea to take a look at the columns that you will use to join queries *before* you start the merge operation itself. Remember that data types do not have to be identical, just similar. So, a decimal number type can map to a whole number, for instance.

You might also have to cleanse the data in the columns that are used for joins before attempting to merge queries. This could involve the following:

- Removing trailing or leading spaces in text-based columns

- Isolating part of a column (either in the original column or as a new column) to use in a join

- Verifying that appropriate data types are used in join columns

Correct and Incorrect Joins

Merging queries is the one data mashup operation that is often easier in theory than in practice, unfortunately. If the source queries were based on tables in a relational or even dimensional database, then joining them could be relatively easy, as a data architect will (ideally) have designed the database tables to allow for them to be joined. However, if you are joining two completely independent queries, then you could face these several major issues:

- The columns do not map.

- The columns map, but the result is a massive table with duplicate records.

Let's take a look at these possible problems.

The Columns Do Not Map

If the columns do not map (that is, you have joined the data but get no resulting records), then you need to take a close look at the data in the columns that you are using to establish the join. The following are the questions you need to ask:

- Are the values in the two queries the same data type?

- Do the values really map—or are they different?

- Are you using the correct columns?

- Are you using too many columns and so specifying data that is not in both queries?

The Columns Map, but the Result Is a Massive Table with Duplicate Records

Joining queries depends on isolating *unique* data in both source queries. Sometimes a single column does not contain enough information to establish a unique reference that can uniquely identify a row in the query.

In these cases, you need to use two or more columns to join queries—or else rows will be duplicated in the result. Therefore, once again, you need to look carefully at the data and decide on the minimum number of columns that you can use to join queries correctly.

Examining Joined Data

Joining data tables is not always easy. Neither is deciding whether the outcome of a merge operation will produce the result that you expect.

So, Get & Transform Query includes a solution to these kinds of dilemma. It can help you more clearly see what a join has done. More specifically, it can show you or each record in the first query exactly which rows are joined from the second query.

Do the following to see this in action:

1. Carry out steps 1 through 8 in the "Merging Data" section.

2. Scroll to the right of the data table. You will see the new column named NewColumn (as shown in Figure 13-7).

3. Click to the right of the word *Table* in the row where you want to see the joined data. Note that you must *not* click the word *Table*. A second table will appear under the main query's data table containing the data from the second query that is joined for this particular row. Figure 13-13 shows an example of this.

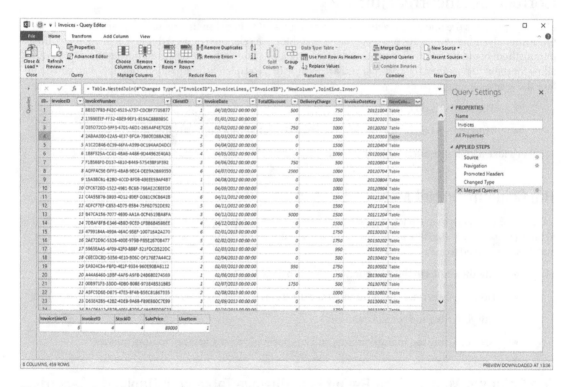

Figure 13-13. *Joined data*

This technique is as simple as it is useful. There are nonetheless a few comments that need to be made.

-   You can resize the lower table (and consequently display more or less data from the second joined table) by dragging the bottom border of the top data table up or down.

-   Clicking to the right of the word *Table* in NewColumn will Expand and Aggregate buttons in the Transform ribbon.

-   Clicking the word *Table* in NewColumn adds a new step to the query that replaces the source data with the linked data. You can also do this by right-clicking inside the NewColumn and selecting Drill Down.

■ **Note** Drilling down into the merged table in effect limits the query to the row (or rows) of the subtable. Consequently, you have to delete this step if you want to access all the data in the merged tables.

The Expand and Aggregate Buttons

Get & Transform offers an alternative to using the NewColumn pop-up menu to expand or aggregate data when merging queries. If you have clicked to the right of the word *Table* in NewColumn, you can then click the newly activated Expand or Aggregate button to display the Expand or Aggregate dialog in the Transform ribbon.

The only real difference between the dialogs and the pop-ups is that the Expand dialog also has an option where you can add a new column prefix that you choose for the additional columns from the second query. You can see this in Figure 13-14.

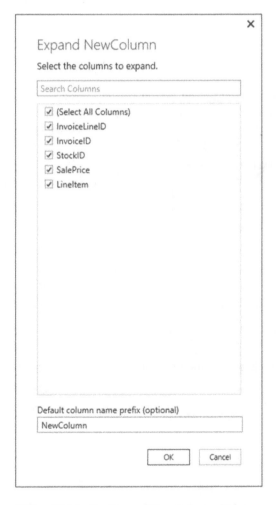

Figure 13-14. The Expand New Column dialog

Appending Data

Not all source data is delivered in its entirety in a single file or as a single database table. You may be given access to two or more tables or files that have to be loaded into a single table in Excel or Power Pivot. In some cases, you might find yourself faced with hundreds of files—all text, CSV, or Excel format—and the requirement to load them all. Well, Get & Transform can handle these eventualities, too.

Adding the Contents of One Query to Another

In the simplest case, you could have two data sources that are structurally identical (that is, they have the same columns in the same order), and all that you have to do is add one to another to end up with a query that outputs the amalgamated content of the two sources. This is called *appending data,* and it is easy, provided that the two data sources have *identical* structures, which means the following:

- They have the same number of columns.

- The columns are in the same order.

- The data types are identical for each column.

- The columns have the same names.

As long as all these conditions are met, you can append the output of queries (which Get & Transform calls *tables*) onto another. The queries do not need to have data that comes from identical source types, so you can append the output from a CSV file to data that comes from an Oracle database, for instance. As an example, you will take two text files and use them to create one single output.

1. Create queries to load each of the following text files into Get & Transform—
   without the final load step, which would output them to Excel or the Excel
   data model. Both files are in the C:\DataVisualisationInExcel2016\
   MultipleTextFiles folder. Name the queries **Colors_01** and **Colors _02**:

   a. Colors_01.txt

   b. Colors_02.txt

   If you want a file with these sources already loaded, you can just open the Excel workbook C:\
   DataVisualisationInExcel2016\Colors.xlsx.

2. Open one of the queries (I use Colors_01, but either will do).

3. Click the Append Queries button in the Get & Transform Query Editor Home
   ribbon. The Append dialog will appear.

4. From the Select The Table To Append pop-up, choose the query Colors_02.

5. Click OK.

The data from the two output tables is placed in the current query. You can now continue with any modifications that you need to apply. You will notice that the column names are not repeated as part of the data when the tables are appended one to the other.

■ **Note**   You can also launch the Merge or Append processes by right-clicking the data grid selector (the icon at the top-left intersection of the row and column headers) or by using the pop-up menu in the peek window.

Adding Multiple Files from a Source Folder

Now let's consider another possibility. You have been sent a load of files, possibly downloaded from an FTP site or received by e-mail, and you have placed them all into a specific directory. However, you do not want to have to carry out the process that you just saw and load files one by one if there are several hundred files. So, here is a way to get Get & Transform to do the work of trawling through the directory and loading only those files that correspond to a file name specification you have indicated:

1.   Open a new Excel workbook

2.   In the Data ribbon, click New Query ➤ From File ➤ From Folder. The Folder dialog is displayed.

3.   Click the Browse button and navigate to the folder that contains the files to load. In this example, it is `C:\DataVisualisationInExcel2016\MultipleTextFiles`. You can also paste in, or enter, the folder path if you prefer. The Folder dialog will look like Figure 13-15.

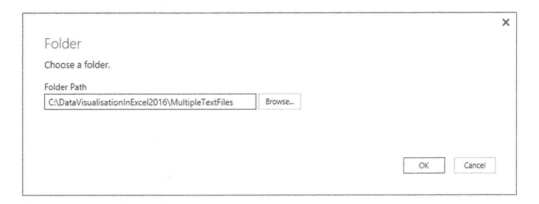

Figure 13-15. The Folder dialog

4.   Click OK. The Get & Transform Query Editor will display the list of files. This is shown in Figure 13-16.

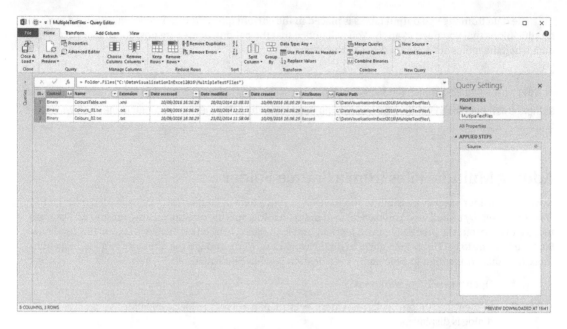

Figure 13-16. *Files listed in the Get & Transform Query Editor*

5. As you want to load only text files and avoid files of any other type, click the filter pop-up menu for the column title Extension and uncheck all elements *except* .txt. This is shown in Figure 13-17.

Figure 13-17. *Filtering file types when loading multiple identical files*

6. Click the Expand icon (two downward-facing arrows) to the right of the first column title; this column is called Content, and every row in the column contains the word *Binary*. Get & Transform loads all the files and displays the result, as shown in Figure 13-18.

⊞▾	Column1	▼	Column2	▼
1	ColourID		Colour	
2	1		Red	
3	2		Blue	
4	3		Green	
5	4		Silver	
6	5		Canary Yellow	
7	ColourID		Colour	
8	6		Night Blue	
9	7		Black	
10	8		British Racing Green	
11	9		Dark Purple	
12	10		Pink	

***Figure 13-18.** All files loaded from a folder*

7. If (but only if) each file contains header rows, then scroll down through the resulting table until you find a title element. In this example, it is the word *ColorID* in the ColorID column.

8. Right-click ColorID and select Text Filters ➤ Does Not Equal. All rows containing superfluous column titles are removed.

The contents of all the source files are now loaded into the Get & Transform Query Editor and can be transformed and used like any other data set. What is more, if you ever add more files to the source directory and then click Refresh in the Home ribbon, *all* the source files are reloaded, including any new files added to the directory.

▓ **Note**   If your source directory contains only the files you want to load, then step 4 is unnecessary. Nonetheless, I always add steps like this in case files of the "wrong" type are added later, which would cause any subsequent process runs to fail. Equally, you can set filters on the file name to restrict the files that is loaded.

Changing the Data Structure

Sometimes your requirements go beyond the techniques that you have seen so far when discussing data cleansing and transformation. Some data structures need more radical reworking, given the shape of the data that you have acquired. I include in this category the following:

- Unpivoting data

- Pivoting data

- Transforming rows and columns

Each of these techniques is designed to meet a specific, yet frequent, need in data loading, and all are described in the next few pages.

Unpivoting Tables

From time to time, you may need to analyze data that has been delivered in a "pivoted" or "denormalized" format. Essentially, this means information that really should be in a single column has been broken down and placed across several columns. Figure 13-19 shows an example of the first few rows of a pivoted data set and can be found in the C:\DataVisualisationInExcel2016\PivotedDataSet.xlsx sample file.

InvoiceDate	Aston Martin	Bentley	Jaguar	MGB	Rolls Royce	Triumph	TVR
02/01/2013	75890	25700	88200	4500	62000	8500	
09/01/2013	31125						
10/01/2013	17500						
02/02/2013	75890	25700	63200	8500	62000	17000	37500
11/02/2013	22500						
02/03/2013	75890	25700	88200	4500	75890	8500	
12/03/2013	17500						
13/03/2013					31125		
14/03/2013	17500						
02/04/2013	75890	25700	99500	8500	62000	17000	37500
15/04/2013					22500		
16/04/2013	17500						
02/05/2013	75890	62000	124500	4500	75890	8500	
17/05/2013	17500						
18/05/2013	17500						
19/05/2013	22500						
02/06/2013	62000	62000	63200	8500	62000	17000	37500
20/06/2013	17500						
02/07/2013	62000	25700	88200	4500	62000	17000	
21/07/2013					17500		
22/07/2013	22500						
02/08/2013	62000	62000	38200	8500	62000	17000	37500
02/09/2013	62000	62000	124500	4500	75890	17000	
23/09/2013	17500						
02/10/2013	62000	62000	63200	8500	75890	17000	37500

Figure 13-19. *A pivoted data set*

To analyze this data correctly, you really need the makes of the cars to be switched from being column titles to becoming the contents of a specific column. Fortunately, this is not hard at all.

1. In a new Excel workbook, load the table PivotedCosts from the C:\ DataVisualisationInExcel2016\PivotedDataSet.xlsx file into Get & Transform. You can use the From Table button in the Data ribbon to do this.

2. Select all the columns you want to unpivot. In this example, this means all columns except the first one.

3. In the Transform ribbon, click the Unpivot button (or right-click with the columns selected and choose Unpivot from the context menu). The table is reorganized, and the first few records look like they do in Figure 13-20. Unpivoted Columns is added to the Applied Steps list.

⊞	InvoiceDate	Attribute	Value
1	02/01/2013 00:00:00	Aston Martin	75890
2	02/01/2013 00:00:00	Bentley	25700
3	02/01/2013 00:00:00	Jaguar	88200
4	02/01/2013 00:00:00	MGB	4500
5	02/01/2013 00:00:00	Rolls Royce	62000
6	02/01/2013 00:00:00	Triumph	8500
7	09/01/2013 00:00:00	Aston Martin	31125
8	10/01/2013 00:00:00	Aston Martin	17500
9	02/02/2013 00:00:00	Aston Martin	75890
10	02/02/2013 00:00:00	Bentley	25700
11	02/02/2013 00:00:00	Jaguar	63200
12	02/02/2013 00:00:00	MGB	8500
13	02/02/2013 00:00:00	Rolls Royce	62000
14	02/02/2013 00:00:00	Triumph	17000
15	02/02/2013 00:00:00	TVR	37500
16	11/02/2013 00:00:00	Aston Martin	22500
17	02/03/2013 00:00:00	Aston Martin	75890
18	02/03/2013 00:00:00	Bentley	25700
19	02/03/2013 00:00:00	Jaguar	88200

Figure 13-20. *An unpivoted data set*

4. Rename the columns that the Get & Transform Query Editor has named Attribute and Value.

The data is now presented in a standard tabular way, so it can be used to create a data model and then produce reports and dashboards.

Pivoting Tables

On some occasions, you may have to switch data from columns to rows so that you can use it efficiently. This kind of operation is called *pivoting data*. It is—perhaps unsurprisingly—similar to the unpivot process that you saw in the previous section.

1. Follow steps 1 through 3 of the previous section so that you end up with the table of data that you can see in Figure 13-18.

2. Click inside the column InvoiceDate.

3. In the Transform ribbon, click the Pivot Column button. The Pivot Column dialog will appear.

4. Select Value (the column of figures) as the values column that is aggregated by the pivot transformation. The Pivot Column dialog will look like Figure 13-21.

Figure 13-21. The Pivot Column dialog

5. Click OK. The table is pivoted and looks like Figure 13-22. Pivoted Column is added to the Applied Steps list.

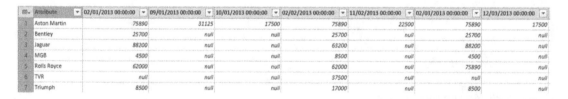

⊞ ▾	Attribute ▾	02/01/2013 00:00:00 ▾	09/01/2013 00:00:00 ▾	10/01/2013 00:00:00 ▾	02/02/2013 00:00:00 ▾	11/02/2013 00:00:00 ▾	02/03/2013 00:00:00 ▾	12/03/2013 00:00:00 ▾
1	Aston Martin	75890	31125	17500	75890	22500	75890	17500
2	Bentley	25700	null	null	25700	null	25700	null
3	Jaguar	88200	null	null	63200	null	88200	null
4	MGB	4500	null	null	8500	null	4500	null
5	Rolls Royce	62000	null	null	62000	null	75890	null
6	TVR	null	null	null	37500	null	null	null
7	Triumph	8500	null	null	17000	null	8500	null

Figure 13-22. Pivoted data

■ **Note** The Advanced Options section of the Pivot Column dialog lets you choose the aggregation operation that is applied to the values in the pivoted table.

The Unpivot button contains another menu option that is displayed if you click the small triangle to the right of the Unpivot button. This is the Unpivot Other Columns option that will switch the contents of columns into rows for all the columns that are not selected when you run the transformation.

Transposing Rows and Columns

On some occasions, you may have a source table where the columns need to become rows and the rows columns. Fortunately, this is a one-click transformation for Get & Transform. Here is how to do it:

1. Load the C:\DataVisualisationInExcel2016\DataToTranspose.xlsx Excel file into the Get & Transform Query Editor. You will see a data table like the one in Figure 13-23.

Figure 13-23. *A data set needing to be transposed*

2. In the Transform ribbon, click the Transpose button. The data is transposed and appears as two columns, just like the CountryList.txt file you saw in Chapter 10.

3. Rename the columns.

Managing the Transformation Process

Pretty nearly all the transformation steps that you have applied so far have been individual elements that can be applied to just about any data table. However, when you are carrying out even a simple data load and transform process, you are likely to want to step through several transformations in order to shape, cleanse, and filter the data to get the result you want. This is where the Get & Transform approach is so clever, because you can apply most data transformation steps to just about any data table. The art is to place them in a sequence that can then be reused any time that the data changes to reprocess the new source data and deliver an up-to-date output.

The key to appreciating and managing this process is to get well acquainted with the Applied Steps list in the Query Settings pane. This list contains the details of every step that you applied, in the order in which you applied it. Each step retains the name that Get & Transform gave it when it was created, and each can be altered in the following ways:

*   Modified

*   Renamed

*   Deleted

*   Moved (in certain cases)

Many steps can also be modified, so you are not stuck with the choices that you initially apply.

■ **Note** Remember that before tweaking the order in which the process is applied, clicking any process step causes the table in the Get & Transform window to refresh to show you the state of the data up to and including the selected step. This is a clear visual guide to the process and how the ETL is carried out.

Modifying a Step

How you alter a step will depend on how the original transformation was applied. This becomes second nature after a little practice and will always involve first clicking the step that you want to modify and then applying a different modification. If you invoke a ribbon option, such as altering the data type, for instance, then you change the data type by simply applying another data type directly from the ribbon. If you used an option that displayed a dialog (such as splitting a column, among others), then you can right-click the step in the Applied Steps list and select Edit Settings from the context menu. Alternatively, and if you prefer, you can click the "gear" icon to the right of any step that was created using a dialog box to display the dialog for modification. This will cause the original dialog to reappear; in it, you can make any modifications that you consider necessary.

A final step that makes it easy to alter the settings for a process is to edit the formula that appears in the formula bar each time you click a step. You will look at this method in greater detail in a later chapter.

■ **Note**   If you can force yourself to organize the process that you are writing with Get & Transform, then a little forethought and planning can reap major dividends. For instance, certain tasks, such as setting data types, can be carried out in a single operation. Not just that, but if you need to alter a data type for a column at a later stage, I suggest you click the ChangedType step before you make any further alterations. This way, you extend the original step, rather than creating other steps, which can make the process more confusing and needlessly voluminous.

Renaming a Step

Because Get & Transform names steps using the name of the transformation that was applied and then, if another similar step is applied later, uses the same name with a numeric increment, you may prefer to give more user-friendly names to process steps. This is done as follows:

1. Right-click the step you want to rename.

2. Select Rename from the context menu.

3. Type in the new name.

4. Press Enter.

The step is renamed, and the new name will appear in the Applied Steps list in the Query Settings pane. This way you can ensure that when you come back to a data transformation process days, weeks, or months later, you are able to understand more intuitively the process that you defined, as well as why you shaped the data like you did.

Deleting a Step or a Series of Steps

Deleting a step is all too easy, but doing so can have serious consequences. This is because an ETL process is often an extremely tightly coupled series of events, where each event depends intimately on the preceding one. So, deleting a step can make every subsequent step fail. Knowing which events you can delete without drastic consequences will depend on the types of process that you are developing as well as your experience with Get & Transform. In any case, this is what you should do if you need to delete a step:

1. Right-click the step you want to delete.

2. Select Delete. The Delete Step dialog might appear, as shown in Figure 13-24.

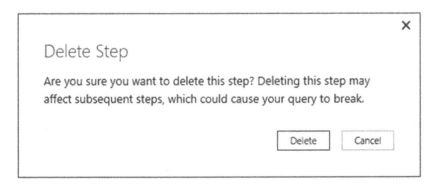

Figure 13-24. *The Delete Step dialog*

    3.   Confirm by clicking the Delete button. The step is deleted.

If—and it is highly possible—deleting this step causes issues for the rest of the process, you will see that the data table is replaced by an error message. This message will vary depending on the type of error that Get & Transform has encountered.

When describing this technique, I was careful to state that you *might* see the Delete dialog. If you are deleting the final step in a sequence of steps, then you will probably not see it since there should not be any potentially horrendous consequences; at worst, you will have to re-create the step. If you are deleting a step in the middle of a process, then you might want to think seriously about doing so before you cause a potentially vast number of problems. Consequently, you are asked to confirm the deletion in these cases.

■ **Note**   If you realize at this point that you have just destroyed hours of work, then (after drawing a deep breath) click the File menu in the Get & Transform window (the downward-facing triangle at the top left) and select Discard And Close. You will lose all work up until the last time you clicked Apply And Close, however. Don't count on using an undo function as you can in other desktop applications. To lower your blood pressure, you may prefer to save a copy of a complex file before deleting any steps.

An alternative technique is to place the pointer over a process step and click the X icon that appears. You may still have to confirm the deletion.

If you realize that an error in a process step has invalidated all your work up until the end of the process, rather than deleting multiple elements one by one, click Delete Until End from the context menu at step 2 in the preceding exercise.

Adding a Step

You can add a step anywhere in the sequence. All you have to do is to click the step that *precedes* the new step that you want to insert *before* clicking the icon in any of the ribbons that corresponds to the new step. As is the case when you delete a step, Get & Transform will display an alert warning you that this action *could* cause problems with the process from this new step on.

Altering Process Step Sequencing

It is possible—technically—to resequence steps in a process. However, in my experience, this is not always practical, since changing the order of steps in a process can cause as much damage as deleting a step. Nonetheless, you can always try it like this:

1. Right-click the step you want to resequence.

2. Select Move Up or Move Down from the context menu.

I remain pessimistic that this can work miracles in practice, as most data transformation processes are a tightly bound sequence of steps. Nonetheless, it is good to know that this possibility is available.

An Approach to Sequencing

Given the array of available data transformation options, you may well be wondering how best to approach a new ETL project using Get & Transform. I realize that all projects are different, but as a rough and ready guide, I suggest attempting you order your project like this:

1. First, of course, load the data into Get & Transform.

2. Second, promote or add correct column headers. For example, you really do not want to be looking at step 47 of a process and wondering what Column29 is, when it could read ClientName.

3. Third, remove any columns that you do not need. The smaller the data set, the faster the processing. What is more, you will find it easier to concentrate on, and understand, the data only if you are looking at information that you really need. Any columns that have been removed can be returned to the data set simply be deleting or editing the step that removed them.

4. Fourth, alter the data types for every column in the table. Correct data types are fundamental for many transformation steps and are essential for filtering, so it's best to get them sorted out early on.

5. Next, filter out any records that you do not need. Once again, the smaller the data set, the faster the processing. This includes deduplication.

6. Then, carry out any necessary data cleansing and transforms.

7. Finally, carry out any necessary column splits or adding custom columns.

Once again, this is not a definitive guide, but I hope that it will help you to see the wood for the trees.

Error Records

Some data transformation operations will cause errors. This can be a fact of life when mashing up source data. For instance, you could have a few rows in a large data set where a date column contains a few records that are text or numbers. If you convert the column to a date data type, then any values that cannot be converted will appear as error values.

Removing Errors

Assuming you do not need records that Get & Transform has flagged as containing an error, you can have all such records removed in a single operation.

1. Click inside the column containing errors, or if you want to remove errors from several columns at once, Ctrl+click the titles of the columns that contain the errors.

2. Click Remove Errors in the Home ribbon. Any records with errors flagged in the selected columns are deleted. Removed Errors is the added to the Applied Steps list.

You have to be careful here not to remove valid data. Only you can judge, once you have taken a look at the data, if an error in a column means that the data can be discarded safely. In all other cases, you would be best advised to look at cleansing the data or simply leaving records that contain errors in place. The range and variety of potential errors are as vast as the data itself. You could see errors because of invalid data types, for instance.

Duplicating Part of a Query

If you have an existing query that you want to reuse—and possibly adapt—inside an existing worksheet, then Get & Transform has a neat way of helping you.

1. Inside an existing query, right-click the step ending the sequence of steps from the start of the query that you want to duplicate.

2. Select Extract Previous from the context menu. The Extract Steps dialog will be displayed.

3. Enter a name for the new, duplicated query. The Extract Steps dialog will look like the one shown in Figure 13-25.

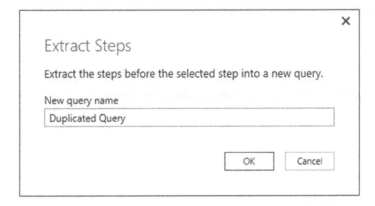

Figure 13-25. Extracting a series of query steps into a new query

4. Click OK. The query will be copied, and you will remain in the source query.

Once you return to Excel, you will see the duplicated query in the Workbook Queries pane.

Managing Queries

Once you have used Get & Transform for any length of time, you will probably become addicted to creating more and deeper analyses based on wider-ranging data sources. Inevitably, this will mean learning to manage the data sources that feed into your data models efficiently and productively.

Fortunately, Get & Transform Query comes replete with a small arsenal of query management tools to help you.

*   Organizing queries

*   Grouping queries

*   Duplicating queries

- Referencing queries
- Adding a column as a new query
- Enabling data load
- Enabling data refresh

Let's take a look at these functions, one by one.

Organizing Queries

When you have a dozen or more queries that you are using in the Get & Transform Query Editor, you may want to exercise some control over how they are organized. To begin with, you can modify the order in which queries appear in the Query List pane on the left of the Get & Transform Query window. This lets you override the default order, which is that the most recently added data source appears at the bottom of the list.

Do the following to change the position of a query in the list:

1. Right-click the query you want to move.

2. Select Move Up (or Move Down) from the context menu.

You have to carry out this operation a number of times to move a query up or down a number of places.

Grouping Queries

You can also create custom groups to better organize the queries that you are using in a Excel workbook. This will not have any effect on how the queries work. Grouping queries is simply an organizational technique.

Create a New Group

The following explains how to create a new group:

1. Right-click the query you want to add to a new group.

2. Select Move To Group ➤ New Group from the context menu. The New Group dialog will appear.

3. Enter a name for the group and (optionally) a description. The dialog will look something like Figure 13-26.

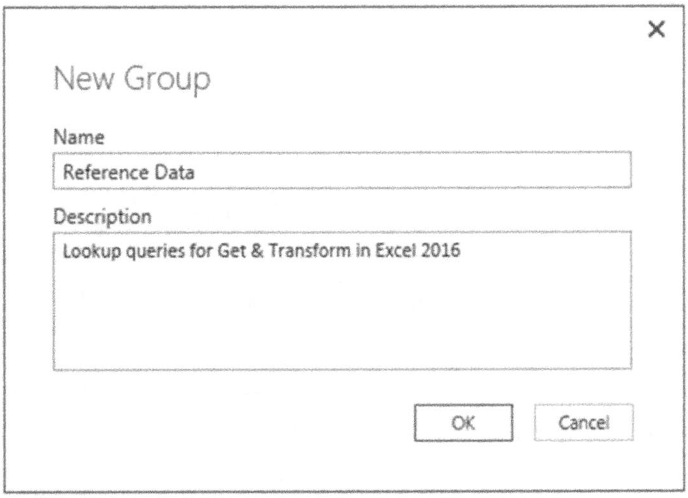

×

New Group

Name

Reference Data

Description

Lookup queries for Get & Transform in Excel 2016

OK   Cancel

Figure 13-26. The New Group dialog

4.   Click OK.

The new group is created, and the selected query will appear in the group. The Query pane will look something like Figure 13-27.

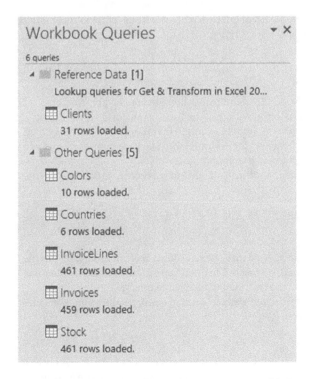

Workbook Queries   ▾ ×

6 queries

▴ ▦ Reference Data [1]
    Lookup queries for Get & Transform in Excel 20...

    ▦ Clients
      31 rows loaded.

▴ ▦ Other Queries [5]

    ▦ Colors
      10 rows loaded.

    ▦ Countries
      6 rows loaded.

    ▦ InvoiceLines
      461 rows loaded.

    ▦ Invoices
      459 rows loaded.

    ▦ Stock
      461 rows loaded.

Figure 13-27. The Query pane with a new group added

■ **Note** By default, all other queries are added to a group named Other Queries.

Add a Query to a Group

To move a query from its current group to another group, you can carry out the following steps:

1. Right-click the query you want to add to another existing group.

2. Select Move To Group ➤ *Destination Group Name* from the context menu.

The selected query is moved to the chosen group.

■ **Note** You can also carry out this operation from inside the Get & Transform Query Editor.

Duplicating Queries

If you have done a lot of work transforming data, you could well want to keep a copy of the original query before trying any potentially risky alterations to your work. Fortunately, this is extremely simple.

1. Right-click the query you want to copy.

2. Select Duplicate from the context menu.

The query is copied, and the duplicate appears in the list of queries. It has the same name as the original query, with a number in parentheses appended. You can always rename it in the Query Settings pane.

Referencing Queries

If you are building a complex extract, transform, and load (ETL) routine, you might conceivably organize your work in stages to better manage the process. To help you with this, the Get & Transform Query Editor allows you to use the *output* from one query as the *source* for another query. This enables you to break down different parts of the process (structure, filters, then cleansing, for example) into separate queries so that you can concentrate on different aspects of the transformation in different queries.

To use the output of one query as the source data for another, you need to *reference* a query. The following explains how to do it:

1. Right-click the query you want to use as the source data for a new query.

2. Select Reference from the context menu.

A new query is created in the list of queries in the Query pane. The new query has the same name as the original query, with a number in parentheses appended. If you click the new query, you see exactly the same data in the referenced query as you can see if you click the final step in the source query.

From now on, any modifications that you make in the referenced (source) query produces an effect on the data that is used as the source for the second query.

Add a Column As a New Query

There are occasions when you might want to extract a column of data and use it as a separate query. It could be that you need the data that it contains as reference data for another query, for example. The following explains how you can do this:

1. In the Query list on the left, edit the query containing the column that you want to isolate as a new query.

2. Right-click the title of the column containing the data that you want to isolate.

3. Select Add As New Query from the context menu. A new query is created. It is named after the original query and the source column.

4. In the Transform ribbon, click To Table. The To Table dialog will appear.

5. Click OK.

6. Rename the query.

Pending Changes

When you are dealing with data sources and switch from the Query Editor to the Get & Transform view, normally you then want to load the full data from the source into the data model.

The downside to this approach is that a huge set of source data can take a long time to load, or reload, when you move back to creating and modifying visualizations. This is why Get & Transform will let you select Close from the Close & Load button in the Query Editor Home ribbon. Doing this will return you instantly to the data view but will not apply any changes that you have made. As a reminder, you will see an alert like the one shown in Figure 13-28 at the top of the data view.

 There are pending changes in your queries that haven't been applied. Apply Changes ✕

Figure 13-28. *The pending changes alert*

You can continue to work in data view as long as you like. Click the Apply Changes button when you have time to reload the modified source data into the data model.

Copying Data from Get & Transform

Get & Transform is designed as a data destination. It does not have any data export functionality as such. You can manually copy data from the Get & Transform Query Editor, however. More precisely, you can copy any of the following:

- The data in the query

- A column of data

- A single cell

In all cases, the process is the same:

1. Click the element to copy. This can be as follows:

   a. The top-left square of the data grid

   b. A column title

   c. A single cell

2. Right-click and select copy from the context menu.

You can then paste the data from the clipboard into the destination application.

■ **Note**   This process is somewhat limited because you cannot select a range of cells. And you must remember that you are looking only at sample data in the Query Editor.

Conclusion

This chapter showed you how to structure your source data into a valid data table from one or more potential sources. You saw how to pivot and unpivot data, to fill rows up and down with data, and to create new columns of data.

Possibly the most important thing that you learned is how to join individual queries so that you can add the data from one query into another. This can involve looking up data from a separate query or carrying the aggregated results from one query into another.

Finally, you saw some of the basic techniques for managing and organizing queries. This way an ETL process can be polished into a structured and maintainable process.

In this chapter and the three previous chapters, you saw essentially a three-stage process: first you find the data, then you load it into Get & Transform Query Editor, and from there you cleanse and modify it. The techniques that you can use are simple but powerful and can range from changing a data type to merging multiple data tables. Now that your data is prepared and ready for use, you can add it to the Excel data model and start delivering truly powerful analysis.

CHAPTER 14

■ ■ ■

Extending the Excel Data Model Using Power Pivot

This chapter shows you how to take some of the data tables that you previously loaded using Get & Transform and convert them into a coherent data set in the in-memory data model using Power Pivot. This data model will enable you to deliver information, insight, and analysis from the data the tables contain.

When creating a complete and coherent data model, you will probably find that there are essentially five steps to follow to mold the tables into a cohesive whole.

1. Load the source data into the Excel data model.

2. Establish relationships between the tables so that Power Pivot understands how the data in one table is linked to the data contained in another table. Chaining one table to another will let you use the data to deliver accurate and cogent results.

3. Prepare the model structure through adding hierarchies and KPIs.

4. Augment the tables with any calculated metrics that you need in the final outputs. These can range from simple arithmetic to complex calculations.

5. Prepare a date table that enables Power Pivot to see how data evolves over time. In the world of data warehousing, such a table is called a *date dimension*, and it is fundamental if there is a date or time element in your analysis.

This chapter covers two of these points: linking source tables and extending the data model with hierarchies and KPIs. Chapters 15 and 16 introduce you to calculations in DAX, the language used to extend an Excel data model with further metrics, and Chapter 17 explains how to create a date table and add and apply time-related calculations.

Admittedly, not every data set in Power Pivot will need all these techniques to be applied. In some cases, you will only need to cherry-pick techniques from the range of available options to finalize a data set. In any case, it probably helps to know what Power Pivot can do and when to use which of the techniques outlined in this chapter. So, it is up to you to decide what is fundamental and what is useful—and to have a suite of solutions available to solve any potential data analysis challenges that you may meet.

© Adam Aspin 2016

411

A. Aspin, *High Impact Data Visualization in Excel with Power View, 3D Maps, Get & Transform and Power BI*, DOI 10.1007/978-1-4842-2400-7_14

▪ **Note** This approach will apply only to data that you have chosen to send from Get & Transform queries into the in-memory data model. You cannot apply any of the modeling techniques that you will see in this chapter to data that you have loaded directly into Excel spreadsheets.

If you want to follow the examples in this chapter, download the `PowerPivotData.xlsx` file from the Apress web site. This file will let you follow the examples as they appear in this chapter.

Power Pivot

One of the first things to remember when creating, modifying, and managing in-memory data models is that you are leaving the traditional Excel framework behind. The new paradigm is based on the following:

- *In-memory data*: You will *not* see or use the source data in Excel workbooks.

- *Power Pivot to manage data*: You cannot manipulate the in-memory data model directly from an Excel worksheet.

- *A separate data management window*: You can create a data model and add KPIs, hierarchies, and calculations.

- *DAX as the formula language*: You use this instead of the Excel functions that you have been used to using.

Fortunately, none of this is particularly difficult. Indeed, if you are a Power Pivot user, then you probably already have a good grasp of these concepts. If not, well, now is the time to have some fun learning them.

Launching Power Pivot

There are a couple of ways that you can open Power Pivot and access the in-memory data model. In Excel 2016, the easiest way is probably as follows:

1. Open the file containing the data model (`PowerPivotData.xlsx` in this example). Do not be surprised if the file seems empty. Remember that it contains Get & Transform queries and in-memory data, both of which are not immediately visible.

2. Switch to the Data ribbon.

3. Click the Manage Data Model button.

Excel will open the Power Pivot window, which will look like the one shown in Figure 14-1.

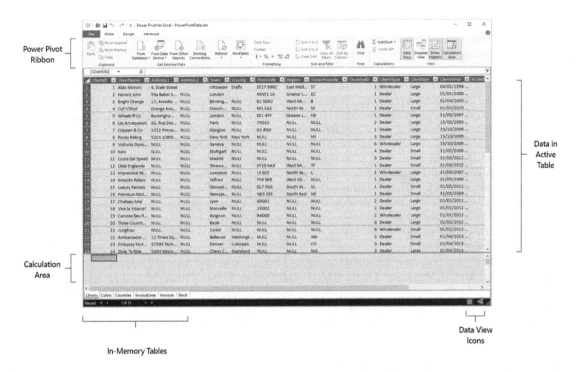

Figure 14-1. *The Power Pivot window*

The Power Pivot Window

If the Power Pivot window is new to you, the principal elements that it contains are outlined in Table 14-1.

Table 14-1. *Elements of the Power Pivot Window*

Element	Description
Power Pivot ribbon	Power Pivot uses three main ribbons: Home, Design, and Advanced.
Selected data table	The data for the selected table is visible in the Power Pivot window.
Calculation area	This is where you can add specific DAX-based calculations. These are explained in Chapter 16.
Tables tabs	This is a list of tabs containing the data for each in-memory data table.
Data view icons	These icons let you switch between the two ways of looking at Power Pivot data: data view and design view.

Data Model or Query?

You could well be thinking that this does not look like very much at all yet. If anything, it looks like an extension of the Get & Transform Query window. However, be reassured, you will soon see what you can do in Power Pivot and exactly how powerful a tool Power Pivot really is when it comes to data modeling. For the moment, it is essential to remember that you have (so to speak) opened a door into the engine room of Power Pivot. Although this new world is part of Excel (and you can return to Excel visualizations instantaneously just by closing this window), it is best if you consider it as a kind of parallel universe for the moment. This universe has its own ribbons and buttons and is distinct from the Excel window so that you can concentrate on enhancing the data without getting distracted by the output produced by the data.

The Power Pivot data view is also different from the Get & Transform Query Editor. For instance, one major difference between the Get & Transform Query window and the data view is that in the data view you are looking at *all* your data. The Query window only ever shows a *sample* of data. Once you load the data into the data model, you finally have access to the *entire* data set (all the data in all the tables), and this is what you can see in Power Pivot.

There are some areas where Get & Transform can do some of the things that can also be done in Power Pivot. For instance, you can create calculated columns in both (you will see how to do this in Power Pivot in the following chapter). My advice is to try to remember that Get & Transform is for finding, filtering, and mashing up data, whereas Power Pivot is for refining and calculating the structure and metrics in your data model. However, each user can take the approach that they prefer and carry out any necessary calculations in either Get & Transform or Power Pivot. After all, it is the result that counts.

The Power Pivot Ribbons

So what, exactly, are you looking at when you start Power Pivot? Essentially, you can see three ribbons, which are all devoted to data management.

- The Home ribbon

- The Design ribbon

- The Advanced ribbon

These three ribbons will remain accessible (and essentially the same) whether you are modeling data or extending the data model with further calculations, hierarchies, or KPIs.

As these interface elements are essential, I prefer to explain them thoroughly from the start. This should make understanding the Power Pivot environment easier. However, if you prefer to skip this section (or possibly use it as a reference later), then feel free to jump ahead.

The Home Ribbon

The first ribbon that you need to understand is (perhaps inevitably) the Home ribbon. You can see its core elements in Figure 14-2; Table 14-2 explains the elements.

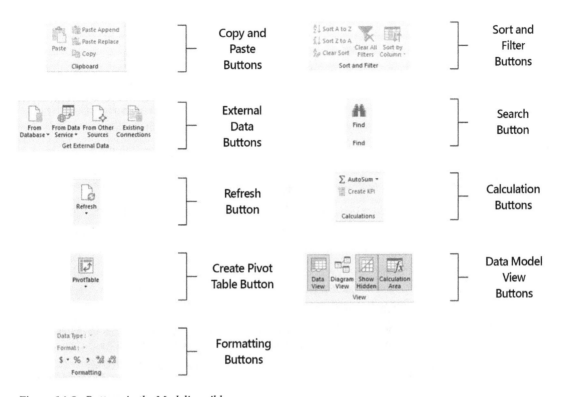

Figure 14-2. *Buttons in the Modeling ribbon*

Table 14-2. *The Home Ribbon Buttons*

Button	Description
Paste	Pastes the clipboard contents
Paste Append	Adds the data from the clipboard
Paste Replace	Adds the data from the clipboard and replaces the selected data
Copy	Copies the selected data to the clipboard
From Database	Adds further data tables from an external database
From Data Service	Adds further data tables from an external data service
From Other Sources	Adds further data tables from other sources
Existing Connections	Adds further data tables from existing connections
Refresh	Refreshes the data in the data model, totally or partially
Pivot Table	Creates a pivot table in an Excel worksheet using the data in the in-memory data model
Data Type	Applies a different data type to the selected column (or columns)
Currency Format	Applies the chosen currency format to the selected column (or columns)
Percentage Format	Applies the percentage format to the selected column (or columns)

(continued)

415

Table 14-2. (*continued*)

Button	Description
Comma-Separated Format	Applies the comma-separated format to the selected column (or columns)
Increase Decimals	Increases the number of decimals in the selected column (or columns)
Decrease Decimals	Decreases the number of decimals in the selected column (or columns)
Sort Ascending	Sorts the data in ascending order using the selected column
Sort Descending	Sorts the data in descending order using the selected column
Clear Sort	Undoes any sort processes that have been applied
Clear All Filters	Removes any column filters that have been applied
Sort byColumn	Defines that a column is sorted on the elements in another column
Find	Searches for metadata in the data model
Autosum	Generates an automatic aggregation-sum, average, and so on
Create KPI	Creates a key performance indicator
Data View	Switches to data view
Diagram View	Switches to diagram (data modeling) view
Show/Hide Hidden objects	Shows or hides any objects (fields or tables for instance) that have been hidden from end user access using client tools like Power View
Show/Hide Calculation Area	Shows or hides the calculation area at the bottom of the screen

The Power Pivot data source buttons are essentially a legacy from previous versions of Power Pivot. I consider that these have been superseded by Get & Transform.

Consequently, I will not be explaining how the Get External Data buttons in the Power Pivot Home ribbon work. Neither will I be explaining how these "classic" Power Pivot technologies can be applied to add data to the data model. This is quite simply because Get & Transform can do not only anything that the old Power Pivot solutions can provide but can deliver much, much more.

So, it is probably best to continue using any existing Power Pivot data connections that you have inherited until you need to upgrade them to Get & Transform. However, I strongly advise adding any new data to existing data models using Get & Transform, as the two approaches can coexist quite happily.

The Design Ribbon

The buttons that contained in the Design ribbon are shown in Figure 14-3 and explained in Table 14-3.

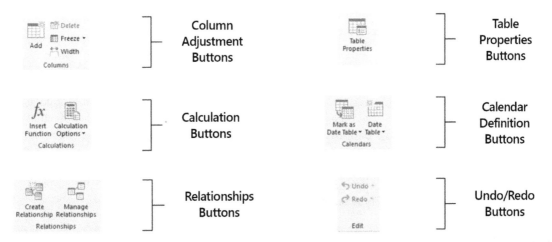

Figure 14-3. *Buttons in the Design ribbon*

Table 14-3. *The Design Ribbon Buttons*

Button	Description
Add	Adds a new column at the right of the existing data
Delete	Deletes the selected column (or columns)
Freeze	Moves the selected column to the left of the data in the table and leaves it visible when scrolling to the right
Width	Sets the width of the selected column (or columns)
Insert Function	Inserts a DAX function from the range of available functions
Calculation Options	Defines the calculation method (automatic or manual)
Create Relationship	Creates a relationship between tables
Manage Relationships	Manages relationships between tables
Table Properties	Defines core table properties
Mark As Date Table	Indicates that a table is to be treated as a date table by DAX
Date Table	Creates a date table
Undo	Undoes the last action
Redo	Redoes the last action that was undone

The Advanced Ribbon

The buttons that contained in the Advanced ribbon are shown in Figure 14-4 and explained in Table 14-4.

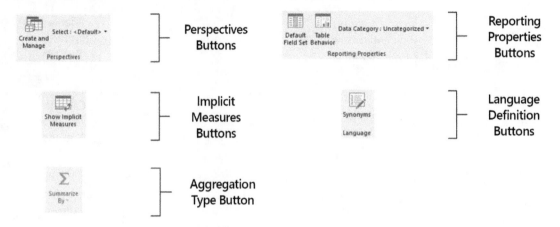

Figure 14-4. *Buttons in the Advanced ribbon*

Table 14-4. *The Advanced Ribbon Buttons*

Button	Description
Create And Manage Perspectives	Creates and modifies views (perspectives) over the data model
Select Perspective	Selects an available perspective
Show Implicit Measures	Displays implicit measures in pivot tables
Summarize By	Sets the default aggregation (sum, average, count, and so on) for end-user tools of the data model
Default Field Set	Defines the default field set and column order for a table in client tools
Table Behavior	Defines core table properties such as row identifier
Data Category	Sets the kind of data in the selected column (or columns)
Synonyms	Lets you define synonyms for fields to allow for natural language queries

Managing Power Pivot Data

Assuming that all has gone well, you now have a Power Pivot data model based on a series of tables. Clicking a table in the sample file PowerPivotData.xlsx will display the data from that table in the central area of the Data View window. It will soon be time to see what you can do with this data, but first, to complete the roundup of overall data management, you need to know how to do the following:

- Rename tables

- Delete tables

- Move tables

- Move around a table

- Rename a column

- Delete columns
- Set column width

Manipulating Tables

Let's begin by seeing how you can tweak the tables that you have imported.

Renaming Tables

Suppose you want to rename a table in the data model that you previously imported using Get & Transform. These are the steps to follow:

1. Right-click the table tab at the bottom of the Power Pivot window.

2. Select Rename.

3. Enter the new name or modify the existing name.

4. Press Enter.

This also renames the query on which the table is based. In essence, Power Pivot will let you rename data sets either as queries in the Get & Transform Query window or in Power Pivot itself. Because the query *is* the table, renaming one renames the other.

Deleting a Table

Deleting a table is virtually identical to the process of renaming one—you just right-click the table name tab and select Delete instead of Rename. As this is a potentially far-reaching operation, Power Pivot will demand confirmation.

■ **Note**   When you delete a table, you are removing it from Power Pivot completely. This means it is *also* removed from the set of queries that you may have used to transform the data. So, you need to be careful because you could lose all your carefully wrought transformation steps as well.

Manipulating Columns

Now let's see how to perform similar actions—but this time inside a table—to the columns of data that make up the table.

Renaming a Column

Renaming a column is pretty straightforward. Follow these steps:

1. Right-click the title of the column that you want to rename. In this example, it is the field InvoiceDate in the Invoices table. The column will be selected, and the context menu will appear. This is shown in Figure 14-5.

Figure 14-5. *The Power Pivot context menu*

2. Select Rename from the context menu. The current column name will be highlighted.

3. Type in the new name for the column and press Enter.

And that is it. Your column has been renamed; it is also selected. You cannot use the name of an existing column in the same table, however. If you try, Power Pivot will name the column *ExistingColumnName2*, for example.

Although renaming a column may seem trivial, it can be important. Consider other users first; they need columns to have instantly understandable names that mean something to them. Then there is the Power BI natural language feature. This works well only if your columns have the sort of names that are used in the queries—or ones that are recognizable synonyms. Finally, you cannot rename columns individually in separate visualizations, so you really need to give your columns the names that you are happy seeing standardized across all the data analysis that is based on this data set.

■ **Note** Excel is forgiving when it comes to renaming columns (or, indeed, tables and calculations too). You can rename most elements in the Get & Transform Query Editor window, the Power Pivot data view, or the diagram view (depending where they were added), and the changes will ripple through the entire in-memory data model. Better still, renaming columns, calculations, and tables generally do not cause Excel any difficulties if these elements have already been applied to dashboards in Power View, for instance, that are also updated to reflect the change of name. Just be sure that if you customize a lot of names and don't document the columns for reference, you will find that reverse engineering a report can be quite a task. In practice, it can save you a lot of effort if you always keep a reference of alias columns back to source in the query.

Deleting Columns

Deleting a column is equally easy. You will probably find yourself doing this when you bring in a column that you did not mean to import or when you find that you no longer need a column. So, to delete a column, you need to do the following:

1. Right-click the title of the column that you want to delete. Alternatively, right-click the field name in the field list. The column will be selected, and the context menu will appear.

2. Select Delete Columns from the context menu. The column will be deleted from the table.

Deleting unused columns is good practice because you will do the following:

- Reduce the memory required for the data set

- Speed up data refresh operations

- Reduce the size of the Excel file

■ **Note**   Deleting a column is not necessarily permanent. You can use the undo function to recover it. If you have deleted a column by accident and it is impractical to recover it with undo, you can choose to close the Power Pivot file without saving and reopen it, thus reverting to the previous version.

Moving Columns

Once in the data model, you cannot move columns around. So if you want to change the column order for any reason, you have to switch to the Get & Transform Query Editor and move the column there. Once you save and apply your changes, the modified column order is visible in the data model.

Setting Column Widths

One final thing that you may want to do to make your data more readable—and consequently easier to understand—is to adjust the column width. I realize that as an Excel or Word user, you may find this old hat, but in the interests of completeness, this is how you do it:

1. Place the mouse pointer over the right limit of the column title in the column whose width you want to alter. The cursor will become a two-headed arrow.

2. Drag the cursor left or right.

■ **Note**   You cannot select several adjacent columns before widening (or narrowing) one of them to set them all to the width of the column that you are adjusting. You can double-click the right limit of the column title in the column whose width you want to alter so that Power Pivot can set the width to that of the longest element in the column.

Power Pivot Data Types

When you are importing data from an external source, Power Pivot tries to convert it to one of the nine data types that it uses. Table 14-5 describes these data types.

Table 14-5. *Power Pivot Data Types*

Data Type	Description
Decimal Number	Stores the data as a real number with a maximum of 15 significant decimal digits. Negative values range from –1.79E +308 to –2.23E –308. Positive values range from 2.23E –308 to 1.79E + 308.
Currency	Stores the data as a number with a fixed number of decimals.
Whole Number	Stores the data as integers that can be positive or negative but are whole numbers between 9,223,372,036,854,775,808 (–2^63) and 9,223,372,036,854,775,807 (2^63–1).
Date/Time	Stores the data as a date and time in the format of the host computer. Only dates on or after January 1, 1900, are valid.
Date	Stores the data as a date in the format of the host computer.
Time	Stores the data as a time element in the format of the host computer.
Text	Stores the data as a Unicode string of 536,870,912 bytes at most.
True/False	Stores the data as Boolean—true or false.
Binary	Stores the data as binary (machine-readable) data.

Formatting Power Pivot Data

Power Pivot allows you to apply formatting to the data in the tables that it contains. When you format the data in the Power Pivot data model, you are defining the format that will be used in all visualizations in all the Power View dashboards and Excel pivot tables that you create using this metric. So, it is probably worth learning to format data for the following reasons:

- You will save time and multiple repetitive operations when creating reports and presentations by defining a format once and for all in Power Pivot.

- It can help you understand your data more intuitively if you can see the figures in a format that has intrinsic meaning.

This explains how to format a column (of figures in this example):

1. Assuming you are working in the Power Pivot data view, click the table name in the field list that contains the metric you want to format.

2. Click inside the column that you want to format (SalePrice from the InvoiceLines table in the DataModeling.xlsx sample file).

3. In the Modeling ribbon, click the Thousands Separator icon (the comma in the Formatting section). All the figures in the column will be formatted with a thousands separator and two decimals.

Table 14-6 describes the various formatting options available.

Table 14-6. *Currency Format Options*

Format Option	Icon	Description	Example
General		Leaves the data unformatted	100000.01
Currency	$ ▾	Adds a thousands separator and two decimals as well as the current monetary symbol	$100,000.01
Date/Time		Formats a date and/or time value in one of a selection of date and time formats	
Decimal Number	⟩	Adds a thousands separator and two decimals	100,000.01
Percentage	%	Multiplies by 100, adds two decimals, and prefixes with the percentage symbol	28.78%
Increase Decimals	⁺.0̥.0̥0̥	Increases the number of decimals	
Decrease Decimals	.0̥0̥ ⁺.0̥	Decreases the number of decimals	

If you want to return to "plain-vanilla" data, then you can do this by selecting the General format. Remember that you are not in Excel and you cannot format only a range of figures—it is the whole column or nothing. Also, there is no way to format nonadjacent columns by Ctrl+clicking to perform a noncontiguous selection. And, you cannot select multiple adjacent columns and format them in a single operation.

By now, you have probably realized that Power Pivot operates on a "format once/apply everywhere" principle. However, this does not mean you have to prepare the data exhaustively before creating dashboards and reports. You can flip between the data model and Power View or pivot tables at any time to select another format, secure in the knowledge that the format you just applied is used throughout all of your outputs wherever the relevant metric is used.

■ **Note**   Numeric formats are not available for selection if the data in a field is a text or data/time data type. Similarly, date and time formats are available only if the column contains data that can be interpreted as dates or times.

Currency Formats

Power Pivot will propose a wide range of currency formats. To choose the currency that you want, follow these steps:

1.   Click the pop-up (the downward-facing triangle) to the right of the currency format icon. This will display a list of available formats.

2.   Select the currency symbol you want or click More Formats to view all the available currency formats, as shown in Figure 14-6; then click OK.

Figure 14-6. *The currency format pop-up list*

Clicking the More Formats option will did play the Currency Format dialog (shown in Figure 14-7) where you can select from a wide range of available formats.

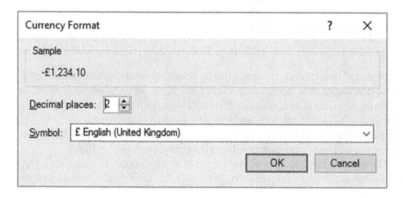

Figure 14-7. *The Currency Format dialog*

___

■ **Note**   The thousands separator that is applied, as well as the decimal separator, depends on the settings of the PC on which the formatting is applied.

___

Preparing Data for Analysis

Corralling data into a structure that can power your dashboards and reports necessitates a good few tweaks above and beyond specifying data types and formats for final presentation. As part of the groundwork for your dashboards, you could also have to do the following:

- Categorize data

- Apply a default summarization

- Define Sort By columns

These ideas probably seem somewhat abstruse at first sight, so let's see them in action to make it clear why you need to add these touches to your data model. Moreover, these adjustments are often of particular relevance when preparing a data model for use in Power View, for instance.

Categorize Data

Power View dashboards are not just made up of facts and figures. They can also contain geographical data or hyperlinks to web sites or documents. While we humans can recognize a URL pretty easily and can guess that a column with postcodes contains, well, postcodes, such intuitions may not be quite as self-evident for a computer.

So, if you want Power View (or any other tool that uses the in-memory data) to be able to add maps or hyperlinks, you will make life easier for both you and the application if you categorize any columns that contain the types of data that are used for maps and links.

For instance, suppose you want to prepare the Country table a potential data source for a dashboard map (and assuming you have loaded the DataModeling.xlsx sample file).

1. Select the Country Table tab at the bottom of the screen. The Country data will appear in the center of the Power Pivot window.

2. Click inside the CountryName column. The column will be highlighted.

3. In the Advanced ribbon, click the pop-up to the right of the Data Category button and select Country/Region from the menu.

The ribbon will show Data Category: Country/Region. This means that Power Pivot now knows to use the contents of this field as a country when generating maps in dashboards.

Table 14-7 describes the data category options that are available.

Table 14-7. *Data Category Options*

Data Category Option	Description
Uncategorized	Applies to data that is not used for hyperlinks or creating maps
Address	Specifies an address for mapping
City	Specifies for mapping
Continent	Specifies a continent for mapping
Country/Region	Specifies a country or region for mapping
County	Specifies a county for mapping
Latitude	Specifies a latitude for mapping
Longitude	Specifies a longitude for mapping
Place	Specifies a location or place for mapping
Postal Code	Specifies a postal (ZIP) code for mapping
State or Province	Specifies a state or province for mapping
Web URL	Indicates a URL for a hyperlink
Image URL	Indicates a URL for an image
Organization	Sets the field as containing an organization
Product	Sets the field as containing a product
Date	Defines the data as dates
Company	Sets the field as containing a company

■ **Note**   Not specifying a data category does not mean that Power Pivot cannot create maps in dashboards or recognize URLs. However, the results cannot be guaranteed of a reasonable chance of success unless you have indicated to the application that a column contains a certain type of data.

If you scroll to the bottom of the list of categories in the Data Category pop-up list, you will see the option More Categories. Clicking this will display the Data Category dialog shown in Figure 14-8. This dialog lets you present the available categories grouped by themes, which can make choosing the correct category easier.

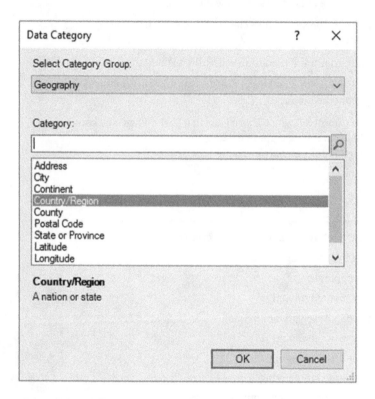

Figure 14-8. *The Data Category dialog*

Apply a Default Summarization

When you are presenting data, you are often aggregating numeric data. Most times, this means adding up the figures to return the column total. However, there could be columns of data where you want another aggregation applied. Do the following to set your own default aggregation (assuming you have loaded the DataModeling.xlsx sample file):

1.   Select the Colors table in the field list. The Colors data will appear in the center of the Power Pivot window.

2.   Click inside the Color column. The column will be highlighted.

3.   In the Advanced ribbon, click the Summarize By button and select Count from the menu.

The ribbon will show Default Summarization: Count.

Table 14-8 describes the default summarization options that are available.

Table 14-8. *Default Summarization Options*

Default Summarization Option	Description
Do Not Summarize	The data in this column is not summarized.
Default	The default aggregation for this data type will be applied.
Sum	The data in this column is added (summed).
Average	The average value for the data in this column is returned.
Minimum	The minimum value for the data in this column is returned.
Maximum	The maximum value for the data in this column is returned.
Count	The number of elements in the column is returned.
Distinct Count	The number of individual (distinct) elements in the column is returned.

Obviously, you can only apply mathematical aggregations to numeric values. However, you can apply counts to any type of data.

▪ **Note**   Specifying a default aggregation does not prevent you from overriding the default in dashboards. It merely sets a default that is applied as a standard when aggregating data from a column. In the real world, this can be really useful because it reduces the time you spend building dashboards.

Define Sort by Columns

Sometimes you will want to sort data in a dashboard visualization based not on the contents of the selected column but on the contents of another column. As an example, imagine that you have a table of data that contains the month for a sale. If you sort by month, you probably do not want to see the months in alphabetical order, starting with April. In cases such as this, you can tell Power Pivot that you want to sort the month *name* element by the month *number* that is contained in another column.

1. Load the C:\DataVisualisationInExcel2016\PowerPivotData.xlsx sample file (unless you have already loaded it, of course).

2. In the data view, select the Calendar table in the field list. The date data will appear in the center of the Power Pivot window.

3. Click inside the Month column. The column will be highlighted.

4. In the Home ribbon, click the Sort By Column button. The Sort By Column dialog will appear.

5. Select MonthNumber from the list of available columns. The Sort By Column dialog will look like the one in Figure 14-9.

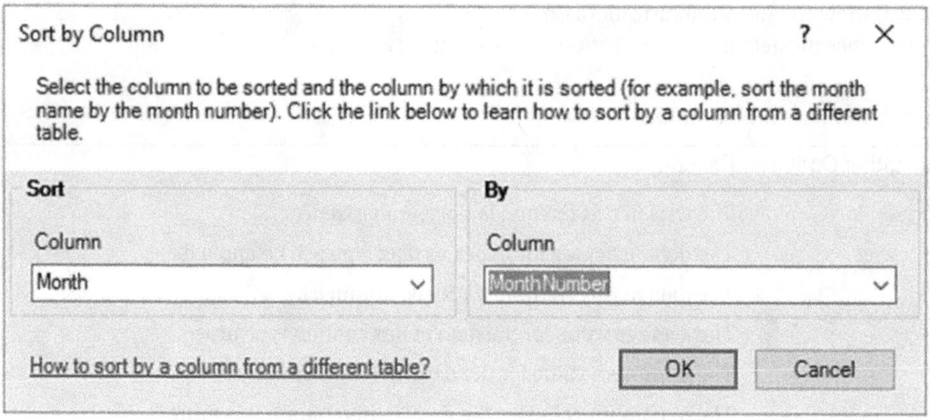

Figure 14-9. *The Sort By Column dialog*

> 6. Click OK.

Now if you sort by MonthFull in a visualization, you see the months in the order that you probably expect—from January to December. Had you *not* applied a Sort By column, then calendar months would have been sorted in alphabetical order, which is from April to September! Once again, this choice applies to *any* visualization that you create in a Power Pivot dashboard that is based on this data model. So, remember to add a numeric sort column alongside textual columns, such as dates and so forth, at the source.

■ **Tip** If you want to see which column has been set as a Sort By column, then all you have to do is to click inside the column to be sorted and then click the Sort By Column button. The pop-up list of columns shows a check mark to the left of the column that is being used to sort the selected column.

The sample file for this chapter (DataModeling.xlsx) already contains columns that you can use as Sort By columns. In the real world, your source data might not always be this instantly usable. So, remember that you can always switch to Get & Transform and enhance source tables with extra columns that you can then use to sort data in data view.

Sorting Data in Power Pivot Tables

A Power Pivot table could contain millions of rows, so the last thing you want to have to do is to scroll down through a random data set. Fortunately, ordering data in a table is simple.

> 1. Right-click inside the column you want to order the data by. I will choose the Make column in the Stock table.
>
> 2. In the Home ribbon, click the Sort A To Z button to sort this column in ascending (alphabetical, smallest number to largest number, or increasing date) order.

The table is sorted using the selected column as the sort key, and even a large data set appears correctly ordered in a short time. If you want to sort a table in descending order (reverse alphabetical, largest to smallest number, or decreasing date order), click the Sort Z To A option in the context menu.

At this juncture, you need to remember that the data model is not really designed for interactive data analysis. That is what dashboards and pivot tables are for. Consequently, you should not expect to use the data tables in Power Pivot as if they were vast Excel spreadsheets.

▪ **Tip**   If you need a visual indication that a column is sorted, look at the right of the column name. You will see a small triangle that faces upward to indicate a descending sort or downward to indicate an ascending sort.

Power Pivot alters the text in the sort icon slightly depending on the data type of the column in which you have clicked. This makes the result even more comprehensible, if anything.

- For a numeric column, the icons read Sort Smallest To Largest and Sort Largest To Smallest.

- For a date column, the icons read Sort Oldest To Newest and Sort Newest To Oldest.

If you want to remove the sort operation that you applied and return to the initial data set as it was imported, all you have to do is click the Clear Sort icon in the context menu for the column.

▪ **Note**   You cannot perform complex sort operations; that is, you cannot sort first on one column and then carry out a secondary sort in another column (if there are identical elements in the first column). You also cannot perform multiple sort operations sorting on the least important column and then progressing up to the most important column to sort on to get the effect of a complex sort. This is because Power Pivot always sorts the data based on the data set as it was initially loaded. Remember that you can add index columns in Get & Transform and then sort on these if you want to reapply an initial sort order.

Designing a Data Model

Congratulations! You are well on the way to developing a high-performance data repository for self-service business intelligence (BI). You have imported data from one or even from several sources into the Excel data model. You have taken a good look at your data using Power Pivot, and you can carry out essential operations to rename tables and columns, as well as to filter the data. The next step to ensure that your data set is ready for initial use as a self-service BI data repository is to create and manage relationships between tables. This is a fundamental part of designing a coherent and usable data set in Power Pivot.

Before leaping into the technicalities of table relationships, I first need to answer a couple of simple questions:

- What are relationships between tables?

- Why do you need them?

Table relationships are links between tables of data that allow columns in one table to be used meaningfully in another table. If you have opened the Power Pivot example file DataModeling.xlsx, then you can see that there is a table of stock data that contains a ColorID column, but not the actual color itself. As a complement to this, there is a reference table of colors. It follows that, if you want to say what color a car was when it was bought, you need to be able to *link* the tables so that the stock table can look up the actual color of the car that was sold. This requires some commonality between the two tables; fortunately, both contain a column named ColorID. So if you are able to join the two tables using this field, you can see which color is represented by the color ID for each car sold, which figures in the sales data.

You can see another example of linking tables if you take a look at the Invoices and InvoiceLines tables. These two tables have been designed using a technique called *relational modeling*. Essentially this means that two tables have been created to avoid pointless data duplication. So, any data that is used to describe an invoice (such as the invoice date or invoice number) is stored in the Invoices table, whereas all the details concerning the vehicles sold are held in a separate table named InvoiceLines. The two tables then share a field that allows them to be joined so that users can see the data from the two tables together if they need to do so.

It is possible to store the data from these two tables as one table. However, this would mean repeating elements such as the invoice date or invoice number each time that an invoice contained more than one item.

■ **Tip** If you have the necessary permissions as well as the SQL knowledge, then you can, of course, join tables directly in the source database using a query. This way you can create fewer "flattened" tables in Power Pivot from the start.

Data View and Diagram View

Up until now, you have worked exclusively in data view; that is, you have looked at tables and the detail of the data. When moving to the design phase of your data preparation in Power Pivot, it is often easier to switch to diagram view, as this allows you to step back from the detail and look at the data set as a whole. To do this, follow these steps:

1. Click the Diagram View button in the Home ribbon. Power Pivot will display the tables in diagram view, as shown in Figure 14-10.

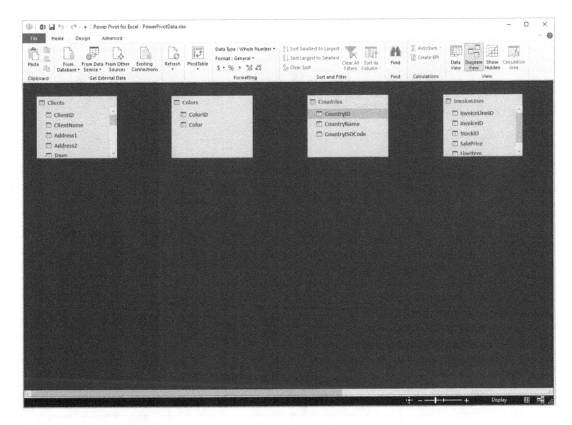

Figure 14-10. *Diagram view*

■ **Tip**   You can also use the Diagram View icon at the bottom right of the Power Pivot window to switch to diagram view if you prefer.

As you can see from Figure 14-10, you are now looking at most or all of your tables, and although you can see the table and column names, you cannot see the data. This is exactly what you need because now it is time to think in terms of overall structures rather than the nitty-gritty. You can use this view to move and resize the tables. Moving a table is as easy as dragging the table's title bar. Resizing a table means placing the pointer over a table edge or corner and dragging the mouse.

Although repositioning tables can be considered pure aesthetics, I find that doing so is really useful. A well-laid-out data set design will help you understand the relationships between the tables and the inherent structure of the data.

Diagram View Display Options

The whole point of diagram view is to let you get a good look at the entire data set and, if necessary, modify the layout in order to see the relationships between tables more clearly.

To this end, a few layout options are worth getting to know. They are shown in Figure 14-11.

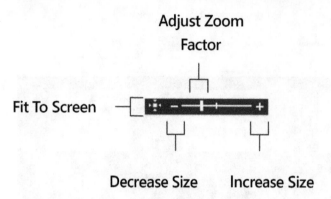

Figure 14-11. *Diagram view display options*

Table 14-9 explains these options.

Table 14-9. *Diagram View Display Options Explained*

Display Option	Description
Zoom	Allows you to zoom into, or out of, the table display
Fit To Screen	Sets the zoom level so that all tables are visible
Increase Size	Increases the size but shows fewer tables
Decrease Size	Decreases the size but shows more tables

Maximizing a Table

If you have many, many fields in a table, then you may occasionally need to take a closer look at a single table. Fortunately, the creators of Power Pivot have thought of this. So, to zoom in on a specific table, follow these steps:

1. Click the table that you want to examine more closely.

2. Click the Maximize button at the top right of the table. The table will expand to give you a clearer view of the fields in the table. You can see an example of this in Figure 14-12.

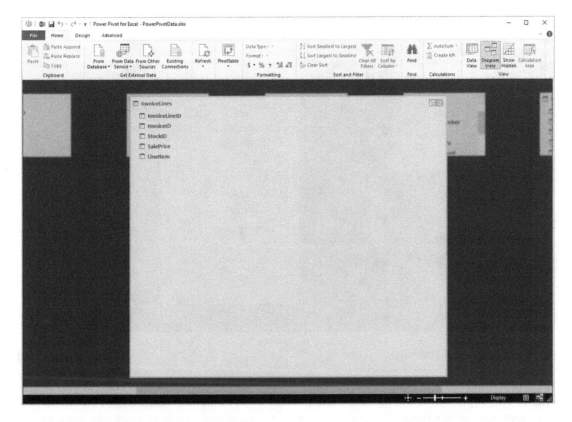

Figure 14-12. *Maximizing the InvoiceLines table*

To reset the table to its previous size, click the same icon—now called the Restore button—at the top right of the table.

Creating Relationships

Creating relationships is easy once you know which fields are common between tables. Since you already agreed that you need to join the Colors table to the Stock table, let's see how to do this.

1. Drag the ColorID field from the Stock table over the ColorID field in the Colors table.

A thin line will join the two tables, as shown in Figure 14-13.

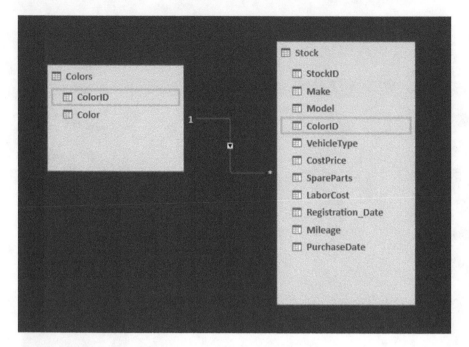

Figure 14-13. *A table relationship*

▪ Note The tiny figure 1 next to the Colors table at the end of the relationship indicates that there will be only a single field for each ColorID in this table. Conversely, the tiny asterisk next to the Stock table indicates that there could be many of the same ColorIDs in this table. This is called a *one-to-many* relationship.

Creating Relationships Manually

You do not have to drag and drop field names to create relationships. If you prefer, you can specify the tables and fields that will be used to create a relationship between tables. What is more, you do not have to be in diagram view to do this. So, just to make a point and to show you how flexible Power Pivot can be, in this example, you will join the Countries and Clients tables on their common CountryID field.

1. Select the Countries table.

2. Click the Create Relationship button in the Design ribbon. The Create Relationship dialog will appear.

3. In the upper row, where the Countries table is already selected (because you started from the Countries table), select the CountryID field. This field will be highlighted.

4. In the lower pop-up, select the Clients table. The CountryID field should appear automatically as the field to join on (it wil be highlighted). If the field is not selected or if Power Pivot has guessed incorrectly, you can always select the correct field in the lower table by clicking it. The Create Relationship dialog should look like Figure 14-14.

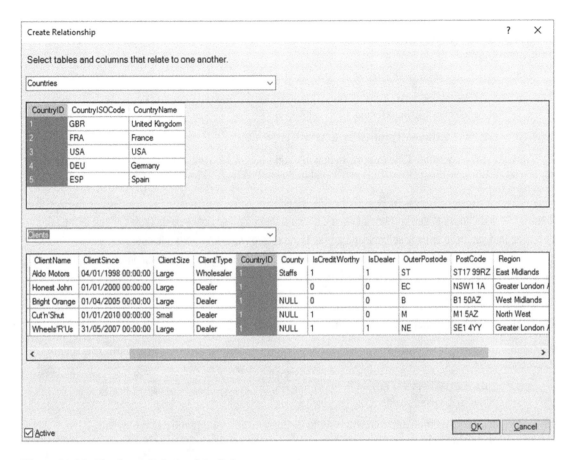

Figure 14-14. *The Create Relationship dialog*

    5.   Click OK. The relationship will be created.

■ **Note**   You can create relationships using the manual method in either data view or diagram view. Creating relationships manually can be easier when you have hundreds of fields or you want Power Pivot to guess which fields to use.

Creating Relationships Automatically

If you are importing several tables from a relational database, then you can have Power Pivot create the relationships during the import process. This approach has a couple of advantages.

- You avoid a lot of manual work.

- You reduce the risk of error (that is, creating relationships between tables on the wrong fields or even creating relationships between tables that are not related).

This technique is unbelievably easy. You carry out an import from a relational database source (say, using SQL Server). When faced with the list of available tables in the source database (as described in Chapter 10), you do the following:

1. Select the major source table.

2. Click the Select Related Tables button. Any tables that are linked to the table you have selected will be selected.

3. Continue the import process as described previously.

Once you have completed the import, switch to diagram view. You will see that the tables you just imported already have the relationships generated in Power Pivot.

■ **Note**   If you choose to select related tables, be aware that doing so only selects tables linked to the table (or tables) that you have already selected. As a result, you may have to carry out this operation several times, choosing a different starting table every time, to force all the existing relationships to be imported correctly.

Deleting Relationships

In addition to creating relationships, you will inevitably want to remove them at some point. This is both visual and intuitive.

1. Click the Design View button in the Home ribbon. Power Pivot will display the tables in diagram view.

2. Select the relationship that you want to delete. The line joining the two tables will be highlighted.

3. Press the Delete key. The Confirmation dialog will appear.

4. Click Delete From Model.

The relationship will be deleted, and the tables will remain in the data model.

Managing Relationships

If you want to change the field in a table that serves as the basis for a relationship, then you have another option. You can use the Manage Relationships dialog. This approach can also be useful if you want to create or delete several relationships at once. If you want to use this, follow these steps:

1. In the Design tab, click Manage Relationships. The Manage Relationships dialog appears, as shown in Figure 14-15.

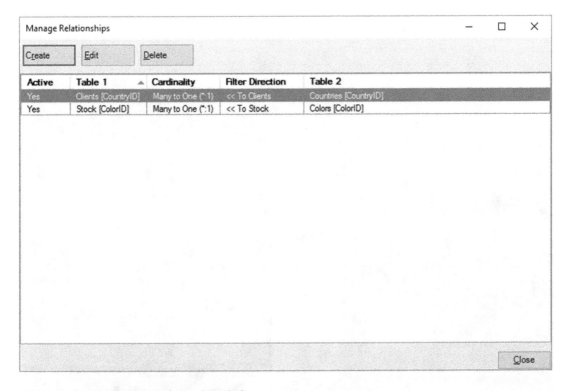

Figure 14-15. *The Manage Relationships dialog*

2. Click the relationship you want to modify.

3. Click Edit. The Edit Relationship dialog appears (it is virtually identical to the Create Relationship dialog shown in Figure 14-4).

4. Continue modifying the relationship as described previously.

As you can see from this dialog, you also have the option of creating or deleting relationships. Since the processes here are identical to those I have already described, I will not repeat them. If you want to practice using the Edit Relationship dialog, you can use it to complete the data model by adding the following final relationships:

- The Invoices to Clients table on the ClientID field in each table

- The InvoiceLines to Invoices table on the InvoiceID field in each table

- The Stock to InvoiceLines table on the StockID field in each table

- The Calendar table to the Invoices table on the Date and InvoiceDate fields, respectively

The data model will then look like the one in Figure 14-16 (after a little juggling to make it look presentable).

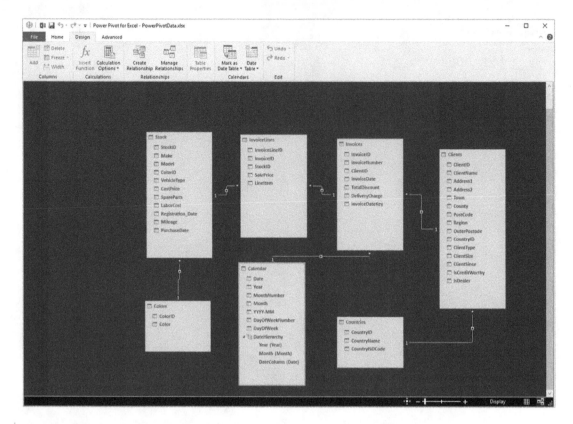

Figure 14-16. *A first data model*

■ **Note**   If you delete a set of related tables and subsequently reimport them without importing the relationships, then Power Pivot will *not* remember the relationships that existed previously. Consequently, you will have to re-create any relationships manually. The same is true if you delete and reimport any table that you linked to an existing table in Power Pivot—once a relationship has been removed through the process of deleting a table, you will have to re-create it.

The techniques used to create and manage relationships are not, in themselves, difficult to apply. It is nonetheless *absolutely fundamental* to establish the correct relationships between the tables in the data set. Put simply, if you try to use data from unconnected tables in a single Power View visualization or Excel pivot table, you will not just get an alert warning you that relationships need to be created; you will also get visibly inaccurate results. Basically, all your analysis will be false. So, it is well worth it to spend a few minutes up front designing a clean, accurate, and logically coherent data set.

Managing relationships in Power Pivot is often the key to creating an efficient data model. It is, however, outside the scope of this book to provide a complete course in data modeling. Nonetheless, here are a few tips to bear in mind when creating your initial data models:

- It can help to think in terms of *main* tables and *lookup* tables. In the data model that you looked at in this chapter, you can consider certain tables as lookup tables for the main data, such as the Colors, Countries, and Clients tables.

- Lookup tables generally contain a series of values that are not repeated in the table (a list of countries, for instance). These values are called the *one* side of a relationship, and they are linked to another table where they are referred to on many occasions. Hence, the table that contains the multiple references is called the *many* side of the relationship. This is also called the *cardinality* of a relationship by database and data warehouse designers.

- If your source data contains many lookup tables that cascade down through a series of relationships (a classic case is the Category ➤ Subcategory ➤ Product hierarchy that you find in many retail environments). To avoid over-complicating the data model, you may prefer to merge multiple tables into a single table using Get & Transform *before* developing the data model in Power Pivot itself.

- Sometimes—and this can be the case when importing data from relational databases—you need to join tables on more than one field. This is not possible in Power Pivot. However, you can often find workarounds to this, again using Get & Transform before modeling the data. In cases like this, you can merge tables by creating joins using multiple columns (as you saw in Chapter13), for instance.

- Data imported from data warehouses can have a built-in structure of facts (main tables containing metrics) and dimensions (containing lookup elements). However, you may want to "flatten" complex hierarchies of dimensions and create single-level tables of lookup elements here, too, using Get & Transform.

- Sometimes you may want to use the same table twice in different contexts. For instance, a date table may be useful to join to a sale date and a purchase date. In cases like this, you can reimport the date table a second time (and give it another name) and then create two separate joins from a lookup table to the two different lookup tables. This allows you to filter and aggregate data by separate date criteria. A lookup table like this is often called a *role-playing dimension*.

Preparing the Data Model

So far in this chapter you learned how to create a valid Power Pivot data model. This data set will allow you to slice and dice your data in many different ways and can be used as is with many tools such as Excel pivot tables and, of course, Power View.

Indeed, there is little to prevent you now from starting to use the data model that you have created in pivot tables or, better still, to deliver stunning Power View visualizations. However, while we are on the subject of finalizing the data model, there are a handful of tweaks that you may want to apply to the tables in the data set. These modifications are not always necessary and in many cases might not be required at all. Yet there could be an equal number of times when you will need to spend a couple of minutes preparing the data so that any output (and specifically Power View reports) can deliver what you expect immediately and flawlessly.

These are the kind of tweaksthat you are looking at:

- Setting a default field set (a predefined subset of columns that can be used by default in tables and charts)

- Setting default table behavior to prevent aggregation

- Defining the default aggregation for a column

- Indicating that a table has a unique identifier, and which field this is

- Indicating that a column contains images

- Indicating that the text in a column is a URL pointing to an image (and so, in effect, it represents an image)

- Indicating to output tools such as Power View that the data in a column is a URL

- Preparing hierarchies

- Setting key performance indicators (KPIs)

- Hiding certain columns from the end user

- Optimizing the file size

None of the techniques that you will see in this chapter is particularly complicated. A few of them take any time at all to apply. Yet, used effectively, they can enhance the output that you present to your audience.

Default Field Set

Some data tables will contain hundreds of fields (or columns, if you prefer); others will contain only a few. Many will contain a subset of columns that you will want to use frequently in Power View visualizations. Power Pivot allows you to define a default field set for each table that "remembers" the frequently used columns so that you can use them all at once in a table or chart, without having to add them individually and potentially laboriously. This subset is called the *default field set*, and it will also be the list of columns that is returned by the Power BI Service natural language query functionality.

What is more, a default field set is easy to apply in Power View, because all you have to do is click the table in the Power View field list. Power View will immediately create a table using *only* the columns in the default field set, in the order in which you defined them when you created the field set. Once this is done, nothing is stopping you from removing any unwanted columns from the table; this is often faster than adding columns individually. Here, then, is how you create a default field set.

1. Click the tab for the table for which you want to define a default field set. I will take Stock as an example.

2. Click the Default Field Set button in the Advanced ribbon. The Default Field Set dialog will be displayed.

3. Add the fields you foresee as being useful as a core group in Power View. I suggest the fields Make, Model, VehicleType, and CostPrice. To add fields, just double-click a field name in the left pane. The Default Field Set dialog will look like it does in Figure 14-17.

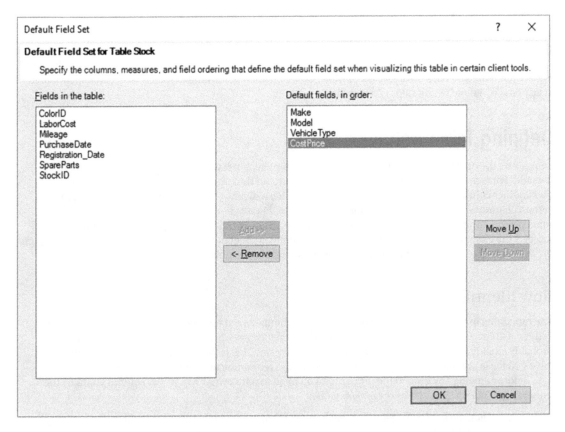

Figure 14-17. *The Default Field Set dialog*

   4.   Click OK.

You will not see any immediate change in Power View. However, the next time that you click the SalesData table in the Power View field list, a table containing the fields Make, Marque, CarAgeBucket, and SalePrice will be created, in this order.

■ **Note**   You cannot create a table in Power View using the default field set by dragging the table name to the Power View canvas.

If you prefer, rather than double-clicking in step 4, you can select a field name in the left pane and click the Add button in the Default Field Set dialog. In addition, to remove a selected field, all you have to do is click a field name in the right pane and click the Remove button in the Default Field Set dialog. If you want to change the order of the fields that make up the default field set, then all you have to do is click the field name in the right pane and click the Move Up or Move Down button. An existing default field set can be modified at any time by following the steps given earlier.

Defining Table Behavior

Sometimes the data in a table may be accurate and complete, but it will not display exactly as you hoped it would. For example, you may want to sort on a column but find that it needs custom sort criteria so that another column actually provides the sort order. Alternatively, you may want to prevent grouping on certain columns—so that Power Pivot does not presume that all your clients named John Smith are the same person, for instance. These and other options are possible and easy to apply so that your final output projects the effect you require in a clear and transparent way. Together these options are known as *modifying the table behavior* and are applied where necessary to individual tables.

Row Identifier

The remaining aspects of table behavior that you can change to enhance output all require that the table contain a unique identifier for each row of data. If your data comes from a relational database, then it probably already has what is known as a *unique primary key*. This is the case for the Countries and Clients tables, so these are the ones that you will use to show the remaining table behavior options.

Before applying any other table properties, you need to tell Power Pivot which column contains the unique key. This is called *setting the row identifier*.

1. Click the tab for the table for which you want to set the table behavior. I will use Countries as an example. If you are in diagram view, click the table.

2. In the Advanced tab, click Table Behavior. The Table Behavior dialog will appear.

3. In the Row Identifier pop-up, select CountryID. The dialog will look like in Figure 14-18.

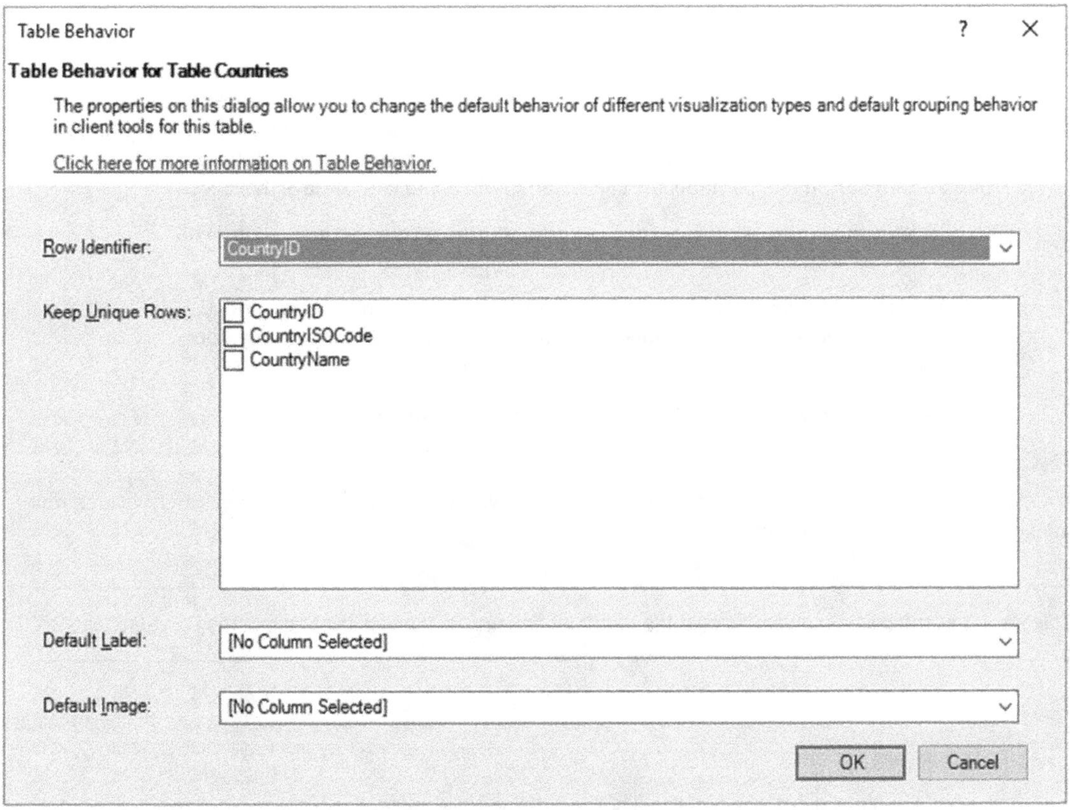

Figure 14-18. *Setting a row identifier for a table in Power Pivot*

4. Click OK.

Once you have successfully set the row identifier, you can proceed to set other table behavior options, as you will see in the next few paragraphs.

░ **Note**   If the column that you chose as the row identifier does not contain unique data, then you will get an error message and will not be able to set table behavior. This is something that will have to be dealt with in the source data itself.

Keep Unique Rows

One table behavior option that can be extremely useful is the ability to prevent Power Pivot (and consequently Power View) from aggregating data for a column. As an example, imagine that you have two clients with the same name. They could be subsidiaries in different states or countries. Anyway, you do not want Power View to display a single total when you analyze data by client. If you tell Power Pivot to keep unique rows for the column that contains the client names, then you can achieve this aim.

1. Click the tab for the table for which you want to stop data aggregating—this will be the Clients table. If you are in diagram view, then click the table.

2. Define the row identifier for the table (ClientID in this example) as described previously. Do not close the Table Behavior dialog. If you have previously done this, then in the Advanced tab, click Table Behavior.

3. In the Keep Unique Rows section of the dialog, check ClientName.

4. Click OK.

Now when you use the ClientName field in Power View, each client will appear separately, even if more than one client has the same name.

■ **Note**   You can select multiple fields if the data that defines uniqueness is spread across several columns.

Default Label

Power View treats all text fields as labels. Such egalitarianism may be laudable in many circumstances, but it can diminish certain visual effects when you are using tiles, for instance. So, one option is to set a default label field. Put simply, any default label field will be given prominence in certain Power View visualizations.

I'll use Countries as an example here, because it contains two fields that might be used in visualizations. However, let's presume that you need the CountryName field to stand out when visualizations are created. Here is how you can set a field to be a default label:

1. Click the tab for the table for which you want to define the column containing the default image (Countries). If you are in diagram view, then click the table.

2. In the Advanced tab, click Table Behavior.

3. Ensure that Row Identifier has been set as CountryID.

4. From the Default Label pop-up, select CountryName.

5. Click OK.

Now, when you create cards in Power View, you get the sort of difference that you can see in Figure 14-19.

Figure 14-19. *Cards in Power View when the default field label is used*

Set a Default Aggregation (Summarize By)

In pivot tables in Excel and visualizations in client tools such as Power View, you will inevitably be aggregating numeric data. Normally, this means summing up the data in a table or matrix. In some cases, however, you may find that you want a different aggregation to be applied when you are analyzing your data. Now, you can certainly override any default aggregations when creating Power View visualizations, as you saw in Chapter 2. But it can get very wearing to override the default time and time again in dozens of visualizations in possibly hundreds of reports. So, to avoid this waste of energy, define the default aggregation for any field in a Power Pivot data set.

1. Click the tab for the table for which you want to define the default aggregation. If you are in diagram view, then click the table.

2. Click the column or field whose default aggregation you want to alter.

3. In the Advanced tab, click Summarize By. A pop-up list of potential aggregations will appear. This is shown in Figure 14-20.

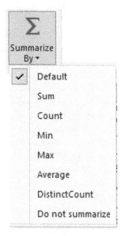

Figure 14-20. *Defining a default aggregation*

4. Click the aggregation you want to apply as the default.

From now on, the selected aggregation will be applied whenever you use this metric in a Power View table, matrix, or chart. This does not mean that you are stuck forever with the default aggregation that you set, just that it will be used by default until you apply another in a specific visualization.

■ **Note**   Setting a default aggregation can just well mean indicating that *no* aggregation must be applied. This is essentially required when a column contains a numeric value that has no meaning if it is summarized. One example is a column containing years; another is a column of IDs. In these cases, you should choose Do Not Summarize as the aggregation.

Preparing Images for Power View

Power Pivot will not display images, but it can reference or contain images so that Power View can use them to impress your audience. You can make Power Pivot return images to Power View in two ways. Both require a column of data containing either of the following:

- The image as binary data in the source table in a relational database

- A URL to files on an accessible network

Both require a small amount of preparation. Indeed, the two methods are slightly different depending on how the image is stored. Yet the result is well worth the small amount of effort required to deliver some impressive results, as I am sure you will agree.

Before walking through the techniques for specifying to Power Pivot that fields contain either images or references to images, I think that it is best to explain what the source data must be. The following are requirements that must be dealt with at the level of the data. Remember that you cannot alter the data itself in Power Pivot.

- Binary data in a database has to be a file stored as binary data. In SQL Server, for instance, this is data of the VARBINARY type. Loading such files into a database could require technical database knowledge and is outside the scope of this book. For further details on this, please consult my book *SQL Server 2012 Data Integration Recipes* (Apress, 2012).

- Image URLs must be a text reference containing the complete path reference to the binary file that contains the image.

I will once again take the Countries table as an example here, as it contains binary images that were previously loaded into the database table—and that consequently have been imported into Power Pivot. To tell Power Pivot that a field actually contains an image, follow these steps:

1. Click the tab for the table for which you want to define the column containing the image (Countries). If you are in diagram view, click the table.

2. Click the column that you know contains the binary data for the image (CountryFlag, in this example).

3. Switch to the Advanced tab (unless it is already active).

4. In the Data category pop-up at the right of the ribbon, select Image.

That is all you have to do. From now on, Power View will recognize this field as an image and display the image in visualizations.

Image URLs

In some cases you may have data that does not contain the image but refers to it, either in a network share or on the Web. In these cases, your source data will (must) have a column that contains the complete path to the image file, including the file name. However, you will need to tell Power Pivot that the text that is imported is not just a label but contains the path to an image. Here is how this can be done for an image on disk:

1. Click the tab for the table for which you want to define the column containing the image (Countries). If you are in diagram view, then click the table.

2. Click the column that you know contains the UNC path to the binary data for the image (CountryFlagURL, in this example).

447

3. Switch to the Advanced tab (unless it is already active).

4. In the Datacategory pop-up at the right of the ribbon, select Image URL.

Default Image

As you know, Power View treats all labels as equal; it does the same with images. However, you can choose to decide that some images are more equal than others, and consequently, you give them preeminence when they are displayed. To do this, follow these steps:

1. Click the tab for the table for which you want to define the column containing the default image (Countries). If you are in diagram view, click the table.

2. In the Advanced tab, click Table Behavior.

3. Check that a row identifier is defined—here it should be CountryID.

4. From the Default Image pop-up, select CountryFlag or CountryFlagURL.

5. Click OK.

Power Pivot now knows that this image is the default image it should use in output and visualizations.

Preparing Hyperlinks for Power View

Another visualization technique that can impress your audience is to include hyperlinks in Power View reports (and those used in certain other tools that can display data from the in-memory data model). Once again, all that this requires is a little preparation.

1. Click the tab for the table for which you want to define the column containing the hyperlink (Clients). If you are in diagram view, click the table.

2. Click the column that you know contains the binary data for the image (ClientWebSite in this example).

3. Switch to the Advanced tab (unless it is already active).

4. In the Datacategory pop-up at the right of the ribbon, select Web URL.

If you use this field in Power View, it will not just display the URL—it becomes a hyperlink.

■ **Note**   You could find that Power Pivot actually recognizes most URLs for what they are and sets them as Web URL (suggested) in the Datacategory pop-up.

Creating Hierarchies

Hierarchies can be an extremely powerful complement to your data set. Although they are rarely strictly necessary, they can make your data set both easier to understand and easier to use.

A *hierarchy* is a set of columns in a table that guide the user through a predefined path from the highest level to the lowest level. As this is probably best understood with an example, consider how you might describe cars when you are analyzing sales. You probably want to start with the make of car and then the model. Let's create a hierarchy based on these two elements.

1. Switch to the diagram view in Power Pivot.

2. Right-click the table title (Stock, in this example) and select Create Hierarchy. A new hierarchy is created under the last field in the table.

3. Right-click the new hierarchy (which will currently be called Hierarchy*n* where *n* is a number) and select Rename.

4. Enter a suitable name (CarDetails, in this example) and press Enter. You will see the new name replace the default name.

5. Drag the first field that you want to add to the hierarchy under the name of the hierarchy. I will use Make. This will become the first level of the hierarchy.

6. Drag the second field that you want to add to the hierarchy under the first level of the hierarchy. I will use Model. This hierarchy will look like Figure 14-21.

Figure 14-21. *A hierarchy in Power Pivot*

7. Save the Excel/Power Pivot file.

Using a hierarchy (in Power View, for instance) is easy. All you have to do is drag the hierarchy onto the Power View canvas; when you do, a table containing all the fields that you defined in the hierarchy will be created in the order in which you created them. So, a single click can convert this table into a matrix with a predefined progression through the data or into a drill-through chart. If you want to use only one of the fields from a hierarchy, then (in Power View again) you just expand the hierarchy and drag the field that you want onto the Power View canvas.

■ **Tip**   Once you are used to creating hierarchies in Power Pivot, you might like to accelerate the process slightly using the following technique. Start by right-clicking the first field that you want to appear in a new hierarchy before you select Create Hierarchy. A new hierarchy will then be created using this field. You can then rename the hierarchy and add other fields as described previously.

You can create a hierarchy of many levels in Power Pivot. However, as this technique is primarily to help and guide the user, I would advise that you not overdo it. You can also rename any level in a hierarchy just as you rename a field. Power Pivot will always place the original field name in brackets after the hierarchy name so that you can see which field was the source.

Modifying Hierarchies

Hierarchies are as easy to modify as they are to create. You can add or remove levels, change the order of levels in a hierarchy, or remove the hierarchy entirely.

Adding a Level to a Hierarchy

To add a level to a hierarchy, all you have to do is the following:

1. Click the name of the field that you want to add to the hierarchy.

2. Drag the new level onto the hierarchy either between existing levels or above or below the top or bottom existing levels.

When you drag a field onto an existing hierarchy, the cursor becomes a thick black line that indicates where the added level will be placed.

Removing a Level from a Hierarchy

To remove a level from a hierarchy, all you have to do is the following:

1. Right-click the level that you want to remove inside the hierarchy at the bottom of the table.

2. Select Remove From Hierarchy.

3. Confirm your choice by clicking Remove From Hierarchy in the confirmation dialog that appears.

■ **Note**   Removing a level from a hierarchy has no effect on the data field, which remains in the field list.

Altering the Levels in a Hierarchy

You do not have to re-create an entire hierarchy to modify the levels that you previously created. Suppose that you want to change the order of the elements in a hierarchy.

1. Right-click the level that you want to reorder inside the hierarchy at the bottom of the table.

2. Select Move Up or Move Down.

If you prefer to use the mouse, then you can simply drag a level in a hierarchy up and down to reorder the hierarchy. The cursor will become a thick black line to indicate where the level will be moved.

Deleting a Hierarchy

To delete a hierarchy, follow these steps:

1. Right-click the level that you want to delete inside the hierarchy at the bottom of the table.

2. Select Delete.

3. Confirm your choice by clicking Remove From Model in the Confirmation dialog.

You can, of course, use the Delete key to remove a previously selected level in a hierarchy, provided that you confirm your action.

■ **Note**   Deleting a hierarchy has no effect on the data fields on which it was based, which remain in the field list.

Hiding the Original Field

If you are using a field in a hierarchy, you probably do not want to see the field name twice in Power View—once as a field and once again in the hierarchy. Power Pivot has a quick trick to help out here.

1. Right-click the hierarchy level whose original field you want to hide.

2. Select Hide Source Column Name.

The field will remain in the hierarchy and in the table, but it will no longer appear in Power View as a separate field.

Key Performance Indicators

Power Pivot is designed to handle large amounts of data. Power View is built to allow you to view the salient points in the data. Nonetheless, it can get hard to track and remember many key numbers in a large data set where you have tens, if not hundreds, of important figures to follow.

This is where key performance indicators step in. KPIs are visual indicators of essential metrics in your data. You set the KPI to indicate whether your sales are on target, for instance. Or you can set a KPI (as you will do now) to keep an eye on gross margins. Then you can display the KPI as a visual alert in Power View, as you saw in Chapter 2.

Creating a KPI

So, what you will do here is create a KPI using the AvgGrossMargin calculated field from some sample data. You will then tell Power Pivot that you are aiming for a gross margin of £15,000.00 and that you will accept a range of £11,000.00 to £16,000.00 as acceptable. Anything less than £11,000.00 is unacceptable and will trigger a visual warning; anything greater than £16,000.00 will be flagged as good news.

1. Open the sample file PowerPivotDataForKPIs.

2. Switch to data view (unless you are already in this view).

3. Select the SalesData tab.

4. Right-click the calculated field AvgGrossMargin in the calculation area at the bottom of the datasheet.

5. Click the Create KPI button in the context menu. The Key Performance Indicator (KPI) dialog will appear. The AvgGrossMargin field will be set at the top of the dialog as the KPI base field (value).

6. Click the Absolute Value radio button.

7. Enter a value of **15000** in the Absolute Value field (it probably shows 100 at the moment).

8. Click anywhere in the middle of the dialog. The Status Thresholds (the funnel indicators separating the red, yellow, and green bands) will change.

9. Drag the upper status threshold to the right of the target until the value is 16000. Alternatively, you can enter the figure in the yellow box above the upper threshold.

10. Drag the lower status threshold to the right until the value is 11000. Alternatively, you can enter the figure in the yellow box above the lower threshold.

11. Select the second icon style from the left (a red X, a yellow exclamation point, and a green check mark). The dialog should look like Figure 14-22.

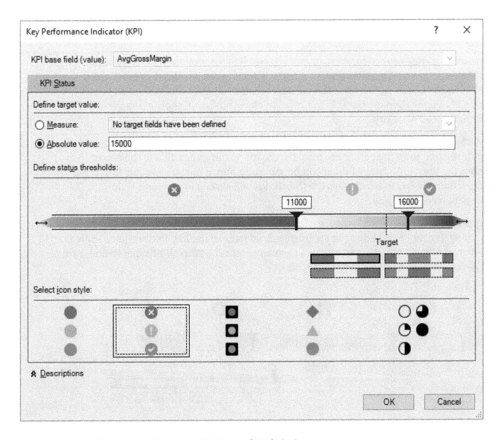

Figure 14-22. *The Key Performance Indicator (KPI) dialog*

12. Click OK.

The KPI has been created, and a small icon with three colors appears to the right of the calculated field that you used as the basis for the KPI. You can now use the Status, Value, and Goal fields in Power View table and matrix visualizations.

■ **Note**   KPIs require that the input data be from a calculated field. You cannot just use a column of data for this.

KPI Options

When building this first KPI, you bypassed some variations on a theme that you may find interesting. It follows that there are a couple of techniques that you could be tempted to apply when developing your own KPIs.

First, there is the question of the number of status thresholds and, consequently, the number of status icons that you can use. The choice is fairly simple.

- Three status icons (using two status thresholds)

- Five status icons (using four status thresholds)

Once you have decided whether to use three or five icons, you can choose how the base field relates to the target.

- *Three icons going from red to green, or green to red*: Red to green implies that a lower number is poor, and a higher number is better. Green to red implies the reverse, and the higher the number, the worse the result. If you have chosen one of the single-color KPI images, then the bar that indicates the thresholds will show a progressive shading instead of colors.

- *Five icons using red at the extremes or red at the center*: Red at the extremes indicates that the further from the center the result is, the worse things are. Red at the center implies the opposite. Once again, if you have chosen one of the single-color KPI images, then the bar that indicates the thresholds will show a progressive shading instead of colors.

You make these four choices by clicking one of the four status threshold icons in the Key Performance Indicator (KPI) dialog. Figure 14-23 shows the status threshold pane of the Key Performance Indicator (KPI) dialog for a five-icon choice. As you can see, you can then adjust the four thresholds that define the five ranges that will be represented by the appropriate icon.

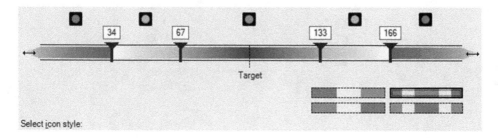

Figure 14-23. The KPI options

Table 14-10 describes the icon selections.

Table 14-10. KPI Options

Indicator	Comments
Circles	Simple colored circles
Indicators in a circle	Symbols in a colored circle
Symbols	Colored symbols
Shapes	Colored shapes
Pies	Progressively filled-in pies of a single color

KPI Descriptions

Creating KPIs is easy, as you have just seen. Remembering the details later can be harder, however. Because of this, Power Pivot lets you add comments to each KPI you create. You can add comments while you are creating a KPI or at a later date, of course. Here, however, I will show you how to add comments to an existing KPI.

1. Right-click the calculated field that you used as the KPI base field.

2. Select Edit KPI Settings. The Key Performance Indicator (KPI) dialog will appear.

3. Click Descriptions at the bottom of the dialog. The dialog will display the Descriptions page.

4. Enter any comments you find useful in describing what your KPI was designed to do. This is shown in Figure 14-24.

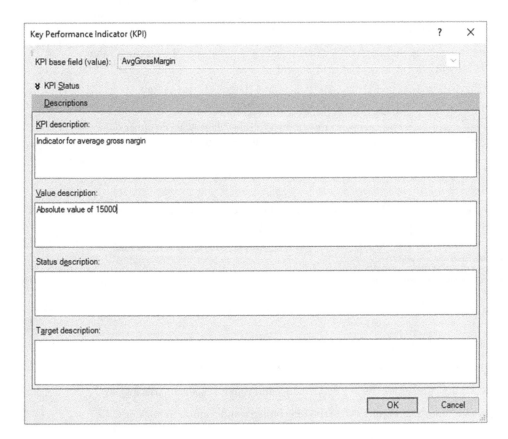

Figure 14-24. *The Key Performance Indicator (KPI) dialog Descriptions pane*

5. Click OK to complete the modification.

To return to the main (status) pane of this dialog, all you have to do is click KPI Status at the top of the dialog.

■ **Note**   The KPI description will be used as a tooltip in Power View.

Calculated KPI Targets

On some occasions you could have a variable rather than a fixed target for a KPI that you are creating. Creating one of these is a virtually identical process to the one that you followed previously in the "Creating a KPI" section, but here are a few minor differences:

- In step 6, earlier in the chapter, click Calculated Field rather than the Absolute Value radio button.

- In step 7, select a calculated field. The data model contains a field named AverageSalePricePreviousYear, and I suggest using this field.

- In steps 9 and 10, set percentages rather than absolute values. You can either enter the values or drag the threshold indicators left and right to do this.

Modifying a KPI

Of course, you may need to tweak a KPI once you have created it. This is why it is so important to be aware of the KPI icon that can appear to the *right* of calculated fields. This icon is shown in Figure 14-25.

AvgGrossMargin: 26,060.68   ▢

Figure 14-25. *The KPI icon for a calculated field*

To modify a KPI, this is all you have to do:

1.   Right-click the calculated field that you used as the KPI base field.

2.   Select Edit KPI Settings. The Key Performance Indicator (KPI) dialog will appear.

3.   Make any adjustments you need to the KPI elements and confirm by clicking OK.

Deleting a KPI

If a KPI has become redundant, you can delete it.

1.   Right-click the calculated field that you used as the KPI base field.

2.   Select Delete KPI.

■ **Note**　The KPI will be deleted without any confirmation or warning. Deleting a KPI will not affect the calculated field (or fields) it was based on.

Perspectives

It is easy, with a little practice, to develop quite complex Power Pivot data models that contain dozens of tables and hundreds of columns. This is fabulous for defining a "single version of the truth"—the Eldorado of business intelligence. The downside is that the sheer complexity and breadth of a large model can become difficult for end users to navigate.

So, the Power Pivot team came up with a solution. The answer is to create and use perspectives. A *perspective* is a subset of the tables and columns that are particularly relevant to a group of users. Once a set of perspectives has been created, users can switch from one to another and thus see only the data that is relevant to a specific type of analysis.

Creating a Perspective

Here is how you can create a perspective:

1. In the Advanced tab, click the Create And Manage button. The Perspectives dialog appears.

2. Click New Perspective. A column appears containing a check box for every table and field in the data set.

3. Replace the current new column name (NewPerspective) with something more appropriate. I will name it **ExecutiveGroup**.

4. Expand all the tables that contain fields you want to retain, and check the boxes for those fields. In this example I will choose the following:

    a. CountryName from the Countries table

    b. Make, Model, and CostPrice from the Stock table

    c. Color from the Colors table

5. The Perspectives dialog will look like Figure 14-26.

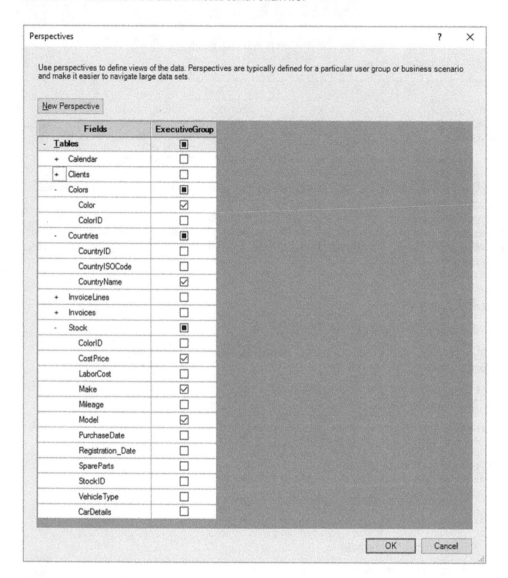

Figure 14-26. *The Perspectives dialog*

    5.   Confirm with OK.

Applying a Perspective

Nothing has happened when you created a perspective—yet. So, now it is time to use the perspective you just created.

    1.   In the Advanced tab, click the pop-up labeled Select. You will see all the available perspectives, including the standard, default perspective, as shown in Figure 14-27.

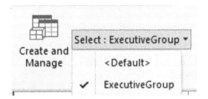

Figure 14-27. *Applying a perspective*

    2.   Select the perspective you just created (ExecutiveGroup).

Any tables that were not selected as part of the perspective will temporarily be hidden, and any columns in the visible tables that you did not select will also be hidden from view. So, you, or your users, can perform any required analyses on a simpler data model. Of course, you can return to the initial, default perspective at any time by selecting it from the list of available perspectives.

■ **Note**   Power View can currently use only the default perspective.

Optimizing File Size

Although it is not something that springs to mind when initially creating a Power Pivot data model, file size can be important. It is altogether too easy to create huge data models in Power Pivot, if only because the existing Excel worksheet limits are no longer a constraint. In practice, though, you are probably better off trying to create the most compact data model that you can.

There are several reasons for this.

- A large data model—despite compression—will take up more memory and more space on disk and can be slower to load and save.

- A data model that contains lots of tables, duplicate data, or unneeded columns will be hard to understand for end users.

So, here are a few techniques and ideas to help you create lean and efficient data models in Power Pivot. This list is not exhaustive, by any means, but it should point you in the right direction.

- *Avoid unneeded tables*: If a table contains a subset of data in an existing table, use the main table only.

- *Avoid unneeded columns*: If a column will likely never be used, remove it. If a column is a duplicate of data in another column but formatted or shaped differently, try to choose only the most useful variant of the data.

- *Avoid unwanted data*: Do not import redundant data in the first place and tweak your connections to source data to exclude unwanted data to avoid re-importing it by mistake when updating.

- *Structure the data set cleverly*: Try to create calculated fields rather than calculated columns, if you can.

- *Avoid redundant data*: Use filters when importing data to exclude unnecessary records.

- *Use short data strings*: Break long, complex columns of data into smaller columns. This allows for better in-memory compression, as more elements are identical in a column, which helps the compression algorithm to work more efficiently.

- *Apply appropriate data types*: Try to use the most suitable data type for each column. For instance, use a date type when you don't need data and time; it takes up less space.

- *Use reference tables*: Do not duplicate the same data inside a table when you can use a lookup table, and save lots of space.

On a more general note, you can also reduce the size of Excel worksheets by removing the following:

- Unused worksheets

- Images and clip art

- Formatting

- Backgrounds

File size optimization is a never-ending cycle of trial and error. However, if you are aware of the basic techniques that can be used, then you should be able to build more efficient data models from the ground up.

Copying Data from Power Pivot

So far when I explained how to subset and order data or when I showed you how to create calculated columns, I suggested that it was in order to get a look at the information that you were using. This is certainly true, but it is only one of the reasons for spending time working on your data. Another valid reason is that you want to use the power and speed of Power Pivot to prepare a data set that you will copy into another application, such as Excel, for further customization.

This operation is as easy as it is fast, and the only limitations are the following:

- The memory of the PC on which you are working

- The capacity of the destination application

So, if you presume you want to copy a subset of data from Power Pivot into Excel and you have checked the row counter to ensure that you have not gone over the million-row Excel limit, all you have to do is the following:

1. Order the columns; filter and sort the data to obtain exactly the subset you want.

2. Click the top-left corner of the grid for the Power Pivot table. The data subset will be selected.

3. Click Copy in the Home ribbon.

4. Switch to Excel and select the destination worksheet.

5. Click Paste.

The data is now standard Excel data, ready to be used as you see fit.

Conclusion

In this chapter, you took the raw data that you successfully imported into Power Pivot and developed it into a coherent and reliable data model. You did this by linking tables to create a cogent whole from the separate tables. Then you saw how to prepare the data set for time intelligence by adding a date table. Finally, you saw how to start adding formulas to the data set to prepare all the metrics that your Power View reports could need.

The data is now almost ready for output. All it needs is some custom metrics to drive data analysis. This will be the subject of the next three chapters.

■ ■ ■

CHAPTER 15

Extending the Data Model with Calculated Columns

This chapter further develops the data model that you began in the previous chapter. It explains how to augment the existing tables by adding new columns containing calculations to the tables that you have imported. You can then apply these additional metrics to the dashboards that you create using Excel and Power View.

Admittedly, not every data model in Power Pivot needs extensive calculations. Frequently, the data can speak for itself without much polishing. Yet, business intelligence is, at its heart, based on figures. Consequently, sooner or later, you need to apply simple math, calculate percentages, or compare figures over time. You may even want to develop more complex formulas that enable you to extend your analyses and illustrate your insights. Fortunately, Excel makes these—and many, many other calculations—amazingly easy. What's more, if you are an Excel user, you will probably find most of the techniques explained in this chapter to be totally intuitive.

In some cases, you only need to cherry-pick techniques from the range of available options to finalize a data set. So, it probably helps to know what Power Pivot can do and when to use the techniques outlined in this chapter. Therefore, I leave it to you to decide what is fundamental and what is useful. The objective in this chapter and the next two is to present a tried and tested suite of core calculation solutions so you are empowered to deal with the range of potential challenges that you may encounter in your data analysis.

All calculations in the Power Pivot data model are written using a simple language named Data Analysis Expressions (DAX). As you will see, DAX is not in any way a complex programming language. Indeed, it is known as a *formula language* because it is a set of some 260 formulas that you can use and combine to extend data models and to create metrics to underpin the visualizations in your dashboards. Fortunately, DAX formulas are loosely based on the formulas in Excel (indeed, a good third of them are identical), so the learning curve for an Excel user is really quite short.

Given the vast horizons that DAX opens up to Excel users, a single chapter could never be enough to give you a decent idea of the practical uses of this formula language. So, the introduction to DAX in this book is spread over three chapters. To apply some structure to a potentially huge and amorphous area, I have broken down DAX into the following areas:

- This chapter covers *column-based calculations* (where the formula appears as a new column in a table).

- Chapter 16 describes *measures* (calculations that are added to a table but that do not add a column of calculated data).

- Chapter 17 describes *time calculations* (measures that are used to aggregate data over time periods or to compare data over time).

© Adam Aspin 2016

A. Aspin, *High Impact Data Visualization in Excel with Power View, 3D Maps, Get & Transform and Power BI*,
DOI 10.1007/978-1-4842-2400-7_15

If you want to continue enhancing the data as it appeared at the end of the previous chapter, download the DataModelForCalculatedColumns.xlsx file from the Apress web site. This file lets you follow the examples as they appear in this chapter.

Types of Calculations

If you are lucky, then the data you have imported contains everything that you need to create all the visualizations and pivot tables you can dream up in Excel and Power View. Reality is frequently more brutal than that, however, and it necessitates adding further metrics to one or more tables. These calculated metrics will extend the data available for visualization. This is fundamental when you are using tools such as Power View that do not allow you to add calculated elements to the output but insist that all metrics—whether they are source data or calculated metrics—exist in the data set. This is less of a constraint and more of a nod toward good design practice because it forces you to develop calculations once and to place them in a single central repository. It also reduces the risk of error because users cannot develop their own (possibly erroneous) metrics and calculations and so distort the truth behind the data.

When creating DAX metrics, you are defining elements that are of practical use for your dashboard visualizations. This can include the following:

- Creating derived metrics that will appear in output.

- Adding elements that you use to filter pivot tables, pages, or visualizations.

- Creating elements that you use to segment or classify data. This can include creating your own groupings.

- Defining new metrics based on existing metrics.

- Adding your own specific calculations (such as accounting or financial formulas).

- Adding weightings to values.

- Ranking and ordering data.

And many, many more...

New Columns

Adding new columns is one of the two ways in which you can extend a data set with derived metrics that you can use in dashboards and pivot tables. There are multiple reasons why you may need further columns, including the following:

- Concatenating data from two existing columns into one new column

- Performing basic calculations for every row in the table, such as adding or subtracting the data in two or more columns

- Extracting date elements such as the month or year from a date column and adding them as a new column

- Extracting part of the data in a column into another column

- Replacing part of the data in a column with data from another column

- Creating the column needed to apply a visually coherent sort order to an existing column

- Showing a value from a column in a linked table inside the source table

Indeed, the list could go on....

Before you start wondering exactly what you are getting yourself into, I want to add a few words of reassurance about the ways in which a data model can be extended.

- First, extending a table with added columns is designed to be extremely similar to what you would do in Excel. Consequently, you are in all probability building on your existing knowledge as an Excel power user.

- Second, the functions that you will be using are, wherever possible, similar to existing Excel functions. This does not mean you have to be an Excel superuser to add a column but that knowledge gained using Excel will help with Power Pivot and DAX, and vice versa.

- Finally, most of the basic table extension techniques follow similar patterns and are not complex. So, the more you work at adding columns, the easier it will become as you reuse and extend techniques and formulas.

Creating columns is a bit like creating a formula in Excel that you then copy down over the entire column. They are even closer to the derived columns that you can add to queries in Access. The key thing to note is that any formula will be applied to the *entire* column.

It is worth noting from the start that a formula that you add to a new column is calculated and applied to a column when it is created. It is recalculated only if you recalculate the entire table or file or if you refresh the source data.

■ **Note**   In this chapter and the next, I frequently emphasize that you need to prepare your metrics *before* building reports. In practice, Excel is extremely forgiving and immensely supple. It lets you switch from the output to the data model at any time so that you can add any new columns or missing metrics. However, it can be more constructive to think through all your data requirements before rushing into the fun part that is creating dashboards. This approach can save you from creating duplicate measures and can help you to adopt a clear and coherent approach to naming metrics as well.

Naming Columns

If you create new columns, then you need to give them names. Inevitably, there are a few minor limitations on the names you can apply. So, rather than have Excel cause problems, I prefer to explain the overall guidelines on the Excel naming conventions earlier rather than later in the course of this chapter.

The first thing to remember is that column names have to be *unique* inside each table. Therefore, you *cannot* have two columns with the same name inside the *same* table. You *can*, however have two columns that share a name if they are in separate tables. However, I generally advise that you try to keep column names unique across all the tables in an Excel file if you possibly can. This can make building output based on the data model easier and safer because you do not run the risk of using a column from the "wrong" table in a chart, for instance, and getting entirely inappropriate results as a consequence.

The essential point of note is that columns cannot contain any of the following:

- Spaces (unless the spaces are enclosed by brackets or single apostrophes)

- The characters . , ; ' : / \ * | ? & % $! + = ( ) [ ] { } < >

Fortunately, column names are *not* case sensitive.

■ **Note**　All the restrictions that concern column names also apply to measures (which you will learn about in the next chapter).

Concatenating Column Contents

As an initial example of a new column, I will presume that when working with Excel to create a dashboard for Brilliant British Cars, you have met a need for a single column of data that contains both the make and the model of every car sold. Because the data you imported contains this information as separate columns, you need to add a new column that takes the data from the columns Make and Model and joins them (or concatenates them, if you prefer) in a new column. The following explains how this is done:

1. Open Power Pivot (by clicking the Manage Data Model button in the Data ribbon, for instance).

2. Make sure that you are in data view.

3. Click the Stock table to select it.

4. In the table of data, click in the blank column at the right of any existing data. This column is currently entitled Add Column.

5. In the formula bar, enter an equal sign.

6. To the right of the equal sign, press [(the square bracket). A list of the fields in the current table will appear, as shown in Figure 15-1.

Figure 15-1. *Selecting a field for a formula*

7. Click the [Make] field. The formula bar now reads =[Make].

8. In the formula bar, add & " " &. The formula bar now reads =[Make] & " " &.

9. Press [. Select [Model] from the list of fields. The formula bar now reads =[Make] & " " & [Model].

10. Press Enter (or click the check mark in the formula bar). The column is automatically filled with the result of the formula, and it shows the make and model of each car sold. The column is now called Calculated Column 1.

11. Right-click the column header for the new column and select Rename Column.

12. Type the word **Vehicle** and press Enter.

The table will now look something like Figure 15-2.

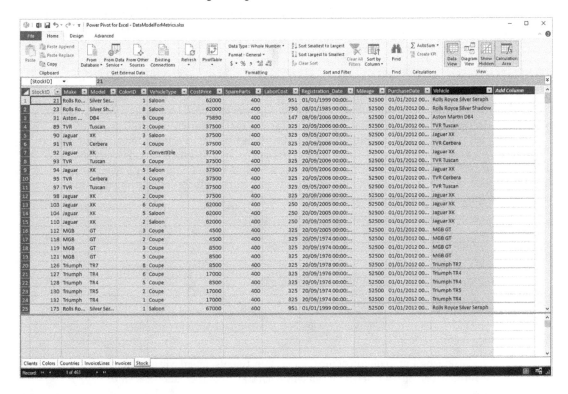

Figure 15-2. *An initial calculated column*

I imagine that if you have been using Excel for any length of time, then you might have a strong sense of déjà vu after seeing this. After all, what you just did is virtually what you would have done in Excel. All you have to remember is the following:

- Any additional columns are added to the *right* of the existing columns. You *cannot* move them elsewhere in the table once they have been created.

- All functions begin with the equal sign.

- Any function can be developed and edited in the formula bar at the top of the table.

- Reference is always made to *columns,* not to cells (as you would in Excel).

- Column names are always enclosed in square brackets.

- You can nest calculations in parentheses to force inner calculations before outer calculations—again, just as you would in Excel.

467

Once a new column has been created, it remains at the right of any imported columns in the table where you added it. It is not possible to move the new column elsewhere in the table. The field that it represents is always added to the bottom of the collection of fields for this table in the field list. This way the available fields will appear in the order they were created. However, fields always appear in alphabetical order in the field list in Power View.

If you look closely at the column that was added, you will notice that the column title is in black. This way you can always visually distinguish calculated columns from source data elements.

■ **Note**   In this example, you selected columns from the pop-up list of the available columns in the table. You can enter the column name in the formula bar if you prefer, but if you do, then you *must* enclose the column name in square brackets. You must also enter it *exactly* as it appears in the field list and column title.

Tweaking Text

In Chapter 11, you learned many techniques that you can apply to text-based columns. If you remember, these included changing the capitalization and removing extra spaces (among other things).

DAX also lets you clean up and modify the text in the tables that you have imported into your data model. Indeed, it offers a wide range of functions that you can apply to standardize and cleanse text in tables. As an example, let's imagine you want to create a column in the Clients table that contains a shortened version of each town. In fact, what you want to do is extract a three-letter acronym from the first letters of the town name, which you can use later in charts.

1. In the Power Pivot window, make sure you are in data view.

2. Click the Clients tab to select the Clients table.

3. In the table of data, click in the blank column at the right of any existing data. This column is currently entitled Add Column.

4. In the formula bar, enter an equal sign.

5. Type **LEFT(**. Once the function appears in the pop-up menu, you can select it if you prefer.

6. Click inside the Town column of the Clients table. Clients[Town] will appear in the formula bar. Alternatively, you can type a left square bracket and select the [Town] field.

7. Enter a comma.

8. Enter the number **3**. This indicates to the LEFT() function that it is the *three* characters on the left that you want to isolate for each row in this column.

9. Add a right parenthesis. The formula bar will read as follows:

    ```
    =LEFT(Clients[Town],3)
    ```

10. Press Enter (or click the check mark in the formula bar). The column is automatically filled with the result of the formula, and it shows the first three letters of every town's name.

11. Right-click the column header for the new column and select Rename Column.

12. Type the word **TownAbbreviation** and press Enter.

As you can see, the LEFT() function takes two parameters:

- First, the field from which you want to extract the leftmost characters

- Second, the number of characters to extract

And that is all you have to do. By applying a simple text formula, you have prepared a column of text for effective use in a visualization.

DAX contains a couple of dozen functions that you can apply to the text in columns. Most of them follow the same principle as the LEFT() function in that they take at least two parameters, the first of which is the column that you want to take as the basis for your new column and the second (or even third) parameters provide information about how the modification is to be applied. Since I do not have space to explain every one of these functions, Table 15-1 contains a succinct overview of a selection of some of the most useful text functions. This table does not explain all the subtleties of every function but is destined to be both a brief introduction and a starting point for your DAX formulas that rework the text elements of your data tables.

Table 15-1. *Core Excel Text Functions*

Function	Description	Example
LEFT()	Extracts a specified number of characters from the left of a column.	LEFT(Clients[Town], 3)
RIGHT()	Extracts a specified number of characters from the right of a column.	RIGHT(Invoices[InvoiceNumber], 12)
MID()	Extracts a specified number of characters (the second parameter) from a specified position defined by the number of characters from the left (the first parameter) inside a column.	RIGHT(Invoices[InvoiceNumber], 10, 4)
UPPER()	Converts the data to uppercase. This function takes no parameters.	UPPER(Clients[ClientName])
LOWER()	Converts the data to lowercase. This function takes no parameters.	LOWER(Clients[ClientName])
TRIM()	Removes any extra spaces (trailing or leading) from the text inside a column. This function takes no parameters.	TRIM(Clients[Address1])
LEN()	Counts the number of characters in a column. This is often used with the MID() function. This function takes no parameters.	LEN(Clients[Address1])
FIND()	Gives the starting point (as a number of characters) of a string inside a column. This function is case sensitive. Interestingly, the first parameter is the text to find, and the second is the column.	FIND('Car',Clients[ClientName])
SEARCH()	Gives the starting point (as a number of characters) of a string inside a column. This function is not case sensitive and disregards accents. Interestingly, the first parameter is the text to find, and the second is the column.	SEARCH('Car',Clients[ClientName])

(continued)

Table 15-1. (*continued*)

Function	Description	Example
SUBSTITUTE()	Replaces one text with another inside the column. This is a bit like the search-and-replace function in a word processor.	SUBSTITUTE(Clients[ClientName], 'Car', 'Vehicle')
VALUE()	Converts a figure in a text column to a numeric data type. This function takes no parameters.	VALUE(Colors[ColorID])
FIXED()	Takes a number, rounds it to a specified number of decimals, and then converts it to a text. The second parameter indicates the number of decimals to apply.	FIXED(Stock[LaborCost], 2)

There are a couple of points to note now that you have seen how to use DAX formulas in Excel.

- Functions need not apply to the entire contents of a column; they can be applied to specific text as part of a more complex formula.

- You can enter functions in uppercase or lowercase.

■ **Note**   If you get tired of renaming columns after you have created a DAX formula, there is an alternative. Simply begin the formula with the column name and := instead of just an equal sign. This will rename the column at the same time that the new column is created.

Simple Calculations

To extend the basic principle and to show a couple of variations on a theme, let's now add a calculation to the Stock table. More precisely, I assume your Excel visualizations frequently need to display the figure for the direct costs relating to all vehicles purchased, which I define as being the purchase price plus any related costs. You obtain this by applying a variation on a technique that you have used before.

1. In Power Pivot, select the Stock table.

2. In the table of data, click in the blank column at the right of any existing data.

3. In the formula bar, enter an equal sign.

4. To the right of the equal sign, enter a left square bracket: [. The list of the fields available in the Stock table will appear in the formula bar.

5. Type the first few characters of the column that you want to reference—**CostPrice** in this example. The more characters you type, the fewer columns are displayed in the list.

6. Click the column name. It will appear in the formula bar (including the right bracket).

7. Enter the minus sign.

8. Enter a left parenthesis.

9. Enter a left square bracket and select the SpareParts column.

10. Enter a plus sign.

11. Enter a left square bracket and select the LaborCost column.

12. Enter a right parenthesis. This corresponds to the left parenthesis before the SpareParts field. The formula should read as follows:

```
= [CostPrice] - ([SpareParts] + [LaborCost])
```

13. Click the check mark in the formula bar (or press Enter). The new column will be filled with the results of the calculation for each row.

14. Rename the column **DirectCosts**.

As you can see, using arithmetic in calculated columns in Excel is almost the same as using calculating cells in Excel. If anything, it is easier because you do not have to copy the formula over hundreds or even thousands of rows as the formula is automatically applied to every row in the table.

When selecting fields in steps 5, 9, and 11, you can (if you prefer) click the field name in the field list rather than enter a left bracket and scroll through a list of fields. Of course, this assumes you have not hidden the field list and that you have expanded the table name so that you can see the fields that it contains.

■ **Note** You can give a new column an appropriate name either when you create the formula initially (by entering the required column name followed by a colon) or when you rename the column once the formula is correct and confirmed. You can include spaces in column names if you want. After all, this is how the name will appear in your dashboards.

Math Operators

For the sake of completeness and in case there are any newcomers to the world of Microsoft products out there, I prefer to recapitulate the core math functions that are available in Excel. These are given in Table 15-2.

Table 15-2. *Core Excel Math Operators*

Operator	Description	Example
+	Adds two elements	[SpareParts] + [LaborCost]
-	Subtracts one element from another	[CostPrice] - [SpareParts]
/	Divides one element by another	[CostPrice] / [SpareParts]
*	Multiplies one element by another	[CostPrice] * 1.5
^	Raises one element to the power of another	[CostPrice] ^ 2

If you are working in BI, then you are certainly able to perform basic math operations. Consequently, I will not explain things you most likely already know. Just use the same arithmetical operators as you would use in Excel, and after a little practice, you should be able to produce calculated columns with ease. Remember that you have to enclose in parentheses any part of a formula that you want to have calculated before the remainder of the formula. This way, you will avoid any unexpected results in your dashboards.

Rounding Values

You already saw in Chapter 12 that Get & Transform can round and truncate values when you are preparing data ready for loading into a data model. In practice, of course, you might not yet be aware that you need to tweak your data at this stage. Fortunately, DAX also contains a range of functions that can be used to round values up and down, or even to the nearest hundred, thousand, or million, if need be.

As an example of this, I take the column Direct Costs that you created previously and round it to the nearest integer. This way, you also learn how to modify a formula in DAX.

1. In the Power Pivot window, select the Stock table.

2. In the table of data, click in the blank column at the right of any existing data.

3. In the formula bar, enter an equal sign.

4. Enter **Round(**. You can also select the formula from the pop-up if you prefer.

5. Click at the right of the formula in the formula bar.

6. Enter a comma.

7. Enter a **0**.

8. Add a right parenthesis to complete the ROUND() function. You will see that the corresponding left parenthesis is highlighted in the formula bar to help you track which pair of parentheses is which.

9. Click the check mark in the formula bar (or press Enter). The formula will be modified, and any decimals will be removed from the data in the column.

This example introduced the ROUND() function. It will round a value (whether calculated or loaded from a data source) to the number of decimals specified as the second parameter of the function, which is zero in this example.

ROUND() is only one of the functions that you can choose when truncating or rounding values. Table 15-3 gives the DAX functions that carry out rounding and truncation.

■ **Note**   Remember that using the ROUND() function *modifies* the data, whereas formatting numbers only changes their appearance.

Table 15-3. *DAX Rounding and Truncation Functions*

Function	Description	Example
ROUND()	Rounds the value to 0 if the second parameter is zero. If the second parameter is greater than zero, the function rounds the value to the number of decimals indicated by the second parameter. If the second parameter is less than zero, the figure to the left of the decimal is rounded to the nearest 10 (for a second parameter of –1, 100 (for a second parameter of –2, and so forth).	ROUND([CostPrice], 2)

(*continued*)

Table 15-3. (*continued*)

Function	Description	Example
ROUNDDOWN()	Rounds the value down to 0 if the second parameter is zero. If the second parameter is greater than zero, the function rounds the value down to the number of decimals indicated by the second parameter. If the second parameter is less than zero, the figure to the left of the decimal is rounded down to the nearest 10 (for a second parameter of –1, 100 (for a second parameter of –2, and so forth). The value is always rounded down, never up.	ROUNDDOWN([CostPrice], 2)
ROUNDUP()	Rounds the value up to 0 if the second parameter is zero. If the second parameter is greater than zero, the function rounds the value up to the number of decimals indicated by the second parameter. If the second parameter is less than zero, the figure to the left of the decimal is rounded up to the nearest 10 (for a second parameter of –1, 100 (for a second parameter of –2, and so forth). The value is always rounded down, never up.	ROUNDUP([CostPrice], 2)
MROUND()	Rounds the value to the nearest multiple of the second parameter.	MROUND((([CostPrice], 2)
TRUNC()	Removes the decimals from a value.	TRUNC([CostPrice])
INT()	Rounds down (or up, if the number is negative) to the nearest integer.	INT([CostPrice])
FLOOR()	Rounds down to the nearest multiple of the second parameter.	FLOOR([CostPrice], .2)
CEILING()	Rounds up to the nearest multiple of the second parameter.	CEILING([CostPrice], .2)
FIXED()	Rounds a value to the number of decimals indicated by the second parameter and converts the result to text.	FIXED([CostPrice], 2)

Calculating Across Tables

If your data model is not complex (particularly if it consists of a single table), then most calculations should be simple. All you have to do is follow the principle of building math expressions using column names and arithmetic operators.

The real world of data analysis is rarely this uncomplicated. In most cases, you have metrics on one table that you need to apply in a calculation in a completely different table. Excel makes these "cross-table" calculations really easy, *if* you have defined a coherent data model. (This can be done even if tables are not joined in a data model, as you will discover in the next chapter.)

As an example, let's look at how to subtract the Stock table's Direct Costs column from the InvoiceLines table's SalePrice column to calculate the margin on sales. To do this, you will add a new column, called Gross Margin, to the InvoiceLines table.

1. In the Power Pivot window, select the InvoiceLines table.

2. In the table of data, click in the blank column at the right of any existing data.

3. In the formula bar, enter an equal sign.

4. To the right of the equal sign, enter a left square bracket: [. The list of the fields available in the InvoiceLines table will appear in the formula bar.

5. Select the SalePrice field. (Remember that you can type the first few characters to limit the pop-up list of fields to those most closely resembling the field that you are looking for.)

6. Enter a minus sign (you can add spaces before or after it, if you want).

7. Start typing the keyword **RELATED**, and select this function once you have limited the selection of functions in the pop-up list. (Alternatively, you can type the whole word and a left parenthesis.)

8. Click the tab for the Stock table.

9. Click anywhere inside the DirectCosts column.

10. Enter a right parenthesis. The formula bar should contain the following formula:

    ```
    = [SalePrice]-RELATED(Stock[Direct Costs])
    ```

11. Click the check mark in the formula bar or press Enter to complete the definition of the calculated column.

12. Rename the column **Gross Margin**.

You can now see a new column added to the right of the InvoiceLines table. This column contains the gross margin for every vehicle sold, even if the sale price is on one table and the sum of the costs is in a separate table. This is all thanks to the RELATED() function, which links fields from different tables using the joins that you defined in the data model.

If you are an Excel user who has spent hours, or even days, wrestling with the Excel LOOKUP() function, then you are probably feeling an immense sense of relief. It really is this easy to look up values in another table in Excel. Once again (and at risk of laboring the point), if you have a coherent data model, then you are building the foundations for simple and efficient data analysis further down the line using DAX.

■ **Note** You can use the related function *only* if a valid link exists between the two tables containing the fields that you are using in the calculated column.

Choosing the Correct Table for Linked Calculations

The nature and structure of a Excel data model controls where you can add new columns from another table. In essence, you can bring data into a table only if it is from another table that

- Contains reference data

- Contains many records that are subelements of the current table

So, tables such as Countries, Clients, and Colors cannot pull back data from another table using the RELATED() function. This is because they are lookup tables and contain reference data that appears only once but is used many times in other tables. In database terms, these tables are the "one" side of a relationship, whereas tables such as InvoiceLines are on the "many" side of a relationship. In Excel (as is the case in a relational database), you can look up data only from the "many" side.

Equally, you can add data to the InvoiceLines table from the Invoices table because the former is considered a "parent" to the latter. However, you cannot pull data into the Invoices table from the InvoiceLines table. Quite simply, when an invoice contains many lines, Excel does not know which row to select and return to the destination table.

In a data model like the sample Brilliant British Cars example, some tables can return data from several tables. For instance, the Stock table can reach into the InvoiceLines table (because there is a single record in the Stock table for each record in the InvoiceLines table). Since the InvoiceLines table is a child of the Invoices table, the Stock table can reach "through" the InvoiceLines table into the Invoices table. Indeed, as the Colors table is a lookup table for the Stock table and the Invoices table looks up data from the Clients table, these are also accessible to the Stock table.

Essentially, the table where you add a new column has the potential to reach through most, if not all, of the data model and return data from many other tables—providing that the data model has been constructed in a coherent manner, of course.

Cascading Column Calculations

New columns can refer to previously created new columns. This apparently anodyne phrase hides one of the most powerful features of Power Pivot: the ability to create spreadsheet-like links between columns where a change in one column ripples through the whole data model.

This implies that you help yourself if you build the columns in a logical sequence so that you always proceed step-by-step and do not find yourself trying to create a calculation that requires a column that you have not created yet. Another really helpful aspect of new columns is that if you rename a column, Power Pivot automatically updates all formulas that used the previous column name and uses the new name in any visualizations that you have already created. This makes Power Pivot a truly pliant and forgiving tool to work with.

So, if you take the DAX formulas that you have created so far, you have the Gross Margin column that depends on the data for the sale price and the calculation of the Direct Costs column, which itself is based on the data for the cost price, spare parts, and labor cost. As a spreadsheet user, you probably won't be surprised to see that any change to the source data for the four elements causes both the Direct Costs and Gross Margin columns to be recalculated.

Refreshing Data

Do the following to force Power Pivot to recalculate the data model:

1. Activate the Home ribbon in data view (or in dashboard view).

2. Click the Refresh button. The Refresh dialog will appear, looking something like Figure 15-3.

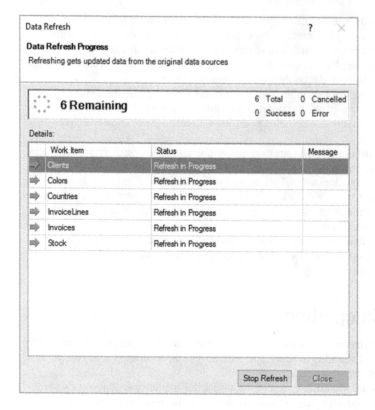

Figure 15-3. The Refresh dialog

3. After a short while (depending on the amount of data that has to be reloaded from the source, or sources, into the data model), the dialog will change to indicate that the data was successfully refreshed.

4. Click Close. The dialog closes, and the data reappears with all the calculated columns updated.

Using Functions in New Columns

You have seen just how easy it is to extend a data model with some essential metrics in Excel. Yet you have performed only simple arithmetic to achieve your ends. Excel can do much more than just carry out simple sums, of course.

Safe Division

I imagine that if you are an Excel user, you have seen your fair share of divide-by-zero (DIV/0) errors in spreadsheets. Fortunately, the Excel team shares your antipathy to this particular issue, and they have endowed Excel with a particularly elegant solution to the problem. This solution also serves as a simple introduction to the world of DAX functions in Excel.

Suppose you want to add a new column that divides the contents of one column by the contents of another. Still using the DataModelForMetrics.xlsx sample file, you can implement safe division like this:

1. With the InvoiceLines table selected, click in the blank column at the right of any existing data.

2. Enter an equal sign. To the right of the equal sign, type **DIVIDE** followed by a left parenthesis.

3. Type the formula **RELATED** and a left parenthesis.

4. Select the Stock[DirectCosts] field from the pop-up list that appears. This will be the numerator (the value that will be divided by another value).

5. Add a right parenthesis (this is to finish the RELATED() function).

6. Enter a comma.

7. Enter a left square bracket: [.

8. Select the SalePrice field from the list. This will be the denominator (the value that divides the first value).

9. Enter a comma.

10. Enter a **0**. This is the figure that will appear if there is a division-by-zero error.

11. Add a right parenthesis to end the DIVIDE() function. The formula bar will look like Figure 15-4.

| [Calculated C... ▼ | *fx* | =DIVIDE(RELATED(Stock[DirectCosts]),[SalePrice],0) |

Figure 15-4. *The DIVIDE() function*

12. Click the check mark in the formula bar (or press the Enter key). The ratio of sales cost to the sale price will be calculated for every row in the table. The column will fill with zeros and will remain highlighted.

13. In the Modeling ribbon, click the percent button and then add a couple of decimals by using the decimals button. As this metric is a ratio, it is best presented as a percentage to be more easily comprehensible, not only in the current table but also in any visualizations that it appears in.

14. Rename the column **SalePriceToSalesCostsRatio**.

In this example, you have used a function at required multiple parameters.

- *The numerator*: The number that is divided by another number

- *The denominator*: The number that is used to divide the first value

- *The error value*: The number that is used if a divide-by-zero error is encountered

You have also seen that there is another way to use fields from another table inside the RELATED() function. You can select the field name from the pop-up list that appears in every field that can be accessed by traversing the data model from the current table.

I imagine that by now you are feeling that DAX formulas are not only relatively easy but also made easier by their close relationship to Excel formulas. So, let's move on to see a few more.

Counting Reference Elements

Data models are often assembled to make the best use of reference elements. The Brilliant British Cars data model has a couple of lookup tables (Clients and Colors) that contain essential information that you could need to analyze the underlying data. So, as an example of how the data model can be put to good use, let's look at how DAX can calculate the number of clients per country.

This challenge introduces two new DAX elements.

- The COUNTROWS() function

- The RELATEDTABLE() function

As its name implies, the COUNTROWS() function counts a number of rows in a table. While you can use it simply to return the number of records in the current table, it is particularly useful when used with the RELATEDTABLE() function. Once again, because the data model has been set up coherently and the Countries table is joined to the Clients table, using the COUNTROWS() and RELATEDTABLE() functions together does not just return the number of records in a table but also calculates the number of records for each element in the table where it is applied. This means any elements from the Countries table that exist in the Clients table can be identified because the Clients table is using the Countries table as a lookup table.

Here is an example of how you can use these two functions to count reference elements:

1. In the Power Pivot window, select the Countries table.

2. In the table of data, click in the blank column at the right of any existing data.

3. In the formula bar, enter an equal sign.

4. To the right of the equal sign, type **COUNTROWS(**. Once the keyword appears in the pop-up list, you can select it to save time (and keystrokes), if you want.

5. Enter (and/or select) **RELATEDTABLE(**.

6. The list of the tables that are related to the Countries table will appear in the formula bar.

7. Select Clients.

8. Add *two* right parentheses. One will close the RELATEDTABLE() function, and the other will end the COUNTROWS() function.

9. The formula bar will contain the following:

   `= COUNTROWS(RELATEDTABLE(Clients))`

10. Click the check mark in the formula bar (or press the Enter key). The number of customers for each country will appear in the new column named Clients Per Country.

11. Rename the new column **Clients Per Country**. The Countries table now looks like what's shown in Figure 15-5.

Count...	CountryName	CountryISOCode	Clients Per Country
1	United Kingdom	GBR	11
2	France	FRA	4
3	USA	USA	11
4	Germany	DEU	1
5	Spain	ESP	1
6	Switzerland	CHE	3

Figure 15-5. *Using the COUNTROWS() function to calculate the number of clients per country*

Statistical Functions

As an intrinsic part of the Microsoft BI offering, DAX can calculate aggregates. After all, analyzing totals, averages, minima, and maxima (among others) is a core aspect of much business intelligence.

However, I do not want just to show you how to create a column containing the average sale price of all vehicles in the data set. This would hardly be instructive. So, instead of this, let's begin with a slightly more interesting requirement. Suppose that, for each vehicle, you want to see how the net profit compares to the average net profit.

1. Select the InvoiceLines table in the Power Pivot window.

2. In the table of data, click in the blank column at the right of any existing data.

3. In the formula bar, enter an equal sign.

4. Enter a left square bracket.

5. Select the Gross Margin field.

6. Enter a minus sign.

7. Start typing the word **Average**. Excel will display the list of available fields. When enough of the function name *Average* appears in the list of functions, select the AVERAGE function.

8. Select the field Gross Margin in the list of available fields in the pop-up list that appears.

9. Add a right parenthesis. The formula will look like this:

```
=[Gross Margin]-AVERAGE(InvoiceLines[Gross Margin])
```

10. Confirm the formula by pressing Enter or clicking the check mark in the formula bar. The new column will display the difference between the net margin for each row and the average net margin.

11. Rename the column **DeltaToAvgNetProfit**.

Once again, if you are an Excel or Microsoft Access user, you are probably feeling quite at ease with this way of working. Even if you are not a spreadsheet or database expert, you must surely be feeling reassured that creating calculations that apply instantly to an entire column is truly easy.

Now that you have seen the basic principles, look at some of the more common available aggregation functions described in Table 15-4.

Table 15-4. *DAX Statistical Functions*

Function	Description	Example
AVERAGE()	Calculates the average (the arithmetic mean) of the values in a column. Any non-numeric values are ignored.	AVERAGE([Mileage])
AVERAGEA()	Calculates the average (the arithmetic mean) of the values in a column. Empty text, non-numeric values, and FALSE values count as 0. TRUE values count as 1.	AVERAGEA([Mileage])
COUNT()	Counts the number of cells in a column that contain numeric values.	COUNT([Mileage])
COUNTA()	Counts the number of cells in a column that contain any values.	COUNTA([Mileage])
COUNTBLANK()	Counts the number of blank cells in a column.	COUNTBLANK([Mileage])
COUNTROWS()	Counts the number of rows in a table.	COUNTROWS(Stock)
DISTINCTCOUNT()	Counts the number of unique values in a table.	DISTINCTCOUNT([Vehicle])
MAX()	Returns the largest numeric value in a column.	MAX([Mileage])
MAXA()	Returns the largest value in a column. Dates and logical values are also included.	MAXA([Mileage])
MEDIAN()	Returns the median numeric value in a column.	MEDIAN([Mileage])
MIN()	Returns the smallest numeric value in a column.	MIN([Mileage])
MINA()	Returns the smallest numeric value in a column. Dates and logical values are also included.	MINA([Mileage])

There are many more statistical functions in DAX, and you can take a deeper look at them in the Excel online documentation. However, for the moment the intention is not to blind you with science but to introduce you more gently to the amazing power of DAX. For the moment, then, rest reassured that all your favorite Excel functions are present when it comes to calculating aggregate values in Excel.

Applying a Specific Format to a Calculation

Sometimes you will want to display a number in a particular way. You may need to do this to fit more information along the axis of a chart for instance. In cases like these, you can, in effect, duplicate a column and reformat the data so that you can use it for specific visualizations. As an example of this and to show how functions can be added to formulas that contain math, you will convert the cost of vehicles and any spare parts from pounds sterling to U.S. dollars and then format the result in dollars.

1. In the Power Pivot window, make sure you are in data view.

2. Click the Invoices table.

3. Click inside the empty column at the right.

4. In the formula bar, enter an equal sign.

5. Type **FORMAT(**. Once the function appears in the pop-up menu, you can select it if you prefer.

6. Enter a left square bracket: **[**.

7. Select DeliveryCharge In Dollars from the list. [DeliveryCharge In Dollars] will appear in the formula bar.

8. Enter *** 1.6**.

9. Enter a comma.

10. Enter the text **"Fixed"** (include the double quotes).

11. Add a right parenthesis.

12. Still inside the formula bar, replace Column with **Invoice In Dollars**.

13. To the right of the equal sign, enter **"$ "** & (include the double quotes). The formula bar will read as follows:

```
DeliveryCharge In Dollars = "$ " & FORMAT([DeliveryCharge] * 1.6, "Fixed")
```

14. Press Enter (or click the check mark in the formula bar). The column will contain the same number as the one in the Cost Plus Spares column. However, it is formatted as text and preceded by a dollar sign. Figure 15-6 shows a few records from this new column.

DeliveryCharge In Dollars
$ 1200.00
$ 2400.00
$ 1600.00
$ 1600.00
$ 2400.00
$ 1600.00
$ 800.00
$ 1600.00
$ 1600.00
$ 1600.00
$ 2400.00
$ 2400.00

Figure 15-6. Applying a custom numeric format

The FORMAT() function can be applied equally well to dates and times as to numeric columns, as you will see later in this chapter. Indeed, it offers a wealth of possibilities. In fact, rather than illustrate all of them, Tables 15-5 and 15-6 contain the essential predefined formats that you can apply to columns of numbers.

Table 15-5. *Predefined Currency Formats*

Format Code	Description	Example	Comments
Currency	Currency	FORMAT(Stock[CostPrice], "Currency"')	The currency indicator will depend on the PC's settings and language used.
Scientific	Exponential or scientific notation	FORMAT(Stock[CostPrice], "Scientific")	This is also called the *scientific format*.
Fixed	Fixed number of decimals	FORMAT(Stock[CostPrice], "Fixed")	This displays at least one figure to the left of the decimal (even if it is a zero) and two decimals.
General Number	No format	FORMAT(Stock[CostPrice], "General Number"')	This displays the number with no thousand separators.
Percent	Percentage (and divided by 100)	FORMAT(Stock[SalePriceToSalesCostsRatio], "Percent"')	This displays the number as a percentage.

Should you want to create your own highly specific date and number formats, you can assemble them using the format code elements in Tables 15-5 and 15-6.

Table 15-6. *Custom Number Formats*

Format Code	Description	Comments
0	The zero placeholder	Adds a zero even if no number is present
#	The digit placeholder	Represents a number if one is present
.	The decimal character	Sets the character that is used before the decimals
,	The thousands separator	Defines the thousands separator
%	Percentage symbol	Adds a percentage symbol

Using the custom number formats is not difficult, but rather than explain all the permutations laboriously, here are a couple of examples to help you to see how they work:

- FORMAT([Cost Plus Spares], "#,#.00") gives you 44,500.00 (and any figure less than 1 will have nothing to the left of the decimal)

- FORMAT([Cost Plus Spares], "0.0") gives you 12250.0 (and any figure less than 1 will have a 0 to the left of the decimal)

Remember that if you want to abandon a formula while you are creating it, all you have to do is click the X in the formula bar or press Escape.

■ **Note** The FORMAT() function actually converts a number to text. Consequently, you might not be able to use a calculated column that is the result of a FORMAT() operation in further calculations.

Correcting and Removing Errors

As the formulas that you create get more and more complex, you run the risk of creating formulas that seem impossible to correct. My advice in these cases is simple. Delete the column containing the error-prone formula and start over.

Simple Logic: The IF() Function

Having data available is always a prerequisite for analysis; however, the raw data may not always lend itself to being used in dashboard visualizations in an ideal way.

DAX can help you to see "the wood for the trees" in the thicket of data that underlies your data model. Let's begin by looking at a series of practical examples that extend your data in ways that use the resources of Excel to do the heavy lifting and let you focus on items that need your attention.

Exception Indicators

As a first example of how to use the IF() function, suppose that you want to highlight any records where the cost of spare parts is greater than £2.000.00. This means comparing the contents of the column PartsCost to a fixed value (3500). If this test turns out to be true (that is, the parts cost is over the threshold that you have set), then you want to display the words *Too High*!

The following steps explain how to add a column that applies this test to the data:

1. In the DataModelForMetrics.xlsx file, click the Data View icon and then click the Stock table tab.

2. In the table of data, click in the blank column at the right of any existing data.

3. Enter an equal sign and, to the right of the equal sign, enter **IF(**. You will see that as you enter the first few characters, the list of functions will list all available functions beginning with these characters.

4. Press the [key. The list of available fields will appear.

5. Scroll down through the list of fields and click the SpareParts field.

6. Enter the greater-than symbol: >.

7. Enter **1000**.

8. Enter a comma.

9. Enter the following text (including the double quotes): **"Too Much!"**.

10. Enter a closing parenthesis:). The code in the formula bar will look like this:

    ```
    = IF([SpareParts]>1000,"Too Much!")
    ```

11. Press Enter or click the check mark in the formula bar. The new column will display *Too Much* in any rows where the cost of spares is greater than £2,000.00.

12. Rename the column **Excessive Parts Cost**.

Like the DIVIDE() function, the IF() function can take up to three arguments (as the separate elements that you enter between the parentheses are called). The first two are compulsory.

- A *test* in this case comparing the contents of a column to a fixed value.

- The outcome if the test is *positive* (or TRUE in programming terms).

The IF() function can also have a third argument, although this is optional, as you can see in the example in this section. The outcome of the test is *negative* (or FALSE in programming terms).

This was a simple test to help you isolate certain records. Later, when building dashboards, you can use the contents of this new column as the basis for tables, charts, and indeed just about any Excel visualization.

Creating Alerts

When using the IF() function, the major focus is nearly always on the first argument—the test. After all, this is where you can apply the real force of Power Pivot. So, here is another example of an IF() function being used, only this time it is to create an alert based on a slightly more complex calculation. This time, the objective is to detect records where the selling price of the vehicle is less than half the average sale price for all cars.

1. In the DataModelForMetrics.xlsx file, click the Data View icon and then click the Stock tab.

2. Click in the blank column at the right.

3. Enter an equal sign.

4. To the right of the equal sign, enter **IF(**. You will see that as you enter the first few characters, the list of functions will list all available functions beginning with these characters.

5. Press the **[** key. The list of available fields will appear.

6. Scroll down through the list of fields and click the CostPrice field.

7. Enter >= (it represents "greater than or equals to").

8. Start typing the word **Average**. Power Pivot will display the list of available fields. When enough of the function name *Average* appears in the list of functions, select the AVERAGE() function.

9. Enter a left square bracket.

10. Start typing the name of the SalePrice field.

11. When the [SalePrice] field is visible in the pop-up list of fields, select it.

12. Add a right parenthesis. This ends the AVERAGE() function.

13. Enter *2.

14. Enter a comma.

15. Enter the following text (including the double quotes before and after the text): **"Price too High"**.

16. Enter a comma.

17. Enter **"Price OK"** (including a pair of double quotes).

18. Enter a closing parenthesis. This ends the IF() function. The code in the formula bar will look like this:

```
= IF([CostPrice] >= AVERAGE([CostPrice]) *2,"Price too high", "Price OK")
```

19. Press Enter or click the check mark in the formula bar. The new column will display Price Too High or OK, depending on whether the cost price is more than half the average cost price.

20. Rename the column **PriceCheck**.

You can then use the results of the cost price test as the basis for a visualization to compare the expensive purchases with the others.

Comparison Operators

When carrying out tests like this, you need to compare values. You may be familiar with the standard comparison operators that many programs and languages use (such as Excel), but for the sake of completeness, Table 15-7 lists the most frequently used operators.

Table 15-7. *DAX Comparison Operators*

Operator	Description
=	Equals (exactly!)
<>	Not equals to
<	Less than
>	Greater than
<=	Less than or equals to
>=	Greater than or equals to

Flagging Data

As a practical example of how you might use an IF() function to validate data, imagine that Brilliant British Cars is embarking on a "know your customer" program and you envisage a chart that compares the clients who have reliable postcodes with those who do not. This way you can make a business case for cleansing the data and potentially rooting out certain clients.

For the moment, the Clients table either has or does not have a postcode (ZIP code) for each customer. What you want is a clear extra column that contains either HasPostCode or NoPostCode to indicate whether there is a postcode present.

In this example, you will not only test numeric values, but you will also look at whether a record contains a value for a row. This means introducing a new DAX function. This is the ISBLANK() function. It allows you to see whether a column contains any data. Technically, this DAX function returns TRUE if the column is empty and FALSE if it contains data. So, you can nest it inside an IF() function to detect the presence of data, rather than looking at the data itself.

The following explains how to create a clear indicator of the presence or absence of a postcode:

1. In the DataModelForMetrics.xlsx file, click the Data View icon and then click the Clients tab.

2. Click in the blank column at the right.

3. Enter an equal sign.

4. To the right of the equal sign, enter **IF(**. You will see that as you enter the first few characters, the list of functions lists all available functions beginning with these characters.

5. Type **IsB**. The list of functions will show ISBLANK().

6. Click ISBLANK() or press the Tab key to select this function. Excel will place the function in the formula bar and add the left parenthesis automatically.

7. Press the [key. The list of available fields will appear.

8. Select [PostCode].

9. Enter a right parenthesis. (This finishes the ISBLANK() function.)

10. Enter a comma and then type **"NoPostCode","HasPostCode"**. These are the outputs that the IF() function will return, depending on whether the column is blank.

11. Enter a final right parenthesis. The formula bar will display this:

    ```
    = IF(ISBLANK([PostCode]),"NoPostCode","HasPostCode")
    ```

12. Press Enter or click the check mark in the formula bar. The new column will display either NoPostCode or HasPostCode for every client.

13. Rename the column **IsPostCode**.

You can now use this new field to filter data in dashboards or in tables and charts to separate the clients who do or do not have postcodes.

Nested IF() Functions

A frequent requirement in data analysis is to categorize records by ranges of values. Suppose, for instance that you want to break down the stock of cars into low-, medium-, and high-mileage models. This requires more than a simple IF() function. However, it is not difficult, as all that is needed is to "nest" one IF() function inside another, thereby extending the test that is applied to cover three possible outcomes.

Here, then, is how to create a simple nested IF() function:

1. In the DataModelForMetrics.xlsx file, click the Data View icon, and then click the Stock tab.

2. Click in the blank column at the right.

3. Enter an equal sign.

4. To the right of the equal sign, enter **IF(**. You see that as you enter the first few characters, the list of functions lists all available functions beginning with these characters.

5. Press the [key. The list of available fields will appear.

6. Select [Mileage]. You can type it fully if you prefer, but remember to add the right square bracket if you do.

7. Enter <= **50000**.

8. Enter a comma.

9. Enter **"Low"** (including the double quotes).

10. Enter a comma.

11. Enter **IF(**.

12. Enter **< 100000**.

13. Enter a comma.

14. Enter **"Medium","High"**. This must include the double quotes and the comma separating the two words.

15. Enter two right parentheses, one for each of the IF() functions. The formula bar will display the following:

    ```
    = IF([Mileage] <= 50000, "Low", IF([Mileage] < 100000, "Medium","High"))
    ```

16. Press Enter or click the check mark in the formula bar. The new column will display Low, Medium, or High for every vehicle in the new Mileage Range column.

17. Rename the column **Mileage Range**.

You have now categorized all the cars in stock by their mileage and can use the category flag in the Mileage Range column to create, for instance, a chart that shows the number of vehicles corresponding to each mileage category.

A nested IF() function works like this:

1. You set up a first test. In this example, the test is to flag all cars that have less than 50,000 miles "on the clock."

2. You specify what the outcome is if this initial test is positive. In this example, the word *Low* appears in the column.

3. You then add a second test. By definition, this will *only* apply to cars that have traveled more than 50,000 miles; otherwise, the formula returns the word *Low*. So, you add a higher threshold for the second test, which is 10,0000 miles in this example.

4. If the record passes the test and the vehicle has traveled less than 100,000 miles, then the word *Medium* will appear in the column. In all other cases (that is, for all mileage that exceeds 100000 miles), the word *High* is displayed in the column.

When writing nested IF() statements, the essential trick is to use a sequence of tests that follow a logical order, from lowest to highest (or in some cases, from highest to lowest). This way, the succession of IF() statements acts like a series of hoops that catch the values and return an appropriate result.

You can nest up to 64 IF() statements in a single DAX expression. In fact, you can nest a maximum of 64 DAX expressions, whatever they are. However, more than half a dozen can be painful to write correctly, and getting the correct number of right parentheses in place can be tricky. Nonetheless, there may be many occasions when you need to segment your data for your visualizations and dashboards, even if it means grappling with complex nested IF() statements. So, let's take a look at one of these to whet your appetite.

Creating Custom Groups Using Multiple Nested IF() Statements

To give you another example of a slightly more complex DAX function (but one that can be necessary), consider the following requirement. Our data now has the car age, but you want to group the cars by age segments (or buckets if you prefer). So, you will use a nested IF() function to do this. Then, to allow you to sort the column in a more coherent way, you will create a Sort By column for the new Vehicle Age Category column that you created. If you remember, you saw how to create and use Sort By columns in the previous chapter.

In this example, I will not explain every step, as you have seen how to select functions and fields from pop-ups in the previous examples. Instead, I prefer to concentrate on the logic itself and explain how complex IF() statements can be built.

The code for the Vehicle Age Category column is as follows:

```
=IF(
    [VehicleAgeInYears] <=5,"Under 5",
    IF(AND([VehicleAgeInYears]>=6,[VehicleAgeInYears]<=10),"6-10",
        IF(AND([VehicleAgeInYears]>= 11,[VehicleAgeInYears]<=15),"11-15",
            IF(AND([VehicleAgeInYears]>=16,[VehicleAgeInYears]<=20),"16-20",
                IF(AND([VehicleAgeInYears]>=21,[VehicleAgeInYears]<=25),"21-25",
                    IF(AND([VehicleAgeInYears]>=26,[VehicleAgeInYears]<=30),"26-30",
                        ">30"
                    )
                )
            )
        )
    )
)
```

The only slight problem with a great technique for segmenting data is that if you sort the Vehicle Age Category column, you will find that the category that corresponds to the highest age appears at the top of the list. So, you need to add a second column that can be used as a sort order column for the new column that you just created. The following is the code for this Vehicle Age Category Sort column:

```
Vehicle Age Category Sort=IF([VehicleAgeInYears]<=5, "1",
    IF(AND([VehicleAgeInYears]>=6, [VehicleAgeInYears]<=10),"2",
        IF(AND([VehicleAgeInYears]>= 11, [VehicleAgeInYears]<=15), "3",
            IF(AND([VehicleAgeInYears]>=16, [VehicleAgeInYears]<=20), "4" ,
                IF(AND([VehicleAgeInYears]>=21, [VehicleAgeInYears]<=25), "5",
                    IF(AND([VehicleAgeInYears]>=26, [VehicleAgeInYears]<=30),"6","7"
                    )
                )
            )
        )
    )
)
```

These formulas could have come straight from an Excel spreadsheet. Indeed, some 80 of the DAX functions are nearly identical to their Excel cousins. Experience and imagination combined have shown me that you have many ways to extend the data you imported by adding calculated columns. Even better, all calculated columns are updated when you refresh the data from the source. The only major caveat is that when you are tweaking the data connection, you must be careful *not* to delete any source columns on which a calculated column depends or you will get errors in Power View.

■ **Tip**   You could have created the formula in this example without creating the VehicleAge column first, as you could have used the formula that calculates the age of the car each time that you need the vehicle age. However, as you can imagine, it is easier to create a column that contains the vehicle age first and then refer to this in the Vehicle Age Category formula. This makes the more complex formula easier to read. It also helps you to break down the analytical requirement into successive steps, which is good DAX development practice. Moreover, you can always hide any "intermediate" columns if you do not need them in dashboards and reports. Indeed, you could even do this kind of calculation in Get & Transform.

Multiline Formulas

By default, all formulas that you create in Excel will be on a single line that overflows onto the next line when there is no more room in the formula bar. This can become an extremely tedious way of working, so it is worth knowing that you can tweak long formulas to force them to display over more than one line. All you have to do is force a line return inside the formula bar by pressing Shift+Enter where you want to force a new line. My experience is that Power Pivot will not let you create line breaks everywhere in a formula. Nonetheless, with a bit of trial and error, a more complicated formula, such as the Vehicle Age Category column that you created, can look as it is shown previously.

Just in case you were wondering, you do *not* have to write formulas over multiple lines as I did just. Indeed, the two formulas used to create complex nested IF() statements could be written as follows:

```
Vehicle Age Category=IF([VehicleAgeInYears] <=5,"Under
5",IF(AND([VehicleAgeInYears]>=6,[VehicleAgeInYears]<=10),"6-10",IF(AND([VehicleAgeInYears]>=
11,[VehicleAgeInYears]<=15),"11-
15",IF(AND([VehicleAgeInYears]>=16,[VehicleAgeInYears]<=20),"16-
20",IF(AND([VehicleAgeInYears]>=21,[VehicleAgeInYears]<=25),"21-
25",IF(AND([VehicleAgeInYears]>=26,[VehicleAgeInYears]<=30),"26-30","Over 30"))))))
```

and as follows:

```
Vehicle Age Category Sort=IF([VehicleAgeInYears] <=5,"1",IF(AND([VehicleAgeInYears]>=6,[Vehi
cleAgeInYears]<=10),"2",IF(AND([VehicleAgeInYears]>= 11,[VehicleAgeInYears]<=15),"3",
IF(AND([VehicleAgeInYears]>=16,[VehicleAgeInYears]<=20),"4",IF(AND([Vehicle
AgeInYears]>=21,[VehicleAgeInYears]<=25),"5",IF(AND([VehicleAgeInYears]>=26-
,[VehicleAgeInYears]<=30),"6","7"))))))
```

I chose to write the formulas over multiple lines, hoping that by doing so, I'd make the nested logic clearer. You can write your formulas in any way that suits you and that does not cause Power Pivot a problem.

Complex Logic

Categorizing data can sometimes involve applying logic that is more complex than a single simple comparison. You could need to apply two or more conditions when evaluating a record, and this more intricate logic could require you to test the contents of more than one column.

Once again, DAX can help you in circumstances like these. To explain by example, consider the following analytical challenge. You want to flag any vehicle that is a red or blue coupe. This example will show the basics of applying complex logic to data analysis with DAX.

1. In the `DataModelForMetrics.xlsx` file, click the Data View icon, and then click the Stock tab.

2. Click in the blank column at the right.

3. Enter an equal sign.

4. To the right of the equal sign, enter **IF()**. Since you are dealing with multiple parentheses in this formula, I prefer to enter both the opening and closing parentheses for each function when adding the function.

5. Click inside the parentheses.

6. Type the **AND()** function and then click inside the parentheses. This function ensures that multiple logical conditions are applied and that all must be satisfied for the test to be successful.

7. Type **[VehicleType] = "Coupe"**, (including the comma). This is one of the conditions that has to be true for the test to be successful.

8. After the comma, type **OR()** and then click inside the parentheses. This is a second condition (it is still part of the AND() function), but it can be one of many different tests.

9. Type (or use the pop-up menus to select as well as partially typing) **RELATED(Colors[Color]) = "Red", RELATED(Colors[Color]) = "Blue"**. This is the second part of the test. However, because the color is in another table, you have to use the RELATED() function to find the color of the vehicle because it is not in the Stock table. Also, there are two alternative conditions inside the parentheses for the OR() expression.

10. Click just inside the final parenthesis at the right of the DAX expression (this is the one that ends the IF() function) and type **,"Special","Normal"**. Be sure to include the commas. The formula should read as follows:

    ```
    = IF(AND([VehicleType] = "Coupe", OR(RELATED(Colors[Color]) = "Red",
    RELATED(Colors[Color]) = "Blue")),"Special","Normal")
    ```

11. Press Enter or click the check mark in the formula bar. The new column will display either Special or Normal for every vehicle in the new Special Sales column.

12. Rename the column **Special Sales**.

I realize that a formula like this can seem daunting at first sight. So, let's take another look at this DAX expression formatted a little differently.

```
Special Sales = IF(
                AND(
                    [VehicleType] = "Coupe",
                    OR(RELATED(Colors[Color]) = "Red",
                        RELATED(Colors[Color]) = "Blue")
                  )
                ,"Special"
                ,"Normal"
                )
```

As you can see, at its heart, the expression is an IF() expression. As such, it consists of three parts:

- A test (the car is a coupe that is either red or blue)

- An outcome for a positive result (displays *Special*)

- An outcome for a negative result (displays *Normal*)

The only tricky bit now is the test itself. Since it is built on logic that is more complex, it requires a little explanation.

- First, you have stated that the test is in several parts, all of which must be true for a record to pass the test. This is done by using the AND() function and then separating each individual test (of which there are two in this example—the vehicle type and the color).

- Second, you have told DAX that the second test (on the color) can be any of several possibilities (two in this example). You did this using the OR() function and separating each individual test by a comma.

Although I prefer to build complex functions from the inside out (that is, by adding all the required parentheses first and adding what goes inside them second), this is not an obligation. You are free to build DAX formulas in any way that works.

■ **Note** This example showed only two alternatives for the AND() and OR() functions. This is because these functions are limited to only *two* parameters. What is important to remember is that you will have to *repeat the field* (and possibly the table name if it is not the current table) for *each comparison*, just as you did here when testing the colors of the cars. If you need more than two alternatives for an AND or OR operation, then you will have to use the logical *operators* (&&, ||, and !) that are described next.

Armed with this knowledge, you can now build extremely complex logical tests on your data. If you are an Excel or Access power user, then the learning curve should be quite short as the principles and functions are similar to those that you are using already. If you have come from the world of programming, then the concepts are probably familiar. If you are just starting out, then just be prepared to spend a little time practicing, and above all, analyze the question that you want DAX to answer *before* starting to write the statement.

DAX Logical and Information Functions

So far in this chapter, you have seen three of the DAX logical functions. In practice, you may need to build formulas that use some of the other functions that DAX provides to apply logic and to test the state and type of information in columns. Table 15-8 describes the essential functions for creating complex data models.

Table 15-8. *DAX Logical Functions*

Operator	Description	Example
IF()	Tests a condition and applies a result if the test is true, and possibly a result if the test is false.	IF([PartsCost]> 500, "Check Parts", "OK")
AND()	Extends the logic to include several conditions *all* of that must be met.	IF(AND([PartsCost]> 500,[LaborCost]>1000), "Repair Cost Excessive", "OK")
OR()	Extends the logic to include several conditions *any* of that must be met.	IF(OR([PartsCost]> 500,[LaborCost]>1000), "Repair or Labor Cost issue", "OK")
NOT()	Extends the logic to include several conditions *none* of that must be met.	IF(NOT([PartsCost]> 500,[LaborCost]>1000), "No Repair or Labor Cost issue", "")
ISERROR()	Tests a value and returns TRUE if there is an error value.	IF(ISERROR([PartsCost]), "Check parts", "")
TRUE()	Returns TRUE.	IF(Stock[Mileage] > 100000, TRUE(), FALSE())
FALSE()	Returns FALSE.	IF(Stock[Mileage] > 100000, TRUE(), FALSE())
ISNUMBER()	Detects whether a column value is numeric.	IF(ISNUMBER([PartsCost]), "", "Data Error")
ISTEXT()	Detects whether a column value is text.	IF(ISTEXT([PartsCost]), "Data Error", "")
ISNONTEXT()	Detects whether a column value is not text and is not a blank.	IF(ISNONTEXT([PartsCost]), "", "Data Error")
ISODD()	Detects whether a value is an odd number.	IF(ISODD([PartsCost]), "Data Error", "")
ISEVEN()	Detects whether a value is an even number.	IF(ISEVEN([PartsCost]), "", "Data Error")
ISLOGICAL()	Detects whether a column value is a true or false.	IF(ISODD([PartsCost]), "Data Error", "")

Logical Operators

If you are writing more complex logical statements when specifying intricate conditions that must be met, then DAX has an alternative to the AND(), OR(), and NOT() functions. These are called *logical operators*, which are explained in Table 15-9.

Table 15-9. *DAX Logical Operators*

Operator	Description	Example
&&	AND	[Color] = "Red" && [VehicleType] = "Coupe"
||	OR	[Color] = "Red" || [Color] = "Blue"
!	NOT	[Color] = "Red" ! [VehicleType] = "Coupe"

As a simple example, you could want a choice of three possible colors in a logical operation. The code for this would read as follows:

```
[Color] = "Red" || [Color] = "Blue" Color] || [Color] = "Green"
```

Formatting Logical Results

Sometimes a logical function might exist only to return a simple true or false. For instance, you could want to test a value and indicate whether it is over a certain threshold, using a formula like the following (added to the Stock table):

```
High Mileage := IF(Stock[Mileage] > 100000, TRUE(), FALSE())
```

This formula simply tests the mileage figure for each record and returns TRUE() if the mileage is greater than 100,000 miles; it returns FALSE() in all other cases.

However, you might not want to display simply TRUE or FALSE in the column. So, DAX also lets you format logical output, whether it is calculated like it is here or imported as a TRUE or FALSE value from a data source. The formula that you just saw can be formatted like this:

```
High Mileage := FORMAT(IF(Stock[Mileage] > 100000, TRUE(), FALSE()),"Yes/No")
```

There are only three logical formats available in DAX. These are explained in Table 15-10.

Table 15-10. *DAX Logical Operators*

Format Code	Description
Yes/No	Formats the output as either Yes or No
True/False	Formats the output as either True or False
On/Off	Formats the output as either Yes or No

▓ **Note**   Different data sources represent True in different ways; however, nearly all represent False as a zero. Consequently, DAX interprets a logical column as a number, any zeros as a False, and anything else as a True.

Making Good Use of the Formula Bar

If you only ever enter simple formulas, then not only will you be extremely lucky, but you can also content yourself with a single line in the formula bar. I doubt that this is likely to be the case, however, because you will want to do great things with Excel. It follows that you may soon be tired of creating long and complex DAX formulas in a limited space. So, here is how to expand the formula bar—pretty much as you would in Excel:

1. Click the Expand icon at the right of the formula bar (the downward-facing chevron).

The formula bar increases in height to allow you to type and see several lines of text. To reduce the height of the formula bar and reset it to a single line, just click the Reduce icon at the right of the formula bar (which has now become an upward-facing chevron). You can see this icon in Figure 15-7.

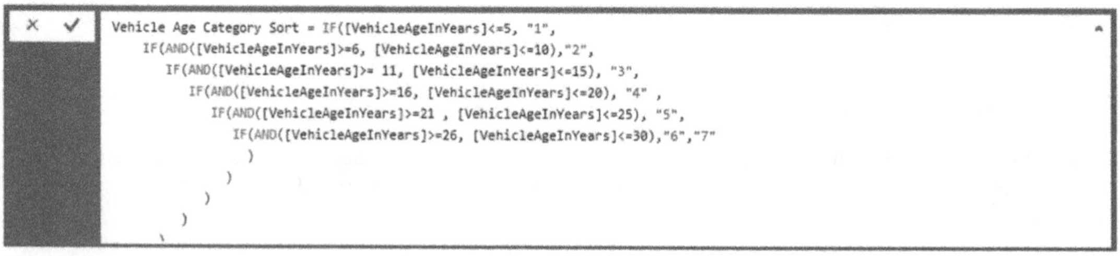

```
Vehicle Age Category Sort = IF([VehicleAgeInYears]<=5, "1",
    IF(AND([VehicleAgeInYears]>=6, [VehicleAgeInYears]<=10),"2",
        IF(AND([VehicleAgeInYears]>= 11, [VehicleAgeInYears]<=15), "3",
            IF(AND([VehicleAgeInYears]>=16, [VehicleAgeInYears]<=20), "4" ,
                IF(AND([VehicleAgeInYears]>=21 , [VehicleAgeInYears]<=25), "5",
                    IF(AND([VehicleAgeInYears]>=26, [VehicleAgeInYears]<=30),"6","7"
                    )
                )
            )
        )
    )
```

Figure 15-7. *Multiline formulas*

Conclusion

This chapter introduced you to some of the core techniques that you can apply to extend an Excel data model with further metrics. These additional elements were in the form of new columns that you added to many of the data tables that you had previously loaded, cleansed, and assembled into a structured data model.

All the added columns were based on DAX, the Power Pivot formula language. As you saw, this language is not especially difficult, and it is fairly close to the Excel formula language.

You also learned how to concatenate fields and how to perform basic arithmetic. Then you practiced carrying out calculations that involve multiple tables. Finally, you learned how to segment records using logical functions.

This brief introduction is nonetheless only a quick taste of the power of DAX. There is much, much more that can be accomplished to prepare the quantitative analyses that you are likely to need to produce telling visuals with Power View or incisive pivot tables in Excel. It is time to move on to the next chapter and take a look at the next feature of DAX: creating measures.

■ ■ ■

CHAPTER 16

Adding Measures to the Data Model

Adding new columns can provide much of the extra data that you want to output in tools like Power View. It is unlikely, however, that this approach can deliver *all* the analyses that you need. Specifically, calculated columns can work *only* on a row-by-row basis; they cannot contain formulas that have to apply to all or part of the records in a table. For instance, counting the number of cars sold for a year, a quarter, or a month has nothing to do with the data in a single row in the Stock table. It does, however, concern the table as a whole.

Generally, you need to add a second type of formula to your tables when you have to look at subsets of the data. These formulas are called, simply, *measures*. These calculations (or measures or metrics—call them what you will) also use DAX. They are applied differently, though, and they can produce some extremely powerful results to help you analyze your data. This is because measures do things that calculated columns simply cannot do. So if you need to work with aggregate values and not on a row-by-row basis, then you will have to create measures to achieve the correct result.

Introducing Measures

Like with so many aspects of Power Pivot and self-service business intelligence in general, measures are probably best introduced through a few examples. Unfortunately, it is impossible to do anything other than scratch the surface of measures in only a few pages, because they are arguably the most powerful element in Power Pivot—one that deserves an entire book to itself. Nonetheless, I hope that this short introduction will whet your appetite and that you will then continue to learn all about DAX and its more advanced application from the many excellent resources currently available.

In this chapter, we will continue to develop the file that you began in the previous chapter. It is now called DataModelForMetrics.xlsx and is available for download from the Apress web site.

A First Measure: Number of Cars Sold

Suppose you want to be able to display the number of cars sold in Power Pivot. Not only that, but you want this figure to adjust when it is filtered or sliced by another criterion, such as country or color. Put simply, you want this metric to be infinitely sensitive to how it is displayed yet always give the right answer.

So, how are you going to achieve this? The following explains how:

1. In Power Pivot, ensure that you are in data view.

2. Select the table to which you want to add a measure. I chose Stock here.

3. Click inside the calculation area under the data.

4. Add the following formula to the formula bar:

```
NumberOfCarsSold:=COUNTROWS(
```

You will see that the pop-up will then suggest a list of DAX formulas interspersed with the names of tables in the current data model. If you scroll down the list, it will look like Figure 16-1.

Figure 16-1. *The pop-up menu showing functions and tables*

5. Select the table Stock and add the right parenthesis. The formula will look like this:

```
NumberOfCarsSold := COUNTROWS(Stock)
```

6. Confirm the creation of the formula by pressing Enter or by clicking the check mark in the formula bar.

The Stock tab in the Power Pivot window will look like the one you can see in Figure 16-2.

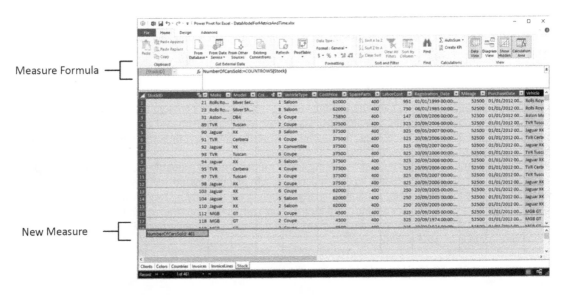

Figure 16-2. *A new measure added to the data model in Power Pivot*

Assuming that you have just read Chapter 15, the first thing that will strike you in comparison with creating a new column is that no column is created for this measure. You can see it in the Power View Fields pane or a pivot table's fields pane once you expand the Stock table, where it appears just like any column of data. In Power View, however, if you look closely at the field (NumberOfCarsSold) that you have just created, you will also see that there is a tiny icon of a calculator to the left of the field name. This allows you to distinguish measures from columns. You will also see this field in the Pivot Table Fields pane of any pivot table that you create based on the data model. Only this time the NumberOfCarsSold field will have an Fx symbol to its left to differentiate it from a column of data.

It's not that difficult, I am sure you will agree. The best is yet to come. Suppose you now use this field in a Power View card (you saw these in Chapter 10), which is also filtered to show the results for green vehicles only. The result is filtered so that only the number of sales for green cars is displayed. In other words, the formula is completely separate from the data in a column but applies any filters that are selected. You can see this applied to a visualization in Figure 16-3.

Figure 16-3. *Using a measure in a card visualization*

The key thing to take away is that a correctly applied measure can be used in an Excel pivot table or a Power View table, chart, or indeed any type of visualization and always shows the correct result of any and all filters and slicers that you have applied. Also, the figures are correct for each intersection of rows and columns in tables. All in all, it is well worth ensuring that you have all the measures that you need for your analytical output in place and that they are working correctly in Power Pivot, because you can then rely on these calculations in the data set in so many different visualizations.

■ **Tip**   You can rename measures by clicking the name of the measure in the field list and altering the name in the formula bar.

When you start out creating measures, it can be a little disconcerting at first not to see the results of a formula immediately, like you can when adding new columns. If this worries you (or if you want to test the result of a new measure), then one approach is to create a table in dashboard view and add the new measure plus any other useful measures that allow you to verify that everything works as you expected. This technique was explained in detail in Chapter 10.

As you are developing metrics and extending a data model, you will probably spend a lot of time testing the results of your measures in Power View visualizations and pivot tables. So, it is probably worth noting that you can leave the Power Pivot window open and switch to the underlying Excel workbook (and back again). This allows you to modify a metric and then use the results that the change produces immediately.

Changing a DAX definition and then switching from the Power Pivot window to Excel will mean that the dialog shown in Figure 16-4 will appear.

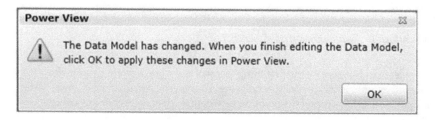

Figure 16-4. *The data model modification alert*

Obviously you will need to confirm that you want the output to be updated with the results of the latest modifications.

Basic Aggregations in Measures

Measures are DAX formulas, so in learning to use measures, you will have to become familiar with some more DAX functions. My intention here, though, is definitely not to take you through all that DAX can offer. Instead, I would like to show you a few basic formulas that can be useful in real-world dashboards and give you some initial DAX recipes that should prove practical.

So, as a second example, let's calculate the total costs of vehicles purchased. Although you can just type in a simple DAX formula, I prefer to show you how you can extend the knowledge that you gained when creating calculated columns and apply many of the same techniques to creating measures.

1. In Power Pivot, ensure that you are in data view.

2. Select the Stock table and click inside the calculation area under the data.

3. Enter the name you want to use (**Total Sales**) for this metric, followed by a colon and an equal sign (:=).

4. Enter **SUM** as the function, followed by a left parenthesis. A list of all the tables and fields in the data model will appear (including any columns and measures that you have added).

5. Enter a left bracket to restrict the pop-up list to fields in the current table.

6. Start typing the field name (**CostPrice** in this example). After a couple of characters, any tables or fields with these characters will be listed, as shown in Figure 16-5.

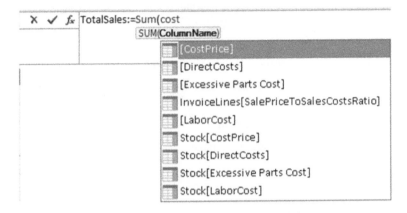

Figure 16-5. Creating a measure containing an aggregation

7. Scroll down and select the [CostPrice] field.

8. Add a right parenthesis. The formula should read as follows:

   `TotalSales:=SUM(Stock[CostPrice])`

9. Press Enter (or click the check mark in the formula bar).

The measure is created, and it appears in the field list. This particular function gives you the total of the SalePrice column. However, when you use it in Power View, it is filtered and applied (or sliced and diced if you prefer) to take into account how the data is subset.

One important thing to note when creating measures is that you should use the table name as well as the field name if there are fields that have the same name in several tables. This is so that DAX is certain that it is using the right field from the right table. What's more, if a table name contains spaces, then the table name needs to be in single quotes. In all cases, the field name has to be enclosed in square brackets.

To practice a little (and to prepare the ground for some eye-catching visualizations in the next few chapters), try creating the average, maximum, and minimum sale prices using the formulas in Table 16-1.

Table 16-1. A Few Elementary DAX Measures

Name	DAX Code
Average Cost Price	AVERAGE(Stock[CostPrice])
Maximum Sale Price	MAX(InvoiceLines[SalePrice])
Minimum Sale Price	MIN(InvoiceLines[SalePrice])

Using Multiple Measures

As you can well imagine, not all metrics are likely to be as simple as those you just saw. You can also create measures that are the result of combining several DAX functions.

For a little practice, you could try adding the ratio of gross margin to sale price to the data model. This measure will then be used in the upcoming chapters on creating dashboards with Power Pivot.

1. In Power Pivot, ensure that you are in Grid view.

2. Select the InvoiceLines table and click inside the calculation area under the data.

3. Enter the name you want to use (**RatioNetMargin Sales**) for this metric, followed by a colon and an equal sign (:=).

4. Enter **SUM** as the function, followed by a left parenthesis.

5. Enter a left bracket to limit the list to fields in the current table.

6. Select the [Gross Margin] field.

7. Enter a right parenthesis.

8. Enter a forward slash (the divide by operator).

9. Enter **SUM** as the function, followed by a left parenthesis.

10. Enter a left bracket to limit the list to fields in the current table.

11. Select the [SalePrice] field.

12. Enter a right parenthesis. The formula should read as follows:

    ```
    RatioNetMargin := SUM([Gross Margin])/SUM([SalePrice])
    ```

13. Press Enter (or click the check mark in the formula bar).

14. In the Modeling ribbon, click the percentage button to apply a percentage format.

The easiest way to see the output of a measure like this is to create a table that uses the measure and another attribute so that you can see how the measure works in practice. Figure 16-6 shows a simple example of this in Power View.

Color	RatioNetMargin
Black	35.73%
Blue	37.26%
British Racing Green	37.00%
Canary Yellow	36.01%
Dark Purple	41.22%
Green	40.13%
Night Blue	25.20%
Red	43.48%
Silver	38.92%
Total	**38.13%**

Figure 16-6. *Applying a measure in a table*

This is an extremely simple example of a composite DAX function, of course. Indeed, you can probably see a distinct resemblance to an Excel formula. However, the key point to take away is that once you have created the measure, it will work in just about any Power View visualization using most, if not all, of the attributes from the data model. Power View can also apply the measure intelligently to hierarchies of data. So, for instance, if you add the Make field to Table 16-1 and switch the visualization to a matrix, you will instantly see the calculations that are shown in Figure 16-7. Here, Power Pivot has automatically calculated the net margin ratio for each vehicle sold without you having to alter the formula in any way. Of course, you can produce the same result in a pivot table in Excel.

Color	Make	RatioNetMargin
Black	Aston Martin	20.24%
	Bentley	44.12%
	Jaguar	43.12%
	Rolls Royce	45.42%
	Triumph	53.73%
	Total	**35.73%**
Blue	Aston Martin	58.50%
	Bentley	40.62%
	Jaguar	4.70%
	MGB	73.75%
	Rolls Royce	36.69%
	Triumph	23.05%
	TVR	6.91%
	Total	**37.26%**
British Racing Green	Aston Martin	29.98%
	Bentley	42.71%
	Jaguar	29.81%
	MGB	70.17%
	Rolls Royce	39.41%
	Triumph	54.35%
	Total	**37.00%**

Figure 16-7. *A hierarchy using a measure*

When you use measures like this one in visualizations, you may well find that some calculations are displayed to many decimal places. If you find this distracting, then you can format measures in the same way that you format Power Pivot columns. Any formats that you apply are used in Power View by default whenever you use this measure.

A final point is that when you insert a table or a field into a DAX formula from the pop-up list shown in Figure 16-1, you see three types of icons to the left of the table or field: the icon with a table outline denotes a Power Pivot table; the table with a selected column icon indicates a column of data or a column that you have added.

Cross-Table Measures

You are not limited to creating measures that refer to the fields in a single table. If anything, measures are designed to apply across *all* the fields in a data model. To start out with a simple example, suppose that you want to create a custom measure that displays the margin for each vehicle once the cost price and any cost of spares have been deducted.

1. In Power Pivot, ensure that you are in Grid view.

2. Select the InvoiceLines table and click inside the calculation area under the data.

3. Enter the name you want to use (**Cost Plus Spares Margin**) for this metric, followed by a colon and an equal sign (:=).

4. Enter **SUM** as the function, followed by a left parenthesis. A list of all the tables and fields in the data model will appear (including any columns and measures that you have added).

5. Select InvoiceLines[SalePrice].

6. Add a minus sign after the formula (you can add spaces before and afterward if you want).

7. Enter **SUM** as the function, followed by a left parenthesis. A list of all the tables and fields in the data model will appear (including any columns and measures that you have added).

8. Select InvoiceLines[CostPrice].

9. Add a minus sign after the formula (you can add spaces before and afterward if you want).

10. Enter **SUM (** and then expand the Stock table in the field list and click the SparesCost field.

11. Add a right parenthesis. The formula will look like this:

    ```
    Cost Plus Spares Margin := SUM(InvoiceLines[SalePrice]) - SUM(Stock[CostPrice]) -
    SUM(Stock[SpareParts])
    ```

12. Press Enter (or click the check mark in the formula bar).

You could then add this new measure to the matrix that you saw previously. If you do, you see something like Figure 16-8. Alternatively, you could create the same result in an Excel pivot table if you prefer.

Color	Make	Cost Plus Spares Margin	RatioNetMargin
Black	Aston Martin	215,550.00	20.24%
	Bentley	176,340.00	44.12%
	Jaguar	143,880.00	43.12%
	Rolls Royce	439,985.00	45.42%
	Triumph	36,750.00	53.73%
	Total	**1,012,505.00**	**35.73%**
Blue	Aston Martin	866,865.00	58.50%
	Bentley	81,220.00	40.62%
	Jaguar	8,490.00	4.70%
	MGB	56,550.00	73.75%
	Rolls Royce	213,710.00	36.69%
	Triumph	30,900.00	23.05%
	TVR	11,100.00	6.91%
	Total	**1,268,835.00**	**37.26%**
British Racing Green	Aston Martin	187,710.00	29.98%
	Bentley	160,980.00	42.71%
	Jaguar	135,390.00	29.81%
	MGB	48,750.00	70.17%
	Rolls Royce	458,400.00	39.41%
	Triumph	36,300.00	54.35%
	Total	**1,027,530.00**	**37.00%**

Figure 16-8. *Applying multiple measures to a matrix*

Creating cross-table measures in DAX is easier than creating new columns that use values from more than one table. From this example, you can see the following:

- You do not need to use the RELATED() function.

- You only have to specify the table name before entering the field name (or select the combination of table and field from the pop-up).

- You can use the field list to refer to fields in other tables (or even in the same table).

- You *must* use aggregation functions on numeric fields. If you do not, you will get an error message.

■ **Note**   A measure is attached to a table so that it appears as a field in the specific table. The measure does not have to use any of the fields in the table that "hosts" it. This means you can attach measures to any table in your data model, which allows for a considerable organizational freedom when extending the model with further metrics.

More Advanced Aggregations

Now that you have seen how to create basic measures, it is time to move on to some more advanced concepts. More precisely, I want to outline a couple of ways to evaluate data on a row-by-row basis yet return the result with any filters and slicers applied. There are many cases where this *cannot* be done using a calculated column and then returning the aggregate of the column data. After all, you need to return the *ratio of the sum* of any values and *not* the *sum of the ratio*. Think of calculating a ratio for each row and then adding up or averaging the results to get the average ratio; it is arithmetically false.

Fortunately, Power Pivot has some simple yet powerful solutions to this kind of conundrum. One principal tool is the use of the "X" functions—AVERAGEX, COUNTX, SUMX, MAXX, and MINX, among others. These functions allow you to specify the following:

- The table in which the calculations apply

- The row-by-row calculation that is to be applied

As an example, consider the requirement for the ratio of the cost of any parts compared to the purchase price of each vehicle. Not only do you need this potentially at the finest level of granularity—the individual record—but you may need it sliced and diced by any number of criteria. The following explains how to create the formula that you could use in Power Pivot reports or pivot tables:

1. In Power Pivot, select the Stock table and click inside the calculation area under the data.

2. Enter the name that you want to use (**Average Parts Cost Ratio**) for this metric, followed by a colon and an equal sign (:=).

3. Enter **AVERAGEX** as the function, followed by a left parenthesis. A list of all the tables and fields in the data model will appear (including any columns and measures that you have added).

4. Select the Stock table.

5. Enter a comma.

6. Add a left parenthesis. This is to ensure that the subtraction is carried out before the division.

7. Enter a left bracket and select the [CostPrice] field or enter the field name, including the square brackets.

8. Add a minus sign after the field name (you can add spaces before and afterward if you want).

9. Enter a left bracket and select the [SpareParts] field or enter the field name including the square brackets.

10. Enter a right parenthesis. This matches the opening left parenthesis in step 7.

11. Add a forward slash (the divide by operator).

12. Enter a left bracket and select the [SpareParts] field or enter the field name, including the square brackets.

13. Enter a right parenthesis. This finishes the AVERAGEX function. The formula will look like this:

```
Average Parts Cost Ratio := AVERAGEX(Stock,([CostPrice]-[SpareParts]) /
[SpareParts])
```

14. Press Enter (or click the check mark in the formula bar).

Just creating the formula is pretty meaningless. So, take a look at the chart created in Power View in Figure 16-9, where you can see how this ratio instantly shows you which models are the most costly as far as spare parts are concerned.

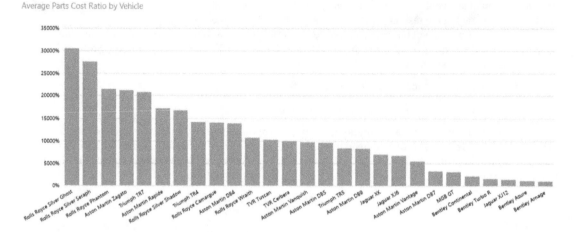

Average Parts Cost Ratio by Vehicle

Figure 16-9. *Using the AVERAGEX() function in DAX*

As you can see from this example—and unlike the AVERAGE function—AVERAGEX takes these two inputs (or parameters as they are technically known):

- The *table* to which the formula is applied

- The *formula* to use, which is just as you would apply it to a calculated column

This formula deducts CostPrice from SalePrice for every row in the table and then returns the average dependent on the filters and selections currently applied. This way, you always get the mathematically accurate result in your visualizations.

The following are the essential points to take away from this example:

- It is essential to wrap any field references in an aggregate function, such as SUM, AVERAGE, or COUNT, for an aggregated result to work. This is because the calculation (depending on the filters used) is not applied to only one record, but potentially several records, so data must be aggregated. That's why you use the SUM function in this example.

- You can (and indeed, must) nest calculations inside parentheses to force Power Pivot to calculate elements in the correct order. This functions exactly as it does in Excel, so I will not labor the point here.

There are many more of these "X" functions (which are generally known as *iterative functions*, as they iterate over an entire table) in DAX. Table 16-2 outlines those that are currently available.

Table 16-2. *DAX Iterative Functions*

Formula	Description	Example
MINX()	Calculates a value for each row in a table and displays the minimum value	MINX(Stock, [SpareParts]+[LaborCost])
MAXX()	Calculates a value for each row in a table and displays the maximum value	MAXX(Stock, [SpareParts]+[LaborCost])
SUMX()	Calculates a value for each row in a table and displays the total	SUMX(Stock, [SpareParts]+[LaborCost])
AVERAGEX()	Calculates a value for each row in a table and displays the average of these values	AVERAGEX(Stock, [SpareParts]+[LaborCost])
COUNTX()	Calculates a value for each row in a table and counts the resulting rows, including nonblank results of the calculation	COUNTX(Stock, [SpareParts]+[LaborCost])
COUNTAX()	Calculates a value for each row in a table and counts the resulting rows, not including nonblank results of the calculation	COUNTAX (Stock, [SpareParts]+[LaborCost])
GEOMEANX()	Calculates a value for each row in a table and displays the geometric mean of these values	GEOMEANX(Stock, [SpareParts]+[LaborCost])
MEDIANX()	Calculates a value for each row in a table and displays the median value of these values	MEDIANX(Stock, [SpareParts]+[LaborCost])
PERCENTILEX.EXC()	Returns the percentile of a record relative to the data set	PERCENTILEX.EXC(Stock, [SpareParts]+[LaborCost])
PERCENTILEX.INC()	Returns the percentile of a record relative to the data set	PERCENTILEX.INC(Stock, [SpareParts]+[LaborCost])
RANKX()	Orders the rows by progressive rank	**RANKX(ALL(Stock[Make]), SUMX (RELATEDTABLE(InvoiceLines), [SalePrice]))**
STDEVX.P()	Calculates a value for each row in a table and displays the standard deviation of the entire population of these values	STDEVX.P(Stock, [SpareParts]+[LaborCost])
STDEVX.S()	Calculates a value for each row in a table and displays the standard deviation of a sample population of these values	STDEVX.S(Stock, [SpareParts]+[LaborCost])
VARX.S()	Calculates a value for each row in a table and displays the variance of the entire population of these values	VARX.S(Stock, [SpareParts]+[LaborCost])
VARX.P()	Calculates a value for each row in a table and displays the variance of the entire population of these values	VARX.P(Stock, [SpareParts]+[LaborCost])

Filter Context

When working with DAX (at least if you want to develop any complex formulas), you need to understand *filter context*. This is the basis of the dynamic data analysis using Power Pivot. It is the basis of the approach where the results of a formula can change to reflect the current row or cell selection and any related filters.

Filter context can become an extremely complicated subject. However, since this is not a book on DAX, I am deliberately simplifying some of the ideas explained later in this chapter. After all, the aim is to get you started with DAX, not to scare you off right at the start.

The following are three key elements that you need to understand:

- Row context

- Query context

- Filter context

Let's take a brief look at these in turn.

Row Context

Row context is essentially the values from the current row. You saw this when creating new columns. This means that any fields that you used in a calculation always use other fields from the same record—or from a linked table. Therefore, this is largely automatic and typically handled by DAX without any intervention on your part.

Query Context

Query context is the combination of the following factors that produce a calculated result:

- Page-level filters

- Visualization-level filters

- Slicers

- Interactive selection

- Row and column filters

The first two are cumulative (page-level filters, and visualization-level filters) and reduce the available data that a visualization can show. They are explained in detail in Chapter 3. For the moment, just consider them as a set of filters that allows only certain data to be used.

Slicers are any interactive filtering that you add for a dashboard. These restrict even further the data set resulting from any report-level filters, page-level filters, and visualization-level filters to reduce even further the data that can be displayed. Interactive selection is a method of filtering data by selecting an element in another visualization. Both of these techniques are explained for Power View in detail in Chapter 8.

Row and column filters are best thought of as the row and column headers in a pivot table (or a cross-tab if you prefer). These define the intersections of data that can be shown.

Query context is the cumulative effect of any filters that you apply when creating Power View reports using the Power View interface elements. The same principles apply to pivot table filters and slicers.

Filter Context

Filter context is added when you specify filter constraints on the set of values allowed in a column or table, by using formulas that expand or reduce the data set that is used to obtain a result. Filter context applies on top of other contexts, such as row context or query context. This is the focus of the next few pages.

Filtering Data in Measures

Inevitably, there will be times when the filters that you apply using the Power Pivot user interface (the query-level filters that were described earlier) are not quite what you are looking for. There could be several reasons for this, including the following:

- You want to apply a highly specific filter to a single metric.

- You want to override the natural result of the query-level filter.

- You are creating a highly complex formula and it has to be tailored to a specific use.

Any of these reasons (and there are many others that you will discover as you progress with DAX) could require you to filter the data in a measure. Let's look at a few circumstances where this could prove necessary. Given the wide-ranging possibilities of DAX, I do not intend to explain anything more than the basics of DAX filtering using a few simple examples that I hope you find practical when building your own dashboards.

Simple Filters

There will probably be many occasions in your career when you need to home in on a specific subset of data. Maybe you need to compare and contrast one sales stream with another. Perhaps you need to highlight one cost compared to a total. Whatever the actual requirement, you need to apply a specific filter to a metric.

There are dozens—if not hundreds—of ways of applying different filters when building measures. However, one function is definitely an essential part of your DAX toolbox: the CALCULATE() function. This function lets you apply a range of filters to a measure that you can then apply in the visualizations that you build into your dashboards.

Text Filters

To begin, let's look at a fairly simple filter requirement. Brilliant British Cars sells to two types of clients: dealers and wholesalers. As part of your ongoing sales analysis, you want to isolate the dealer sales stream. The following steps explain how you can do this:

1. Select the InvoiceLines table and click inside the calculation area under the data.

2. Enter the name you want to use (**DealerSales**) for this metric, followed by a colon and an equal sign (:=).

3. To the right of the equal sign, enter (or select) **CALCULATE(**.

4. Enter (or select) **SUM(**.

5. Select the InvoiceLines[SalePrice] field.

6. Add a right parenthesis. This will terminate the SUM() function.

7. Enter a comma. This tells the CALCULATE() function that you are about to add the filters.

8. Select the Clients[ClientType] field.

9. Enter an equal sign.

10. Add the word **"Dealer"** (include the double quotes).

11. Add a right parenthesis. This will terminate the CALCULATE() function. The formula should now read as follows:

```
DealerSales := CALCULATE(SUM(InvoiceLines[SalePrice]),Clients[ClientType]="Dealer")
```

You could then add this new measure to a simple table of sales by make. If you do, you will see something like Figure 16-10.

Make	SalePrice	DealerSales
Aston Martin	10686040	7,943,930.00
Bentley	4998000	3,509,000.00
Jaguar	6319000	4,787,500.00
MGB	1011000	839,750.00
Rolls Royce	7356900	5,599,300.00
Triumph	925500	718,000.00
TVR	542750	389,750.00
Total	**31839190**	**23,787,230.00**

Figure 16-10. *Using a simple filter*

You can see from this table that the SalePrice column is not filtered in any way. However, the DealerSales column always shows a smaller figure for the sales per make, as it is displaying only the filtered subset of data that you requested. The new measure that you created can be applied to any visualization and can be filtered and sliced and diced like any other data column, calculated column, or metric.

Now let me explain. Here you are using a function in DAX called CALCULATE(). This function does what its name implies; it calculates an aggregation. However, the calculation is nearly always a *filter* operation. This is because of the way in which its two parameters work.

- The first parameter defines the *function* to use (SUM() and AVERAGE() here) and the table and column that is aggregated; it could have been potentially a much more complex formula.

- The second parameter is a *filter* to force DAX to show only a subset of the data. In this specific case, it returns the sum of sales *only* when the client is a car dealership.

The filter that is applied here comes from another column. Indeed, it comes from another table altogether. When using the CALCULATE() function, you can use just about any column (either an original data column or a calculated column) as the source for a filter.

> **Note** When you are filtering on some text (such as the type of dealer in this example), you *must* always enclose the text that you are searching for in double quotes.

Numeric Filters

You are not restricted to filtering on text-based data only in Power Pivot. You can also subset data by numeric values. As an example, suppose you want to see totals for sales for lower-priced models so that you can target the higher end of the market. The following explains how you can do this:

1. Select the InvoiceLines table and click inside the calculation area under the data.

2. Enter the name that you want to use (**LowPriceSales**) for this metric, followed by a colon and an equal sign (:=).

3. To the right of the equal sign, enter (or select) **CALCULATE(.**

4. Enter (or select) SUM(.

5. Select the InvoiceLines[SalePrice] field.

6. Add a right parenthesis. This will terminate the SUM() function.

7. Enter a comma. This tells the CALCULATE() function that you are about to add the filters.

8. Select the InvoiceLines[SalePrice] field again.

9. Enter a less than sign: <.

10. Enter **50000**.

11. Add a right parenthesis. This will terminate the CALCULATE() function. The formula should now read as follows:

```
LowPriceSales := CALCULATE(SUM(InvoiceLines[SalePrice]),InvoiceLines[SalePrice] < 50000)
```

Comparing the low price sales with the unfiltered sales for make and model produces a table like the one in Figure 16-11.

Make	Model	SalePrice	LowPriceSales
Aston Martin	DB4	793000	
Aston Martin	DB7	1023480	325,980.00
Aston Martin	DB9	5423860	646,110.00
Aston Martin	DBS	465500	
Aston Martin	Rapide	455500	
Aston Martin	Vanquish	1506750	
Aston Martin	Vantage	658200	313,700.00
Aston Martin	Zagato	359750	
Bentley	Arnage	90750	90,750.00
Bentley	Azure	489500	266,750.00
Bentley	Continental	3709000	1,357,750.00
Bentley	Turbo R	708750	263,250.00
Jaguar	XJ12	618000	172,500.00
Jaguar	XJ6	1239750	1,017,000.00
Jaguar	XK	4461250	3,757,500.00
MGB	GT	1011000	1,011,000.00
Rolls Royce	Camargue	4116900	216,650.00
Rolls Royce	Phantom	359750	
Rolls Royce	Silver Ghost	1315500	
Rolls Royce	Silver Seraph	582500	
Rolls Royce	Silver Shadow	622500	
Rolls Royce	Wraith	359750	

Figure 16-11. *Using a numeric filter*

In this simple example you saw how to use the less than (<) comparison operator. You can use any of the standard logical comparison operators (=, <. >, <=, >=, <>) that you saw in the previous chapter.

■ **Note** When you are filtering on a number, you must *not* enclose the number that you are searching for in quotes. Neither must you format the number in any way.

More Complex Filters

In the two previous examples, you saw the basics of creating filtered measures using either text or a number to subset the data returned by the CALCULATE() function. In the real world of data analysis, filters can get a lot more complex. Indeed, allowing you to create specific and complex filters for metrics is one of the ways that DAX can help you tease out real insight from your data. So, without attempting to get overly complicated, next are a few examples of the ways that you can define more complex filtered metrics in your data models.

Multiple Criteria in Filters

The CALCULATE() function is not limited to a single filter. Far from it. You can add multiple filters to the second part of this function each separated by a comma.

For example, imagine that you didn't just want to see dealer sales when you look at your data but also want to see the (slightly lower) figure for dealer sales where the client has a good credit status. This means combining two filter criteria.

1. Click the InvoiceLines table in the tabs at the bottom of the Power Pivot window.

2. Click inside the calculation area under the data.

3. Enter the name that you want to use (**DealerSales**) for this metric, followed by a colon and an equal sign (:=).

4. To the right of the equal sign, enter (or select) **CALCULATE(**.

5. Enter (or select) **SUM(**.

6. Select the InvoiceLines[SalePrice] field.

7. Add a right parenthesis. This will terminate the SUM() function.

8. Enter a comma. This tells the CALCULATE() function that you are about to add the filters.

9. Select the Clients[ClientType] field.

10. Enter an equal sign.

11. Add the word **"Dealer"** (include the double quotes).

12. Enter a comma. This indicates you are adding another filter criterion.

13. Select the Clients[IsCreditWorthy] field.

14. Enter an equal sign.

15. Add the word **TRUE()**. This is a logical value; it does not need to be enclosed in quotes, and it has an empty parenthesis added.

16. Add a right parenthesis. This will terminate the CALCULATE() function. The formula should now read as follows:

```
Creditworthy DealerSales := CALCULATE(SUM(InvoiceLines[SalePrice]),Clients[ClientType]="Deal
er",Clients[IsCreditWorthy]=TRUE())
```

If this column is added to the table that you saw in Figure 16-9, you will see a result something like the one in Figure 16-12.

Make	SalePrice	DealerSales	Creditworthy DealerSales
Aston Martin	10686040	7,943,930.00	5,086,050.00
Bentley	4998000	3,509,000.00	2,192,500.00
Jaguar	6319000	4,787,500.00	3,187,250.00
MGB	1011000	839,750.00	519,750.00
Rolls Royce	7356900	5,599,300.00	3,671,550.00
Triumph	925500	718,000.00	488,000.00
TVR	542750	389,750.00	324,750.00
Total	**31839190**	**23,787,230.00**	**15,469,850.00**

Figure 16-12. *Using a more complex filter*

If anything, this was a simple example. The filters that you add to any measure that uses the CALCULATE() function can contain multiple elements. Also, you can create a series of filters where each filter element compares data from different tables and mixes both text-based and numeric filters.

■ **Note**   You can only apply a logical test for a true or false value (such as the test on the IsCreditWorthy column) if the column's data type is True/False.

Using Multiple Filters

For a final filter example, imagine that you want to isolate the percentage of creditworthy dealer sales relative to dealer sales. You can do this by using the two measure calculations (DealerSales and CreditworthyDealerSales) in a single measure to obtain the desired result.

Since you just saw how to create these calculations, I will only show you the formula here:

```
Creditworthy DealerSales Percent := CALCULATE(SUM(InvoiceLines[SalePr
ice]),Clients[ClientType]="Dealer",Clients[IsCreditWorthy]=TRUE()) /
CALCULATE(SUM(InvoiceLines[SalePrice]),Clients[ClientType]="Dealer")
```

As you can see (as you would in Excel), you can combine functions—even complex filtered functions—in a single metric to deliver powerful analysis. Using this measure in a simple table displaying sales by make produces the results shown in Figure 16-13.

Make	SalePrice	Creditworthy DealerSales Percent
Aston Martin	10686040	64.02%
Bentley	4998000	62.48%
Jaguar	6319000	66.57%
MGB	1011000	61.89%
Rolls Royce	7356900	65.57%
Triumph	925500	67.97%
TVR	542750	83.32%
Total	**31839190**	**65.03%**

Figure 16-13. *Using multiple filters in a measure*

Now that you have learned how to create filtered measures, you have mastered the building blocks of an extremely powerful technique that you can adapt and extend in your own data models.

Calculating Percentages of Totals

The filters that you have applied up until now in this chapter merely delivered subsets of data. Sometimes you need filters to do the opposite and apply a calculation to an entire data set. In other words, you need filters that *remove* filters. This is often because calculating a total means telling DAX to aggregate a column without applying any of the filtering by row that would normally be applied. In other words, you need to *prevent* the automatic filters that have proved so useful thus far.

A Simple Percentage

Imagine a table where you want to calculate the percentage of a total that each row represents. This could be the total of sales by make, for instance. Here you need to simply divide the sales by the total sales.

1. Click the InvoiceLines table in the list of data tabs.

2. Click inside the calculation area under the data.

3. Enter the name you want to use (**MakePercentage**) for this metric, followed by a colon and an equal sign (:=).

4. To the right of the equal sign, enter (or select) **DIVIDE(**.

5. Enter (or select) **SUM(**.

6. Select the **InvoiceLines[SalePrice]** field.

7. Add a right parenthesis. This will terminate the SUM( ) function.

8. Enter a comma.

9. Enter or select **CALCULATE(**.

10. Enter (or select) **SUM(**.

11. Select the InvoiceLines[SalePrice] field.

12. Add a right parenthesis. This will terminate the SUM( ) function.

13. Enter a comma. This tells the CALCULATE() function that you are about to add the filters.

14. Enter or select **ALL(**.

15. Select the Stock[Make] field.

16. Add a right parenthesis. This will terminate the ALL() function.

17. Add a right parenthesis. This will terminate the CALCULATE() function.

18. Add a right parenthesis. This will terminate the DIVIDE() function. The formula should now read as follows:

```
MakePercentage := DIVIDE(SUM(InvoiceLines[SalePrice]), CALCULATE(SUM(InvoiceLines[SalePrice]), ALL(Stock[Make])))
```

In Power Pivot the result of this calculation will be 1, that is, 100 percent. This is logical, as for all the data the total percentage of all makes should equal 100 percent. However, if you create a simple table of sales per make and add this new measure, it should look like Figure 16-14.

Make	SalePrice	MakePercentage
Aston Martin	10686040	33.56%
Bentley	4998000	15.70%
Jaguar	6319000	19.85%
MGB	1011000	3.18%
Rolls Royce	7356900	23.11%
Triumph	925500	2.91%
TVR	542750	1.70%
Total	**31839190**	**100.00%**

Figure 16-14. *Using the ALL() function to calculate a percentage per attribute*

So, it is important when creating measures not to worry about the result that appears in the calculation area of the Power Pivot window. Instead, it is probably better to get into the habit of testing the metric in Power View or a pivot table to see a more coherent result.

This formula and the concept behind it probably seem a little peculiar. So, let me explain the ALL() function in greater detail. In essence, the ALL() function says, "Remove all the filters concerning any specified fields." Consequently, in this example, the make is *not* filtered when calculating the total sales. This means that the unfiltered total can now be calculated—and so can the percentage of each make relative to this grand total.

It is important to note that the ALL() function only removes filters for the fields that you have specified. For instance, look at Figure 16-15, which shows a matrix for the sales and the percentage by make for two colors.

Color	Black		Blue		Total	
Make	SalePrice	MakePercentage	SalePrice	MakePercentage	SalePrice	MakePercentage
Aston Martin	1173500	37.25%	1556250	41.16%	2729750	39.38%
Bentley	473000	15.01%	297250	7.86%	770250	11.11%
Jaguar	416000	13.21%	818000	21.63%	1234000	17.80%
MGB			81250	2.15%	81250	2.15%
Rolls Royce	1014750	32.21%	615750	16.28%	1630500	23.52%
Triumph	73000	2.32%	154250	4.08%	227250	3.28%
TVR			258500	6.84%	258500	6.84%
Total	3150250	100.00%	3781250	100.00%	6931500	100.00%

Figure 16-15. *The ALL() function lets all other filters be applied*

You can see here that the measure MakePercentage is correctly applied independently to sales for Red, Blue, and the grand total. This is because all other filters (the year in this case) are applied as you have come to expect with DAX; *only* the make is not filtered when calculating the total sales.

Removing Multiple Filter Elements

If your visualization is more complex than the simple example that you just saw, then you have to craft your measures appropriately to handle any complexity. For instance, take the case where you want to see sales by make and color and display the percentage of each row compared to the total. You need to calculate a total that discards the filters for make *and* color so that DAX can arrive at the correct figure for the overall total. Here is the formula that can do this:

```
MakeAndColorPercentage := DIVIDE(SUM(InvoiceLines[SalePrice]), CALCULATE(SUM(InvoiceLines[SalePrice]), ALL(Stock[Make]), ALL(Colors[Color])))
```

Since this code snippet is only an extension of the previous one, I have not explained how to construct it in detail. All you have to do is to follow the steps from the previous example and add a second filter to the second CALCULATE() function (the one that returns the grand total of sales). As you saw earlier in this chapter, the CALCULATE() function can take multiple filter parameters. It follows that it can also take multiple "unfilter" parameters, as it is doing here. The key is in the following part of the measure:

```
ALL(Stock[Make]), ALL(Colors[Color])
```

This piece of DAX is simply saying, "Don't apply any make or color filters when calculating." The consequence is that this measure now calculates the total sales whatever the make or color. This then becomes the basis for the percentage calculation, as you can see in Figure 16-16, where the results are filtered only to show sales in France.

Make	Color	SalePrice	MakeAndColorPercentage
Aston Martin	Blue	141250	5.60%
Aston Martin	British Racing Green	181250	7.18%
Aston Martin	Canary Yellow	284440	11.27%
Aston Martin	Green	108990	4.32%
Aston Martin	Night Blue	165600	6.56%
Aston Martin	Red	450300	17.84%
Aston Martin	Silver	155380	6.15%
Bentley	Blue	44000	1.74%
Bentley	British Racing Green	39500	1.56%
Bentley	Canary Yellow	110000	4.36%
Bentley	Dark Purple	44000	1.74%
Bentley	Red	110000	4.36%
Bentley	Silver	46750	1.85%
Jaguar	Black	84500	3.35%
Jaguar	Canary Yellow	88000	3.49%
Jaguar	Night Blue	39500	1.56%
Rolls Royce	Black	48250	1.91%
Rolls Royce	Blue	72000	2.85%
Rolls Royce	Canary Yellow	207250	8.21%
Rolls Royce	Night Blue	45800	1.81%
Triumph	Silver	28000	1.11%
TVR	Silver	29750	1.18%
Total		**2524510**	**100.00%**

Figure 16-16. *Using the ALL() function to calculate a percentage per attribute*

Admittedly, preparing highly specific measures like those that you have seen in the last few pages can take a few minutes. Clearly, these measures are tightly linked to the data that you are displaying in the visuals that use them. However, the ability to compose highly focused metrics like these is often key to using your dashboards to highlight the insights that you want to deliver.

Visual Totals

Users (meaning the target audience for your reports and dashboards) do not like anomalies or apparent contradictions. So, you have to be sure that the data they see is visually coherent. This is especially true when displaying tables and matrices with subtotals and grand totals.

One technique that can help you here is the ALLSELECTED() function. This only applies any filters that have been added (either at report-, page- or visualization-level, or as slicers or cross-filters from other visuals) *without* you having to specify the fields that you do not want to filter as you did in the previous examples.

SalesPercentage is a measure that uses the ALLSELECTED() function as the filter for the CALCULATE() function that returns the total much like you did earlier.

```
SalesPercentage := DIVIDE(SUM(InvoiceLines[SalePrice]), CALCULATE(SUM(InvoiceLines[SalePri
ce]), ALLSELECTED()))
```

If you look at Figure 16-17, you see that the subtotals for the sales percentage (and indeed the grand total) are accurate, despite that the country (Spain) is selected in a slicer and the creditworthiness in a filter.

Make	Color	SalePrice	SalesPercentage
Bentley	Canary Yellow	46750	22.50%
	Total	**46750**	**22.50%**
Jaguar	Green	39500	19.01%
	Red	29750	14.32%
	Total	**69250**	**33.33%**
Triumph	Canary Yellow	47750	22.98%
	Total	**47750**	**22.98%**
TVR	Blue	44000	21.18%
	Total	**44000**	**21.18%**
Total		**207750**	**100.00%**

Figure 16-17. Using the ALLEXCEPT() function to calculate a percentage per attribute per group

The ALLSELECTED() function says to DAX "don't filter on any filters applied by the user, whatever the technique used to apply them." This can make creating percentage totals much easier, as this function removes the need to create highly specific measures that are tied to specific types of calculation.

The ALLEXCEPT() Function

In practice, you could find yourself having to write extremely targeted measures that need to remove filters from all the elements in a calculation except one or two. So, to save you writing long lists of ALL() functions, you can say "All but" a field using the ALLEXCEPT() function.

As an example of this (although it is extremely simple), suppose you want to see the percentages of sales grouped by a subclassification. You know that you want to have Make as the main grouping element, but then you might want to use Color, Client, or even Model as the subgroup. So to save you from having to write a measure specifically for each of these combinations, you can write the following:

```
AllButMakePercentage := DIVIDE(SUM(InvoiceLines[SalePrice]), CALCULATE(SUM(InvoiceLines[Sale
Price]), ALLEXCEPT(Stock, Stock[Make])))
```

If you use this measure in a matrix where Make is the leftmost column, you can then add subgroups using any other field to get the kind of output that is shown in Figure 16-18, for France this time, creditworthy customers only.

Make	Color	SalePrice	AllButMakePercentage
Aston Martin	Blue	141250	9.50%
	British Racing Green	181250	12.19%
	Canary Yellow	284440	19.13%
	Green	108990	7.33%
	Night Blue	165600	11.13%
	Red	450300	30.28%
	Silver	155380	10.45%
	Total	**1487210**	**100.00%**
Bentley	Blue	44000	11.16%
	British Racing Green	39500	10.02%
	Canary Yellow	110000	27.90%
	Dark Purple	44000	11.16%
	Red	110000	27.90%
	Silver	46750	11.86%
	Total	**394250**	**100.00%**
Jaguar	Black	84500	39.86%
	Canary Yellow	88000	41.51%
	Night Blue	39500	18.63%
	Total	**212000**	**100.00%**
Rolls Royce	Black	48250	12.93%
	Blue	72000	19.29%
	Canary Yellow	207250	55.52%
	Night Blue	45800	12.27%
	Total	**373300**	**100.00%**
Triumph	Silver	28000	100.00%
	Total	**28000**	**100.00%**
TVR	Silver	29750	100.00%
	Total	**29750**	**100.00%**
Total		**2524510**	**100.00%**

Figure 16-18. *Using the ALLEXCEPT() function to calculate a percentage per attribute per group*

In this example, other filters (color here) are applied, but not make. So, you are displaying the percentage for each color compared to the aggregate total for the make.

> ■ **Note**   ALLEXCEPT() does what it says and removes all filters except the one you specify. This can have the effect of preventing other filters from working as you expect.

Filtering on Measures

The CALCULATE() function is without a doubt one of the most powerful functions that you will use in DAX. However, there are a few things that it cannot do. One of these is to filter data by comparing to a *measure* rather than to a column. If you cast your mind back to the examples where CALCULATE() was applied, you will remember that a data column or a calculated column was used every time that a comparison (text-based or numeric) was invoked. Indeed, if you try to use CALCULATE() with a measure rather than a column, you will get an error.

Fortunately, DAX has a solution to this conundrum, which is to use the FILTER() function. You may well wonder what the differences are between FILTER() and CALCULATE(). Well, at its simplest, FILTER() can use *measures* as part of a comparison, whereas CALCULATE() must use columns—or calculated columns. Also, FILTER() *must* use an iterator function (such as SUMX()) rather than a simple aggregation function to produce a correct result.

Let's see this in action. Suppose you want to isolate sales where the ratio of net margin is more than 50 percent. Fortunately, you have a measure—RatioNetMargin—that calculates the percentage. The following explains how you can use this measure in a filter so that you can display these lucrative sales:

1. Click the InvoiceLines tab and click inside the calculation area under the data.

2. Enter the name that you want to use (**HighNetMarginSales**) for this metric, followed by a colon and an equal sign (:=).

3. To the right of the equal sign, enter (or select) **CALCULATE(**.

4. Enter (or select) **SUM(**.

5. Select the InvoiceLines[SalePrice] field.

6. Add a right parenthesis. This will terminate the SUM() function.

7. Enter a comma. This tells the CALCULATE() function that you are about to add the filters.

8. Enter or select **FILTER(**.

9. Select the InvoiceLines[RatioNetMargin] field. This is the field to filter on.

10. Enter a comma. This tells the FILTER() function that you are about to enter the filter criteria.

11. Enter the greater than symbol: >.

12. Enter the figure **0.5**.

13. Add a right parenthesis. This will terminate the FILTER() function.

14. Add a right parenthesis. This will terminate the CALCULATE() function. The formula should now read as follows:

```
HighNetMarginSales := CALCULATE(SUM(InvoiceLines[SalePrice]),FILTER(InvoiceLines,
[RatioNetMargin]>0.5))
```

If you use this measure in a table of sales by make and model for Switzerland, you should see something like Figure 16-19.

Make	Model	SalePrice	HighNetMarginSales
Aston Martin	DB7	228000	111,500.00
	DB9	118570	37,690.00
	Vantage	196600	131,350.00
	Total	**543170**	**280,540.00**
Bentley	Azure	110000	110,000.00
	Continental	112750	112,750.00
	Total	**222750**	**222,750.00**
Jaguar	XJ12	152250	112,750.00
	XJ6	138500	
	XK	159500	120,000.00
	Total	**450250**	**232,750.00**
Rolls Royce	Camargue	192300	192,300.00
	Total	**192300**	**192,300.00**
TVR	Cerbera	32500	
	Total	**32500**	
Total		**1440970**	**928,340.00**

***Figure 16-19.** Applying a filter to a measure*

In this example, you filtered data on a measure (RatioNetMargin) rather than a column. Be aware, however, that the FILTER() function can be slow when applied to large data sets.

Displaying Rank

DAX can do so much when it comes to preparing metrics for BI delivery that it is hard to know exactly what you need and when. The final example in this short tour of DAX measures explains how to rank sales by make. I realize that you can do this just by sorting records, but should you need a clear and unequivocal indicator of ranking, then here is how it can be done:

1. Click the InvoiceLines tab and click a blank cell in the calculation area.

2. Enter the name you want to use (**SalesRankByMake**) for this metric, followed by a colon and an equal sign (:=).

3. To the right of the equal sign, enter (or select) **RANKX(**.

4. Enter (or select) **ALL(**.

5. Select the Stock[Make] field.

6. Add a right parenthesis. This will terminate the ALL() function.

7. Enter a comma. This tells the RANK() function that you are going to enter the calculation of how to order the data.

8. Enter or select **SUMX(**.

9. Enter or select **RELATEDTABLE(**.

10. Select the InvoiceLines table. This is the table where the data is to be sourced.

11. Add a right parenthesis. This will terminate the RELATEDTABLE() function.

12. Enter a comma. This tells the RELATEDTABLE() function that you are about to enter the field to use.

13. Enter or select [SalePrice].

14. Add a right parenthesis. This will terminate the SUMX() function.

15. Add a right parenthesis. This will terminate the RANKX() function. The formula should now read as follows:

```
SalesRankByMake := RANKX(ALL(Stock[Make]),SUMX(RELATEDTABLE(InvoiceLines), [SalePrice]))
```

If you apply this measure to a simple table that lists the makes sold (in 2014, for instance) and then sort by the SalesRankByMake field, you will see something like Figure 16-20.

Make	SalesRankByMake ▲
Aston Martin	1
Rolls Royce	2
Jaguar	3
Bentley	4
MGB	5
Triumph	6
TVR	7

Figure 16-20. Using the RANKX() function to classify data

As its name implies, RANKX() ranks the first field using the order returned by the descending output of the second field.

A Few Comments and Notes on Using Measures

Measures are an immense subject. The breadth and depth of the calculations that can be delivered using DAX are little short of astounding. Consequently, it is impossible in an introductory chapter on measures to do anything other than give you a taste of what can be done and provide a few useful starter functions for you to adapt to your own requirements.

As you move on with DAX, a few things might help you on your way. The first concerns the use of calculated columns. Sometimes they are such an easy solution that it is a shame not to create them. However, they are stored in the table and do take up space. This means more space on disk and more space in memory. This is particularly true for a table containing tens of millions of rows. Measures, on the other hand, are calculated only at run time, so they take up virtually no space. So, if you are considering creating many calculated columns, perhaps some of them could become measures instead.

Managing Measures

Once you have a collection of suitable measures, you will probably want to manage them coherently and have them evolve with your changing requirements. Fortunately, managing measures is extremely intuitive, as you will see. Indeed, deleting, copying, and pasting measures needs no explanation for an Excel user as each measure is, in effect, a cell in the calculation area.

There are nonetheless a couple of techniques that are useful. These include the following:

- Annotating measures

- Formatting measures

- Hiding measures

Measures are so powerful that you can soon end up with a considerable number of highly complex matrices in your Power Pivot model. Adding a description to each measure is not only good practice, it can make your life easier when you return to a workbook weeks or months after you developed it and need to remind yourself what the DAX that you wrote really means.

To add a description to a measure, follow these steps:

1. Right-click the measure that you want to annotate.

2. Select Description from the context menu. The Measure Description dialog will appear.

3. Enter a suitable description. The dialog will look something like Figure 16-21.

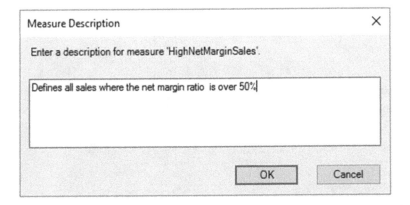

Figure 16-21. *Annotating a measure*

> 4. Click OK.

Formatting Measures

You have created a range of measures in this chapter. If you take a look at the measures in the InvoiceLines table, you can see that they are all presented as raw output. Unless you want to have the output formatted like this, it is usually a good idea to format each measure as you want to see it in any visualizations where you add it.

Measures are formatted in the same way that you formatted columns of data. Only here, inevitably, you click the measure (or measures) to format in the calculation area before selecting the required format. As I have described this technique previously, I will not repeat it here. As an Excel power user, you probably need little guidance at this point as the approach is similar to the one you use in Excel itself. You can even Ctrl+click and Shift+click to select contiguous or separate cells in the calculation area before applying a format.

Formatting Measures

As I mentioned earlier in this chapter, you can format measures so that the selected format will be applied in your Power View visualizations and pivot tables. Apart from using the formatting buttons in the Home ribbon, you can do the following:

> 1. Right-click the measure you want to format.
>
> 2. Select Format from the context menu. The Formatting dialog will appear, as shown in Figure 16-22.

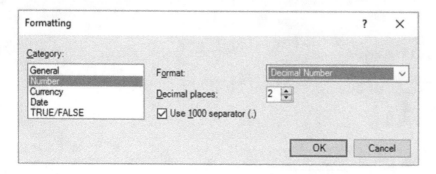

Figure 16-22. *The formatting dialog for measures*

3. Select the appropriate formatting options.

4. Click OK.

After a few minutes formatting, the measures that you have created could look like those in Figure 16-23.

InvoiceLines table measures

RatioNetMargin: 38.13%	Creditworthy DealerSales: 15,469,850.00	SalesRankByMake: 1
Cost Plus Spares Margin: 10,830,265.00	Creditworthy DealerSales Percent: 65.03%	
DealerSales: 23,787,230.00	MakePercentage: 100.00%	
LowPriceSales: 10,907,190.00	MakeAndColorPercentage: 100.00%	
HighNetMarginSales: 13,954,480.00	SalesPercentage: 100.00%	
	AllButMakePercentage: 100.00%	

Stock table measures

NumberOfCarsSold: 461
TotalSales: 20,510,095.00
Average Parts Cost Ratio: 8211.18%

Figure 16-23. *Formatted measures*

Hiding Measures

Some measures may exist only to be "staging" or "intermediate" measures that feed into other measures (possibly to simplify an otherwise overly complex calculation). It follows that you probably do not want these measures to encumber the list of measures that end users can see. To do this, follow these steps:

1. Right-click the measure that you want to hide from end users.

2. Select Hide From Client Tools from the context menu.

Calculation Options

I imagine that you have not had to worry about recalculating Power Pivot workbooks if you have been using relatively small data sets like the sample data for this book. If you are using vast amounts of data (after all, this is what Power Pivot was designed for), however, then recalculation could become a subject that you need to master.

By default, Power Pivot recalculates all calculated columns and measures when there is a change in the data set. These are the main operations that can trigger a recalculation:

- The data from an external data source (of any kind) has been updated.

- The data from an external data source has been filtered.

- You have changed the name of a table or column.

- You have added, modified, or deleted relationships between tables.

- You have altered any formula for a calculated column or a measure.

- You have added new calculated columns or measures.

More generally, if you want to be sure that your data is up-to-date, you should probably update the data. You can do this by clicking the Refresh button in the Home ribbon.

Conclusion

In this chapter, you took a first look at one of the most powerful features in DAX: measures. These let you develop custom calculations for the Power Pivot data model. You then use these metrics in your visuals to deliver specific insights based on your data.

First, you saw how to apply iterator functions so that you can apply a calculation to a set of rows and return an aggregation, be it a sum, average, or any other available aggregate function. Then you saw how to apply specific filters to your calculations. Finally, you saw how to prevent filters from being applied so that you can display percentages and calculate advanced ratios.

This chapter was only a brief introduction to measures in DAX. Yet I hope that it has whetted your appetite and that you can now develop the analyses and metrics that you need for your own data.

It is time to move on to having some real fun with Power Pivot and DAX: analyzing data over time. This is the subject of the next chapter.

CHAPTER 17

▨ ▨ ▨

Analyzing Data over Time with DAX

Most data analysis—and nearly all business intelligence—involves looking at how metrics evolve over time. You may need to aggregate sales by month, week, or year, for instance. Perhaps you want to compare figures for a previous month, quarter, or year with the figures for a current period. Whatever the exact requirement, handling time (by which I nearly always mean dates) is essential in Power Pivot.

Initially, using time functions in Power Pivot may be limited only to extracting time intervals from the available data and grouping results by units of time, such as days, weeks, months, quarters, and years. As you will find out in the first part of this chapter, DAX makes this kind of analysis really simple.

However, Power Pivot can also add what is called *time intelligence* to data models. This massively useful capability can take your analysis to a fundamentally higher level. This approach involves adding a separate table (called a *date* or *time dimension*) to the data model and then adding DAX functions that enable you to see how data evolves over time. Consequently, this chapter also includes an introduction to time intelligence using a wide range of DAX formulas that are available to help you create time-based calculations quickly and easily.

In this chapter, we will continue to develop the file that you extended in the two previous chapters. Should you need it, a complete version of this file is available on the Apress web site, including the extensions added in the previous chapter, as `DataModelForMetricsAndTime.pbix`.

Simple Date Calculations

Data analysis often involves looking at how key metrics evolve over time. Power Pivot can help you group and isolate date and time elements in your data. Since dates (and time) are often a continuous stream of dates in a data set, it can be useful to isolate the years, months, weeks, and days in a table alongside the date that a row contains so that you can create tables or visuals that group and aggregate records into these more comprehensible "buckets." You can then display and compare data over years and months, for instance, to tease out the real insights that your raw data contains.

For the first example of how DAX can help you to categorize records using date-based criteria, let's imagine that you envisage creating a couple of charts. First, you need one that lets you track sales over the years that Brilliant British Cars has traded. Then you want a second graphic that looks at sales for each month over the years. Unfortunately (for the moment at least), your data model does not contain columns that show the year or the month of a sale, and Power Pivot does not let you create metrics as part of a visualization. You need to have the metric available in the data model if you plan to use it in a dashboard element. Moreover, as you saw in Chapters 2 through 8, it is best if you have all the metrics in place before you create any visualizations. Indeed, this is precisely the reason you are learning how to extend the data model with new columns using DAX. The following explains how to create these two new columns in the Invoices table:

1. Select the Invoices table in the field list.

2. Click in the empty column at the right of the data.

© Adam Aspin 2016
A. Aspin, *High Impact Data Visualization in Excel with Power View, 3D Maps, Get & Transform and Power BI*,
DOI 10.1007/978-1-4842-2400-7_17

3. Enter an equal sign.

4. Enter (or start typing) and then select **YEAR(**.

5. Enter a left square bracket: **[**.

6. Select the InvoiceDate field.

7. Add a final right parenthesis to complete the YEAR() function.

8. Confirm the formula by pressing Enter or clicking the check mark in the formula bar. The new column will display the year of each sale.

9. Rename the column **Sale Year**.

10. Repeat steps 2 through 9 to use only the DAX formula MONTH() instead of YEAR() and name the new column **Sale Month**.

The formula for the two new columns is as follows:

```
= MONTH([InvoiceDate])
= YEAR([InvoiceDate])
```

Figure 17-1 shows what the Invoices table looks like with these two new columns added.

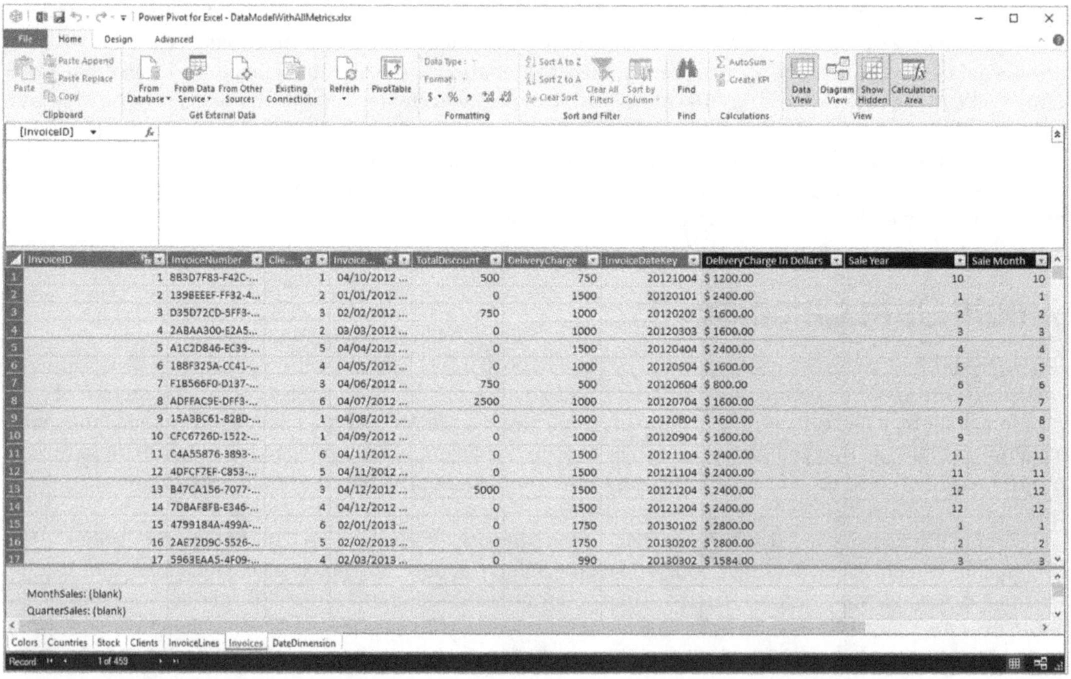

Figure 17-1. *The YEAR() and MONTH() DAX functions*

■ **Note**   To extract part of a date like this, the column that you are using for the original data must be of the date data type or be capable of being interpreted as a date by Power Pivot.

This example illustrated two of the DAX date and time functions. Inevitably, there are many other functions that you can apply to extract a date or time element from a date field. Since they all follow the same principles as those that you have just seen (with the exception of the NOW() and TODAY() functions that are explained in a couple of pages), it is easier to list them in Table 17-1 rather than provide a set of nearly identical examples.

Table 17-1. *DAX Date and Time Functions*

Function	Description	Example
YEAR()	Extracts the year element from a date.	YEAR([InvoiceDate])
MONTH()	Extracts the month number from a date.	MONTH([InvoiceDate])
DAY()	Extracts the day number from a date.	DAY([InvoiceDate])
WEEKDAY()	Extracts the weekday from a date. Sunday is 1, Monday is 2, and so forth.	WEEKDAY([InvoiceDate])
WEEKNUM()	Extracts the number of the week in the year from a date.	WEEKNUM([InvoiceDate])
HOUR()	Extracts the hour from a time or datetime column.	HOUR([InvoiceDate])
MINUTE()	Extracts the minutes from a time or datetime column.	MINUTE([InvoiceDate])
SECOND()	Extracts the seconds from a time or datetime column.	SECOND([InvoiceDate])
EOMONTH()	Returns the last day of the month from a date.	EOMONTH([InvoiceDate])
NOW()	Returns the current date and time.	NOW()
TODAY()	Returns the current date.	TODAY()
DATE()	Lets you enter a date as year, month and day.	DATE(2015, 07, 25)
TIME()	Lets you enter a time as hours and minutes.	TIME(19, 57)
DATEDIFF()	Calculates the difference between two dates and/or times expressed as a number of specified periods.	DATEDIFF([InvoiceDate], DATE(2025, 07, 25), YEAR)
STARTOFMONTH()	Selects the first day of the month for a date.	STARTOFMONTH(Invoices[SaleDate])
STARTOFQUARTER()	Selects the first day of the quarter for a date.	STARTOFQUARTER(Invoices[SaleDate])
STARTOFYEAR()	Selects the first day of the year for a date.	STARTOFYEAR(Invoices[SaleDate])
ENDOFMONTH()	Selects the last day of the month for a date.	ENDOFMONTH(Invoices[SaleDate])
ENDOFQUARTER()	Selects the last day of the quarter for a date.	ENDOFQUARTER(Invoices[SaleDate])
ENDOFYEAR()	Selects the last day of the year for a date.	ENDOFYEAR(Invoices[SaleDate])

■ **Note** If you define a field as having a date or datetime data type, then Power Pivot always creates a hierarchy of Year ➤ Quarter ➤ Month ➤ Day in the visual that you are creating. This can become annoying when all you need is the day. So, it is well worth creating a well-structured date dimension table, as described later in this chapter, so that you use only the exact date element that you want, rather than have Power Pivot make assumptions for you.

Date and Time Formatting

When dealing with dates and times in Power Pivot, you may not need to go to the lengths of extracting a part of a date field but may simply need to display a date in a different way. Rather like Excel, DAX can help you to do this quickly and easily.

Suppose you want to have the InvoiceDate field displayed in a specific date format for use in certain visualizations. The following steps explain how you can do this:

1. Select the Invoices table in the field list.

2. Click in the empty column at the right of the data.

3. In the formula bar, enter an equal sign.

4. Enter (or start typing and then select) **FORMAT(**.

5. Enter a left square bracket: **[**.

6. Select the InvoiceDate field.

7. Add a comma.

8. Enter the format code **"D-MMM-YYYY"** (include the double quotes).

9. Add a final right parenthesis to complete the FORMAT() function. The formula bar will display the following code:

   ```
   = FORMAT([InvoiceDate], "D-MMM-YYYY")
   ```

10. Rename the column **UKDate**.

11. Confirm the formula by pressing Enter or clicking the check mark in the formula bar. The new column will display the sale date in a different format.

    If you look at Figure 17-2, you see what the newly formatted invoice data field looks like in the new column.

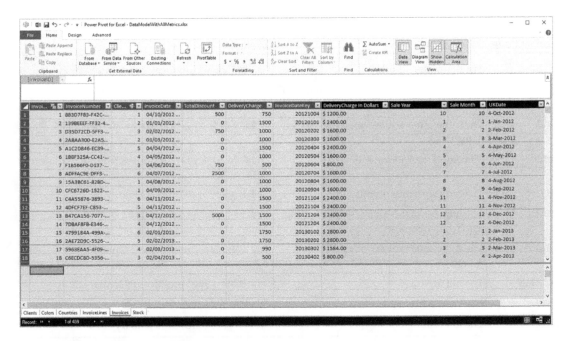

Figure 17-2. Applying the FORMAT() function

■ **Note**   To reformat a date like this, the column that you are using for the original data must either be of the date data type or be capable of being interpreted as a date by Power Pivot.

The date format that you applied in this example was not predefined by DAX in any way. In fact, it was assembled from a set of available day, month, and year codes that you can combine to create the date format you want. Table 17-2 explains the codes that are available.

Table 17-2. *Custom Date Formats*

Format Code	Description	Example
d	The day of the month	"d MMM yyyy" produces 2 Jan 2016
dd	The day of the month with a leading zero when necessary	"dd MMM yyyy" produces 02 Jan 2016
ddd	The three-letter abbreviation for the day of the week	"ddd d MMM yyyy" produces Sat 2 Jan 2016
dddd	The day of the week in full	"ddd dd MMM yyyy" produces Saturday 02 Jan 2016
M	The number of the month	"dd M yyyy" produces 02 1 2016
MM	The number of the month with a leading zero when necessary	"dd MM yyyy" produces 02 01 2016
MMM	The three-letter abbreviation for the month	"dd MMM yyyy" produces 02 Jan 2016
MMMM	The full month	"dd MMMM yyyy" produces 02 January 2016
yy	The year as two digits	"d MMM yy" produces 2 Jan 16
yyyy	The full year	"MMMM yyyy" produces January 2016

If you do not want to build your own date formats, then you can choose from the four predefined date and time formats that Power Pivot has available. These are explained in Table 17-3.

Table 17-3. *Predefined Date Formats*

Format Code	Description	Example	Comments
Short Date	The short date as defined in the PC's settings	FORMAT([InvoiceDate], "Short Date")	Formats the date using figures only
Long Date	The long date as defined in the PC's settings	FORMAT([InvoiceDate], "Long Date")	Formats the date with the month as a text and the day of the week
Long time	The long time as defined in the PC's settings	FORMAT([InvoiceDate], "Long Time")	Formats the datetime or time column with the hour and minutes of the day
Short time	The short time as defined in the PC's settings	FORMAT([InvoiceDate], "Long Date")	Formats the datetime or time column with the hour and minutes and seconds of the day

■ **Note** The FORMAT() function converts a field to a text, so you need to be aware that this has the potential to restrict its use if further calculations are applied to the result produced by this formula. In my opinion, it is essentially useful when applied to modify the way that dates are displayed.

Calculating the Age of Cars Sold

To continue with elementary DAX formulas—and as an admittedly extremely simple example—I will presume that you need to calculate the age of every car sold relative to the current date. As the source data contains the registration date for each vehicle, this will not be difficult. So, you have to do the following:

1. With the Stock table selected, click inside the new column at the right of the data.

2. Type =**(NOW()**. Make sure you add the left and right parentheses even if these remain empty.

3. Enter a minus sign.

4. Click inside the column PurchaseDate.

5. Enter a right parenthesis. This corresponds to the left parenthesis before the NOW() function.

6. Enter a forward slash (the division symbol).

7. Enter **365**.

8. The formula should look like this:

```
=(NOW()-[PurchaseDate])/365
```

9. Press Enter or select the check box in the formula bar.

10. Format the column as a whole number.

11. The formula will be added to the entire new column.

12. Rename the column **VehicleAgeInYears**. Figure 17-3 shows you a small sample of the result of this operation.

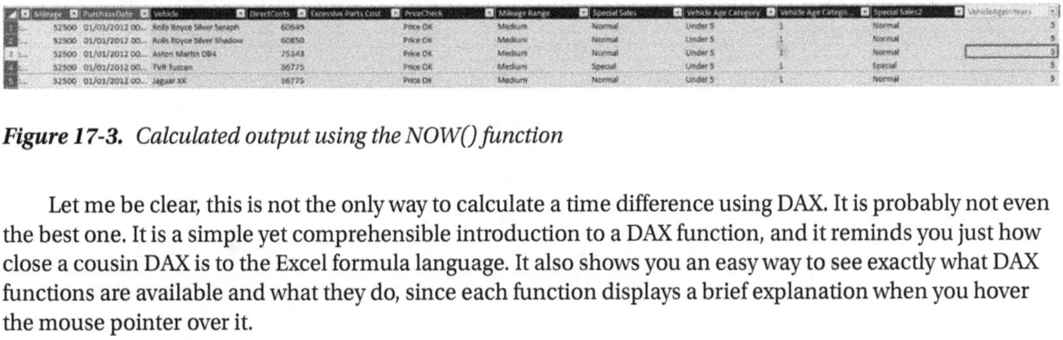

***Figure 17-3.** Calculated output using the NOW() function*

Let me be clear, this is not the only way to calculate a time difference using DAX. It is probably not even the best one. It is a simple yet comprehensible introduction to a DAX function, and it reminds you just how close a cousin DAX is to the Excel formula language. It also shows you an easy way to see exactly what DAX functions are available and what they do, since each function displays a brief explanation when you hover the mouse pointer over it.

Calculating the Difference Between Two Dates

As you would probably expect, DAX can do more than just specify a number of days. As befits a formula language that is designed to aid in business analysis, it can deduce the time between two dates expressed as the following:

- Years
- Months

- Weeks

- Days

- Hours

- Minutes

- Seconds

This can be extremely useful when you want to classify records according to a duration and can be calculated using the DATEDIFF() function. The DATEDIFF() function expects you to apply three parameters when calculating an interval.

- The start date for the calculation of the interval.

- The end date up until when the interval will be calculated.

- The interval to calculate. This could be in years, days, or minutes, for example.

As an example, imagine that you want to display the number of weeks that each vehicle remained in stock, as this will help you to determine the fastest-selling models and consequently optimize the company's cash flow. As the data contains both the purchase date for each vehicle as well as its sale date (even if the two are in different tables), this can be done using the DAX DATEDIFF() function.

1. In the DataModelForMetricsAndTime.xlsx file, click the Data View icon and then click the Stock table in the field list.

2. Click inside the empty column at the right of any existing columns.

3. Enter =**DATEDIFF(**. You will see that as you enter the first few characters, the list of functions will list all available functions beginning with these characters. You can click the function name to have it appear in the formula bar.

4. Press the [key. The list of available fields from the current table will appear.

5. Select the [Registration_Date] field.

6. Enter a comma.

7. Select the [PurchaseDate] field.

8. Enter a comma. A pop-up list of available intervals will appear.

9. Select WEEK.

10. Add a final right parenthesis. The formula will look like this:

    ```
    =DATEDIFF([Registration_Date],[PurchaseDate],WEEK)
    ```

11. Press Enter or select the check box in the formula bar. The formula will be added to the entire new column. You can now rename it **Weeks To Purchase**. Figure 17-4 shows you a small sample of the result of this operation.

Vehicle Age Category	Vehicle Age Catego...	VehicleAgeInYears	Weeks To Purchase
Under 5	1	5	679
Under 5	1	5	1408
Under 5	1	5	278
Under 5	1	5	276
Under 5	1	5	243
Under 5	1	5	276
Under 5	1	5	243
Under 5	1	5	276
Under 5	1	5	276
Under 5	1	5	276
Under 5	1	5	243
Under 5	1	5	276

Figure 17-4. The results of a DATEDIFF() function

You can now see the number of weeks that each vehicle was in stock before being sold and use this figure in Power View dashboards or Excel pivot tables. Only *complete* intervals are displayed. In other words, if you have selected YEAR as the interval, then the difference between the two dates must be fractionally more than one year for the function to return 1. Notice that you used the RELATED() function again to compare elements from separate tables. Once again, Power Pivot listed only the tables that were correctly linked to the destination table when you applied this function.

■ **Note** When you use the DATEDIFF() function, you must always add the lower date (the Purchase date in this example) as the first date that the function uses. If you do not, you will get an error message.

As you saw in the pop-up in step 10, the DATEDIFF() function lets you choose from a range of available intervals. These are explained in Table 17-4.

Table 17-4. Date Difference Intervals

Function	Description
YEAR	Returns the time difference in complete years
QUARTER	Returns the time difference in complete quarters
MONTH	Returns the time difference in complete months
WEEK	Returns the time difference in complete weeks
DAY	Returns the time difference in complete days
HOUR	Returns the time difference in complete hours
MINUTE	Returns the time difference in complete minutes
SECOND	Returns the time difference in complete seconds

■ **Note**   DAX cannot currently handle negative date differences, so you need to ensure that your data has been correctly prepared in Power Pivot Query *before* you calculate date and time differences.

Adding Time Intelligence to a Data Model

I want now to explain the vital set of functions that concern time or, rather, the dates used in analyzing data. Power Pivot calls this time intelligence (even though it nearly always refers to the use of date ranges). Applying this kind of temporal analysis can be a fundamental aspect of data presentation in business intelligence. After all, what enterprise does not need to know how this year's figures compare to last year's and what kind of progress is being made?

Time intelligence always requires a valid date table, which is one of the reasons why you will now spend a certain amount of time creating this core pillar of a successful data model. Then the date table has to be joined to the table containing the data you want to compare over time on a date field. The good news is that once you have a valid date table and have acquainted yourself with a handful of data and time functions in DAX, you can deliver some extremely impressive results. These kinds of calculations can cover (among other things) the following:

- YearToDate, QuarterToDate, and MonthToDate calculations

- Comparisons with previous years, quarters, or months

- Rolling aggregations over a period of time, such as the sum for the last three months

- Comparison with a parallel period in time, such as the same month in the previous year

An introduction to time intelligence in Power Pivot gives you a taste of some of the DAX functions that you are likely to use when analyzing data over time. To begin with, you will learn how to create a date table. Then you look at some of the different types of calculations that you can create to analyze data over time.

Creating and Applying a Date Table

For time intelligence to work, you need a table that contains an *uninterrupted* range of dates that begins at least at the *earliest* date in your data and that ends with a date at least equal to the *final* date in your data. In practice, this will nearly always mean creating a date table that begins on January 1 of the earliest date in your data and that ends on December 31 of the last year for which you have data. Once you have your date table, you can join it to one of the tables in your data model and then begin to exploit all the time-related analytical functions of Power Pivot.

The good news is that you can use Power Pivot itself to create a date table. It is also possible to import a contiguous range of dates from other applications such as Excel.

Creating a Date Table in Excel

One way of creating a date table is to use your Excel skills to create a large list of dates that encompasses all the dates for sales, or whatever you are analyzing. This date table can then contain other columns that in turn contain information about each date record. These other columns could, for instance, contain the following:

- Which **Year** the date is
- Which **Quarter** the date is
- What the **Weekday** is
- What the **Month** is

These four examples are only an extremely superficial subset of all the columns that you will probably need in a data table. A good data table will contain every date-based element that you are likely to need in every visualization that you will create using the data model. So, you need to foresee every combination of year, day, month, quarter, and possibly week that you are likely to want in every table and chart you will create.

You can then use these complementary columns in visualizations to display the year, quarter, or month (and so on) and to display them exactly as you have prepared them in the date table. So, what you are doing is avoiding the need to format and subset dates in a visualization by preparing the elements that you will use in Power View. Then, once you have such a table, you can link it to the date field in your core data, which will be the basis for time analysis.

So, where are you going to get such a table? Well, if you already have such a table in your source data (and corporate data warehouses nearly always contain date tables), then you no longer have a problem. However, if this is not the case, there is nothing to worry about. In Power Pivot there is an easy solution for creating a date table. You simply create the table in an Excel worksheet and then import it using the techniques I described in the previous chapter.

However, when preparing a date table, the last thing you want to do is enter the month, the quarter, and the day of the week for several hundred rows manually. Table 17-5 contains some selected Excel formulas that will help you create a fairly standard date table easily. Each date element will be a separate column in an Excel table. This table is not meant to be exhaustive, but you can always use this as a starting point and develop it further to correspond more exactly to your requirements. Remember to start with the earliest date that you will be using for all time-based analysis in the table that contains your metrics; then drag the row down in Excel to create as many rows as there are days in the date range that ends at the end of the year corresponding to the last date in your metrics. After you have done this, add the formulas that return the data elements to the first row of the table and copy this row down until you reach the bottom of the date column.

Table 17-5. *Preparing a Date Table*

Column	Formula	Description
DateKey		The unique date.
Year	=YEAR(A2)	The year element.
MonthNum	=MONTH(A2)	The month of the year, as a number. This can be useful for sorting dates.
MonthFull	=TEXT(A2,"mmmm")	The full name of the month.
MonthAbbr	=TEXT(A2,"mmm")	The abbreviated name of the month.
QuarterNum	=ROUNDUP(MONTH(A2)/3,0)	The quarter of the year, as a number. This can be useful for sorting dates.
QuarterFull	="Quarter " & ROUNDUP(MONTH(A2)/3,0)	The full name of the quarter.
QuarterAbbr	="Qtr " & ROUNDUP(MONTH(A2)/3,0)	The abbreviated name of the quarter.
YearAndQuarterNum	=YEAR(A2) & ROUNDUP(MONTH(A2)/3,0)	The year and the quarter in digits. This can be useful for sorting dates.
MonthAndYearAbbr	=TEXT(A2,"mmm") & " " & YEAR(A2)	The abbreviated month of the year and the year.
QuarterAndYearAbbr	=TEXT(A2,"mmm") & "-" & RIGHT(YEAR(A2),2)	The quarter of the year in short form and the year.
MonthAndYear	=TEXT(A2,"mmmm")& " " & YEAR(A2)	The abbreviated month and the year in two digits.
MonthName	=TEXT(A2,"mmmm")	The full name of the month.
MonthNameAbbr	=TEXT(A2,"mmm")	The short name of the month.
QuarterAndYear	="Quarter " & ROUNDUP(MONTH(A2)/3,0) & " " & YEAR(A2)	The quarter and the year fully laid out.

Once you have created a date table, it could look something like Figure 17-5.

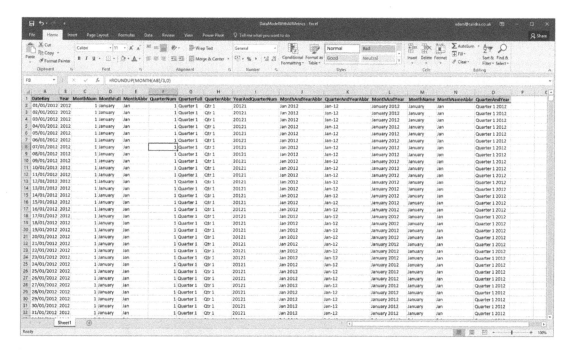

Figure 17-5. *A date table in Excel*

A small date table is in the sample files that you can find on the Apress web site. Once the table is finished, you can then import it into Power Pivot. I will not repeat here how to import a table from Excel; please refer to Chapter 10. Anyway, once you have imported the date table into Excel, you still have a couple of things to do, and then your date dimension will be ready to add time intelligence to your Power Pivot data set.

Marking a Table as a Date Table

Power Pivot now needs to know that the table you have imported is, in fact, a date table that it can use to add time intelligence. This is easier to do than to talk about.

1. Click the DateTable tab (in data view) or the table itself (in display view).

2. In the Design tab, click the Mark As Date Table button.

3. Switch to the data view.

4. Click the tab for the DateTable.

5. Select the column that contains the contiguous list of dates. In the example used in this book, it is the DateKey column.

6. To make sure everything has gone well, click the lower part of the Mark As Date Table button (the small downward-facing triangle) and select Date Table Settings from the pop-up menu. The Mark As Date Table dialog will appear.

7. The selected (date key) column should appear in the Date pop-up. If this is not the case, select it from the pop-up. The Mark As Date Table dialog should look like the one in Figure 17-6.

Figure 17-6. *The Mark As Date Table dialog*

    8.   Click OK.

Now Power Pivot knows that this table is slightly special and that it contains only a list of dates that can be used to add time intelligence to your analyses. The final thing to do is define a relationship between the DateKey column in the date table and a date field in the table that contains the data you want to analyze over time. In the sample data you are using, this will be the InvoiceDate field in the SalesDate table. This way the data set knows that you may be looking at sales by invoice date but that the DateTable will provide the list of days, months, quarters, and years used to display metrics over time.

Creating the Date Table in Power Pivot

Another way to create a date table is to do everything in Power Pivot. This lets you use and extend your newly acquired DAX skills.

    1.   In data view, activate the Design ribbon and click the Date Table button.

    2.   Select New from the Date Table menu. DAX analyses every date column in the current data tables and creates a new table named Calendar that creates a record for every date from the earliest to the latest in the entire data.

    3.   Rename the table **DateDimension**.

    4.   Click the Date Table button and select Update Range from the Date Table menu.

    5.   Enter **1/1/2012** as the starting date for a table of dates. I am assuming here that your computer is configured for the UK or European date format. If this is not the case, then enter the date as you would normally using your local date format.

    6.   Enter **31/12/2017** (or the equivalent date format that represents December 31, 2017, in your local date format). This is the end date for a table of dates.

7. Click OK. Power Pivot will create a table containing a single column of dates from January 1, 2012, until December 31, 2016.

8. In the field list, right-click the Date field in the DateDimension table and select Rename. Rename the Date field to **DateKey**. The date table will look like Figure 17-7.

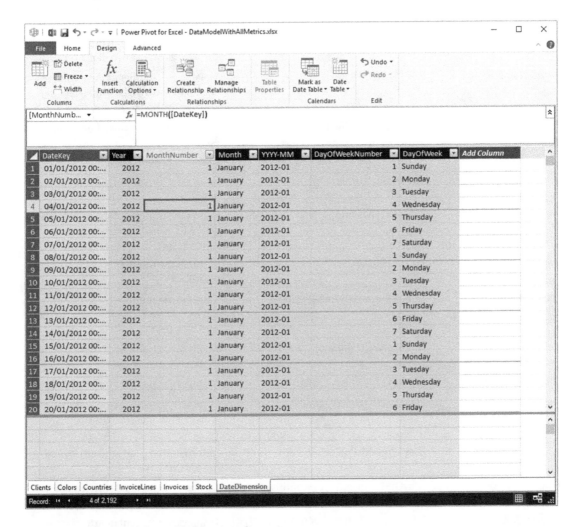

Figure 17-7. *An initial date table for a time dimension*

9. Delete the columns Year through DayOfWeek, leaving only the DateKey columns.

10. Add 20 new columns containing the formulas explained in Table 17-6. Because Chapter 15 provided an exhaustive explanation covering the techniques that you need to apply when you want to add new columns, I will not repeat the process in detail here.

Table 17-6. *DAX Formulas to Extend a Date Table*

Column Title	Formula	Comments
FullYear	YEAR([DateKey])	Isolates the year as a four-digit number.
ShortYear	VALUE(Right(Year([DateKey]),2))	Isolates the year as a two-digit number.
MonthNumber	MONTH([DateKey])	Isolates the number of the month in the year as one or two digits.
MonthNumberFull	FORMAT([DateKey], "MM")	Isolates the number of the month in the year as two digits, with a leading zero for the first nine months.
MonthFull	FORMAT([DateKey], "MMMM")	Displays the full name of the month.
MonthAbbr	FORMAT([DateKey], "MMM")	Displays the name of the month as a three-letter abbreviation.
WeekNumber	WEEKNUM([DateKey])	Shows the number of the week in the year.
WeekNumberFull	FORMAT(Weeknum([DateKey]), "00")	Shows the number of the week in the year with a leading zero for the first nine weeks.
DayOfMonth	DAY([DateKey])	Displays the number of the day of the month.
DayOfMonthFull	FORMAT(Day([DateKey]),"00")	Displays the number of the day of the month with a leading zero for the first nine days.
DayOfWeek	WEEKDAY([DateKey])	Displays the number of the day of the week.
DayOfWeekFull	FORMAT([DateKey],"dddd")	Displays the name of the weekday.
DayOfWeekAbbr	FORMAT([DateKey],"ddd")	Displays the name of the weekday as a three-letter abbreviation.
ISODate	[FullYear] & [MonthNumberFull] & [DayOfMonthFull]	Displays the date in the ISO (internationally recognized) format of YYYYMMDD.
FullDate	[DayOfMonth] & " " & [MonthFull] & " " & [FullYear]	Displays the full date with spaces.
QuarterFull	"Quarter " & ROUNDDOWN(MONTH([DateKey])/4,0)+1	Displays the current quarter.
QuarterAbbr	"Qtr " &ROUNDDOWN(MONTH([DateKey])/4,0)+1	Displays the current quarter as a three-letter abbreviation plus the quarter number.
Quarter	"Q" &ROUNDDOWN(MONTH([DateKey])/4,0)+1	Displays the current quarter in short form.

(continued)

Table 17-6. (*continued*)

Column Title	Formula	Comments
QuarterNumber	ROUNDDOWN(MONTH([DateKey])/4,0)+1	Displays the number of the current quarter. This is essentially used as a sort by column.
QuarterAndYear	DateDimension[Quarter] & " " & DateDimension[FullYear]	Shows the quarter and the year.
MonthAndYearAbbr	DateDimension[MonthAbbr] & " " & [FullYear]	Shows the abbreviated month and year.
QuarterAndYearNumber	[FullYear] & [QuarterNumber]	Shows the year and quarter numbers. This is essentially used as a sort by column.
YearAndWeek	VALUE([FullYear] &[WeekNumberFull])	Indicates the year and week. The VALUE() function ensures that the figure is considered as numeric by Power Pivot.
YearAndMonthNumber	Value(DateDimension[FullYear] & DateDimension[MonthNumberFull])	A numeric value for the year and month.

The first few columns of the DateDimension table should now look like Figure 17-8.

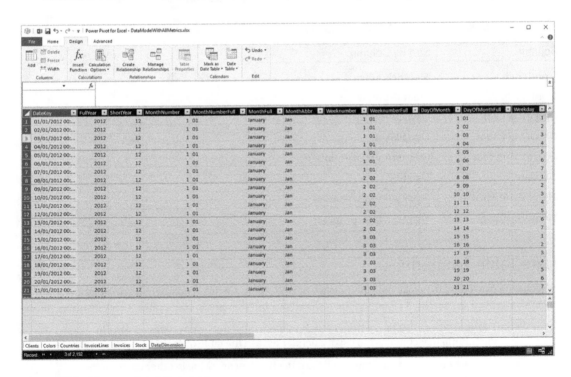

Figure 17-8. *The completed Date table*

The point behind creating all these ways of expressing dates and parts of dates is that you can now use them in your tables, charts, and gauges to aggregate and display data over time. Any record that has a date element can now be expressed visually—not just as the date itself, but shown as and aggregated as years, quarters, months, or weeks. The trick is to prepare all the time groupings that you are likely to need in the date table of your dashboards. However, you do not need to worry if you find yourself needing an extra column or two further down the line, because you can always add columns that contain other date elements.

Note   You do not have to override the date range suggested by Power Pivot when creating a date table in DAX. You might prefer to leave the date range that is suggested by Power Pivot.

Adding Sort By Columns to the Date Table

In Chapter 15, you saw how to sort a column using the data in another column to provide the sort order. This technique is essential when dealing with date tables, as you want to be sure that any visualizations that contain date elements appear in the right order. The classic example is months. As things stand, if you were to use the MonthFull or MonthAbbr column in a chart or table, then you would see the month names appearing on an axis or in a column in alphabetical order.

To avoid this, you have to add one final tweak to the date table and apply a Sort By column to certain date elements in other columns. Since you saw how this is done in Chapter 13, now I will only provide the list of columns that need this extra tweak, rather than reiterating all the details. Table 17-7 gives you the required information to extend the data table so that all date elements are sorted correctly.

Table 17-7. *The Sort By Columns Needed for the Date Table*

Column	Sort By Column
MonthFull	MonthNumber
MonthAbbr	MonthNumber
DayOfWeekFull	DayOfWeek
DayOfWeekAbbr	DayOfWeek
Quarter And Year	QuarterAndYearNumber
FullDate	DateKey
MonthAndYearAbbr	YearAndMonthNumber
MonthAndYear	YearAndMonthNumber

Date Table Techniques

When using date tables to invoke time intelligence in DAX, there are two fundamental principles that must always be applied. I realize that I mention them elsewhere, but they are so essential that they bear repetition.

- The date range must be *continuous*; that is, there must not be any dates missing in the column that contains the list of calendar days in the table of dates.

- The date range must encompass *all the dates* that you are using in other tables in the data model.

Creating a data table can be fun but nonetheless takes a few minutes. So, here's a tip that I can give you: create a Power Pivot file that contains nothing but a date dimension table (using a manually defined start date and end date, just as you saw at the beginning of this example) with all the other columns added. You can then make copies of this "template" file and use them as the basis for any new data models that you create. This can include replacing the fixed threshold dates with references to the data in tables, as mentioned previously.

Adding the Date Table to the Data Model

Now that you have a date table, you can integrate it with your data model so that you can start to apply some of the time intelligence that DAX makes possible.

1. Click the Relationships View icon to display the tables in the data model.

2. In the Home ribbon, click the Manage Relationships button. The Manage Relationships dialog will appear.

3. Click the New button. The Create Relationship dialog will appear.

4. At the top of the dialog, select the DateDimension table from the pop-up list.

5. Once the sample data from the DateDimension table is displayed, click inside the DateKey column to select it.

6. Under the DateDimension table sample data, select the Invoices table from the pop-up list.

7. Once the sample data from the Invoices table is displayed, click inside the InvoiceDate column to select it. The dialog will look like Figure 17-9.

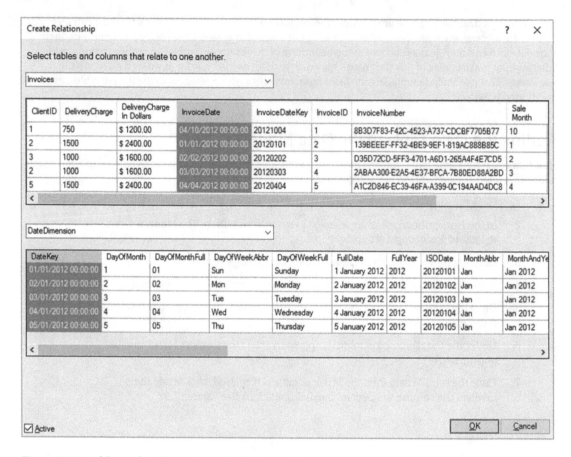

Figure 17-9. *Adding a date dimension to the data model*

8. Click OK. The relationship will appear in the Manage Relationships dialog.

9. Click Close. The DateDimension table will appear in the data model joined to the Invoices table.

■ **Note** For time intelligence in Power Pivot to work correctly, the fields used to join a date table and a data table must both be set to the *date* or *datetime* data type.

Applying Time Intelligence

Now that all the preparations have been completed, it is (finally) time to see just how DAX can make your life easier when it comes to calculating metrics over time. This is possible only because you have a date table in place and it is connected to the requisite date field in the table that contains the data you want to aggregate. However, with the foundations in place, you can now start to deliver some really interesting and persuasive output.

YearToDate, QuarterToDate, and MonthToDate Calculations

To begin, let's resolve a simple but frequent requirement: calculating month-to-date, quarter-to-date, and year-to-date sales figures.

The three functions that you will see in this example are extremely similar. Consequently, I will explain only the first one (a month-to-date calculation) and then will let you create the next two in a couple of copy, paste, and tweak operations.

1. In the data view, select the Invoices table and click in the calculation area.

2. In the formula bar, enter **MonthSales** and then a colon followed by an equal sign; then enter (or type and select) **TOTALMTD(**. This will apply the month-to-date aggregation for a field.

3. Enter (or type and select) **SUM(**. This specifies the actual aggregation you want to apply.

4. Select the InvoiceLines[SalePrice] field from the pop-up list of available fields.

5. Enter a right parenthesis to end the SUM() function.

6. Enter a comma.

7. Type the first few characters of the date table (DateDimension in this example) and select the date key field (**DateKey** in this example).

8. Enter a right parenthesis to end the TOTALMTD() function. The formula should read as follows:

```
MonthSales := TOTALMTD(SUM(InvoiceLines[SalePrice]),DateDimension[DateKey])
```

9. Press Enter or click the check mark to complete the measure definition.

In the calculation area, the result will be like the one in Figure 17-10. In other words, the calculation will return (blank). This is perfectly normal, as all time-intelligence-based metrics need a time element to return data. You will only see the results in your final output.

MonthSales: (blank)

Figure 17-10. *A first DAX time-intelligence function*

Now copy the formula that you just created and use it as the basis for two new measures. These will be quarterly sales to date and annual sales to date, as follows:

```
QuarterSales := TOTALQTD(SUM(InvoiceLines[SalePrice]),DateDimension[DateKey])
YearSales := TOTALYTD(SUM(InvoiceLines[SalePrice]),DateDimension[DateKey])
```

The three formulas that you have used are TOTALMTD() for the month-to-date aggregation, TOTALQTD() for the quarter-to-date aggregation, and TOTALYTD() for the year-to-date aggregation. All three functions take the following two parameters:

- *The aggregate function*: Depends on the actual metric that you want to deliver and the table and column that is aggregated. (SUM() was used here, although it could have been AVERAGE(), or COUNT(), or any other of the aggregate functions that you saw in Chapter 15.)

- *The key field of the date table*: Since the Invoices table is linked to the date table in the data model using the InvoiceDate field, DAX can apply the correct calculation if—and only if—you have added a date table to the data model and then specified the key field of the date table.

Since you have created these measures, I imagine that you would like to see them in action. Figure 17-11 shows the quarter-to-date and year-to-date sales (along with the aggregated sales from the initial SalePrice column in the InvoiceLines table) in a simple Power View table like the one you created in Chapter 2. This table is filtered to show the results for 2014 only.

MonthFull	SalePrice	QuarterSales	YearSales
January	555500	$555,500.00	$555,500.00
February	359500	$915,000.00	$915,000.00
March	372500	$1,287,500.00	$1,287,500.00
April	367500	$367,500.00	$1,655,000.00
May	529500	$897,000.00	$2,184,500.00
June	544500	$1,441,500.00	$2,729,000.00
July	565500	$565,500.00	$3,294,500.00
August	584500	$1,150,000.00	$3,879,000.00
September	606500	$1,756,500.00	$4,485,500.00
October	554940	$554,940.00	$5,040,440.00
November	657000	$1,211,940.00	$5,697,440.00
December	689000	$1,900,940.00	$6,386,440.00
Total	**6386440**	**$1,900,940.00**	**$6,386,440.00**

Figure 17-11. The quarter- and year-to-date functions in DAX

As you can see, you have each month's sales figures along with the cumulative sales for each quarter to date (and restarting each quarter). The final column shows you the yearly sales total for each month to date. Also, note that the months appear in calendar order because the MonthFull field has used the MonthNumber field as its Sort By column.

Conceptually, the three functions that are outlined—TOTALMTD(), TOTALQTD(), and TOTALYTD()—can be considered as CALCULATE() functions that have been extended to deliver a specific result for a time frame. You can always calculate aggregations for a period to date using the CALCULATE() function if you want. However, since this "shorthand" version is so practical and easy to use, I see no reason to try anything more complicated when there is no real need.

> **Note** In this example, I suggest starting the process of adding a new measure with the Invoices table selected, merely because this table seems a good place to store the metric. You can create the metric in virtually any table in practice—provided that you have a coherent data model to build on.

Analyze Data As a Ratio over Time

Looking at how data aggregates over time is only one of the ways that time intelligence can enable you to deliver time-based analysis. On occasion, you may well want to see how a day's sales relate to the total sales for a period. So, in this example, you will calculate the daily percentage of sales for Brilliant British Cars relative to the total sales for the year 2014.

1. In the data view, select the InvoiceLines table and click in the calculation area.

2. In the formula bar, enter **PercentOfYear** and then a colon followed by an equal sign; then enter (or type and select) **SUM(**.

3. Select the [SalePrice] field from the pop-up list of available fields.

4. Enter a forward slash to indicate division.

5. Enter (or type and select) **CALCULATE(SUM(**. This tells DAX that you want a filtered calculation and that the specific aggregation you want to apply is a SUM() function.

6. Select the [SalePrice] field from the pop-up list of available fields.

7. Enter a right parenthesis to end the SUM() function.

8. Enter a comma. This tells the calculate function that you have chosen the aggregation that you want and will now apply a filter.

9. Enter (or type and select) **DATESBETWEEN(**.

10. Start typing the name of the date table (**DateDimension**) and then select the DateKey field from the pop-up. This tells the DATESBETWEEN() function which field in the time dimension should be used as its first parameter.

11. Add a comma. This ends the first parameter for the DATESBETWEEN() function.

12. Enter (or type and select) **STARTOFYEAR(**.

13. Start typing the name of the date table (**DateDimension**) and then select the DateKey field from the pop-up. This will be the lower boundary of the time span that will be used to filter the CALCULATE() function.

14. Add a right parenthesis to close the STARTOFYEAR() function.

15. Add a comma. This ends the second parameter for the DATESBETWEEN() function.

16. Enter (or type and select) **ENDOFYEAR(**.

17. Once again, start typing the name of the date table (**DateDimension**) and then select the DateKey field from the pop-up. This will be the upper boundary of the time span that will be used to filter the CALCULATE() function.

18. Add a right parenthesis to close the ENDOFYEAR() function.

19. Add a comma. This ends the third and final parameter for the DATESBETWEEN() function.

20. Add three right parentheses. The first one ends the ENDOFYEAR() function, the second ends the DATESBETWEEN() function, and the final parenthesis closes the CALCULATE() function. The formula should look like this:

```
PercentOfYear := sum([SalePrice]) / CALCULATE(sum([SalePrice]),DATESBETWEEN(DateDimension[Da
teKey],STARTOFYEAR(DateDimension[DateKey]),ENDOFYEAR(DateDimension[DateKey])))
```

21. Press Enter or click the check mark to complete the measure definition.

22. In the Modeling ribbon, click the percentage icon to format this measure as a percentage.

This formula was a little more complex than those you have seen so far in this chapter. So, let me explain it in a bit more detail. At its heart, this formula consists of two main elements.

- The sales total for the time element that will be used in a visualization. This could be the day, week, month, or quarter, for instance.

- The total sales for the entire year that will be used in a visualization. This has to be calculated independently of the actual date element that will be displayed. Consequently, the CALCULATE() function is used to extend the aggregation—the SUM() in this case—to the whole year. This is done by setting a range of dates as the filter for the aggregation. The date range is set using the DATESBETWEEN() function. This requires a lower threshold (defined by the STARTOFYEAR() function) and a higher threshold (defined by the ENDOFYEAR() function). This way, the date range runs from the first to the last days of the year.

Finally, the calculation divides the specified time span's total by the total for the year; the percentage for that sales period is displayed.

So that you can see the outcome of your formula, you could create a Power View table that contains the following three fields:

- DateKey

- SalePrice

- PercentOfYear

You should see something like Figure 17-12 if you have applied a page-level filter to restrict the FullYear field to 2014, as described in the previous example.

DateKey	SalePrice	PercentOfYear
01 January 2014	555500	8.70%
01 February 2014	178000	2.79%
02 February 2014	181500	2.84%
01 March 2014	189000	2.96%
03 March 2014	183500	2.87%
01 April 2014	178000	2.79%
04 April 2014	189500	2.97%
01 May 2014	319000	4.99%
04 May 2014	210500	3.30%
01 June 2014	319000	4.99%
04 June 2014	225500	3.53%
01 July 2014	310000	4.85%
04 July 2014	255500	4.00%
01 August 2014	319000	4.99%
04 August 2014	265500	4.16%
01 September 2014	451000	7.06%
04 September 2014	155500	2.43%

Figure 17-12. *Displaying the sales per day as a percentage of the yearly sales*

You may be thinking that this was a lot of work just to get a percentage figure. Well, perhaps it is at first. Yet you can now capitalize on your effort and see how time intelligence is worth the effort. For instance, if you replace the DateKey field with the MonthFull field in the table shown in Figure 17-9, you instantly see the sales percentages for each month. The same applies if you replace MonthFull with Quarter. This is because you have created an extremely supple and fluid formula that can adapt to any time segment. The formula says to "Take the time segment (day, month, quarter, or year) and then find the date range for the whole year. Use this to calculate the total for the year and then divide the figure for the time span by this total to display the percentage."

Comparing a Metric with the Result from a Range of Dates

Let's push the time-based data analysis a little further and imagine that you need to look at how figures have evolved compared to a specific time interval in the past. By this I mean that you want to see how sales for the current month have fluctuated compared to, say, the previous month. The following formula shows you how to do just this. Once you understand the principles that this technique can be extended to, compare the data over many different time spans.

1. In the Data View, select the InvoiceLines table and click in the calculation area.

2. In the formula bar, enter **PercentOfPreviousMonth**, a colon followed by an equal sign, and then enter (or type and select) **SUM(**.

3. Type a left bracket and select the [SalePrice] field from the pop-up list of available fields.

4. Enter a right parenthesis to end the SUM( ) function.

5. Enter a forward slash to indicate division.

6. Enter (or type and select) **CALCULATE(SUM(**.

7. Select the [SalePrice] field from the pop-up list of available fields.

8. Enter a right parenthesis to end the SUM() function.

9. Enter a comma. This tells the calculate function that you have chosen the aggregation that you want; it will now apply a filter.

10. Enter (or type and select) **PREVIOUSMONTH(**.

11. Start typing the name of the date table (**DateDimension**) and then select the DateKey field from the pop-up. This tells the PREVIOUSMONTH() function the time dimension field that should be used as its parameter.

12. Enter a right parenthesis to end the PREVIOUSMONTH() function.

13. Enter a right parenthesis to end the CALCULATE() function. The formula should look like this:

```
PercentOfPreviousMonth := sum([SalePrice]) / calculate(sum([SalePrice]),PREVIOUSMONTH(DateD
imension[DateKey]))
```

14. Press Enter or click the check mark to complete the measure definition.

Figure 17-13 shows you the output that can be obtained by using the MonthFull field to give the month of a year (2014 in this example) alongside the PREVIOUSMONTH() function. To stress that time intelligence can adapt to different circumstances, you can also see the PERCENTOFYEAR function from the previous example—only it has automatically returned the percentage for the month this time.

MonthFull	SalePrice	PercentOfYear	PercentOfPreviousMonth
January	555500	8.70%	110.60%
February	359500	5.63%	64.72%
March	372500	5.83%	103.62%
April	367500	5.75%	98.66%
May	529500	8.29%	144.08%
June	544500	8.53%	102.83%
July	565500	8.85%	103.86%
August	584500	9.15%	103.36%
September	606500	9.50%	103.76%
October	554940	8.69%	91.50%
November	657000	10.29%	118.39%
December	689000	10.79%	104.87%
Total	**6386440**	**100.00%**	**1271.57%**

Figure 17-13. *Comparing values with a previous period of time*

Once again, the "magic" in the formula was the use of the CALCULATE() function. Yet again, this function required you to enter two elements.

- An aggregation to carry out (the sum of the Sale Price in this case).

- A filter to apply (the previous month in this example). Once again, the function uses the date key from the date table to apply the time intelligence.

With these two parameters in place, DAX was able to take the time element used in the visualization (the month) and say, "Give me the aggregation for the previous month."

As you can probably imagine, DAX does not limit you to comparing only month-by-month data. Indeed, it can help you compare data for a wide range of time spans. Now that you understand the basic principles, it is probably easiest to appreciate the related DAX functions as they are shown in Table 17-8.

Table 17-8. *DAX Date and Time Formulas to Return a Range of Dates*

Formula	Description	Example
PREVIOUSDAY()	Finds data for the previous day	CALCULATE(SUM(InvoiceLines[SalePrice]), PREVIOUSDay(DateDimension[DateKey]))
PREVIOUSMONTH()	Finds data for the previous month	CALCULATE(SUM(InvoiceLines[SalePrice]), PreviousMonth(DateDimension[DateKey]))
PREVIOUSQUARTER()	Finds data for the previous quarter	CALCULATE(SUM(InvoiceLines[SalePrice]), PreviousQuarter(DateDimension[DateKey]))
PREVIOUSYEAR()	Finds data for the previous year	CALCULATE(SUM(InvoiceLines[SalePrice]), PREVIOUSyear(DateDimension[DateKey]))
NEXTDAY()	Finds the date for the following day	CALCULATE(SUM(InvoiceLines[SalePrice]), NextDay(DateDimension[DateKey]))
NEXTMONTH()	Finds data for the following month	CALCULATE(SUM(InvoiceLines[SalePrice]), NextDay(DateDimension[DateKey]))
NEXTQUARTER()	Finds data for the following quarter	CALCULATE(SUM(InvoiceLines[SalePrice]), NextDay(DateDimension[DateKey]))
NEXTYEAR()	Finds data for the following year	CALCULATE(SUM(InvoiceLines[SalePrice]), NextDay(DateDimension[DateKey]))
DATESMTD()	Finds data for the month to date	CALCULATE(SUM(InvoiceLines[SalePrice]), DATESMTD(DateDimension[DateKey]))
DATESQTD()	Finds data for the quarter to date	CALCULATE(SUM(InvoiceLines[SalePrice]), DATESQTD(DateDimension[DateKey]))
DATESYTD()	Finds data for the year to date	CALCULATE(SUM(InvoiceLines[SalePrice]), DATESYTD(DateDimension[DateKey]))

Comparisons with Previous Time Periods

While the various DAX functions that return a "previous" time span are extremely useful, it could be argued that they are a little rigid for some types of calculation. After all, comparisons to the previous month typically require you to display data by month. So, DAX has alternative methods of comparing data over time that do not require you to specify exactly which time element (day, month, quarter, or year) you want to compare with. Instead, you can merely say that you want to go back a defined period in time, and then depending on the choice of time element that you use in a visualization, DAX automatically calculates the correct figure for comparison.

As a first example, let's imagine that you want to compare current sales with sales for the current period— be it a day, week, month, quarter, or year. There might be several ways of doing this, but there is one fairly simple approach that returns the total car sales for the same time span for the previous year. Once the principle is clear, I will show you how to extend this to calculate the following:

- The average car sales price for the previous year

- The number of cars sold in the previous quarter

Initially, you should carry out the following steps to calculate sales for the previous year:

1. In the data view, select the Invoices table and click in the calculation area.

2. In the formula bar, enter **PreviousSalesYear** and then a colon followed by an equal sign; then enter (or type and select) **CALCULATE(.**

3. Enter (or select) **SUM(.**

4. Select the InvoiceLines[SalePrice] field.

5. Enter a right parenthesis to close the SUM() function.

6. Enter a comma.

7. Enter (or select) **DATEADD(.**

8. Select the DateDimension[DateKey] field. This indicates to DAX the correct date table and date key field.

9. Enter a comma.

10. Enter **-1**. This will cause the time comparison to apply to a *previous* period of time.

11. Enter a comma.

12. Enter (or select) **YEAR.** This indicates to the DATEADD() function that it wants to compare figures with the previous year.

13. Enter two right parentheses. The first one closes the DATEADD() function; the second one closes the CALCULATE() function. The formula will look like this:

```
PreviousYearSales := Calculate(Sum(InvoiceLines[SalePrice]),
dateadd(DateDimension[DateKey],-1,YEAR))
```

14. Press Enter or click the check mark in the formula bar to finish the measure.

Figure 17-14 shows how the sale price (at the quarter level in this instance) is compared to last year's sale price when you add the PreviousYearSales measure to a table. In this example, the table shows only sales for 2014. Consequently, the previous year's sales are those for 2013. What is so impressive is that if you filter the table on another year (2015 for example), you will see that the previous year's figures are now those for 2014.

QuarterAndYear	SalePrice	PreviousYearSales
Q1 2014	1287500	2001550
Q2 2014	2007000	2412090
Q3 2014	2402940	2242820
Q4 2014	689000	502250
Total	**6386440**	**7158710**

Figure 17-14. *Calculating metrics for a previous year*

The formula sums or averages the data in a column, but only for the previous year, compared to the date field for each row. (This is the InvoiceDate in the sample data, because the date field is linked to the date table in the sample data model.) Note that you do not use the InvoiceDate field in these formulas. This is because it is the field that is linked to the DateKey field of the date table. Power Pivot knows which field to use in the Stock table as the basis for time comparisons. To labor the point, it was essential to create a coherent and complete data model to make time intelligence work perfectly.

In this example, you set the "time shift" to a negative value so that DAX would go back one year in time. You can also use positive numbers if you are looking at data from a past viewpoint and want to compare with data from later dates.

■ **Tip** The DATEADD function lets you replace YEAR with MONTH or DAY if you need to compare with data from days or months previously.

Once you have the mastered this technique, you can extend and enhance a formula such as this to provide a multitude of metrics that will adapt to the time-based filters on tables and charts. As a second example, try creating the following measure. It will calculate the average sale price for the selected period (or periods) in the preceding year. I hope that by now you have become used to writing DAX formulas, so I will not explain how to create this formula, step by step. Instead, I will let you create is unaided. This should provide you with some good practice in creating DAX formulas by yourself.

```
AverageSalePricePreviousYear := CALCULATE(
                                    AVERAGE(InvoiceLines[SalePrice]),
                                    DATEADD(DateDimension[DateKey],-1,YEAR)
                                    )
```

■ **Note** I have formatted the code for these formulas for greater readability on the page and ideally to make the logic of the functions more comprehensible. You might not be able to use the code formatted like this in Power Pivot without simplifying the presentation.

Alternatively, perhaps you want to see the number of sales for the previous quarter relative to the date that is used to filter a visualization. This formula would be as follows:

```
NumberOfSalesPreviousQtr := CALCULATE(
                                    COUNT(InvoiceLines[InvoiceID]),
                                    DATEADD(DateDimension[DateKey],
                                            -1,QUARTER)
                                    )
```

Now that you have seen the principle, you are free to adapt it to your specific requirements. You can use any of the DAX aggregation functions that were described in the previous chapter. You can mix these with the four interval types (Year, Quarter, Month, and Day) that the DATEADD() function uses to deliver a truly wide-ranging set of time comparison metrics that automatically adapt to the time span of your Power Pivot visualization.

Comparison with a Parallel Period in Time

Looking at metrics from the past can be key indicator of how a business is progressing. Clearly identifying the extent (or lack) of progress is even more telling. There are several ways that you can perform these types of calculation in DAX. In this section, you will see a couple of techniques that you may find useful.

Comparing Data from Previous Years

So, the YearOnYearDelta and YearOnYearDeltaPercent measures calculate the increase or decrease in sales compared to a previous year and also that change is expressed as a percentage. These measures extend the logic of the last few formulas using functions that you have already met. I will presume that after two chapters on DAX, you do not really need a step-by-step explanation on how to enter a formula. So, I will only present and then explain the code from now on. The following is the code to add YearOnYearDelta and YearOnYearDeltaPercent as new measures to the Invoices table:

```
YearOnYearDelta:=IF(
                ISBLANK(
                        SUM(InvoiceLines[SalePrice])
                        ),
                BLANK(),
                IF(
                    ISBLANK(
                            CALCULATE(
                                    SUM(InvoiceLines[SalePrice]),
                                    DATEADD(DateDimension[DateKey],
                                            -1, YEAR)
                                    )
                            ),
                    BLANK(),
                    SUM(InvoiceLines[SalePrice])
                    - CALCULATE(
                            SUM(InvoiceLines[SalePrice]),
                            DATEADD(DateDimension[DateKey], -1, YEAR)
                            )
                    )
                )
```

```
YearOnYearDeltaPercent:=IF(
                        ISBLANK(
                                SUM(InvoiceLines[SalePrice])
                                ),
                        BLANK(),
                        IF(
                           ISBLANK(
                                   CALCULATE(
                                             SUM(InvoiceLines[SalePrice]),
                                             DATEADD(DateDimension[DateKey],
                                                     -1, YEAR)
                                             )
                                   ),
                            BLANK(),
                            (
                              SUM(InvoiceLines[SalePrice])
                              - CALCULATE(
                                SUM(InvoiceLines[SalePrice]),
                                   DATEADD(DateDimension[DateKey],
                                           -1, YEAR)
                                          )
                            )
                            /CALCULATE(
                                      SUM(InvoiceLines[SalePrice]),
                                      DATEADD(DateDimension[DateKey],
                                              -1, YEAR)
                                      )
                           )
                        )
```

These two formulas are a lot easier than they look, believe me.

The formula for YearOnYearDelta is this:

```
SUM(Stock[SalePrice]) Excel data model, PowerPivotcalculated fieldsYearOnYearDelta
- CALCULATE(SUM(InvoiceLines[SalePrice]), DATEADD(DateDimension[DateKey], -1, YEAR))
```

All the code says is "Subtract last year's sales from this year's sales." Everything else is wrapper code to prevent a calculation if either this year's or last year's data is zero.

Equally, this is the core code for the YearOnYearDeltaPercent formula:

```
SUM(InvoiceLines[SalePrice]) - CALCULATE(SUM(InvoiceLines[SalePrice]),DATEADD(DateDimension
[DateKey], -1, YEAR)) / CALCULATE(SUM(InvoiceLines[SalePrice]),DATEADD(DateDimension[DateK
ey], -1, YEAR))
```

In other words, "Subtract last year's sales from this year's sales and divide by last year's sales."
Everything else in the complete formula that is given in full earlier exists to prevent divide-by-zero errors or unwanted results for the first year where there is no previous year's data!

The logic "wrapper" around the core formula uses two functions that you saw in Chapter 7, but it is worth taking another look at them here. They are as follows:

- ISBLANK(): This function tests whether a calculation returns nothing and allows you to specify what to do if this happens. This is a bit like an IF function that tests only for blank data.

- BLANK(): Returns a blank (or Null). This is useful for overriding unwanted results and replacing them with a blank.

Using these functions lets you handle the case where there is no data for a previous period of time. Because you are using the ISBLANK() function to test for inexistent data, you are able to replace any missing data with a BLANK()—rather than letting Power Pivot display an unsightly error.

You have seen a couple of fairly complex formulas in a short section. So, I think that it is a good idea to see how they look when you apply them. In this case, I will use a Power View table to show the results, as shown in Figure 17-15. As you can see, the appropriate formats have been applied to each metric to enhance readability.

MonthFull	SalePrice	PreviousYearSales	YearOnYearDelta	YearOnYearDeltaPercent
January	$555,500.00	£737,500.00	-£182,000.00	-24.68%
February	$359,500.00	£610,750.00	-£251,250.00	-41.14%
March	$372,500.00	£653,300.00	-£280,800.00	-42.98%
April	$367,500.00	£642,800.00	-£275,300.00	-42.83%
May	$529,500.00	£691,240.00	-£161,740.00	-23.40%
June	$544,500.00	£558,000.00	-£13,500.00	-2.42%
July	$565,500.00	£520,050.00	£45,450.00	8.74%
August	$584,500.00	£455,000.00	£129,500.00	28.46%
September	$606,500.00	£534,690.00	£71,810.00	13.43%
October	$554,940.00	£638,250.00	-£83,310.00	-13.05%
November	$657,000.00	£614,880.00	£42,120.00	6.85%
December	$689,000.00	£502,250.00	£186,750.00	37.18%
Total	**$6,386,440.00**	**£7,158,710.00**	**-£772,270.00**	**-10.79%**

Figure 17-15. *Power View output for year-on-year comparisons*

Once again, these formulas only scratch the surface of the myriad possibilities that DAX has on offer. However, you can adapt them to create comparisons by quarter, month, or day if you prefer simply by changing the specified time interval from YEAR to QUARTER, MONTH, or DAY.

Comparing with the Same Date Period from a Different Quarter, Month, or Year

In the last couple of sections, you saw various ways to compare data from a prior year or month. DAX offers one alternative method for these kinds of calculations that can be both easy to implement and extremely powerful. Moreover, it can serve as the basis for comparison with years, quarters, or months. This is the PARALLELPERIOD() function. Suppose you want to use it to find average sales for the previous quarter.

Because this function is fairly similar to the DATEADD() function that you saw previously, I will not explain it step-by-step; instead, I prefer to give you three examples of measures that you can add to the InvoiceLines table directly.

Here are the sales for the preceding month:

```
SalesPrevMth := Calculate(Sum(InvoiceLines[SalePrice]), parallelperiod(DateDimension[DateK
ey],-1,MONTH))
```

Here are the sales for the preceding quarter:

```
SalesPrevQtr := CALCULATE(SUM(InvoiceLines[SalePrice]), PARALLELPERIOD(DateDimension[DateK
ey],-1,QUARTER))
```

Here are the sales for the preceding year:

```
SalesPrevYear := CALCULATE(SUM(InvoiceLines[SalePrice]), PARALLELPERIOD(DateDimension[DateK
ey],-1,YEAR))
```

You see two examples of these functions displayed as simple visualizations in Figure 17-16.

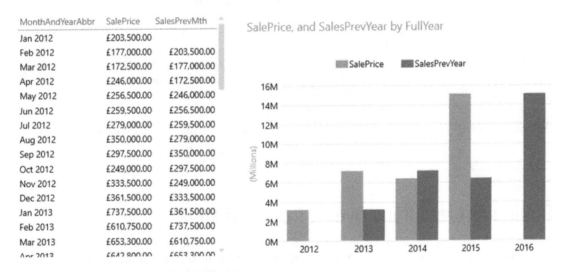

Figure 17-16. *Using the PARALLELPERIOD() function*

■ **Note** You need to be aware that the PARALLELPERIOD() function compares the current data, not just up to the same data in the previous period (be it a year, a quarter, or a month), but for the entire previous time.

There are further DAX functions that you can also use when comparing data over time. These are outlined in Table 17-9.

Table 17-9. *DAX Date and Time Formulas to Compare Values over Time*

Formula	Description	Example
PARALLELPERIOD()	Finds dates from a "parallel" time frame defined by a certain number of set intervals. The first parameter is the source data; the second is the number of years, quarters, months, or days; and the third is the definition of the interval: years, quarters, months, or days. A positive number of intervals looks forward in time, and a negative number goes backward in time.	CALCULATE(SUM(InvoiceLines [SalePrice]), PARALLELPERIOD (DateDimension[DateKey],-1, MONTH))
SAMEPERIODLASTYEAR()	Finds the date(s) for the same time range one year before.	CALCULATE(SUM(InvoiceLines [SalePrice]), SAMEPERIODLASTYEAR (DateDimension[DateKey])
DATEADD()	Used to return data from a past or future period in time compared to a specified date. The date difference can be in years, quarters, months, or days.	CALCULATE(SUM(Inv oiceLines[SalePrice]), DATEADD(DateDimension[DateKey], -1, YEAR))
DATESBETWEEN()	Calculates a list of dates between two dates. The first parameter is the start date, and the second parameter is the end date.	DATESBETWEEN(Stock[PurchaseDate], Invoices[SaleDate])
DATESINPERIOD()	Calculates a list of dates beginning with a start date for a specified period.	DATESINPERIOD(DateDimension[D ateKey], DATE(2015,06,30),-90,day))

Rolling Aggregations over a Period of Time

You are now getting into the arena of more complex DAX formulas. So, since returning the rolling sum (or average) of a specified period to date necessitates several DAX functions and some in-depth nesting of these functions, I will take this as an example of a more complicated DAX formula. I will begin by outlining some of the functions that are used to deliver a result that is reliable and efficient.

- DATESBETWEEN(): Lets you select a range of dates. The three parameters are the date key field from the date table, then the starting date, and then the ending date.

- FIRSTDATE(): Allows you to get the first date from a range. Since you are using this momentarily to go back a defined number of months, it will get the first day of the month.

- LASTDATE(): Allows you to get the last date from a range. Since you are using this momentarily to go back a defined number of months, it will get the last day of the month.

You can now create two measures (3MonthsToDate and Previous3Months) using some fairly sophisticated logic to ensure that only blank cells are returned if there is no previous year's data using the following formulas:

```
3MonthsToDate :=IF(
                ISBLANK(SUM(Stock[SalePrice])),
                        BLANK(),
                        CALCULATE(
                                SUM(Stock[SalePrice]),
                                DATESINPERIOD(
                                        DateDimension[DateKey],
                                        LASTDATE(DateDimension[DateKey]),-3,MONTH
                                )
                        )
                )
```

```
Previous3Months :=IF(
                ISBLANK(
                    CALCULATE(
                            SUM(Stock[SalePrice]),
                            DATEADD(DateDimension[DateKey],-1,MONTH)
                    )
                ),
                BLANK(),
                CALCULATE(
                        SUM(Stock[SalePrice]),
                        DATESBETWEEN(
                                DateDimension[DateKey],
                                FIRSTDATE(DATEADD(DateDimension[DateKey],
                                  -4,MONTH)),
                                LASTDATE(DATEADD(DateDimension[DateKey],
                                  -1,MONTH))
                        )
                )
            )
```

The 3MonthsToDate formula essentially evaluates the code that is in boldface. This says, "Add up the sales for a time period ranging from three months ago to now," using the InvoiceDate field as the date to evaluate. The IF function detects whether there are sales for the current date and whether there are none (ISBLANK), then the calculation is not attempted, and a BLANK is returned.

The Previous3Months formula is pretty similar, except that the time span uses the DATESBETWEEN function to set a range of dates—from the first day of the month four months ago to the last date in the preceding month.

DAX contains a couple of functions that you can use to return a specific date when aggregating data over time. These are shown briefly in Table 17-10.

Table 17-10. *DAX Date and Time Formulas to Return a Date*

Formula	Description	Example
FIRSTDATE()	Finds the first date that an event took place	FIRSTDATE(Invoices[InvoiceDate])
LASTDATE()	Finds the last date that an event took place	LASTDATE(Invoices[InvoiceDate])

Conclusion

This chapter has taken you on a short tour of some of the ways that you can use DAX in Power Pivot to extract meaning from your data by analyzing its evolution over time.

First, you saw how to extract date and time elements from columns that contain dates. The new columns that you create based on dates can then be used to filter or group data in your visualizations. This way you can provide a daily, weekly, monthly, quarterly, and yearly breakdown of your source data. These date elements can also help you to filter the data sets that you are using by dates, date elements, and date ranges.

Then you saw how to prepare the data set for time intelligence by adding a date table and joining this table to the other tables in the data model. Finally, you saw how to start adding formulas to the data set to prepare all the time-based metrics that your Power Pivot reports could need. This can include analyzing sales to date or comparing data from previous time periods with current data.

Explaining all the possibilities of DAX would take an entire book, so all I wanted to do in this and the previous two chapters was explain how you can use core DAX functions in a handful of useful calculations. I sincerely hope that this brief overview helps you on your road to mastery of DAX and that you are able to apply these formulas to deliver stunning visualizations using Power Pivot.

Your data is now ready for output. It can be used as the basis for multiple dashboards and reports. Should you want to see examples of all the time functions created in this chapter, then please download the file `DataModelWithAllMetrics.xlsx` from the Apress web site.

■ ■ ■

CHAPTER 18

Self-Service Business Intelligence with PowerBI.com

You are now approaching the end of your journey into the world of self-service business intelligence with Excel. Up until now in this book you have seen how to use Get & Transform and Power View to prepare and visualize your data. All that remains is to learn how to share your insights with your colleagues. This is where PowerBI.com comes into the frame.

PowerBI.com is an online service that lets you do the following:

- Share your Excel files and Power View reports in the cloud. This will allow your co-workers to view and interact in real time with Power View reports in a browser window.

- Use the new Power BI app for mobile devices to view and interact with Power View reports on tablet devices.

- Configure any Excel files that you have loaded into PowerBI.com so that they connect to on-premises data and so they refresh the data that they contain from onsite data sources at regular intervals. This way you can be sure that your colleagues are always using the most recent available data.

- Create new reports in the cloud if you want.

However, the truly amazing thing about PowerBI.com is that it is absolutely *free* (for up to 1 GB of data at the moment). If this threshold is too low (and to access many other possibilities, especially where group collaboration is concerned), you can upgrade to the PowerBI.com enterprise service and raise the limit to 10GB of data (as well as obtaining other advantages) for $9.99 per month. (This was the price when this book went to press.)

PowerBI.com is a vast product in its own right and worthy of a book in itself. So, in this chapter you will only be taking a quick look at some of its features and will not be examining everything that this service can do in detail.

Create a Power BI Account

Before you can use PowerBI.com, you need to create a Power BI account. Here is how:

1. In your browser, navigate to the following URL: www.microsoft.com/PowerBI. You should see a web page like the one in Figure 18-1.

© Adam Aspin 2016

A. Aspin, *High Impact Data Visualization in Excel with Power View, 3D Maps, Get & Transform and Power BI*, DOI 10.1007/978-1-4842-2400-7_18

565

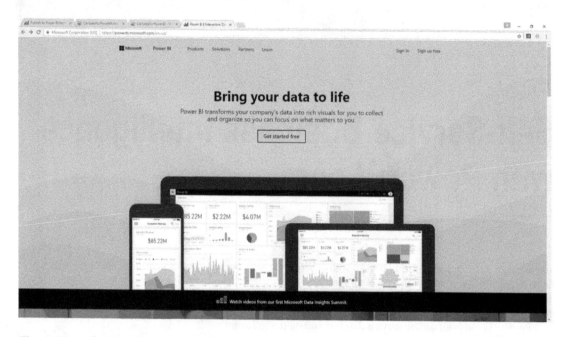

Figure 18-1. *The PowerBI.com connection page*

2. Click Get Started Free. You will see the getting started page, as shown in Figure 18-2.

Choose how to get started with Power BI

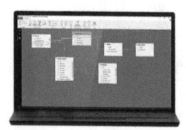

Power BI Desktop for Windows

Analytics tools at your fingertips

Connect and transform data, create advanced calculations, and build stunning reports in minutes.

Download

Power BI

The easy way to see your important data in one place

With a few clicks, connect to data from applications you use and get started with pre-built dashboards from experts.

Sign up

Figure 18-2. *The getting started page*

3. Click Sign Up. You will see the sign-up page.

4. Enter your work e-mail. The page will look like the one displayed in Figure 18-3.

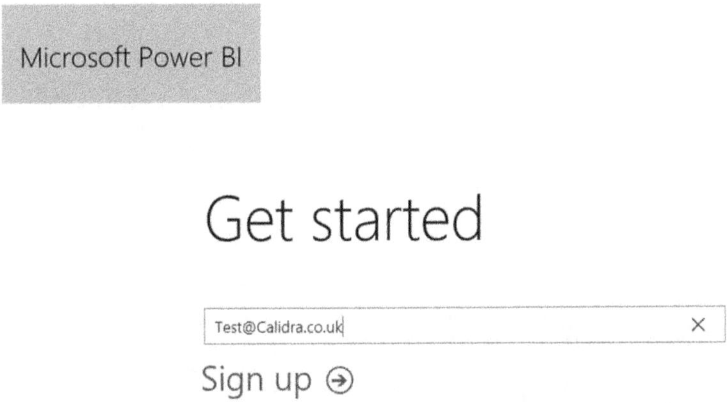

Microsoft Power BI

Get started

| Test@Calidra.co.uk | × |

Sign up ⊖

Figure 18-3. *Entering your e-mail*

5. Click the arrow. PowerBI.com will display the screen shown in Figure 18-4 and send you an e-mail confirming the creation of your account.

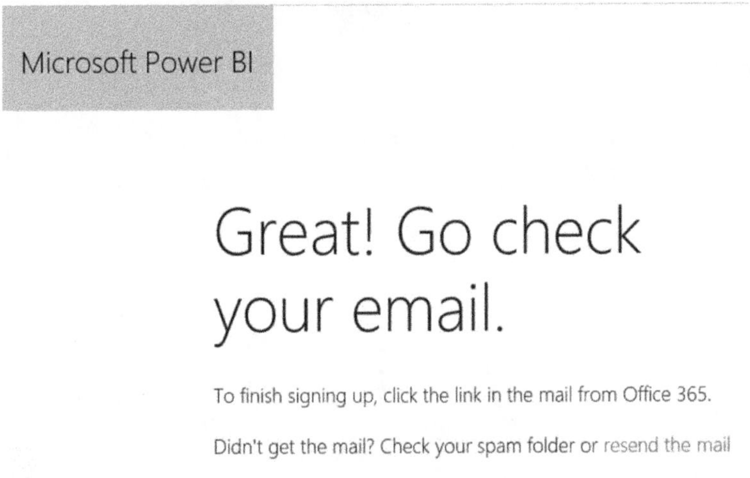

Microsoft Power BI

Great! Go check your email.

To finish signing up, click the link in the mail from Office 365.

Didn't get the mail? Check your spam folder or resend the mail

Figure 18-4. *The e-mail confirmation screen of PowerBI.com*

6. Go to your e-mail client and open the mail from Power BI. It should look like Figure 18-5.

Figure 18-5. *The e-mail from PowerBI.com*

7. Click Yes, That's Me. You will be connected to the PowerBI.com service and will see a web page like the one in Figure 18-6.

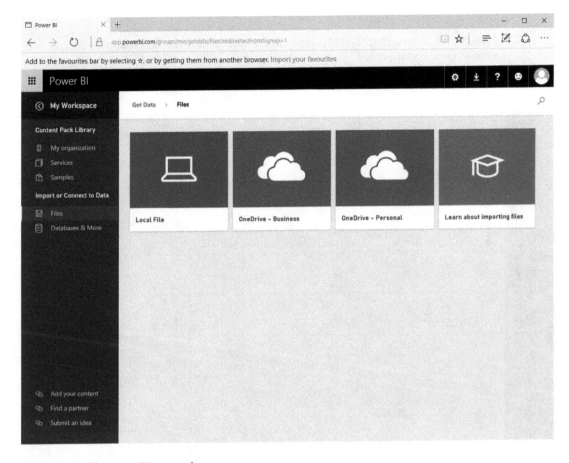

Figure 18-6. *The PowerBI.com web page*

That is all you have to do. You now have a PowerBI.com account and can start sharing your insights with colleagues and friends.

Publish Excel Files to Power BI

Now that you have a Power BI account, you can export data and Power View reports to Power BI. Before starting, you need to be aware of these key limitations:

- You have to use the same online account for Office, OneDrive for Business, and Power BI.

- You cannot publish an empty workbook or a workbook that doesn't have any Power BI–supported content.

- You cannot publish encrypted or password-protected workbooks.

Here is how:

1. Open the file CarSalesForPowerBI.xlsx from the sample data. This file contains a Power View worksheet.

2. Click File ➤ Publish. You will see the Publish window, as shown in Figure 18-7.

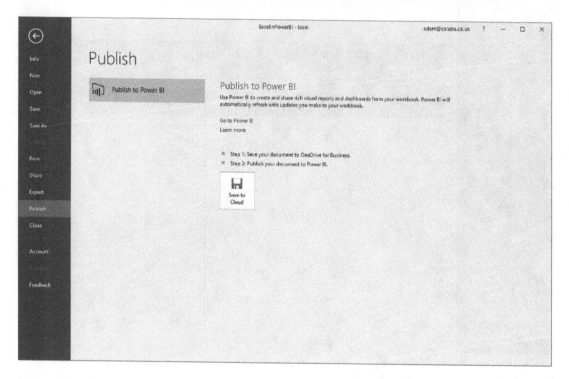

Figure 18-7. The Excel Publish window

3. Click Save To Cloud. The Save As window will appear.

4. Select your OneDrive for Business account and the required folder. Alter the file name if necessary.

5. Click Save. You will return to the Publish screen, which now looks like Figure 18-8.

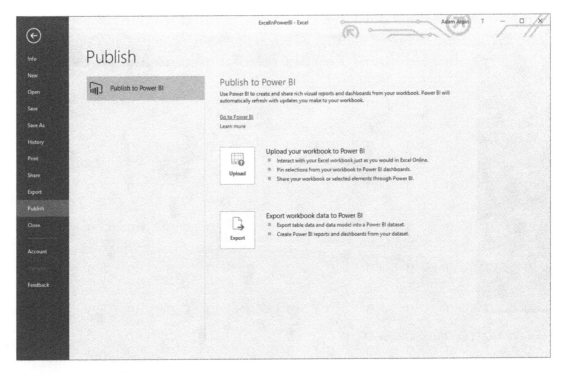

Figure 18-8. The Publish screen ready to upload to Power BI

6. Click Upload your workbook to Power BI. The workbook will be uploaded, and after a short time, you will return to the Excel workbook and see the alert that appears in Figure 18-9.

Figure 18-9. The successful upload alert

7. Click the Go To Power BI button to open the Power BI service.

8. Click Reports in the left pane.

9. Click the report CarSalesForPowerBI that you just loaded.

10. Click the SalesData tab. You will see the Power View sheet that was created in Excel, just as it is shown in Figure 18-10.

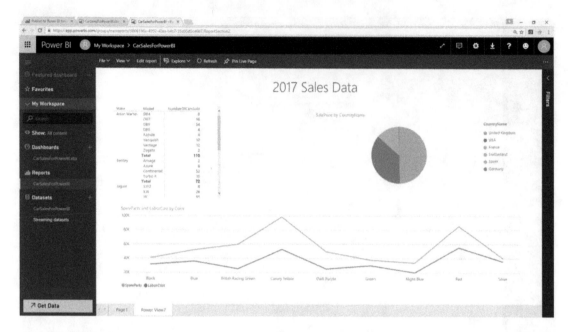

Figure 18-10. *Power View in Power BI*

Work with Reports on PowerBI.com

Now that you have uploaded a report to PowerBI.com, it is worth asking what you can do with reports now that you are no longer in Excel. The answer is quite simple: you can do nearly everything that you can do in Power View. Specifically, you can do the following:

- *Filter data* in the filter pane on the right of the PowerBI.com report, just as you would using Power View. Note that you cannot add further filters but that any existing report, page, or visualization filters are accessible, and you can switch between basic filtering and advanced filtering just as you can in Power View.

- *Highlight data* by clicking chart elements, for instance (again just as you can in Power View).

- *Switch between pages* using the tabs at the bottom of the report.

- *Zoom* in to a specific visual by clicking the Focus icon in the top-right corner of a visual (yes, once again just as you can in Power View).

- *Sort data* in a visual, in the same way that you can in Power View.

- *Pan and zoom* in map visuals.

- *Use any custom visuals* that you have downloaded from the PowerBI.com site.

I imagine that by now you have understood that the Power View reports that you have loaded from Excel are virtually identical to the originals. The only major differences is that you cannot extend a report by adding new data or visuals. Indeed, if you have read the chapters explaining how to filter, sort, and highlight data, then you will find that PowerBI.com uses almost the same techniques as Power View, so you do not need any further explanation to help you on your way to interacting with your Power View reports in the cloud.

Printing PowerBI.com Reports

Although PowerBI.com is built for sharing information interactively using the Web, it will let you print reports directly from a PowerBI.com site. To print a report, follow these steps:

1. In the report menu, click File. The File menu will appear.

2. Select Print. The Print options dialog of your PC or tablet will appear from where you can select a printer and print the report.

Nearly all of this book has been devoted to explaining how you can create powerful interactive analytical reports using Power View. Moreover, as I mentioned at the start of this chapter, PowerBI.com then comes into the frame to let you share your reports. However, a large part of the knowledge that you have acquired so far in this book can also be used in PowerBI.com to create reports directly in the cloud.

Creating Reports in PowerBI.com

Should you need to, you can also use existing cloud-based data—or Excel, PowerBI desktop, or CSV files as data sources to create new reports. As a simple example, here is how to use the data in the Excel file that you loaded earlier in this chapter to create a new report:

1. In the My Workspace tab, click the data set CarSalesForPowerBI. A new, blank report canvas, similar to those you have been using in Power View, will be displayed. You can see this in Figure 18-11.

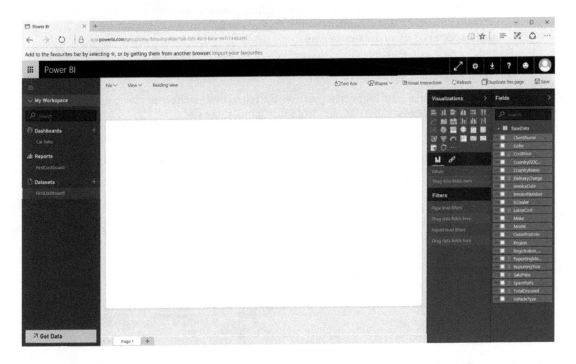

Figure 18-11. *The new report canvas*

2. Build your report in PowerBI.com. This includes creating any of the visualizations that you explored in earlier chapters. You can format the visuals just as you would in Power View as well as adding filters and shapes and defining visual interactions much as you saw previously in this book.

Well, I have to warn you that PowerBI.com is not identical to what you have learned so far. This is because PowerBI.com uses the same interface as Power BI Desktop. This interface is different from the Power View interface.

■ **Tip**   If you want a guide to the PowerBI.com interface, then I suggest my book *Pro Power BI Desktop* (Apress, 2016).

As well, it is probably worth outlining the essential differences between creating reports directly in PowerBI.com and developing reports in Power View.

- *Data*: This is currently limited to Excel, Power BI Desktop, CSV files, or data that is accessible from a cloud-based source such as the following:

    - Azure SQL database

    - Azure SQL Data Warehouse

    - SQL Server Analysis Services

- *Calculated columns and measures*: It is not currently possible to extend the data set with calculated columns and measures. So, you will have to ensure that all the metrics you need are in the source data.

- *Custom visuals*: You can import any of the custom visuals that are available on the PowerBI.com site, just as you can when using Power BI Desktop.

One final thing that you need to know is how to save the report that you have made. In reality, you create a new report by saving the canvas in the data set. To do this, follow these steps:

1. At the top right of the Datasets page, click Save.

2. Enter a name for the report. I have chosen PowerBIReport for this example. The save dialog will look like the one in Figure 18-12.

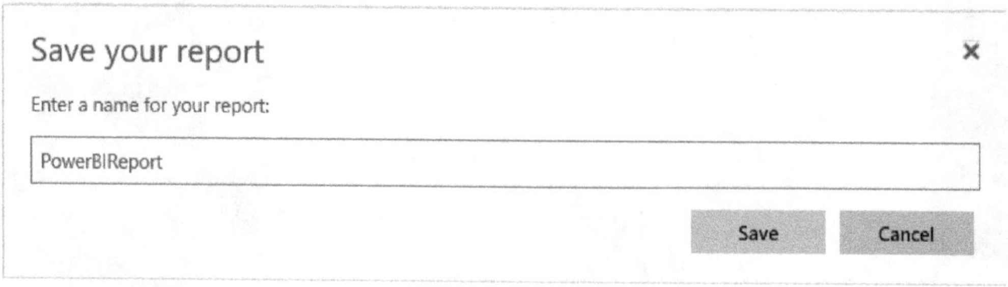

Save your report   ✕

Enter a name for your report:

PowerBIReport

Save   Cancel

Figure 18-12.   *The save report dialog*

3. Click Save. The report will be displayed in the Workspace pane in the Reports tab with an asterisk to indicate that it is a new report. You can see this in Figure 18-13.

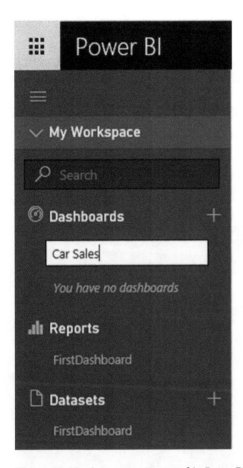

Figure 18-13. *A new report created in PowerBI.com*

Uploading Excel Workbooks Without OneDrive for Business

Although seamless publishing from Excel to the Power BI service requires a OneDrive for Business account, there is nothing stopping you from loading Excel files into the Power BI service in other ways. This is because the Power BI service can accept data from various sources. These include both local files and personal OneDrive accounts.

Here is how to load an Excel workbook containing Power View reports directly into the Power BI service:

1. In Power BI, click the yellow Get Data button at the bottom of the left pane. The Get Data window will appear, like the one you can see in Figure 18-14.

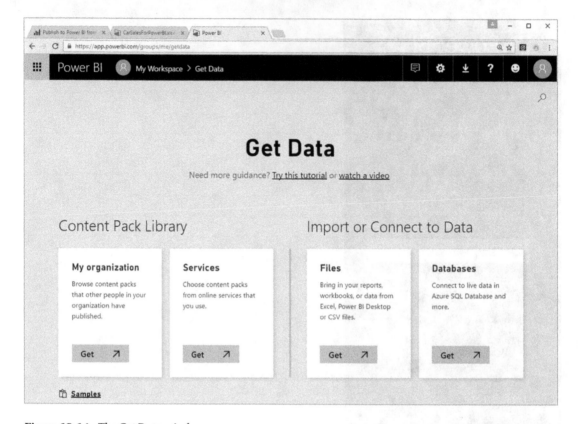

Figure 18-14. *The Get Data window*

    2.   Click Files. The Files window will appear. You can see this in Figure 18-15.

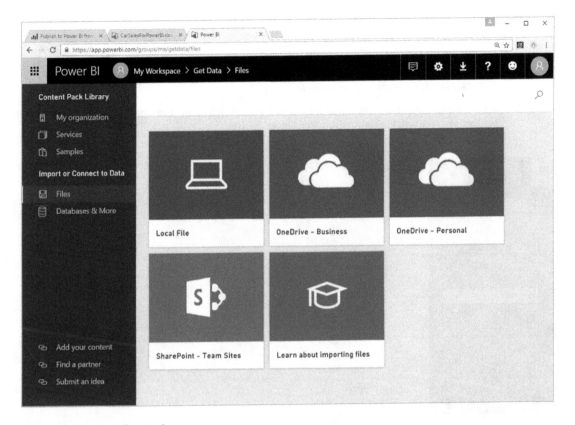

Figure 18-15. *The Files window*

3.   Click Local File and browse to select the Excel workbook that you want to load.

4.   Click Open. The file will be loaded into Power BI.

Creating PowerBI.com Dashboards

In PowerBI.com the term *dashboard* has a slightly different meaning than the one you have been using so far in this book. In PowerBI.com a dashboard is a central point of focus where you can do the following:

- Add visuals from any report that you have loaded into PowerBI.com

- Jump straight from a dashboard to the report hosting a visual in a dashboard

- Enhance dashboards with specific annotations.

Let's take a look at how this works by creating a dashboard and adding a visual to it from the report that you loaded previously.

Creating a New Dashboard

Adding a new dashboard is really simple.

1. In the navigation pane, click the plus icon to the right of the Dashboards heading. A new empty dashboard field will appear.

2. Enter a name for the new dashboard. I will call it **Car Sales** in this example. The navigation pane will look something like Figure 18-16.

Figure 18-16. *Creating a new dashboard*

3. Press Enter or click outside the navigation pane.

You have just created a new, empty dashboard. Now you will learn how to add elements (that PowerBI. com calls *tiles*) from reports that you have previously loaded into PowerBI.com.

Adding Tiles to PowerBI.com Dashboards

Now that you have a dashboard ready and waiting, here is how to add some content from an existing report:

1. In the navigation pane, click the report you have already loaded. This will be CarSalesForPowerBI, assuming that you followed the example given earlier. Click the SalesData tab containing the Power View report. The report will appear, looking like it does in Figure 18-10.

2. Hover the mouse pointer over the chart (with the title SalePrice by CountryName) on the top left of the report. Three small icons will appear at the top right of the chart.

3. Click the pin icon. This will display the Pin To Dashboard dialog that you can see in Figure 18-17.

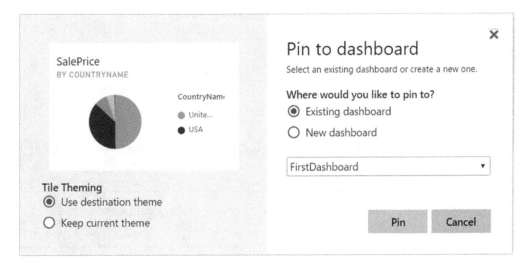

Figure 18-17. *The Pin To Dashboard dialog*

4. Ensure that the radio button Existing Dashboard Is Selected and that the dashboard FirstDashboard is selected in the pop-up list of available dashboards.

5. Click Pin.

The chart is now added to the FirstDashboard dashboard. If you click the name of this dashboard in the navigation pane, you will see that the dashboard looks like it does in Figure 18-18.

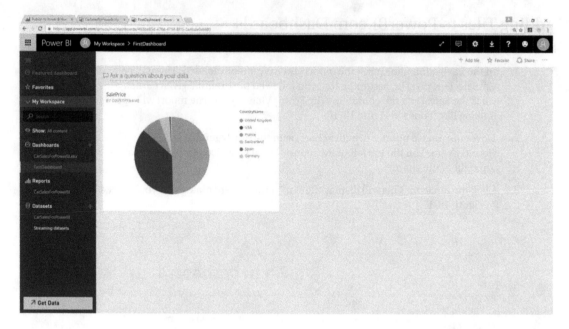

Figure 18-18. *A dashboard with a visual added*

If you now click the chart in the dashboard, you will immediately jump to the source report (and page) for this visual.

■ **Note**   You can also create a new dashboard when you pin a visual by selecting New Dashboard as the destination in the Pin To Dashboard dialog.

Editing Dashboard Tiles

There are a few interesting things that you can do to tiles once you have added them to dashboards. These are the available options:

- Deleting tiles
- Modifying tile details
- Exporting the data behind the tile
- Pinning the tile to another dashboard

Let's look at each of these in turn.

Deleting Tiles

To delete a tile from a dashboard (while leaving the source visual intact on the original report), follow these steps:

1. Click the tile menu icon (the ellipses at the top right of the tile). The tile options will appear, overlaying the tile data, as you can see in Figure 18-19.

Figure 18-19. *The tile menu*

2. Click the trash icon on the right. The tile will be removed from the dashboard.

■ **Note** If you delete a tile by mistake, you cannot undo the action. However, as the original visual is still in the source report, you can add it back easily enough.

Modifying Tile Details

There are a few details that you can modify when adding tiles to dashboards. Here is how:

1. Click the tile menu icon to display the tile menu options.

2. Click the pencil icon. The Tile Details pane will appear on the right of the screen, looking rather like the one in Figure 18-20.

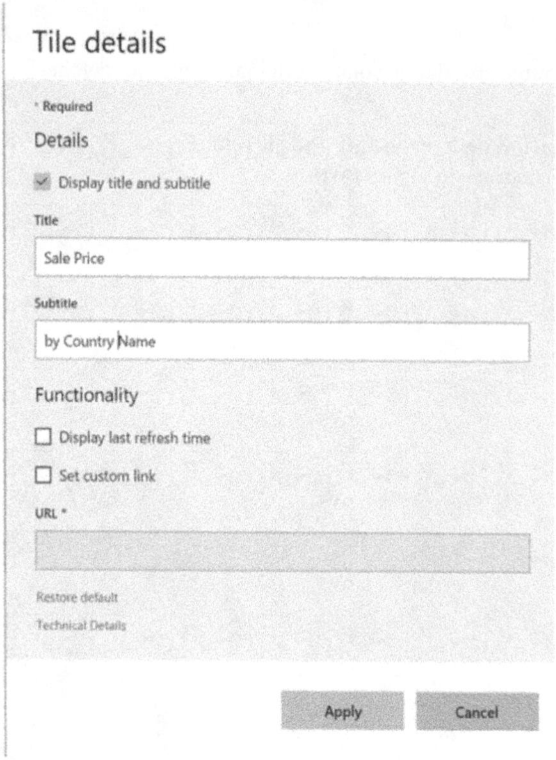

Figure 18-20. *The tile details pane*

The available options are largely self-explanatory, so I will not take you through all the possibilities but will simply explain what can be done to tweak a tile in a dashboard.

- *Title and subtitle*: If you edit the elements in these fields, you can change the title and subtitle that were inherited from the source visualization.

- *Display last refresh time*: Checking this option will add the latest refresh date and time to the tile title.

- *Set custom link*: Adding a URL to this field will define a hyperlink to a completely different web page (rather than the original report containing the source visual) when you click the tile in PowerBI.com.

Exporting the Data Behind the Tile

You can export the data that a visual is based on at any time. It will be exported as a CSV file to your Downloads folder. To do this, follow these steps:

1. Click the tile menu icon to display the tile menu options.

2. Click the page icon.

The data will be exported, and a confirmation message will appear. The CSV file will have the same name as the tile title.

■ **Note** PowerBI.com will not export the entire data set that a report is based on. It will only export the subset of data that is used in a visualization.

Pinning the Tile to Another Dashboard

Just as you pinned a visual to a dashboard, you can extend the process by pinning a tile to another dashboard. Here is how:

1. Click the tile menu icon to display the tile menu options.

2. Click the Pin icon; this will display the Pin To Dashboard dialog that you saw previously in Figure 18-17.

3. Select a new or existing dashboard and click Pin. The tile will be added to the selected dashboard.

Modifying Dashboards

Apart from adding tiles, there a several other things you can do with dashboards.

- Resizing tiles

- Adding other tiles (which can be images, text boxes, or other web content)

- Displaying dashboards in full-screen mode

- Printing dashboards

Let's take a quick look at each of these in turn.

Resizing Tiles

As you might expect, tiles can be resized (and moved) on dashboards. All you have to do to move a tile is to click inside the tile and drag it elsewhere on the dashboard pane. To resize a tile, you click the bottom-right corner of the tile and drag the mouse either up and left (to shrink the tile) or down and right (to enlarge a tile).

Adding Other Tiles (Images, Text Boxes, or Other Web Content)

Dashboards are not limited to displaying only visuals from existing reports. To enhance your message, you can add other web content or existing images. You can even add text boxes to make a specific point.

1. At the top right of the PowerBI.com screen, click Add Tile. The Add Tile pane will appear, as you can see in Figure 18-21.

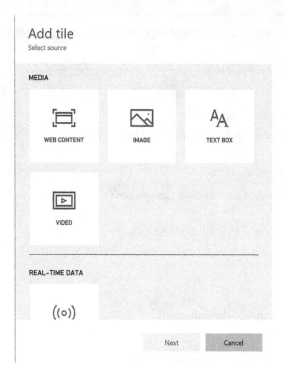

Figure 18-21. *Dashboard tiles*

2. Select one of the available tile options. The appropriate Tile Details pane
    will appear at the right of the web page where you can enter any necessary
    information.

Table 18-1 outlines the currently available options for tiles.

Table 18-1. *Tile Options*

Tile Type	Comments
Image	Clicking Image allows you to set a URL for the image that you want to display. You cannot add images from a local disk.
Video	Clicking Video allows you to set a URL for the YouTube video that you want to display. Only YouTube videos can be added to PowerBI.com dashboards as of the time of writing.
Web Content	Clicking Web Content displays the Tile Details pane where you can add any code that you want to embed in the dashboard page.
Text Box	Clicking Text Box displays the Text Box pane where you can enter and format the text that you want to display in a dashboard.
Real-Time Data	Clicking this lets you add data from streaming data sets.

■ **Note**   If you have begun to add a tile and want to abandon it before you have finished, then simply click the Close icon at the top right of the Tile Details pane.

Displaying Dashboards in Full-Screen Mode

If you are using PowerBI.com as a presentation tool or if you simply want to see the contents of a dashboard without any of the other panes or menus, you can always display the dashboard in full-screen mode.

1.   Click the Enter Full Screen Mode icon (the diagonal two-headed arrow) in the PowerBI.com title bar. The dashboard will appear in full-screen mode, as shown in Figure 18-22.

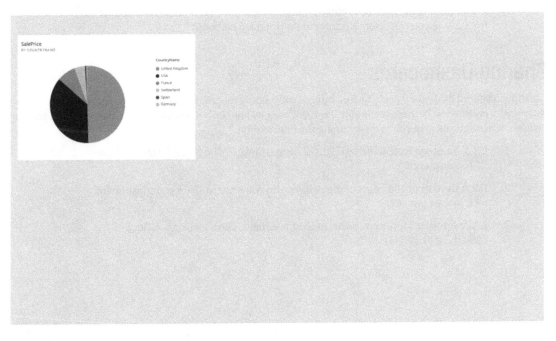

Figure 18-22. Displaying a dashboard in full-screen mode

To exit full-screen mode, simply press Escape, or click the Exit Now button in the toolbar at the bottom of the web page.

Print Dashboards

Although PowerBI.com is built for sharing using the Web, it will also let you make paper copies of your dashboards. To print a dashboard, follow these steps:

1.   Click the More Options button (the ellipses at the top right of the web page). The options menu will appear as shown in Figure 18-23.

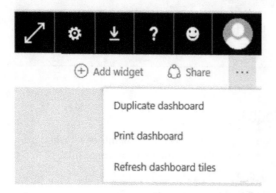

Figure 18-23. *The More Options menu*

2. Click Print Dashboard. The Print options dialog of your PC or tablet will appear from where you can select a printer and print the dashboard.

Sharing Dashboards

Creating insightful dashboards may be fun, but it is only a truly meaningful activity if the information can be shared with colleagues. Perhaps inevitably, PowerBI.com will not only allow your co-workers to share your insights, it will actively help you to disseminate the information.

1. Click the Share icon at the top right of the dashboard. The Share Dashboard pane will be displayed.

2. Enter the e-mail addresses of the people who you want to share your dashboard with in the upper field.

3. Add a message for the recipients in the lower field. The web page will look something like Figure 18-24.

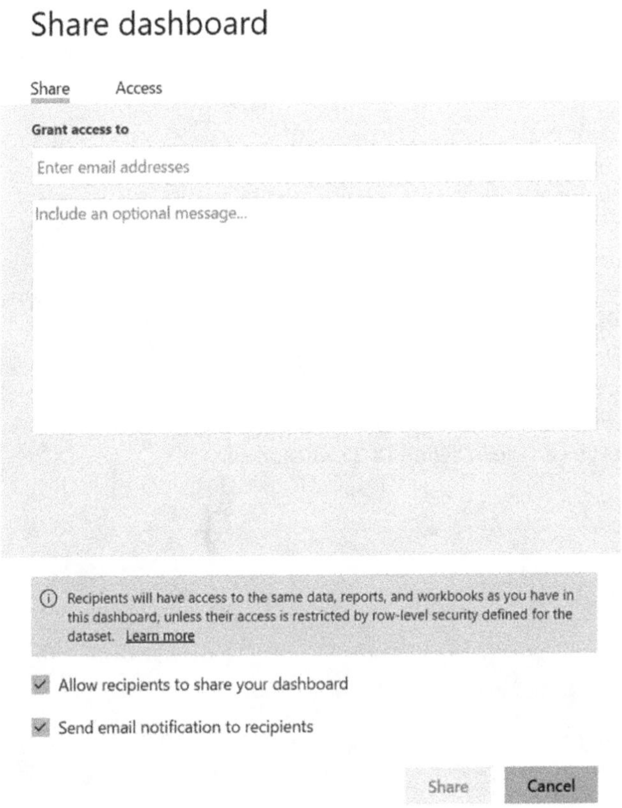

Share dashboard

Share   Access

Grant access to

Enter email addresses

Include an optional message...

ⓘ Recipients will have access to the same data, reports, and workbooks as you have in
this dashboard, unless their access is restricted by row-level security defined for the
dataset. <u>Learn more</u>

☑ Allow recipients to share your dashboard

☑ Send email notification to recipients

Share   **Cancel**

Figure 18-24. Sharing dashboards

4.   Click Share.

Your colleagues will receive an e-mail containing the link to the dashboard that you have shared.
Clicking this link will display the dashboard.

If you do not want to send an e-mail with a link, you can click the Shared With tab in the Share
Dashboard page and simply copy and paste the link into a file or a Microsoft Lync message (for instance)
and enable your co-workers to access your dashboard in this way.

The Power BI App on Tablet Devices

Self-service business intelligence with PowerBI.com is not limited to PCs or web browsers. Indeed, Microsoft has released a set of apps that are tailored to mobile devices on the following platforms:

- iPad and iPhone

- Android

- Windows

So, if you have an Android or Windows phone (or an iPhone for that matter) or an iPad or Windows or Android tablet, then you are in luck. You can download the app that is specific to the device you are using and access reports, dashboards, and data on PowerBI.com using the app. All the apps are specifically adapted to their specific platforms and make interacting with the data and visuals even easier and more intuitive.

To download the app for your device, follow these steps:

1. Point the browser on your phone or tablet to `https://powerbi.microsoft.com/en-us/mobile/`. The web page that you can see in Figure 18-25 will appear.

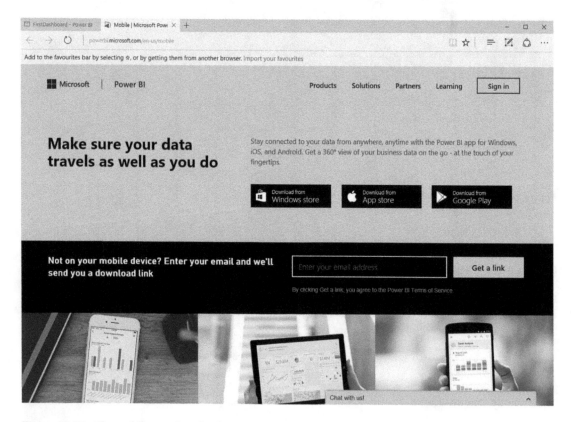

Figure 18-25. *The mobile app download page*

2. Download the app as you would any other app for your mobile device.

3. Run the app. You will be asked to sign in, so do this using the account that you created for PowerBI.com. Once you have signed in, you should see a screen rather like the one in Figure 18-26 (this example is on a Windows 10 tablet).

Figure 18-26. *The mobile app screen*

4. Click the tile FirstDashboard. You will switch to the report that you loaded previously, which will look like it does in Figure 18-27.

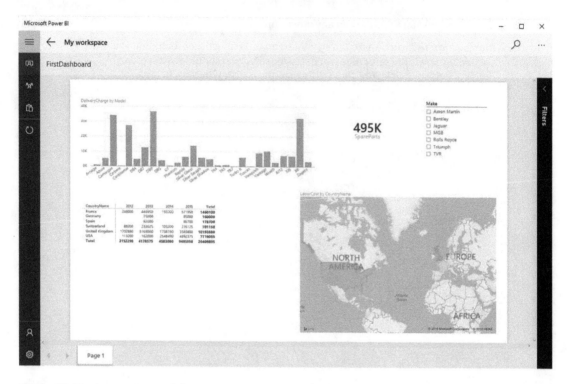

Figure 18-27. *A report in a mobile app*

From now on you can interact with your reports on PowerBI.com much as you would using Power View or PowerBI.com.

Conclusion

Over the course of this book you have seen how to develop the data discovery, modeling, and visualization capabilities of Get & Transform, 3D Maps, Power Pivot, DAX and Power View. As the culmination of your journey into self-service BI, this chapter has shown you the new ways you can share discoveries and collaborate from anywhere using PowerBI.com. This has meant publishing Excel files to PowerBI.com and interacting with Power View reports on the Web.

Once you master and implement these techniques and technologies, PowerBI.com could really become a dynamic online hub for insight and collaboration, data reuse, and interaction among your colleagues. I sincerely hope you will have fun using Excel 2016 and develop some really awesome uses for this amazing technology.

Index

A

Advanced charting
  bubble (*see* Bubble charts)
  multiple charts
    bar/column, 121–122
    drill down approach, 130
    grid, 124–126
    horizontal multiples creation, 124
    line charts, 126–128
    pie charts, 128–129
    vertical and horizontal selections, 123
    visualizations, 121
  play axis, 140–142
  scatter charts
    drill down approach, 133
    fields list, 132
  techniques, 121
  types, 142
Aggregations, 550
  AVERAGEX() function, 506
  essential points, 506
  iterative functions, 506–507
  Power Pivot reports/pivot tables, 505
ALLEXCEPT() function, 519–520
ALLSELECTED() function, 519
Appending data
  adding multiple files, source folder
    file name specification, 395
    files loaded, 397
    filtering file types, 396
    Folder dialog, 395
    FTP site, 395
    Get & Transform, 395–396
    process, 395
  conditions, 394
  identical structures, 394
  Oracle database, 394
AVERAGE() function, 484
Azure sources, 283

B

Background images
  adding, 190
  families, 188
  fitting, 191–192
  Light 1 Solid, 188
  popup menu, 187
  removing, 192
  report, 187–188
  transparency, 193
  usage, 190
Bing Maps, 205, 225
Brilliant British Cars, 475
Bubble charts
  creation, 135–136
  data labels and legend, 137
  definition, 135
  field list, 136
  multiple charts, 139–140
  multiple elements, 138–139
Bubble maps
  creation, 241
  multiple values, 243
  pie chart, 242
  pie-style, 242–243
  settings, 252
  subdivisions/categories, 240–241

C

CALCULATE() functions, 550–551
Calendar popup, 77
CarAgeBucket field, 212
Card visualizations, 497
  callout style, 52
  card-type tables, 49–50
  multiple non-numeric
    fields, 50–51
  sorting cards, 53

© Adam Aspin 2016

A. Aspin, *High Impact Data Visualization in Excel with Power View, 3D Maps, Get & Transform and Power BI*,
DOI 10.1007/978-1-4842-2400-7

591

Charts
    adjustments
        color pallete, to bar and
            column charts, 100
        element sorting, 97–99
        font size, 100
        repositioning, 97
        resizing, 96–97
    column charts, 93
    data labels, 107–109
    data values
        clustered bar chart, 102, 104
        clustered column chart, 101
        introductory line chart, 103
        stacked bar chart, 103
    deletion, 91
    drilling down
        clustered bar chart, 112
        data analysis, 109
        drill-Up icon, 111
        fields list layout section, 112
        inside chart, 113
        lower level in, 110
        top level in, 110
    elements, 87
    filters
        data visualization, 117
        individual charts, 118
        pie charts, 115–117
    first chart, 88–91
    Layout ribbon, 105
    legends, 106
    line charts, 94
    modification, 92
    pie charts, 94–95
    popping charts out and in, 113–115
    title, 107
Clients per country, 478
Column-based calculations, 463
Column charts, 93
Column maps
    clustered columns, 244–245
    geographical element, 244
    settings, 253
    stacked columns, 245–246
Comma-separated values (CSV), 289–292
Comparison operators, 485
Completed Date, 545
Complex filters
    CALCULATE() function, 513
    DealerSales and CreditworthyDealerSales, 514
    multiple criteria, 513
Complex Logic, 489
Connection security, 315, 317
COUNTROWS() function, 478–479
Custom number formats, 481–482

■ **D**

Dashboard
    adding tiles, 579–580
    creation, 578
    deleting tiles, 581
    editing tiles, 580
    exporting, data behind tiles, 582
    full-screen mode, 585–586
    images, text boxes/web content tiles, 583, 585
    modifying tiles, 581, 583
    pinning tiles, 583
    print, 586
    resizing tiles, 583
    sharing, 587–588
Data analysis expressions (DAX), 4, 463, 563
    logical and information functions, 491
    metrics, 464
    rounding and truncation functions, 472
    time-intelligence function, 549
Data and aggregations, 29–30
Databases sources, 281–282
Data card, 257–258
Data cleansing
    changing datatype, 351–352
    context menus, 350–351
    description, 349
    Detect Data Type, 353
    filling down, 363–365
    grouping records, 366–368
    headers
        column headers, 366
        FirstRowAsHeader element, 366
    replacing values, 353, 355
    transforming column contents
        date and time transformations, 360–362
        duration, 362–363
        leading and trailing spaces, remove, 357
        numbers calculation, 358–359
        number transformations, 357–358
        text transformation, 355–356
Data discovery, 279, 293
Data loading, 279
Data management, Power Pivot, 428
    columns
        deletion, 421
        manipulation, 419
        moving columns, 421
        renaming column, 419–420
    series of tables, 418
    setting column widths, 421
    sorting data, 429
    tables
        deletion, 419
        manipulation, 419
        renaming, 419

Data mashup
    appending (*see* Appending data)
    changes, structure
        pivoting tables, 399–400
        rows and columns transpose, 401
        unpivoting tables, 398–399
    copying data, 409–410
    data merging (*see* Merging data)
    extending data
        custom columns, 377–379
        description, 372–373
        duplicating columns, 373
        merging columns, 376–377
    extending data sets, 371
    extending datasplitting columns (*see* Splitting
        columns)
    Get & Transform View ribbon, 372
    index columns, 379–381
    joining data sets, 371
    pending changes, 409
    pivoting and unpivoting data, 371
    queries (*see* Queries management)
    stages, 410
    transformation process
        adding, 403
        altering process, 403
        application, 401
        deleting, 402–403
        error records and removal, 404
        extracting series of query, 405
        modification, 402
        Query Settings pane, 401
        renaming, 402
        sequencing, 404
DataModelForMetrics.xlsx, 477, 484–485, 495
Data model modification alert, 498
Data modification, 279
Data operations, 236
Data selection
    approaches, 143
    characteristics, 143
    filters (*see* Filters)
    fundamental difference, 171
    highlighting (*see* Highlighting data)
    interactive elements and presentations, 143
    Power View, 174
    slicers (*see* Slicers)
    tiles (*see* Tiles)
Data sources
    Azure, 283
    connection security, 315, 317
    databases, 281–282
    description, 279
    ETL, 280
    file sources, 281
    less corporate sources, 283

    loading (*see* Loading data)
    modifications, 318–319
    old data, 315
    relational database (*see* Relational databases)
    reuse, 314
    types of data, 280–281
Data transformation, 321–322, 325–326, 332, 347
Data types, 29
    date and time data, 69, 71
    excluding outliers, 69
    list filter mode, 68–69
    range filter mode, 66–67
DATEADD() function, 556, 561
Date and time formatting, 532
Date calculations, 529
DATEDIFF() function, 536–537
DATESBETWEEN() function, 552
Date table, PowerPivot
    columns, 539
    in Excel, 541
    marking table, 541–542
    preparation, 540
Date table techniques, 538, 542, 546
DAX. *See* Data analysis expressions (DAX)
2D charts
    classic visualization, 268
    creation, 268
    types, 269
DeltaToAvgNetProfit, 479
DirectCosts, 471
DIVIDE() function, 477, 484
3D Maps
    aggregations, 239
    Bing Maps, 225
    bubble maps, 240, 242, 244
    column maps, 244–246
    custom regions, 277
    data area, 234–235
    data card, 257–258
    data model, 225
    data operations, 235–236
    geographical representation, 225
    heat maps, 247
    insert ribbon, 225
    layers, 269
    map visualization, 227
    movies
        exporting, 275–276
        managing scenes, 274
        multimedia file, 272
        transitions, 274
    PowerMapSample.xlsx, 225
    region maps, 230–231, 248–249
    ribbon, 228–229
    satellite image, 255
    settings view, 250–253

3D Maps (*cont.*)
  source data, 232–233
  task panel, 227
  text boxes, 256–257
  themes, 255
  timelines (*see* Timelines, 3D Maps)
  tours
    deletion, 271
    Editor, 227
    Excel workbook, 270–271
    Excel worksheet, 272
    multiple layers, 269
  types, 240
  visualization type, 240

■ E

Extract, transform, and load (ETL), 280
ETL. *See* Extract, transform, and load (ETL)
Excel BI Toolkit
  Power Map, 5, 11
  PowerPivot, 3–4, 6–8
  Power Query, 3, 10
  Power View, 4–5, 8–9
Excel data model, PowerPivot
  Brilliant British Cars, 13
  calculated columns
    data set, 464–465
    DAX formulas, 475, 488–489
    SalesData tab, 466–468, 470
    sample file, 469, 471, 480, 485, 492–493, 499,
      507, 531, 537, 544, 546, 555, 562–563
  calculated fields
    advanced aggregations, 505
    annotating, 525
    basic aggregations, 498, 503, 506
    comments and notes, 524
    creation, 499
    DAX, 495
    displaying rank, 522–523
    filtering, 521–522
    formatting, 525–526
    hiding, 526
    managing, 524
    number of cars sold, 495–496
    previous years/quarters/months,
      comparisons, 556
    rolling aggregations, 562
    time-dependent, 538
    YearOnYearDelta, 558
    YearToDate, QuarterToDate and
      MonthToDate, 549
  calculation options, recalculation, 527
  column calculations, 475
  copying data, 460
  correcting and removing errors, 483
  correct table, linked calculations, 474
  CostPrice, 470
  creating relationships, 14, 433
    automatic, 435
    manual, 434–435
  cross-table, 473, 503–504
  data and diagram view, 430
  date table
    in Excel, 541
    marking table, 541–542
    preparation, 540
  DAX, 468
  deletion, relationships, 436
  description, 12
  designing, 429
  diagram view display options, 431
  DirectCosts, 471
  discovering data, 14
  entire column, 465
  existing excel BI and sharing, 14
  format, 480
  formula bar
    description, 494
    multiline formulas, 489
  geodata delivering, 14
  IF() function, 483
  management, relationships, 436–438
  maximizing table, 432
  mobile devices, 14
  multiple measures, 500–502
  naming columns, 465
  outputs, 14
  products, 15
  refreshing data, 475
  relational modeling, 430
  rounding values, 472
  safe division, 476
  self-service business intelligence (BI), 429
  statistical functions, 479
  technicalities, table relationships, 429
  tweaking text, 468

■ F

File size, optimization, 459–460
FILTER() function, 521–522
Filter context
  elements
    filter context, 509
    query context, 508
    row context, 508
Filtering data
  complex, 512, 514
  simple, 509–512

Filters, 61
  advanced filters
    applying, 72–73
    clearing, 73
    complex filters, 78–79
    date and time filters, 76–77, 80
    numeric filter options, 75–76, 79–80
    text filter options, 79
    wildcard filters, 74
  annotation techniques, 85
  bubble chart, 165–166
  clearing filters, 61
  column and bar charts, 167, 169–170
  data types, 66–69
    date and time data, 69–71
    excluding outliers, 69
    list filter mode, 68–69
    multiple filters, 71
    range filter mode, 66–67
  deleting filters, 62
  drill-down and, 84–85
  expanding and collapsing
    filters, 62–63
  filtered table, 60
  filter element search clearing, 66
  filter hierarchy, 81–82
  granularity, 171–174
  hiding and displaying areas, 58
  "large" filter list, 63
  levels, 57
  modification, 61
  scatter chart, 166–167
  sections, 166
  specific elements search, 63–64
  subset clearing, 64
  type of data, 57
  types, 59
  visualization-level filters
    filter hierarchy, 81
    in power view, 80–81
  wildcard search, 64–65
Flagging data, 485
FORMAT() function, 482, 533–534
Formatting logical results, 493
Formula language, 463

G

Geographical data
  3D Maps, PowerPivot, 232
  types, 232–233
Get & Transform queries
  data cleansing
    sorting data, 340–341
    editing, 323

Editor
  elements, 325–326
  ribbons, 327–331
ETL, 322
filtering data
  approaches, 342
  date and time ranges, 344–345
  filter list, 343
  numeric ranges, 344
  PowerPivot, 342
  text ranges, 344
  values, 342–343
headers
  keep rows, 337–338
  merging columns, 334–336
  remove rows, 338–339
  removing columns, 334
  removing duplicate
    records, 336, 339–340
  renaming columns, 332
  reordering columns, 333
before loading, 324
Gross margin, 474

H

Heat map
  colored bubble, 247
  settings, 253–254
Hierarchies
  adding level, 450
  altering evels, 451
  definition, 449
  deletion, 451
  hiding original field, 451
  Power Pivot, 449
  removing level, 450
Highlighting data
  bubble charts, 163–164
  COLOR and SLICES boxes, 160
  cross-chart, 161–163
  definition, 160
  map data, 214–216
  remove, 160
  stacked bar chart of costs, 160

I, J

IF() statements, 487
Images
  background (*see* Background images)
  context menu, 179, 181
  file format, 202
  font used, 181
  free-form images, 200

Images (*cont.*)
    free-form text elements, 203
    independent, 197–198
    layering visualizations, 199–200
    logo adding, 198
    overloaded, 201
    Power View, 175, 189
    preparation, 202
    slicers, 195–196
    sources, 189
    tables, 194–195
    textboxes (*see* Text boxes)
    rext ribbon (*see* Text ribbon)
    text size, 182
    themes, 182–186
    tiles, 196–197
    titles (*see* Titles)
Initial calculated column, 467
Initial date table, 543
In-memory data model. *See* Power Pivot
Interactive selection, 508
InvoiceLines table, 475
ISBLANK() function, 485, 560

K

Key performance indicators (KPIs), 54
    calculation, targets, 456
    creation, 452–453
    deletion, 456
    descriptions, 454–455
    modification, 456
    options, 453–454

L

Layer pane. *See* Task panel
Layers, 3D Maps
    2-D charts, 268–269
    map visualizations, 265
    multilayered map, 267
    show/hide layer icon, 268
Layout ribbon, 105
LEFT() function, 468
Line charts, 94
Loading data
    CSV files, 289–292
    excel, 295–296
    Microsoft access databases, 297
    relational database-SQL Server, 285
    text files, 292–293
    web pages, 285–289
    XML files, 293–294
Logical operators, 492
LOOKUP() function, 474

M

Mapping data
    Bing Maps service, 205
    CarAgeBucket field, 212
    creation, 208
    drilling down, 221, 223
    filtering, 211–212
    highlighting, 214–216
    latitude and longitude, 205
    legend placement options, 217
    modification, map
        background, 209–210
    multiple maps, 219
    pie charts, 213
    positioning, 208
    Power View, 206, 208, 216–217, 223
    by region, 219–220
    removing/adding title, 209
    sections, 208
    tiles, 217–218
    trellis visualizations, 218
    zooming in/out button, 209
Math operators, 471
Matrix tables
    column hierarchies, 47–49
    column matrix, 40, 42
    drill-down approach, 45–46
    drill-up approach, 46
    matrix visualization, 47
    row matrix, 38–39
    sorting data, 43–44
Merging data
    adding, 381–383
    aggregate data, 381, 384–387
    columns map, 391
    correct and incorrect joins, 391
    examination, joined data, 391–392
    expand and aggregate buttons, 393
    individual query, 381
    joining multiple columns, 389
    join types, 388–389
    look up data, 381
    preparing data sets,
        joins, 390–391
Microsoft access databases, 297
Multiline formulas, 494
Multiple filters, 71

N, O

Naming columns, 465
Nested IF() functions, 486
NOW() function, 535
NumberOfCarsSold field, 497

▨ P

Parallel period, 558
PARALLELPERIOD() function, 560–561
Percentages calculation
    ALLEXCEPT() function, 519–520
    ALL() function, 516–518
    removing multiple filter elements, 517–518
    total sales, 515
    visual totals, 518
PercentOfPreviousMonth, 553
PERCENTOFYEAR function, 554
Pie charts, 94–95, 115–117
Power BI
    cloud-based data sharing environment, 5
    corporate BI/self-service BI, 11
    tablet devices (*see* Tablet devices)
PowerBI.com
    creation
        connection page, 566
        e-mail confirmation, 567
        entering e-mail, 567
        getting started page, 566
        web page, 569
    dashboard, modifying tiles, 582
    group collaboration, 565
    online service, 565
    publish excel files, 569–572
    reports
        creation, 573–575
        Power View, 572
        printing, 573
        uploading Excel workbooks without
            OneDrive Business, 575, 577
Power Pivot, 3–4, 6–8, 473, 496
    access, 412
    advanced ribbon, 417–418
    complete and coherent data model, 411
    creation, hierarchies, 448
    creation, modify and managmenting,
        in-memory data models, 412
    data analysis
        categorization, 425–426
        default aggregation, 426
        default summarization options, 427
        Sort by columns, 427
    data model, 414, 439
    data types
        currency format dialog, 424
        currency format pop-up list, 424
        description, 422
        formatting options, 423
        formatting tables columns, 422
    default field set, 440–442
    default image, 448

designing a data model (*see* Excel data model,
        Power Pivot)
    design ribbons, 416–417
    elements, 413
    Excel 2016, 412
    file size, optimizing, 459–460
    formatting tables, columns, 422
    hierarchies, 450–451
    home ribbon
        buttons, 415–416
        Get & Transform, 416
        modeling, 415
    hyperlinks, 448
    KPIs, 451–457
    managing data (*see* Data management,
        Power Pivot)
    perspectives, 457
        applying, 458–459
        creation, 457
        dialog, 458
    preparation, images for power view, 447
    sorting data, 428
    table behavior, 446
    tweaks, 440
    URLs images, 447
    window, 412
Power Query, 3, 10
    appending data, 394, 397
    data cleansing (*see* Data cleansing)
    datasource (*see* Data sources)
    Get & Transform (*see* Get & Transform queries)
    unpivoting tables, 399
Power View, 4–5
    card visualizations, 49–53
    data aggregation, 29–30
    data types, 28–29
    Excel data model, 17
    Excel workbook, 18
    field list, 21–22
    interface, 18
    KPIs, 54
    report, 23
    ribbon, 19–21
    switch table types, 53
    table granularity, 37–38
    usage, 17
    without data model, 54
Predefined Currency formats, 482
Predefined Date formats, 534

▨ Q

Queries management
    add columns, 408
    duplication, 408

Queries management (*cont.*)
  Get & Transform query, 405
  grouping
    adding, 408
    creation, new group, 406–407
    technique, 406
  organizing, 406
  reference, 408
  tools, 405

■ R

RANKX() function, 523
Reference elements, 478
Refresh dialog, 476
Region maps, 248
RELATED() function, 475, 477, 537
Relational databases
  CarSalesData, 298, 301–302
  connection options, 301
  database security, 305
  description, 298
  server connection, 302–303
  SQL database, 299–300
  SQL statement, 305–307
  SSAS (*see* SQL server analysis
    services (SSAS))
ROUND() function, 472

■ S

SalePriceToSalesCostsRatio, 477
Scatter charts
  definition, 131
  design area, 131
  drill down approach, 132–133
  fields list, 132
  flattened hierarchies, 133–134
  multiple, 134–135
  Power View, 131–132
Self-service business intelligence (BI)
  Excel BI Toolkit, 2–4
  Power View, 4–5
  universe, 2
Settings view, 3D Maps
  bubble map settings, 252
  column map settings, 253
  heat maps, 252–253
  region map, 253
  task panel, 250–251
Simple filters
  DAX toolbox, 509
  numeric, 511–512
  text, 509–510

Slicers
  adding, 155
  applying, 156–157
  charts, 158–159
  clearing, 157
  deletion, 157–158
  modification, 158
  Power View report, 154
Source data
  Excel data model, 232
  geographical data types, 232–233
  geographical information, 232
  network drive, 232
Splitting columns
  classic cases, 373
  custom columns, 378
  delimiter, 374–375
  number of characters, 376
SQL server analysis services (SSAS)
  attributes and measurement, 310
  collapse columns, 313
  cube tools, 311
  multidimensional database, 309
Statistical functions, 479

■ T, U, V

Table behavior
  default aggregation, 445–446
  default label, 444–445
  row identifier, 442–443
  unique rows, 444
Table relationships, Power Pivot
  creation
    automatic, 436
    colours table, 434
  diagram view display options, 432
  management, 437
Tables
  column order, 27
  column widths, 34–35
  copying table, 36
  creation, 23–24, 26
  default formatting, 34
  deletion, 26
  design ribbon, 30, 32
  field list, 24–25
  font sizes, 36
  granularity, 37
  matrix (*see* Matrix tables)
  number formatting columns, 33–34
  removing columns, 27–28
  row totals, 32
  size and position, 26

sorting by column, 36
without data model, 54
Tablet devices
mobile app download page, 588
mobile app screen, 589
self-service business intelligence, 588
steps, 588–590
Task panel
3-D globe, 238
elements, 234
find location, 238
flat Map button, 238
map visualization, 236
showing and hiding, 233
zoom and pan, 237
Text boxes
chart visualization, 178
deletion, 179
3D map, 256–257
Power View report, 178
Text files, 292–293
Text ribbon, 177–178
Tiles
adding, 146–147
creation, 146
deletion, 149
display, 145
filtering, 151–152
modification, 147
and multiple charts, 154
pie chart, 153–154
re-creation, 148
removing, 149

types, 150
usage, 151
visualizations, 144
with no data, 152–153
Time calculations, 463
Time intelligence, 529, 548
Timelines, 3D Maps
date and time formats, 265
date range, playback, 264
duration, 263
elements, 261
hiding, 264
play and pause, 262
playback settings, 259
progression, 262
time decorator, 259–260, 264
Titles
adding, 176
audience's attention, 175
formatting, 177
moving and resizing, 176

■ **W**

Wildcard search, 64–65

■ **X**

XML files, 293–294

■ **Y, Z**

YEAR() and MONTH() DAX functions, 530

Get the eBook for only $4.99!

Why limit yourself?

Now you can take the weightless companion with you wherever you go and access your content on your PC, phone, tablet, or reader.

Since you've purchased this print book, we are happy to offer you the eBook for just $4.99.

Convenient and fully searchable, the PDF version enables you to easily find and copy code—or perform examples by quickly toggling between instructions and applications.

To learn more, go to http://www.apress.com/us/shop/companion or contact support@apress.com.

CPSIA information can be obtained
at www.ICGtesting.com
Printed in the USA
LVHW02s2322080818
586377LV00003B/15/P